LAW AND TRADE

IN ANCIENT MESOPOTAMIA AND ANATOLIA

sidestone press

LAW AND TRADE

IN ANCIENT MESOPOTAMIA AND ANATOLIA

SELECTED PAPERS BY K.R. VEENHOF

Published by Sidestone Press, Leiden
www.sidestone.com

Lay-out & cover design: Sidestone Press

Photograph cover:

- Image: General Research Division, The New York Public Library. (1849). A winged human-headed lion. (Nimroud) [Calah]. By Austen Henry Layard (1849). Retrieved from http://digitalcollections.nypl.org/items/510d47dc-46e5-a3d9-e040-e00a18064a99
- Background: Detail of cuneiform inscriptions (Code of Hammurabi), Louvre, Paris (photo: John S.Y. Lee | Flicr.com)

ISBN 978-90-8890-915-3 (softcover)
ISBN 978-90-8890-916-0 (hardcover)
ISBN 978-90-8890-917-7 (PDF e-book)

Contents

	Foreword	7
	Abbreviations	11
1.	Justice and Equity in Babylonia	15
2.	Old Assyrian And Old Babylonian Law: Some Comparative Observations	27
3.	Ancient Assur: The City, its Traders and its Commercial Network	55
4.	The Archives of Old Assyrian Traders: Their Nature, Functions and Use	83
5.	"In Accordance with the Words of the Stele". Evidence for Old Assyrian Legislation	109
6.	Trade and Politics in Ancient Assur. Balancing of Public, Colonial and Entrepreneurial Interests	129
7.	Silver and Credit in Old Assyrian Trade	159
8.	Old Assyrian and Ancient Anatolian Evidence for the Care of the Elderly	185
9.	Redemption of Houses in Assur and Sippar	211
10.	Old Assyrian *Iṣurtum*, Akkadian *Eṣērum* and Hittite GIŠ.ḪUR	225
11.	A Deed of Manumission and Adoption from the Later Old Assyrian Period	245
12.	Before Hammurabi of Babylon. Law and the Laws in Early Mesopotamia	267
13.	The Interpretation of Paragraphs t and u of the Code of Hammurabi	285
14.	The Relation between Royal Decrees and 'Law Codes' of the Old Babylonian Period	297
15.	Fatherhood is a Matter of Opinion. An Old Babylonian Trial on Filiation and Service Duties	329
16.	The Dissolution of an Old Babylonian Marriage According to *CT* 45, 86	345
17.	Three Old Babylonian Marriage Contracts Involving *Nadītum* and *Šugītum*	355
18.	Trade with the Blessing of Shamash in Old Babylonian Sippar	369
19.	Assyrian Commercial Activities in Old Babylonian Sippar. Some New Evidence	395
	Bibliography of Publications by Klaas. R. Veenhof	413

Foreword

In Klaas Veenhof's long scholarly career, legal and commercial aspects of Old Babylonian and Old Assyrian society are a key topic. This interest is reflected in a large number of articles published in journals, conference proceedings and collective volumes over the past fifty years. Many of these are of lasting value and of fundamental importance to the study of these subjects.

The present selection of nineteen papers, made in close cooperation with Klaas himself, focuses on law and trade in the Old Babylonian and Old Assyrian society of the early second millennium B.C. This unavoidably entails that it was not possible to include the numerous other fields of interest Klaas has written about, such as Akkadian grammar and lexicon, chronology, and his editions of cuneiform texts.

Within these confines, both "broad" papers have been selected, which give an introduction to or an overview of a specific subject, and "narrow" papers that give an in-depth study of a single issue or a single text. The first two papers provide a general introduction to the subject; the next nine papers focus on Old Assyrian society, and the final eight papers concern Old Babylonian.

The papers were basically reprinted in their original form, with just some typographical errors silently corrected. However, especially the older ones were updated by Klaas himself.

Small additions – mainly additional references to the bibliography and to newly published texts – have not been marked as such. Substantial additions to the main text have been put in a separate indented paragraph and marked "Addition" or "Addendum". Those in the footnotes have been put between square brackets and introduced by a bold face "**Add.**". The original numbering of footnotes has been maintained and the page numbers of the original publications have been inserted in the text in bold print between square brackets.

The publication of this volume is made possible by a generous subsidy of The Netherlands Institute for the Near East. Our special thanks go to Prof. C. Waerzeggers, its present director, and C. H. van Zoest, its secretary, for their practical support.

Moreover, we are much indebted to the following publishers, institutions and editors for their permission to reprint the papers included in this volume:

Brill (Leiden/Boston) for:

"A Deed of Manumission and Adoption from the Later Old Assyrian Period", originally published in G. van Driel *et al.*, *Zikir šumim. Assyriological Studies Presented to F. R. Kraus on the Occasion of his Seventieth Birthday*, 1982, pp. 359-385.

"Ancient Assur. The City, its Traders, and its Commercial Network", originally published in the *Journal of the Economic and Social History of the Orient* 53 (2010) 39-82.

"Old Assyrian and Ancient Anatolian Evidence for the Care of the Elderly", originally published in M. Stol and S. P. Vleeming (eds.), *The Care of the Elderly in the Ancient Near East*. Studies in the Culture and History of the Ancient Near East, vol. 14, 1998, pp. 119-60.

"Before Hammurabi of Babylon. Law and the Laws in Early Mesopotamia", originally published in F. J. M. Feldbrugge (ed.), *The Law's Beginnings* (proceedings of a symposium held in Leiden May 2002), 2003, pp. 137-159.

The Netherlands Institute for the Near East (Leiden) for:

"Silver and Credit in Old Assyrian Trade", originally published in J.G. Dercksen (ed.), *Trade and Finance in Ancient Mesopotamia*, MOS Studies 1, 1999, pp. 55-83.

"Old Assyrian *iṣurtum*, Akkadian *eṣērum* and Hittite GIŠ.ḪUR", originally published in Th. P. J. van den Hout and J. de Roos (eds.), *Studio Historiae Ardens. Ancient Near Eastern Studies Presented to Philo H. J. Houwink ten Cate*, 1995, pp. 311-332.

"The Relation between Royal Decrees and 'Law Codes' of the Old Babylonian Period", originally published in the *Jaarbericht van het Vooraziatisch-Egyptisch Genootschap Ex Oriente Lux* 35-36 (2001) 52-83.

"Trade with a Blessing of Šamaš in Old Babylonian Sippar", originally published in J.G. Dercksen (ed.), *Assyria and Beyond. Studies Presented to Mogens Trolle Larsen*, 2004, pp. 551-582.

Harrassowitz (Wiesbaden) for:

"Fatherhood is a Matter of Opinion. An Old Babylonian Trial on Filiation and Service Duties", originally published in W. Sallaberger *et al.* (eds), *Literatur, Politik und Recht in Mesopotamien. Festschrift für Claus Wilcke*, 2003, pp. 313-332.

"Old Assyrian and Old Babylonian Law. Some Comparative Observations", originally published in the *Zeitschrift für Altorientalische und Biblische Rechtsgeschichte*, 18 (2012) 141-174.

"L'Erma" di Bretschneider (Roma) for:

"Trade and Politics in Ancient Aššur. Balancing of Public, Colonial and Entrepreneurial Interests", originally published in C. Zaccagnini (ed.), *Trade and Politics in the Ancient World*. Saggi di Storia Antica 21, 2003, pp. 69-118.

Ugarit-Verlag (Münster) for:

"Redemption of Houses in Assur and Sippar", originally published in B. Böck, E. Cancik-Kirschbaum, and Th. Richter (eds), *Minuscula Mesopotamica, Festschrift für Johannes Renger*. AOAT 267, 1999, pp. 599-616.

EUT (Edizioni Università di Trieste) for:

The Archives of Old Assyrian Traders, their Nature, Functions and Use, originally published in M. Faraguna (ed.), *Archives and Archival Documents in Ancient Societies. Trieste 30 Sept. – 1 Oct. 2011*. Legal Documents in Ancient Societies IV, Graeca Tergestina, Storia e Civiltà 1. Triest 2013: EUT, pp. 27-61,

The *Chicago-Kent Law Review* (Chicago) for:

"In Accordance with the Words of the Stele": Evidence for Old Assyrian Legislation, originally published in *Chicago Kent Law Review* 70/4 (1995) 1717-44

Zerobooks (Istanbul) and S. Dönmez for:

"The Interpretation of Paragraphs t and u of the Code of Hammurabi", originally published in S. Dönmez, (ed.), *Studies Presented to Veysel Donbaz*, 2010, pp. 283-294.

Presses Universitaires de France for:

"The Dissolution of an Old Babylonian Marriage according to CT 45, 86", originally published in *Revue d'assyriologie et d'archéologie orientale* 70 (1976) 153-64.

Peeters (Leuven) and M. Tanret for:

Three OB Marriage Contracts involving *nadītum* and *šugītum*, originally published in M. Lebeau and Ph. Talon (eds), *Reflets des deux fleuves. Volume de mélanges offerts à André Finet*. Akkadica Supplementum 6. Leuven, 1989, pp. 181-89.

ADPF (Paris) and D. Charpin for:

"Assyrian Commercial Activities in Old Babylonian Sippar – Some New Evidence, originally published in D. Charpin and F. Johannès (eds), *Marchands, Diplomates et Empereurs, Études sur la civilization mésopotamienne offertes à Paul Garelli*, 1991, pp. 287-303.

Bloemendaal, November 2019
N.J.C. Kouwenberg

Abbreviations

Abbreviations for current editions of cuneiform texts are those used by the *CAD*. The following additional abbreviations used in this volume:[1]

AbB	*Altbabylonische Briefe in Umschrift und Übersetzung*, Leiden 1964-.
AC	P. Garelli, *Les Assyriens en Cappadoce*, Paris 1963.
Ad	Ammi-ditana (in OB year names).
Ae	Abi-ešuḫ (in OB year names).
AfO	*Archiv für Orientforschung*, Vienna.
AfO Beiheft 13/14	H. Hirsch, *Untersuchungen zur altassyrischen Religion*, AfO Beiheft 13/14, Osnabrück 1961; 2nd ed. 1972.
AHw	W. von Soden, *Akkadisches Handwörterbuch*, Wiesbaden 1959/81.
AKT	*Ankara Kültepe Tabletleri / Ankara Kültepe Texte / Kültepe Tabletleri*
AKT 3	Bilgiç, E. and Günbattı, C., *Ankaraner Kultepe-Texte* III: *Texte der Grabungskampagne 1970*. FAOS Beiheft 5, Stuttgart 1995.
AKT 4	Albayrak, İ., *Kültepe Tabletleri* IV (*Kt. o/k)*, TTKY VI/33b, Ankara 2006.
AKT 5	Veenhof, K.R., *The Archive of Kuliya, son of Ali-abum (Kt. 92/k 188-263), Kültepe Tabletleri* V, TTKY VI/33c, Ankara 2010.
AKT 6a-c	Larsen, M.T., *The Archive of the Šalim-Aššur Family.*Vol. 1. *The First Two Generations. Kültepe Tabletleri* VIa, TTKY VI/33d-a, Ankara 2010-2014.
AKT 7a	S. Bayram and R. Kuzuoğlu, *Aššur-rē'ī Ailesinin Arşivi, I. Cilt, Kültepe Tabletleri* VII-a, Ankara 2015.
AKT 8	K.R. Veenhof, *The Archive of Elamma, son of Iddin-Suen, and his Family* (*Kt. 91/k 285-568 and Kt. 92/k 94-187*), *Kültepe Tabletleri* VIII, Ankara, in the press.
AlT	D.J. Wiseman, *The Alalakh Tablets*, London 1953.
AMMY	*Anadolu Medeniyetleri Müzesi Yıllığı*, Ankara.
ANET	J.B. Pritchard, *Ancient Near Eastern Texts relating to the Old Testament*, Princeton 1950.
AnStud	*Anatolian Studies*, London.
AOAT	Alter Orient und Altes Testament, Münster.
AOATT	K. R. Veenhof, *Aspects of Old Assyrian Trade and its Terminology*, Leiden 1972.
AoF	*Altorientalische Forschungen*, Berlin.
AOS	American Oriental Society, New Haven.
ArAn(at)	*Archivum Anatolicum*, Ankara.
ArOr	*Archív Orientální*, Prague.
AS	Assyriological Studies, Chicago.
ASJ	*Acta Sumerologica*, Heroshima.
Assur	*Assur*, Monographic Journals of the Near East, Malibu.
AulOr	*Aula Orientalis*, Barcelona.

1 Lists of abbreviations can also be found in C. Michel, *Old Assyrian Bibliography* (OAAS 1, PIHANS 97, Leiden 2003), and in the *Reallexikon der Assyriologie und vorderasiatischen Archäologie* 13 (Berlin 2011-13), pp. III-LXV (and also in earlier volumes).

AulOrS 1	D. Arnaud, *Textes Syriens de l'Age du Bronze Recent.* Aula Orientalis Supplementa 1, Barcelona 1991.
BBVOT	Berliner Beiträge zum vorderen Orient. Texte, Berlin.
CAD	*The Assyrian Dictionary of the Oriental Institute of the University of Chicago*, Chicago, 1956-2010.
CBQ	*Catholic Biblical Quarterly*, Washington D.C.
CH	The Code of Hammurabi.
CMK	C. Michel, *Correspondance des marchands de Kaniš au début du IIe millénaire avant J.-C.*, LAPO 19, Paris 2001.
CRRAI	*Compte rendu des Rencontres Assyriologiques Internationales.*
CTMMA	M.T. Larsen, "Old Assyrian Texts", in I. Starr (ed.), *Cuneiform Texts in the Metropolitan Museum of Art*, Vol. 1. *Tablets, Cones and Bricks of the Third and Second Millennia*, New York 1998, 92-142, nos. 71-98.
CUSAS	Cornell University Studies in Assyriology and Sumerology, Bethesda Md.
DTCFD	*Dil ve Tarih-Coğrafya Fakültesi Dergisi*, Ankara.
EA	F.R. Kraus, *Ein Edikt des Könings Ammi-ṣaduqa von Babylon*, SD 5, Leiden 1958; 2nd ed. 1958.
EG	E. Grant, *Babylonian Business Documents of the Classical period*, Philadelphia 1919.
EL	G. Eisser and J. Lewy, *Altassyrische Rechtsurkunden vom Kültepe*, I-II. MVAeG 33 and 35/3, Leipzig 1930-1935.
ELTS	I.J. Gelb, P. Steinkeller, and R. M. Whiting, Jr. *Earliest Land Tenure Systems in the Near East: Ancient Kudurrus*, OIP 104, Chicago 1991.
Emar 6.3	D. Arnaud, *Recherches au Pays d'Astata. Emar 6.3. Textes sumeriens et accadiens*, Paris 1986.
FAOS	Freiburger Altorientalische Studien, Freiburg.
FAOSB	Freiburger Altorientalische Studien, Beihefte, Freiburg.
GAG	W. von Soden, *Grundriss der akkadischen Grammatik*, AnOr. 33, Rome 1952; 3rd ed. 1995.
GKT	K. Hecker, *Grammatik der Kültepe-Texte*, AnOr. 44, Rome 1968.
Ḫa	Hammurabi (in OB year names).
HdO	Handbuch der Orientalistik/Handbook of Oriental Studies.
Ḫḫ	Lexical Series *Ḫar-ra = Hubullu* (*Materialien zum sumerischen Lexicon* 5-11).
HUCA	*Hebrew Union College Annual*, Cincinnati.
HW	J. Friedrich *et al.*, *Hethitisches Wörterbuch*, Heidelberg 1975-
IEJ	*Israel Exploration Journal*, Jerusalem.
IFAO	Institut Français d'Archéologie Orientale, Cairo.
JA	*Journal Asiatique*, Paris.
JAOS	*Journal of the American Oriental Society*, New Haven.
JCS	*Journal of Cuneiform Studies*, New Haven/Boston.
JEOL	*Jaarbericht van het Vooraziatisch-Egyptisch Genootschap Ex Oriente Lux*, Leiden.
JESHO	*Journal of the Economic and Social History of the Orient*, Leiden.
JNES	*Journal of Near Eastern Studies*, Chicago.
JSOT	*Journal for the Study of the Old Testament*, Sheffield.
KLR	*Chicago-Kent Law Review*, Chicago.
Kt	Sigla of texts from Kültepe found in *kārum* Kanesh since 1948 and kept in the Anatolian Civilizations Museum at Ankara (in Kt a/k or Kt 73/k followed by a number, *Kt* stands for Kültepe, *a* or *73* identifies the year of excavation (*a-z* for 1948-1972, thereafter (19)73 etc., and *K* denotes the commercial quarter or lower town, *kārum* in Assyrian).
LAPO	Littératures anciennes du Proche Orient, Paris.
LAPO 16-18	J.-M. Durand, *Documents épistolaires du palais de Mari*, 3 vols, Paris 1997-2000.
LAPO 19	C. Michel, *Correspondance des marchands de Kanish*, Paris 2001.

LCMA — Martha T. Roth, *Law Collections from Mesopotamia and Asia Minor*, SBL Writings from the Ancient World Series 6, Atlanta 1995.

LE — Laws of Eshnunna (R. Yaron, *The Laws of Eshnunna*, 2nd edition, Jerusalem/ Leiden 1988.

LH — Laws of Hammurabi.

MA(ss) — Middle Assyrian.

MARI — *Mari, Annales de Recherches Interdisciplinaires*, Paris.

MDOG — *Mitteilungen der Deutschen Orientgesellschaft*, Berlin.

MHEO — Mesopotamian History and Environment, Occasional Publications, Ghent.

MHET — *Mesopotamian History and Environment. Texts*, Ghent.

MDP — *Mémoires de la Délégation en Perse*, Paris.

MSL — *Materialien zum sumerischen Lexicon*, Rome.

MSL 1 — B. Landsberger, *Die Serie ana ittišu. Materialien zum Sumerischen Lexikon*, 1, Roma 1937.

MVAeG — Mitteilungen der Vorderasiatisch-ägyptischen Gesellschaft, Leipzig.

NABU — *Nouvelles assyriologiques brèves et utilitaires*, Paris.

NH — E. P. Laroche, *Les noms des Hittites*, Paris 1966.

NHAI — Nederlands Historisch-Archeologisch Instituut, Istanbul.

NINO — Nederlands Instituut voor het Nabije Oosten, Leiden.

NKRU — P. Koschaker, *Neue keilschriftrechtliche Urkunden aus der El-Amarna-Zeit*, Leipzig 1928.

NRVU — M. San Nicolò and A. Ungnad, *Neubabylonische Rechts- und Verwaltungsurkunden*, Leipzig 1935-37.

OA(ss) — Old Assyrian.

OAA 1 — M.T. Larsen, *The Aššur-nādā Archive*, OAAS 1, PIHANS 96, Leiden 2002.

OAAS — Old Assyrian Archives, Studies, Leiden 2003-.

OACC — M.T. Larsen, *The Old Assyrian City-State and its Colonies*, Mesopotamia 6, Copenhagen, 1976.

OALP — Th.K. Hertel, *Old Assyrian Legal Procedures. Law and Dispute in the Ancient Near East*, OAAS 6, Leiden 2013.

OB — Old Babylonian.

OBO — Orbis Biblicus et Orientalis, Fribourg/Göttingen.

OBRED — L. Dekiere, *Old Babylonian Estate Documents from Sippar in the British Museum*, Ghent 1994-.

OLA — *Orientalia Lovanensia Analecta*, Leuven.

OLA 6 — E. Lipiński (ed.), *State and Temple Economy in the Ancient Near East*, vol. II, Leuven 1979.

OLA 21 — K. van Lerberghe, *Old Babylonian Legal and Administrative Texts from Philadelphia*, Leuven 1986.

OLZ — *Orientalistische Literaturzeitung*, Berlin.

Or(NS) — *Orientalia* (Nova Series), Roma.

PIHANS — Publications de l'Institut historique-archéologique néerlandais de Stamboul.

PN — personal name.

POAT — W.C. Gwaltney Jr., *The Pennsylvania Old Assyrian texts*, HUCA Supplements, 3, Cincinnati 1983.

Prag I — Siglum for the texts edited in K. Hecker, G. Kryszat, and L. Matouš, *Kappadokische Keilschrifttafeln aus den Sammlungen der Karlsuniversität Prag*, Prague 1998.

PRU — *Le palais royal d'Ugarit*, Paris.

RA — *Revue d'assyriologie et d'archéologie orientale*, Paris.

RAI — *Rencontres Assyriologiques Internationales*.

RB — *Revue biblique*, Jerusalem.

RIMA 1	The Royal Inscriptions of Mesopotamia. Assyrian Periods, vol. 1: A.K. Grayson, *Assyrian Rulers of the Third and Second Millennia BC (to 1115 BC)*, Toronto 1987.
RlA	*Reallexikon der Assyriologie und vorderasiatischen Archäologie*, Berlin.
RSO	*Rivista degli Studi Orientali*, Rome.
SAAB	*State Archives of Assyria Bulletin*, Padua.
SAOC	Studies in Ancient Oriental Civilization, Chicago.
SCCNH	*Studies on the Civilization and Culture of Nuzi and the Hurrians*, Winona Lake.
SD	*Studia et Documenta ad Iura Orientis Antiqui Pertinentia*, Leiden.
SD 5	F.R. Kraus, *Ein Edikt des Könings Ammi-ṣaduqa von Babylon*, 1958.
SD 6	W.F. Leemans, *Foreign Trade in the Old Babylonian Period as Revealed by Texts from Southern Babylonia*, 1960.
SD 9	J. Brugman *et al.*, *Essays on Oriental Laws of Succession*, 1969.
SD 10	K.R. Veenhof, *Aspects of Old Assyrian Trade and its Terminology*, 1972.
SD 11	F.R. Kraus, *Königliche Verfügungen in altbabylonischer Zeit*, 1984.
SEL	*Studi epigraphici e linguistici sul Vicino Oriente antico*, Verona.
Si	Samsu-iluna (in OB year names).
SKIZ	W.H.Ph. Römer, *Sumerische 'Königshymnen' der Isin-Zeit*, Leiden 1965.
SLB	*Studia ad tabulas cuneiformes a F.M.Th. de Liagre Böhl collectas pertinentia.*
SLB 4	R. Frankena, *Kommentar zu den altbabylonischen Briefen aus Lagaba und anderen Orten*, Leiden, 1978.
Studies Donbaz	S. Dönmez (ed.), *Studies Presented to Veysel Donbaz*, Istanbul 2010.
Studies Garelli	D. Charpin and F. Joannès (eds.), *Marchands, diplomates et empereurs. Études sur la civilisation mésopotamienne offertes à P. Garelli*, Paris 1991.
Studies Lands-berger	H.G. Güterbock and Th. Jacobsen (eds.), *Studies in Honor of Benno Landsberger on his Seventy-Fifth Birthday, April 21, 1965*, AS 16, Chicago 1965.
Studies Larsen	J.G. Dercksen (ed.), *Assyria and Beyond. Studies Presented to Mogens Trolle Larsen*, PIHANS 100, Leiden 2004.
Studies N. Özgüç	M.J. Mellink *et al.* (eds.), *Aspects of Art and Iconography. Anatolia and its Neighbors. Studies in Honor of Nimet Özgüç*, Ankara 1993.
Studies T. Özgüç	K. Emre *et al.* (eds.), *Anatolia and the Ancient Near East. Studies in Honor of Tahsin Özgüç*, Ankara 1989.
Studies Veenhof	W.H. van Soldt *et al.* (eds.), *Veenhof Anniversary Volume. Studies Presented to Klaas R. Veenhof on the Occasion of his Sixty-fifth Birthday*, PIHANS 89, Leiden 2001.
Studies Günbattı	İ. Albayrak, H. Erol, and M. Çayır (eds.), *Studies in Honour of Cahit Günbattı*, Ankara 2015.
ThWAT	*Theologisches Wörterbuch zum Alten Testament*, Stuttgart.
TLB	*Tabulae Cuneiformes a F. M. Th. de Liagre Böhl Collectae*, Leiden, 1954-.
TPAK	C. Michel and P. Garelli, *Tablettes paléo-assyriennes de Kültepe*, 1 (*Kt 90/k*), Paris 1997.
TVE	G. Beckman, *Texts from the Vicinity of Emar in the Collection of Jonathan Rosen*, Padova 1996.
UAR	H. Hirsch, *Untersuchungen zur altassyrischen Religion*, AfO Beiheft 13/14. Osnabrück 1961; 2nd ed. 1972.
VAB 5	M. Schorr, *Urkunden des altbabylonischen Zivil- und Prozessrechts*, Leipzig 1913.
WO	*Die Welt des Orients*, Göttingen / Tübingen.
WZKM	*Wiener Zeitschrift für die Kunde des Morgenlandes*, Vienna.
YNER	Yale Near Eastern Researches, New Haven.
ZA	*Zeitschrift für Assyriologie und vorderasiatische Archäologie*, Berlin.
ZAR	*Zeitschrift für Altorientalische und Biblische Rechtsgeschichte*, Wiesbaden.

Justice and Equity in Babylonia*

Around 1700 BC, during he reign of Hammurabi's son Samsu-iluna, a Babylonian man, called Sherum-ili got into serious financial problems for reasons unknown to us. The only way out he saw was to borrow a few shekels of silver (one shekel is a decent monthly wage) at an annual interest of 20%. When his creditor asked for a security, he ceded his field to him, formally by means of a tenancy contract in which the loan received counted as advance payment of the tenancy fee, but in fact as a pledge to be used by the creditor. In due time he expected to receive in due time still some barley, to wit that part of the harvest that according to legal custom would accrue to the owner of the field, naturally after deduction of the silver borrowed plus the interest due on it. But this was a miscalculation, for the creditor appropriated the complete harvest. He then turned to a protector or superior of his for help, who wrote a letter of protest to the creditor that has recently been published, which acquaints us with this case.[1]

Such letters are an important source of information on the social and economic history of Babylonia. The Department of Assyriology at Leiden since the arrival there of my teacher and predecessor Fritz Rudolf Kraus, has devoted much attention to the reconstruction and understanding of Babylonian and has edited a corpus of Old Babylonian letters that are an important source for this study.[2] Letters complement the usually short and businesslike contracts that by their very nature offer a snapshot. They may reveal something of the background and effects of such a transaction, of its economic context and of the personal aspects of it, in particular if we can study them as part of a family archive. Moreover, they allow a comparison of the rulings laid down in the Mesopotamian law collections on such matters with what, at least from the viewpoint of those directly involved, was the reality.

The above-mentioned letter was part of a group of texts excavated in the previous century by illegal diggers in a little Babylonian town called Lagaba. Through antique dealers part of the collection arrived in the Yale Babylonian Collection (among them the above mentioned letter) and another part in the Ashmolean Museum at Oxford, and a group was confiscated while still in Iraq and is now in the Baghdad Museum. Some sixty years ago about 125 texts of it were purchased by Professor De Liagre Böhl, the first full professor of Assyriology in Leiden. They were edited in 1968 by Böhl's former student R. Frankena,[3] as vol. 3 of the series "Corpus of Old Babylonian Letters". My first task, when I was appointed as research-assistant in Assyriology, was to assist in editing them.

The above-mentioned letter is a document that allows us to look behind the scenes of the legal system, where what the Babylonians called "justice" and "equity" met. They are two related and partly overlapping concepts that together embody what the notion "righteousness" comprises. Babylonian theology knows them as hypostases, sons of the

* English translation (made in 2015) of the public lecture delivered in Dutch, entitled Recht en Gerechtigheid in Babylonië, at Leiden University on 12-12-2000, on the occasion of my retirement as professor in the Languages and History of Babylonia and Assyria. My daughter Martine helped me to improve the quality of my English.

1 Published by O. Tammuz, in *RA* 90 (1996) 125f.

2 Edited in the series *Altbabylonische Briefe in Umschrift und Übersetzung* (Leiden, Brill; abbreviated as *AbB* in what follows), in which thirteen volumes with together ca. 2400 letters have been published since 1964 [in 2005 the present writer published vol. 14, *Letters in the Louvre*].

3 After he had been appointed at the University of Utrecht.

sun god Shamash, the god of justice.[4] But their content, purpose and practical implications differ. According to its etymology "justice" (*kittum*) is what is fixed and stable, what is true. Among others things it qualifies measures, weights and words. "Justice" is the basis of law and falls under the sun god, who grants it to the king he has mandated and so prepares him for his task.[5] It materializes in verdicts, which may acquire the status of laws, and has to be maintained and applied by judges. According to its etymology "equity" (*mīšarum*) is what is correct, sincere, fair and normal. It qualifies rulers, verdicts, actions and prices and refers to the social order and welfare that have to be maintained or restored. Practicing "equity" results in what is just and fair, also from the social perspective.[6]

On the basis of the information provided by the plaintiff we would expect the writer of our letter, to ask that the "law" be maintained and justice be done to him. The law collection of Hammurabi had been published only some twenty years earlier and been made accessible on imposing diorite stelae placed in various cities of his empire. And in their epilogue (col. 48:3-19) the king had invited everyone who had suffered injustice to (have) read out (to him) the texts of his "righteous verdicts", to get insight into his case and (so we believe), armed with this knowledge, bring his opponent to court. This expectation seems justified, because § 49 of the collection deals precisely with the case described in our letter. We read:

> "If a man borrows silver from a merchant[7] and gives him a field prepared for planting with either barley or sesame (as pledge) and declares to him: 'You cultivate the field and collect and take away as much barley or sesame as will be grown' – if the cultivator should produce either barley or sesame in the field, at the harvest it is only the owner of the field who shall take the barley or the sesame that is grown in the field, and he shall give to the merchant the barley (or sesame) equivalent to his silver which he borrowed from the merchant and the interest on it and also the expenses of the cultivation".

By means of this regulation the king wished to prevent that "the mighty wrongs the weak" (col. 47:59f.). The surplus resulting from a fair balancing of the size of the debt with the yield of the harvest from the pledged field should accrue to the debtor who is its owner.[8]

I assume that our plaintiff may also have thought of this regulation, for when he complains about the appropriation by his creditor of the complete harvest he uses the technical term found in the laws, "to collect and take away", a hendiadys for "to take along everything.[9] The Assyriologist is most willing to follow his view, because lawsuits about conflicts that are identical to cases described in Hammurabi's instructive and learned law collection (that cotains many specific and exceptional, perhaps construed cases) are

---

4 Just like in Greece Δίκη, the personification of penal justice, is a son of the sun god [see D. Holwerda, *Helios en Dike bij Heraclitus* (public lecture, Groningen 1969)].

5 Codex Hammurabi col. 48:95ff.: "I am Hammurabi, the righteous king (*šar mīšarim*), to whom Shamash has granted the truth (*kīnātim*)." A contemporary royal inscription from Mari states that this "truth" has been granted to Shamash himself (by whom is left open). Just as Hammurabi wishes to be a "righteous king", so "justice" is also the lot or share, the assigned task (*isqum*), of Shamash.

6 The word pair *kittum u mīšarum* has an exact parallel in later Hebrew *'èmèt weṣedāqā*.

7 The word translated "merchant" (*tamkārum*) can also mean moneylender and creditor, since merchants, who had silver at their disposal, usually were the ones to give out loans.

8 The same purpose is served by § z, where in the case of a silver debt paid by handing over goods (*datio in solutum*) the value of the latter ("what they yield") is taken into account. In Middle Assyrian times this could be stipulated by contract, if pledged goods had to be sold (see *Assur* 3/1 (1980) no.2:1f.).

9 In Babylonian *esip tabal*. This expression is also used when a tenant, because he has opened up new land or for other reasons, is entitled to retain part of the yield as compensation for the additional labor he has had to perform (see *SOAC* 44 no. 32; TIM 5, 42; TLB 1, 206; YOS 12, 401). For the use of this terminology in connection with pledging a field, see G. Mauer, *Das Formular der altbabylonischen Bodenpachtverträge* (München 1980) 78f., and earlier P. Koschaker, *Über einige griechische Rechts-urkunden aus den östlichen Randgebieten des Hellenismus* (Leipzig 1931) 93f.

extremely rare. Practical application of § 49 then would become a valuable argument in the still unresolved discussion about the nature, authority and function of what are usually called the "Laws of Hammurabi".

The writer of the letter, unfortunately, disappoints us by not appealing to the law. He chooses a different strategy, because in the mean time king Samsu-iluna (Hammurabi's son and successor) had taken a legal measure – probably not yet known to the plaintiff – in order, as he states in an official letter sent around when he succeeds his father on the throne of Babylon, to "provide justice to the land" and "to make strong" his subjects.[10] The writer refers to his royal decree and confronts his correspondent (the creditor) with its substance: "As you know, according to the decree of my lord, the king, whoever has collected a debt has to pay it back!"

Such a decree meant that the arrears of servants of the crown and interest bearing loans contracted by citizens in economic distress were remitted and their collection was forbidden.[11] Apparently the decree also applied to Sherum-ili's debt and appropriation of the yield of the pledged field was tantamount to collecting a debt and therefore unjustified and punishable.[12] Therefore the writer of the letters concludes by: "Is this the way you have executed the ruling of the decree of my lord the king, (by) depriving him in his absence of his barley? Give the barley you took back to its owner!"

To stick to the terminology of the title of this lecture, the writer of the letter does not ask to maintain "justice" by applying the law, but to assure "equity" by obeying a decree that remits debts. One could argue that this choice was based on calculation, because the decree that cancels the whole debt would yield a few shekels more than an application of the law, which would guarantee the plaintiff only the (small) part of the harvest to which he was entitled. But the matter is not as simple as that, for while appeals to such royal decrees restoring equity regularly occurring in letters (which occasionally even quote them), none of the letters, nor the hundreds of Old Babylonian judicial records contain a single appeal to or a quotation from the law. This raises the question why none of their writers failed to do so, what was the idea behind their action and what was their aim.

The Babylonian king was the manager or governor of the god of his city or land. His duty was not only to care for the god's temples and cult, but also to guard, as a shepherd for his flock, for the welfare of his subjects, the people of his god. Welfare meant safety, prosperity and maintenance of justice. Therefore official inscriptions proclaim therefore, also to future generations, that the king has performed this duty. They report on the building of temples and the fashioning and dedication of statues of the gods, on military successes and fortifications, they mention the digging of irrigation canals and also the concern for just prices and the maintenance of justice and equity.

The most eloquent phrasing of this last task is found in the prologue to Hammurabi's law collection, the rulings of which are presented as obtaining during his reign. The king "has to rise over his people as the sun (god)", in order "to make justice and equity appear in the land, to eradicate who is wicked and evil and to prevent the strong from oppressing the weak" (col. 1:27ff.). We are inclined to summarize this as "maintaining justice by preventing or punishing evil", and what better way to achieve this than by putting the

10 See for this letter F.R. Kraus, *Königliche Verfügungen in altbabylonischer Zeit* (SD 11, Leiden 1984) 66f. [In the mean time this letter has been edited as *AbB* 14, 130 (see above note 2)].

11 I simplify by not dealing with the case of servants of the crown who have arrears in delivering what they owe. The debtor in our case is called "musician" (possibly in the service of the palace) and he may have been such a servant. In that case we have to assume that the pledged field had been given him as a "sustenance field", which provided him his livelihood and part of yield of which he had to deliver to the palace. However this may be, this is not important for my argument here.

12 This is probably the reason why the tenancy contract AO 9080, mentioned by Kraus *op. cit.* (see note 10) 69, B S-i 4, contains the note "after the decree"; a royal decree was only retroactive and did not apply to new contracts.

king's "just verdicts (*dīnāt mišarim*) into the mouth of the land" (col. 5:14f.)? [13] Still, this is only part of the truth as the king explains in the epilogue. His goal is not only to punish perpetrators and solve conflicts, but also to provide "justice and equity for the waif and the widow", to help those who are weak.[14]

The king here uses words that are at least six hundred years old by then. As far as we know they were first used by the ruler Uru'inimgina of Lagash, according to the title of a Dutch novel "the good shepherd, who slays the wolves", and according to Thierry, the first scholar to occupy the (by then still special) chair of Assyriology in Leiden, "an energetic reformer ... guided by sublime seriousness and noble insight".[15] He promised the god of his city under oath "that he would not surrender waif and widow to the mighty".[16] And these words, which have made history, mean more than maintaining justice and enforcing the law. As is clear from the texts called "Uru'inimgina's reform edicts", they aim at abolishing abuse and protecting the weak.[17]

Of old the weak have suffered from the mighty, which were helped by customary law, which rigorously protected property rights and allowed forcing debtors to pay back what they owed at any cost. Without a family as safety net the weak could in adverse times easily loose their property in adverse times and subsequently also their freedom. Redeeming family members and property was a traditional right, but its realization was often difficult.[18] Therefore the king had to come into action and intervene to "restore equity", that is to restore the previous, just situation But helping the weak was difficult to realize by means of laws and courts-of law only.[19] This is the reason why kings, in times of crisis, especially during the first centuries of the 2nd mill. BC, intervened to prevent social disruption. Not only arrears in deliveries to the crown, but also private, consumptive debts were cancelled. Family members and dependents that had been pledged or sold (into debt slavery) could return to their homes.[20] Using a metaphor that we can understand the texts speak of "washing away debts", which allows citizens, after "their debt-notes have been thrown away / broken", to start again with a clean slate.

Of course such measures were popular and good for the king's reputation, an instrument to earn the sympathy of large sections of the population. The memory of them was kept alive by recording them in royal inscriptions and mentioning them in year names ("Year in which the king..."). It does not come as a surprise that such measures were regularly enacted when a new king ascended the throne (as shown by the letter of Samsu-iluna, *AbB* 14, 130, quoted above). Once (*AbB* 12, 172) it is said that the king at his accession "has washed away the dirt of the country", an expression which probably refers

---

13 In her edition *Law Collections from Mesopotamia and Asia Minor* (Atlanta, 1997^2), Martha Roth translates these words as "I established the declaration of the land", which probably means that the "just verdicts" were proclaimed in the land. I believe that these words state the ideal that all subjects will be just and fair when they speak (and what they speak should come from the heart). This ideal is comparable to that voiced by the prophet Jeremiah (31:31f.), that the law is written in man's heart, which implies its knowledge and secures its application.

14 "Weak" (*enšum*) also has a clear economic connotation. The Laws of Eshunnah in § 39 deal with a man who, because "he has become weak (Roth: impoverished) sells his house".

15 G J. Thierry, *Vorsten uit Oud-Babylonië tijdens de eerste bloeiperiode van de stad Lagasj* (Leiden 1913) 25. The novel by the well-owner author Theun de Vries was published in 1946.

16 His predecessor Entemena, fifty years earlier, had taken similar measures in order to realize "freedom" (amargi, see below note 19) and canceled interest bearing grain loans.

17 See the translation by Th.J.H. Krispijn, in K.R. Veenhof (ed.), *Schrijvend Verleden. Documenten uit het Oude Nabije Oosten vertaald en toegelicht* (Ex Oriente Lux, Leiden 1983) 126-130.

18 See e.g. my "Redemption of Houses in Assur and Sippar", in: B. Böck *et al.* (eds.), *Munuscula Mesopotamica. Festschrift für Johannes Renger* (AOAT 267, Münster 1999) 599-616 [= pp. 211-223 in this volume].

19 The king realized or restored *andurārum* (a term that lives on in Hebrew *derōr*), which is used in connection with the manumission of slaves and in the Hebrew Bible with the "sabbatical year". Its Sumerian precursor is the above mentioned amargi, lit. "return to the mother", which means restoration of the previous/original good situation. "Freedom" as its result is only one aspect of it and may evoke a wrong picture, see D. Charpin, "Les décrets royaux à l'époque paléo-babylonienne", *AfO* 34 (1987) 36-44.

20 See for the texts describing such measures, Kraus (*op. cit.*, note 10).

both to the cancellation of debts and to the termination of a period of mourning after the death of his predecessor.[21] Such measures were also proclaimed after the conquest of a city, apparently in order to reassure its population and to win support for the new ruler. For it was from the population at large that rulers, from Uru'inimgina until Samsu-Iluna, recruited their soldiers, laborers, tenants, craftsmen and clerks, who were the backbone of their power. Restoring justice and social equilibrium therefore also served the palace's own interests.

But this is no reason for a cynical perspective on these measures, because social justice and palatial interest can go together. By remitting arrears the palace indeed gave up income and claims, but it also meant writing off in many cases claims that could not be collected. And the measures also concerned private consumptive debts, including the consequences of bankruptcy. Their social effects are also clear from the fact that merchants, moneylenders and people exploiting economic problems of others could not profit from them.[22] Careful descriptions of what was affected by the royal measure, possible exceptions and the ways in which the measures should be executed, were meant to prevent their misuse or attempts by clever people to get around them.[23]

Maintaining the law and striving for equity need not be antipoles. Application of the law also serves and restores justice, by punishing crimes and repairing wrongs. King Hammurabi himself also makes this connection, for the stela inscribed with his laws also features a relief, which shows the sun god giving him the symbols of his office and his mandate, and he calls its "my image as king of equity" (*šar mīšarim*). The rules of law inscribed under this relief, which have to prove that he indeed lives up to his mandate, are called "equitable/righteous verdicts" (*dīnāt mīšarim*), they exhibit both justice and equity.

Babylonia in Hammurabi's time was indeed a state in which justice ruled in spite of its social imperfections. The hundreds of judicial records document that justice was administered conscientiously, centrally and locally. The king was also accessible for complaints by subjects who had suffered private or administrative injustice. His letters order his civil servants to pass verdicts in accordance with the royal decrees and to treat the plaintiffs honestly, and undoubtedly the righteous rulings inscribed on the stele are partly based on precedents created by actual royal jurisdiction.

But social justice was also done. While most laws on the stela lay down how justice has to prevail in a great variety of cases, there are also regulations that aim at helping weak citizens, also in cases where they are not the victims of crimes or injustice. According to § 47 a tenant farmer, who has been unable to bring in a harvest due to the flooding of his fields, is entitled to see his tenancy term extended by a year, so that he gets the opportunity to recover. And if this happens to him due to lack of irrigation water, while he needs the harvest to pay off a debt, he is also entitled to pay back one year later, the next paragraph states. And we have already seen how § 49, quoted above, protects the rights of farmer who had to pledge his field. In these cases – which could be multiplied – the principle of "equity" prevails over the right of a creditor, who normally has the law on his side. And if such a debtor for lack of any other option but to sell family members into

---

21 See D. Charpin, *RA* 87 (1993) 87, and also his study "Les prêteurs et le palais", in A.C.V.M. Bongenaar (ed.), *Interdependence of Institutions and Private Entrepreneurs* (MOS Studies 2, Istanbul, 2000) 185 note 1. The date of this letter suggests that it refers to the death of Samsu-iluna and the accession of Abi-ešuh.

22 See § 20 of the Edict of Ammi-ṣaduqa. Its § 9 does cancel default interest due by trading agents that have exceeded their terms, but here too the weaker one – the commission agent – is protected against the mighty, his capitalist and investor.

23 § 4 of the edict even deals with what happens if the year has an intercalary month, which affects the due date of debts and may lead to their premature collection.

debt-slavery or to make them serve his creditor as "antichretic pledges", then, as § 117 stipulates, they regain their freedom after three years.[24]

The ruler also tries to come to the aid of the weak by protecting them against the harmful effects of he market. At times people in economic problems could only borrow grain by accepting that their debt in silver was to be paid back at harvest time "at the then current rate of exchange". In this way creditors, using the market mechanism, could get back more than they had given, because the silver loaned late in the year would yield more grain at harvest time, when it was cheaper. Royal legislators tried to prevent this and the Laws of Eshnunna (perhaps two generations older than those of Hammurabi) stipulate in § 19 that the creditor at harvest time only receives what he has actually loaned, irrespective of the rate of conversion of grain to silver.[25] And Hammurabi even goes a step further by stipulating that an actual silver loan can also be paid in grain if the debtor is unable to pay back in silver. The amount of grain is then increased by interest according a standard rate of conversion, which must also apply to the loan itself.[26] These rulings protect debtors, who has to pay pack with a substantial interest anyhow, against what in German is called "verhüllte Fruchtwucher", disguised usury that exploits the seasonally fluctuating rates of exchange.

The righteous king, just like Solon in Athens much later, in this way wishes to include stipulations in the law that promote equity in cases where there is no question of crimes or law breaking, but of social injustice due to the merciless law of obligations. The program includes the offer of a second chance, extension of payment for unlucky debtors and tenants, rules about the usufruct of goods pledged, prevention of valuta manipulations in the interest of the creditor, prohibition of excesses in the case of debt bondage, and limitation of the duration of the loss of freedom due to defaulting on debts.

What did this mean in practice? Unfortunately, records hardly ever reveal how these new regulations were applied. Only a few tenancy contracts (in which a debt had to be paid from the yield of the harvest), predating Hammurabi's time,[27] give us some information. In them the indebted (tenant) farmer has to promise that he will not refuse payment on account of forces of nature (such as flooding of his fields). Creditors who drew up such contracts apparently took such potential excuses into account and in a few contracts of the Ur III period (ca. 250 years before Hammurabi) the debtor is also forbidden to appeal to the king or the head of the temple in such cases, which suggests that the latter could intervene and enforce extension of payment. Hammurabi thus raised the legal status of such escape mechanisms by integrating them in his law collection and by trying to make them independent of judicial decisions. Moreover, he broadened their range by including

---

24 In the Hebrew "Covenant Code" (Ex. 21:2) the slave only becomes free after six years and girls do not get free at all, but may be redeemed (Ex. 21:7-8). Protection of the weak is also found in § 106f. of Hammurabi's Code, where a trading agent who has received silver as credit, but denies this, has to pay back three times the amount as penalty. But if his boss, the trader or capitalist, denies that he has received back payments, he has to pay six times the amount borrowed. Financial power and status make a difference in what are rather similar crimes.

25 The "loan converted into silver" is contrasted with the previously mentioned one that had been in silver right away (*ana panišu*).

26 The regulation in question, § u, is only known from two damaged manuscripts and the current reading and edition have to be corrected [see now my article "The Interpretation of Paragraphs t and u of the Code of Hammurabi", in Ş. Dönmez (ed.), *DUB.SAR É.DUB.BA.A. Studies presented in Honour of Veysel Donbaz* (Istanbul 2010) 283-94 = pp. 285-296 in this volume]. The "royal decree" referred to in paragraphs u and 51 in my opinion also applies to the "rate of exchange" (*mahīrum*) mentioned.

27 Some are from the Ur III period (21st century BC), analyzed by C. Wilcke in his article "Flurschäden verursacht durch Hochwasser, Unwetter, Militär, Tiere und schuldhaftes Verhalten zur Zeit der 3. Dynastie von Ur", in: H. Klengel and J. Renger (eds.), *Landwirtschaft im Alten Orient. Ausgewählte Vorträge der XLI. Rencontre Assyriologique Internationale, Berlin 1994* (Berlin 1999) 301-339. Old Babylonian examples are UET 5, 212 (see H.P.H. Petschow, *ZA* 74 (1984) 189f.) and E.C. Stone, *Nippur Neighborhoods* (SAOC 44, Chicago, 1987) pl. 73, no. 66.

flooding and lack of irrigation water as valid reasons for not paying.[28] Such a measure is typical for a lawgiver and reformer: exceptions and possibilities become normative rulings and more general regulations are grafted on specific cases.[29] In this way an amount of "equity" was integrated in the law.

But however well meant these rulings were, their impact, assuming that they were effectuated, must have been very limited; they were changes in the margin. Paying debts with the normal interest – 20% for silver loans, 30% for grain – remained a legal obligation, for property rights were inviolable and a creditor was entitled to take hard measures against a defaulting debtor. In the case of poor harvests, illness or disasters (ecological or caused by war) the victim ended up in a downward spiral, that easily led to poverty, loss of property and servitude.[30] The soft loans that temples occasionally provided to persons in distress only offered limited and temporal solace.[31]

For a conscientious Babylonian ruler it was difficult to reconcile this reality with his divine mandate and it could also be harmful for his empire. Therefore, when a crisis disturbed the economic order and the social equilibrium, he intervened by means of a "decree of equity", which could work as a safety valve to reduce the pressures. He did so at irregular times, but not infrequently. During Samsu-iluna's thirty-eight years long reign this happened four times.[32] First at his accession, eleven years after the previous decree of his father, and the last time, in his final year, while his son and successor Abi-ešuh followed his father's example eleven years later, at his accession. This is an average of about once every ten years.

Such decrees were drastic events with considerable administrative consequences that generated quite some written documentation. Canceling debts and annulling contracts required checks to establish to which transactions the edict did apply and to which it did not. Usually judges were involved in getting back immovable property sold because of now canceled debts and we know that once an official conference was held to implement the remission of arrears due to the palace and the return of alienated crown land.

Such a measure was also drastic for another reason. It meant nothing less than invalidating by royal intervention, loans and sales contracted according to the rules of common law and sealed by parties and witnesses. The king derived the authority to do so from his divine mandate. One letter (*AbB* 7, 153) writes that by means of such a decree the king "restored equity for the god Shamash, who loves him". When it was proclaimed, the king "raised a golden torch",[33] a symbolic action that refers to the sun (god). In my opinion the king hereby wished to show that he would rise like the sun over his subjects and bring light in their darkness, as Hammurabi had stated in his law collection and Ammi-ṣaduqa in his year-names. [34] Judging from what year-names of various Babylonian kings, from Samsu-iluna till Ammi-ṣaduqa, say about these decrees one can say that at the beginning

28 Ur III texts (see Wilcke, *op. cit.*, previous note, 334f.) show that the administration also helped subjects (usually servants of the crown, who had received "sustenance fields") who had been unable to harvest due to lack of irrigation water, by advancing them money.

29 Compare the by now almost classical example of a royal regulation of the rules concerning property owned by a class of unmarried, religious women, dedicated to the sun god. The ruling originated from a decision evoked by a concrete complaint, cf. S Lafont, "Les actes législatifs des rois mésopotamiens", in: S. Dauchy *et al.* (eds.), *Auctoritates. Xenia R.C. van Caenegem Oblata* (Iuris Scripta Historica XIII, Bruxelles 1997) 22f., with my analysis in *JEOL* 35-36 (1997-2000) 56ff., § 3.

30 The various phases of such a fate have been well described in M. Stol, *Een Babyloniër maakt schulden* (inaugural lecture at the Free University, Amsterdam 1983).

31 See for such loans R. Harris, *JCS* 14 (1968) 126-37, and A. Skaist, *The Old Babylonian Loan Contract* (Ramat Gan 1994) 171f.

32 The decree of his 17th year was discovered by E. Woestenburg, cf. *AfO* 44/45 (1997/8) 355. See for the various Babylonian decrees Kraus, *op. cit.* (note 10), 50-85, and for their frequency Charpin, *op. cit.* (note 21) 202f., § 4.4.

33 Cf. also *AbB* 12 172, Kraus, *op. cit.* (note 10) 55, 71f., and presumably ARM 8, 6:17'f. (cf. *MARI* 6 (1990) 294f.).

34 In *NABU* 1997/116 B. Lion makes the interesting suggestion that this happened in spring, when nature renewed itself and new expectations arose.

of his rule the king presents himself as the divinely appointed good shepherd, who makes his subjects happy by canceling their debts and restoring good relations. It was divine authorization that made it possible to let such decrees prevail over current contractual law.[35] In a letter from Mari it is the sun god himself who instructs the king, via his prophet, to let the whole population of a conquered city benefit from such a measure.[36]

Did such royal measures not create legal uncertainty and confusion? This is difficult to assess, for we have seen that they were taken with considerable intervals and that they applied primarily to private, consumptive debts of modest size. Large debts and those due to commercial transactions (loans, credit, investment) were not affected. Of course, they were not welcomed by moneylenders and creditors who lost money, nor by those who had bought pledged and auctioned property of defaulting debtors at attractive prices. The temptation to circumvent the effects of such a decree by tampering with debt-notes (changing their date or stated purposes) or by intimidating debtors is documented, but the texts of the decrees (*e.g.* Edict of Ammi-ṣaduqa § 4-7) anticipate such attempts by stipulating heavy penalties for such actions. Judicial records and letters prove that the authorities monitored their correct implementation.

Other countries or states – Assyria, Nuzi and Mari – followed the example of Babylonia and its impact is also noticeable in Anatolia and Northern Syria, areas subject the influence of "cuneiform law".[37] We do not have the texts of such measures there – usually designated by the term *(an)durārum / uddurārum*[38] – but we know of their existence from letters and especially from two kinds of notes in deeds of sale and debt acknowledgments. The first states that the transaction recorded took place "after the decree", which meant that the decree could not cancel the transaction, since it had only retroactive force. The second tries to protect buyers and creditors contractually against the effects of such decrees. The first type is well known from Babylonia itself and an understandable notification to show that the contract is valid; in fact, a buyer or creditor may even have waited until after the decree before concluding the contract.

The second type is unknown from Babylonia and therefore deserves special attention. It stipulates that debt claims and acquisitions of fields or slaves in consequence of pledging or forced sale are "not liable to cancellation", and even may write explicitly that debts have to be paid "even when the king washes away the debts". This type is an attempt to frustrate the effect of an expected royal measure. Some Neo Assyrian debt-notes also write that the creditor who has to give back the fields or manumit the slaves he has acquired, nevertheless retains a claim (the verb used is *dagālum*) on his silver, that the debt has to be paid back.[39] In Nuzi we come across a creditor who, when a debt-slave of his had regained her freedom, demands another woman in her place. A loan contract from Alalakh (in Northern Syria) stipulates that the creditor will not claim interest and that (therefore) cancellation will not take place.[40]

---

35 A comparable measure in ancient Assur, meant to facilitate the redemption of family houses sold because of debts (not to cancel debts, because the royal measures did not apply to commercial debts such as those of the Old Assyrian traders) and taken by the City Assembly is nevertheless designated as "an act of mercy of the god Assur for his city" (see Veenhof, *op. cit.*, note 18).

36 See Charpin, *op. cit.* (note 19) 40f.

37 See for Mari and Northern Syria, D. Charpin, "L'*andurārum* à Mari", *MARI* 6 (1990) 253-70. For younger period also E. Otto, "Programme der sozialen Gerechtigkeit. Die neuassyrische *(an)duraru*-Institution sozialen Ausgleichs und das deuteronomische Erlassjahr in Dtn 15", *ZAR* 3 (1997) 26-63 [and for some additions and corrections P. Villard, "L'*andurāru* à l'époque néo-assyriene", *RA* 101 (2007) 107-124].

38 In Old Assyrian contracts we find the expression "to wash away debts" [and once (unpublished) also "to release (by means of) an *andurārum*". In a treaty between Assyrian traders and an Anatolian ruler the (possible) "manumission of slaves" is rendered by "to realize their *andurārum*"]. Neo Assyrian records [see Villard *op. cit.*, previous note] write about the king restoring the (good) previous situation (*da/urāru*).

39 Cf. *State Archives of Assyria* VI (Helsinki 1991) 226 and *Cuneiform Texts from Nimrud* II, 248. In *State Archives* VI, 259, a contract passed "after the *darāru*", stipulates that the debtor can only redeem the field he lost by pledging, if he pays the creditor the double of the original debt [see now Villard, *op. cit.*, note 37].

40 *Alalakh Texts* no. 42.

Attempts to frustrate or circumvent such royal decrees of equity are not restricted to the cultures employing the cuneiform script. The are known also from ancient Israel with its sabbatical year; after seven years debt-slaves became free and debts were cancelled. But the fact that one knew in advance when such a measure was due, created specific problems. Deut. 15 warns the Israelites not be merciless when such a seventh year was approaching by refusing to give loans to poor fellow men. Israel's law, moreover, differs from the Babylonian one by not making an exception for commercial loans. Rabbinic Judaism tried to solve the problems, *e.g.* by temporarily ceding ownership and, following the initiative of Rabbi Hillel, it developed the institution called *prosbul* (derived from the Greek προσβουλή). It meant that before a loan was extended the creditor declared before judges that he would collect his debt claim under all circumstances, which meant he could also cede its collection to the court, since the law, phrased in the singular ("you shall ...") did not apply to such a plural body. It also led to a casuistic definition of who was "poor" (a person without immovable property) and thus should benefit from the measure.[41]

According to Kraus private contracts that stipulated payment of a debt notwithstanding a royal decree were legally invalid. They merely served to intimidate the debtor, so that he would not try to obtain remission of his debt. But I agree with Otto[42] that it is very unlikely that one would insert such a clause in a contract if it could not have any effect. Unfortunately, we know very little about the content and effects of the royal measures outside Babylonia and about the judicial complications they might cause.[43] Their impact and the way they were implemented may have differed from those of the decrees in Babylonia, just as there were differences in this respect between the Old Babylonian period and Neo Assyrian times, thousand years later.

In Babylonia, where we know the text of royal "decrees of equity" and have many references to them in letters, contracts and judicial records, we never meet a contractual clause aimed at frustrating their implementation. There was no doubt about legal force of the decrees and they were enforced by stipulated penalties. Creditors and moneylenders could only resign themselves to them,[44] for they prevailed over contractual law. Whether one considers this a specific Babylonian feature[45] or not, it was a serious attempt to intervene when "justice" and "equity" were incongruent. By force of his divine mandate the king took action to remedy undesirable social effects by canceling valid contracts. In Babylonia his sacral function and authority, sanctioned by tradition, allowed him to do so, but this may have been somewhat different elsewhere, perhaps even in Assyria, where we meet respect for the "decree of freedom" alongside attempts of creditors to maintain their claims.

According to Otto it was only in Israel that this dilemma between "justice" and "equity" was solved. Manumission of debt-slaves after six years, stipulated in the Covenant Code (Ex. 21:2f.) in Deut. 15 is extended by the obligation to cancel debts and also broadened. For it demands the Israelite to help his poor fellow man not by means of an interest-bearing loan, but by making it a gift. It becomes a matter of social conscience, without legal sanctions. There are however – although we are unable to monitor individual deeds of

---

41 See for the prosbul, *Encyclopedia Judaica* vol. 13 (1972) 1182.

42 E. Otto, "Soziale Reformen und Vertragsrecht", *RA* 92 (1998) 125-60, esp. 138f., reacting to Kraus, *op. cit.* (see note 10), 105. But Otto does not realize that the few Old Assyrian examples he adduces (rare in comparison with the large number of preserved Assyrian debt-notes) concern measures taken by Anatolian rulers in favor of Anatolian debtors. That their "washing away of debts" was inspired by the Mesopotamian example does not mean that the legal procedure was identical in both countries.

43 Knowledge where the relevant debt-notes were found is important, for after payment a debt-note was normally given back to its debtor to be destroyed, while unpaid ones remained in the archive of the creditor.

44 This is shown by the presence of groups of debt-notes from the same years in the archive of a creditor. They are not proof of the date of the destruction of the house where they were found, but result of a royal cancellation of debts whose creditor nevertheless preserved the relevant contracts.

45 Otto (*op.cit.*, note 42) writes about "eine zeitliche und örtliche Sonderentwicklung" and elsewhere of "patrimoniale Willkür wohlfahrtsutilitaristischer Akte"!

mercy, – no indications that these rules were implemented. The manumission of Hebrew (debt-)slaves at the time of the siege of Jerusalem by Nebukadnezzar was cancelled and hundred-fifty years later, in the time of Nehemiah (Neh. 5: 1-5), indebted Israelites were forced to yield not only fields and vineyards as pledges, but also their sons and daughters, some of whom were even sold into debt-bondage.

Apparently, it has always been so that an ethical appeal for a moral behavior by resigning legal claims in order to practice mercy must be buttressed by a fitting legal framework and relevant regulations, as our society also realizes. Therefore Hammurabi also incorporated in his law collection a number of rulings to protect and help the poor, but it is difficult to find proof that they were applied. Help for defaulting debtors and manumission of debt-slaves after three years (twice as fast at Deuteronomy prescribes for Israelite boys!) looks rather idealistic and we know that customary law often made redemption difficult.[46] Apparently royal "decrees of equity" were more important and were enforced, but they were only issued from time to time and had only retroactive force. There was never a fundamental change of the traditional law of obligations ruled the system of debts, securities and forfeiture, which was also incorporated in the law collections. That royal measures to restore equity were issued time and again and apparently were necessary, proves that the problem remained basically unsolved.

Nevertheless, it is remarkable that the serious problems created by the fact that ordinary citizens often could not pay off their debts, was acknowledged, formulated and addressed in Mesopotamia already more than four thousand years ago. Increase of social differences between mighty and weak, rich and poor in a hierarchical society gave rise to the realization that if the problems grew serious customary law could generate social injustice. And that it was the task of the king, mandated by the gods, to prevent, restrict or repair it.[47] Without real legal reforms one tried to provide remedies for and some protection against certain evils by special measures and a few new legal rulings. Financial regulations were also used to this effect, such as the right to pay back in a different valuta, with standard rates of exchange and interest, to guarantee the debtor the value of what he had pledged and to protect him against the forces of the market and seasonal fluctuations in price, that could easily be exploited by creditors.

The Babylonian notion of "equity" also had an impact also outside Mesopotamia, *e.g.* in the laws of ancient Israel, where more legal features of Babylonian origin can be detected. Just as in Mesopotamia, "equity" (*ṣedāqā*) as liberation and solidarity with the poor was expected from the king. He was the one who "rules his people with justice and equity ... and must do justice to those who are oppressed and come to the aid of the poor" (Ps. 72). But the pious Israelite counts primarily on God, who had liberated his enslaved people from Egypt and whose "righteousness" one expects and praises. It is remarkable that Daniel 4:24 promises Nebukadnezzar, punished and humiliated for his hubris, return to his royal dignity "if he expiates his sins by equity (*ṣedāqā*) and his misdeeds by mercy towards those in distress". The biblical writer here speaks the same language as a prophet of the great Levantine weather god Haddu (Adad) did fifteen hundred years earlier. He tells the king of Mari that the only thing he asks from him is "to do justice to the oppressed who calls to you and to give him what he is entitled to".[48]

This ideal of social equity in the Old Testament also applies to the future messianic king, who "will do justice and righteousness in the land" and will be called "Jahu is

46 The redemption of houses in ancient Assur (see above note 35) was realized by a special measure that allowed payment in three installments, whereby the debtor got his house back after the first payment of half of the price (that would equal the debt covered by its transfer or forced sale) had been paid.

47 See S. Lafont, "Nouvelles données sur la royauté mésopotamienne", *Revue historique de droit francais et étranger* 73 (1995) 473-500, esp. 491f., "le roi de justice".

48 See J.-M. Durand, *MARI* 7 (1993) 43f., on the important letter A 1968, to be compared with the letter edited by B. Lafont, "Le roi de Mari et les prophètes du dieu Adad", *RA* 78 (1984) 7f., lines 45f. Cf. also the positive judgment of the prophet Jeremiah (22:15f.) on king Josiah of Judah, because "he maintained righteousness and equity and did justice to the distressed and poor.".

our righteousness". It is certainly not by accident that Jesus Christ, at his first public appearance in a synagogue (Luc. 4:18f.) presented himself with the proclamation about the new, just king of Is. 61. He has been anointed and is sent "to bring good tidings to the poor … to give prisoners their freedom and to announce their liberation (*derōr*) to those bound", thereby ushering in a year of grace. This notion of "equity" that prevails over conviction by the law belongs to the core of the New Testament message, elaborated in particular in the epistles of Paul. This notion forbids to contrast mercy with justice, for "justice" includes or even is "equity".[49]

Our modern concept of "social justice" as an ethical standard owes much to the just-mentioned biblical notion, which again is clearly related to and was inspired by the example of ancient Mesopotamia, where it was first phrased, given legal form and applied by kings. The preservation of ancient cuneiform texts that document this notion allowed me to confront you this afternoon with its historical and ideological roots and with the legal problems created by its implementation. These problems still exist, on a national and an international level, as the discussion about poverty, the shady sides of the market and remission of debts of poor countries proves.

49 As happens in question and answer 11 of the so-called "Heidelberger Catechism", a classic protestant textbook, whose first part, on human sins, debt and atonement, argues on the basis of the traditional law of obligations.

Old Assyrian And Old Babylonian Law: Some Comparative Observations*

The study of Old Babylonian law is a well-established branch of the "Keilschriftrecht" that grew during the last quarter of the 19th century, matured after the publication of the Laws of Hammurabi in 1902 and was developed by many assyriologists and legal historians, among whom the scholar to whose memory this colloquium pays tribute. They edited and analyzed a great variety of sources, including practice documents and law collections, royal decrees and scholastic compositions, and reconstructed and interpreted the underlying law, legal terminology and judicial procedures. This is in many respects different with the study of Old Assyrian law. It started much later, its students are nearly all philologists, and its sources are exclusively practice documents, contracts, judicial records and letters, while laws, decrees and scholastic texts are missing. The great majority of the sources are records dealing with commercial issues, while those documenting other areas of law, apart from several dozens dealing with marriage, inheritance and the sale of slaves and houses, are absent or rare. This is somewhat compensated by the abundance of contracts dealing with trade and commerce, notably records dealing with credit, security, commission, partnership and investment, by a few commercial treaties, and by a rich variety of judicial records that give insight into legal procedures. In addition many letters exchanged between Assur and Anatolia report on legal actions, conflicts and lawsuits (often referring to or quoting from verdicts and legal decisions), among them a few dozen official letters written by the rulers of Assur as executive officers of the City Assembly and correspondence between the authorities in Anatolia, both the Assyrian ones and the local rulers.

1. RESEARCH ON OLD ASSYRIAN LAW

1.1. A short history

The study of OA law, after a few pioneering text editions,[1] only started around 1920, when the first volume of *Tablettes cappadociennes* in the Louvre (TCL 4), by Georges Contenau, had become available, a year later followed by Sidney Smith's first volume of *Cuneiform Texts from Cappadocian Tablets in the British Museum* (CCT 1). Around that time also **[142]** enough of the orthography and the grammar of the archaic OA dialect had become sufficiently understood to produce more or less reliable translations of legal documents.[2] Thanks to the efforts of three pioneers, G. Eisser, B. Landsberger and J. Lewy, this lead to

1 By W. Golénisheff in 1891, V. Scheil in 1898, Th. Pinches in 1908, and by A.H. Sayce in 1911. F. Thureau-Dangin, who had published four copies of "Cappadocian" texts as TCL 1, 239-242, edited 242 (now *EL* 5) in *Florilegium M. de Vogüe* (1909) 591-597, as "Une acte de répudiation sur une tablette cappadocienne". See for these early editions of OA texts the bibliography in Michel 2003, Ch. 1.1.1, "Texts from illicit diggings of Kültepe".

2 At least by those who studied them and their language systematically, see the criticism by B. Landsberger in *ZA* 38 (1929) 275-280 of G.R. Driver's translation of OA texts.

* Originally published in the Zeitschrift für Altorientalische und Biblische Rechtsgeschichte 18 (2012) 141-174.

a promising start of the study of OA law, but due to various circumstances it came to a halt soon after 1935.

A first pioneer of OA studies was Julius Lewy, whose dissertation on *Das Verbum in den altassyrischen Gesetzen* of 1921[3] had raised his interest in the so-called "Cappadocian tablets". Already a year later, when he had become Privatdozent in Giessen,[4] he published his *Studien zu den altassyrischen Texten aus Kappadokien* (Berlin, Selbstverlag), which includes the edition of eleven selected legal records. Legal comments, with some elements of an "Urkundenlehre", and discussions of technical terms were given in lengthy footnotes that deal with security for debt (p. 49, note 1), judicial procedure (p. 58, note 1), marriage law (p. 68 note 1), and the Assyrian form of the so-called "Inhaberklausel" (*wābil ṭuppim šut tamkārum*).

A second pioneer was Benno Landsberger, who in 1924, in *ZA* 35, 22-26, published the first article on OA law, "Solidarhaftung von Schuldnern in den babylonisch-assyrischen Urkunden", based on a number of OA debt-notes. In the same year his *Assyrische Handelskolonien in Kleinasien* (Landsberger 1924) appeared, which in good thirty pages presented a concise and brilliant sketch of the OA world, including a three-page paragraph (§ 6) on the main features of "Der Kredit" and an even shorter one (§ 7) on "Die Gerichtsbarkeit". The next year he published a long critical review of Lewy's *Studien.*[5]

A third pioneer was Georg Eisser, a legal historian who, stimulated by Lewy, in 1925 produced a Habilitationsschrift for the Law Faculty in Giessen on the legal documents from Kültepe known by that time.[6] Exploiting the rapid publication of new OA texts he and Lewy in 1930 (after Eisser had acquired a chair in Tübingen) completed their admirable and still valuable *Die altassyrischen Rechtsurkunden vom Kültepe* (here abbreviated as *EL*), a massive volume with an edition of 340 legal documents, accompanied by a detailed commentary, that dealt with many legal issues and procedures and their terminology.[7] The volume includes contracts dealing with a great variety of issues (nos. 1-237), judicial records and of various types (nos. 238-309) and finally 30 "interrelated records", provided with a rich and lengthy commentary on 138 pages. Noteworthy are nos. 288-290, published as **[143]** appendix on p. 334-340, designated as *tašīmtum*, ca."wise ruling", in Assyrian and labeled "Gesetzesfragmente" in *EL.*[8]

EL divided the texts in a large number of groups and categories "in einer den Urkunden-aufbau berücksichtigenden systematische Reihenfolge", which, as their titles show, reflects a rather formal approach. It was the work of Eisser, who was also responsible for the introductions to the groups and the individual texts, while Lewy took care of the transliterations, translations and the philological notes.[9] The volumes laid a solid foundation for the study of OA law and for decades nearly all students based themselves

---

3 Prepared in Berlin under F. Delitzsch; the degree was obtained under B. Meissner. Its title shows that the distinction between Middle and Old Assyrian still had to be made.

4 See for a sketch of Lewy's life, K. Hecker, "Julius Lewy (1895-1963) / Assyriologe", in H.G. Gundel *et al.* (eds.), *Giessener Gelehrte in der ersten Hälfte des 20. Jahrhunderts* (Lebensbilder aus Hessen, Bd. 2), 626-633.

5 *OLZ* 1925, cols. 229-233.

6 Unpublished, but its substance was no doubt incorporated in Eisser's legal comments in *EL*.

7 Due to its size the manuscript was published in two volumes, as *MVAeG* 33 (1930) and 35/3 (1935). The delay in the publication of the second volume allowed Lewy to add 30 pages of important "Berichtigungen und Nachträge", that reflect the progress of Old Assyrian studies. A long "Verzeichnis der in den Anmerkungen und Nachträgen besprochenen Worte und Termini technici", contributed by Lewy (vol. II, 197-205), proved to be an important research tool. The first volume was reviewed by M. David in *Savigny Zeitschrift* 52 (1932) 496-503.

8 With important "Nachträge" in vol. 2, p. 191-2. See for literature on these "laws", that were included in G.R. Driver and J.C. Miles, *The Assyrian Laws* (Oxford 1935), 1-3, 376-379 and 455-457. A new edition and interpretation was offered in Larsen 1976, 283-332, who designated them as "The Statutes of the Kanesh Colony". We now know that the *awīlū ša nikkassē*, "men with accounts", mentioned in them, were prominent traders, also called "*dātum*-payers", who contributed to the funds of the *kārum*, where they kept accounts that allowed them to use book transfers instead of paying certain taxes cash.

9 In the preface the authors thank Landsberger for having critically read the manuscript and for making "in gewohner Hilfsbereitschaft ... eine größere Zahl von Änderungsvorschlagen".

on them.[10] It served a function similar to M. Schorr's *Urkunden des altbabylonischen Zivil- und Prozessrechts* (*VAB* 5, 1913), but offered much more comments on and analysis of both the legal and the commercial contents of the texts and their terminology.

The earliest focus of the study of OA law was the issue of "joint liability" (or "Solidarhaftung"), the subject of Landsberger's above-mentioned article of 1924 and which was subsequently also studied in Eisser 1931. Unfortunately, after the publication of *EL* the study of OA law for various reasons did not make much progress. The "juristische Erläuterungen", which the preface of *EL* describes as "eine zusammenfassende rechtsvergleichende Darstellung des in den Urkunden enthaltenen altassyrischen Rechts" and to which *EL* repeatedly refers, even by paragraph numbers, were never published. The "Urkundenlehre", embodied in the categorization of the texts in *EL*, was published much later, as Eisser 1939, but it focused on formal aspects of the records and not on the substance of law. It was, apart from Eisser 1931, his only contribution to OA law after *EL* and for more than forty years no other legal historian worked on it. Moreover, Julius Lewy, who between 1926 and 1935 had published hundreds of Kültepe texts in small private and public collections (notably those in Istanbul, Jena and Paris), after that devoted most of his time to studying historical and religious issues, geography and grammar.[11] Landsberger, who kept an interest in the "Kültepe texts",[12] focused on different texts and subjects, notably the reconstruction of the lexical series.

[144] An important factor was that neither Assur, nor the main Assyrian colony in Kanesh in Anatolia, yielded an OA counterpart of the Codex Hammurabi, which had so stimulated the study of OB law, also because its editions and translations made OB law accessible to law students outside the narrow circle of Assyriologists. The study of OA law had to be based exclusively on hundreds of records (legal records and letters) written in a difficult dialect, a peculiar orthography and a rather technical jargon, most of which (apart from those edited in *EL*) were published only in cuneiform copies. This must have discouraged legal historians, as regretted and criticized by Koschaker,[13] and it was made worse by the fact that the grammatical sketch of Old Assyrian, foreseen for the end of *EL*, was never published. It only changed with the publication of the Akkadian grammar of W. von Soden (1952) and especially K. Hecker's *Grammatik der Kültepe Texte* (1968), and that of the great dictionaries, von Soden's *AHw* and in particular *CAD*.[14] But some of the OA terminology still presents problems of understanding and the knowledge of the orthography and grammar can be refined, as shown by the recent

---

10 After seventy-five years many, mostly minor, corrections are now possible, due to improved lexical and grammatical knowledge, the enormous increase of new texts, collations of originals, joining of tablet fragments and the re-uniting of a few tablets and envelopes. A list of them would be very useful.

11 He developed the theory of "ein altassyrisches Großreich", that would have included Central Anatolia, called "Halys Assyria", an idea fiercely criticized and rejected by Landsberger (see *ZA* 35 (1924) 220-228), which is one of the reasons for their estrangement. Later (1950) they still crossed swords about the meaning of *Hattum*, "land of the Hittites", in the Kültepe texts, in contributions to successive volumes of the Festschrift for B. Hrozný in 1950 (*ArOr* 18/1-3). In the field of religion Lewy developed a special interest in the relations between the OA world and the Old Testament, where the occurrence in both of "the god of the fathers" and a possibly shared "Amorite" background were his favorite topics.

12 Revived when he worked at Ankara University from 1935 until 1948, where he trained young Assyriologists, studied "Kültepe texts" that private owners showed him, and wrote the important article Landsberger 1940. Since 1948, when the Turkish excavations at Kültepe started, he kept in close contact with the excavator Tahsin Özgüç and the epigraphist Kemal Balkan, his former student; together they edited the important new inscription of Irišum I, which also deals with the administration of justice, Landsberger and Balkan 1950, now accessible in *RIMA* 1, as A.0.33.

13 In *NKRU*, VIII-X, where he declares himself lucky to have enjoyed the "interest and support" of Landsberger.

14 It covers Old Assyrian very well, due to contributions, during its long history, by most of the OA specialists, beginning with J. Lewy, who supplied texts, read manuscripts or worked for longer periods in Chicago.

studies of N.J.C. Kouwenberg.[15] Not surprisingly, many Assyriologists and of course legal historians, to quote the title of Erica Reiner's contribution to the Festschrift I received, "are afraid of Old Assyrian".[16] She is, unfortunately, right and it is not rare to come across legal interpretations of OA records that are based on wrong readings or translations of cuneiform texts.[17] Some interpretations are also not acceptable because they start from too theoretical and dogmatic legal considerations, without a sufficient knowledge of the underlying, complex OA commercial procedures and goals. For OA records and the legal rules and devices they embody are instruments in the service of the trade and commerce, meant to prevent or solve problems that might occur and they have to be understood against that background.

1.2. Prospects for the future

After the second world war publication of new texts, notably those from Hrozný's excavations at Kültepe,[18] and Paul Garelli's masterful synthesis *Les Assyriens en Cappadoce* (Paris 1963) aroused new interest in Old Assyrian and its law. It manifested itself in due time in a scattering of articles and comments accompanying editions of selected, "interesting" **[145]** texts. Only much later a legal historian, J. Hengstl, again ventured into OA (Hengstl 1987, cf. Hengstl 2008), but books on OA law are rare.[19] Judicial procedure received much attention in Larsen's monograph *The Old Assyrian City State and its Colonies* (Larsen 1976), but Rosen's dissertation on the Old Assyrian loan contracts of 1977 remained unpublished.[20] The only published monograph was Kienast's *Altassyrisches Kaufvertragsrecht* (Kienast 1984), who also wrote articles on "Pfandrecht" (1976) and the so-called "*be'ūlātu*-loans" (1989). This was the beginning of a series of articles by various authors, which can be easily traced in the bibliography Michel 2003 and in Veenhof 2008a, part II, Ch. 2.5. The present writer offered a general overview of OA Law (Veenhof 2003; the original manuscript was longer than the printed version), dealt with the issue of laws and legislation (Veenhof 1995 and 2008b, 262-269) the commercial treaties (Veenhof 2008a, part V; 2008b, 254-262), and OA testaments (see below § 2.3, b).

There is a future and certainly a need for the study of OA law, now that the complete archives of the OA traders, excavated since 1948, which contain so much fascinating new material, are gradually being edited and progress can be made. To mention one example, in Veenhof 1991 I tackled the issue of private summons and arbitration, because I had discovered that *EL*'s interpretation (vol. I, p. 245) of the procedural key-phrase of the OA "Gerichtsprotokolle" – "for this case the *kārum* gave us and before the dagger of Assur we gave our testimony" – was not correct and that the role of mediation and arbitration had been underestimated. This subject has now been thoroughly investigated in Th. K. Hertel's dissertation *Old Assyrian Legal Practice*. He broadens and in some respects corrects my attempts and investigates all aspects of OA judicial procedure, also with the help of insights acquired by legal anthropology on dispute strategies, which constitutes a methodological progress. He could use many new texts excavated in 1994, which are being edited by M.T. Larsen in AKT 6, notably a group of ca. 70 records that emanated

---

15 See for their titles Veenhof 2008a, 112 note 497, and now his book *The Akkadian Verb and its Semitic Background* (Languages of the Ancient Near East, 2. Winona Lake, 2010), which pays much attention to Old Assyrian.

16 In *Studies Veenhof*, 389-394.

17 Occasionally also with specialists in Old Assyrian, such as Kienast's proposal to find the verb *baqārum* in OA (see below note 80). Note the re-interpretation of the important letter on the redemption of houses sold for debts, TPAK 1, 46, in Veenhof 1999a.

18 ICK 1 and 2, published in 1952 and 1962.

19 My own dissertation, *Aspects of Old Assyrian Trade and its Terminology* (Leiden 1972), treated some legal issues and according to my promotor, F.R. Kraus, it was included as vol. 10 in the series *Studia et Documenta ad Iura Orientis Antiqui Pertinentia* also because its chapter on smuggling had aroused interest.

20 B. L. Rosen, *Studies in Old Assyrian Loan Contracts*, defended at Brandeis University in 1977 (UMM 77-22.827). He edits and studies 105 new loan contracts published since *EL*, mostly in cuneiform copies only.

from a serious conflict about an inheritance between two brothers in the family of the archive owner. His material and approach made it possible to supplement a legal and terminological interpretation, as presented *e.g.* in Dombradi 1996, with an analysis of the roots of conflicts and the identity and goals of the parties. He suggests that the commercial background of a dispute and the status of the parties may have had a bearing on the dispute strategy followed, which can range from private summons and mediation to arbitration and – if no solution is reached – adjudication in a formal lawsuit before the *kārum* as court of law or the City-Assembly of Assur. The publication of this book,[21] together with the overview of OA Law I wrote for R. Westbrook's *History of Ancient Near Eastern Law* (2003) should stimulate others to venture into this fascinating and still developing field of ancient law.

[146] 2. PROBLEMS IN COMPARING OLD ASSYRIAN AND OLD BABYLONIAN LAW

2.1. Availability and nature of the sources

Certain types of legal records, prominent in OB times, are absent or rare in the OA Period. This applies to those concerning real estate transactions, such as sale, exchange, rent, and tenancy, numerous in OB and "Schlussklauseln" of which have been thoroughly studied. Houses were of course bought and sold in Assur, as we know from references in letters, but the contracts we have all concern property in Anatolia and most are purchases from Anatolians, many of which were studied in Kienast 1984. We have only three house sale contracts from Assur, dating to the end of the Late OA period,[22] which makes the reconstruction of the OA law and its comparison with OB difficult (see below § 4). Records on the sale and exploitation of fields around Assur, not surprisingly, are missing in the colonial archives, but it is striking that they also do not occur among the assets divided in the last wills we have.

The situation is similar with adoption contracts. We know a few Anatolian contracts from Kanesh,[23] but not a single Assyrian one, apart from one contract from the end of the late OA period, presumably from Assur (Veenhof 1982). There is no reason to doubt that children were adopted in ancient Assur, but the relevant records were apparently not brought to Kanesh and must have remained in the family archives in Assur.

Legal records of commercial nature are very numerous in OA and they show a great variety. Comparing loans and debt-notes, including their security clauses, with similar OB contracts is rewarding, as shown by Landsberger 1964, a comparative analysis of the payment clause *ana ittišu*, and my own observations on the so-called "Kursklausel" or "tablet bearer clause" (*wābil/nāši ṭuppim*), which facilitated the cession of debt claims.[24] The most interesting OB category is the contract about a commercial partnership (*tappūtum*) between one or more investors and a trading agent (*šamallûm*, lit. "the carrier of the bag"; also treated in Codex Hammurabi §§ 100-107), who will do business with the capital or merchandise provided by the investor(s) and after the completion of his journey will settle accounts with them, and they will receive back the capital, while the

21 Th.K. Hertel, *Old Assyrian Legal Practices. Law and Dispute in the Ancient Near East.* OAAS 6, PIHANS 123, Leiden 2013: Nederlands Instituut voor het Nabije Oosten. See also Hertel and Larsen 2010.

22 See for these late house sales, Veenhof 2011, § 5.

23 See for an edition of these contracts, Veenhof 2016/17.

24 Veenhof 1997: 351-364.

profit will be divided.[25] In OA, which uses *tappā'um*, "partner, business associate",[26] there are only a few occurrences of a partnership (*tappā'uttum*) between Assyrians, of which the best known is the one made (*tappā'uttam epāšum*) by four Assyrians for buying iron in Anatolia with capital of 20 **[147]** minas of silver provided by an investor, documented in ICK 1, 1 and BIN 6, 181 and 214.[27] We also have a late, damaged deposition about a mutual clearance (l. 13, *zakû*) to end a partnership with a capital of 9 minas of silver, between two Assyrians, carried out before a committee of five arbitrators,[28] and also some evidence on partnerships with and between Anatolians.[29] As Larsen 1977:123 has suggested, there may have been much informal business cooperation that functioned without a written partnership contract. The Assyrians also knew a kind of partnership in which a number of traders cooperated by entrusting their merchandise to a caravan lead by an important trader, after whom it was called (*ellat* PN) and who took care of the expenses, taxes and possible losses, which were shared proportionally on the basis of the value of each participant's merchandise.[30] These "partnerships" were for one particular trading enterprise or caravan journey, as were OB partnerships, where the accounts would be settled "upon the successful completion of the journey".[31] OA knew various types of commercial loans, some also for longer periods (called *ebuṭṭum* and *bulātum*),[32] but the main instrument of OA commercial investment was the so-called *naruqqum*, a substantial joint-stock fund brought together by ten of more investors and entrusted to a manager or *tractator*, called *tamkārum*, for a number of years; as Larsen pointed out it is comparable to the early medieval *commenda*. The relevant contracts (see Larsen 2001) had a special format and specific clauses on sharing profits, paying dividend, withdrawal, a final settlement of accounts, and on the assets (called *šalṭum*) of the tractator that served as security. Some of the terminology typical for such contracts occurs occasionally in OB,

---

25 See Eilers 1931 and Westbrook 2003, 411f., with previous literature; add W.F. Leemans, *The Old Babylonian Merchant* (Leiden, 1950), Ch. 3. The dissertation of G.F. Dole, *Partnership Loans in the Old Babylonian Period* (Harvard, 1965), has unfortunately never been published. See for some partnerships between a trader and a temple/god, Veenhof 2004a, 556ff. Skaist 1994, 46-51 only treats some OB *tappūtu*-contracts in connection with *qīptu*-loans and fails to make the comparison with OA data (his note 53 is wrong, since I defined *bābtum* not as "loss", but as "outstanding goods / claims").

26 Examples in *CAD* T, 184f., a, 1', a'. Note in particular OIP 27, 57:5f., where Buzāzu, son of Pūšu-kēn, designates the dead Puzur-Assur as "partner of our family" (*tappā bēt abini*). In OIP 27, 59:9-11 an Assyrian has a debt claim on the Anatolian and on his *tappā'um*. But, as Larsen 1977, 123 has stressed, it is usually not clear what the legal basis for the use of this term is, which might denote "(mutual) representation", "partnership" and "agency". Also persons who at a particular occasion had acted as witnesses and had to render a joint testimony designated each other as *tappā'um*.

27 It was analyzed by B. Landsberger and J. Lewy in *ArOr* 18/3 (1950) 331-336 and 423-440. Kt 89/k 231 (courtesy of Y. Kawasaki) deals with seven traders, designated as "I. and his partners" (*I. u tappā'ūšu*), who wanted to sell a large amount of iron identified as "our joint property" (*ša barini*). A kind of partnership, where the term *tappā'uttum* is not used, recorded in ICK 1, 83 (tablet) + ICK 2, 60 (case), is the arrangement whereby the capitalist I. borrows 4 ½ minas of silver to the agent A., who is in his service and has to use it to make a profit (*takšītam kaššu'um*) of which I. will receive two-thirds and A. one-third.

28 Kt n/k 28b, published by V. Donbaz in Michel 2008, 49f. Read in lines 9f., "They seized us by mutual agreement and we concluded their case" (*ina migr[ātišunu i]ṣ-bu-tù-[ni-a-tí-ma] / a-wa¹-tí-šu-nu nu-[ga-me-er]*. Lines 19-21 mention wool, carnelian and necklaces as their joint property (*ina barišunu*).

29 Kt d/k 14 records that Peruwa gave W. silver that would "be doubled in partnership" (10f., *ina tappā'uttim uštanna*) and be paid back in annual installments, to be deducted from (the debt recorded on) his tablet. Kt n/k 32 (edited by Dercksen in *Studies Larsen*, 166f.) records the termination of a commercial cooperation (the term "partnership" is not used) between an Assyrian and two Anatolians to trade silver, gold, cups of iron, tin, textiles, slaves and lapis lazuli.

30 See for this feature Dercksen 2004a, Ch. 9.

31 *Ina šalām / sanāq* (BE 6/1, 115:7) / *erēb* (MDP 22, 124:7 and frequently in late OB contracts, VS 22, nos. 35 and 40ff.) *harrānim / gerrim*; cf. also W.W Hallo in *Studies Landsberger*, 199f.

32 See Dercksen 1999.

such as *šipkātum*, "investment",[33] and the tractator, in OA usually *tamkārum*, **[148]** can probably also be called *šamallā'um*, although this term is rare.[34] There are some other lexical similarities,[35] but the *naruqqu*-contract as such has no OB analogues.

Here I must also mention the fact, noted above, that Old Assyrian laws, written on a stele, are not preserved, although we have a few references to them. It means that for most areas and issues we have to reconstruct OA law on the basis of a large number and great variety of practice documents. This is a challenge, because they are usually a mixture of customary and perhaps written law and individual agreements and solutions resulting from negotiations, which are probably more frequent in a commercial context, and it is not easy to separate the two. When trying to do so and comparing OB data one realizes to what extent the reconstruction of OB law is influenced by the data found in law collections such as those from Eshnunna and Babylon. Even when one does not accept (all of) them as binding laws, they still are a great help in understanding the issues at stake, a help which is not available for OA law.

2.2. Anatolian law?

We have quite a number and some very interesting of contracts in which the parties are Anatolians and this raises the question whether the formulary and/or legal substance of these records reflect Assyrian and/or (also) Anatolian law. The texts are written in Assyrian, the only written language then available, so that possible Anatolian elements appear in Assyrian linguistic garb. Even badly written texts that betray the hand of native scribes[36] do not necessarily imply that the type of contract and its clauses are basically Anatolian. These Anatolian contracts concern sales of slaves and houses, marriage and divorce, and in particular loans and debts. Many of the latter are provided with a variety of payment and security clauses, frequently similar to those found in contracts between Assyrian creditors and Anatolian debtors. Anatolian debtors usually have to provide more securities[37] and that the due dates are the times, seasons and festivals of the Anatolian agricultural year (no Anatolian month-names are known) is an understandable adaptation to the local situation, but does not **[149]** mean different legal norms.[38] When the texts are written in good Assyrian they must be the work of Assyrian scribes employed by Anatolians, and they may have known enough of the native language to make, when

---

33 See the last two texts quoted in *CAD* Š/III, 70, 2, b; the verb also occurs sporadically in OB as "to invest", in UET 5, 25:22 and in the reciprocal Gt-stem (very common in OA) in F.H.H. al-Rawi and S. Dalley, *Old Babylonian Texts from Private Houses at Abu Habbah, Ancient Sippir* (É-DUB-BA-A 7; London 2000) 26:4, ½ *mana ½ mana kaspam / ša* N. / *u* G. / *iš-ta-ap-ku-ú*, and in BM 80365:9'f. (OB Sippar, unpubl.), silver *ahum mala ahim / iš-ta-ap-ku-ma / ana gerr*[*im illikū* ...].

34 The term, always with a following genitive for designating the trader for whom he works, occurs only in legal confrontations, see *CAD* Š/I 291, 1, a (ATHE 48, a deposition(!), *šībuttum*; kt c/k 697, courtesy Dercksen, in connection with the death of a *š*.), where a person is identified as or denies to be somebody's *š*. The close relation between *EL* 327 and 328 suggests that man trading with money invested by *ummeānū* in his joint-stock capital could also be called *šamallā'um*, see already Landsberger 1940: 22.

35 At the end of the journey or partnership accounts were settled, for which the OA *naruqqu*-contract Kt 91/k 482:23f. uses simply *nikkassē tadānum*. OB partnership contracts frequently show that, because in overland trade not everything (sales, expenses, taxes, losses) could be proved by records, this happened in the temple, where oaths were sworn. CT 2, 22 (*VAB* 5 no. 282) speaks of *nikkassīšu mahar Šamaš epēšum*, an expression also used in the legal handbook *Ana ittišu* VI, col.I:22f. According to BE 6/1, 15:17f. (*VAB* 5, 170) this resulted in a sealed record "written by the judges at the place of the purification (*ašar tēbibtim*) in the temple of Šamaš" (cf. "to give *tēbibtum*" to the creditor, *Studies Landsberger*, 200:8-10), while VAS 8, 8 (*VAB* 5, 169) writes *bāb Šamaš nikkassam epēšum*. But one also writes *ṭēmšu mahar ummiānim šakānum* (S. Greengus, *Studies in Ishchali Documents* (Malibu 1986), p. 185:8 and 189:10-12).

36 Irregular orthography, ignorance of certain signs, grammatical mistakes in distinguishing masculine and feminine verbal prefixes and object suffixes, mixing up of pronominal accusative and possessive suffixes, problems with the subjunctive and the use of the tenses, etc.

37 See the survey in Veenhof 2001a,124-137 (pledges), 148-152 (joint liability).

38 See for the due dates and their names, Veenhof 2008a, 234-245. That the debtor, in addition to the interest due, at times had to provide some additional gifts ("Zugaben"), such as sheep, barley, bread, honey, onions (cf. L. Matouš in *Studies Landsberger*, 180f.) may have been an Anatolian custom.

necessary, good Assyrian translations of Anatolian clauses. In such cases we can only detect Anatolian elements if the relevant clauses and rules of law are unknown from Assyrian (or even Mesopotamian) sources, but this is difficult since our knowledge of Assyrian contracts outside the commercial sphere is limited and we cannot rule out still unknown OA legal customs and formularies. I have previously suggested (Veenhof 1998, 45-160) that a special category of Anatolian contracts about the establishment of brotherhood, between natural and apparently adopted brothers, who join the household of the parents and will live and work in it and for it, are probably of Anatolian inspiration since nothing similar is known from Mesopotamia. That we have to be careful is shown by the fact that a few Anatolian debt-notes, edited and studied in Balkan 1974, mention the possibility that the local ruler "washes off the debt" (*šumma rubā'um hubullam imassi*). Such measures must be of Mesopotamian inspiration, even when Assyrian debt-notes register nothing similar, which is understandable, since such royal acts (as we know from Babylonia) apply only to non-commercial, consumptive debts that are not normally found in the archives of the traders. And the use of the Babylonian technical term *andurārum* in Anatolian contracts and in the new treaty with Kanesh supports this conclusion.[39]

The situation could be similar in other contracts for which we have no Assyrian parallels. An example is Kt 84/k 169, which I studied in Bayram / Veenhof 1992, 92-96, a contract between Anatolians on the sale of a field to be exploited for five years by the creditors, who then will give it back if the original owners pay back the price paid. This is obviously the conditional sale of a field by defaulting debtors for the amount of their debt. It does not state what happens when they do not pay back, but the use of the sale terminology suggests that the field was then simply forfeited. We have no OA parallels for it, because the colonial archives do not contain any document dealing with Assyrian fields, but it seems to be a precursor of similar Middle Assyrian contracts, whereby fields of debtors, handed over as security or pledge for a period of several years, could become the property of the creditor. Another example is the sale of some fields and a garden between Anatolians, recorded on the sealed tablet (an Anatolian feature) Kt o/k 52:5-19,[40] which reads:

> "Four fields with a garden next to his fields K. sold to A. for 7 minas of silver. [9b] All the irrigation water that comes belongs to both of them. [12] If K. breaks the contract (*ibbalakkat*) he will pay to A. 14 minas of silver; [15] if A. breaks the contract he takes (*i.e.* keeps, *itabbal*) the 7 minas of silver, the price of the field, and pays to K. 7 minas of silver".[41]

For lack of parallels (also in Middle Assyrian) we can only speculate whether the unique clause about sharing the irrigation water and the penalty for breaking the agreement are of Assyrian inspiration or reflect Anatolian customary law. The penalties imply that the fields return to their previous owner, if the seller wants them back or the buyer wants to get rid of them. Both have to pay a fine equal to the sale price, the seller pays its double

---

39 An unpublished Anatolian debt-note (communicated to me by Y. Kawasaki) uses the expression *andurāram waššurum*, "to remit *a*.," i.e. to remit (debts by means of) an act of *a*."; this combination is also attested in Mari (see *Florilegium marianum* VII [2002], no. 47:17-25), where it refers to the liberation of people by "the washing of the workhouses" (*neparātim mesûm*). The treaty with Kanesh (see Günbattı 2004, 253, lines 82-84) uses *addurārum* for the manumission of slaves (the missing verb could be *waššurum* or *šakānum*).

40 See Albayrak 2001, 308f. We have no evidence of Assyrians purchasing fields in Anatolia, not, as Kienast 1984, 6 believed, because the Assyrians were not permitted to do so (in Kt a/k 583 an Assyrian even refuses to accept "fields and gardens" which the palace wants to make available instead of paying a large debt in copper), but simply because they preferred to invest their money in the trade and they could easily buy the agricultural products they needed.

41 Lines 5-11: 4 *eq[lātim] / u kiriam ša ṭehi / eqlātišuma* K. / *ana* A. *ana 7 mana / kaspim iddiššina mimma* (10) *ma'ē šiqītum*[sic] / *ša illukuni ša kilallēšunuma*.

and gets the field back, the buyer the sale price, but looses the field. The remarkable formulation may have been chosen to show the 'mirror character' of the fine. The *duplum* as a fine for violating the no-contest clause is well known from Mesopotamia, already during the Sargonic Period,[42] and we have also OA occurrences of it, but the remarkable formulation might be of Anatolian origin. Note that the writer does not use *tuārum*, "to come back on (a transaction)", so dominant in OA and used both of sellers (and their relatives) and of third parties,[43] but *nabalkutum*, "to break an agreement", which is occasionally attested during the Sargonic, Ur III and OB periods (including Mari, Susa and Alalakh), but is very rare in OA.[44] The contract thus reflects Mesopotamian and therefore probably also Assyrian legal traditions, but it might also contain Anatolian elements in Assyrian linguistic garb rendered by an Assyrian scribe, a well-trained one considering the quality of the language.[45] (including the use of *tabālum* in the sense of "to take (legally), to keep", well-known in OB legal texts). A comprehensive study of the many "Anatolian" contracts is necessary to evaluate these legal issues and to obtain better insights into Anatolian society and law.[46]

2.3. Different types of contracts in Old Babylonian and Old Assyrian

A third problem is that contracts dealing with similar or at least comparable issues can be rather different in OA and OB. I mention four examples.

[151] 2.3.1. Hiring personnel

In OA we have no contracts of the type known from OB, which uses the verb *agārum*, stipulates the hireling's wage with additional provisions (on clothing, days off, etc.) and the period of his employment.[47] This could be accidental, because the type of contract for engaging caravan personnel does use *agārum* and the noun "hire" (*igrū*) in a contingency clause describing that the employer can hire a substitute if the person contracted leaves prematurely. But we have no contract where it is the main verb, with provisions similar to those in OB, perhaps because this was done by oral agreement.[48] For contracting the services of a "harnesser" (*kaṣṣārum*), who took care of a trader's donkeys that traveled in a caravan, OA used a so-called *be'ūlatu*-contract, which recorded that the harnesser had received an interest free silver loan for his free use (*be'ālum*), which he could put to commercial use (usually by buying a few textiles in Assur that he sold with profit in Anatolia) to earn his own wage. This witnessed contract must have been recorded in writing to have evidence of the receipt of this repayable loan. "With this silver he is held" (*išti kaspim uktâl*), that is, by accepting the loan he is bound to work for his creditor (in letters and transport contracts he is usually identified by mentioning the name of

---

42 See Steinkeller 1989, 56, and for the Ur III Period, H. Limet, *OrNS* 38 (1969) 520-532 and H. Neumann, *CRRAI* 35 (Philadelphia), 171f. with notes 66ff. The *duplum* occurs in particular if a promise to pay is not kept, as in *NRVU* I no. 49.

43 See Kienast 1984, Ch. IV, both in the "Verzichtklausel" and in the "Eviktionsgarantie". It occurs also in Anatolian field sales, such as Kt d/k 6b:13, 10b:8, 27:14 (sale of a field with a well), and 52a:10 (where the penalty for *tuārum* is a fine amounting to the double of the purchase price).

44 See *CAD* N/I, 13, b) and for bala in the Ur III period Steinkeller 1989, 47f. The only other OA occurrence I know is again *šumma ibbalakkat* in kt c/k 672:10 (courtesy Dercksen), in a payment contract.

45 Note in particular the nominal predicate with added *-ma* in line 11. The contingency clause about breaking the agreement uses *šumma* + present tense, to describe the intention.

46 See for the time being Dercksen 2004b, on "Some Elements of Old Anatolian Society", with an appendix that contains translations of two dozen Anatolian records.

47 See M. Stol, *RlA* 8 (1993-1997) 170ff., Miete. B. Altbabylonisch, § 3.

48 For hiring an attorney (*rābiṣum*), apparently on the basis of a written contract, OA used *aḫāzum*; *agārum* is also used for renting porters, messengers, donkey-drivers, houses, boats, donkeys and oxen; once (in BIN 4, 98:9; by mistake?) a letter uses it for hiring a harnesser.

his employer, "the *kaṣṣārum* of PN"[49]) and forbidden to leave or to rent his services to somebody else (*ana igrē alākum*, ICK 1, 83:18). The terminology is similar to that used for the antichretic personal pledge, who is also "held" by his creditor to work off his debt (or the interest on it), but the status of the "harnesser" was different. A personal pledge was usually provided when a debtor had defaulted on an existing debt, but the "harnesser" voluntarily entered a service-relationship by accepting the loan.[50] Kienast may be right that the use of *išti kaspim uktâl*, 'borrowed' from antichretic pledging, identifies the *be'ūlātu*-contract as a "nachgeformtes Rechtsgeschäft", but it had a structure and purpose of its own. The contract also features a special clause about the consequences when the person hired "rebels", "breaks the contract" (for which the verb *šamāhum* is used, see below note 76) by disappearing or entering into somebody else's service.

[152] It is interesting to observe that this type of contract shows a gradual development during the ca. 180 years that separate the oldest and youngest specimens, especially in the penalty clause. The oldest, *EL* 97 (from ca. 1930 BC), which already uses the expression "he is held with the silver" (its earliest dated occurrence!), contains detailed clauses (also quoting *verbatim* what the harnesser might say in such a case) on breaking the contract prematurely, ("in the middle of a voyage") or terminating it regularly ("in Kanesh or Assur"), on the penalty for absconding (*puzram ṣabātum*) without paying back the loan (a fine of 1 shekel of silver per month) and on the employer's right of seizing and enforcing payment "wherever I see him". The youngest one, Kt n/k 30 (from ca. 1750 BC), uses much less words and ends with (lines 15-19): "He will not abscond somewhere; if he does so I will hire in his stead a donkey-driver as hireling and he shall compensate the wages of the hireling at a rate of 1 shekel of silver per double hour". The distance covered by the hired substitute, which must be translatable into the number of days he was employed, determines the size of the penalty.[51] There are further developments or differences, since some older contracts speak of the harnesser "leaving somewhere else" (*ajēma dappurum*), while others use "go into hiding" (*puzram ṣabātum* or *pazārum*) or "to move in with somebody else" (to work for him) (*išti šanîm wašābum*).

2.3.2. Inheritance law

Inheritance in OB was by intestate succession, with prerogatives (first choice, plus ten percent or a double share) for the eldest son and it resulted in large tablets detailing the division of the inheritance. In OA inheritance was apparently always on the basis of a testament or last will of the *pater familias* (*šīmtašu* / *šīmti bētišu išīm*), that laid down the division of his possessions between the members of his nuclear family. It allowed, within certain limits, a more flexible division, tuned to specific wishes, such as securing financial position of the widow and his unmarried daughter who was priestess. For this purpose they received a share in the inheritance (frequently a house, money and some assets), alongside the sons, who were liable for their father's debts and would receive the remaining assets in order to be able to continue their business. The widow, who is

---

49 The contracts usually do not stipulate how long the relationship will last and it is clear that many "harnessers", who occur frequently in caravan documents, served for many years as trusted servants and during all this time could use their interest free "*be'ūlātu*-loan".

50 See for the *be'ūlātu*-loan Kienast 1989, supplemented and corrected in Veenhof 1994. Kienast, impressed by the pledging terminology (*uktâl*), believes that the loan was called *be'ūlātum* because the recipient thereby came under the control (*be'ālum*) of his employer/creditor. But the texts clearly state that the employee himself "becomes boss of/will manage the silver" (*kaspam ibe''el*, cf. AKT 1, 9:7; Kt 91/k 473:6, etc.), he receives it *ana be'ālim*, which cannot to be taken as a passive infinitive, as Kienast tries. This does not mean that there were no OA cases where defaulting debtors (or their dependents) were "held by the silver (owed)" and obliged to work for their creditors. In TPAK 156 a woman pays silver to redeem – read in l. 6, *tapṭur*! – a man, who is now "held by the silver" and has to serve her for five years. Some contracts say that the hireling "holds the silver" in his possession (*kaspam ukâl*) and thereby "is held by the silver"; a few others add "with the creditor" (*išti kaspim išti* creditor *uktâl*, ICK 2, 73 and 109).

51 *Ajēmma* (16) *ula ipazzar ajēmma ipazzarma* / *pūhšu agram sāridam* / *aggaršumma igrē agrim*! / *bērā* 1 GÍN. TA *kaspam umalla*. See V. Donbaz, in Michel 2008a, 52f.

once said to be "father and mother of the silver that was her share", that is to say had full power of disposition over it, in turn could bequeath what she had inherited and left behind (called her *warkatum*) to her children.[52] See more in detail on OA testaments Veenhof 2012.

2.3.3. Marriage law

OA marriage law has been well studied recently, in particular bigamy with two wives of different rank in different places (see Veenhof 2003a, 450-455, with literature, and Michel 2006). I note here the completely different format of the marriage contracts, since OA does not know contracts whose main part is an itemized list of the goods making up the bride's **[153]** dowry[53] and in general rarely mention the transfer of goods. Also what the groom (or his father) paid for acquiring the bride, in OB *terhatum*, is rarely mentioned, but it now appears a few times as "her price", "what is paid for her" (*šīmūša*), which might rekindle the discussion about "Kaufehe".[54] The OA contracts usually also do not mention the transfer of the bride, marriage ceremonies or *verba solemnia*. Both OA and OB marriage contracts contain stipulations on a potential divorce, which was legally possible for both and with the same penalty or fine (apparently if it was without grounds). But while this was the general rule in OA – where divorcing can be rendered by the reciprocal N-stem of *parāsum (ittaprusū)* or *ezābum (innezibū, ittēzibū)* – in OB this was restricted (to quote Westbrook) to "the old cities of the South".[55] Elsewhere in OB the penalties for the wife were heavier and could vary from higher fines to being drowned or killed by being cast from a tower in the more "patriarchal" North.

Another difference concerns the marrying of a second(ary) wife or a slave as concubine, if the main wife does not (or is not allowed to) bear children. In OB the evidence is mainly found in marriage contracts and stipulations in the Laws of Hammurabi that concern *nadītums*. In OA we have three marriage contracts from *kārum* Kanesh that stipulate (as other contracts do) that the husband cannot marry a second(ary) wife there,[56] but also lay down how this, if the couple stays childless for two or three years, can be remedied. In ICK 1, 3 the wife herself buys a slave-girl for that purpose which, if she has produced a child,

---

52 See for the widow as "father and mother", Michel 2000.

53 For "the gift" to a daughter OA uses the noun *iddinū*, see the references in Veenhof 1998:150 with note 66. Kt 75/k 44:14' (fragment of a last will, courtesy of C. Michel) mentions eight textiles *ša iddinē*, "of the gift", and in CCT 5, 43:29 a share in a joint-stock company figures as "the gift of Waqqurtum".

54 E.g. in TPAK 1, 161:1-3, "15 shekels of silver, the price of (*šīm*) ᶠH. ᶠŠuppi'elka received (*talqe*) from Assur-mālik for ᶠH."; she was married as his 'maid' (l. 16, *amtum*, of different status than an *aššatum*) and he is forbidden to marry a wife (*aššatum*) in Anatolia. Kt 94/k 156:1-6, "1/2 mina of silver, the price (*šīmīša*) of ᶠAsulka, Irma-Assur paid to Anarila"; he will take her along on his trips, but is forbidden to sell her (Kt 94/k 154 documents her divorce from her husband and Anarila acknowledges to be satisfied with the divorce payment [*ēzibtum*] for Asulka). In Kt 94/k 487 (courtesy of Barjamovic) a couple sells *(ana šīmim tadānum)* their daughter as wife (l. 14f. allows the husband to marry a second wife if she remains childless) to an Assyrian for 15 shekels of silver. It seems likely that in such marriages between Assyrian traders and Anatolian girls the financial aspects, and hence the mentioning of the price paid for the girl, was particularly important, because the Assyrian husbands might in due time return to Assur, without taking their Anatolian wife along. She then would be divorced ("left behind"), after payment of the divorce settlement, the amount of which must have been conditioned by the price paid for her.

55 Westbrook 1988, 83f. He maintains that in the OB period the law of marriage was one and the same, but that the marriage contract could contain terms that survived as contingency clauses, which could contain an element of deterrent. Among them the penalty for divorcing, whose purpose in the case of the wife was transformed in North Babylonia by raising the deterrent element to a point where it renders the contingency itself virtually impossible. Whether this only meant a difference between theory and practice and not a conflict within the legal system (or even between two legal systems) – as Westbrook states, p. 85.3 – is another question, especially if the heavy penalty for the wife is not an individually negotiated feature, but a general trend in a particular period and area.

56 In ICK 1, 3 La-qēpum marries Hatala as *aššatum*, "he shall not marry a second(ary) wife/slave-girl in the land" (of Kanesh; DAM/GEME *šanītum ina mātim la ehhaz*), but marrying a *qadištum* in Assur is allowed. In Prag I 490 Puzur-Ištar marries Ištar-lamassī as *amtum*, no (*aššatum*) *šanītum* is allowed, apart from the *aššatum* he has in Assur.

can be sold again; in Prag I 490 a slave-girl will be bought and married (l. 22: *ehhaz*) by the **[154]** husband for that purpose; and in Kt 94/k 487:1-5 (see note 54) the husband of an Anatolian girl is only allowed to marry a second wife (*šanītam ehhaz*) if she does not bear children. Similar stipulations are found in contracts from Alalakh, which might suggest a "northern" feature.

Some of the peculiarities of marriage law and customs were due to the complication of the colonial life. In the OA society marriage promises or engagements apparently could be made early, before sons would leave for the colonies and some of these, as letters show, in due time were not kept. There are also a few verdicts by the *kārum* by which such an engagement or perhaps inchoate marriage was cancelled and they may state that the girl's parents "as of today (*ūmamma*) can give her to a husband (of their choice) (*EL* 275 – read in line 5 *me-er-a-sú*, "his daughter" – and Kt 88/k 1095:8-10). Other contracts reflect the realities of a commercial society, with traveling husbands, *e.g. EL* 1, which demands that if the new husband shows no care for (= visits) his new wife (an inchoate marriage?) within two months, the girl can be given to another husband. The (copy of a) verdict Kt 88/k 269 (see Çeçen 1995, no. 5) obliges a husband to give his wife during his absence each month 8 minas of *šikku*-copper for buying food, oil and fire-wood and one garment per year. Several contracts lay down the husband's right to take his wife along (*radā'um*) on his trips, if he also brings her back.[57] Such clauses may well have been negotiated by the parents of a bride who wished to protect a daughter married to a traveling trader and this also holds good of the clause that forbids a husband to deliver his wife as pledge to creditors (*EL* 2:12, the verb is *errubum*), or to sell her as a slave (Kt 94/k 156, above note 54). Some parents apparently were more successful in this than others.

2.3.4. *Guarantee*

OA has a specific type of contract by means of which a creditor obliges a "Gestellungsbürge", who guarantees the availability of his debtor on the due date to make him pay. This type of contract (Veenhof 2001a, 109-112) begins by stating that "creditor gives debtor to the guarantor" and demands him to "bring the/my man back" (*awīlam/awīlī ta''urum*) in due time. The debtor normally was a man who traveled and his departure some time before his due date is only acceptable if the risk is covered by a guarantor, who also accepts a subsidiary liability for the paying the debt. We have a few contracts where this is agreed before witnesses, and a published example is Prag I 478, where the creditors are the Assyrian authorities, represented by their secretary, because the debt is a fine imposed by the city of Assur. More numerous are depositions by witnesses, seized by the creditor, who have to testify on the words spoken by the parties, because the contract apparently had been frustrated or the debtor had protested, which had led to a law-suit before the *kārum*. Published examples are *EL* 238, 306 (where the debtor denied his liability and probably protested against being detained),[58] TPAK 1, 171, O 3684,[59] and AKT 6a, 87 (where the debtor protests **[155]** and the creditor is ready to cancel the tablet if a quittance is produced). That texts of the second type are more numerous is understandable, for when the debt was paid in time the guarantee-contract could be cancelled, while complications generated judicial records preserved in archives.

---

57 See for these features Michel 2008b, and for Kt 94/k 156, above note 54.

58 Read in line 1 the name of the creditor as [*Pu*]*zur*$_4$*-Assur* and in l. 22 presumably [*sí-ki uk-ta-n*]*a-lu-ni*.

59 In TPAK 1, 171 the creditor first addresses the guarantor M. in the usual way ("you shall bring [my man] back ..."; read in lines 7-8, [*awīlī tutarr*[*ram šumma*] / *la tut*[*a''eraššu*]), whereupon the debtor addresses his creditor about the guarantor (l. 15, *bēl qa*[*tātišu*]), perhaps stating that the latter had paid him (*šabbu'um*), but the passage is broken. In the late (ca. 1755 BC) deposition O 3684 (published in Garelli and Homès Fredericq 1987), the guarantor declares that if he fails "I will be responsible for / guarantee to you " (*ana ... azzazakkum*) the silver debt.

2.4. New and special features

A number of features require special attention, because they are innovative devices or shed some light on the purpose and writing of the records, their formulary and style.

2.4.1. The formulary of debt-notes

Nearly all OA *debt-notes* use the formulation "x silver (etc.) creditor *iṣṣēr* debtor *išû*", which does not record the act of borrowing or receiving goods, but simply the existence of a debt claim. The current OB formulary, "debtor *itti* creditor *ilqe*" (ŠU BA.AN.TI), is extremely rare. This was probably due to the fact that in most cases the debt-notes do not record loans, but result from transactions in which merchandise was given in commission to agents (*iṣṣēr tamkārim nadā'um*, "to lay on an agent"), or sold on credit (*qiāpum*), whereby the debt-note recorded how much silver the debtor owed to the creditor.[60] Once this formulary had become common it was apparently also used for real commercial loans, when a trader "borrowed silver at interest with a money-lender" (see below § 2.4.3). Only when there was the desire to fix the time a debt became interest bearing and the date was narrowed down beyond the usual week-eponymy, *ilqe* appears. An example is OIP 27, 56:22-25, "In month IV, when the (moon)god had reached the full moon stage, from the week-eponymy of A., the year eponymy of A, they received the silver (*kaspam ilqe'ū*)".[61] The commercial background of these debt-notes also explains differences in the interest clauses. Some, presumably mainly real loans, stipulate that the debt is interest bearing right from the beginning, most others, which are credit arrangements, state the date before which the agent has to pay, lest default interest starts to accrue. They show that the agent needed and received time to sell his merchandise before being able to pay and it is likely that the price he had to pay for the merchandise was also conditioned by the length of this credit term.[62]

[156] 2.4.2. "Harsh words" and "contracts"

A new feature is "to speak a strong word / harsh terms" (*dannātam qabā'um*), when in a confrontation between creditor and debtor a claim is contested. It amounted to "binding a party by a contract" (*rakkusum*), also called "to take a contract against somebody" (*tarkistam laqā'um* with dative suffix), which meant that the one who would be proved wrong would pay the double or triple (*šušalšum*, an adverb in the locative) of the amount involved. The resulting record is called *ṭuppum ša tarkistim* (*e.g.* CCT 5, 9b:23) and was

60 This formulary also occurs in OB and M. Stol in his Dutch inaugural lecture, *Een Babyloniër maakt schulden* (Free University, Amsterdam 1983) 7, qualifies them as "debts with a prehistory", occurring in debt-notes about the remainder of a partially paid debt or a down payment. He follows Koschaker in assuming that *hišum* is the Akkadian term for such a "Verpflichtungsschein". See also H. Lutzmann, *Die neusumerischen Schuldurkunden*, I (1976) 13, § 18, on the reality behind the Ur III "Verpflichtungsschein" (creditor – e debtor – ra in.da.tuku).

61 See for more examples in *CAD* Š/II, 450, 1, b); note also ICK 1, 178:2'ff., "they took the silver when Labarša became ruler", and ICK 2, 45, case, "from the week of A., when the god appeared (*ina nāmarti ilim*) they took it".

62 Many of these debt-notes were excerpted in long memoranda that give an overview of a trader's claims. That most of the excerpted debt-notes are usually absent in the archives in question suggests that they were paid, whereupon, as custom demanded, the debtor received "his tablet" back. The remaining ones could be bad debts, debt-notes rendered invalid by issuing a quittance (a tablet of satisfaction, which usually stipulated that if the debt-note turned up it would be invalid, *sar*), or debt-notes kept after their envelopes with the seal impressions that gave them their legal force had been removed. This procedure could allow creditor or debtor to preserve the tablet inside as source of information. Requests in such situations "to split" (*latā'um*) the tablet, which turned up in new texts, must refer to this practice; see for occurrences Larsen, AKT 6c, 671, comment on line 16.

preserved for potential future action.[63] Many letters give the instruction to do so and we have also records and letters that imply that this has taken place by stating that the double or triple of a disputed sum has to be paid. In AKT 3, 49:10-15, K., questioned whether he has paid to the person who has summoned him, answers: "I will not open my mouth. Give me silver and then speak your strong word to me as soon as you hand over the silver" *(ina rēš kaspim / dannatka qibiam)*. The letter KTS 5a:21-26 writes, "As for H. (apparently one of some jointly liable debtors – K.R.V.), interrogate him and set witnesses against him and validate their record (testimony). Let who is reliable (*kēnum*) give you the silver and speak the strong word to the one who denies you(r claim)" (*ana ša inakkiruka / dannatam qibišum*)." CCT 4, 5b:19-27 instructs "Seize him and make him pay the gold ... I have here his valid tablet. If he protests, take a contract against him (*tarkistam liqišum*) and then make him pay the gold." This ingenuous solution could break a stalemate during a confrontation (when neither party could prove his claim, if witnesses or records where not at hand) and prevent legal complications, as is also shown by the promise to pay "without resorting to a lawsuit" (see note 63). The one who accepted such a "contract" would almost certainly be in his right, so that the obligation or refusal to pay could be accepted. A full analysis of this device is offered in Th. K. Hertel's book on OA legal practices (Hertel 2013).

2.4.3. Borrowing at the expense of the debtor

Another legal device with a similar purpose was inserting in a debt-note a clause that authorized the creditor, if his debtor defaulted, "to enter a money-lender's house and to borrow the money at interest" *(ana bēt tamkārim erābum kaspam ana ṣibtim laqā'um)* at the debtor's expense.[64] Some occurrences add that the action could be undertaken *ana bitiqtim / bitqātim*, "for what is missing", presumably when only part of a financial obligation could be met, in which case the debtor "shall supply what is missing" (*bitiqtam šut umalla*; cf. *EL* 87 and 185, AKT 1, 34). This frequently attested clause[65] is also known from a few OB **[157]** letters (*AbB* 9, 64:10f. and 11, 12: 12f.) and from a letter from Mari, ARM 14, 17 rev:2'f., where a man who needs silver to save his life declares: "I will enter the house of a merchant and borrow [the silver]".[66] Its rarity must be due to the fact that we have much less commercial texts from the OB period. In OA it was a very useful legal device and *EL* 309 describes how things went in such a case. A debtor told his creditor that his representatives would pay his debt, adding "if they do not pay, take/call for it for me (= at my expense; *liqi'am / šisi'am*) with a money-lender at an interest of 3 shekels per month" (double the normal one, an example of the *duplum* as a fine). At the end of this record the creditor in the first person singular adds: "I asked them and when they did not give it, in accordance with his promise (*mala pīšu*) I called for it at his expense". One expects that the creditor had to produce evidence to be able to borrow money at his debtor's expense and this is perhaps implied by the verb "to call" (*šasā'um*), which could mean a public, formal action. But this is not certain because the verb, much used in OA, also occurs as simply "to borrow", "to contract for a loan" (for making purchases), as shown by the first references quoted in *CAD* Š/II, 159f., 6.

---

63 Tablets can be identified as such, e.g. the envelope Kt k/k 67a (courtesy of K. Hecker), which after the mention of the seals is said to be *ša tarkisti* PN. But the tablet inside does not use this term and only states that if a contested payment indeed had been made, the party proved wrong would pay, without resorting to a lawsuit (*balum dīnim*), three times the disputed amount, which *de facto* means *šušalšum šaqālum*, but this technical term is also not used.

64 See Veenhof 1999b, 81f.

65 It is possible that some of the many debt-notes where the creditor is not mentioned by name, but is identified as *tamkārum* reflects such loans, but the use of *tamkārum* can also be explained as a device to keep the name of the creditor secret (to avoid claims but third parties), to facilitate the transfer and cession of a debt (obvious in the clause *wābil ṭuppim šut tamkārum*), or perhaps to refer to the *tractator* of a joint-stock company.

66 Restore *ana bīt tamkārim lu-[ru-ub-ma 2 mana kaspam] / lulqêm*, cf. *MARI* 1 (1982) 149f.

2.4.4. First person clauses

The clause that authorizes a creditor to borrow money at the expense of his debtor is always in the first person singular, "I will enter with a money-lender and borrow silver". The debt-note Kt 91/k 544 uses more first person verbal forms; after stating the creditor's claim and the mention of the witnesses, it adds that the debtor "will send it to me or I will take it from his outstanding claims. The remainder of the silver I will borrow at interest and I. (the debtor) will compensate the silver and the interest on it". There are more contracts, formulated in the objective third-person style, in which one party is quoted in the first person singular, which is rare in OB contracts. One may find it in a slave sale, such as Kt 91/k 286:15-22, "If somebody raises a claim, saying 'The slave-girl is mine!', *I will lay claim to* (*adaggal*) D. and Š. (the sellers) and their house. Should they not give me my silver (*i.e.* the sale price), than the slave-girl K. is *my slave-girl and I can sell her*".[67] The *be'ūlātu*-contract Kt 91/k 403 starts in the third person, but adds in lines 8-11, "*If I send him* to Kanesh, no creditor of his father shall touch him".[68] Most occur in debt-notes, such as the clause that allows a creditor to collect his claim from his debtor wherever he turns up/they meet, which is a very useful device in a society of traveling traders. It appears in the third person formulation, but also regularly in the first person, with either the creditor as subject, "wherever **[158]** I see him", or both, in the reciprocal N-stem, "wherever we will meet" (*ašar ninnammuru*), followed by a third person "he will pay" or a first person "I will collect my silver".[69] In the Anatolian debt-note Kt d/k 34b:14, after the interest clause, we read *šalmam u kēnam nišaqqal*, "*we* (the debtors), (who of us) is solvent and available, *will pay*". Kt 91/k 515 (unopened case) contains the standard text recording a debt claim, but after the date and the clause of joint liability, it states "If they do not pay at their due date, *I will lead off* Tuwatuwi", where the singular form *ušeṣṣa* (l. 22) must have the creditor as subject, who will take the debtor's wife as pledge. In ICK 1, 193 (a rather curiously formulated contract) the clause about what happens when the debtors default is: "*I will sue* (*aše'e*) A. and E. for the silver and the interest on it". The last examples are security clauses and here the first person forms are frequent, especially in the statement "the house/slave-girl/object is my pledge" (*erubbātū'a*).[70] Similarly, the creditor's claim on a hypothecary pledge is expressed by the first person verbal form *adaggal*,[71] although third person forms also occur.

Eisser 1939, 121 already called attention to this interesting feature, but I am not sure that his explanation: "Der ... Übergang in die direkte Rede ist wohl durch die Besonderkeit bedingt, was in aller Kürze ausgedruckt werden sollte" is correct. I would rather assume that scribes traditionally used the objective, third person formulary for the standard clauses, especially in debt-notes, but could add specific stipulations, usually those recording securities, in the first person. This may indicate that at the meeting where the contract was drawn up the creditor claimed a security and that his claim was included as a quotation. That in many cases such security clauses nevertheless were in the third person must be due to the trained scribe and where this was not the case the creditor

---

67 (15) *šumma mamman iturram / umma šutma amtum / jātum* D. / *u* Š. *u bēssunu / adaggal* : *šumma kaspī* (20) *la ittadnūnim / amtum* K. *amtī / ù aššīmim addašši*. The last lines show that the sale was conditional, probably of a pledge provided by defaulting debtors, which the sellers could get back if they paid "my silver", the debt owed to the creditor. If they fail to do so, the girl was forfeited and became the creditor's chattel slave, which is shown by the last words: the right to sell is proof of unrestricted ownership.

68 There is no first person form in the marriage contract *EL* 1:19, since we have to read *a-hi-sà*! (< *āhiz-ša*) *la ukassa*, "he (the original husband) will not bind the one who (now) marries her".

69 Interesting is TC 3, 219, whose scribe used the first person in lines 12-14 of the tablet, *alī ammurušu kaspī alaqqe*, but converted this in lines 10-11 of the case into the third person, *alīma emmurušu* [KÙ.BABBAR-*p*]*í-šu* (mistake for *kasapšu*?) *ilaqqe*. Note in BIN 6, 237:3-4 the qualification of the silver owed by "the (weight of) silver has been established by means of my weights of 1/3 mina and 10 shekels".

70 TC 3, 222:9; 232:9; AKT 1, 44:8, etc., but one also finds the noun without suffix (Prag I 475:11) with a third person suffix (*EL* 227:38) or the construct state (*erubbāt kaspim*). Note that *šapartum*, "pledge", does not occur with a first person suffix.

71 See *EL* 14:16, Kt c/k 181:16, d/k 43:18, f/k 160:10, k/k 14b:13, Kt 91/k 286:19, etc.

himself, a trader who had mastered the basics of the scribal craft, may have written the contract. He may have been more prone to state his own rights and claims as he had uttered them, in the first person, which seems likely for cases like Kt 91/k 515 and ICK 1, 193. In a few cases also statements by the debtors might be quoted literally, as happened in Kt d/k 34b:14.

2.4.5. Terminological variation

From the examples give above it is clear that frequently the formulary is not fully standardized and that *variations* occur. At times this is only in the choice of a particular word, such as in the clause of the "Eviktionsgarantie", which states that the seller will "clear" the new owner from claims by others, where OA normally uses *ebbubum* (cf. Kienast 1984, 59), but without any difference in meaning also *šahhutum* occurs (both verbs even alternate on the envelope and tablet of *EL* 215). The same is the case in the verb used for "to divorce", mentioned above, under c). In other cases the variation is greater, *e.g.* in the **[159]** formulary of the sale contracts, as noted in Kienast 1984, for which various explanations are possible. Some scribes may have decided to record only the essentials of a contract; some variation is probably due to the fact that alongside a few professional scribes also traders who had mastered the art of writing were active, and there must have been developments in the formulation over time, as the example of the *be'ūlātu*-contracts has shown (above § 2.3, a).[72] Moreover, each language offers the possibility, as the terminology for the "clearance" shows, to use synonyms in descriptions and statements, apart from the fact that some variation in the order of the elements of a contract formulary is usually possible. For the study of law it is essential to establish which variations are meaningful. The absence or presence of a clause in contracts of the same type cannot be simply taken as evidence that a new rule has been introduced or an old one abolished. Even in the few extremely important *naruqqu*-contracts we know there is variation. Kayseri 313[73] mentions in lines18f. that the trader "will trade (with it) for 12 years", while Kt 91/k 482:19f. simply states that "the gold will go into Elamma's *naruqqum*", and adds that after 10 years "he will render account (*nikkassī iddan*)", an obligation not mentioned in Kayseri 313.

2.5. Terminological differences between Old Babylonian and Old Assyrian

A third problem, already mentioned, is that while OA and OB have many legal terms in common (*ahāzum*, "to marry", *ezābum*, "to divorce", *qatātum*, "guarantor", *ṣabātum*, "to seize, to summon", *hubullum*, "interest bearing debt", *qīptum*, "trust", *tadmiqtum*, a specific type of loan, *ummiānum*, "investor"), there are also differences. OA terminology which is different from OB at times agrees with that attested elsewhere Northern and peripheral Mesopotamia and in the Middle Assyrian period. "Supporting" one's parents is expressed by the Gtn-stem of *wabālum* (also used in Alalakh, in Middle Assyrian and in the "Syrian texts" from Emar) and by the Gtn-stem of *našûm* in Babylonian.[74] The same difference

---

72 As an example I mention that the way of recording the rate of interest shows a development. Older contracts, like the very old *be'ūlātu*-contract *EL* 97, for smaller amounts of silver use the formulation "1 shekel (etc.) per 10 shekels" (*10* GÍN-*um* / *ešartum 1* GÍN.TA) – with variation in using the locative ending -*um* or a prepositional construction with *ana* or *ina*. In addition, alongside the predominant expression *ṣibtam uṣṣab*, "he will add interest", one finds (as in *EL* 97:21) *illak*(*šum*), "it accrues (for him)", while a few texts also use the verb *sahārum*, presumably to express the idea that the interest is added to the capital, e.g. Kt o/k 40:18, (if they do not pay) *1 manā'um ½ mana isahhuršunūti*, "per mine ½ mina is added for them"; KKS 6:15, *1 manā'um ½ mana i-sà*(ZI)-*hu-ur*; Kt 91/k 490: 31f. (I cannot pay the copper) *aṣṣibtim lishuram*; Kt 94/k 451: 26f. (courtesy Barjamovic), (the silver we borrowed) *šinišu isahhurniāti*, "will become the double for us", etc. Not registered in *CAD* S s.v. *sahārum*, but the quote of TCL 20, 87:21, under 2, d, 1', most probably also refers to interest that accrues.

73 Recently re-edited by K. Hecker in *ArOr* 67 (1999) 558-560.

74 See Veenhof 1998, 123-134.

exists between the OA and OB versions of the so-called "Inhaber-" or "Inkassoklausel", whereby the "bearer of the tablet (*wābil ṭuppim* versus *nāši ṭuppim/kanīkim*) is said to be the one who entitled to a payment (*tamkārum*) and can collect a debt.[75]

Such lexical differences create no problems when the terms used are inter-dialectic variants and some differences indeed have only lexical interest, *e.g.* that divorce money in OB **[160]** is called *uzubbûm*, but *ēzibtum* in OA, and the "gift" to a daughter, the dowry, *iddinū* in OA, but *nudunnûm* and *šeriktum* in OB. In the formulary of the deeds of sale the "satisfaction" of the buyer and/or seller in OB is expressed by "he is content", *libbašu ṭāb*, while OA only uses *šabā'um* in the D-stem, "to satisfy" (in the stative, *šabbu'u*, and as fientic verb), which also occurs in the name for a quittance (*ṭuppum ša šābā'ē*), although *ṭubbum*, "to satisfy", is used in letters, also for "satisfying a creditor" (see *CAD* Ṭ, 41, h). Another difference is that OA has a specific verb for "to rebel against, to break an agreement", *šamāhum* (frequent in *be'ūlātu*-contracts),[76] for which rarely also *nabalkutum* is used (see above, note 44).

Problems arise when OA uses two nouns, such as those for "pledge", *šapartum* and *erubbātum*, while OB has only one, and we have to establish the difference in meaning and use, whereby also its uses in Assyrian and purely Anatolian contracts have to be distinguished. Such problems occur more often with verbs used in security clauses to describe the rights of the creditor vis-à-vis his defaulting debtor, such as "to seize" (*ṣabātum*), "to lay one's hand on" (*qātam šakānum ina*), "to hold" (*ka''ulum*), and "to look at" (*dagālum*, either having a claim on or to own).[77] They may refer to rights stipulated in contracts and to those not mentioned, but apparently by custom granted to a creditor, such as "seizing" (*ṣabātum*) objects or persons of the latter's household, "levying a distress", for which OA uses *katā'um* (which the derived noun *kutu'utum*)[78], which is the equivalent of OB *nepûm*, and different from OB and later *kattûm*, which is used for the guarantor.

The presence of a rich OA terminology in matters of security is understandable, because investments, loans, credit sale, commission and consignment created financial liabilities that asked for securities. This also led to a measure of commercial and legal creativity, because OA letters and contracts seem to have been the first where some of these features and devices were described or stipulated, which resulted in assigning new, technical meanings to existing words and to new expressions. An example of a new meaning is the use of the D-stem of the verb *erābum*, "to enter", for "to pledge", not yet registered in the dictionaries. An "old" example is in the marriage contract *EL* 2:12, where a concubine is married off and her husband and others promise that "they will neither sell her nor pledge her" (11-12, *ula iddunūši*[!] *ula urrubūši*[!]); other examples have a slave and a house as its object.[79]

---

75 See Veenhof 1997, 351-362. I can add that "the holder of a tablet" in this clause is occasionally also designated in OA by *muka''il ṭuppim* (AKT 4, 26:11; TPAK 1, 120a:6; Kt 91/k 195:27). The OA "Inkassoklausel" was already noted by Landsberger 1924, 27.

76 The verb that occurs also in a few other situations, may have a more general meaning "to be insolent, to resist, to rebel", but the hesitation of *CAD* Š/I, 290, s.v. *šamāhu* B "(mng. uncertain)", as its translations show, is not necessary (there are now several more occurrences).

77 See my survey in Veenhof 2001a,128-131.

78 There are now a few more occurrences than the single one recorded in *CAD* K s.v. *kutūtu*. The plural, *kutu'ātum*, is used with the corresponding verb in the iterative Gtn-stem, to refer to repeated attempts to obtain this security, but there is now also an occurrence of the singular, AKT 5 no. 74*:23, *ku-tù-a-sú ... lublūnim*, which shows that the noun is **kutu'atum*, with vowel harmony.

79 Cf. in the slave sale Kt c/k 701:14-16 (courtesy Dercksen*) aššīmim la iddašši / ana tamkārim / la ú-ra-áb-ší*; the statement in Kt n/k 543:12-14, "myself and my father's house *ana bēt tamkārim lu-ri-ib*" to obtain the silver that has to be paid; TPAK 1, 106:2, "They pledged [the house of A.] to I. (*ana* I. *ú-ri-bu*), to be connected with TPAK 1, 194:13-1, for a debt of S. to I_1 the house of A. / they pledged (*ú-ri-bu*). I_2 paid x silver to I_1 and the house is held (as pledge) by the silver (owed; *išti kaspim bētū uktallū*). Not that *ú-ru-ub* in *ú-ru-ub a*-WA-*tim / kaspim* (CCT 2, 35:45; 3, 38:9; 40b:11; AKT 3, 98:29) cannot be from this verbal stem (the infinitive should be *errub*), but probably is a construct state of a noun *urbum*, "what has come in, arrived".

[161] In the so-called no-contest clause or "Verzichterklärung" both OA and OB use the verb *tuārum*, "to come back, "to go back on an agreement". But OA knows a much wider use of this verb, also in the so-called "no-claim clause" that covers vindication (including redemption of a person sold into debt-slavery) and litigation. This happened because OA contracts do not use *baqārum*, "to claim"[80] and *ragāmum*, "to complain, litigate.[81]

3. SECURITIES FOR DEBTS

The first example of a comparative use of OA legal material was Landsberger's already mentioned study on "Solidarhaftung von Schuldnern" of 1924, written when only a limited number of OA texts were available. A few years later Koschaker in *NKRU* § 10, used the OA evidence in his investigation of the liability of the debtor in Middle Assyrian loan documents, where he accepted Landsberger's new interpretation (*NKRU* 118[3]) that the so-called '*šalmu-kēnu* clause', used with more than one debtor, does not mean the one who is "unversehrt und ehrlich" (which would imply "seine materielle Solvenz"), but is a *hendiaduoin*, expressing that the debtors are "forever indivisible", hence joint liability. We find this view in his comments on *HG* VI no. 1536 and it was also adopted in *EL* (p. 14), to be elaborated a few years later in Eisser 1931, who uses the translation "wohbehalten und (orts)beständig". Koschaker (p. 119) nevertheless[82] maintains that the clause originally expressed the debtor's "persönliche Exekutionsbereitheit", a view he supported by referring to the situation in OA, where the standard terminology for describing a debt, "creditor has a claim on (the back of, *iṣṣēr*) the debtor" already would imply "körperliche Haftung", while the "*šalmu* – *kēnu* clause" only occurs when there are more debtors. He also referred to the OA expression that a debt is "bound on the head (person) of the debtor" *(ina qaqqad* debtor *rakis*) as proof of "persönliche Haftung im engsten Sinne", "mit dem Leibe".[83] But he admitted that in describing the right of a creditor vis-à-vis his defaulting debtor the clause implied that he could not only seize him as pledge or distress, but could also "take" the amount due from him, presumably by seizing his property. This means a "Vermögenshaftung", as shown by the OA examples, where the debt can also be "bound on" members of his family, his house and his other possessions (*alānišu*).[84] He shared with **[162]** Landsberger the idea that the clause was "formelhaft erstarrt" and also used in a different context, as shown *e.g.* by an OA contract (now *EL* 94:19) where *šalmam u kēnam* qualifies the copper to be paid back by the debtor, clearly the complete amount, without deduction of expenses for transport and fees.[85]

Landsberger in *MSL* 1, 121ff. again discussed the clause, starting from the OB version, in which the original meaning was no longer understood. The words of TCL 10, 98:6-7, "the one (of the three debtors) who is *šalmum* will pay the silver" (lú.silim.ma kù ì.lá.e), made him modify his interpretation mentioned in *NKRU* 118[3]. Maintaining that the expression reflects the idea of "einer für alle", *i.e.* the "Integrität (Unteilbarkeit) der Schuld", he now tries to explain how the notion "ganz auf jeden einzenen der für das

80 Kienast 1984, 73, with note 78, mentions three occurrences of the verb, but only the one in a very late OA tablet, WAG 48/1464:17, where its object is a couple sold into (debt) slavery, is correct. Read in his text no.13B:7' *ipaṭṭar*, "he redeems", and the same verb is used in BIN 4, 65:42, where it means "to unpack".

81 *Ragāmum* is used in OA in letters and judicial records, with personal dative *ana* + impersonal object, for "to lodge a claim against, to sue for" (also *rigmam nadā'um*, and the noun *rigmātum*, *CAD* R 334, b)), but it does not occur in contracts.

82 Impressed by Cuq's idea that the clause meant to help a creditor if one debtor had died, fled or denied his liability, by allowing him to dun the one who was safe and sound (*šalmu*) and honest (*kēnu*).

83 He stated that the notion of a debt bound on all debtors "als Ganzheit" was too abstract and that, if the notion of "Ganzheit" of the hendiaduoin was original, it should have referred rather to the debt, "die ganze Schuld".

84 In OA the "*rakis*-formula" could even amount to a kind of "Generalhypothek", see Veenhof 2001a, 148-152. This parallels the fact that the above-mentioned *iṣṣēr* ... *išû* formula not only includes the debtor (and his family) but also his property (e.g. his house) (*NKRU* 120[2]).

85 Landsberger, *MSL* 1, 121, called it a clause whose "ursprünglichen Wortsinn nicht mehr verstanden worden ist".

ganze aufkommenden Partner übertragen worden ist".[86] But this exceptional case does not make him give up his conviction that the clause refers to "joint liability", in particular on the basis of the OA occurrences quoted in 1924, to which he now adds its use in CCT 2, 50:16.[87] He rejects Cuq's and Koschaker's idea that the clause expresses "persönliche Exekutionsbereitschaft" as anachronistic, because these contracts do not refer to "Haftung" and it would be strange if the threat of "Personalexekution" would only appear when there were more debtors. According to him the inclusion (in OA contracts) of the debtor's person, family and property in the clause leads to a new interpretation of the notion of "Ganzheit" (*šalmum*) and so gave it a new meaning, which indeed fits the OA occurrences well.

Interesting is Koschaker's observation (*NKRU* 118) that the '*šalmu-kēnu* clause' is exceptional in having an exact Old Babylonian and Sumerian equivalent (also in the lexical series *ana ittišu*: ki lú silim.ma.ta ù lú gi.na.ta šu ba.ab.te.gá), which makes him suggest that it may rather be an OA borrowing from OB than the other way around (p. 199 note 1) and that the Sumerian version, not attested in earlier Sumerian sources, could be "eine Lehnübersetzung aus dem Akkadischen" (an idea accepted by Landsberger, *MSL* 1, 123).[88] Though this is difficult to prove, it is true that the OA examples are the oldest ones attested, followed by occurrences from Northern Babylonia, while attestations in texts from Ur and Larsa are about half a century later.[89]

[163] Koschaker also mentions the case of two closely related records (CCT 1, 9a + TC 1, 77), one of which lists two men as debtors (*i-qaqqad šalmišunu rakis*), while the other states that the second man actually is the guarantor.[90] But this feature, of which we now have more examples (cf. Veenhof 2001a, 150f.), was no Assyrian innovation, since it had precursors in the Ur III period (see P. Steinkeller in Westbrook / Jasnow 2001, 50, on the guarantor as "co-obligor"). Indeed, being co-debtor or guarantor with a subsidiary liability for paying the debt probably did not make much difference in practice, although a guarantor would normally have the right of regress on the real debtor. Uncertainty about the precise implications of a '*šalmu-kēnu* security clause' might cause confusion, as was the case in a conflict concerning a capital managed by two traders and invested by others (*EL* 328:17-30; Veenhof 2001a, 150), where the solution proposed by arbitrators betrays uncertainty. It mentions both possibilities, shared and subsidiary or individual liability, and spells out the consequences of both. Such uncertainty is also clear in a settlement between the creditors and one of two presumably jointly liable debtors, recorded in Kt c/k 680, where the representatives of the missing debtor are granted the right to inspect the original tablet of the agreement to find out whether the shares (in the debt) of both are

---

86 His ingenious explanation is that an original A B *u* C *hubullam šalmu u kēnu*, via an abstracted singular version, A *hubullam šalim u kēn*, could result in the designation of the single partner as *šalmu u kēnu*.

87 "For the 30 *kutānu*-textiles that you gave (on credit) to E. and for which you drew up a tablet stating our joint liability (17f., *ṭuppam ana qaqqad / šalmini talputu*) of paying for them 10 pounds of silver within 5 weeks and which textiles E. / took, (20) you must sue E. From the tablet mentioning my name you must remove my name and write only (*-ma*) E.'s name." However, this letter does not, as claimed by Landsberger, show that the size of the amount to be paid depended on the presence of the *šalmu*-clause. The writer of this letter protested against being registered (and possibly sued) as co-debtor, since he had not received any textiles.

88 He notes that Sumerian version lú.silim.ma *ù* lú.gi.na implies that two different persons are meant, while the use of the Akkadian copula *ù* shows it not to be "good, old Sumerian".

89 See now Skaist 1994, Ch. 8 (who ignores the OA evidence). He points out the existence of two versions, one with the creditor and the other with the debtor as subject and notes that the second (which according to Koschaker and Landsberger indicates that the original meaning of the clause was no longer understood), is primarily attested in southern Babylonia and also later (after 1841 BC).

90 Koschaker also mentions the letter BIN 4, 4, which describes a substantial credit sale to two men, secured by a pledge and "bound to the head of who of them is sound" (*šalmišunu*), but adds that one of them is guarantor.

really separate shares or "the silver is bound to the person of both (jointly)".[91] In another case of a debt apparently recorded as owed by two jointly liable debtors – actually two brothers, as we know from other texts of their archive – a special record (Kt 94/k 551, courtesy of G. Barjamovic) was drawn up (perhaps later) to state that one brother is the debtor, while the other is "not concerned"; his liability, probably as guarantor, must have been only subsidiary.[92]

These uncertainties may be due to the variety of such commercial arrangements and to the fact, stressed recently by Hengstl 2008, that they could be based on oral agreements. This matches the fact than in many lawsuits not only written evidence, but also oral testimonies are necessary, especially in cases where a trader has died and his sons and heirs have to declare "we are the sons of a dead man, we do not know whether ...". This is also reflected in a few references to or short quotes from OA laws that occur in verdicts of Assur's City-Assembly, that demand "proof by witnesses" (*ina šībēšu ikuan*).[93] Another explanation could be that records were not only written by professional scribes, but also by traders, men with a basic training in writing, who may have been more focused on substance than on form. This may also explain the variation, even in a standard clause such as the *šalmu-kēnu* one, where not only the order of both adjectives can vary, but also *kēnum* is frequently omitted. It may also show that what *šalmum* expresses, "financial solvency", was **[164]** considered essential and sufficient, as already noted by Landsberger, also because readers knew what was meant, while an abbreviated formula saved room on the tablet.[94]

But there are in OA also some examples of wrong use of these adjectives, which suggests that their specific meaning was at times misunderstood, as was the case in OB, where we meet the grammatically strange construction *kaspam šalmam u kēnam išaqqal*, with the debtor as subject and the adjectives qualifying the debt. In OA both adjectives are used correctly in Kt k/k 14:10 (courtesy of K. Hecker), as object of the verb *dagālum*, where the creditors will "look at, have a claim for the silver on them jointly" (*ana kaspim šalmam u kēnam idaggulū*). But when *EL* 94:17-21, ATHE 75:19 and Kt d/k 34b:14 stipulate that the Anatolian debtor(s) will pay *šalmam u kēnam* (to which *EL* 94 adds, "in Kanesh, without (deduction of) transport fees") the addition of *kēnum* makes no sense, in particular because in the first two contracts there is only one single debtor. Less experienced scribes (Assyrian traders?) apparently used the combination instead of *šalmum* alone, "the complete, the whole (amount)", without deductions for expenses, taxes, etc., as used correctly in Kt c/k 809, rev:1-3 (courtesy of Dercksen), "He shall pay the silver [without deduction of] fees and excise to the whole amount" ([*balum*] *da'atim u nishātim šalmam išaqqal*).[95]

Studying the OA evidence one also has to distinguish – as advocated by Landsberger at an early stage – between records of legal actions in which only Anatolians figure and those were Assyrians are involved. TC 1, 68, mentioned earlier, where two jointly liable,

---

91 Edited in Balkan 1967, 401f., no. 14. The text is closely related to *POAT* 12, see Veenhof 2001a, 150. [The reading of Balkan of Kt c/k 680:15ff., quoted in my original foonote, has to be corrected according to Dercksen, who now reads *šumma* / *qātum ša* E. / *šál-ṭá-at* .. etc.].

92 Lines 5-10, *kaspum hubul* / A. / I. *ula ṭahhū*.

93 See Veenhof 1995, 1729, for this unusual intransitive form, "it becomes certain, is confirmed"; it also occurs in AKT 6, 29:14f. (in a verdict of the City of Assur), the existence of a silver debt in Anatolia *ina ṭuppēšu* / *u šībēšu ikuan*.

94 MSL 1, 121: adding *kēnum* did not add a new conceptual element. See for some OA examples *CAD* Š/I, 260, left column. Note TC 3, 218, whose tablet has only *šalmišunu*, while the case adds *kēnišunu*.

95 See for examples *CAD* Š/I, 258, 2'. Note also the single occurrence of the combination *kēnum u balṭum* in ICK 2, 43, recording a debt claim by an Assyrian on an Anatolian couple, where we have to read in line 20 (collation in Donbaz and Joannès 1982, 33 and 40) *ina qaqqad* (20) *kēnišunu ù ba-al-ṭí-šu-/nu* (21) *ra-ki-sá*. This must be a scribal mistake, because this combination refers to persons who receive a loan when they are in difficult straits (impoverished or ill) and are allowed to pay when they have recovered (see the OB examples in *CAD* Š/I, 257, 3', where the word order is always *balṭum – šalmum*, and the observations in Veenhof 1987, 58ff., and Skaist 1994, 172-180), which is not the case here.

defaulting debtors will both enter (*erābum*) the house of their Anatolian creditor (*NKRU* 120 note 3) is such a purely Anatolian record, written in Assyrian, but possibly reflecting Anatolian legal custom. Koschaker's observation that in Middle Assyrian debt-notes the *šalmu-kēnu*-clause never occurs in combination with a pledge, apparently does not apply to such Anatolian records, since we have examples where it occurs in combination with the pledging of a daughter (*EL* 15), and with a guarantor. Such records, as I have shown in Veenhof 2001a, 148-152, more often stipulate a combination of different securities,[96] but they occur also in purely Assyrian transactions. In Veenhof 2001a, 98f. I mentioned a case, detailed in a letter, where a substantial commercial silver debt, resulting from commission sale and payable in one month, is secured by default interest, joint liability, a guarantor and a valuable pledge. Such combinations may defy legal logic, but probably reflect the creditor's desire to obtain maximum security and leave him the choice which device he would actually use when his debtor defaulted. It is clear that we have to be very careful in reconstructing law on the basis of such documents. We have to isolate basic legal customs or law from variations due to individual negotiations and specific circumstances and/or to a less strict notarization of legal records by the traders themselves.

[165] The OA state of affairs regarding pledges is complex, not only because we have to distinguish between Assyrian and Anatolian contracts, but also because two nouns are used for pledge. The one is *šapartum*, well-known from later Assyrian, called "Fahrnispfand" or Faustpfand"[97] and used of movable objects, but in Anatolian records persons and houses also figure as *šapartum*. The second noun is *erubbātum*, used in OA only, from the verb "to enter" (*erābum*), from which various Semitic languages derive nouns for "pledge" and the derivative D-stem of which occurs in OA as "to pledge" (see above note 79). This suggests that what was pledged – objects, persons, real estate – entered into the power or the household of the creditor.

Kienast 1976, quoting *NKRU* 99, does not believe that "das Grund- und Personenpfand in aAss. Zeit noch generell mit Besitzübertragung verbunden war" and would have served as antichretic pledge. For *erubbātum* he distinguishes between Anatolian law, where the "Eigentumspfand" was known, and Assyrian law, where this would not be the case. He argues for the latter from the absence of clauses protecting the creditor against risks and because "Haftungskonkurrenz" is not acceptable: no "Besitzpfand" when alongside it also joint solidarity and/or a guarantor and default interest are stipulated. But, as shown above, such combinations do occur and in my opinion Kienast's approach is too theoretical. It even leads him to consider the clause that the creditor "will leave" (*waṣā'um*) a house pledged (*šapartum*) if the debtor pays, "trotz des Wortlautes als ein Garantieklausel" mentioning a "Sicherheitspfand".

Several new texts provide additional evidence for the fact that the pledge comes into the physical power of the creditor and for combinations of securities. In Kt 91/k 228:13'-14' defaulting debtors have to accept that "their pledges will be taken along" (*šaprātušina ittabbalā*) and in addition they will have to pay interest. In TPAK 1, 194 an Assyrian "pledged" (*urrib*) a house, which is now "held with the silver (owed)" (*išti kaspim uktâl*) and when the debtors pay "they will take their house (back)" (*ilaqqe'ū*). In *EL* 180 a storehouse is held (*ka''ulum*, Dtn) as pledge and the female creditor will "leave it" (l. 14: *ina huršim tuṣṣi*) when the debtor pays. In TPAK 1, 88: a house is "held" (as pledge) for a debt of three Assyrians and (lines 7-11), "if they want to expel him (the creditor), they must give him back his silver and then he will leave" (*šumma iṭarrudūšu kasapšu utarrūšumma u uṣṣi*). A girl held by an Assyrian (as pledge, or simply "seized" as distress) must be released

96 See the observations in Veenhof 2001a, 148-152.

97 A German rendering by "Sendepfand" is better abandoned, because *šapārum*, "to send", has as object persons, letters and instructions, not objects; *šapartum* probably means something that the creditor "can control, manage", another meaning of *šapārum*. OB uses *šipirtum*, which, contrary to what *CAD* Š/III, 69 s.v. *šipirtu* B suggests, is not restricted to Nuzi; see for OB occurrences D. Charpin, *NABU* 2009/59.

(*waššurum*) if silver is paid; if not the person holding her pays the double as fine (Kt v/k 157). The Assyrians clearly knew and used the "Besitzpfand".

4. SALE

The OA "Kaufvertragsrecht" was analyzed in great detail in the monograph Kienast 1984 and the picture he drew on the basis of ca. 40 contracts of sales of houses and slaves is complicated. He assumed the existence of a Babylonian, an Assyrian and a Cappadocian **[166]** "Kaufformular', all three "zweiseitig", that is, consisting of a combination of a "Kaufvermerk" (buyer bought / seller sold) with a "Kaufpreisquittung" (buyer paid, seller is satisfied / received the price). While the so-called Cappadocian formulary was always "zweiseitig", the Babylonian and Assyrian ones could be "*ex latere venditoris*" or "*ex latere emptoris*". In addition, he pointed out the existence of some variation in the sequence of certain elements, while there are also records that consisted only of a "Kaufpreisquittung" (x silver, price for object, seller *šabbū* / buyer *išqul*), followed by some "Schlussklauseln".

His use of ethnic labels requires some comment. Babylonian for him does not imply borrowing from the south but similarity, Cappadocian is used because the parties in the relevant contracts are all Anatolian, and Assyrian means that it occurs in contracts between Assyrians only, notably in one of the few deeds of sale (of a house) from Assur itself. But there is some overlap between the three, the enormous formulaic variety is rather confusing, and the Cappadocian formulary is of course in the Assyrian language. Most relevant records must have been written by Assyrians and we have no possibility of proving that the Cappadocian formulary was a basically correct Assyrian rendering of a putative native one. My earlier observations about the activity of non-professional scribes and the evidence for terminological and structural variety in many contracts, raises the question whether such a detailed analysis – with subdivisions and differentiations within each type – however informative, is fully justified.

The ideas about the historical development of the formulary have changed since Kienast wrote and we also have more OA deeds of sale that confirm the picture of formulaic variation.[98] More importantly, Steinkeller 1989, 22-29 and 139-149 has changed our understanding of the sale documents of the last centuries of the 3rd millennium, which Kienast had used only sparingly, because he focused on the comparison with the OB contracts. Steinkeller demonstrated that the idea that the buyer in the third millennium BC received two different documents, one recording the purchase and one recording the payment and its receipt (which I had originally also accepted, following my teacher F. R. Kraus), which would have merged in the OB period, was wrong. Both "served exactly the same purpose", both were real "sale documents". The use of the verbs "to buy" or "to pay" and "to receive the price" did not reflect two different legal realities, but "was purely a matter of phraseology". The purpose of the records was always to furnish the seller with a document of title. Steinkeller showed that in these early times contracts with a one-part operative section, only mentioning either the purchase of the object from the seller or the receipt of the price by the seller, were much more common than the bipartite ones. The frequent OA "Kaufvermerk" *ex latere emptoris* (Kienast 1984, 40), just like some early OB contracts from Eshnunna and OB ones from Alalakh, followed the dominant type (80%) of the Ur III period (type A): "object y for the price of x from seller buyer bought", which did not mention the payment of the price. Alongside it there existed a less frequent type (E) **[167]** with a two-part operative section, already rarely attested in the Pre-Sargonic and Sargonic periods, which used both "he bought" and "he paid" (or "he – the seller – received").

98 See e.g. Veenhof 2003b, 693ff., no. 1, a sale of a house, mentioning that the seller gave the buyer "the tablet of the purchase (price) of this house, provided with the seal of the Anatolian who was the previous owner of the house"; no 2, the sale of an Anatolian slave in the form of a "Kaufpreisquittung *ex latere emptoris*" (x silver, the price of the slave, buyer paid to seller), but without any clause protecting the buyer, which all similar records have.

Kienast is right that the typically Assyrian formulary is the one where mention of the sale (*ana šīmim tadānum*) to the buyer is followed by the statement that the seller has satisfied him (*ušabbišu*) and by a one-sided clause of non-vindication (*la tuārum*) of the item bought and/or the price paid for it. It is a precursor of the Middle Assyrian formulary and occurs in the single house sale from Assur known to him (Kienast 1984, no. 1), but it has now turned up in a second one from Assur; both are 'Late Old Assyrian', presumably from the 17th century BC.[99] The first is said to be a copy of the text of an official *tuppum dannatum*, "a validated tablet", whose issue, according to MALaws, tablet B § 6, was preceded by publicizing and validating the transaction by public officials. The second one uses the same terminology, but adds that the sale was "voluntary" (*ina migrātišu*), a clause more common in Middle Assyrian times, but omits the phrase of the satisfaction of the buyer. A further variation in OA is that when the clause of satisfaction is present, it is not in the form of a fientic past tense (*ušabbišu*), but as a stative, *šabbu'u*, comparable to the OB *libbašu ṭāb / ṭīb*, which is not used in Assyrian.

In view of the situation prevailing during the preceding Sargonic and Ur III-periods it does not surprise to find in OA a variety of formulations. It also fits the more general picture of a certain fluidity in the redaction of OA legal documents, combined with a tendency to keep them short and factual, without what has been called narrative elements and without reference to symbolic actions or *verba solemnia*, a feature which is also noticeable in the judicial records, in particular in verdicts.[100] And there must have been also certain developments in OA law during the period of ca. two centuries during which Old Assyrian records were written. Unfortunately the number of legal texts from the earliest period, roughly before eponymy year 65 (ca. 1910 BC) and from the so-called later OA period, contemporary to level Ib of *kārum* Kanesh, roughly from the last quarter of the 19th century BC (middle chronology), is still very limited. Above (§ 2.3, a) I called attention to the development in the formulary and substance of the so-called *be'ūlātu*- or service-contract, used for engaging caravan personnel and a broader investigation of such changes is a desideratum.

[168] 5. LAWS AND LEGISLATION

The last comparative feature I wish to raise here relates to what are commonly called "laws". As mentioned above, we have no OA laws, but only some of references to or short quotes from them.[101] Assur's City Assembly passed some verdicts whose substance is provided with the qualification "in accordance with the words of the stele". As their formulation ("whoever .."), syntax (a simple indicative) and in one case a sanction in the form of a death penalty show, they prove the existence of authoritative legal regulations inscribed on a stone monument, hence published. That the references in texts found in the archives of traders refer to commercial and financial issues is understandable, but does not mean that these laws could not also have dealt with other matters.

99 See for both contracts Veenhof 2011, 219, § 5.

100 Kt 91/k 410:7-9 (Veenhof 2003b, no. 3) mentions as proof of the sale of a slave that the buyer "cut the stalk" (*hāmam ibtuq*), apparently a symbolic action to mark the change of status or owner. The record is not a deed of sale, but occurs in a testimony of witnesses summoned when the sale was contested, in whose presence (*mahrini*) the action was performed. It shows that symbolic actions did take place without being recorded in the contract, but were mentioned when witnesses had to testify. In the case of a marriage or divorce the accompanying symbolic actions "knotting / cutting the hem of a garment" (*sissiktam kaṣārum / batāqum*) are not mentioned in the relevant contracts, but reported in judicial records by witnesses, because they apparently stuck better in their memory than the words spoken.

101 Veenhof 1995 supplemented by Veenhof 2008b, 262-269, § 3, where I could mention two additional references. In AKT 3, 98:18 somebody writes to his opponent "Has a separate stele been written for you, that you dare to... ?" (*naru'a'um ku'a'um ina battim lapitma mā ...*), which means "Does the law not apply to you?". In Kt 94/k 543:22f. (courtesy of G. Barjamovic) a trader writes: "You have violated/ignored what the stele stipulates (*ša naru'a'im tukkiš*) by interrogating me in a trial", which must refer to a rule of procedural law.

What is important in comparative respect is the mere fact *that* verdicts do refer to them and quote them. This contrasts with the lack of such references in OB contracts and judicial records,[102] which has been an argument in the discussion on whether the laws had binding legal force and the courts had to apply them. The force of this argument has been played down in various ways,[103] but OA quotations of rules of law in official verdicts show that they were referred to. And we cannot ignore the fact, stressed by Westbrook 1989, 214f., that royal edicts (*ṣimdat šarrim*) were regularly quoted or referred to (in the same way as OA laws, "in accordance with ...") in OB contracts and letters. This suggests that the latter, royally imposed rules and regulations for frequent legal issues, at times also to supplement existing rules,[104] are comparable in substance and application to the OA laws. OA laws dealt with very concrete, frequent legal issues – the liquidation of a dead trader's business, payment of debts, compensation for merchandise lost in a collective caravan, the use of gold in commercial operations – and aspects of judicial procedure, both relevant for the life and business of citizens of Assur and thus applicable and quoted in verdicts. They were not a scholarly composition, but the result of the actual jurisprudence of the City Assembly and the ruler,[105] who had drafted and published them. In both respects they are different from **[169]** Hammurabi's "laws", which also embodied tradition, scholarship and ideology. If this is right, the comparison shows that the laws in both countries were rather different in origin, substance and coverage, which this may explain the lack of quotations from laws in OB records.

6. CONCLUSION

The study of the law and legal records of the OA period is fascinating and notwithstanding their specific commercial background a comparative approach is necessary and enlightening. Assyriology has gradually entered a period of high specialization, in which broad, comparative investigations are difficult to realize and individual research strongly focuses on particular periods, areas or text types. This makes cooperation, joint efforts and specialized workshops valuable and they may produce volumes where the presentation of the evidence for various periods, areas and cultures by a number of specialists is preceded by a general introduction. Good examples are the volumes *Rendre justice en Mésopotamie. Archives judiciaires du Proche-Orient ancien (IIIe-Ier millénaires avant J.-C.)* (Joannès 2000), and *Security for Debt in Ancient Near Eastern Law* (Westbrook / Jasnow 2001).[106] It shows that comparison is possible and fruitful, certainly for the largely contemporary OA and OB periods. It is rather unsatisfactory to see that in the rich volume on *The Old Babylonian Loan Contract* (Skaist 1994) the at times relevant and enlightening comparative OA evidence is almost completely absent.

---

102 There is one reference to a stele that stipulated the wages of a hired worker (cf. *CAD* N/I, 364, 1), but it occurs in a letter.

103 See e.g. R. Westbrook, *Revue Biblique* 92 (1985) 204, on three reasons why we lack evidence on its actual consultation, but in his "Cuneiform Law and the Origins of Legislation", *ZA* 79 (1989) 213-215, he rejects the traditional explanations for the lack of quotations in antiquity – that citation was not required in antiquity and that trial records never give legal grounds for their decisions, – pointing to texts from the "post-cuneiform period of classical antiquity" in which laws are indeed quoted. This proof is not convincing, because legal customs may have been different then and there (in a later period and in different cultures). Moreover, quotations in a legal work, in *Mishna*, tractate Ketubot, and in a speech of Demosthenes, are quite different from quotations in practice documents such as contracts or verdicts.

104 They have been collected and explained in Veenhof 2001b.

105 This is clear from the verdict (*dīnum*) on the sale of gold to non-Assyrians, recorded in Kt 79/k 101, communicated in a letter of the ruler of Assur (Veenhof 1995, 1733). It states that the City, contrary what was implied by the text of a recent verdict sent to Kanesh, "had not fixed anything (*iṣurtam la nēṣur*) about gold; the earlier regulation (*awātum pāniātum*) is still in force" and the text then quotes what is "in accordance with the words of the stele".

106 This volume was the result of a colloquium of the Society for Ancient Near Eastern Law, a form of cooperation that, unfortunately, has come to an end.

In a review of J. Lautner's *Die richterliche Entscheidung und die Streitbeendigung im altbabylonischen Prozessrechte* of 1922, Julius Lewy (*OLZ* 1925, 656f.) voiced his regret that in the discussion of the "Privatladung" the OA evidence was not considered, "veilleicht nur deswegen weil es altassyrisch war". This complaint, in the early stages of OA studies, was perhaps a little unfair, but one may regret that in Eva Dombradi's analysis of the meaning and implications of this feature and its key-verb *ṣabātum* in OB she pays much attention to the comparative evidence of Roman law,[107] while the nearly contemporary OA data, which have been studied,[108] are only referred to in two footnotes. In OA legal procedure private summonses, expressed by stating that one person "seized" (*ṣabātum*) another person (usually his debtor) and more fully by *sikki* PN *ṣabātum*, "to seize a person's hem", are very numerous. And we are also well informed about a different (and in some cases perhaps next) step, in which the plaintiff "seized" arbitrators against his opponent, who then work out a solution to settle the case (*awātam gamārum*).[109] Dombradi does not use the OA **[170]** evidence, because "im benachbarten assyrischen Raum anscheinend andere Verhältnisse herrschen",[110] but notwithstanding the differences, due to the commercial background and the nature of the colonial society which came up with some original procedural devices, there is also similarity, which warrants a more thorough comparative analysis. The OA evidence in my opinion would also have been useful for her in refuting Lautner's view that such a "Ladung", somewhat like the Roman *manus iniectio*, would force the person seized to start a formal lawsuit in order to free himself. This is also not true in OA, although each of the two parties, if dissatisfied, could always appeal to the judicial authorities.[111] This happened in particular when the one initiating the seizure would "hold the hem" (*sikkam ka''ulum*) of his opponent, which meant that he could not leave, unless he satisfied his opponent in some way, which must have been very detrimental for a traveling trader.[112] I admit that the forms and procedures of these OA summonses or "seizures" are complicated, but they can be studied in detail in Hertel 2013.

And such summonses are of course not the only aspect of judicial procedure where comparison is rewarding, not to mention the area of debts and loans, with their modes of payment, rates of interest and various security devices. The source material has increased considerably since Rosen 1977 (see note 20), also from officially excavated archives that allow a better analysis of these records on the basis of more knowledge of the parties, their status and interests.[113] Especially the many contracts in which Anatolians figure as debtors and/or creditors, with partly deviating and original features, deserve a special investigation, also to trace possible native Anatolian elements. And such studies would

---

107 Dombradi 1996, I, §§ 393-399, with notes 1789, 1792, 1795-98, 1800 and 1803-4.

108 In Veenhof 1991 and before that in M. Mallul, *Studies in Mesopotamian Legal Symbolism* (AOAT 221, 1988), Ch. X, who focused on the legal symbolism embodied in the acts called "to seize / to hold the hem" of a person's garment.

109 In addition OA knows cases where the person seized inverts the action by himself "seizing" his opponent, cases where two parties "seized each other mutually" (reflexive N-stem, *naṣbutum*), and cases where both parties "in mutual agreement" *(ina migrātišunu)* "seized" arbitrators. The frequency of "seizures" is related to the fact that both debtors and creditors were traveling and that credit sales were very frequent. "Seizures" (in combination with security stipulations) tried to prevent or solve the problems of actual or feared delays in payment due to defaulting or absent debtors.

110 Footnote 1814. In footnote 1794 she admits that in OA *ṣabātum* means "einen Akt der Ladung", but adds: "Dieser Akt is allerdings anders definiert und hat auch andere Wirkungen", quoting Larsen 1976, 173f.

111 E.g. in CCT 5, 44b rev.: 2'-10', "Here we seized [PN] and we said: Pay the silver!. He appealed to the plenary assembly of the *kārum* and said: I do owe 2 ½ minas of silver, but I have been given a term." (*ettum šaknam*).

112 Larsen 1976, 316 quotes two texts where the action of a creditor in such a case is designated both by the verb "to seize" and by "to approach (with a claim)" (*ṭahā'um*): *tamkārum ula iṣabbassu / iṭahhiaššunūti* (ICK 1, 26a:9 and OIP 27, 12:19), cf. *CAD* Ṭ, 1, a,1',b' and 3', a' (*ArAn* 1, 54, no. 3:50), *šumma* .. PN *rigmam ittidima a-mimma iṭṭihi*. Compare Dombradi 1994, § 396, where she states that *ṣabātum* as "Geltendmachung eines Begehrens" is not essentially different from *ragāmum* and *baqārum*.

113 Some new insights have been offered in Dercksen 1999 and Veenhof 1999b in the volume *Trade and Finance in Ancient Mesopotamia*.

certainly benefit from a cooperation between philologists and legal historians, as successfully exemplified for the Old Assyrian material by the joint efforts of G. Eisser and J. Lewy, embodied in *EL*.

Bibliography

Albayrak, I. 2001. Kültepe Merinlerinde Geçen *mā'û*, "su" Kelimesi, *AMMY* 2000, 300-311.

Bayram, S., and Veenhof, K.R. 1992. Unpublished Kültepe Texts on Real Estate, *JEOL* 32, 87-100.

Balkan, K. 1967. Contributions to the Understanding of the Idiom of the Old Assyrian Merchants of Kanish, *OrNS* 36, 393-415.

–. 1974. Cancellation of Debts in Cappadocian Tablets from Kültepe, in: *Anatolian Studies Presented to Hans Gustav Güterbock on the Occasion of his 65th Birthday*. Istanbul, 29-42.

Çeçen, S. 1995. *Mutānū* in den Kültepe-Texten, *ArAn* 1, 43-72.

Dercksen J.G. 1999. On the Financing of Old Assyrian Merchants, in: J.G. Dercksen (ed.), *Trade and Finance in Ancient Mesopotamia*, Istanbul, 85-99.

–. 2004a. *Old Assyrian Institutions*. MOS Studies 4, PIHANS 98. Leiden.

–. 2004b. Some Elements of Old Anatolian Society in: *Studies Larsen*, 137-177.

Dombradi, E. 1996. *Die Darstellung des Rechtsaustrags in den altbabylonischen Prozessurkunden*, I-II. FAOS 20/1-2. Stuttgart.

Donbaz, V. and Joannès, F. 1982. Nouvelles lectures de textes cappadociens, in: *Mémorial Atatürk*. Istanbul, 27-41.

Eisser, G. 1931. Zur Deutung der Gesamthaftungsklausel des altassyrischen Rechts, *Archiv für Civile Praxis*, Beilageheft (Tübingen) 157-177.

–. 1939. Beiträge zur Urkundenlehre der altassyrischen Rechtsurkunden vom Kültepe, in: *Festschrift für Paul Koschaker*, III. Weimar 1939, 94-129.

Garelli, P., and Homès-Fredericq, D. 1987. Une tablette de la couche Ib de Kaniš, in: F. Rochberg-Halton (ed.), *Language, Literature, and History. Philological and Historical Studies Presented to Erica Reiner*. AOS 67. New Haven, 107-124.

Günbattı, C. 2004. Two Treaty Texts Found at Kültepe, in: *Studies Larsen*, 249-268.

Hengstl, J. 1987. Zum Kauf under Rückkaufsvorbehalt in den altassyrischen Urkunden aus Kanesh, *ZA* 77, 98-116.

–. 2008. Rechtsgeschäfte im Rahmen des altassyrischen Handels, *AoF* 35, 268-295.

Hertel, Th.K., and Larsen, M.T. 2010. Situating Legal Strategies. On reading Mesopotamian law cases, in: S. Dönmez (ed.), *Veysel Donbaz'a Sunulan Yazilar. DUB.SAR É.DUB. BA.BA. Studies Presented i Honour of Veysel Donbaz*. Istanbul, 167-180.

Landsberger, B. 1924. *Assyrische Handelskolonien in Kleinasien. Der Alte Orient*, Heft 24/4.

–. 1940. Vier Urkunden vom Kültepe, *Arkeologya Dergisi* 4, 7-31.

–. 1964. Einige unerkannt gebliebene oder verkannte Nomina des Akkadischen 5. Exkurs: *ana ittišu, WdO* 3, 62-77.

Landsberger, B., and Balkan, K. 1950. Die Inschrift des assyrischen Könings İrişum gefunden in Kültepe 1948, *Belleten* 14, 219-268.

Larsen, M.T. 1976. *The Old Assyrian City-State and its Colonies*. Mesopotamia 4. Copenhagen.

–. 1977. Partnerships in the Old Assyrian Trade, *Iraq* 39,119-145.

–. 2001. *Naruqqu*-Verträge, *RlA* 9, 181-184.

Michel, C. 2000. À propos d'un testament paléo-assyrien: une femme de marchand "père et mère" des capitaux, *RA* 94, 1-10.

–. 2003. *Old Assyrian Bibliography*. OAAS 1. Leiden.

–. 2006. Bigamie chez les Assyriens au début du IIe millénaire avant J.-C., *Revue historique de droit francais et étranger* 84, 155-176.

–. 2008a. C. Michel (ed.), *Old Assyrian Studies in Memory of Paul Garelli*. OAAS 4. Leiden.

–. 2008b. Femmes au foyer et femmes en voyages, in: *Voyageuses. Histoire, femmes et sociétés* 28, 17-38.
Skaist, A. 1994. *The Old Babylonian Loan Contract. Its History and Geography*. Bar-Ilan.
Steinkeller, P. 1989. *Sale Documents of the Ur-III-Period*. FAOS 17. Stuttgart.
Veenhof, K. R. 1982. A Deed of Manumission and Adoption from the Later Old Assyrian Period, in: G. van Driel e.a. (eds.), *Zikir šumim. Assyriological Studies Presented to F.R. Kraus on the Occasion of his Seventieth Birthday*. Leiden, 359-385 [= pp. 245-265 in this volume].
–. 1987.'Dying Tablets' and 'Hungry Silver'': Elements of Figurative Language in Akkadian Commercial Terminology, in: M. Mindlin *et al.* (eds.), *Figurative Language in the Ancient Near East*. London, 41-76.
–. 1991. Private Summons and Arbitration Among the Old Assyrian Traders, *Bulletin of the Middle Eastern Culture Center in Japan* 5, 437-460.
–. 1994. Miete. C. Altassyrisch, *RlA* 8, 181-184.
–. 1995. "In Accordance with the Words of the Stele". Evidence for Old Assyrian Legislation, *Chicago-Kent Law Review* 70, 171-1744 [= pp. 109-127 in this volume].
–. 1997. "Modern" Features in Old Assyrian Trade, *JESHO* 40, 336-366.
–. 1998. Old Assyrian and Ancient Anatolian Evidence for the Care of the Elderly, in: M. Stol and S.P. Vleming (eds.), *The Care of the Elderly in the Ancient Near East*. Studies in the History and Culture of the Ancient Near East 14. Leiden-Boston, 119-160 [= pp. 185-210 in this volume].
–. 1999a. Redemption of Houses in Assur and Sippar, in: B. Bock *et al.* (eds.), *Munuscula Mesopotamica. Festschrift für Johannes Renger*. AOAT 267. Münster, 599-616 [= pp. 211-223 in this volume].
–. 1999b. Silver and Credit in Old Assyrian Trade, in: J.G. Dercksen (ed.), *Trade and Finance in Ancient Mesopotamia*. Istanbul, 56-84 [= pp. 159-184 in this volume].
–. 2001a. The Old Assyrian Period, in: Westbrook – Jasnow (eds.) 2001, 93-159.
–. 2001b. The Relation between Royal Decrees and 'Law Codes' in the Old Babylonian Period, *JEOL* 35-36, 49-83 [= pp. 297-328 in this volume].
–. 2003a. Old Assyrian Period, in: R. Westbrook (ed.), *A History of Ancient Near Eastern Law* (HdO section I, vol. 72), vol. I. Leiden-Boston, 431-485.
–. 2003b. Three Unusual Old Assyrian Contracts, in: G.J. Selz (ed.), *Festschrift für Burkhart Kienast zu seinem 70. Geburtstage*. AOAT 274. Münster 2003, 693-705.
–. 2004a. Trade with the Blessing of Šamaš in Old Babylonian Sippar, in: *Studies Larsen*, 551-582 [= pp. 369-393 in this volume].
–. 2008a. The Old Assyrian Period, in: M. Wäfler (ed.), *Mesopotamia. The Old Assyrian Period. Annäherungen* 5. OBO 160/5. Fribourg-Göttingen, Teil 1.
–. 2008b. Aspects of Old Assyrian Commercial Law: Treaties and Legislation, in: M. Liverani and C. Mora (eds.), *Il diritti del mondo cuneiforme (Mesopotamia e regioni adiacenti, ca. 2500-500 a.C.)*. Pavia. Istituto Universitario di Studie Superiori di Pavia, 247-269.
–. 2011. Houses in the Ancient City of Assur, in: B.S. Düring *et al.* (eds.), *Correlates of Complexity. Studies in Archaeology and Assyriology dedicated to Diederick J.W. Meijer* (PIHANS 116). Leiden, 211-232.
–. 2012. Last Wills and Inheritance of Old Assyrian Traders with Four Records from the Archive of Elamma. Pp. 169-202 in K. Abraham and J. Fleishman (eds), *Looking at the Ancient Near East and the Bible through the Same Eyes. A Tribute to Aaron Skaist*. Bethesda, Maryland: CDL Press.
–. 2016/17. Some Old Assyrian and Old Babylonian Adoption Contracts. *JEOL* 46, 3-43.
Westbrook, R. (ed.). 2003. *A History of Ancient Near Eastern Law*. Handbook of Oriental Studies, Section One, vol. 72 /I-II. Leiden-Boston.
Westbrook, R. and Jasnow, R. (eds.). 2001. *Security for Debt in Ancient Near Eastern Law*. Culture and History of the Ancient Near East 9. Leiden-Boston.

Ancient Assur: The City, its Traders and its Commercial Network*

1. Trade in ancient Mesopotamia

As the alluvial plain of southern Iraq, where the Mesopotamian civilization arose, lacked most natural resources (metals, stones and good wood) essential for the development of a complex society, they had to be obtained from neighboring and more distant regions. Throughout Mesopotamian history we therefore notice a variety of strategies to acquire them from Iran, the Persian Gulf, the Northern Levant, and Anatolia.

A very early practice meant to achieve this, which has been termed an early, perhaps embryonic colonial system, existed shortly before 3000 BC, on the fringes of Northern Mesopotamia, between the Upper course of the Euphrates in the west and the Zagros mountains in the east. It was a network that comprised at least one impressive city on the Upper Euphrates[1] and a number of enclaves in existing towns, clearly recognizable by their purely South-Mesopotamian material remains. This system is thought to have served to secure exchange relations with, and trade routes through, areas from which the highly developing urban culture of the South-Mesopotamian 'Late-Uruk Culture' obtained metals, lumber and stones. Because it dates to the centuries immediately before the invention of script, we only have archaeological data, which makes its interpretation and function **[41]** somewhat hypothetical. I will not dwell on this, however, and refer those interested to a fascinating book on this so-called "Uruk World System".[2]

Occasionally military means, such as conquests, campaigns and raids, were used to obtain essential materials as booty.[3] In a few periods (mainly during the last centuries of the third millennium BC) powerful Mesopotamian empires managed to subdue and temporarily control some neighboring cities and lands, and at times they also tried to secure the flow of goods by imposing the payment of tribute on vassals or by establishing a more permanent military or commercial presence in vital fringe areas. Susa, in southwestern Iran, during the last centuries of the 3rd millennium BC, was frequently

---

1 The city, whose ruins are called Habuba Qabira/Tell Qannas, was submerged by Lake Assad before it could be completely excavated. With its size of 15 ha, its walls and lay-out (with temples and an administrative quarter) on an Euphrates terrace, it goes far beyond a trading colony and suggests a massive effort to dominate this important region and to defend the Mesopotamian economic interests, if necessary also by force.

2 G. Algaze, The Uruk World System. The Dynamics of Early Mesopotamian Civilization (Chicago-London: University of Chicago Press, 1993). See for an analysis also G.J. Stein, Rethinking World-Systems. Diasporas, Colonies, and Interaction in Uruk Mesopotamia (Tuscon: University of Arizona Press, 1999), and G. J. Stein "The Political Economy of Mesopotamian Colonial Encounters." In The Archaeology of Colonial Encounters, Comparative Perspectives, ed. G.J. Stein (Santa Fe-Oxford: School of American Research Press – James Currey, 2002) Ch. 5, where he compares the "Uruk world system" with the Old Assyrian colonial system.

3 The Old Akkadian king Manishtusu (ca. 2300 BC) boasts of having campaigned in southern Iran, subdued towns on the far side of the Persian Gulf, reached the "silver mines" and quarried precious "black stones" (diorite?) that were shipped by boat to his capital. Naram-Sîn and his son claim to have cedars cut in the Amanus for the temple of their goddess Ishtar.

* Originally published in the Journal of the Economic and Social History of the Orient 53 (2010) 39-82.

under the rule of Mesopotamian kings and harbored Mesopotamian merchants. The Old Akkadian empire built the fortress Nagar (Tell Brak) in the north of the Jazira, from where it could monitor southern Anatolia. But before the rise of the Neo-Assyrian empire, in the 1st millennium BC, most of these areas were rarely conquered and dominated, and several materials originated from regions usually (*e.g.* the Lebanon with its cedars, Cilicia with its silver mines) or always (Oman with its copper, Northeastern Afghanistan with its lapis lazuli and tin) beyond Mesopotamian reach or control.

This meant that during most of Mesopotamian history and certainly during the first centuries of the second millennium BC, which are the focus of this contribution, trade was the preferred, most efficient and presumably also cheapest way of obtaining the materials essential for its highly developed and urbanized culture. It was practiced in the form **[42]** of interregional exchange, via entrepreneurs,[4] who ventured abroad with their donkey caravans and boats, preferably to emporia, market towns and ports of trade, such as Bahrain in the Persian Gulf, Susa in southwestern Iran, or Emar and Karkemish on the Upper Euphrates, where traders from various regions met. The importance of trade also meant that foreign traders, especially from the area of the Upper Euphrates and from that of the Persian Gulf, were welcomed as sellers and buyers to the cities and quays of Mesopotamia.

In the Babylonia of the early second millennium BC we witness a system emerged which allowed groups of merchants from various trading cities to settle in other cities,[5] occasionally even – presumably on the basis of political agreements – in those of neighboring territorial states. These merchants were usually[6] concentrated, often together with the local traders, in a special area, called *kārum*, "quay, harbor",[7] where they conducted their business in the interest of themselves, their mother-city and their host-city. According to a famous statement in a letter from that period they **[43]** could even travel between areas at war, just like pastoral nomads during the transhumance, because their activities were appreciated and they enjoyed a special status that offered protection. This arrangements did not only apply to their trips, but it also protected them from service duties for which a ruler could summon his citizens. The *kārum* of the city of Mari on the Middle Euphrates, *e.g.* also included traders from Sippar (the main Babylonian trading city on the Euphrates), whose designation as "the *kārum* of Sippar that is in Mari" identifies it as an organized, corporate group, under its own "head", who stood in contact with the mother-city, an arrangement, which probably also existed in other

---

4 Rulers occasionally also sent out envoys for the sake of gift exchange, diplomatic operations of at times limited direct economic importance, but valuable for establishing and fostering international contacts with strategic foreign states or cities, from which their traders could profit. In the early 18th century BC Mari (on the Euphrates) sent envoys with gifts in gold to the ruler of Susa, to secure the import on tin. See C. Michel, "Le commerce dans les textes de Mari". In *Amurru* 1, ed. J.-M. Durand (Paris: Éditions Recherche sur les Civilisations, 1996): 385-425, esp. 390-1.

5 A royal edict from ca. 1640 BC, edited in F.R. Kraus, *Königliche Verfügungen in altbabylonischer Zeit* (Leiden: Brill, 1984): 169-83, in § 10 enumerates the *kārums* of eleven cities in southern Mesopotamia which were affected by a measure of a Babylonian king and therefore consisting (in part?) of traders originating from the Babylonian state.

6 Not always. Traders from Sippar lived in Susa, without reference to a *kārum*, and we meet traders from Isin settled in Sippar in "the street of the men of Isin", and traders from Assur operating from "quarters" (called *bēt napṭarim*, a term denoting a secondary or temporary facility outside one's home town) bought or rented in that city or in the *kārum*. See for similar observations on Mari, C. Michel, "Le commerce": 413-26.

7 Because the main Babylonian cities were situated on watercourses and most bulk transport was by water, their "quays" (*kārum*) played a key role in the distribution and transfer of domestic and imported goods. "Quays" became "commercial districts", with public and private buildings where suppliers and domestic and foreign traders would meet, goods were exchanged and also their exchange values became established (one could speak of "the current *kārum* of barley", or state that "the *kārum* of dates is x shekels of silver per kor"). In its derived meaning of "commercial district" the term was also used in connection with cities outside Babylonia, not situated on a watercourse, such as the commercial settlements or colonies in Upper Mesopotamia and even Anatolia (see below).

cities and *kārums*, must have been based on formal agreements,[8] and there is evidence that the activities of the foreign traders could be monitored by the local "Overseer of the traders", a government official. Cities that needed imports and wished to convert their own surpluses and products into goods they lacked apparently welcomed foreign traders in their *kārums*, because commercial exchange was not normally undertaken by "the state" itself. They not only supplied essential goods, but also stimulated economic activity, generated income in the form of import taxes (called *miksum*, usually at a rate of 10%), paid in the towns where their boats or caravans entered a state's territory.[9]

[44] This so-called "*kārum*-system" was very important for the trade and for exploiting the economic potential of the cities and their countryside and even for trade across some territorial boundaries. But, as far as the evidence now available goes, it never developed, not even under powerful states such as Babylon, Larsa or Mari, into a real "colonial system", that is a more or less coherent network of traders settled in market-cities and emporia to serve the economic interests of a particular empire. What we are rather dealing with here were in essence we are dealing with commercial arrangements that facilitated regional, inter-city trade, in some cases also across territorial boundaries, by groups of merchants from various cities operating in, and from, other cities, preferably capitals and strategically located emporia and market-towns. While these merchants were thus important for palaces and rulers in supplying them with goods required or converting their mostly agricultural surpluses – tasks also performed by local traders and occasionally by officials of the palace sent out with particular commissions – they were basically private entrepreneurs.

2. The Assyrian Commercial Network and Colonial System

The only well-documented commercial network, consisting of a series of interconnected trading colonies from one single state in strategic towns in a target area was that of the city of Assur during the first centuries of the 2nd millennium B.C. It served the massive import of expensive woolen textiles, tin (essential in the Middle Bronze Period) and also lapis lazuli by donkey caravans into Anatolia, where the Assyrians sold them, directly and indirectly (via their participation in the internal Anatolian trade in copper, wool and grain) for silver and gold that was shipped back to Assur.[10] In its fully developed form it comprised ca. forty commercial settlements of two kinds. The bigger and presumably more independent and administratively more equipped ones, attached to politically and

---

8 The "commercial quarter" of the city of Apum (Tell Leilan), in Northern Mesopotamia, comprised merchant communities (*kārums*) from three neighboring towns and from Assur, and the position of the latter was regulated in a treaty concluded between the local king and the city of Assur; see K.R. Veenhof, "Old Assyrian Period" (2008a): Ch. V, on treaty B. Unfortunately, the few other surviving international Old Babylonian treaties focus on diplomacy and military matters and do not mention trade. A much later, instructive example from a neighboring area is provided by the Biblical story of 1 Kings 20:21ff., (9th century BC), in which king Barhadad of Aram-Damascus, defeated by Achab of Israel, offers him permission "to set up 'streets' (*ḥuṣōt*, the equivalent of a *suq*) in Damascus, as my father did in Samaria", whereupon Achab lets him go "with a treaty". Such agreements of course could also be concluded without war, in the economic interest of both parties.

9 My focus on Assur does not allow me to go into details for Babylonia and I refer to the recent documentation and discussion (with bibliographical references) by M. Stol, "Wirtschaft und Gesellschaft in altbabylonischer Zeit." In P. Attinger, W. Sallaberger, and M. Wäfler, eds., *Mesopotamien. Die altbabylonische Zeit. Annäherungen* 4 (Orbis Biblicus et Orientalis 150/4; Fribourg-Göttingen 2004): Ch. 15, "Der Handel", esp. p. 893-9. See for the *kārum* of Mari and other *kārums* mentioned in the texts from Mari, Michel, "Le commerce" (above note 4): 413-17, and J.-M. Durand, *Documents épistolaires du palais de Mari*, III (Paris: Le Cerf, 2000): Ch. 12, "Les activités commerciales".

10 It is impossible to describe the Old Assyrian trade here in detail and I refer the reader to my recent overview in Veenhof, "Old Assyrian Period" (2008a) and the bibliography presented there. Other valuable introductions are M. T. Larsen, *The Old Assyrian City-State and its Colonies* (Copenhagen: Akademisk Forlag, 1976), the introduction to C. Michel, *Correspondance des marchands de Kanish au début du IIe millénaire avant J.-C.* (Paris: Le Cerf, 2001) [and now M.T. Larsen, *Ancient Kanesh. A Merchant Colony in Bronze Age Anatolia* (Cambridge: Cambridge University Press, 2015)].

economically important Anatolian cities, frequently capitals of city-states, were called *kārum* or "colony", of which at least 23 are known. Alongside these there existed **[45]** ca. 15 so-called *wabartums* or "trading stations", usually in smaller or economically less important cities and road-stations.[11]

Of the *kārums* that of Kanesh, an important city in Central Anatolia, northeast of Kayseri, just south of the Halys/Kızılırmak, was the most important (and presumably oldest) one and our knowledge of Old Assyrian trade is due to the fact that is was identified in 1925 and has been continuously excavated by Turkish archeologists since 1948. It was the seat of the corporate administration of the whole colonial system, led by a committee of "big men", a plenary assembly, a secretary, with archival, storage and meeting facilities, and it features a shrine of the god Assur, where oaths were sworn. All these facilities must have been concentrated in the so-called "*kārum* house" that, unfortunately, has not yet been found. Other colonies and trading stations were subject to its authority, with the smaller "trading stations" (*wabartum*) administratively being under the nearest "colony" (*kārum*). Although *kārum* Kanesh had a fair measure of autonomy with respect to internal affairs – thanks to the extra-territorial rights guaranteed by a treaty with the king of Kanesh – and could issue orders, render verdicts, and make regulations (it had fixed the rate of default interest, for example), it was essentially an extension of the government of the city of Assur. Its city assembly, the highest political and judicial authority, could steer and correct the colonial administration and the behavior of its traders by directives, decisions, formal verdicts, decisions, and laws. They usually concerned conflicts and judicial issues related to the trade, financial problems, and occasionally matters of family law (in particular matters of inheritance, after the death of a trader),[12] **[46]** but occasionally also matters of commercial policy. They were communicated by means of official letters sent to *kārum* Kanesh, who had to make their contents known to the other colonies (occasionally by "messengers of the *kārum*") and to supervise and enforce their implementation. More direct control by, and contact with, the mother-city was secured by the "Envoys of the City", regularly present in Anatolia, and in particular involved in regulating the diplomatic relations with the local Anatolian kings.

The Assyrian colonial system accordingly was rather tightly knit, characterized by good coherence and much mutual communication. And while the journey from Assur to Kanesh (more than 1000 km) took about six weeks, the links with Assur always remained close on all levels. Members of the same trading families regularly lived in one of the colonies and in Assur – caravans, traders, messengers, and mail regularly traveling both ways – while traders based in the colonies paid occasional visits to Assur to see their wives and family and to pay homage to the god Assur. This regular communication, even though many traders lived for many years in the colonies and some also died there, prevented the rise of a "diaspora situation", which seems to be more likely for a commercial community abroad in a system of maritime trade. Only in the later phase of the trade, in the 18th century BC, some "diaspora features" may be detected, when the number of Assyrians in Anatolia became smaller and contacts with Assur less regular,

---

11 The network existed during a period of ca. 240 years, with a small gap (when *kārum* Kanesh was destroyed) in ca. 1837 BC (middle chronology), which separates the older level II (which yielded the bulk of the textual sources) from the younger, still poorly documented (ca. 500 texts) level Ib of *kārum* Kanesh. During the level II period the number of Assyrian settlements grew and a few developed from *wabartums* into *kārums*. But it seems to have shrunk during level Ib, from which thus far 23 settlements are attested. In that period also changes occurred: 3 settlements known as *wabartums* during level II came to figure as *kārums*, while two important *kārums* in the west, Wahshushana and Burushhattum, no longer occur. See Veenhof, "Old Assyrian Period" (2008a): 154-167.

12 Important lawsuits, started in the colonies, could end up by being tried by the City Assembly, to which traders could appeal from decisions of *kārum* Kanesh with the words: "Bring my affair before the City and the ruler!" The Old Assyrian sources are very important for ancient legal history and I may refer to my overview of these matters in K.R. Veenhof, "The Old Assyrian Period". In *History of Ancient Near Eastern Law*, ed. R. Westbrook (Leiden-Boston, 2003): 431-84. [See now Th.K. Hertel, *Old Assyrian Legal Practices. Law and Dispute in the Ancient Near East* (Leiden: NINO, 2013)].

but they did not lead to the emergence of politically more autonomous Assyrian trading communities in Anatolia.[13]

Of the Assyrian commercial settlements ten were spread out over Northern Mesopotamia (the so-called Jazira, between the upper courses of the Tigris and the Euphrates) and they enabled the Assyrian caravans to traverse that region unharmed on their way to the crossings of the Euphrates.[14] Another thirty were established in Anatolia, ranging from the Black Sea to the Euphrates and from Malatya to at least the line between Konya **[47]** and Ankara.[15] Their number grew over the years due to the development of the trade, a growing turnover, a wider range of action, made possible by the employment of more people as traveling agents and representatives in more peripheral settlements. The settlements had been established on the basis of treaties (called "oaths") concluded between the Assyrian authorities and many local rulers, who allowed the Assyrians to settle, travel and do business in the various Anatolian "countries" in ex change for the right to levy taxes on the imported tin (ca. 3 %) and textiles (5 %) and a pre-empt part (10%) of the latter. These treaties in combination with the efficient colonial organization, commercial skills, good transport and information facilities, agency and representation, and the administrative support from the mother-city of Assur, were the basis of the Assyrian commercial success.

This highly developed, coherent and well documented commercial system seems a good choice for an attempt to shed some ancient Near Eastern light on "Empires and Emporia", the topic of *JESHO*'s jubilee conference, but there are nevertheless some problems to be mentioned at the outset.[16] The first, which applies generally to the study of dead cultures, is a complete dependence on written sources that have survived and that have their limitations and biases.[17] In the case of Assur nearly all our extensive written documentation (nearly 25.000 cuneiform texts, less than half of which are accessible) consists of the archives of ca. eighty Assyrian traders who had settled in *kārum* Kanesh (excavated since 1948), while Assur itself has yielded very little data, also archaeologically. **[48]** The lower town of our period, with the houses and archives of the traders, has not been reached by the German excavators and there are only very few inscriptions from the contemporary palace in the upper town and nothing remains from the "City Hall", the financial and economic centre of the city.[18] Our data, although we have many letters and official documents sent from Assur to the colonies and traders in

13 In this case "diaspora features" indicate weakening ties of the Assur traders with their mother city. Although specific cultural, legal and religious features nay linger on, this implies that there is an increasing degree of assimilation into the host society e.g. through local economic transactions and marriage.

14 Whilst en route some Assyrians – as reports about transactions, payment of taxes, and legal conflicts show – also engaged in some commerce, for which they probably could use, apart from the inns in several towns, the facilities and know-how of colleagues who belonged to the commercial settlements there or owned houses in the relevant towns. The above-mentioned treaty between Assur and the ruler of Apum distinguishes between Assyrian traders living in, and members of, the local *kārum* and those visiting the city while traveling back and forth.

15 See for a list of the cities with Assyrian commercial settlements Veenhof, "Old Assyrian Period" (2008a): 153-67.

16 My choice is of course also conditioned by the fact that ancient Assur and its trade are my main research interest. But the fact remains that data on the emporia linked with and serving some of the well-known ancient Mesopotamian empires (the empire of Ur III, of the 21st century BC; the empires of Larsa and Babylon of the beginning of the 2nd millennium BC) are much more limited and haphazard. Data on and from Mari, a kingdom from the same period on the Middle Euphrates, and its trading connections with the areas and cities north and northwest of it, are richer (see above note 10). But they are less numerous than those on Assur and mostly from the palace only, so that we have only limited documentation from and on its traders and *kārum*, which are vital for dealing with the role of emporia.

17 Archaeological evidence, bearing on material culture, is usually less informative for issues of political and economic history.

18 See for the last attempt to identify it and to analyze its functions, J.G. Dercksen, *Old Assyrian Institutions* (Leiden: NINO, 2004): Part 1, "The City Hall at Assur".

Anatolia, therefore have a distinctly "colonial" bias. A second problem is that although ancient Assur was the strategically located (near an important crossing of the Tigris), fortified capital of a prosperous city-state of some size (guesses about the number of its inhabitants usually range between five and eight thousand), with important temples and an efficient administration, it was not the capital of an empire. Assyria as a country did not yet exist; the city-state covered a limited territory of unknown size, just north of the fertile Mesopotamian flood plain, with a restricted subsistence potential (agriculture, husbandry, crafts). Niniveh (near present-day Mosul, 100 km north of Assur) was still an independent city-state with a different ethnic affiliation. Assur's successful, well organized, and to some extent monopolized trade on Anatolia did give the city a substantial economic power – in Anatolia and presumably also in relation to its more immediate neighbors. But Assur was not an "imperial" city, with a strong military and a ruling elite supported and supplied by a large producing territory and with income from subjected fringe areas. Its commercial presence in Anatolia and the trade routes through Northern Mesopotamia had not been enforced by and could not be backed by military power, but were based on mutual commercial interests, sealed by treaties.

3. Assur as an Emporium

Assur was a trading city and itself an important emporium, inhabited by many trading families, with a market and public and private warehouses The former was the "City Hall", where merchandise to be exported to Anatolia (it seems to have had a monopoly on the sale of lapis lazuli and the expensive meteoric iron) could be bought by "Kanesh traders", at times at credit, which could result in substantial debts owed to this institution, with possible dire consequences in case of default (ultimately the sale of a **[49]** trader's house), which are mentioned in the texts. In addition, merchandise was bought in the "(ware)houses" of individuals, presumably successful traders, merchants and investors living in Assur, and we read that silver arriving by caravan from Anatolia for such purposes "entered their houses".

Rather little of what was traded was produced in Assur itself, only part of the woolen textiles, presumably produced in a well-developed home industry, run by women. Each year people also raised a few hundred expensive caravan donkeys (20 shekels of silver apiece) and manufactured their harness, for which there was a constant demand, because most them stayed in Anatolia, where part of them were also sold. The bulk of the merchandise exported to Anatolia was first imported into Assur and to all appearances not by the Assyrians themselves: wool by the nomads to the southwest and perhaps east of Assur, textiles and copper by the Babylonians, and tin and lapis lazuli to all appearances by Elamites from Susa.[19] This made Assur a trading city and an international market with a large turnover and presumably stocks, where foreigners knew they could sell their goods and buy what they required, because there was a constant demand of merchandise for export to Anatolia. Unfortunately, due to the "colonial bias" of our sources, we know very little of these imports in Assur, because texts take their presence for granted. They only mention (rarely) that occasionally no expensive "Akkadian textiles" could be bought, because the Babylonians had not come to Assur, or that the arrival of tin from the "low country" was delayed, but one normally expected the problems to be of a temporary nature. Assur was an important port of trade and market town where different streams of goods met and could be exchanged. As such it was part of a much wider commercial network that included Anatolia, Babylonia and Iran, and operated by means of indirect exchange and relay trade, of which the caravan traffic between Assur and Anatolia was

---

19 The provenance of the copper is a very likely assumption, since no Anatolian copper was imported and we know that traders of Southern Mesopotamia (e.g. of the city of Ur) imported it by boat from the Persian Gulf. Tin arrived by caravan from "the low country", the area southeast of Baghdad, via the road that skirted the Zagros mountains, and texts from Mari reveal that it originated from Susa, where it must have be brought (how and by whom is unknown) all the way from northeastern Afghanistan.

one particular circuit.[20] Without the regular import of tin and textiles from elsewhere the Assyrian trade on Anatolia would have been impossible.

[50] We do not know for certain what the merchants and warehouses of Assur offered the foreign traders in exchange for what they imported, but it is very likely that they were paid silver, universally valued of means of payment, especially in the trade. It was imported en masse from Anatolia by the "Kanesh traders", who used it to buy in Assur the merchandise for their next caravan.[21] Tin imported in Assur, except for what the Assyrian metal craft needed to produce bronze tools and weapons, was exported to Anatolia and it amunted to several tons each year. The tin Babylonia and the regions more to the west (such as Mari on the Euphrates and Qatna, Aleppo and Ugarit in North-Syria) needed also came from Susa, via caravans who turned westward far south of Assur, to reach Babylonia via Eshnunna (on the Diyala) and across the Tigris, to proceed further to the south or via the Euphrates to the west.

How Assur came to play this strategic role is only partly known. As a city in the northern periphery of the empire of Ur III (21st century BC) it may already have played a role in the commercial contacts with the north. When it became independent one of its first rulers, Ilushuma (ca. 1980 BC), mentions in an inscription that he "established the freedom of the Akkadians (= Babylonians) and their sons; I washed their copper from the border of the marshes and Ur (in the far south, at the head of the Persian Gulf) until the City". This probably means, as stated by Larsen, that the ruler "attempted to attract traders from the south to the market of Assur by giving them certain privileges". The "washing of the copper" seems to mean the removal of obstacles for the trade, possibly the cancellation of debts or the abolition of taxes.[22] The measure supports the conviction that the city obtained its copper from the south, via Babylonian traders, who by Ilushuma's measure would gain easier access to city, where they could sell it for the silver the Assyrians obtained in Anatolia. Ilushuma's successor, Erishum I, ca. 1950 BC, went a step further and "established the freedom of silver, gold, copper, tin, barley and wool, down **[51]** to bran and chaff", where "freedom of" most probably means that he opened the city for import of and trade in the goods mentioned. It reveals the wish to increase the importance of Assur as a trading town and international market, because the first products mentioned are not subsistence goods, but imports, especially metals and also wool (necessary for the textile production), which were both essential for the Assyrian overland trade. The institution of the *līmum*, an annually appointed official who managed the important City Hall and was responsible for the City's finances, was created at the beginning of his reign,[23] and thus fits this interpretation of Erishum's measures. Considering the position of the ruler, it is very likely that these measures were based on decisions taken by him in conjunction with the City Assembly, which implies that important traders in Assur, as members of that Assembly, must have helped to develop its commercial policy.

A difficult to find out what this policy implied for foreign traders coming to Assur. It is remarkable that the sources never mention a *kārum* of Assur, where such traders could

---

20 See M.T. Larsen, "Commercial Networks in the Ancient Near East." In *Centre and Periphery in the Ancient World*, eds. M. Rowlands – M.T. Larsen – K. Kristiansen (Cambridge: Cambridge University Press, 1999): 47-56.

21 The uncertainty stems from the fact that the numerous so-called "caravan reports" only mention the amounts of tin and textiles bought in Assur and the prices paid, but do not state where they came from and from whom they were bought, but data in letters indicate that this happened in the above mentions public and private warehouses. Since the latter were in Assyrian hands, they must have been the ones to acquire the goods from those who imported them in Assur.

22 See the interpretation of this inscription and the one of Ilushuma's successor in Larsen, *Old Assyrian City-State* (see note 10): 63-80, and Veenhof, "Old Assyrian Period" (2008a): 126-30.

23 The office rotated among the citizens of Assur, presumably members of the main families. It is better known because the dating system of Assur identified years by the name of the officiating *līmum*, who thus serves as "(year) eponym". All lists of eponyms we have start with the first year of Erishum I.

work and settle down, a facility many other cities of that period had. Considering the mass of textual evidence we may conclude that there was no special commercial district or *kārum*. Assur, being trading city, may not have needed a special *kārum*, because foreign traders could settle inside its walls in houses rented or bought. But there is no evidence for this and if we are not mislead by the "colonial bias" of our sources, we must assume that foreign traders were welcome to supply and buy and perhaps stay for a few days (in an inn or *khan*), but were not granted their own facilities and could not operate from Assur. In that case it could be explained as a deliberate attempt to protect and monopolize Assur's own commercial activities, primarily those of the caravan trade on Anatolia. In support of this conclusion I can point at two official measures to restrict or ban competition, especially from other Mesopotamian cities and traders. A treaty concluded with a town near the Euphrates, in the area where one enters Anatolia proper, stipulates that the local ruler is forbidden to let Babylonian traders enter his town and, if they do, has to seize and extradite them to the Assyrians to be killed. And a remarkable verdict of the City Assembly in Assur asserts **[52]** the validity of a law (inscribed on a stone stele) that forbids Assyrians, on penalty of death, to sell gold to other traders from the north or south, mentioning Amorrites, Subaraeans and Akkadians.[24] These pieces of evidence reveal the will to protect Assur's commercial interest, even by extreme measures. Barring foreign traders from settling in and working from Assur could be explained along the same lines, but more evidence is needed to substantiate this conclusion.

The nature of Assyrian trade and especially the massive imports of silver from Anatolia resulted in a rather specific economy, in which the many citizens involved in the trade cold buy all they needed with silver, also the very expensive houses of the merchant class, which seem to have been a mark of status. That also barley, oil, wool and bronze utensils were bought, of course implies the existence of an agricultural sector and of crafts (which also produced the equipment of the caravan donkeys) and in addition there must have been a militia, city-administrators, temple personnel and a work force employed in building operations. But this cannot change the picture of a predominantly trading city, with a powerful merchant class that also played an important role in its administration. A rough guess, considering the number of Assyrians traveling on and working in Anatolia and of the merchants active in Assur as money-lenders, investors, administrators and craftsmen, is that perhaps as much as half of its citizens was directly or indirectly (*e.g.* those supplying the material needs of the caravans, equipment, food and donkeys) involved in trade.[25]

The political structure of ancient Assur was remarkable, no doubt due to its nature of independent trading city in which the families of powerful merchants and bankers played a big role, although calling it "a trading republic" (as a colleague of mine recently did) may go too far. In other trading cities too, the autonomy and political authority of the city, embodied in a City Assembly (its composition, whether it **[53]** merely consisted of "city elders" or was a popular assembly, is unfortunately unknown) was prominent, presumably at the expense of that of a ruler, *e.g.* in Emar (on the Middle Euphrates)[26] and in Babylonia's main trading city, ancient Sippar.

---

24 See for the evidence Veenhof, "Old Assyrian Period" (2008a): 211 (on treaty C), and 88-9 (on gold). The reason for asserting the law on gold must have been that active traders would like to use it as means of payment, but that the City authorities wished to reserve the gold for specific purposes (which are not stated).

25 This also involved persons attached to the temples, since the latter invested in the trade, also by using the numerous votive gifts they received, and we even meet a priest as owner of a warehouse and another who officiated as *līmum*, that is manager of the City Hall. The ruler of the city too bought merchandise there, which he gave in commission to agents traveling to Anatolia and some records mention the silver earned for him that was sent back to Assur.

26 See J.-M. Durand, "La cité-état d'Imar à l'époque des rois de Mari", *MARI* 6 (1990): 39-92, especially 55-64, 'Le statut politique d'Imar". In ancient Sippar the oath was sworn by the gods, the ruler, and the city, and the *kārum* played a role in the city administration.

The ruler of Assur seems to have played a limited role, which is confirmed by the fact that a palace and thus by definition a strong palace organization is completely absent from the documentation. The main administrative powers rested in the "City Assembly", simply called "the City", which was ultimately also in charge of the important "City Hall" (*bēt ālim*), the financial and economic centre of the city. The latter was managed by an annually appointed official, called *līmum* (hence its alternative designation as "*Līmum*-Office"), whose power may have balanced that of the ruler. He was chosen by casting lots (as we know from later times) from among persons belonging to the main families or lineages, apparently in order to spread power. According to his seal, the ruler called himself the "steward" (*ensi*) of the city-god Assur, the true king of the City, which lent his office a religious and ideological character and implied that he was responsible for the care of the god and the well being of the citizens by securing peace, prosperity and justice. His prestige must have been buttressed by the fact that his dynasty, which started to reign around 2000 BC, remained in power for two centuries, during nine successive generations. The ruler is usually designated as *rubā'um*, "the great one", perhaps identifying him as *primus inter pares*, but his real power remains rather unclear. We meet him primarily as chief judge, together with the "City Assembly", whose verdicts and decisions he communicated by means of official letters, written in his capacity of "Overseer" (*waklum*) of the community. A few inscriptions, usually in the form of inscribed bricks, document his concern for the administration of justice and record that he built (or restored) temples and walls and opened springs. Ambitions, however, were not lacking, since two of Assur's rulers chose the names of Sargon and Naram-Sîn, the two most powerful and deified kings of the Old Akkadian empire (of four centuries earlier). And it is probably no coincidence that this happened during the hey-day of the trade on Anatolia, between ca. 1900 and 1850 BC, when Assur must have been very prosperous and rich.

[54] 4. The Old Assyrian Merchants and Traders

While calling the city-state of Assur an "empire" is problematic, focusing on its "merchants and brokers", the sub-theme of the conference, offers better prospects. The two terms in the heading of this paragraph try to distinguish between two categories of persons, both private entrepreneurs, involved in Assyrian trade. First we have the "traders", the men active as leaders of caravans and who had settled in, or were moving between the colonies abroad, several of whom were also heads of the Anatolian branches of Assyrian firms; the Assyrians called them *tamkārum*, I also use the designation "Kanesh traders", and in some Anatolian texts from Anatolia "trader" simply means Assyrian, as distinguished from "native" Anatolians (*nuā'um*).[27] Then there are the "merchants", persons commercially active in Assur as investors, moneylenders and owners of warehouses, some of whom could be the superiors (also as senior relatives) of traders active in Anatolia. Some "merchants" can also be designated as *tamkārum*, especially in their capacity as "creditors" and "money-lenders". Those who had invested in joint-stock funds (*naruqqum*) or had supplied substantial, long-term loans were called *ummiānum*, "boss'. They were the financial backers of young "Kanesh traders" considered old and experienced enough to start their own business as manager (*tamkārum*) of a fund consisting of capital invested by relatives, Assur based merchants and other rich citizens (see below note 28).

---

27 *Tamkārum* is a notoriously difficult term whose meaning is determined by its context. It is used to designate traveling retail agents, who receive lots of merchandise on credit for sale elsewhere, and the manager of a joint-stock fund, in classical terms a *tractator*, for his agents and personnel "the boss". The term is frequently used in caravan texts to denote "the owner" of merchandise, who wishes to remain anonymous. Because traders/merchants were the ones who extended credit and loaned money, the term frequently means "creditor", especially when there is mention of "borrowing money (at interest) in the house of a *tamkārum*". In many loan contracts a debt is said to be owed to *tamkārum*, "the owner, creditor", a formulation which allows their transfer or cession See the observations in K.R. Veenhof, "'Modern' Features in Old Assyrian Trade," *JESHO* 40 (1997): 351-364.

In Anatolia

Traders working in Anatolia settled down in and became members of the various colonial settlements. During the first two generations they usually were married men, whose wives stayed in Assur to manage the household **[55]** and raise the children. Later more wives would accompany or follow their husbands to the colonies, at times with adolescent children (who might marry in Anatolia, occasionally also with native Anatolian traders), and in some case even two sons of the same family would move to Anatolia, each basically working for his own interests. This gave rise to a real 'colonial society', which also included hired Assyrian caravan personnel, retail agents and those who acted as messengers and scribes.

The main and probably most successful traders in Kanesh were usually involved in many transactions, at times also together with partners, and many also carried out commission sales and purchases for relatives, friends an women in Assur. Many of these traders had become more independent by having become managers of a "joint-stock fund" (called *naruqqum*, "money bag"), usually set up in Assur. This device appeared for the first time around 1900 BC and seems to have been an Old Assyrian invention that went beyond individual partnerships and cooperation in a joint caravan. The arrangement, rather similar to that of the early medieval *compagnia*, meant enlisting a number (usually about a dozen) of investors (*ummiānum*, "financiers"), who supplied a capital rated in gold, usually in all ca. 30 kilos, ideally consisting of shares of 1 or 2 kilo's of gold each. It was entrusted to a trader (the *tractator*), usually for ca. ten years, for the generally formulated purpose of "carrying out trade."[28] The contract contained stipulations on a final settlement of accounts, on paying dividends, on the division of the expected profit, and on fines for premature withdrawal of capital (meant to secure the duration of the business). Investors or shareholders mostly lived in Assur, but successful traders in Anatolia too did invest in such funds managed by others, perhaps also as a way of sharing commercial risks. In such case a contract was drawn up in Anatolia that obliged the *tractator* "to book in Assur x gold in his joint-stock fund in the investor's name". Among the investors we find members of the *tractator*'s family, but also business relations and others, probably a kind of "merchant-bankers" and other rich citizens, who aimed at fairly safe, long-term investments.[29]

[56] Some successful traders, long established in Anatolia and perhaps more independent thanks to their "joint-stock fund", might be tempted to depend more on their own commercial contacts and network and also pursue, alongside the import trade from Assur, more local business interests, such partaking in the trade in local goods, such as copper, wool, grain, meteoric iron and Anatolian textiles. This could mean more integration into the Anatolian host community, at times cemented by marriage links with an Anatolian family, not surprising since the Assyrian "quarter" in the lower city of Kanesh (and presumably also in other main cities with a *kārum*) was not isolated and Anatolian business men lived nearby. This process entailed the risk of differences in business interests between the colonial traders and the City of Assur and its establishment, a feature to which I will return.

In Assur

In Assur other, frequently senior members of trading families, including some "Kanesh traders" who had returned home in their old age, dominated the scene together with

28 See for the joint-stock funds, M.T. Larsen, "*Naruqqu*-Veträge". In: *Reallexikon der Assyriologie und Vorderasiatischen Archäologie*, vol. 9 (Berlin, Walter de Gruyter, 1999): 181-184. The verb used is *makārum*, from which the noun "trader", *tamkārum*, is derived.

29 A remarkable feature was that the shares invested or bought for silver were said to be in gold, at an exchange rate of gold:silver = 4:1, while the real rate was ca. 8:1. It meant that after the term stipulated the investor would anyhow receive back 200% of his investment, augmented, when the business had been successful, by one third of the profit.

the above-mentioned "merchants". They played an important role in different, at times partly overlapping aspects of the city's commercial life. One was to meet the constant need of capital for the expensive and expanding trade on Anatolia, necessary to maintain its infrastructure, for paying contributions and taxes to the *kārum* organization, the financing the many caravan trips there, and the various gifts made to local rulers and officials to create goodwill or solve problems. A "Kanesh trader" was supposed to invest his own money in his business, but its size and costs made investments, financing by others necessary. This could be achieved in three different ways, perhaps in part by the same persons in different roles. Money could in the first place be obtained as interest bearing long-term loans or commercial credit granted *in natura*, which for those who supplied them were fairly risk-free and yielded a substantial interest of 30% per year. More important, however, was a second possibility, described in the previous paragraph, the acquisition of capital in the form of a "joint-stock fund" (*naruqqum*, "money bag") supplied by investors, among which we meet male (rarely also female) members of the *tractator*'s family, and others, rich and commercially interested citizens who aimed at fairly long-term investments with safe returns and a good chance of a share in the profit. Because many traders managed to create such funds, some investors and traders had "shares" in several of **[57]** them, which could be inherited and sold; such investments, to quote Larsen, "crisscrossed the entire community" and made them "a factor in the creation of social cohesion".[30] Finally, there were merchants who acted (perhaps it was their specialization) as moneylenders, who supplied commercial loans,[31] when traders experienced temporal shortages of cash, due to delayed caravans, arrears of commission agents, or special expenses (*e.g.* the purchase of a house). Such loans were in general fairly risk-free, since the silver normally could be counted on to arrive in Assur in the foreseeable future and could be protected by securities, while the legal system also offered possibilities to enforce payment of debts. Such investors and money-lenders thus could be called "merchant bankers"

To the category of the "merchants", as defined above, also belonged the persons into whose "houses" the silver arrived from Anatolia would "enter," in order to purchase merchandise for equipping a new caravan. This was important, not only because of the profit to be made on the sales, but also because an excise or commission (*nishatum*) was paid there. These "houses" must have functioned as a kind of warehouses, with merchandise in stock and we can consider their owners "wholesale dealers," although we know very little of how they functioned and how they acquired their merchandise. Their owners must have been rich citizens, possibly including some of the "merchant bankers" mentioned above. They may have been identical to the owners of the "houses" where the "joint-stock funds" were "established", because it is unlikely to assume that too many related but different "mercantile groups" were active in a not very big trading city. Unfortunately, it is difficult to prove these suggestions, due to a general lack of informative descriptions of the commercial procedures and the anonymity of many "merchant bankers" and of some "investors". The letters dealing with these matters usually only mention that merchandise was purchased and loans were obtained from a *tamkārum*, **[58]** restricting the information to the bare facts, without mentioning names, which

30 See above note 28 and more in general J.G. Dercksen, "On the Financing of Old Assyrian Merchants". In *Trade and Finance in Ancient* Mesopotamia, ed. J.G. Dercksen (Istanbul: NHAI, 1999): 85-99 [and now also Larsen 2015, Ch. 17, "Where Did the Money Come from?"].

31 To obtain them, according to the contracts, a trader "entered the house of a *tamkārum* to take out silver at interest", see K.R. Veenhof, "Silver and Credit in Old Assyrian Trade". In *Trade and Finance in Ancient Mesopotamia*, ed. J.G. Dercksen (Istanbul: NHAI, 1999): 55-83, esp. 66-9 [=. pp. 159-184 in this volume]. Note that "Kanesh traders" in some letters also ask their representatives in Assur, when a shipment with silver arrived and (due to the season or for other reasons) no purchases could be made, to loan the silver at interest, again a proof of the constant demand for "money".

should have been mentioned in the relevant contracts that were apparently usually kept in Assur and therefore have not been found.[32]

Relations and cooperation between traders in Kanesh and merchants in Assur were frequently based on family ties, not rarely through several generations, and "Kanesh traders" could enjoy the support and advice of fathers, brothers or uncles in Assur. They might also figure as their representatives in business and legal matters and in contacts with the city administration, and could provide help to overcome a financial crisis, *e.g.* by soft loans or acting as guarantors. But Larsen has recently shown that "family firms" as a formal institution did not exist; no "family" occurs as creditor or debtor and ownership of funds – apart from formal partnerships – was basically individual. After the death of a *pater familias* and the division of the inheritance, the sons carried on separately, even in separate houses in the same colony. [33] This development was perhaps stimulated by the fact that each son acquired his own "joint-stock fund" or inherited part of his father's shares in one, although we occasionally observe that they continue to work with their father's business relations, partners or agents.

5. Colonies and Emporia in Anatolia

The main traders were, certainly during the first generations, active in the large *kārum* Kanesh, probably the oldest Assyrian colony and (therefore) the administrative center of the Assyrian colonial system. It was situated in the lower town of what was an important emporium and market town with an imposing palace, which has been revealed by the excavations. The importance of the city is also clear from a treaty between the Assyrians and its king, from the younger period of the colonial phase, which mentions the trade in tin, textiles (imported and Anatolian ones), lapis lazuli and iron.[34] **[59]** Kanesh could play this role, even though the main items the Assyrians bought in Anatolia – silver, copper and wool – did not originate there,[35] because it was the capital of a strategically located old city-state, located at a road junction just south of the Kızılırmak, which counted many native traders among its inhabitants. Its importance was enhanced by the fact that most of the caravans coming from Assur and elsewhere (there is evidence of visits of traders from North-Syria) would arrive here, which in turn must have attracted traders and goods from elsewhere in Anatolia.

In *kārum* Kanesh the resident Assyrians traders organized the sale of the goods arriving by caravan, part of which was sold to the local palace, its officials and to native traders, while the rest was sent on to destinations north and west of the city, or entrusted to retail agents who went into the countryside. From Kanesh also most of the silver and gold, collected there or arriving from elsewhere (including that earned by indirect exchange, via copper and wool), would be shipped to Assur. Several traders in Kanesh also carried out commissions for people in Assur who used their expertise, and by means

---

32 The few contracts we have of the setting up of a joint-stock fund do mention the names of the investors, some of whom are family and business relations of the trader, but others are unknown and some are registered as *tamkārum*, probably again in order to enable the transfer of shares, e.g. in cases of disputed ownership or in connection with the division of an inheritance.

33 M.T. Larsen, "Individual and Family in Old Assyrian Society". *Journal of Cuneiform Studies* 59 (2007): 93-106. [See now also K.R. Veenhof, "Families of Old Assyrian Traders". In *La famille dans le Proche Orient ancien: réalités, symbolisms et images. Proceedings of the 55th Rencontre Assyriologique Itnernationale, Paris 6-9 July 2009*, ed. L. Marti (Winona Lake: Eisenbrauns, 2014): 341-371, esp. § 5.2, "Relation Building"]

34 Veenhof, "Old Assyrian Period" (2008a): 190-3 (treaty D). It also secured the freedom of movement (even during war) and the protection of the Assyrian traders and their property (compensation in case of robbery and bloodshed), also against royal measures (summons for service duties and manumission of slaves). In the time of this treaty the importance and political power of Kanesh had increased and its ruler bore the title "the great king", which meant that he ruled a territorial state of some size and counted a number of petty kings as his vassals.

35 Texts and/or archaeology yield evidence of local metallurgy (during the excavations quite a number of moulds for ingots, tools and weapons were found) and of production textiles and beautiful pottery, products that were also marketed.

of their partners, representatives (occasionally their grown-up sons) in other important colonies, they could cover a wide area. The patterns were not uniform and we know cases where a trader in due time returned to Assur and his son took over in Anatolia, and of sons settled in Anatolia, whose father always remained in Assur.[36] As the range of the trade expanded and the trade in copper gained importance some traders decided to settle, temporarily or for good, in other colonies, especially those in the capital cities to the north and west that were at the same time nearer to the main production areas of copper and silver and important Anatolian centers of trade and emporia. This development may have turned *kārum* Kanesh increasingly into the administrative center of Old Assyrian colonial system.

[60] Since thus far none of these Anatolian emporia has been identified and excavated we therefore have to rely on the Assyria written evidence; it primarily documents the Assyrian mercantile activities there and as a rule tells us rather little about the political and economic structures of these cities. Moreover, because our sources only reflect the fully developed colonial system, we encounter difficulties in reconstructing its development, in particular in finding out when and why colonial settlements were established in particular towns and in several cases also why one became a "trading station" (*wabartum*) and an other a "colony" (*kārum*). We can understand that certain towns must have been less important and "interesting" for the Assyrians due their size, location, commercial potential, or the proximity of an important city with a *kārum*, but we cannot give explanations for individual cases. That the system was dynamic is indicated by the fact that during the main period of *kārum* Kanesh level II (but we do not know exactly when) at least four *wabartum*s (those of Shaladuwar, Shamuha, Timilkiya and Tuhpiya) seem to have been "upgraded" to become *kārum*s, while three others of this period (Kuburnat, Shuppiluliya and Washhania) became *kārum*s during the later period of level Ib. These developments may be due to political developments in Anatolia, but also to the fact that in the course of time more Assyrian traders moved from Kanesh to the economic centers in the north and west.[37]

The large number of settlements reflects the concern to "cover" Anatolia well and some *wabartum*s may have served more as road stations for passing caravans or as Assyrian pieds-à-terre that allowed visiting traders to conduct business in the area. In general, Assyrian commercial settlement was of course conditioned by the possibilities to sell and buy what they wished, but the texts show that textiles could be sold (at times in smaller numbers) almost everywhere, and this also seems to have been the case with tin. It was not sold en masse in the areas where copper was mined, as one might expect, because the production of bronze seems to have been a rather local affair, with blacksmiths presumably alloying tin to copper in every city or major town, where tin could accordingly be sold as well.[38] Assyrian involvement in the internal Anatolian trade in copper and **[61]** wool[39] (the latter was acquired especially in some cities to the south and southeast east of Kanesh, notably Mamma and Luhusaddiya, but for the latter town no Assyrian trading station is attested) also must have made some towns and routes more important than others. In general big and important cities, with an interesting countryside and a well developed palace system and good facilities (a market or *kārum*) for traders must have been attractive, and we can indeed single out a few of these that must have been important emporia.

---

36 An example is Aššur-idī in Assur, whose son Aššur-nādā lived and worked in Anatolia. See the edition of the latter's archive in Larsen, *Aššur-nādā*.

37 See also footnote 11.

38 See Dercksen, *Copper Trade*: 151, "There was no commercial demand for ready bronze, only for its two components, copper and tin". He also notes that Assyrian did not trade in bronze, although bronze artifacts were valued and turn up in inventories of households.

39 See for the wool trade in Anatolia, Dercksen, *Institutions*: Ch. 10. [See now also A.W. Lassen, "The Trade in Wool in Old Assyrian Anatolia". *JEOL* 42 (2010) 159-179].

The first is Hahhum, a market town (with a local textile production and wool trade) and important road-station in the area where most caravans crossed the Euphrates to enter Anatolia proper. Here they could be split (to travel to Kanesh or via a more easterly route, bypassing Kanesh, to the north of Hattum) or their final destination could be decided on the basis of information arriving from Kanesh, and in the city itself merchandise was sold, bought or stored. Many Assyrians records mention the city as the goal or stop for passing caravans and specify travel expenses "until Hahhum", or report that goods were bought there. A very damaged, large treaty (originally ca. 250 lines) concluded between the administrators of this city (there was no king at that time) and "the *kārum* Hahhum and any Assyrian of a caravan traveling up or down" shows its importance as emporium and as road station. It stipulates the safety of the traders "in your city, in your mountains and in your land" and contains a special paragraph dealing with the local ferryman who might try to harm traders whom he brought across the river.[40]

In northern Anatolia, probably in the area between Tokat and Amasya, the city of Durhumit, the center of the copper trade, was an emporium with an important *kārum*, where many Assyrian traders had a house. The copper was most probably mined in the area between Ankara and Çankırı, often "in small, localized deposits, and smelted in the vicinity of the mine where the supply of fuel was sufficient. The raw copper resulting from this primary smelting was cast into ingots and transported out of the mining regions",[41] in particular to Durhumit. Its market provided the link between the copper producing areas and the Assyrian and native merchants who **[62]** wished to buy it, usually in exchange for tin and textiles, but at times also for silver and wool. Moreover, poor copper arriving from the mines could be exchanged or converted there for refined copper that was exported, in at times in enormous quantities, to the south and southwest, across the Kızılırmak and also to Kanesh, for which the Assyrians used their donkeys caravans. Texts mentions "the rate of exchange of copper of Durhumit", normally 120:1 against silver at purchase and 60:1 at sale elsewhere (with variations determined by the quality of the metal and the costs of transport). Several Assyrian traders settled down in its *kārum*, because they considered the trade in copper, which they shipped and sold elsewhere in Anatolia, profitable and it was apparently easier (perhaps also more profitable) to sell their imports in northern Anatolia for copper than for silver.[42]

Important emporia more to the west, again with large Assyrian colonies, were the cities of Wahshushana, probably in the area just north of the Tuz Gölu, and Burushhattum, still further to the southwest.[43] The former, the most city frequently mentioned city after Kanesh, with a king, a palace and a large Assyrian trading community, was an important city west of the Kızılırmak, strategically located where the road coming from Hattum (inside the bend of the river) and the area of the copper trade crossed the one (skirting the river) coming from Kanesh. It was in a way also the gate to the most western emporium, Burushhattum, and there is evidence that heavy loads (*e.g.* of copper) could be shipped there from Wahshushana on ox-drawn wagons. But Wahshushana was not only a gate to the west, it was also a place where goods imported by the Assyrians, in particular many expensive textiles and occasionally also wool imported from southwestern Anatolia, were

---

40 See for this city K. R. Veenhof, "Across the Euphrates." In *Anatolia and the Jazira during the Old Assyrian Period*, ed. J.G. Dercksen (Leiden: NINO, 2008): 3-29, esp. 7-8, and for the treaty, Veenhof, "Old Assyrian Period" (2008a): 194-200.

41 Quoting Dercksen, *Copper Trade*: 32.

42 See for this city C. Michel, "Durhumid, son commerce et ses marchands." In *Marchands, diplomats et empereurs. Études sur la civilisation mésopotamienne offertes à Paul Garelli*, eds. D. Charpin – F. Joannès (Paris: Recherche sur les Civilizations, 1991): 253-73.

43 The dissertation of G. Barjamovic, *A Historical Geography of Ancient Anatolia in the Assyrian Colony Period* (defended in 2005 [and published in Copenhagen in 2011 as CNI Publication 38], discusses these cities and make proposals for their location [in Ch. 5.15 and 17, where he proposes a more western location of Burushhattum in what the Hittites called the "Lower Land", possibly "due north of Sultan Dağ, at Akar Çay"].

sold for silver. A few texts indicate that in the last phase of the first period of Assyrian colonial activity serious problems arose in this area, perhaps due to a military conflict that caused upheaval in the city, which seems to have resulted in the disappearance of the Assyrian traders. City and *kārum* do no longer occur in the Assyrian sources from the later period.

Burushhattum, probably southwest of Wahshushana, may have harbored what after Kanesh was the most important Assyrian colony, in a city **[63]** that was an important market for tin, textiles and copper, shipped there from Kanesh and Durhumit. It was in Burushhattum that the Assyrians obtained important quantities of silver, the goal of their trade, which was shipped from there to Kanesh. Again, our knowledge of the city itself is rather limited, but it lived on in the period of the Hittite empire under de name Parsuhanda, as a city in the "Lower Lands", with an important storm-god. A legendary tale tells about how the Old Akkadian king Sargon (24th century BC) would have come to the rescue of Mesopotamian traders in that city, but there is no further evidence for such an early settlement of traders abroad and the tale may have been construed in the context of the role of the city in Old Assyrian times.[44] That the city was important is confirmed by the so-called "Anitta text" (found in the later Hittite capital), which mentions how the king of Parsuhanda accompanied the victorious Anitta (who ruled a.o. over Kanesh) and offered him a throne and a scepter of iron, gifts that acknowledged his status as "great king", a title the ruler of Kanesh also bears in the above-mentioned treaty.

The mention of these five emporia does not imply that there were not more important market towns and perhaps emporia in Anatolia. That several others also had a *kārum* in which Assyrians had settled, may hint at this possibility, but too little is known of them and, as said earlier, we do not really know why they were chosen as "colonies.[45]

6. The Economic and Political Scene of Assur

The importance of the trade for the city at large

The "Kanesh traders" and the city of Assur had shared interests, because the success of the trade meant prosperity for both and commercial failures also **[64]** affected the city. Not only the families and especially the wives of the "Kanesh traders" were involved – they could be forced to sell valuable property, even houses, to pay private and institutional creditors – but of course also their commercial partners, creditors and investors, and the owners of the warehouses suffered if revenues diminished and debt claims mounted. And the gradually developing trade had a much wider impact, because it employed many people who were needed to accompany the caravans, serve as retail agents in Anatolia, and man the growing number of trading stations. The trade also created (as explained above) a constant need of new caravan donkeys, a few hundred of which had to be raised, trained and provided with harness every year, which happened outside Assur in a special paddock (*gigamlum*) and must have created a lot of work and income. The trade was especially important for the Assyrian textile production, a home industry by women (wives, daughters and slave-girls), which supplemented the import from the south and

44 See for this text Veenhof, "Old Assyrian Period" (2008a): 121-2. Note that the cities of Hahhum and Kanesh also occur in tales dealing with the Old Akkadian period, as enemies of king Naram-Sîn of Akkad.

45 The later capital of the Hittite empire, Hattush (Boğazköy) also had a *kārum*, with Assyrian inhabitants, but very little is known about the early city and the excavations in the lower town have only yielded evidence for Assyrian presence in the phase contemporary with *kārum* Kanesh level Ib. See for the evidence, J.G. Dercksen, "'When we met in Hattush'. Trade according to the Old Assyrian texts from Alishar and Boğazköy". In *Veenhof Anniversary Volume. Studies Presented to K.R. Veenhof on the Occasion of his 65th Birthday*, ed. W.H. van Soldt *et al.* (Leiden: NINO, 2001): 39-66.

supplied the women with private income.[46] Successful traders and merchants apparently bought what they consumed and needed on the local market with the silver earned in Anatolia, which meant income for local farmers, shepherds and craftsmen. And part of the silver was also invested in jewels, slaves and sumptuous, expensive houses, which must have created work.

The city of Assur and its institutions also profited from the trade. The City levied an "export tax" (*waṣītum*) of 0.85 % on all caravans leaving for Anatolia and collected a tithe on the lapis lazuli and iron it sold. The "City-Hall," as a kind of public warehouse, probably made profit on its the sales, especially on credit sale (at an interest of 10%) of merchandise to "Kanesh-traders", and its activities must have provided work and income for its staff and employees (scribes, accountants, porters, etc.). There is no evidence that the palace – which is absent from our sources – as such was involved in the trade, but the rulers profited from it by entrusting their own consignments of export goods to their agents and befriended traders for sale in Anatolia.[47] Temples too were involved, because important lots of merchandise and perhaps capital, designated as *ikribū* – meaning "votive **[65]** gifts", but regularly used to designate goods as "temple property" – were entrusted to traders, often for longer periods and therefore rather functioned as investments than as retail goods.[48] Some priests were also involved in trade, one had a "(ware)house", where merchandise could be bought; another, administrator of the temple of Assur, even served a term as *līmum*, that is as director of the "City Hall," a truly financial and commercial occupation. But they seem to have played these roles rather as rich and commercially minded citizens than *qualitate qua*, as members of the clergy representing their temples.

The City Assembly

The trade was of course also important for and an issue in the deliberations and decisions of Assur's main administrative institution, the City Assembly. It must have counted important traders and merchant bankers among its members, although we are unable to identify them because "the City" always appears as an anonymous collective. The City Assembly was the highest judicial authority, to which "Kanesh traders" could appeal with regards to verdicts passed by the court of the *kārum*. Such cases and the resulting verdicts passed in commercial conflicts between traders, regularly put issues of the trade on the agenda of the Assembly.[49] But there were also decisions that were important for the trade as such, which reveal elements of a commercial policy. Apart from the measures of two early rulers of Assur, mentioned above (§ 3), meant to stimulate the city's commercial role, we have a few explicit pieces of evidence for this role of the City. In § 3, footnote 24, I already mentioned a clearly protectionist stipulation in a treaty that wished to prevent competition by Babylonian traders. We may assume that such treaties with Anatolian rulers, which no doubt reflected the experiences and wishes of *kārum* Kanesh, were also approved by the City, whose Envoys probably were involved in negotiating and drafting them. This explains why the City Assembly in official letters warns against smuggling, that is the **[66]** dodging of the taxes that by treaty were due to the Anatolian rulers, because it would endanger the trade relations.[50]

---

46 See already K.R. Veenhof, *Aspects of Old Assyrian Trade and its Terminology* (Leiden: Brill, 1972): 103-23, and now C. Michel, "Femmes et production textile à Aššur au début du IIᵉ millénaire avant J.-C." In *Techniques et culture* 46, *Spécialisation des tâches et sociétés*, eds. A. Averbough, P. Brun *et al.* (Paris, 2006): 281-97.

47 See M.T. Larsen, *Old Assyrian City-State*: 131-138.

48 See J.G. Dercksen, "The Silver of the Gods. On Old Assyrian *ikribū*," *Archivum Anatolicum* 3 (1997): 75-100.

49 This also resulted also in decisions with a more general validity that set down more or less standard rules for frequent issues (e.g. the liquidation of a dead trader's business, compensation for losses of a collective caravan, modes of collecting certain debts), some of which acquired the status of laws, engraved on a stone monument; see K. R. Veenhof, "In Accordance with the Words of the Stele": 1717-44.

50 See for the evidence, Veenhof, "Old Assyrian Period" (2008a): 214-5.

That the fostering of good relations with the towns along the route through the North-Mesopotamian Jazira was a concern of the City is confirmed by a late treaty (ca. 1750 BC) concluded by Assur with the city-state of Apum in that area (see above, footnote 8). This concern is also clear from a letter written by father in Assur to his son traveling with a caravan in the Jazira, in which he advises him to avoid the city of Hahhum and to test whether entering a particular the town on the route to Kanesh is safe. He mentions that the City has ordered to split the large caravan he had joined into three parts, which have to cross the area involved one after the other, as soon as the first one has arrived safely.[51] This concern and the knowledge required to give such orders implies that the City was well informed, probably by official (from a *kārum*) and private letters arriving from Anatolia or by traders who visited Assur. In another letter one trading station tells another that it has received "a letter of the City" ordering them not to collect taxes due to *kārum* Kanes from traders passing, because the money is needed to ransom colleagues held (perhaps kidnapped) by Anatolians. Assur must have reacted on information received from the trading station in question and the letter with the City's decision was then used to inform another trading station. The latter is asked to implement this decision immediately, without waiting for written confirmation by *kārum* Kanesh (which would normally make such decisions known in the colonial network), which, however, was duly informed about the issue, because the letter we have was a duplicate found in Kanesh.[52]

The City Assembly presumably reached its decisions both in consequence of appeals by individual traders or a *kārum*, or of its own accord, in order to solve problems it encountered. There must have been deliberations to reach an agreement or a decision by majority vote, if we may assume that the decision making procedures we know from to the so-called "Statutes of *kārum* Kanesh[53] were applied in Assur. Deliberations on difficult issues are also implied by an official letter of the ruler of Assur addressed to *kārum* **[67]** Kanesh, which told them that the City Assembly (reacting to an appeal by traders?) had first decided to change the regulation concerning the sale of gold, but had later changed its opinion and now insisted that that no new rule had been drafted and that the old one, inscribed on a stone stele, remained in force.[54] The letter is not only interesting as evidence of decisions on commercial policy, *in casu* on selling gold to other Mesopotamians (already mentioned in § 3), but also because it betrays differences of view and probably clashes of interests in the assembly.

The role of the City Hall and its director, the līmum

The policy of the City must also have conditioned the commercial role of the City Hall, which, according to Dercksen's recent analysis,[55] included:

- collecting taxes, notably the export tax paid by caravans leaving for Anatolia;
- checking measures and weights and the purity of metals;
- acting as custodian of the treasury of Assur and of the archive of the City;
- storing, selling (and perhaps distributing) barley stocked in its granaries;
- marketing all kind of commodities, including textiles and copper, and some luxury items such as lapis lazuli and iron, on which it had a monopoly so that it could control their circulation.

---

51 See for this letter M.T. Larsen, *Aššur-nādā*: no. 18.

52 See for this letter, Michel, *Correspondance des marchands*: no. 58.

53 See for these "Statutes", Larsen, *Old Assyrian City State*: 283-86. The assembly of the *kārum* was convened by the "secretary" (scribe), and if its committee of "big men" could not decide, the plenary assembly was convened, which could be divided into seven groups to solve an issue by majority vote.

54 See Veenhof, "In Accordance with the Words of the Stele": 1733-5.

55 Dercksen, *Institutions, part I*: Ch. 2.

Its tasks, especially the first three, and the monopoly on the sale of lapis lazuli and iron, must have been based on a mandate of the City Hall. As a market it may have enjoyed more freedom in deciding on quantities, prices and credit terms. This was important for the trade, since it seems to have served as entrepôt or warehouse (alongside private ones) to which also foreign traders probably sold what they imported and where or through which "Kanesh traders" could buy, if necessary at credit, what they wished to export.[56] Its possibility to influence the flow and perhaps prices of **[68]** certain goods is important here, but our knowledge is still limited and it is very unclear which role it played in the sale of tin. However, it could also steer the purchases by "Kanesh traders", as is shown by an interesting verdict of the City;[57] it described that – at a certain time – they should buy tin for only one third of the silver imported, which implied that for the rest, two thirds, textiles had to be bought, which is more than usual, since in caravan reports we repeatedly meet a fifty-fifty division. The measure apparently intended to promote export of textiles, which had an added importance because there existed a local Assyrian textile industry. The "City Hall" as a main warehouse, where both items could be bought, might have simply implemented such a measure, but it is clear that the traders could and did buy their goods also elsewhere, at times also "on the market", so that an order of the City would have been necessary.

Commercial credit granted to traders by the City Hall played an important role, as is shown by the many cases where they owe it large amounts of silver. Parts of these debts could be the result of arrears in paying the "export tax" (*waṣītum*) as shown in a dramatic case, reported in a letter written from Assur to Kanesh. The houses of four traders were seized by city officials (called *bērū*) because of "the various amounts of export tax of our father/boss, that amounted to 5 pounds of silver in the City Hall, the payment of which The City imposed on us". Three of them paid their share in the debt and when the house of the fourth was put on sale by the officials they quickly borrowed what he owed with a money lender "and we paid it to the officials who brought it into the City Hall". The case shows how that City Assembly and City Hall cooperated; for, although the debts are said to have mounted in the City Hall, the City, probably after having evaluated the case, "imposed" the payment, and the silver paid eventually "entered the City Hall".[58] This reveals the power of the City and the City Hall, and also that of its director, the *līmum*, which is well-documented.[59] Debts owed to the City (Hall) **[69]** were taken very seriously and the leaders of colonies and trading stations are occasionally also warned by *kārum* Kanesh to collect taxes and debts of traveling traders – in fact their colonial colleagues – "without favoring anybody".[59a]

Who were the *līmums* and what was their relationship to the traders, the merchants and the City administration? Since we do not know the number and names of the members of the City Assembly and thus are unable to know whether (which is rather likely) and

56 The considerable amounts, frequently many kilos of silver, for which traders were regularly indebted to the City Hall, are too big to be only arrears in paying the modest export taxes and therefore rather reflect credit sales. The sale of (imported) copper and the stocking and sale of barley show that the City Hall also served other commercial or domestic interests; the handling of grain probably was a separate "department," since the texts acquaint us a special "*līmum* of the barley".

57 See K.R. Veenhof, "Trade and Politics in Ancient Assur. Balancing of Public, Colonial and Entrepreneurial Interests." In *Saggi di Storia Antica, vol. 21: Mercanti e Politica nel Mondo Antico*, ed. C. Zaccagnini (Roma: L'Erma di Bretschneider, 2000): 90-4 [= pp. 129-157 in this volume].

58 The text was studied in Veenhof, "Trade and Politics": 98-9.

59 His powers – taking pledges, sealing a debtor's house and eventually selling it – probably were not basically different from those the legal system granted every creditor. But in the case of liquidations, paying debts to the City Hall seems to have enjoyed priority and their size could made things worse. That a *līmum*, who was personally responsible for running the City Hall, had to hand over his task after one year to his successor must have increased his urge to collect arrears in time. But we have to admit that the debt policy of the City Hall is far from clear, see Dercksen, *Institutions, part 1*: Ch. 3.

[59a See now K.R. Veenhof, *The Archive of Kuliya, son of Ali-abum. Kültepe Tabletleri V* (Ankara: Türk Tarih Kurumu, 2010): 82-90, "Kuliya's task and the system of taxation".]

how many of the future, acting and previous *līmum*s were among them. As we know the *līmum*s primarily from the 'Eponym List'[60] and from entries in records ("during the eponymy of PN"), we usually now nothing about their profession or background. In the eponym list a few of them, especially early ones, are not identified by the name of their father, but by their profession. One is designated as "boatman" and he may have been involved in shipping on the Tigris, another, a very late one is called "trader" (*tamkārum*). Since such qualifications must have been distinctive, we might conclude that in this late period *līmum*s normally were not active overland traders, a profession indeed difficult to combine with that of head of the City Hall, which must have required continuous presence in Assur during his year of office. A *līmum* must have had experience in commercial, financial, and administrative matters and it is not surprising that during the heyday of the trade at least two of the *līmum*s (nos. 102 and 104 of the list) are known to have spent many years as traders in Anatolia, where they also served as week-eponyms in *kārum* Kanesh, one before and the other after his turn of office in Assur. Various others traveled there and spent some time in the colonies, where they must have engaged in trade, since they occur in financial transactions or figure as witnesses, but not *ex officio*.[61]

This means that, apart from the importance of the trace as such for the city, the interests and problems of the "Kanesh traders" were well known in the City Assembly and that the city administration counted several members who had close links with the colonial society. Its measures to promote trade and reduce problems and dangers (pointed out in §6.2) will **[70]** have taken these interests into account, but other measures concerned the traders as well. Remarkable in this respect was one taken in order to alleviate the consequences of financial problems at a time when "many Assyrians" had been forced to pledge and sell their family houses (under which their ancestors were buried). This danger must have threatened in particular the families of "Kanesh traders", who apparently had run into serious financial problems, which is the reason why the story is told in a letter sent from Assur to relatives in Anatolia. The use of the words "many Assyrians" indicates that it must have been due to a more general, unfortunately further unknown and undated crisis. In this situation "the God Aššur had mercy with his city", which meant that debtors could redeem and recover their family houses by paying half of their sale price, while the rest could be paid in three annual installments. This decision, no doubt taken by the City Assembly, is presented as an act of mercy on the part of the god Assur. But since care for the citizens was a traditional duty of the ruler of a city-state, who was considered to be the steward of the god Assur, the measure must have been taken by its ruler in conjunction with the City Assembly.[62]

7. Diverging Interests in Assur and in the Colonies

There are also some indications that the interests of the "Kanesh traders" did not always coincide with those of the City or the administrative establishment there. However, this does not apply to the colonial *kārum* organization as such, which was ultimately under the authority of the City and always took care to implement it decisions and instructions, also in the other colonies and in relation to its members.

Problems could arise with individual "Kanesh traders," who, as private entrepreneurs, were very focused on the financial success of their own business in the Anatolian circuit. Some traders, although rather dependent on the *kārum* organization in commercial and legal matters and for help in conflicts with local rulers, occasionally ignored its instructions and policy. This could concern an injunction not to smuggle, to avoid a

---

60 Published in K.R. Veenhof, *The Old Assyrian List of Year Eponyms from kārum Kanish* (Ankara: Türk Tarih Kurumu, 2003).

61 See Dercksen, *Institutions*: 58-9, and Veenhof, "Trade and Politics": 80-2.

62 See for an analysis of this case, K.R. Veenhof, "Redemption of Houses in Assur and Sippar." In *Munuscula Mesopotamica. Festschrift für Johannes Renger*, eds. B. Böck et al. (Münster: Ugarit Verlag, 1999) (eds.): 599-607 [= pp. 211-223 in this volume].

particular area or town, to boycott an important defaulting Anatolian creditor, to pay arrears in taxes or to appear in court without delay. Some "Kanesh traders" **[71]** might also act in a way that harmed the interests of the City, both local concerns of Assur and its interests as part of a much wider commercial network, whereby it also served as market for traders from Babylonia and Iran and perhaps visiting Bedouins. A few few decisions of the City reveal such clashes of interest.

Two decisions were taken to protect and stimulate the sale of woolen textiles imported in Assur or produced by the Assyrian home industry. In the first verdict the City imposed heavy fines on "many merchants" in Anatolia who had been trading in various types of locally produced woolen textiles, especially a type called *pirikannum*.[63] The second, already mentioned in § 6.3, stipulated that in a particular period two thirds of the silver arriving from Anatolia should be used to purchase textiles, which is more than is usual according to the "caravan accounts" and its purpose must have been to boost their export. A quite different and rather surprising decision, important enough to have been made a rule of law, published on a stone monument, also already mentioned above (§3, with note 24) was that Assyrians, on penalty of death, were forbidden to sell gold imported from Anatolia to the various non-Assyrian population groups of Mesopotamia. Its motive is not stated, but must reflect the importance of this metal for (the god or the city of) Assur, perhaps for the benefit of its treasury of Assur or in the interest of the City Hall, because gold may have been a preferred means of payment for certain highly desirable imports in Assur, such as the tin from Susa.[64] This rule must have restricted its use by Assyrian traders, either on the way back from Anatolia or in Assur itself, and we can understand that it was not welcome to the "colonial traders".

Another, minor clash of interests is mentioned in a unique letter that reveals another aspect of the relation between Assur and the colonial society. It reveals that the city had told the colonies to contribute 5 kilos of silver in the costs of the upkeep or repair of the city-wall. This decision apparently had been accepted without protest (it may not have been the first time such a contribution was asked) and the subject of the letter is the City's decision to send a special messenger to Kanesh, at the expense of the colonies, to collect this sum and bring it Assur, apparently because the *kārum* had been lax in doing so. *Kārum* Kanesh must have decided to prevent this and asked persons in Assur to intervene. **[72]** They are called *nībum* and in their letter they report how they had pleaded with "the Elders" (a synonym for the City Assembly or a committee of seniors)[65] not to do so and urged the *kārum* to send the silver without delay.

The appeal to "the Elders" may imply that the *nībum* had not been not present in (or were no members of) the Assembly when the decision was taken and now tried to counter the measure by a special appeal. The issue is fairly trivial, but it is interesting to learn that there was in Assur an otherwise unknown group of persons (the verb of which *nībum* is the subject is in the plural) that looked after the interests of the colonial society and of which we know almost nothing; it might have acted in other situations too. We do not know who was member of it and its very name is unclear; a tentative translation "the appointed" (from the verb *nabā'um*, "to name") suggests a formal body, with appointed members, but further evidence is needed.[66]

Diverging interests between "colonial traders" and the city are understandable. The former, getting more integrated into the host community – by business contacts and intermarriage – might have focused more on the internal Anatolian trade in copper, wool

---

63 See Veenhof, "Trade and Politics": 89-90.

64 Suggested by the fact that the king of Mari sent there an emissary with an amount of gold to Susa to acquire tin; see above note 4.

65 A bicameral system would make a parallel with the functioning of the assembly of *kārum* Kanesh. There is in fact one reference to "the city, small and big" (i. e. its plenary assembly) and several texts mention verdicts by "the Elders" in Assur.

66 The letter was edited and commented upon in Dercksen, *Institutions, part 1*: § 4.2.

and grain, or the trade in the highly desirable and expensive Anatolian meteoric iron, which was difficult for the Assyrian the authorities to monitor. Successful traders there could become rich and might start to operate more independently as heads of an Anatolian trading firm, by getting more involved in purely Anatolian commercial transactions, so that the financial successes in Anatolia could become at least as important for them as the benefits of the merchants and institutions of their mother-city, which could cause frictions. We also observe that some traders in Anatolia took risks that might have brought them in conflict with local rulers, who might put them in jail, which cost ransom and kept him out of business, at times for many months, as some dramatic letters written in such situations show. Others might run into financial problems by acquiring or granting too much credit, by employing unreliable retail agents, by suspension of commercial traffic due to local political unrest,[66a] and by commercial failures. This would make it impossible to pay their (interest bearing) debts to Assyrian **[73]** financiers and to the City Hall, and prevented them even to give the gods in Assur the votive gifts promised, which must have alarmed their family, creditors and investors there. It is therefore not surprising to find among the decisions of the City regulations for liquidations, for the proportional sharing losses of a joint caravan, and for the collection of debts, interest and compound interest, whereby a clear distinction was made between transactions concluded in Anatolia or in Assur. But regardless of how annoying such problems may have been, they nevertheless need to be distinguished from more general ones, that affected the trade as such, because they were more often due to strained relations with certain local rulers and cities, than to problems between the city of Assur and the colonial society. The "colonial traders" knew how much they depended on maintaining good relations with their kārum organization and their mother-city and how essential it was to stick to the rules, because Assur could not intervene militarily in Anatolia to help its traders, as the great Sargon of Akkad would have done in the past according to a legendary tale.[67]

8. Assyrian traders as brokers?

The role of Assur's traders in Anatolia as cultural brokers is a fascinating, but difficult topic, which requires a monograph, but some remarks can be made here.[67a] The civilization of the Assyrians traders living in Anatolia was in various ways more complex than their of the native Anatolian kingdoms, although we should not underestimate the latter, as its developed palace organization shows.[68] Assyrian cultural superiority cannot be observed in the remains of their houses, which exhibit the Anatolian material culture. The use of donkey caravans for contact with Assur – a situation quite different in maritime trade – allowed the transfer small personal items only, some of which were found in graves. The traders, judging from request to send them, may have dressed in Assyrian **[74]** style garments, but no remains of them have survived. Contact with Anatolian elites is responsible for the use by the Assyrians of a number of loanwords, including titles and a few terms referring to social and political institutions that apparently were difficult to translate.[69]

[66a See now K.R. Veenhof, "Old Assyrian Traders in War and Peace". In *Krieg und Frieden im Alten Vorderasien, Alter Orient und Altes Tesamen Bd. 401*, eds. H. Neumann *et al.* (Münster: Ugarit Verlag, 2014):837-849.]

67 See above, note 44. Illustrative is a recently discovered, but not yet published official letter, from the late Old Assyrian period, in which the ruler of an Anatolian city via *kārum* Kanesh asks for military support from Assur in his conflict with a rival. But the request is refused. [See now C. Günbattı, *The Letter Sent to Hurmeli King of Harsamna and the Kings of Kaniš* (Ankara: Türk Tarih Kurumu, 2015): 87-100].

[67a See now Larsen 2015, Ch. 19, "Cultural Interaction", in a book which deals with many of the issues raised in this article.]

68 J.G. Dercksen presented a fascinating study: "Old Anatolian Society." In *Assyria and Beyond. Studies Presented to Mogens Trolle Larsen*, ed. J.G. Dercksen (Leiden: NINO, 2004): 137-177, but many questions of course remain.

69 See now J.G. Dercksen, "On Anatolian Loanwords in Akkadian Texts from Kültepe." *Zeitschrift für Assyriologie* 97 (2007): 26-46.

The main and best observable cultural impact was the introduction of the Assyrian cuneiform script and language, the earliest written language attested in Anatolia. Assyrians and Anatolians spoke radically different languages, but were able to communicate thanks to interpreters (called *targumannum*)[70] and by gradually picking up elements of each other's language, especially in the *kārums*, where both Assyrian and Anatolian traders lived and contacts became more intensive by mixed marriages. Fairly soon we meet some records of legal transactions between Anatolians, especially contracts about debts and family-law, written in Assyrians. Their structure and formulary seem to have been inspired by Assyrian examples, but some must haven been written by Anatolian scribes who had mastered the cuneiform script, but betrayed their background by a number of typical mistakes. In many cases we have to assume that Assyrians – not necessarily scribes, but also traders, some of which had mastered the art of writing – wrote texts for Anatolian, probably at times also for Anatolian rulers.[71] The use of seals for validating records and as "signature" of parties and witnesses also must have been inspired by the Assyrian example, especially the use of cylinder seals in Anatolian style, produced locally and often exhibiting a mixture of Mesopotamian and Anatolian iconographic motifs and styles. Use of the Assyrian script and seals by local palaces and rulers (the evidence is very restricted, due to the utter destruction of the palace of Kanesh) comes only later and the best examples are a few personnel lists from the palace of Kanesh and a famous letter sent to its king by a king of Mamma.[72]

[75] It is difficult to decide which legal, commercial and administrative features documented in records in which only Anatolians figure are of Assyrian inspiration, because there are no Anatolian precursors. Some must be of Assyrian origin, *e.g.* joint liability for debts, forms of surety, cancellation of consumptive debts by the ruler, but others – especially in the area of family law, such as rules of divorce, brotherhood contracts, death penalty for eviction – probably are of native origin. In all cases native legal customs are formulated in a different language and thus appear "under Assyrian linguistic garb" which makes it difficult to discover them. Many titles and professional designations are furthermore problematic as most of them must be Assyrian translations of Anatolian terms, for which underlying local designations are not attested. The same applies to some extent to the mention of deities by means of Mesopotamian cuneiform logograms, such as those for the sun-god and the storm-god, which may have been read as Akkadian ones by Assyrians, but as Anatolian ones by the local people.

Anatolia did not take over the Assyrian system of dating records (by year eponym and month) and used its own weights and measures (called "of the land") and some Assyrian texts reveal or state how they related to each other. In loan contracts between Assyrians and Anatolians or in those where both parties were Anatolian, payment clauses occur that mention as due dates the phases of the local agricultural year (plowing, the picking of the grapes, the spring, the ripening of the grain, the seizing of the sickle, etc.) and the festivals of the main local deities, which were also related to the seasons, and this custom was unknown in Assur.[73] Although the impact of the Assyrian traders and their culture

---

70 We have to assume that the treaties between the local rulers and the Assyrians, which were written in Assyrian and were formulated as an address to these rulers (in the second person singular), were read to them in translation, so that they knew what was expected from them and could propose changes in their own interest.

71 A still unpublished record mentions an Assyrian "who had taken up the position of scribe in the town of Mamma", apparently a trader who had mastered the art of writing and probably was employed by the local palace; see Veenhof, "Old Assyrian Period" (2008a): 48.

72 K. Balkan, *Letter of King Anum-Hirbi of Mamma to King Warshama of Kanish* (Ankara: Türk Tarih Kurumu, 1957).

73 See for the titles, professions and payment terms, Veenhof, "Old Assyrian Period" (2008a): Ch. VI, and more in general for the relations between Assyrians and Anatolians, K.R. Veenhof, "The Old Assyrian Merchants and their Relations with the Native Population of Anatolia." *In Mesopotamien und seine Nachbarn*, ed. H.J. Nissen – J. Renger (Berlin: Dietrich Reimer, 1982): 147-55.

was important, Dercksen concludes,[74] perhaps a little too defensively, that Anatolia took over only those cultural elements that it lacked itself and which did not affect the essence of their native culture.

The Assyrian impact, however, did not last, although we cannot exclude that certain elements survived in the legal sphere, perhaps also in commercial procedures, but this is difficult to document for lack of written sources. When in the last quarter of the 18th century BC the **[76]** Assyrian colonial system and presence broke down, visible traces of Assyrian influence, including the use of their script, language and cylinder seals, disappeared. And when, about a century later, during the Hittite Old Empire, the cuneiform script was again introduced, it was of Syrian/Babylonian inspiration.

Conclusion

Many questions remain, as usual when dealing with an ancient culture on the basis of written sources, and the situation in Assur for lack of sources from the administrative institutions of the city, can only be described in rather general terms. Over the years new texts have repeatedly led to adaptations of current ideas[75] and have surprised us by information and data we had not expected. The fact that some interesting features (*e.g.* the action of the *nībum*, the measure allowing redemption of sold houses) are thus far only documented by own or two sources, allows room for new ones and several of the interpretative suggestions put forward in recent literature still are in need of confirmation.[76]

The role of Assur as emporium and interregional market town, focused on a particular circuit in a much wider commercial network is clear, but we would like to know more about the situation in the city. In particular the role and facilities of the foreign traders who supplied it with tin and textiles and the questions what they obtained in exchange and the nature or their dealings with the local warehouses remain areas of speculation. The role of the City Hall also needs more clarification, as does the relation between the warehouses and "the market", where one could buy textiles (the local production), but which is never mentioned in connection with tin. We also lack information on commercial activities outside Anatolia and the routes leading there and I find if difficult to assume that Assyrian traders were so focused on Anatolia that they did not engage in trade with Babylonia. A few pieces of evidence from the later period, the first half of the eighteenth century BC, show that Assyrian traders were active in the Babylonian city of Sippar and had contacts with **[77]** Mari on the Middle Euphrates and one wonders whether this was not also the case a century earlier.[77]

There can be no doubt that "mercantile groups" played an important role in the Old Assyrian society, not only in the colonial community but also at home, in Assur, both on a private and on an institutional level. In the sources we meet different "groups," identified by their specific tasks, competence and interests – "Kanesh traders", caravan leaders, retail agents, merchant-bankers, investors in joint-stock funds, owners of warehouses, and even priests – but we cannot describe their distinctive roles in the administration because the texts always refer to the actions and decisions of collectives ("the big men" and "the (plenary) *kārum*" in Kanesh, "the Elders" and "the City Assembly" in Assur). It is

74 "Loanwords": 43 with note 80.

75 The best example is the now refuted idea about the existence of an Old Assyrian empire in Anatolia, called "Halys Assyria".

76 See especially some of the highly interesting interpretations suggested in Dercksen, *Institutions*, for administrative and financial procedures.

77 See K. R. Veenhof, "Assyrian Commercial Activities in Old Babylonian Sippar." In *Marchands, diplomates et empereurs. Études sur la civilisation mésopotamienne offertes à Paul Garelli*, eds. D. Charpin – F. Joannès (Paris: Recherche sur les Civilisations, 1991): 287-301, and J.-M. Durand, "Une alliance matrimoniale entre un marchand assyrien de Kanesh et un marchand mariote." In *Veenhof Anniversary Volume. Studies Presented to K.R. Veenhof on the Occasion of his 65th Birthday*, eds. W.H. van Soldt *et al.* (Leiden, NINO, 2001): 119-132.

clear that the main traders, investors, and merchants were important and rich citizens, many of which must have qualified as members of the City Assembly and, considering the restricted role of the ruler, we might qualify them as a kind of "mercantile oligarchy" that played a prominent role in the administration of the city, that is in the decisions of the City Assembly and via the policy of the City-Hall, many of whose directors must have been recruited from their ranks. But the colonial bias of our sources may hide that the City Assembly was also involved in other issues and may have counted among its members landowners, members of the militia, priests, and eminent craftsmen, etc. They may well have profited from the trade and invested in it, but probably also had other interests. The lack of sources from Assur must be responsible for the fact that verdicts and decisions reflecting issues regarding them are unknown, because there was not reason to send such documents to Kanesh.

Among the directors of the City Hall we also find a few experienced Kanesh traders, but their relatively small number shows that many prominent and rich Assyrians, though somehow involved in the trade or its financing, were not active (colonial) traders. They too may have harbored other interests, either local Assyrian ones or those related to the imports from the south. It may have induced them and the City Assembly to foster of good relations with foreign traders visiting Assur and perhaps with the **[78]** cities from which the latter originated, but we lack all evidence to prove it. Even a city like Eshnunna, the capital of a small territorial state ca. 250 km south of Assur and important as emporium for the provision of Babylonia with tin, is never mentioned in our texts and this is also the case with Susa, from where the tin caravans came to Assur. We also know very little of the institutional fabric and economic role of the temples of Assur that invested in the trade and provided facilities for storing silver and gold,[78] and where many oldest daughters of "Kanesh traders" served priestesses of the god Assur.

That the interests of "Kanesh traders" could and did diverge from those of the City, is therefore not surprising, but notwithstanding the evidence for a few painful decisions and clashes, we should not overestimate the problems. Under the guidance of the *kārum* organization, which faithfully followed the rules and decisions of the City, the colonial mercantile groups on the whole abided by the rules set by the City and embodied in the treaties. As traders had to declare in lawsuits, "they subjected themselves to the City and its ruler", which probably was also the best way of being successful as a member of the colonial society.

Assur and its colonies, without political power in Anatolia, could not ignore developments there, in particular in the later period of the trade, when the number and influence of the Assyrian traders diminished and more powerful territorial states started to emerge in Anatolia. This becomes clear from the treaties of the later period, mentioned above, in which the Assyrians tried hard to protect themselves against misuse of power by the Anatolians and in doing so *de facto* admitted changes in the situation. The system of import taxes and pre-emption, from which the local rulers profited, by that time had been adapted and the rulers could now also collect the tithe on *pirikannu*-textiles traded by the Assyrians, the very same Anatolian textiles whose trade had been forbidden in the past and had been heavily fined by the City! The Assyrian authorities, no doubt on the basis of the experiences of the "colonial traders", were willing and able to adapt their policies to new realities.

How successful these adaptations were remains unknown due to the lack of written data. My impression is that in the later period some traders gradually came to figure less as Assyrian merchants in Anatolia and more **[79]** as Anatolian merchants with Assyrian roots. Their smaller number and reduced importance and economic power inevitably led

78 See the interesting observations on "the treasury of divine Assur" in Dercksen, *Institutions*: 77-81, on which we need more evidence.

to more integration in the host communities.[79] Less frequent contacts with Assur and a less clear presence of the City in the colonial community – during the later period "Envoys of the City" no longer appear – make the Assyrian trading communities in Anatolia acquire some traits of a "trade diaspora," with features of intermarriage, more local business contacts and a measure of mutual acculturation. Closer contacts with the host community provided opportunities for more cooperation and the setting up of partnerships with Anatolians (not attested for the earlier period),[80] but also entailed certain risks, because Assyrians now figure more frequently as debtors of Anatolian traders. It is revealing that two treaties of this later period, with the cities of Hahhum and Kanesh, contain so many detailed stipulations to guarantee the freedom of action of the Assyrian traders and to protect them in legal conflicts and against high-handed Anatolian creditors. They also want to safeguard them from legal measures by Anatolian rulers, such as manumission of slaves and recruitment for service duties, dangers that seem to have been absent and difficult to envisage during the well-documented main period of the trade, one century earlier,[81] and may thus reveal that the position of the Assyrians was less secure than before. But the existence of these treaties shows that the Assyrians still believed that they had sufficient influence and that their commercial presence was attractive enough to secure their trading system by such treaty stipulations, accepted under oath by the Anatolian parties. And this was also the case in the probably slightly younger treaty with Apum, in the Jazira, much closer to Assur.

Although the colonies by then were less numerous, becoming smaller and lost some of their economic power, the links with the **[80]** mother-city remained too important to allow them to become independent "diaspora settlements". What really happened during the last generations remains unclear, because we can neither follow the fates of individual traders nor discover how the City of Assur reacted to these developments. Trade eventually collapsed, possibly due to the breakdown of the caravan system under a different political constellation in Northern Mesopotamia, the disruption (or perhaps shift) of the import of tin from Elam, the increasing struggle for political power between a few expanding Anatolian territorial states, and (perhaps in consequence of all this) the decline of Assur itself, which by that time had entered a "dark period", from which we have almost no written sources. Thus a unique, structurally and legally highly advanced system of commercial colonization came to an end.

---

79 See for an impression of the situation during the later period J.G. Dercksen, "'When we met in Hattuš'. Trade According to Old Assyrian Texts from Alishar and Boğazköy". In *Veenhof Anniversary Volume. Studies Presented to Klaas R. Veenhof on the Occasion of his Sixty-fifth Birthday*, eds. W. H. van Soldt *et al.* (Leiden: NINO, 2001): 39-66, and K.R. Veenhof, "Old Assyrian Period" (2008a): 32-5 and 140-6.

80 See for a partnership between an Assyrian trader in Kanesh and an Anatolian one in Mamma the text kt n/k 32 (which records its termination), edited in J.G. Dercksen, "Some Element of Old Anatolian Society in Kaniš." In *Assyria and Beyond. Studies Presented to Mogens Trolle Larsen*, ed. J.G. Dercksen (Leiden: NINO, 2004): 166-7.

81 This idea is based on the general picture of the economic power and influence of the Assyrians; the administrators of *kārum* Kanesh were actually called "our fathers" by some Anatolian rulers. But I admit that we do not have the text of one single a treaty with an important city during the main period of *kārum* Kanesh level II, which leaves the possibility open that similar stipulations occurred already earlier – and worked well, so that letters did not have to report on problems encountered in this respect.

Bibliography

See in general: C. Michel, *Old Assyrian Bibliography* (Leiden, NINO, 2003), with supplements in *Archiv für Orientforschung* 50/51 (2005/2006): 436-49, and 52 (2011): 417-437.

Algaze, G. 1993. *The Uruk World System. The Dynamics of Early Mesopotamian Civilization.* Chicago-London: University of Chicago Press.

Balkan, K. 1957. *Letter of King Anum-Hirbi of Mamma to King Warshama of Kanish.* Ankara: Türk Tarih Kurumu.

Barjamovic, G. 2005. *A Historical Geography of Ancient Anatolia in the Assyrian Colony Period* (thesis, published in 2011: Carsten Niebuhr Publications No. 38, Copenhagen: Museum Tusculanum Press).

Dercksen, J.G. 1996. *The Old Assyrian Copper Trade in Anatolia.* Istanbul: NHAI.

–. 1997. The Silver of the Gods. On Old Assyrian *ikribū*, *Archivum Anatolicum* 3: 75-100.

–. 1999. On the Financing of Old Assyrian Merchants. In *Trade and Finance in Ancient* Mesopotamia, ed. J.G. Dercksen. Istanbul: NHAI: 85-99.

–. 2001. "When we met in Hattush". Trade according to the Old Assyrian texts from Alishar and Boğazköy. In *Veenhof Anniversary Volume. Studies Presented to K.R. Veenhof on the Occasion of his 65th Birthday*, eds. W.H. van Soldt *et al.* Leiden: NINO: 39-66.

–. 2004a. Some Elements of Old Anatolian Society in Kaniš." In *Assyria and Beyond. Studies Presented to Mogens Trolle Larsen*, ed. J.G. Dercksen. Leiden: NINO: 166-7.

–. 2004b. *Old Assyrian Institutions.* Leiden: NINO.

Durand, J.-M. 1990. La cité-état d'Imar à l'époque des rois de Mari. *MARI* 6: 39-92.

–. 2000. *Litératures anciennes du Proche-Orient, vol. 18. Documents épistolaires du palais de Mari*, III. Paris: Le Cerf.

Günbattı, C. 2015. *The Letter Sent to Hurmeli King of Harsamna and the Kings of Kaniš.* Ankara: Türk Tarih Kurumu.

[Hertel, Th.K., 2013. *Old Assyrian Legal Practices. Law and Dispute in the Ancient Near East.* Leiden: NINO 2013.]

Kraus, F.R. 1984. *Königliche Verfügungen in altbabylonischer Zeit.* Leiden: Brill, 1984.

Larsen, M.T. 1976. *The Old Assyrian City-State and its Colonies.* Copenhagen: Akademisk Forlag.

–. 1987. Commercial Networks in the Ancient Near East, In *Centre and Periphery in the Ancient World*, eds. M. Rowlands, M. T. Larsen, and K. Kristiansen. Cambridge, Cambridge University Press: 47-56.

–. 2001. *Naruqqu*-Veträge, In: *Reallexikon der Assyriologie* 9. Berlin, Walter de Gruyter: 181-184.

–. 2002. *Old Assyrian Archives, vol. 1: The Aššur-nādā Archive.* Leiden, NINO.

–. 2007. Individual and Family in Old Assyrian Society. *Journal of Cuneiform Studies* 59: 93-106.

[–. 2015. *Ancient Kanesh. A Merchant Colony in Bronze Age Anatolia* Cambridge: Cambridge University Press.]

[Lassen, A.W. 2010. The Trade in Wool in Old Assyrian Anatolia. *JEOL* 42 (2010) 159-179.]

Michel, C. 1991. Durhumid, son commerce et ses marchands. In *Marchands, diplomats et empereurs. Études sur la civilisation mésopotamienne offertes à Paul Garelli*, eds. D. Charpin and F. Joannès. Paris: Recherche sur les Civilizations: 253-73.

–. 1996. Le commerce dans les textes de Mari. In *Amurru* 1. *Mari, Ebla et les Hourrites*, ed. J.-M. Durand. Paris: Éditions Recherche sur les Civilisations, 413-26.

–. 2001. *Litératures anciennes du Proche-Orient, vol. 19: Correspondance des marchands de Kanish au début du IIe millénaire avant J.-C.* Paris: Le Cerf.

–. 2006. Femmes et production textile à Aššur au début du IIe millénaire avant J.-C. In *Spécialisation des tâches et sociétés, Techniques et culture, vol. 46*, eds. A. Averbough, P. Brun *et al.* Paris: 281-97.

Stein, G.J. 1999, *Rethinking World-Systems. Diasporas, Colonies, and Interaction in Uruk Mesopotamia*. Tuscon: University of Arizona Press.

–. 2002. The Political Economy of Mesopotamian Colonial Encounters. In *The Archaeology of Colonial Encounters. Comparative Perspectives*, ed. G.J. Stein. Santa Fe-Oxford: School of American Research Press – James Currey: Ch. 5.

Stol, M. 2004. Wirtschaft und Gesellschaft in altbabylonischer Zeit. In *Annäherungen* 4. *Orbis Biblicus et Orientalis vol. 150/4. Mesopotamien. Die altbabylonische Zeit.* eds. P. Attinger, W. Sallaberger, and M. Wäfler. Fribourg-Göttingen: Academic Press-Vandenhoeck & Ruprecht: Teil 3, 643-975.

Veenhof, K.R. 1972. *Aspects of Old Assyrian Trade and its Terminology.* Leiden: Brill.

–. 1982. The Old Assyrian Merchants and their Relations with the Native Population of Anatolia. In *Berliner Beiträge zum Vorderen Orient, vol. 1/1, Mesopotamien und seine Nachbarn*, ed. H.J. Nissen and J. Renger. Berlin: Dietrich Reimer: 147-55.

–. 1991. Assyrian Commercial Activities in Old Babylonian Sippar. In *Marchands, diplomates et empereurs. Études sur la civilisation mésopotamienne offertes à Paul Garelli*, eds. D. Charpin and F. Joannès. Paris: Recherche sur les Civilisations: 287-301 [= pp. xxx-xxx in this volume].

–. 1995. "In Accordance with the Words of the Stele". Evidence for Old Assyrian Legislation. *Chicago-Kent Law Review* 70: 1717-44 [= pp. xxx-xxx in this volume].

–. 1997. 'Modern' Features in Old Assyrian Trade. *JESHO* 40: 336-66.

–. 1999a. Silver and Credit in Old Assyrian Trade. In *Trade and Finance in Ancient Mesopotamia*, ed. J.G. Dercksen. Istanbul: NHAI: 55-83 [= pp. xxx-xxx in this volume].

–. 1999b. Redemption of Houses in Assur and Sippar, In *Munuscula Mesopotamica. Festschrift für Johannes Renger*, eds. B. Böck et al. Münster: Ugarit Verlag: 599-616 [= pp. xxx-xxx in this volume].

–. 2000. Trade and Politics in Ancient Assur. Balancing of Public, Colonial and Entrepreneurial Interests. In *Saggi di Storia Antica, vol. 21. Mercanti e Politica nel Mondo Antico*, ed. C. Zaccagnini. Roma: L'Erma di Bretschneider: 69-118 [= pp. xxx-xxx in this volume].

–. 2003a. *The Old Assyrian List of Year Eponyms from kārum Kanish.* Ankara: Türk Tarih Kurumu.

–. 2003b. The Old Assyrian Period. In *Handbook of Oriental Studies, Section I, Vol. 72. History of Ancient Near Eastern Law*, vol. I, ed. R. Westbrook. Leiden-Boston: 431-84.

–. 2008a. The Old Assyrian Period. In *Annäherungen 5, Orbis Biblicus et Orientalis 160/5: Mesopotamia. The Old Assyrian Period*, ed. M. Wäfler. Fribourg-Göttingen, Academic Press-Vandenhoeck & Ruprecht: Part I, 13-263.

–. 2008b. Across the Euphrates. In *Anatolia and the Jazira during the Old Assyrian Period*, ed. J.G. Dercksen. Leiden: NINO: 3-29.

[–. 2010. *The Archive of Kuliya, son of Ali-abum (Kt. 92/k 188-263), Kültepe Tabletleri 5*, Ankara: Türk Tarih Kurumu.]

[–. 2014. Families of Old Assyrian Traders. In *La famille dans le Proche Orient ancien: réalités, symbolisms et images. Proceedings of the 55th Rencontre Assyriologique Inter-nationale, Paris 6-9 July 2009*, ed. L. Marti. Winona Lake: Eisenbrauns: 341-371.]

[–. 2014. Old Assyrian Traders in War and Peace. In *Krieg und Frieden im Alten Vorderasien, Alter Orient und Altes Tesamen Bd. 401*, eds. H. Neumann *et al.* Münster: Ugarit Verlag: 837-849.]

The Archives of Old Assyrian Traders: Their Nature, Functions and Use[*]

The Old Assyrian archives are private archives. They were found in the houses of traders who in the early centuries of the second millennium BC lived in Kanesh, an ancient city in Central Anatolia, not far from modern Kayseri.[1] The houses are situated in the commercial district of the lower town, called *kārum* Kanesh, which flourished for more than a century during the period of level II, which came to an end by destruction around 1835 BC (middle chronology). The Assyrian settlement in Kanesh is not only nearly the only source of our documentation, thanks to more than fifty years of excavations, it was also the administrative capital of an Assyrian colonial network, that comprised ca. 30 commercial settlements and small trading stations, spread over the whole of Central Anatolia. The archives were kept in what they called the "sealed room" (*maknukum*) or "guarded room" (*maṣṣartum*), where also valuables were stored. They vary considerably in size and range from few hundred to a few times ca. 2000 cuneiform documents, variations that must reflect the importance and status of a trader, the history of the **[28]** house and presumably also the administrative habits of the owner. The archives consist of the written documents accumulated – drawn up, received, acquired, accepted for safe-keeping, or deposited there for other reasons – during the period of activity of a trader, which usually covered many, occasionally up to thirty, years. In several cases the house had been taken over or inherited by his son, who added his own records to those left behind by his father and there are also a few examples of archives with records of three generations of traders. The archives brought to light by the excavations, first by the villagers and after 1948 by Turkish archeologists, reflect what they contained when the houses were destroyed.

1. TRADERS, ARCHIVES AND RECORDS

Some general information on the traders, their archives and the types of records they contain is necessary before I can focus on the subject of this paper. This is not easy, because the archives of Kanesh have yielded more than 20.000 cuneiform documents (half of which are more or less known or accessible) of an at times bewildering variety, which reflect an extensive and very sophisticated overland trade, carried out by perhaps ca. 60 trading families. Moreover, most of the texts available were unearthed and sold by the local villagers, so that their archival background and coherence in unclear. Only the publication of officially excavated archives, in TPAK 1 and the volumes of the series AKT offers better insights, but much work still remains to be done.

Status, wealth and family situation of the traders vary considerably and their archives, all of which contain the usual variety of business documents, reflect these differences in

* Originally published in M. Faraguna (ed.), Archives and Archival Documents in Ancient Societies. Trieste 30 Sept. – 1 Oct. 2011. Legal Documents in Ancient Societies IV, Graeca tergestina, Storia e Civiltà 1. Triest, pp. 27-61.

1 See for general information on the excavation at Kanesh and on the Old Assyrian trade LARSEN 1976, Özgüç 2003, and VEENHOF 2008a, mentioned below in the bibliography, and see also C. MICHEL, *Old Assyrian Bibliography* (OAAS 1), Leiden 2003. In the following text I have simplified the rendering of the names, not indicating long vowels and typical Semitic consonants, writing Ishtar instead of Ištar, Assur, etc.

the nature and numbers of commercial records and correspondence and to some extent also in the presence of certain types of legal documents. And most traders also had a family house in Assur, with an archive, but we know little from Assur, because the layers of this period in the lower town were not reached by the German excavators.

In general archives of traders whose family had stayed behind in Assur contain more letters of their wives and more correspondence with relatives, business associates and representatives, who took care of their legal and economic interests in Assur. Archives of traders living in Assur, whose grown-up sons lived and worked in Anatolia, include letters exchanged between them, while those of traders settled in Kanesh with their family comprise letters exchanged with their wives when they were traveling around. Important family documents – marriage contracts, testaments, title deeds, last wills, and joint-stock contracts that supplied the trader with his capital – were usually kept in the archive in Assur, but may turn up in Kanesh when a whole family lived there. Many of the older traders focused on the import of tin and textiles from Assur and their sale for silver and gold in Anatolia, so that their archives contains many letters and records relating to the caravan trade. Others were more involved in the internal **[29]** trade in copper and wool inside Anatolia, and we also meet traders who traveled a lot in Anatolia and were engaged in commission sale and agency for colleagues in Assur and Kanesh.

For a good appraisal of the archives several facts have to be taken into account. The first is that several traders also had houses – apparently with archives – in other trading settlements in Anatolia, where they stayed temporarily and even could move. This can only be discovered by a comprehensive analysis of an archive and as an example I mention some features of the large archive of Shallim-Assur and his family (more than 1100 texts), which has been analyzed in an exemplary way by Larsen. In the first volume of its edition (AKT 6a) he writes:

> "It seems clear that his main archive must have been stored in the city of Durhumit,[2] where he stayed during the last years of his life and where eventually he died and was buried. (...) The texts from the Kanesh archive, relating to his work and his actions are probably to be understood as a scattered sample that happened to end up here, presumably because he was staying in this house occasionally and received letters and engaged in other activities that lead to the writing of texts." (AKT 6a, p. 8-9).

His house also contained many documents of his elder brother Iddin-abum, although he must have had his own house with a separate archive. The dates and subject matter of these documents made Larsen conclude that "when he was a very young man he may have shared a house and archive with his brother" (from where his texts were never removed) and that, much later, after his death, "collected documents relating to his affairs were brought to the house of his brother, who was the executor of his estate". Shallim-Assur's eldest son, Ennam-Assur, probably was the main inhabitant of the house, but he was murdered only a few years after his father's death, in ca. 1865 BC.[3] Next we have ca. 200 texts associated with the affairs of the latter's younger brother, Ali-ahum, who "must have been the last person to use this house and to deposit texts here", several of which deal with attempts to obtain blood money for his murdered brother. But since none of them is later than ca. three years after this murder, while he must have lived considerably longer, "the later texts were not stored in this house, where he probably did not live, so that the documentation for his last years is no longer extant". In fact no dated records from the last 25 years, before Kanesh was destroyed in ca. 1835 BC, have been found and Larsen considers it likely that the house was in fact not lived in during this

2 An important city and colony, ca. 250 km north of Kanesh, the center of the Anatolian copper trade.

3 The texts are dated, according to the Assyrian custom, by means of the name of an important eponymous official in the City of Assur, head and manager of the "City Hall", who was elected annually. This institution was created during the first year of king Erishum I, according to the Middle Chronology ca. 1870 BC.

period and may have been used exclusively for storage. Fortunately, the texts it contained were not removed (AKT 6a, 11-13).[4]

[30] A second feature is that, as mentioned in some records, groups of texts for a variety of reasons could be taken out of an archive and brought elsewhere, frequently to Assur. A trader could move to Assur in old age and take records along, as shown by the witnessed record *EL* 141:1-10, "The containers with tablets of Enlil-bani and the containers with copies we entrusted to Iddin-Kubum and he brought them to Enlil-bani." When a lawsuit, by appeal, was transferred from *kārum* Kanesh to the court of the City of Assur, records to be used as evidence were shipped there. *EL* 298:9ff. describes how in a conflict about a debt the authorities of *kārum* Kanesh entrusted to an attorney of the plaintiff a sealed box with ten sealed documents, including four formal letters (*našpertum*, "missive") of *kārum* Kanesh, four missives of a trader sealed by the *kārum* and two records dealing with the debt in question, which (lines 35-36) "he will submit to the City and our Lord (the ruler)". When a trader died and his business had to be liquidated and his inheritance divided on the basis of his last will – which was always kept in Assur – this had to take place after heirs and relevant records had been brought together in Assur, as a ruling of the City stated (VEENHOF 1995, pp. 1725-1727). And we have seen in the previous paragraph how a large file on the affairs of a dead trader was brought to the house of his brother, who was the executor of his estate.

In some cases, after a trader had died, particular records in his archive could be required to prevent unfinished transactions from being frozen and to pay or collect debts. In such a case formal authorization could be given to open his safe and take out assets and tablets. Two records inform us about what happened in this way with the archive of Elamma. CCT 5, 3 reports that after his death the sons of his partner "had opened the strong-room and taken out a sealed debt-note for 12 pounds of silver", declaring: "We act at the order and under the responsibility of his investors". They were, as usual in such situations, accompanied by a committee of impartial outsiders (*ahiūtum*), who looked on and afterwards sealed the door of the strong-room together with those who had entered. And in Kt m/k 145 people declare: "On the basis of a verdict of the plenary *kārum* the scribe seized us and we entered Elamma's house and broke the seals of the strong room, which we left there. Agua took two coffers with tablets." In the deposition BIN 6, 220+, that is part of a large file, studied by MATOUŠ 1969, about what happened when the trader Puzur-Assur died, his sons state: "When our father Puzur-Assur had died the investors and creditors of our father, having entered his sealed strong-room, took 12 boxes with tablets and entrusted these to you".

The destruction of the houses in *kārum* Kanesh in ca. 1835 BC did not come as a complete surprise, no unburied skeletons were found, nor valuables (silver, gold, items of bronze) in the strong-rooms. This suggests that the inhabitants managed to flee in time and it is reasonable to assume that they took along a number **[31]** of records, in particular those recording valid debt-claims and investment contracts, perhaps also title deeds. This situation helps to explain why in general records of the last twenty years of *kārum* Kanesh level II are fairly rare. But there must have been other reasons too, perhaps the move of traders from Kanesh, the administrative centre of the trade, to cities and colonies in the north and west, which were the centers of economic activity. Larsen, in the introduction to AKT 6b points to "the apparent collapse in the commercial activities of the Assyrian businessmen [that] probably had its roots in legal and economic problems associated with the death of a whole generation of important merchants".[5] Whatever was the case, there is no evidence that, when a number of years after 1835 BC the rebuilding

4 Concerning the archive excavated in 1993 in grid LVII/127-128, with texts from three generations of traders, Michel 2008b, p. 58 observes that the number of texts of the second owner, Ali-ahum, son of Iddin-Suen, is not substantial (ca. 50 letters, 11 loan contracts), presumably because he also had a house in Burushhattum, and one in Assur.

5 The issue is studied in Barjamovic, Hertel, and Larsen 2012.

of what became *kārum* Kanesh level Ib started, Assyrians tried to retrieve records from the earlier ruins.

Finally, we have to assume that the enormous number of written records accumulating in the archives made traders from time to time decide to remove texts that were no longer valid or necessary. Most commercial transactions were finished in a few years[6] and their records did not have to be preserved, as happened with title deeds or marriage contracts. Only in particular cases, such as with a joint-stock company that would run for ten years, did records have to be preserved for longer periods. This explains why records from the oldest period, when the scope of the trade was also more limited, are relatively rare,[7] but we know almost nothing about the removal of records, apart from returning debt-notes when they were paid. We occasionally meet references to records we would expect to find, but which are missing, but we do not know why. The archive of Kuliya (AKT 5) contained eight, in part overlapping lists (texts nos. 62-69) that enumerated in all 50 tablets of various kinds, apparently present there; the biggest one lists "27 tablets placed in a big box". Since none of these tablets was found in the archive, the list may have been drawn up to select and identify documents that were removed, but we do not know why and where. In general one gets the impression that outdated records were not systematically discarded and that much depended on the habits and zeal of the archive owner, who usually had room enough to store them, while reading and selecting them may have been a cumbersome task. Some old documents, such as large memoranda enumerating all outstanding claims, may have been preserved for their informative value, letters from relatives and wives for emotional reasons. The archaeological record unfortunately is not clear enough to show whether old, outdated records **[32]** may not have been stored in separate containers or even rooms. No hoards of discarded tablets were found outside the archival rooms and houses, used as fill or for paving a floor, as happened in Babylonia.

Every archive also contains groups of records that cannot be linked with the owner or related to his business, which I have called elsewhere (VEENHOF 2003, p. 115, § 5.2) "strange records". Various explanations for their presence are possible. There were people without a house in the *kārum*, *e.g.* caravan personnel, traveling agents and relatives who stayed in Kanesh for some time. They may have deposited their records in the archive of their boss, as is clear for an employee of the trader Imdilum. Traders traveled a lot and might temporarily move to other places and in such cases they might give valuable records in safe-deposit (*ana nabšēm ezābum*) to a friend or colleague. The most impressive piece of evidence is a large tablet in New York (CTMMA I, 84), where a trader, whose strong-room had been emptied out by a partner, enumerates and describes 25 records of all kinds, including "tablets of others, which they had left in deposit with me" (l. 40),... "all contained in two sealed containers" (lines 60f.).[8] In several cases such deposited records were apparently never retrieved by their owners, who may have died or disappeared. As already mentioned above in connection with the archive of Shallim-Assur, traders did move and could live only temporarily in a house, judging from the presence of groups of records belonging to them alongside the more substantial archive of the owner or main inhabitant of the house. Cécile Michel observed that the archive edited in TPAK I, basically that of Shumi-abiya, also contained 25 letters of a certain Assur-mutappil, some still in unopened envelopes, but not a single debt-note of his. She assumes that he deposited his letters with Shumi-abiya when he left Kanesh, but did not

---

6 The terms of commercial loans, actually the consignment of merchandise given on credit to traveling agents, usually did not exceed one year. Also the notes and accounts of expenses paid en route by leader of a caravan lost their value after the accounts had been settled.

7 The absence of early dated records (the oldest one preserved is from eponymy year 47) is not surprising, since nearly all are debt-notes and they were returned or destroyed when the debt was paid (see also below note 34).

8 That the victim could give a long, detailed description of all these tablets implies that he had kept a list of them.

return; some letters addressed to him that had arrived after his departure were never opened and read (pp. 33-34).

2. TRADERS IN DIFFERENT SITUATIONS AND CONTEXTS

The circumstances under which traders lived and worked in Kanesh could be different and this had a bearing on their archives. We may distinguish the following situations:

a. A trader as the head of a family who had moved to Kanesh, while leaving his family, that means his wife and young children, behind in Assur. All important family records are in Assur and this situation generates a correspondence between husband and wife. The lively business correspondence is with the trader's male relatives, investors and especially his representatives in Assur, **[33]** who take care of his interests, receive his silver, buy merchandise for export and equip his caravans. His sons in due time might join him, assist him in the business and when they were grown up develop their own commercial activities, to be continued after his death.
   A good example is Pushuken, father of four sons, who was active in Kanesh for more than 20 years and died there. His business was continued mainly by his son Buzazu, who lived in his house, where his father's archive was left in place,[9] to which he added his own records. It contained i. a. letters sent to Pushuken by his wife in Assur and also many texts dealing with the division of Pushuken's inheritance among his children, in which his eldest daughter, a priestess in Assur, played a prominent role.

b. A variant to this type is the successful trader who after many years returns to Assur and leaves the business in Kanesh in the hands of his by now experienced son, whom he assists and advises in letters sent from Assur, while also carrying on some business of his own. The son took over his father's house and archive, apart from the records his father had taken along when he returned to Assur, presumably records of affairs that still had not been finished, although this not easy to prove, for we have no texts from Assur.
   The best example is the prominent trader Imdilum, – whose father Shu-Laban was already active in Anatolia, – who led the business there at least 17 years, returned to Assur around 1880 BC and was succeeded by his son Puzur-Ishtar. The latter is attested for fifteen years, the last seven after his father had died. The father in Assur kept writing letters to his son, which we have to distinguish from copies of letters written by him when he still lived in Kanesh.

c. A young man who moved to *kārum* Kanesh to trade there in the service of or in co-operation with his father who remained in Assur. The latter, the boss of the family business, conducts a lively correspondence with him and also supplies him with merchandise, money, advice and information and in return receives the silver sent back from Anatolia, which he used to pay debts and taxes and to equip a new caravan.
   A good example is Assur-nada, son of Assur-idi, whose archive was published in Larsen 2002. It shows us a father much concerned about what his son does, such as the latter's failure to meet promises (of votive gifts) made to the gods, and also burdened with the task of caring for his son's children, after the latter's wife, who had stayed in Assur, had died. Another example is Ennum-Assur, the oldest son of Shalim-ahum, a merchant and capitalist living in Assur and the main business associate of Pushuken (mentioned under a). He **[34]** lived, temporarily perhaps in a house in Kanesh together with his brother Dan-Assur. Ennum-Assur's archive was excavated in 1970 and partially published (without the tablets still in sealed envelopes) as AKT 3.

---

9 All texts dealing with Pushuken were unearthed and sold by the local villagers early in the 20th century and there exists no general description of his (reconstructed) archive, although we can now identify almost 350 letters and dozens of legal documents that belonged to it.

The archive, not surprisingly, contained letters of the father to his son(s) and letters written by Ennum-Assur when the traveled and worked elsewhere in Anatolia, to his wife Nuhshatum. She had to take care of and "guard" his house and the archive and was occasionally instructed to retrieve documents from the archive for particular purposes.

d. A grown-up son who had moved to Kanesh with his wife, when he had become independent or his father in Assur had died and he had inherited his share in his fortune. He started a business and family life there and his sons in due time would work with him and get married. In his archive we may also find contracts and records relating to their family life and the business correspondence is with male relatives, his representatives and his investors in Assur.
A good example is Elamma, the younger son of Iddin-Suen, an energetic importer of merchandise from Assur (which he occasionally visisted), whose archive, excavated in 1991 and 1992, I am publishing. He lived in Kanesh for more than thirty years (opposite the house of his elder brother Ali-ahum) and had a lively correspondence with his representatives in Assur. His business was carried on after his death by some sons and his energetic widow, Lamassatum, who continued to live in the house for several years and conducted some business of her own. The archive also contains records dealing with the division of his father's, his own and his wife's inheritance and records about and letters from various family members living in Kanesh or Assur, such as a file about the death, funeral and inheritance of a twice married daughter,[10] and letters of his favorite daughter, who was priestess in Assur.

e. e) In some cases an archive contains a number of records of the father of the trader, but this depended on his age and where he lived, in Assur or Anatolia. We have *e.g.* no records of Pushuken's father Suejja, who lived in Assur, and only a few of Imdilum's father Shu-Laban, of whom it is not certain that he lived in or visited Kanesh.[11] In Ali-ahum's house in Kanesh, excavated in 1993, with an archive of more than 900 texts, a few dozen letters addressed to his father Iddin-Suen were found, but no debt-notes. Cécile Michel[12] assumes that these letters, which all have low excavation numbers, had been stored separately after his death, when his son Ali-ahum (active there since ca. 1895 BC) became **[35]** the owner of the house and the archive. This contrasts with the archive of Iddin-Suen's second son, Elamma (who lived across the street in Kanesh), whose house, which he must have acquired or built when he became an independent trader,[13] did not contain documents of his father. The archive of Shallim-Assur, son of Issu-arik contained a few letters to and records of his father, but no letters written by him after he had returned to Assur, presumably because he died there soon (AKT 6a, 6). After the death of a *pater familias* his inheritance was apparently divided and his "firm" liquidated, whereupon his sons could start their own business.[14] In most cases one of the sons acquired the house in Kanesh, where his mother might continue to live, with his father's archive left in place, to which his own and his mother's records would be added.

---

10 I studied this file in VEENHOF 2008b.

11 LARSEN 1982, p. 224 assumed that the father, who appears already in ca. 1910 BC (ICK 2, 104), died early and that Imdilum's uncle Assur-imitti, who lived in Assur, took care of the interests of the family, before Imdilum himself is attested in the sources, 18 years later.

12 MICHEL 2008b, p. 58, footnote 1.

13 The oldest dated text in which he occurs, as creditor, is from ca. 1905 BC, much earlier than his elder brother, but the latter apparently first operated from Assur, before coming to Kanesh, perhaps after the death of their father.

14 See LARSEN 2007 for this development.

3. THE KĀRUM ORGANIZATION

The archives excavated, while clearly those of private entrepreneurs and their families, also reflect that the Old Assyrian traders belonged to a community and organization of traders. They all originated from the same city, Assur, and had all settled abroad, far from home, in a completely different environment and society, without military protection. This stimulated forms of cooperation (mutual aid, business partnerships, representation, etc.), but it also took a more structural form. The totality of the Assyrian traders in Kanesh formed a kind of corporation, called *kārum*. This term originally meant the "quay, harbor district" that every Mesopotamian city had, where bulk goods arrived by boat, and then also the commercial quarter where traders met and finally its inhabitants as a group. A *kārum* could comprise foreign traders, who might organize themselves as a group, at times with a leader (called "its head"), to cooperate and to be better equipped to deal with the local powers. *Kārum* Kanesh was a well-organized, hierarchical organization, which comprised a plenary assembly, "the *kārum* great and small" that met as an "assembly" (*puhrum*), and knew a committee, designated as "the big men", who ran the daily affairs. The plenary *kārum* appears frequently as court-of-law to solve the many, mostly commercial conflicts between its members.

The *kārum* as organization had a building, "the *kārum* house", where meetings were held, its secretary worked, which housed a cella with the statue of the god Assur (by whose dagger members would swear), and had storage facilities and an archive. The *kārum* arranged and supervised the presumably semi-annual general "accounting of *kārum* Kanesh" (*nikkassū ša kārim Kaneš*), which involved both individual traders and the *kārum* as such. They were necessary because of **[36]** the many credit operations and book transfers between members, for accounting the results of collective commercial transactions organized by the *kārum* to which its members could subscribe, and for settling accounts (on taxes and credit sales) with the local palace, whereby payments and transfers were regularly channeled via the *kārum* organization.

Kārum Kanesh was also the administrative head of the colonial network that consisted of at least 25 other *kārum*s and trading stations (*wabartum*), spread over central Anatolia. As such it functioned as an extension of the government of the City of Assur, to which it was responsible and whose directives it had to apply. It maintained the diplomatic relations with the many city-states and rulers in Anatolia, with whom treaties had been concluded, and stepped in when problems arose. It could also issue orders and rulings and traders in other colonies could appeal to the authorities of *kārum* Kanesh for justice.

The archive of the *kārum* probably contained records (or their copies) emanating from these activities, such as official letters and verdicts, and we have references to tablets of/in the *kārum*-house on which traders were "booked/registered" for certain amounts, which they owed the organization or it owed to them.[15] Since the "*kārum*-house" has not been found, we do not have the archives of *kārum* Kanesh, but many texts it produced and also received (letters from other colonies and from the City of Assur and its ruler) are known and give us a welcome insight into its workings. They are frequently referred to or quoted in the business correspondence and several (copies) of them were found in the archives of the traders. As a self-governing institution the *kārum* had its members perform various administrative, commercial and judicial tasks and in doing so they produced or were given records and letters, some of which (in part duplicates) ended up in their archives. The orders and verdicts of the *kārum* were sealed by members who administered them and acted as its court-of-law and special members (called *līmū*) could represent the *kārum* in financial transactions. Messengers in temporary service of the *kārum*, sent out to other colonies with official letters and orders, might take their copy of such texts home when

15 See VEENHOF 2003, § 1.1. There is e.g. mention of a "big tablet of the *kārum*-house" and of a trader's "deposits [booked] on the third and sixth tablet of the *kārum*-house", but we do not know the system.

they returned.[16] The traders in whose cases the *kārum* intervened by letters, orders and verdicts apparently could acquire duplicates of these records. And this was also the case with official letters of the City, addressed to *the kārum*, which dealt with an issue that involved a particular trader. The texts of three treaties concluded between the Assyrians and some Anatolian rulers were all found in private archives, presumably **[37]** because their owners had represented the *kārum* when they were negotiated and concluded and had retained a copy of the text.

4. A CLASSIFICATION OF THE TEXTS

The records in the archives can classified in several broad categories:

a. *Letters*, which comprise usually ca. 30-50% of the texts of an archive. The main types are letters related to the caravan system, letters that report on a variety of commercial and legal problems (frequently small files around a particular incident), letters from and to family members, and official letters, by the authorities in Assur in Kanesh and their agents. An overview is offered by MICHEL 2001, who presents 400 of them in translation, divided into seven chapters, each with its introduction, dealing with the Assyrian and the Anatolian authorities, the caravan trade, smuggling, commercial partnerships and joint-stock companies, family firms (three samples), and the correspondence of women.[17]

b. *Legal documents*, usually ca. 30% to 40% of the texts, an important older sample of which (340 records) was published long ago in *EL* in a careful classification. They can be distinguished in two types. The first consists of contracts of various types, of which debt-notes, service contracts with personnel, transport contracts, contracts on settling accounts, and quittances are most numerous. Next there is limited number of contracts concerning family life (marriage, divorce – especially when a trader married an Anatolian bride – and inheritance) and a large variety of other contracts, *e.g.* concerning securities, joint-stock companies, partnerships, and contracts that served as title deeds, about the purchase of houses and slaves in Anatolia (frequently from defaulting debtors, whose pledges were forfeited)[18]. The second comprises a great variety of records that emanate from and reflect the administration of justice, such as protocols of private summonses, testimonies, oaths sworn, interrogations, agreements, records of arbitration, mediation and adjudication, together with protocols of lawsuits and of verdicts by the various colonial authorities. In addition verdicts by the City Assembly of Assur, which issued also "strong letters of the City (Assur)", written to help a plaintiff whose case has been considered valid by the legal authorities. **[38]**

c. *Lists, memorandums and notes*, usually ca. 20-30% of the texts, ca. 600 of which, mostly unearthed before the official excavations by the local villagers and therefore devoid of their archival context, was edited in ULSHÖFER 1995. Alongside a variety of short notes about expenses, distributions of bread and meat, small payments, settlements, deposits, etc., the more important categories are:
   - lists of packets of silver and gold, the yield of the trade, but also gifts for various persons, entrusted for shipment to Assur;

16 The role of the messengers of the *kārum* is described in VEENHOF 2008c, pp. 224-246, and there one finds samples of official letters carried by messengers. A large selection of official letters of the Assyrian authorities is offered by MICHEL 2001, Ch.1.

17 Other collections of published letters are those related to the caravan system, studied in LARSEN 1967, the letters in Prague, published in Prag I, those in the Assur-nada archive edited in LARSEN 2002, and translations of letters in the recent volumes in the AKT-series.

18 See for such contracts B. KIENAST, *Das altassyrische Kaufsvertragsrecht*, FAOS Beiheft 1, Stuttgart 1984.

- large memorandums (*tahsistum*) that register all a trader's transactions that had resulted in debt-claims that still had to be paid;
- lists of records present in his archive at a particular moment, probably drawn up as inventory or because they were transferred.

5. THE FUNCTIONS OF THE TEXTS

Old Assyrian documents are not only very numerous, but there is also no body of cuneiform texts that contains so many references to the writing, reading, sending, transfer, use and storage of written pdocuments. That is because the success of the OA trade depended on them and they were indispensable for three reasons:

a. In the system of overland trade based of a colonial network there was a constant need of communication, of passing on information between traders living or working at home (in Assur), traveling in the caravans (six weeks from Assur to Kanesh), living in Kanesh or in one of the many commercial settlements spread over Anatolia. Oral communication did take place, but the trade would have been very difficult and much less successful without this written communication.

b. The trade was so sophisticated and "dense" – that is there were so many simultaneous transactions of an at times complex nature – that the human memory was unable to remember all the data. They had to be written down to aid the memory, to prevent problems and in the interest of good accountability.

c. The nature of the trade and the value of the goods traded on many levels and in many situations required "valid records" (*ṭuppum harmum*), that is a record whose contents are certified by the seals of parties and witnesses impressed on its envelope. By issuing "valid records" traders could obtain and use capital of investors and money-lenders, buy on credit from the City Hall in Assur, and they used them to contract caravan personnel, employ commission agents, sell on credit, and provide and obtain securities. They not only informed them on transactions, but also provided evidence to be used if problems arose that had to be solved by private summons, arbitration or formal lawsuits.

[39] Written documents therefore had three partly overlapping functions, as means of communication, as aid to memory and as evidence. These functions must also have determined the preservation of the records, but here many things are uncertain. Many letters may have been preserved because they contained important business or other information, but others, such as letters from wives and family, presumably often for emotional reasons. Most letters of both categories must have lost their informative or evidentiary value after a few years and were or could have been thrown away, but we cannot establish to what extent that happened. The preservation of records with a lot of valuable data (*e.g.* the large memorandums) and records with evidentiary value (*e.g.* of contracts, investments, etc.) is understandable, but most of the commercial records too lost their value after the transactions recorded had been completed and accounts had been settled, for they are different from marriage contracts, title deeds, or records of the division of an inheritance. Such texts, including judicial records confirming rights that had been contested, had a lasting value, as OB archives show, which occasionally contain records more than a century old. Most OA loans and credits were for a year or less and only investment loans (*ebuṭṭum*) and contracts for joint-stock companies (in which trader used capital made available by investors) could have a longer duration, up to 10 years in some cases. And even though we find some very old debt-notes, possibly never paid and therefore preserved, and we meet a few references to credit not paid back for a very long period, this does not change the fact that the great majority of the records in the archives no longer had any practical or legal value. We have to assume that once deposited in an archive, as long as there was space available to store them, records had a good chance of remaining there. Sifting, which required reading and classifying them, presumably did not have priority. When a son succeeded his father and inherited his house or when a trader moved elsewhere, to Assur or another colony, their records (or at least part of them) would be left behind. It seems rather likely that groups of older records that were no longer needed and were not thrown away were stored in separate containers. Some of the inscribed (but not sealed) bullae may have identified them, such as AKT 6a:16, "Tablets concerning our Iddin-abum's debts", which could be related to groups of records of Shallim-Assur's elder brother, found in his archive (see above § 1). Unfortunately the excavation reports never identify the tablets that were found together in a particular container or as a group, nor where exactly such bullae were found.[19]

The three functions mentioned of course obtain whenever texts are written, but they apply in particular in the framework of the OA overland trade and its colonial system.

[40] *5.1. Communication*

The colonial system meant that members of the same family and firm were regularly and at times for long periods separated by considerable distances, not only between Assur and Kanesh, but also between the nearly forty colonies and trading stations spread out over the whole of Central Anatolia and Northern Mesopotamia. In this situation letters were of vital importance. We can distinguish business letters, private letters – especially those exchanged with wives and other relatives – and official letters, written by the Assyrian authorities, both in Kanesh and in Assur.

Among the business letters an important category are those required by the system of overland trade by donkey caravans. They were called "notifying messages" and "caravan reports" by LARSEN 1967. The first type – sent from Kanesh and from Assur – reports that a caravan with silver and gold or one with tin and textiles had left Kanesh or Assur and summarily mentions its load, the persons involved, also with instructions about what to do with the goods. Those dealing with caravans with silver and gold leaving for Assur must be archive copies kept in Kanesh. The second type reports on the arrival of the caravan at its destination, Those sent from Assur, Larsen's "caravan accounts", mention the arrival of the money and describe in detail how it was used to make various payments and in particular for equipping a new caravan: the purchase of merchandise and donkeys (with numbers and price) and the hiring of personnel; the Assyrians themselves called them "letter of purchases". Those written in Kanesh, again archive copies, report on the safe arrival of the merchandise from Assur, its clearance in the palace (payment of taxes, etc.), the expenses incurred en route and the first sales made. Such letters may well have been sent ahead of the caravans they describe, to inform their recipients in time about what was coming. Known duplicates may indicate that a second copy was given along with the caravan. These letters must be used in combination with the transport contracts drawn up for these caravans and the detailed accounts of the expenses made by the leader of the caravan. The few cases where we have all four texts for one caravan are informative in showing to what extent requests and orders were or could be followed up. Such letters were also used to check whether the goods arriving matched the data of the caravan accounts. A nice example is TC 3, 36:16-23, "We opened the packet (with silver) in the presence of five traders and broke your seals. One took out of it the excise and checked the remainder of the packet: it contained 14 pounds and 37 ½ shekels, which is 1 pound less than your letter mentioned. They must have erred when weighing it there (in Kanesh)".

The bulk of the letters was written in a large variety of situations, usually to inform about business matters, to make requests or give orders, or to report on a variety of

---

19 More such bullae were found in Shallim-Assur's archive, e.g. Kt 94/k 879, "Memorandums concerning agents", and Kt 94/k 1062, "Validated records of my witnesses concerning the sons of Iddin-abum", see Özgüç and Tunca 2001, pp. 347-9.

problems – political, economic, social, personal – that interfered with the trade. Many were exchanged between traders and their sons, agents or partners who traveled around in Anatolia or were based in another colony. They **[41]** could contain warnings for war, unrest, blockades, difficult customers, or problems with the market, stating that no silver was available, that textiles were in demand, or that there was too much supply of tin (which affected the price). It allowed the recipient to redirect a caravan or to keep merchandise for some time in store. Other letters, at times of a more personal kind, but always also with business information, were exchanged between a trader traveling in Anatolia and his wife staying in Kanesh. Many such letters received elsewhere or en route were apparently taken along when the trader returned to his base in Kanesh and ended up in his archive.

A remarkable sample of communication via various channels is provided by the letter edited in LARSEN 2002 as no. 18. On his journey in Northern Mesopotamia, heading for Hahhum, where caravans would normally cross the Euphrates, Assur-nada receives a letter from his father in Assur, who writes: "If you are afraid to go to Hahhum, go to Urshu (more to the southwest, across the Euphrates) instead. Please, travel alone. Do not enter Mamma (across the Euphrates, northwest of Hahhum) together with the caravan. And in accordance with the orders of the City Assembly your brother's caravan must be split into three. Then let the first leave Mamma and as soon as it has reached Kanesh, the second can leave Urshu, and then the third can leave in the same way." This letter implies that information on the problems in the area of Hahhum-Mamma had reached Assur, either directly from there or from Kanesh, where incoming caravans had told about it. This information then had made the City Assembly issue an order on the behavior of the caravans and when Assur-nada's father learned about it he wrote a letter to his son, who must have received it en route and have taken it along to Kanesh, where it ended up in his archive.

Interesting information on letters is found in CCT 2, 6:6-15, written when Imdilum is accused by an angry partner of constantly writing him heated, incendiary letters (*himṭātum*), which from now on he will no longer read. Imdilum reacts by writing: "If I have written you any incendiary letter of mine and you have preserved it, send it under your seals to your representatives to show it to me and put me to shame. Or show it to my representatives there so that they can put me to shame. I have copies of all letters I have sent you over time!" We know copies or duplicates, also of letters, but this statement is surprising and if Imdilum was not an exception or exaggerating, we may assume that most copies were due time discarded, for few were found.

While letters were indispensable, the long distances (it took at least five weeks to travel from Assur to Kanesh) and the time it took to receive a reply, let alone when the addressee was lax in answering, were at times felt as frustrating. One trader wrote in an unpublished letter "What? Must we be hurling big words at each other over a distance of many miles (as) with a sling?" Several traders complain of having written many letters without getting an answer and some even protest that "they have used up all the clay in the town" for their letters **[42]** without getting an answer, or ask "Is there no clay in GN that you do not keep me informed?" (see VEENHOF 2009, p. 195, with Kt 94/k 497:15).

Official letters played an important role in the administrative and juridical sphere. Official letters, at times circular letters of the *kārum* organization ("to each colony and trading station") and of the City of Assur could impose regulations and order or forbid certain transactions. *Kārum* Kanesh could also order other colonies to take or abstain from certain actions. Official letters of standardized types served the administration of justice by ordering the transfer of a party or witnesses in a trial (LARSEN 1976, pp. 255-258; VEENHOF 2008c, pp. 230-234). So-called "strong tablets of the City", sent from Assur, could grant rights to plaintiffs, *e.g.* to summon or interrogate an opponent, to engage an attorney, to get access to certain tablets in an archival room, etc. Official letters of the *kārum* were also instrumental in establishing or renewing agreements or "treaties" ("sworn oaths") with local rulers or in solving problems, when caravans were detained, goods got lost, traders were apprehended or killed, or palaces delayed payment for merchandise bought.

We know these official letters only because they were found in private archives, presumably because, as mentioned, people serving the *kārum* organization apparently did take such letters home after they had accomplished their job. This was *e.g.* done by "Kuliya, messenger of the *kārum*", whose archive was published in AKT 5. It contained several such letters, some clearly circular letters, whose address not only mentioned the colonies and persons to whom it was addressed, but also Kuliya himself as "our messenger", which turned such a letter into his credential, which he apparently took home. The address of AKT 5, 2:1-6 reads: "Thus *kārum* Kanesh, to the *dātum*-payers, our messenger Kuliya and the *kārums* of Durhumit, Hattush, Tamniya and Tuhpiya, all the way until Nenassa", and 5:1-6 begins with: "Thus *kārum* Kanesh, to Kuliya, our messenger, the *kārum* Tegarama and wherever I. son of K. is staying".

Letters with decisions of the City Assembly in Assur, addressed to *kārum* Kanesh, must also have arrived in more copies, meant for the *kārum* and for the person with whom it dealt, usually a plaintiff whose case had been considered strong. Some were even found in unopened envelopes and since not opening such an important letter is unthinkable, it must have been a duplicate of a letter used by the *kārum* organization in the relevant lawsuit, meant for the party involved ICK 1, 182 is a letter addressed to *kārum* Kanesh by the ruler of Assur, which communicated the decision reached by the City to grant Imdilum the right to hire an attorney and to send him to Kanesh to gain his case. The copy we know was found in the archive of Imdilum, whom it concerned, but there must have been another copy in the archives of the *kārum*.

[43] *5.2. Aid to memory*

The importance of written records as an aid to memory is obvious. Traders were usually involved in many simultaneous transactions, for their own family or firm, for investors, for friends and partners for whom they sold merchandise in Anatolia. They worked with representatives and agents, who received merchandise in commission or bought it on credit, and many were also involved in transactions with or via the *kārum* organization. It must have been difficult to keep track of all activities, to remember the size of debts, claims, and investments, due dates, rates of interest, names of debtors and witnesses. There was, moreover, a concern about whether agents would pay in time or had to be summoned and charged default interest. The best aid was drawing up a memorandum[20] – whose Assyrian name, *tahsistum*, from the verb "to remind", has exactly that meaning – especially one that listed all a trader's outstanding claims by excerpting his debt-notes. Since the claims were often on agents who had received merchandise on credit, one could also call them "memorandums of outstanding claims" (*ša ba'abātim*, CCT 3, 19b:3-4) or "memorandums concerning agents" (*ša tamkaruttim*), the term used on the bulla Kt 94/k 879. They were valuable as a means to collect outstanding debts, even in the absence of the original debt-notes, because they provided the essential data, including the due date and the witnesses so that the debtor, confronted with them, would not normally refuse payment. In CCT 3, 19b:3-10, Pushuken's wife complains, "your representatives have taken away and keep in their possession the memorandum with the outstanding claims that you have left behind in your house (in Assur, when leaving for Anatolia). I cannot get at anything and do not know at all whether they have paid your creditors or not. It is up to you!" The biggest such memorandum I know is a tablet with 113 long lines that registers in abbreviated from 62 different transactions from a period of 18 years.[21] Such memos were drawn up from time to time or updated and the fact that in most cases

---

20 The expression *tahsistam nadā'um* means "to draw up a memorandum", or more simply "to note down". Memorandums are frequently mentioned in surveys of available documents (see for references *CAD* T s.v.) and BIN 6, 18:18-20 asks: "Bring the boxes (*tamalakkū*) with memorandums along".

21 See VEENHOF 1985.

the original debt-notes excerpted in them are not present in the archive shows that the debts had been paid; only the contracts of a few bad debts remained.

Memorandums could be kept in a strong room in a "box" (*tamalakkum*), as mentioned in BIN 6, 19:18, and some bullae attached to containers mention "memorandums" among their contents, *e.g.* Kt 84/k 878, "My tablets in sealed envelopes, my copies, and memorandums".[22] While in general memorandums **[44]** as private records were not sealed – one calls them "open memorandum" (*t. patîtum*; AKT 6b, 375:11; 446:19-20), we occasionally also meet a memo with seals. In Kt n/k 176:4-10, I. asks B. "Does this memo not carry your seals? B. answers: 'They are my seals'. They opened the memo and 45 shekels of silver proved to be written in the memo". And BIN 4, 32:34-36 asks: "Encase a memo in an envelope (*harāmum*) and write in it ...". Though not a valid legal record a memo might contain important or confidential data, that had to be protected by a sealed envelope and therefore Ka 24b:31-33 asks to send a memorandum of witnesses under seal.

Because most transactions concerned valuable goods or money and entailed liabilities it was customary to carry them out in the presence of witnesses and to record them in writing. But in some situations no witnessed record was drawn up, but a private note or memo in the first person singular ("I gave, entrusted, paid..."), where the mention the witnesses in whose presence the action had taken place did suffice, since one could summon them when necessary. An example of how this worked is found in the letter Kt 94/k 769 (courtesy of M.T. Larsen):

> I left (as credit) 32 shekels of silver in city B. with E. When we met on the road I said to him: "Give me the silver I gave you!". He answered: "I have sent it to you with A." I then seized A. and said: "The silver E. gave you, give that to me!" A. answered: "E. did not give me any silver!" If E. can produce witnesses that he gave it to me, I will pay you". Now seize E. and let him give you the 32 shekels of silver. If he refuses to pay confront him with strong conditions.[23] If E. says: "I really gave it to A.", then let him give you the name of his witnesses, assist him to get a tablet with (the testimony of) his witnesses in 'the gate of the god' and let him bring it to me.

"Memorandums" were drawn up in many situations, dealt with a variety of issues and could vary greatly in size and complexity. Archives usually contain groups of small tablets with up to a dozen lines of script (often only partially inscribed), that register one or a few transactions, usually payments (to be) made and transfers of goods, which were probably drawn up during a business trip, as an aid to memory, presumably by the traders themselves, many of which were able to read and write; some of them exhibit a non-professional hand. The few groups I found in the archive of Elamma, judging from their excavation numbers probably were kept together and perhaps still had to be digested or submitted for accounting. A very small, with one of only four lines of script (Kt 91/k 338 = AKT 8, 134) reads, "3 shekels of silver due from the man of Ebla, who took the wool". That such texts were called *tahsistum*, "memo", is shown by Kt 91/k 339 = AKT 8, 141 (an oblong tablet of only 1 ½ by 2 ½ cm and with seven small lines of script): "1 mina 2 shekels of tin S. borrowed from me; this *tahsistum* is a later one (*warkiat*)", perhaps an addition to a previous lot. A particular type memo is of the following type: "I am entitled to a share of 1 ½ **[45]** mina of silver in the 'holding' (and) of 45 shekels in the 'one-thirds-fund' of the caravan of A and B." (Kt 91/k 323, and variations) = AKT 8, 52). They state a trader's share in the proceeds from a particular caravan (*ellutum*) and were no doubt submitted when the accounts were settled.[24] Why and when memos were drawn up is shown *e.g.*

---

22 See Özgüç and TUNCA 2001, p. 347; note also Kt n/k 1460:24-26, "*ṣiliānu*-containers made of rush in which memos have been placed".

23 They usually were that if the person refusing payment was proved wrong he would pay the double or triple of the disputed sum.

24 See for the system and the terminology used, Dercksen 2004, Ch. 9.

by the letter ATHE 30:17-23, written by a transporter: "22 ½ shekels of silver, the price of 2 ½ *kutānu*-textiles of D., which you charged to me, you have (already) deducted from the transport fee due to me. Do not forget it over there, draw up a memo about it".[25] The writer of TC 3, 100 had promised to do so, saying "when the two textiles I gave you have been converted into silver, I will draw up your memo," but has to confess "I forgot it when the caravan was leaving".

Apart from the big memorandums of outstanding claims, there were "memorandums of witnesses", too all appearances a list of witnesses that had been involved in a particular case. Those "concerning the payment for the wool of Ushinalam", mentioned in the bulla Kt 94/k 1664, must have been attached to a container that held the memos published as AKT 6a, nos. 91-103. LARSEN describes them as "small, square tablets, ca. 3,5 to 4 cms in size (...) which give an amount of silver which has been received from the proceeds of Ushinalam's wool and conclude with a list of witnesses" (AKT 6a, 17).[26] The use of a memo of witnesses is shown by CCT 5, 17a: "We gave our testimony before Assur's dagger and I now send you a copy of the valid tablet drawn up in the Gate of the God. Read it and make up your mind and then submit a notification[27] to the gentleman, which he has to confirm or to deny and also draw up a memo of your witnesses." The testimony under oath, rendered by the writers, is sent to the addressee, who has to use it to force his opponents to accept or deny the claim. This is done in a formal confrontation, in the presence of (court) witnesses and the writers ask the addressee to send them a note on who they were (so that they could be summoned later, if the problem was not solved). Another example is in the letter CCT 4, 14b:15-18, where the creditor A. has to be paid: "He (Hanaya) still owes me [x] minas 15 shekels of silver. And when I departed on my trip I left you a memo with my witnesses, saying: Draw up a valid record (of their testimony), then intervene and take (it) from the silver of Hanaya and satisfy A."

[46] *5.3. Evidentiary value*

Most transactions, which frequently concern valuable merchandise or substantial sums of money, took place before witnesses and were recorded in writing, usually on a "valid tablet" *(ṭuppum harmum)*. This term qualifies a tablet by the verbal adjective *harmum*, lit. "covered (by a clay envelope)", which has the meaning "valid(ated)", because the envelope carries the seal impressions of parties, witnesses, etc., that gives a record its legal, evidentiary power.[28] The inscriptions on the bullae, attached to various containers with tablets, mention among their contents "valid tablets",[29] which were carefully preserved so that, if problems arose, they could be "produced", "shown" or "submitted". "Valid tablets" could record a variety of contracts concluded before witnesses, ranging from simple debt-notes to contracts about a joint-stock company (*naruqqum*), with many investors and a large capital. Others are settlements of accounts, agreements, records of deposit, acquisition of securities, sale of houses and slaves, etc. They were used during private summonses and lawsuits and could settle conflicts, unless it was claimed and

---

25 In Assyrian: *ina libbika e ūṣi tahsistaka idi* (correct the *editio princeps*).

26 These memorandums mention in all ca. 2 talents 18 pounds of silver, the proceeds from the sale of ca. 25 tons of wool, received by 13 different traders, which shows the size and complexity of this commercial operation.

27 The expression is *nudu'am nadā'um*, perhaps "to make a note, to serve somebody a notice" (one also finds "to give somebody a *n*."). The noun, from the verb *nadā'um* that is used for "to put down, draw up" (e.g. a memorandum), occurs a few times in the combination *ina tahsisātim u nudu'ātim*, "among (a person's) memorandums and notifications" (see *CAD* N/II 312 s.v. *nudu'u*), as the place where one has to look for a particular tablet, but we are as yet unable to differentiate the two types.

28 The verb is also used in abbreviated expressions, such "witnesses *harrumum*", short for drawing up a valid record of a testimony sealed by the witnesses".

29 Ten occurrences in Özgüç and Tunca 2001, pp. 319-350. Note Kt m/k 100, with the text "Copies of valid tablets of the debt of A. and I., whose originals are in the strong room of Ş.," and Kt 93/k 273, "Valid tablet with the verdict of the *kārum* concerning S." In AKT 3, 106:11-13, a trader asks his wife to send him "the boxes (*tamalakkū*) with valid records which A. left behind with you".

proved that a record was no longer valid.[30] The awareness of their existence and warning statements such as "I have in possession a valid tablet" (*ṭuppam harmam ukâl*), scil. as proof of my claim, must have induced people to meet their obligations. The importance of such a "valid record" is also clear from Kt n/k 470 (courtesy of C.Günbattı), drawn up to "revive", to replace a lost quittance as proof of the payment of a debt. Lines 1-9 presumably repeat the original text, stating that the debt has been paid, and they are followed by the phrase that the *kārum* organization summoned those who had sealed the record, who then "revived (l. 15, *balluṭum*) the tablet before Assur's dagger" by their testimony under oath.[31]

Various types of "valid records" were generated by granting credit and extending loans, due to complications met in collecting or paying them, in forcing **[47]** defaulting debtors to pay or provide a security. They were meant to safeguard the interests of the creditor, as is shown by some cases where in the objectively styled contracts in the third person singular clauses in the first person singular were inserted, (as) spoken by the creditor during the transaction and by which he had claimed (additional) security.[32] They occur in various type and situations and the most important types are the following.

a. A debtor denying or disputing a claim, promising a (delayed) payment and in some other situations could be forced to accept a "binding agreement" (*tarkistum*) in which he promised to pay a fine (frequently the double or triple) if he was subsequently proved wrong or did not live up to his promise. A similar "contract" could be imposed upon a person who shifted a debt claim to somebody else and therefore had to "confirm" (*ka''unum*) this presumed debtor on penalty of a fine. The result in such cases was a witnessed "valid tablet of his binding agreement", on which he impressed his seal.[33]

b. If a debtor paid his creditor or his creditor's representative and they did not have the original debt-note available to return it, the debtor received a "tablet of satisfaction", a quittance (*ṭuppum ša šabā'ē*). It recorded the payment in the presence of witnesses and invariably stated that if later the debt-note should turn up it was invalid (*sar*; examples in *EL* nos. 191ff., and see above note 30). Letters mention that such a quittance could be exchanged for the original debt-note, whereupon both records could "die" (*muātum*) or "be killed". This is usually interpreted as "be cancelled", which was done by breaking the sealed envelope, which deprived the tablet inside

---

30 OA expresses this by the stative of the factitive stem of the verb *akāšum*, *ukkuš*, not yet recognized in *CAD* A/I s.v., meaning 3, which mentions only one occurrence and translates "mislaid". The now more than a dozen references leave no uncertainty about its meaning, e.g. in *POAT* 2:24-26, where as a result of a comprehensive settlement of accounts "all the earlier valid tablets of the debt of I. are (now) cancelled" (*ú-ku*!*-šu*), and such a fact can also be the consequence of a verdict (CCT 5, 18d:3-5). In Kt r/k 17:5-6 a man is accused of having given "invalid tablets" as pledges. In younger variants of the clause in quittances, that if the missing debt-note still turns up it is "invalid" (see below under b), *ukkuš* may replace *sar*, e.g. in *Ugarit-Forschungen* 7 (1975) 318, no. 4:15 (read: *a*!*-ku-uš*).

31 "Reviving" lost legal records is attested in other periods too, see VEENHOF 1987, pp. 49-50 for some Old Babylonian examples.

32 E.g. clauses where the creditor states "item/person x is my pledge" (VEENHOF 2001, pp. 127-8), or where he grants himself the right, if the debtor defaults, to borrow the amount owed at the latter's expense with a money-lender (see below type c).

33 See for the procedure Kt 91/k 242:3'-11', "They drew up a valid tablet of his contract(ual obligation), that he promised to confirm PN. If he does not confirm PN, he will pay in accordance with the contract of his valid tablet to the creditor [...]" (remainder missing). An example of such a "contract" is TC 3, 262, dealing with a man who denied the accusation of not having paid his share in the purchase price of a slave. The envelope, after mentioning the seals, begins with "Contract (*tarkistum*) of S. ..., that he will pay 12 shekels of silver for 6 shekels of silver", hence a conditional penalty of 100%.

of legal force[34] (but allowed its preservation for administrative purposes, see below § 6 on "splitting a tablet"). That several quittances have turned up in archives suggests that the exchange and perhaps the return of the original debt-note did not always take place or perhaps at times was impossible. While it is true that a debt-note became harmless if its envelope was removed and the existence of a quittance **[48]** neutralized its validity, the debtor must have wanted his debt-note back to destroy it.

c. A loan contract with the creditor as debtor, because, as he had stipulated in the debt-note, he was authorized to borrow the debt owed by a defaulting debtors at the latter's expense with a moneylender and to charge the debtor compound interest (Veenhof 1999, pp. 66-69).

d. Debt-notes, usually for smaller debts, which are stated to be owed to "the *tamkārum*", that is an unnamed creditor. This allowed cession of the claim and we have letters where somebody writes in such a case: "I have a record stating that I am the *tamkārum*". In about a dozen cases we meet the clause stating that "the bearer [twice "the holder"] of the tablet is the creditor" (*wābil ṭuppim šut tamkārum*). It turned debt-notes into bearer's cheques – the earliest occurrence of this device – and this made it possible to cede and perhaps to sell debts (see VEENHOF 1997, 351-364).

The procedure described under d) explains the existence of a particular type of debt-note, and means that it may turn up in an archive without (for us) obvious connection with its owner, and there are more OA devices that have such consequences. One is that debt-notes and similar records had a monetary value and could function as a kind of (clay) money. They could be handed over as pledges, alongside valuable property,[35] and at the division of a trader's inheritance his widow and children could be assigned bonds, which they could exchange or convert into silver. Shares in a joint-stock company (formulated as a debt owed to the investor) could be inherited and sold, and I even found a case where a man was ready to draw up an (in my opinion fictive) contract whereby he owed to his brother's creditor exactly the same amount of silver as his brother and so provided him a security. It is only in officially excavated archives that can one identify such "strange" tablets and search for an explanation of their presence.

Alongside witnessed contracts also "testimonies" (*šibuttum*) play an important role in the OA commercial society as evidentiary records, for several reasons. One is that commercial transactions inside Anatolia could be cash, that in the trade promises and oral agreements were used, and that in general in trade not all payments, expenses and losses could be recorded in writing before witnesses.[36] Therefore they had to be accounted for by statements, oral declarations, not infrequently under oath. In OB commercial partnerships too, the final settlement of accounts about yields, losses, and profit frequently took place by **[49]** clearance (*tēbibtum, ubbubum*) in the temple of the Sun god, apparently under oath. Testimonies could become necessary if a trader died and not all his assets and debts could be proved, records turned up whose status was uncertain and if his sons and heirs had to declare "We are sons of the dead, we do not know ..." In such situations oral witnesses are produced and testify, and we have two verdicts of the City Assembly in Assur that refer to an existing procedural law, written

---

34 See for "dying tablets", VEENHOF 1987, pp. 46-50, where some occurrences are discussed. In Prag I 446, an arrangement between the sons of debtor and creditor, states that if the former produces a sealed quittance, the latter will release the debt-note, whereupon "the one tablet will smash the other". The exceptional use of this verb (*mahāṣum*) indicates physical destruction.

35 See for this feature, VEENHOF 2001, pp. 132-3.

36 Not necessarily because no *writer* was available, for there are indications that traders could read and write, as shown by less professionally written texts and the information that a son of a trader was learning the scribal craft in Assur.

on a stele, that states that a debt-claim on a dead trader will only be honored "if it is confirmed by witnesses".[37]

Most testimonies appear in the course of the administration of justice and this was a consequence of the judicial practice, because it was often not easy to recover the facts due to the complications of the trade and because parties, witnesses and evidence could be in different places.[38] One usually tried to solve conflicts, especially on the payment of debts and similar claims, first on a private level by summoning a debtor or opponent "before witnesses" or mediators. The latter were "seized" (at times by mutual agreement of the parties) in order to "finish, settle the affair" (*awātim gamārum*). Letters frequently mention these matters and ask "to set witnesses against" (*šībē šakānum ana*) a person who refuses to meet his liabilities. When such a private attempt failed or when the opponent did not stick to what he had promised, the plaintiff could appeal to the *kārum* court to obtain satisfaction. In such a case this court first made the witnesses and mediators who had been present at the earlier confrontations render testimony of what had happened and had been said. Occasionally the testimony of these witnesses and mediators had already been recorded in writing, in which case we read, "We gave our tablet". In most cases they gave an oral testimony "before the dagger of Assur" or "in the gate of the god", which was then recorded in writing in the form of a deposition in the first person, which the witnesses signed (by impressing their seals) and which was given to the court.

To do so certain complications might have to be surmounted, because the usually two or three witnesses were expected to deliver a single testimony, one of "witnesses in agreement" (*šībū etamdūtum*; BIN 4, 70:17-18, "until I obtain a tablet of two witnesses in agreement so that we do not come to shame"). And this final testimony, recorded in writing, was at times apparently preceded by and based on drafts, which we find in the archives, alongside (provisional) copies **[50]** of testimonies, probably prepared for the benefit of the plaintiff or of those who had rendered it. The unique judicial record *POAT* 9, drawn up because one party contested a testimony given, describes how it had been drafted. In a formal appeal D. said to M.:

> "I did not arrange to let you give testimony. Why have you given a tablet with your testimony?" M. answered: "I did not give the tablet at my own initiative. The gentleman (who needed the testimony) appealed for us with *kārum* Tawiniya and the *kārum* made us testify, whereupon we, I and my companion, gave the tablet (with our testimony)". M. added: "When we drew up the tablet in the gate of the god my companion reminded me of a few things ("words") that I did not know. And after I had made him swear an oath ("made him raise his hands") we added them". D. repeated: "I did not arrange to let you give testimony!".

The administration of justice by formal courts also gave rise to a variety of records. The *kārum* authorities and the City Assembly could both issue "strong tablets" that granted plaintiffs whose case had been considered strong, the right to hire an attorney, who had powers that enabled him to search for the truth. Parties could be forced to swear an oath in which they had to confirm or deny a variety of facts. Such formal, substantive oaths were apparently carefully formulated and written down in advance by the court and the other. They started with a formal invocation, "Listen, god/goddess of the oath", followed by verbal forms in the mode (subjunctive) of the oath" (*e.g. EL* 284, and CCT 5, 14b). Such

37 See VEENHOF 1995, 1729, on the use of the verb *kuānum*, "to be confirmed", as used in Kt a/k 394:17 and Kt n/k 1925:16f. This is not a general law applying in all situations, for the verb as such can be used of both oral and written evidence, as shown by another verdict of the City Assembly, quoted in AKT 6a, 294:16-17, which demands that a disputed debt, contracted in Anatolia, "shall be confirmed by his tablets or his witnesses". There was no difference between the value and power of oral and written evidence, their use was conditioned by their availability and the situation.

38 See for the details and the variation in the procedures and testimonies, Hertel 2013.

formal oaths were sworn while holding the dagger of the god Assur, in "the gate of the god", and in such cases the court could appoint special witnesses to attend the swearing of these oaths. The tablet with the text of the oath sworn was put in an envelope, which the seals of the persons "who heard his oral statement" (*ša pi/ašu išme'ū*) to confirm its authenticity. It usually ended up in the archive of the party that had won the case.

The complexity of the issues and the fact that persons and evidence could be located in Assur, Kanesh or elsewhere, frequently prevented a quick solution and verdict. It resulted in various so-called 'procedural verdicts', that prescribe steps to be taken to collect the evidence and find the truth, such as gaining access to tablets, summoning witnesses, interrogating people, making statements, and they can be conditional ("if ... then ..."). The final verdict, frequently passed many months later, is usually rather short and restricted to the main issue. OA did not produce verdicts of the Old Babylonian type, which present a short history of the case, describe the various steps taken to find the truth and even occasionally mention the reason for the verdict. Difficult cases, in particular those concerning the liquidation of a business after a trader's death and the division of his inheritance, could generate large files of at times of dozens of texts of different type, most of which are undated. The challenge to reconstruct such cases can only be met if such a file can be reconstructed or is found in an excavated archive.

[51] 6. FUNCTIONAL OVERLAP

The three functions of written records overlap. Information in letters, in particular in the long caravan accounts, is a valuable aid to memory and it can be used to claim that a caravan upon arrival proves to contain less than had been mentioned in the letter that also functioned as a kind of bill of lading. Long memorandums listing outstanding claims can be more than an aid to memory. CCT 2, 8-9, a letter of 75 lines written by Imdilum to his brother, his son and an agent, consists mainly of a long list of his outstanding claims, which quotes two memorandums we have (CCT 6, 9a and KTS 2, 42), but it ends with the request: "Please, make all these agents (*tamkārē*) pay!". The data from the memorandum transmitted in the letter apparently enabled the addressees to dun the debtors, even without the original debt-notes at hand, because they must have been aware of their liabilities and knew that with the data available the witnesses could always be summoned to buttress the claims.

Letters can also have evidentiary value, especially those called *našpertum*, "missive". The word is very common, but refers especially to letters that are not simply communications, but in which orders and authorizations are given, facts are stated or acknowledged, or claims established. They have a kind of legal force and are sent under seal to the person (a partner, agent, representative) who can use them to realize something in the name of the sender. A *našpertum* can bring about the release of a tablet held as security for a debt and they play a role when more persons are involved in a transaction, *e.g.* when debts, claims, securities or merchandise have been transferred and an authorized "missive" is required to be able to proceed. In ICK 2, 150, where E. had probably ceded his debt-claim or entrusted its collection to his partner, we read: "If E. says: 'I. owes ten pounds of copper to P.' and if P. indeed brings a *našpertum* with E.'s seal stating that I. does owe 10 minas of copper to P., then I. will pay the copper to P." The text adds that "if the *našpertum* is supplied, I. shall not make E. swear an oath", *i.e.* I. is not entitled to request further proof. Kt 91/k 368:20-25 = AKT 8, 166 states that "if A. (to whom E. had entrusted merchandise for transport) protests against releasing it to P. (the addressee of the letter), then let him hear the *našpertum* of E. that he must entrust the textiles in their sealed bags to you."

Because of their evidentiary value such missives were preserved in their sealed envelope or in a packet. Archives have yielded more than forty inscribed bullae with the text "*našpertum* of PN", apparently a label attached to such a tablet or a packet containing it, stored in the archive. They remind me of OB letters in which superiors give instructions, which at the end may state: "Keep/guard this letter of mine as testimony /

proof of me /my word". It is not by accident that these words occur especially on a rare category of sealed Old Babylonian letters, called *ze'pum*, which may be compared to the equally sealed Sumerian "letter orders", kept by administrators as proof of the discharge of an order, of the delivery **[52]** of goods.[39] I also mention here that when the ruler of Assur wrote a letter to Pushuken to ask him for a favor (*POAT* 18) and promises that he will take action for him in a undisclosed matter, he adds in lines 17-21: "Now look, one brings you two tablets. Read one of them and keep the other with you". The second must be *POAT* 18, found in its sealed envelope and I assume that it was preserved as proof of the promises made by the ruler.

Legal documents, both contracts and judicial records, with a primary evidentiary function, of course at the same time can be valuable sources of information and this may have been a reason to preserve them, also when their legal value no longer mattered. This is particularly true of debt-notes, occasionally true loans, but more frequently recording the amount of silver an agent has to pay for merchandise received in commission. Upon payment of the debt they had to be given back to the debtor – they are called "his tablet" – to annihilate this proof of a discharged liability (see above, § 5.3, b). But for a trader, creditor or debtor, the information provided by a debt-note could be valuable for his administration, in particular if he had to render account of his business to investors or partners. I have suggested that, upon payment, one could break the sealed envelope (which gave it its legal force) and preserve the tablet inside, now devoid of any legal value. This would explain why so many debt-notes without envelopes are found in archives, not all of which we can simply consider proof of unpaid debts. This is now confirmed by a few occurrences of the verb *laṭā'um*, "to split", with a tablet as object, *e.g.* AKT 6c, 561:7-15: "Pay this silver to E. and obtain the release of my tablet (debt-note) and split it and deposit it with A., among my tablets" (cf. AKT 6c, 671:14-16 and Larsen's note on these lines). It means separating envelope and tablet, destroying the former, which carries the seal impression of the debtor and gives it its legal force, and keeping the tablet inside.

7. COPIES AND DUPLICATES OF RECORDS

The preceding pages have made clear for which purposes written records were used, but some additional data must be added. Insight into the use of tablets is also provided by the many references to copies or duplicates (*mehrum* or *mehertum*). The inscription on the sealed bulla Kt 94/k 878 identifies the contents of the container it was attached to as "my valid records, my copies and memorandums", and TTC 21:1-7 states "we entrusted the boxes with tablets of E. (and) the boxes with copies (*tamalakkī mehrī*)" for transport. Inbi-Ishtar in CCT 2, 17b:3-6 **[53]** asks his correspondent to take along "both valid records and copies and memorandums that you have in your possession" and KTS 40:33 mentions "tablets of my witnesses and their copies". We also read requests to make and send copies overland,[40] for which one used a specific term, *mehram šubalkutum*, as discovered by LARSEN. It is used in AKT 6a, 231:8-17:

> "On the day my father left Assur he made his testament in your presence. Please, my fathers and lords, have a copy of my father's will made, what he decided for us. Give this tablet, as it has been cleared (?), to A. and send him here with the first caravan".

---

39 The OB letters write *ṭuppī anniam ana šībūtia* (variants *šībūt awātia* and *qīp awātia*) *kil(lam)* or *uṣur*, cf. Veenhof 1986, p. 33 note 125; see for *ze'pum*, F.R. Kraus, in: J.-M. Durand and J.-R. KUPPER (eds.), *Miscellanea Babylonica. Mélanges offerts à Maurice Birot*, Paris 1985, 141f., 7. An unpublished Old Babylonian letter order writes "preserve my tablet as (if it were) a sealed document" (*kīma kanīkim*).

40 See references in *CAD* M/II, s.v. *mihru*, 1, a, 2', a'-b'. Cf. TC 3, 9:14-16, "send overland to me a copy of the record stating that my affair is terminated"; TC 3, 44:14'-19', "they have removed the copy (of the caravan account), there is no copy of the textiles they have been depositing here. We have made and sent copies of the valid records and they are under seal in the house".

We have to distinguish between copies and duplicates, although Old Assyrian does not have separate terms for them. A duplicate is a document that was immediately produced in more copies, an example of which is the letter of the ruler of Assur sent to Pushuken (*POAT* 18, see § 6), both copies of which apparently were in an envelope sealed by the ruler and hence "valid". With "valid deeds" we can easily identify copies made later, because they can only reproduce the text on the envelope, which begins by listing the persons who had sealed it, while on the tablet inside they are mentioned at the very end, as those "in whose presence" (*mahar*) the contract had been concluded. An example is AKT 6a, 123, a copy of the text on the envelope of an original debt-note, referred to in other texts, but not preserved in the archive. Such copies of debt-notes (also of quittances and service contracts) make sense, because the sealed envelope usually reproduces the text of the contract inside, occasionally with minor differences, also due to limitations of space alongside the seal impressions. Of many "valid tablets", notably depositions, the text on the envelope is usually short and limited to mentioning the witnesses and the so-called "procedural formula", "for this affair the *kārum* gave us and we gave our testimony before Assur's dagger". Copies of such envelopes are useless, since they do not contain the substance of the testimony or agreement. If copies of such texts are needed they have to be made before the tablet is encased in the sealed envelope and this is indeed what we can observe. I mention some examples of copies of depositions from the archive of Shallim-Assur, now accessible in AKT 6a. First copies made from (indicated by =) tablets before they were encased in envelopes: 10 = 10a inside envelope 10b; 56 = 58 inside 57; 77 = 79 inside 78; 84 = 83 inside 82; 191 = 191a inside 191b; 194 = 195b inside 195a. Other tablets, on the basis of the identity of the witnesses and the 'procedural formula' must be copies of tablets still inside their unopened envelopes: 46 and 47 = 48, 53 = 54, 104 = 105, 106 and 107 = 108, 118 and 119 = 117, 195 = 196a. And we also have copies of depositions whose sealed original is not preserved in the archive: 63 = 64 (settling accounts), 221 = 222 (summons), 227 = 228 (interrogation), 257 = 258 (interrogation), 270 = 271 (answer to an attorney, called 'witnessed statement'). **[54]** The same applies to verdicts of a *kārum*, where the text on the envelope starts with "Seal of *kārum* GN", while the (copy of the) tablet inside begins with "The *kārum* passed the following verdict: .." This applies to AKT 6a, 66 (copy) and 67 (unopened envelope), cf. the tablet 80 from the opened envelope 81.

Shallim-Assur's archive also contained three virtually identical copies of a contract for the transport of a large amount of silver to Assur, AKT 6b, 478-480, whose purpose it not clear, but the background might have been a conflict. This is suggested by texts 495-497, three identical copies that start with the text of such a transport contract, but presented as testimony by the persons who had witnessed the transfer of the silver, given because, as the 'procedural formula' shows, because the *kārum* had made them testify.

I am not able to offer a general picture of the making and use of copies, which requires much more research and has to take into account the numerous references in letters. But I note that the edition of an excavated archive shows that copies, especially of depositions and at times several of the same record, were fairly numerous and apparently considered useful. Their presence in Shallim-Assur's archive probably has to do with the long and at times bitter fights between members of the family, which generated and required a lot of written evidence, in addition to the presence of large file concerning a dead brother, whose executor Shallim-Assur was (see above § 1). All copies mentioned above were found in this archive and therefore had been kept in store. Copies certainly will also have been sent out to provide others, members and associates of the family/firm living elsewhere (including Assur), with records of evidentiary and informative value. Many letters do indeed mention the making and dispatching of copies and we have information on their uses during summonses and lawsuits.

For the existence of copies of letters various explanations are possible and some reasons have already been mentioned in § 5.1. Copies or duplicates are also likely for important letters addressed to more than one person, if they lived not in the same place. While most copies we know are of legal documents, we cannot assume that every person who sealed a contract or deposition as a witness received a copy of it. Copies of debt-notes are fairly rare, but they were occasionally made to allow a partner or representative to collect a debt. In CCT 2, 38:3-9, Puzur-Assur writes to Pushuken: "I told you that I wished to stay here one month longer in order to collect all my outstanding claims. But you said: 'Leave me your copy, then I will collect the silver and send it after you'". Such a copy therefore is comparable to a memorandum with excerpts of debt-notes. Some of the latter state why they were made, *e.g. EL* 225:47-48, "Copy of valid records (made because) they went overland", similarly *EL* 224:37-38, ICK 1, 187:63, TC 3, 13:45-47, each time at the end of a long memorandum. It is understandable that this was done for reasons of security, considering the value of the original debt-notes. Security is also suggested as a reason for making a copy in CCT 3, 14-19, whose writer orders to bring all his belongings into a new house, "lock it up and give a copy (listing) all you left behind to the maid and leave a second one behind in the main dwelling". Some **[55]** of the copies of testimonies or depositions must be due, as mentioned above (§ 5.3), to the fact that several witnesses together had to give one single testimony, which generated drafts and copies to be checked and approved. But they also appear in connection with important legal cases, apparently to provide witnesses with written evidence of what they had testified and for which they might be held responsible. An interesting example are the two copies of a long deposition in connection with a conflict between the *kārum* organization and an Anatolian ruler, who had accused and jailed an Assyrian trader for conspiring with a rival ruler. The deposition reports how the *kārum* negotiated with the ruler to obtain the release of its member, but we do not know how the affair ended. The deposition is given by five traders, apparently appointed to negotiate for the *kārum* organization, and they testify before the *kārum* of what had happened. That this was done "in accordance with a tablet of the City" (of Assur), shows that the matter was important enough to get the City involved. One copy of this long text was found in the archive of the family of the victim, Assur-taklaku, excavated in 1993 (see MICHEL 2008b), apparently supplied in order to inform his relatives. The second turned up in that of Usur-sha-Ishtar, excavated in 1962, who was one of the traders who had negotiated and testified.[41] One might expect other copies of this deposition, made for the other members of the delegation, for the archive of the *kārum* and one to be sent to Assur. This is a rare example, because we know the origin of the two copies, but it suggests that there were more such cases, also in less serious affairs, where copies of a deposition may have been made and distributed, but they are difficult to identify if we are dealing with records from illicit excavations, scattered by the antiques trade.

8. FINDING ONE'S WAY IN A LARGE ARCHIVE

The use of a large archive with more than thousand cuneiform tablets is only possible to somebody who knows what it contains, where particular texts are to be found, and who is able to read them. This was obviously in the first place the owner of the archive and we know that many traders could read. But others too had to be able to do it, *e.g.* if in the absence of the trader a debt-note had to be retrieved (*šēṣu'um*) to be returned to a debtor who had paid or to be shown to a reluctant one, when a tablet handed over as pledge or given in safe deposit was asked back, or when a trader had died and particular records needed to be inspected or used.

The use of an archive by its owner is taken for granted and we regularly read that he inspects, selects, takes, removes and adds documents, which are "placed among his tablets" (*ina libbi ṭuppēšu šakānum*). More information is occasionally **[56]** given when an absent owner asks others, such as his wife, employee or partner, to do so and he gives some details, or when he shows his concern about the safety of his records. The writer of AKT

41 See for the copy excavated in 1962, C. Günbatti, "The River Ordeal in Ancient Anatolia", in: W.H. van Soldt *et al.* (eds.), *Veenhof Anniversary Volume*, Leiden 2001, pp. 151-160, where one also finds the data on the other copy, Kt 93/k 145.

3, 112, hearing about A.'s departure writes: "I had entrusted to him the boxes with tablets under my seal and he was to guard my seals (...) Ask his representatives there whether he has left the tablets somewhere (?) or has taken them out personally". Good examples of requests to wives are in the letters addressed by Ennam-Assur to his wife Nuhshatum, who is in charge of his house in Kanesh and has to guard it and its archive. "Do not give any tablet to anybody until you see me", he writes to her in Kt 91/k 563:10-14.[41a] It is probably not by accident that in the address of his letters she usually figures alongside what must be his representatives, friends or agents, presumably because she has to allow them to find and identify the tablets he asks for, since she could not read them. He asks her and a certain Alaku in AKT 3, 84:4-23:

> "Look (plural) for the tablet in which I certified (the testimony) of my witnesses A. and E. in the gate of the god, which is placed in the container with the tablets of the gate of the god. Take it out of it, pack it solidly in leather, seal it and entrust it to H. or S. to bring it to me".

In AKT 3, 82:4-13 he asks her and her husband's representatives:

> "In the *hušālu*-container[42] a memorandum without envelope, listing the witnesses on behalf of P., has been deposited among the tablets. Inspect it and if the witnesses in question are staying there, lead them down to the gate of the god and validate the tablet with their testimony and inform me about it."

In AKT 106:11-13 she is asked to send him immediately "the boxes with valid records that A. left behind for you".

These letters and many other texts show the existence of various containers, the most frequent one called *tamalakkum/tamalākum*, a word only attested in OA, whose meaning is unknown, perhaps a kind of wooden box, usually protected by sealings.[43] Such a box can be identified by its position in the archive ("the upper *t.*", of a stack or on the shelve? Kt 93/k 69:18), by its size (we meet a small one with six tablets and a big one with more than twenty tablets; cf. also AKT 3, 104:17), and by its cover or encasing. Kt 93/k 69:18-27 (courtesy of C. Michel) states: "We opened the upper *tamalakkums* that were covered by (or: encased in) leather (*ina maškim harmū*) and removed the tablet"[44]. But one also identifies boxes by their specific **[57]** contents and we meet "a *t.* with tablets with certified testimonies" (*ša šībē*), "*t.*s with memorandums", "*t.*s with valid records", "a *t.* with copies" (*ša mehrē*, TTC 21:1f.), "a *t.* with big tablets of the caravan(s)" (*ša ṭuppē rabûtim ša harrānim*, AKT 3, 77:7), "7 *t.*s with tablets of agents (*ša tamkārim*, TPAK 1, 77:3), etc. Note also Kt 91/k 147:29-32, "In all 12 tablets, placed in a *t.* with new tablets, not in envelopes".

If tablets in an archive were stored and arranged in groups of various types, in different containers, one would expect the excavations to have revealed their material traces. This is true and in addition the archives have produced a large number of inscribed, frequently sealed bullae, originally attached to packets or containers with tablets,

---

41a For Nuhshatum, see now Veenhof 2015.

42 Attested only in OA, also in Kt 91/k 446:18, which mentions the sealing of a *hušālum*.

43 See *AKT* 5 p. 174 and *CAD* T s.v. Other frequently mentioned containers used for tablets (and other items) are *ṣiliānum* and *huršiānum*, both only attested in OA, exact meanings unknown, see *AKT* 5, 175. BIN 4, 90:14-16 mentions "three *t.*s with tablets put under seal in a *ṣilliānum*", and according to Kt k/k 53:12-15, a *huršiānum* is to be taken out of a *t.* Both *t.* and *h.* are also used for transporting tablets. Note a *ṣ.* made of rushes (*ša ašlātim*) in Kt n/k 1460:26, which suggests a basket-like container. Kt f/k 11:5-6 mentions "small *ṣ.*s" containing sealed records, and BIN 6, 218:5-6, 13 *t.*s with tablets alongside a pouch (*zurzum*) with tablets. See for the rare *hušālum* footnote 42.

44 Kt f/k 11:23 (courtesy of L. Umur) mentions a *ṣiliānu*-container with a leather cover/casing *(maškam harim)*, containing tablets.

whose contents or nature they mention.[45] Most numerous is the designation *našpertum*, "missive" (already mentioned above), followed by the name of the person who had sent it or for whom it was meant. Some inscriptions start with the word "tablet(s)" followed by qualifications, such as "of PN", "of the debt of PN"; other mention "valid tablets" (in sealed envelopes) or "quittances". Fuller descriptions are: "copies of tablets by which I sent silver to PN," "my encased tablets, my duplicates and my memorandums," "certified tablets of my witnesses," "tablets of the city," "tablets of the testament of A.," "tablets of native Anatolians," "testimony of A. and B.," "tablet of the gate of the god concerning A.," and "memorandums of witnesses of the price of wool of A." It would be too much to describe this as a classification system, but it is clear that groups of tablets, often files or tablets of similar type, were kept together, stored and labeled so that they could be found more easily.

The excavator, Tahsin Özgüç, in several publications has described how he found the tablets and the bullae. On the archive found in 1994 (in the house in grid LXIV/LXV-130/131, now being published as AKT 6) he writes (Özgüç 2001, p. 370):

> "In the conflagration the thin partition wall between rooms nos. 5-6 fell down to its foundations and the tablets kept in the two rooms were mixed up. An archive of 947 tablets and unopened envelopes and pottery were found in these two small rooms. They were evidently kept on wooden shelves against the walls and the tablets found along the walls are those that fell off the shelves in the fire. The tablets that had been packed in bags, in straw wrappings and sacks were discovered in piles in the middle of the rooms. A group of tablets, as usual, were kept in pots. The pottery was set along the base of the walls".

On the archive excavated in 1991/2 (in the house in grid LVI-LVII/128-129, the archive of Elamma, which I am publishing) he wrote:

> "The archive of the merchant was found along the base of the east wall of room 3 and in rooms 4-5 in groups once packed in boxes, bags, sacks and straw mats. On top of each group lay one or two bullae. Unopened envelopes were placed at the bottom, tablets on top. In contrast to other archives [58] here we did not find tablets stored in jars".[46]

Elsewhere he mentions the discovery in a room of "two groups of 50 unopened envelopes, lying side by side" and observes that the shape of a rectangular pile of tablets and fragments of carbonized wood suggests that they were kept in some kind of wooden box.

Unfortunately, these observations are rather general, with few photos of the tablets in situ (but see Özgüç 2003, pp. 71-75, ills. 13-18) and the ground plans of the houses do not show the exact positions of the hoard of tablets. Moreover, we almost never learn the excavation numbers of the tablets found in such groups or in jars, so that it is impossible to identify them. The bullae attached to or belonging to containers or packets with tablets in most cases were numbered and published separately, so that it is extremely difficult to establish – in the few cases when the archive in question is published – to which groups of tablets or packet they belonged. It is regrettable that the unique opportunity to discover more about archival classification and storage is lost, also due to the absence of an epigraphist at the dig where every year so many written documents were found.

One would expect that tablets in current use were stored on the shelves along the walls (on which the *tamalakkum*-containers could have been placed) or on benches

45 The inscribed bullae were edited by O. Tunca, "Inscriptions on the Bullae", in: Özgüç and Tunca 2001, pp. 319-350.

46 T. Özgüç, "A Boat-shaped Cult-vessel from the Karum of Kanish", in: H. Gasche *et al.* (eds.), *Cinquante-deux réflexions sur le Proche-Orient ancien offertes en homage à Léon De Meyer*, Leuven 1994, pp. 369-376.

covered with reed mats, perhaps in open bowls, to be easily accessible. Since retrieving and selecting tablets stored in jars is rather difficult, jars may have contained older tablets, preserved but rarely used, but we cannot prove it. The excavator has suggested for the archive excavated in 1990, in the 'Avant-propos' (p. 8) of TPAK I, that the position in which tablets were found in the ruined archival room might indicate that some groups were kept on a second floor. One part, whose excavation numbers he mentions, was found on the floor, the rest mixed with the debris that filled the room. But the distinction is not very convincing, for I found that the envelope of text 10 was found in the debris, but the tablet it contained on the floor. That certain groups of tablets were kept on a second floor, where the living quarters were, is not impossible, but would be surprising, since the strong room on the ground floor, closed with a heavy, sealed door was better and safer.

These last observations show that there are still many questions, but the potential of the material is huge. Because the textual data are so rich and diversified and their philological analysis already yields important insights, a good correlation between epigraphic and archeological data will yield more. Moreover, publication of the many still unpublished archives (with more than 12.000 texts) will help to solve some of the remaining epigraphic and lexical problems, including the precise nature of the various containers. This will throw more light on the customs of the remarkable Old Assyrian traders, energetic and creative businessmen and at the same time industrious writers of records and careful keepers and users of their archives.

BIBLIOGRAPHY

Barjamovic, G., Hertel, Th., and Larsen, M. T. 2012. *Ups and Downs at Kanesh. Chronology, History and Society in the Old Assyrian Period.* OAAS 5. PIHANS 120. Leiden: NINO.

Dercksen, J.G. 2004. *Old Assyrian Institutions*, MOS Studies 4, PIHANS 98. Leiden: NINO.

Hertel, Th. K. 2013. *Old Assyrian Legal Practices. Law and Dispute in the Ancient Near East.* OAAS 6, PIHANS 123. Leiden: NINO.

Kryszat, G. 2004. *Zur Chronologie der Kaufmannsarchive aus der Schicht 2 des Kārum Kaneš*, OAAS 2, PIHANS 99. Leiden: NINO.

Larsen, M.T. 1967. *Old Assyrian Caravan Procedures*, Istanbul: NHAI.

–. 1976. *The Old Assyrian City-State and its Colonies*, Mesopotamia 4, Copenhagen: Akademisk Forlag.

–. 1982. Your Money or Your Life! A Portrait of an Assyrian Businessman, in N.J. Postgate (ed.), *Societies and Languages of the Ancient Near East. Studies in Honour of I.M. Diakonoff*, Warminster, 215-245.

–. 2002. *The Aššur-nādā Archive.* OAA 1, PIHANS 96. Leiden: NINO.

–. 2007. Individual and Family in Old Assyrian Society. *Journal of Cuneiform Studies* 59, 93-106.

–. 2008. Archives and Filing Systems at Kültepe, in C. Michel (ed.), *Old Assyrian Studies in Memory of Paul Garelli*, OAAS 4, PIHANS 112. Leiden: NINO, 77-90.

–. 2010. *The Archive of the Šalim-Aššur Family.* Vol. 1: *The First Two Generations*, Kültepe Tabletleri VI-a, Ankara (= AKT 6a).

Matouš, L. 1969. Der Streit um den Nachlass des Puzur-Aššur, *Archiv Orientálni* 67, 156-180.

Michel, C. 1995. Validité et durée de vie des contrats et reconnaissances de dettes paléo-assyriens, *Revue d'Assyriologie* 89, 15-27.

–. 2001. *Correspondance des marchands de Kaniš au début du IIe millénaire avant J.-C.* Littératures Anciennes du Proche-Orient 19. Paris: Les Éditions du Cerf.

–. 2008a. La correspondance des marchands assyriens du xixe s. av. J.-C., in L. Pantalucci (ed.), *La lettre d'archive. Communication administrative et personelle dans l'antiquité proche-orientale et égyptienne.* Actes du colloque de l'Université de Lyon 2 (2004), IFAO, 117-140.

–. 2008b. The Alāhum and Aššur-taklāku archives found in 1993 at Kültepe Kaniš, *Altorientalische Forschungen* 35, 53-67.

Özgüç, N. & Tunca, O. 2001. *Kültepe-Kaniš. Sealed and Inscribed Clay Bullae*, TTKY V/48, Ankara.

Özgüç, T. 2001. Observations on the Architectural Peculiarities of the Archive of an Assyrian Trader of Karum Kanesh, in W.H. van Soldt (ed.), *Veenhof Anniversary Volume. Studies Presented to Klaas R. Veenhof on the Occasion of the Sixty-Fifth Birthday*, Leiden: NINO, 367-372.

–. 2003. *Kültepe Kaniš/Neša. The Earliest International Trade Center and the Oldest Capital City of the Hittites*. The Middle Eastern Culture Center in Japan, Tokyo.

Ulshöfer, A. M. 1995. *Die altassyrische Privaturkunden*, FAOS Beiheft 4, Stuttgart.

Veenhof, K. R. 1985. Observations on Old Assyrian Memorandums, with particular reference to Kt c/k 839, *Jaarbericht Ex Oriente Lux* 28, 10-23.

–. 1986. Cuneiform Archives. An Introduction, in K. R. Veenhof (ed.), *Cuneiform Archives and Libraries. Papers read at the 30e Rencontre Assyriologique Internationale, Leiden 1983*, Leiden, 1-36.

–. 1987. 'Dying tablets' and 'Hungry Silver'. Elements of figurative language in Akkadian Commercial Terminology, in M. Mindlin *et al.* (eds.), *Figurative Language in the Ancient Near East*, London, 41-76.

–. 1991. Private Summons and Arbitration among the Old Assyrian Traders, *Bulletin of the Middle Eastern Culture Center in Japan* V, Wiesbaden: Harrassowitz, 437-459.

–. 1995. 'In Accordance with the words of the stele': Evidence for Old Assyrian Legislation, *Chicago-Kent Law Review* 70/4, 1717-1745 [= pp. 109-127 in this volume].

–. 1997. "Modern" Features in Old Assyrian Trade, *Journal of the Economic and Social History of the Orient* 40, 336-366.

–. 2001. The Old Assyrian Period, in R. Westbrook and R. Jasnow (eds.), *Security for Debt in Ancient Near Eastern Law*. Culture and History of the Ancient Near East, vol. 9, Leiden/Boston: Brill, 93-159.

–. 2003. Archives of Old Assyrian Traders, in M. Brosius (ed.), *Ancient Archives and Archival Traditions. Concept of Record-Keeping in the Ancient World*, Oxford: Oxford University Press, 78-123.

–. 2008a. The Old Assyrian Period, in M. Wäffler (ed.), *Mesopotamia. The Old Assyrian Period. Annäherungen* 5, Orbis Biblicus et Orientalis 160/5, Fribourg/Göttingen, Teil 1, 13-264.

–. 2008b. The Death and Burial of Ishtar-lamassi in Karum Kanish, in R.J. van der Spek (ed.), *Studies in Near Eastern World View and Society Presented to Marten Stol on the Occasion of his 65th Birthday*, Bethesda: CDL Press, 97-120.

–. 2008c. Communication in the Old Assyrian Trading Society by Caravans, Travelers and Messengers, in C. Michel (ed.), *Old Assyrian Studies in Memory of Paul Garelli*, OAAS 4, PIHANS 112, Leiden, 199-246.

–. 2009. A New Volume of Old Assyrian Texts from Kārum Kanesh, *Jaarbericht Ex Oriente Lux* 41, 179-202.

–. 2015. Nuhšatum, the Wife of an Old Assyrian Trader. Her Status, Responsibilities and Worries (With Two New Letters). Pp. 271-88 in İ. Albayrak, H. Erol, and M. Çayır (eds), *Studies in Honour of Cahit Günbattı*. Ankara: Ankara Üniversitesi Basımevi.

"In Accordance with the Words of the Stele" Evidence for Old Assyrian Legislation*

I. INTRODUCTION

Thus far the only tangible evidence of Assyrian legislation are the so-called Middle Assyrian Laws. They have come down to us as a series of rather damaged cuneiform tablets, numbered A to O by modern editors.[2] A least the first three tablets were of large size and the best preserved one, A, measures more then 20 by 30 cms, with four columns of writing on each side and it totals more then 800 lines of script. This large, presumably incomplete corpus, considered a legal handbook by some scholars and a true code by others, lacks a prologue and epilogue and hence cannot be associated with a particular king nor exactly dated. Only manuscript A is dated, by an Assyrian year eponym and is now placed around 1175 B.C.[3] This suggests that the laws themselves (probably a compilation of material from the reigns of several kings) are somewhat older and may go back to the thirteenth and/or fourteenth centuries B.C., when the Middle Assyrian state established itself under series of able kings.

The Old Assyrian period (twentieth to eighteenth centuries B.C.) thus far has not yielded a collection of laws comparable to those known from several states of contemporary Babylonia, such as Isin (Lipit-Ishtar), Eshnunna (Dadusha?), and Babylon (Hammurabi). Assur, before becoming an independent city-state around 2000 B.C., had been a province of the empire of the Third Dynasty of Ur, the laws of whose first king, Ur-Nammu, might have served as an example of legislation. The Old Assyrian city-state was prosperous and well administered.[4] From the hundreds of contracts and records of private **[1719]** summonses, arbitrations, testimonies, and verdicts[5] we know that judicial procedures and jurisprudence needed for solving the at times rather complicated conflicts between the members of its commercial class were well-developed. The highest judicial authority of Assur, the City Assembly (*ālum*), which acted in conjunction with the ruler, passed many verdicts and its consultations and decisions might well have led to the promulgation of a body of legal rules for dealing with important issues frequently submitted to its judgment.

The Assyrians of this period, in fact, did formulate rules and lay down procedures, as records of the community of Old Assyrian traders in Anatolia, excavated in the commercial quarter (*kārum*) of the city of Kanesh, demonstrate. Among the thousands of

---

1 Footnote lapsed.

2 See now *LCMA* 153ff. Some new readings and interpretations in H. Freydank, *Altorientalische Forschungen* 21 (1994) 203-211.

3 See H. Freydank, *Beiträge zur mittelassyrischen Chronologie und Geschichte* (Schriften zur Geschichte und Kultur des Alten Orients 21, Berlin 1991) 68, 73ff.

4 See for an analysis *OACC*.

5 See the older, but still reliable edition in *EL*. See for a typological analysis of part of the material, K.R. Veenhof, Private Summons and Arbitration among the Old Assyrian Traders, in*: Near Eastern Studies Dedicated to H.I.H. Prince Takahito Mikasa* (Bulletin of the Middle Eastern Culture Center in Japan 5, Wiesbaden 1991) 437 – 459.

* Originally published in Chicago-Kent Law Review 70 no. 4 (1995). Symposium on Ancient law, Economics & Society, part I, 1718-1744. Paragraph V of the original version has been rewritten and expanded.

tablets discovered there are three fragments which have been called "the Statutes of the Kanesh Colony". Larsen, who has provided a detailed analysis of their contents, describes them as "the rather pitiful remains of what must have constituted a corpus of rules governing the correct procedure of the assemblies of the Kanesh colony".[6] Moreover, the Assyrians used to conclude treaties (sworn agreements) with the various Anatolian rulers in whose territory they traded, which stipulated the rights and duties of both parties as the legal framework for the overland trade.[7]

While the frequency of judicial activities might have called for a collection of legal rules and the scribal tradition and skills, together with the administrative experience, certainly would have enabled the Old Assyrians to draft laws, yet, thus far no code or legal handbook from that period has surfaced.

Our knowledge of law codes of ancient Mesopotamia is, to some extent, a matter of luck. The famous stele which contains the Laws of Hammurabi, was not excavated in Babylonia, but in surprise discovery by the French in Susa (south western Iran), where it had been carried **[1720]** of by an Elamite conqueror of Babylonia of the 12th century B.C. to be subsequently buried there. All other sources of laws, with the exception of a single fragment of a stone monument of Lipit-Ishtar of Isin, are clay tablets. Many originate from Babylonian schools, where these "classic" texts were copied and studied. A few may have been copies made for, and kept in, administrative centres for consultation.

No Assyrian law stele, however, was discovered in Susa, and the German excavators of Assur have reached Old Assyrian levels only in certain parts of the upper city (the area with the palaces and temples), where they discovered only a limited number of usually short royal inscriptions. Old Assyrian schools, which certainly existed, probably were located (as was the case in Babylonia) in the houses of expert scribes in the lower city, whose levels were not reached by the excavators. Nevertheless, if a collection of laws did exist, one would expect to have discovered a copy of it in the administrative center of the network of trading colonies, called *kārum*, in the lower city of Kanesh. There, in the so-called "*kārum* house", the colonial authorities met and administered justice, close to the cella of the god Assur, where oaths were sworn on his divine dagger. But this building has not yet been discovered by the Turkish excavators. Overall, the lack of a collection of Old Assyrian laws, disappointing as it may be, is less surprising than the absence of a list of year eponyms indispensable for public and private administration. There is, however, some reason to remain hopeful, since excavations at Kanesh continue and archaeologists certainly will return to Assur in due time.

II. LAWS ON STELAE

Official "publication" of laws by kings, as the examples of Lipit-Ishtar's and Hammurabi's collections (columns XLVIII:9f. and XLIX:4 of the Code of Hammurabi) show and explicitly state, could be achieved by carving them into a stone monument. This was usually a stele (Akkadian *narûm*, "inscribed stone"), which was erected, just like other royal inscriptions, for display. Thus, references to "the words of the stele" in a legal context can be taken as proof of the existence of a "published" law code. While no references to or quotations from the stele with Hammurabi's Laws are known, there are two references to texts of

6 See *OACC* 287-332; the second text has the title *tašīmtum*, "(wise) rule".

7 See P. Garelli, *Les Assyriens en Cappadoce* (Paris 1963) 321-61, "Les relations politiques entre Assyriens et indigènes d'Anatolie". See for a draft of a treaty text S. Çeçen and K. Hecker, "*Ina mātika eblum*. Zu einem neuen Text zum Wegerecht in der Kültepe-Zeit", in: M. Dietrich and O. Loretz (eds.), *Vom Alten Orient zum Alten Testament (Festschrift W. von Soden)*, (Alter Orient und Altes Testament vol. 240, Neukirchen-Vluyn 1995) 31-41. The text mentions losses by Assyrians, bloodshed, the barring of Babylonian traders, the amounts of merchandise the local ruler will receive from every caravan passing his town, and his revenues when due to hostilities no caravan traffic is possible. Cf. also the Old Assyrian treaty found at Tell Leilan (dated to ca. 1750 B.C.), published by Jesper Eidem in: D. Charpin and F. Joannès (eds.), *Marchands, diplomates et empereurs. Études sur la civilisation mésopotamienne offertes à Paul Garelli* (Paris 1991) 185-207.

other Old Babylonian steles, which themselves are unknown to us. A contract from Ur records the liability of a person hired for supervising the cultivation of a field, stating: "For the shortfall which occurs one will treat him in accordance with the text of the **[1721]** stele" (*kīma pī narêm*)[8]. The second reference is in a still unpublished letter in Chicago, where a person is warned that "the wages for a hired worker are written on the stele".[9]

In the light of these occurrences two references to "the words of the stele" (*awāt naru'ā'im*) in Old Assyrian texts, known for many years, arouse interest. In the one, found in two closely related records, a plaintiff, in the course of lawsuit, asks his opponent "to swear him with/by the three words of (variant: which are written on) the stele".[10] Though royal steles, also those containing laws, usually end with a series of curses meant to protect the monument and to deter anyone who might wish to damage it, we have no example of a collection of laws formulating or prescribing a particular oath formula. Balkan and Landsberger therefore have suggested that the reference was to an inscription of king Irishum,[11] where the god Assur is described as "a reed swamp not to be traversed, terrain not to be trodden upon, canals not to be crossed" (lines 35-38). They assume that the rather independent second part of this inscription (lines 26-74), which contains this passage and is devoted to matters of establishing justice, preventing false testimony, and ensuring correct judicial procedures, had been copied from a stele. They suggest that it been erected in the so-called "Step-Gate" (*mušlālum*), behind the temple of Assur,[12] near the chapel of the seven divine judges (whose names are enumerated in the inscription), where justice was administered. Proof for this view, however, is lacking, since the lines in question are not a real curse formula, as one would expect as the core of an oath. If a curse formula were contained in this inscription, it is more likely to be found in lines 39ff., where the terrible fate of the false witness is described: "[The demon] of the ruins will seize his mouth and hindquarters, he will smash his head like a shattered pot, he will fall like a broken reed and water will flow from his mouth". Yet, this identification is a hypothesis and can we cannot prove that the reference is to Irishum's inscription, or that it indicates the existence of a stone monument inscribed with laws.

[1722] It is also odd that, although letters and court records contain numerous mentions of judicial oaths sworn or demanded, the texts quoted in note 10, known for a long time, are still the only ones referring to the stele. It has been suggested that in this court case the plaintiff demanded from his opponent a very solemn and heavy oath to confirm or to deny the plaintiff's claim of a large amount of silver paid by the latter as his guarantor. But the case is not essentially different from many others where oaths were sworn. We could assume that the scribe of the documents in question for some reason took great pains to record *verbatim* what the plaintiff said, while in all other judicial records the simple mention of the oath would have been deemed sufficient. This assumption would mean that all oaths in fact were sworn "by/with the three words of the stele" and that the three texts are our somewhat lucky evidence for this state of affairs. Unfortunately, without more evidence the issue cannot be decided[13].

---

8 UET 5, no. 420, see *CAD* N/1, 365a, a, 1 (collated text).

9 A 3529:10, see *CAD* N/1, loc.cit., and *LCMA* 6, with a full translation.

10 The texts are *EL* no. 325 (VS 26, 112): 34f. (long variant) and *EL* no. 326 (BIN 4, 114):3lf. // BIN 6, 211: 31f.; for "to swear" the verb *zakārum* is used.

11 B. Landsberger and K. Balkan, "Die Inschrift des assyrischen Königs Irišum gefunden in Kültepe 1948", *Belleten* XIV (1950) 218-268, esp. 262, c; see for a recent edition of this inscription, A.K. Grayson, *Assyrian Rulers of the Third and Second Millennia BC. The Royal Inscriptions of Mesopotamia, Assyrian Periods* 1, (Toronto 1987) 20f.

12 This location results from a comparison of two unpublished texts, Kt n/k 511:30 and n/k 1365:36 (courtesy C. Günbattı and S. Çeçen).

13 See for the oath in Old Assyrian, H. Hirsch, *Untersuchungen zur altassyrischen Religion (Archiv für Orientforschung*, Beiheft 13/14, Osnabrück 1972) 68ff. [and now *OALP* passim and K.R. Veenhof in: R. Westbrook (ed.), *A History of Ancient Near Eastern Law* (*Handbuch der Orientalistik*, section I, vol. 72/1 (Leiden-Boston 2003) 445-6.]

[*Add.* New evidence has since turned up and Hertel in *OALP* 80-1 argues that "'the oath of the three words' appears indeed to have been a very solemn and heavy oath of a special kind, which could be sworn in the colonies by litigants who disqualified the colonial jurisdiction and instead demanded their suit transferred to the jurisdiction of the City and the King, *i.e.* the High Court in Assur". He uses a new source, *Kültepe Tabletleri* VIa (Ankara 2010) 115:37-40 (quoted in his footnote 438), a verdict of the City Assembly, which states that if somebody makes a formal statement about a deposition (*nadītam izakkar*), "if it (involves) the three [words], he shall come to the City, if it does not involve the three words he must not come to the City. He who comes anyway will not stay alive". Which "three words" he pronounced is still unknown].

A. Compound Interest and the Stele

The second reference to "the words of the stele" deals with the issue of taking compound interest (*ṣibat ṣibtim*, "interest on interest"). One occurrence on the "second page" of a letter has been known since 1935. A second, in a damaged judicial record, was published in 1962.[14] Yet, since their contents were not well understood, they have received little attention. H. Lewy, in 1947, concluded that "the cases in which compound interest could be charged were determined by law".[15] Balkan and Landsberger admit that the reference suggests the existence of a law stele which regulates the rates of interest and compound interest, but they consider this evidence too weak a basis for assuming the existence of an "extensive law stele" and suggest as alternative a moral exhortation: "(charge interest) as honestly and brotherly as the stele teaches!".[16] This solution, however, is very unlikely in the light of both old and new evidence.

A stipulation about (compound) interest in itself is not surprising, especially not in a commercial society. Rates of interest were of great economic and social relevance in Mesopotamia and along with prices and other rates are dealt with in the law **[1723]** corpora of Eshnunna (§ 18A), Babylon (§§ t and u) and in the laws of X § m.[17] But stipulations about tariffs could also occur separately, in royal decrees (*ṣimdat šarrim*), as the one to which § u of Hammurabi's laws may refer. An Akkadian inscription of the Elamite king Attahuššu, from the Old Babylonian period, states that he had fashioned and erected on the market "a statue of justice, in order that the sun god would instruct him who did not know the just price".[18] One of the two Old Babylonian references to a stipulation on a stele (see note 9) in fact mentions a rate, that of the wages of a hired labourer. Hence, the Old Assyrian stipulation on compound interest, when interpreted as a rate regulation is not necessarily proof of the existence of a complete law code. Instead, one could consider it a separate ruling, comparable to the one which prescribes "interest in accordance with the stipulation of the *kārum*" (*ṣibtum kīma awāt kārim*), which is frequently mentioned in debt-notes and demonstrates that the *kārum* authorities had fixed the interest to be charged among Assyrians at thirty per cent per year by a separate decree.

New occurrences, however, of references to a rule about compound interest, found in clear texts, leave no doubt as to its meaning and show that the law is not concerned with its rate or term.[19] They occur in a series of letters, all addressed to the same trader, Mannu-ki-Assur (henceforth M.). The letters are part of the very large archive Kt n/k (ca. 2000 texts), excavated in 1962, which is studied by my Turkish colleagues in Ankara,

---

14 VAT 11509 = VS 26,76:6f (*EL* II p. 75 note c) and ICK 2,147:21'f.; both are listed in *CAD* N/1 , 365a.

15 In a review article in *JAOS* 67 (1947) 305-310, where the method of computing compound interest was discussed.

16 *Loc.cit.* (note 11).

17 See *LCMA* 38, 61, 97.

18 Published as *MDP* 28 no. 3, see *AOATT* 353 with note 470.

19 This implies that it is still unknown when, in the case of a normal loan, the simple interest was added to the capital to be recapitalized. Mrs. H. Lewy (above, note 15), on the basis of Old Babylonian mathematical texts, assumed this happened when interest and capital had become equal, which would normally be after three to five years. The situation in the Old Assyrian period needs a fresh investigation.

who kindly allowed me to use some of their data. All the letters deal with the payment of a debt of more than twenty pounds of silver, owed by M. to the "city-office" or "*līmum*-office" in Assur. Unable to pay it in full M. is helped by Dadaja (henceforth D.), who as M.'s guarantor was obliged to pay in his place. Since D. himself did not have the silver available, he had to take out a loan to meet his obligation as guarantor. In the letters K/t nk 431 and 515 (both courtesy C. Günbattı) M. is told: "You now have become indebted to D. for 8 pounds of silver." D. declared: "I am his guarantor, I will charge him, in accordance with the words of the stele, interest and compound interest!" (431:12-17). And Kt n/k 515:7-16 complements the picture by stating: "D. called at the house of a moneylender for 8 pounds of silver for your **[1724]** sake and paid it for your debt to the city-office. Next D. appealed to the City saying: 'City, my Lord! I have indeed been registered as guarantor of M. and I have now paid (his debt) to the *līmum*(-office). Now give me a tablet (stating) that, wherever silver of M. is available I can go for it'. Moreover, he will charge you compound interest".[*Add.* An additional example is found in *Kültepe Tabletleri* VIa (Ankara 2010) 60:8-12, "I paid the debt of your father at the order of I., I am the guarantor, I sue you for the silver, the interest on it and the compound interest"].

Hence, the rule about compound interest stipulated in which specific situation a creditor was authorized to charge it: when a guarantor had to borrow money to meet his obligations, which turned him into a creditor of the original debtor and a debtor of his moneylender at the same time. In such situations he had recourse against the original debtor by charging him interest, because he had paid for him, and compound interest, because he himself had to pay it to his creditor. The two older references support this conclusion. In VS 26,76, the mention of compound interest is followed by the statement: "And the tablet recording my guarantee (which the original creditor kept) will become my tablet" (lines 8f.). And in ICK 2,147, three guarantors, who had failed to make the brother of a (dead?) debtor pay back to them, stated before witnesses: "Keep in mind that we talked to him, but that he refused to pay! We will now enter the house of a moneylender and borrow silver and the interest on it [at his expense], (satisfy the creditor) and get back our tablet (the contract whereby they had been registered as guarantors, kept by the creditor – K.R.V.) and he shall pay us interest and compound interest according to the words of the stele" (lines 17-23). The guarantors here borrow "silver and the interest on it", to recover both the capital they had paid and the interest on it to which they were entitled.

Since all references known to me connect the rule with payments by guarantors,[20] this connection seems to be the essence of the legal stipulation, although it is not impossible that the law mentioned other cases in which charging compound interest – a novel feature, not earlier attested in ancient Mesopotamia – was authorized.

B. Rules for paying debts

Paying debts was of vital importance in the community of Old Assyrian traders. The term "debt" covers a variety of contractual financial obligations and is not limited to real loans taken out **[1725]** with a moneylender. It also means the liability of paying for merchandise bought on credit, received in consignment, or entrusted to partners, representatives, and agents. It may also refer to what is owed as capital, profit and dividend to people who had invested in a trader's capital (called *naruqqum*, "money-bag"), and to financial obligations to the Assyrian authorities, in Assur or Kanesh, such as fees, taxes, excise and even fines. Most of the records of private summonses, arbitrations and lawsuits deal with problems

---

20 See for the role of guarantors in Old Assyrian, *EL* I 175-183, *CAD* Q under *qātātum* 3, *bēl qātātim* and *ša qātātim*, my remarks in *Jaarbericht Ex Oriente Lux* 28 (1983-4) 20 with note 19, and P. Garelli in: F. Rochberg-Halton (ed.), Language, Literature and History. Philological and Historical Studies Presented to Erica Reiner (*AOS* 67, New Haven 1987) 111f. [and in great detail my observations in The Old Assyrian period, in: R. Westbrook and R. Jasnow (eds.), *Security for Debt in Ancient Near Eastern Law* (Leiden-Boston 2001), 93-159, esp. ch. II, "Guarantee"].

connected with the payment of such debts. Thus far, I have found two references to a rule on the stele.

1. Payment in Assur or in Anatolia

The first reference is a verdict of the City of Assur, which, as usual, was communicated to the authorities of *kārum* Kanesh by means of a formal letter written by the ruler of the City, presumably acting as its chairman and chief executive officer.[21] The letter reads after the address:

> The City has passed the following verdict: 8 "If anyone has given A. in Anatolia (lit. "the countryside") a capital investment (*naruqqum*) or investment loans (*ebuṭṭū*), he shall take it (or: it shall be taken) back together with his (other) investors, by means of his witnesses, in the City. 14 If he has promised any silver in Anatolia, in accordance with the words of the stele, when it is confirmed by his witnesses, 18 he shall take it (or: it shall be taken) back only there. 19b Nobody shall touch the silver, it shall be brought together in the City."[22]

The verdict distinguishes between two types of claims. On the one hand those resulting from investments, either by taking a share in a trader's capital,[23] or by granting him a special type of long term loan (presumably interest free and rewarded by a share in the profits).[24] On the other hand claims resulting **[1726]** from commercial activities in Anatolia such as transactions engaging partners, representatives or agents. The former have to be paid back in Assur, the latter must be settled in Anatolia. This distinction between Assur an Anatolia was vital for a trade whose goal it was to acquire in Anatolia, in exchange for tin and textiles imported from Assur, silver and gold. Due to transport costs and the difference between its exchange value in Anatolia and Mesopotamia, silver in Assur was much more valuable than in Anatolia. This important distinction is also made in a letter, where the writer, after discussing a settlement of accounts, concludes with the question: "Don't you know the rule ('words') of the City: Items of Anatolia shall only be collected in Anatolia, those of the City only in the City (of Assur)?".[25] But this letter appears to contradict the ruling of our verdict, since only its second part agrees, which states that financial obligations assumed in Anatolia have to be settled there. The first part, which looks like an adaptation or extension, stipulates that capital investments not made in the City (as they usually were), but in Anatolia, also had to be settled in Assur. The rich evidence on *naruqqum*-investments shows that, not infrequently, successful traders living in Anatolia gave silver to a trader there on the condition that he would

21 The ruler in such letters uses his title *waklum*, "overseer", "head (of the community)". See for his titles and his position in relation to the City, *OACC* 109-159.

22 Kt a/k 394, published by H. Sever in *DTCFD* 34 (1990) 258f., lines 5-22: *ālum dīnam* [6] *idīnma ana* A. [7] DUMU A. [8] *šumma ina eqlim* [9] *lū naruqqum*[!] *lū ebuṭṭē* [10] *mamman iddin* [11] *qādē ummiāniš[u]ma* [12] *ina šībēšu ina* [13] *ālim i-lá-qé* [14] *šumma kaspam ina eqlim* [15] *ēpul kīma* [16] *[a]wāt naru'ā'im* [17] *iššībēšu ikuanma* [18] *ašrakamma kasapšu* [19] *i-lá-[qé ana] kaspim* [20] *mamma[n lā] iṭahhe* [21] *ana ālim* [22] *ipahhuram*. Because Old Assyrian spelling does not indicate double consonants, *i-lá-qé* in lines 13 and 19 can be parsed both as active (*ilaqqe*, "he will take") and as passive (*illaqqe*, "it will be taken"). In the text quoted in footnote 25, where no personal subject occurs, the form has to be passive.

23 See for such investments, always rated in gold, M. T. Larsen, "Partnerships in the Old Assyrian Trade", *Iraq* 39 (1977) 119-145.

24 See for this type of loan, *CAD* E 21, discussion. There are many new references that warrant a fresh analysis which will correct and supplement *CAD*. [See now J.G. Dercksen, in: J.G. Dercksen (ed.), *Trade and Finance in Ancient Mesopotamia* (*MOS Studies* 1, Istanbul 1996), 97-99]. Such loans were recorded in written contracts and they entail a share in the profits (Kt n/k 1841). The text Kt n/k 460 explicitly mentions *naruqqum* and *ebuṭṭum* as alternative ways of investing in the trade.

25 L 29-571, edited by W. C. Gwaltney, *The Pennsylvania Old Assyrian Texts* (*HUCA* Suppl. no.3, Cincinnati 1983) no.16: 34-37: *awāt ālim lā tidē ša eqlim ina eqlimma illaqqe ša ālim ina ālimma illaqqe*.

inscribe their name among his shareholders on the "*naruqqum*-tablet" in Assur.[26] Hence, the verdict goes beyond the "rule of the City" in looking not only at the place of origin of a transaction, but also at its nature: capital investments by nature have to be settled in Assur, where the contracts recording the foundation of and investment in a *naruqqum* were kept.

[*Addendum.* A new verdict of the City in connection with the payment of debts, in *Kültepe Tabletleri* VIa (Ankara 2010) 294:12-22, contains the same ruling: "The City passed the following verdict: If Š. owes silver in Anatolia (*ina eqlim*), if it is proved (*ikuan*) by his tablets and witnesses he will take his silver [16] *i-na sá-bi-tí-šu*. For the debt Š. owes in the City nobody shall take silver in Anatolia. Who has taken it shall give it back, [who has not given it] back will be considered a thief". This verdict does not refer to "the words of the stele", which indicates that more rulings in verdicts and quotes in letters may reflect laws, without being identified as such].

Our verdict adds that settlements concerning investments – which usually were long term – should take place in Assur "together with (all) the investors" (line 11), at the same time, to ensure a fair division of all assets among all partners. For this purpose, as the last lines state, all assets (silver) shall be brought together in Assur; nobody is allowed to touch (lit. "to approach") any silver before the final, general settlement.

This last stipulation has parallels in several other texts, which deal with the liquidation of a firm or household after its head, a trader, had died. A trader's death usually prompted his relatives, partners, creditors and investors to try to recover the money to which they were convinced **[1727]** they were entitled. The authorities apparently had ruled that all such individual, uncoordinated actions were forbidden and that a general settlement of accounts had to take place in Assur itself, where all debts and assets could be balanced. We know this rule from several judicial records and letters, which use almost the same words as our verdict: "Nobody, either in Assur or in Anatolia, shall touch anything, all his silver shall be brought together in Assur".[27] Several other texts add: "Whoever has taken anything shall give it back, he who does not give it back, will be considered a thief" (lit.: "it will be [considered as having been] stolen by him").[28] But none of its occurrences refers back to "the words of the stele" as its source, so what can we derive from our verdict?

The words "in accordance with the words of the stele" only appear in line 15, in the middle of the second alternative and therefore do not seem to cover lines 6-13. Was this because the first part of the verdict was an extension of an existing rule? If so, it is important to note that this "new" ruling closely parallels the second part of the verdict in syntactic structure and in wording ("If..., by means of his witnesses it shall be taken")[29] and convinces by its analogy. New rules could be derived from and patterned after existing ones, but it is difficult to prove that this new rule was also inscribed on the stele.

The next question is whether the reference to the stele covers all of the second part of the verdict (lines 14-22). The scribe inserted the reference to the stele only after presenting the case ("If he has promised...", *šumma ēpul*), and this suggests that only the verdict in a narrow sense (lines 17ff.) is based on the stele. It contains three elements: 1) the necessity of proof by testimony; 2) obligations assumed in Anatolia have to be paid there; and 3) nobody shall touch anything, all assets of the dead trader have to come to Assur before there can be a division. Most likely, element 3 was part of customary

26 See Larsen, *op. cit.* (note 23).

27 TCL 14, 21:8-10, cf. J. G. Dercksen, *Bibliotheca Orientalis* 49 (1992) 794.

28 See the references in *CAD* Š/2, 56, 4, a. The verb is *šarāqum*, "to steal" (in the passive, with a pronominal suffix in the dative, *iššarriqšum*) and it states that individual, unauthorized collection of claims is considered theft.

29 The omission of "when it is confirmed" (*ikuanma*) in line 12 is accidental or for the sake of brevity. Its occurrence in line 17 may support the view that this is the quote from the stele, which could not be abbreviated.

law, due to its remarkable, concise formulation which shows almost no variation, but I hesitate to consider it a rule inscribed one the stele based solely on the evidence of this verdict. While elements 1and 2 immediately follow the reference to the stele and form a logical unit (linked by enclitic *-ma*), element 3 follows as a new, unconnected sentence. **[1728]** Therefore I conclude the reference to the stele covers these two elements.

Element 1 imposes the necessity of proof by witnesses before claims can be realized. This necessity is also stated, again with reference to the stele, in my second reference (see note 33), which shows the importance attached to it. However, the necessity of proof (by witnesses or written texts) in settlements of accounts appears so obvious, that stressing it by referring to the law seems odd [note that the verdict quoted in the Addendum above, mentions the necessity of proof without referring to the stele]. Mesopotamian laws, moreover, do not contain abstract rules such as "financial claims have to be proved by testimony", but present such conditions in the framework of concrete examples, as the first paragraphs of Hammurabi's Laws show. The necessity of proof (oral or written) is usually stressed in particular situations, such as in commercial transactions, as §§104-106 of the same laws reveal. I would therefore consider it likely that the rules inscribed on the Assyrian stele laid down the condition of proof by witnesses for specific cases where it was essential. Our verdict and the one to be discussed presently probably were such cases, because the debtor to all appearances had died. And the death of a trader, engaged in a variety of transactions, always created legal problems, because, however careful he may have been in securing written proof, there were always dealings with relatives, partners and friends, which by nature were oral or had not yet been formalized by written contract. Many letters and records acquaint us with the problems caused by such deaths and show that oral testimony was needed to recover the truth. We read that sons, who had to answer for their fathers' liabilities, at times were badly informed and had to confess "I am the son of a dead man, I don't know...".[30] In such situations, probably covered by some of our verdicts, the necessity of witnesses was obvious and was stressed. The fact that all transactions that according to our verdict had to be accounted for had taken place in Anatolia may have added to the problems. We do not know whether the nature of the *ebuṭṭum*-loan made oral testimony important, but this was certainly the case with the action mentioned in line 15, designated by the verb *apālum*. Its basic meaning is not simply "to pay", but "to answer (for)". In a commercial context it frequently means to accept responsibility for, to promise, or to guarantee a delivery or payment which still has to be **[1729]** effectuated, usually for or on behalf of somebody else.[31] It does not surprise that the financial consequences of such actions by a trader who had died in Anatolia needed confirmation by witnesses and that the law prescribes this.

The way the condition of confirmation by witnesses is formulated may also hint at its legal character. The rule uses an impersonal, intransitive form of the verb *kuānum*, "to become firm, proven, confirmed", which is rare. The dictionaries does not list Old Assyrian examples and only quote a few Old Babylonian ones, with "the matter, the case" as subject.[32]. The verb also occurs in an official letter of a *kārum* (Kt 91/k 219:12f.)), dealing with an indebted trader: "When it is confirmed (*līkūnma*) by [his records] and/or his witnesses he will collect his silver". This statement strongly reminds us of the formulation on the stele. The use of such impersonal forms, which focus not on the creditor or debtor but on the procedure (just like the impersonal form *illaqqe*, "it shall be collected", in some

30 See e.g. the study by L. Matouš, Der Streit um den Nachlass des Puzur-Aššur, *Archiv Orientální* 37 (1969) 156-180 (we now can add four more texts to the file), J. G. Dercksen, *loc.cit.* (note 27), C. Michel, Le decès d'un contractant, *Revue d'Assyriologie* 86 (1982) 113 – 119, and *CAD* M/2, 140b, a, 1, for some occurrences of "I am the son of a dead man".

31 The dictionaries do not single out this meaning. The comments in *EL* p. 196 mention that the verb is frequently used when someone else pays for the debtor.

32 *CAD* K 161b, e.

of the texts quoted above) may well be a feature of stipulations which phrase general, normative rules, hence the law.

[Addendum. We now have a reference in a letter (*Ankaraner Kültepe Texte* 3 [Stuttgart 1995] no. 98), which suggests that the laws included a rule how to behave when a trader had died. A man reproaches a partner for the latter's behaviour after the death of his father. Both had promised under oath "not to turn to anything the latter had left behind, either in the city or in the countryside", but the addressee, nevertheless, had done so. The writer asks him: "What claims do you have on me? Don't tell me 'I am an appointed representative!' Has a stele of yours been inscribed separately (*naru'ā'um kuā'um ina ba*?*-tim lapit*), that you dare to act as representative?" (lines 16-20). From the context I interpret the sentence quoted as: "Have special rules been drafted for you separately?", that is: "How dare you act as if you are above the law?" In this ironic question "the law" appears as "an inscribe stele" which suggests the existence of a statuary ruling about the liquidation of a dead trader's assets.]

2. Payment in Particular Situations

The second reference to a stele in connection with the payment of debts is in kt n/k 1925, also a letter by the ruler of Assur to the authorities of *kārum* Kanesh, in which he informs them about a verdict of the City.[33] It reads:

> The creditors of Šu-Kūbum, will (each) take from whatever Šu-Kūbum possesses, in accordance with the words of the stele, when it is confirmed by witnesses, his silver in / at/ from his ...[34]

The rule referred to or quoted grants the creditors (the text uses the plural in line 8, but switches to the individual singular in lines 16 and 19f.) the right to indemnify themselves by taking their silver "from whatever the debtor possesses". This rule is similar to the one we met in the case of the guarantor D.,[35] where this right was the result of an appeal to the City, which issued him a "valid tablet" to that effect. By sheer coincidence we possess a letter, published seventy years ago, CCT 2, 22, which deals with the **[1730]** same case as kt n/k 1925. Its writer states in lines 16ff.: "As for Šu-Kūbum, I have acquired a tablet of the City (stating) that, from whatever Šu-[Kūbum possesses], in accordance with the words of the st[ele], I can take my silver in/at his ...".[36] The continuation of this letter makes it highly likely that Šu-Kūbum had died, since it mentions the sale of his house to cover the debts of (that is: inherited by) his sons. It adds that the writer has acquired a "powerful tablet of the City", which stipulates that the buyer has to give it back or else will be considered a thief. This shows that the rule of law quoted in these two texts indeed deals with the liquidation of a dead trader's business.

Both texts mention that the creditor is allowed to recover his money in a particular way or at a particular moment. This expression, which is now a few more times attested, has been read *i-na-sà bi-tí-šu* and translated "when the house(hold) is transferred",[37] but this makes no sense, because in our text the pronominal suffix does not refer to the dead

33 I am grateful to the Director of the Anatolian Civilizations Museum in Ankara, Dr. Ilhan Temizsoy, for his permission to open and study this letter that was still in its envelope. [This verdict is published in K.R. Veenhof, "A Verdict of the Assembly of the Old Assyrian City-State", in a Festschrift for H. Freydank (in the press)].

34 Lines 8-20: *tamkarū* [9] [p]*Šu-Kūbim* [10] *mer'a Aššur-bēl-awātim* [11] *ina mimma* [12] [p]*Šu-Kūbum* [13] *išūni* [14] *kīma awāt* [15] *na-ru-wa-ú* (for *naruwā'im)* [16] *ina šībēšu* (final *-nu* erased) [17] *ikuanma* [18] *i-na sà-bi-tí-šu* [19] *kasapšu* [20] *ilaqqe.*

35 See above, § IIA.

36 The text was edited by C. Michel, *Innāya dans les tablettes paléo-assyriennes* (Paris 1991), II no. 155; read at the end of line 18 *i[šûni*] and in line 20 [*alaqqe'u*].

37 See *CAD* N/2, 188a, d.

trader, but to the creditor. There is a new occurrence, in Kt n/k 1684 13f., where the son of a debtor asks his father's creditor, who is about to leave Anatolia for Assur, to submit evidence about his father's debts in silver or tin, "then I will pay you *i-na sà-bi-tí-ni*, "in/ at our ...", where the division of the signs over two lines shows how to parse the word. I suspect an expression which designates an occasion or situation suited for payment or for collecting the money.[38]

C. A Rule about Compensation of Losses During Caravan Journeys

The next reference to the words of the stele is in the badly-damaged tablet Kt n/k 1570, again a letter of the ruler communicating a verdict of the City, also published by H. Sever. I propose to restore in lines 9 and 18 the key word *huluqqā'ū*, "losses", which fits the space available. [39] This restoration is also suggested by the verb in the last line, *mallu'um*, "to compensate", which is also used, again with "losses" as object, in **[1731]** the verdict published as *EL* no. 278 and in some letters.[40] It also occurs in the unpublished memorandum Kt 91/ k 451:1-5 [see now *Kültepe Tabletleri* VIII, 127, with comment], where we read: "For the 17 *kutānu*-textiles which got lost in Badna, the caravan has paid us a compensation (*mallu'um*) of 1⅓ mina of tin apiece". This allows us to read our verdict as follows:

> [The loss]es of PNl-5 (five broken personal names with patronyms), their [loss]es, [in accordance with (the words of)] the stele, [either t]in or silver [or] textiles, the caravan of Kurub-Ištar, son of Puzur-ili, shall compensate to them.

While losses during caravan transport were infrequent, they did occur, and thus it makes sense to have a rule about compensation, but the simple reference to a stele which we do not possess does not reveal us to what it amounted. Most probably simple compensation when the loss was due to force majeure (robbery, bad weather, accidents with donkeys, etc.), a rule found in many law collections. That a rule existed and was incorporated in the law must be due to the nature of the transport. The word translated "caravan", basically "traveling company" (*ellutum*), refers to a large caravan, which comprises merchandise of many of people, organized by an important trader after whom the caravan is called. A famous example is the "caravan/company of Imdī-ilum", mentioned in VS 26, 155, which lists merchandise of 35 traders, with a total value of more than 400 talents of tin, or some 30 kilos of silver, in which Imdī-ilum himself is the biggest participant, with 47 talents of tin. Such caravans functioned as a single unit: the calculated value (*awītum*) of all the merchandise and the donkeys was expressed in one single valuta, tin, as were all expenses, taxes and losses. This allowed the organizer or leader of the caravan, who must have been responsible for the safety of the transport, to add, divide and apportion costs

38 Kt n/k 1684:13-14, *šēliāma i-na* [14] *sà-bi-tí-ni lašqulakkum*. [*Add.* There are now several additional references, including *Kültepe Tabletleri* VIa, 294:16 – quoted in the addendum to § B.1 – where the spelling with DI=*sá* reveals the nature of the sibilant; the noun could be *sab/pa/utum*, with vowel harmony, or *sa/pbitum*. In a few more texts it qualifies a payment, notably in the memorandum Kt c/k 623:36, where the obligation to pay a debt within one year is followed by: He shall not say: 'I will pay *ina sabitia*'. Other texts use it in combination with the verb *atawwum*, "to discuss, to negotiate" (VS 26, 8:23; *Kültepe Tabletleri* VIb, 528:34; Kt 92/k 554:9-10 // 557a:19-20, *ina sabitišunu*), or with *awātam tadānum*, "to render account", VS 26, 112:43-4, cf. 80:4'-5')].

39 *Op.cit.* (note 22) 264f.: [9] *[hu-lu-qá]-e* [10-17] PN_{1-5} (with their patronyms)[18] *[hu-lu-q]á-e-šu-nu 19 [ki-ma] na-ru-a-im* [20] *[lu* AN].NA *lu* KÙ.BABBAR [21] *lu* T]ÚG.HI.A ILLAT-*at* [22] *[Kur-u]b-Ištar* DUMU *Puzur*$_4$*-i-lí* [23] *[ú]-ma-lá-šu-nu-tí* (in l. 19 there is no room for *[a-wa-at]*)

40 "To compensate (for losses)" is also attested in KTHa 3:29 and CCT 2,11:15ff., where a caravan is mentioned: "The 36 *kutānu*-textiles of Aššur-emūqī's caravan, which Aššur-ṭāb exported, got lost in the mountains of Mamma. Let your message reach me whether the caravan has compensated them, yes or no". [The *kārum* verdict *EL* 278 demands that a trader submits (evidence of additional) costs of transportation, underweight and losses (*taššiātum bitqāt abnim huluqqā'ū*) and then will compensate half of it].

and losses among the participants. For that reason, it was rational to have strict rules for apportioning and compensating losses fairly among the many participants, rules which eventually were incorporated into statutary law.[41]

[1732] III. LEGISLATION

A. Trade policy and legislation

Trade appears to have been the backbone of Assur's economy and prosperity. It occupied a substantial part of its population, and many of its habitants had invested in it, as well as the temples and the ruler. Assur, in fact, served as a strategic market city and entrepôt in a commercial network that linked Iran, Babylonia, Assyria, Anatolia, and Syria. Consequently, Assyrian politics engaged itself with the trade and tried to promote it by means of political measures. King Ilushuma, around 1980 BC, proclaimed: "I established the freedom of the Babylonians ('Akkadians') and their sons. I washed their copper",[42] adding that this freedom (*addurārum*) was established all the way from Ur, on the northern shore of the Persian Gulf, to Assur. And his successor, Irishum, followed his steps by "establishing the freedom of silver, gold, copper, tin, barley, wool, until(?) bran and chaff".[43] Larsen, after a thorough analysis of these inscriptions, suggests "that the Old Assyrian commercial expansion under the later kings of the dynasty to a large extent rests on a clear policy which took its beginning (as far as we can see) under Ilushuma, who attempted to attract traders from the south to the market in Assur by giving them certain privileges. Whether this meant abolition of old taxes or of a previous state monopoly remains undecided".[44]

Access to the profitable markets of Anatolia required political decisions and skills, resulting in treaties with the various local rulers. Lacking military power in Anatolia, the Assyrians managed to secure free trade by negotiations, well aware of the economic importance of what the imported for the Anatolian upper class and the metallurgical industry. But the Assyrian authorities also checked their own traders who, by treaty, were not permitted to dodge local import and transit taxes by smuggling. *Kārum* Kanesh once issued a written order to a trader in charge of a large caravan: "Nobody shall smuggle tin or textiles. Who smuggles will be caught by the order (*awātum*) of the *kārum*!"[45] In another case a verdict of the *kārum* called for a commercial boycott of a high Anatolian palace official who had failed **[1733]** to pay his Assyrian creditor: "Nobody shall give any textile whatsoever to the 'head of the stairway'. Who does shall pay all the silver the 'head of the stairway' owes to Ikunum!".[46]

Politics also affected the Assyrian trade itself by means of decisions of the City Assembly and powers granted to the "city-office". The latter institution seems to have held a kind of monopoly on the trade in a few luxury items, notably the rare and very expensive meteoric iron. The City also passed verdicts aimed at protecting the interests of the Assyrian trading establishment (which must have been well represented among the "elders", the heads of the powerful families, which made up the Assembly), also when

---

41 See the study by C. Michel, "Transporteurs, responsables et propriétaires de convois dans les tablettes paléo-assyriennes. Réflexions sur les expressions *šēp* NP et *ellat* NP", in: D. Charpin and F. Joannès (eds.), *La circulation des biens, des personnes et des idees dans le Proche-Orient ancien* (Paris 1992) 137-156. She lists two occurrences of *ellat* Kurub-Ištar. The purely commercial aspect of these caravans still needs further analysis. [See now J.G. Dercksen, *Old Assyrian Institutions* (Leiden 2004), ch. 9, The 'Caravans'].

42 A.K. Grayson, *op. cit.* (note 11) 18, lines 49-65.

43 A.K. Grayson, *ibid.* 22f., lines 49-65.

44 See *OACC* 63-80.

45 Kt c/k 1055, quoted by K. Balkan, in: *Anatolian Studies Presented to Hans Gustav Güterbock on the Occasion of his 65th Birthday* (Istanbul 1974) 29 note 2. The leader of the caravan is the same Kurub-Ishtar mentioned in note 41 [and in *Kültepe Tabletleri* VIII, 127]. See for smuggling in the framework of the Old Assyrian trade, *AOATT* part IV, 305ff.

46 *EL* 273. Read in line 3, with Larsen, *1* TÚG.

these were at odds with those of the entrepreneurs based in Anatolia. Once traders doing brisk business in local Anatolian textile products were convicted and heavily fined, which resulted in a general decree or ukase (*awātum*) to refrain from all such transactions. The letter reporting this incident ends with the warning: "The ukase of the City is binding (strong)!"[47]

Even to those aware of these facts, the official letter Kt 79/k 101, sent by the ruler to *kārum* Kanesh, recently published by H. Sever[48], comes as a surprise. It reads in translation (lines 4-25):

> The tablet with the verdict of the City, which concerns gold, which we sent to you, 8 that tablet is cancelled. 9 We have not fixed any rule concerning gold. 11 The earlier rule concerning gold still obtains: 13 Assyrians may sell gold among each other, (but) 16, in accordance with the words of the stele, 18 no Assyrian whosoever shall give gold to any Akkadian, Amorrite or Subaraean. Who does so shall not stay alive!.[49]

I have to limit myself to a succinct analysis of this remarkable document, without being able to dwell on is economic aspects. The reader also is asked to take the translation of *iṣurtum* by "fixed rule" for granted,[50] and to be content with the information that the people mentioned in lines 19-21, attested since the end of the third millennium B.C., belong to the population of Mesopotamia, listed from south to north, with whom the Assyrians had commercial contacts, perhaps even in the city of Assur itself.

The following is my interpretation of the meaning of this letter. Sometime before the letter was sent, the ruler had sent a letter **[1734]** to *kārum* Kanesh to inform it about a verdict passed by the City. The verdict dealt with the sale of gold and presumably declared as illegal a transaction in gold in Anatolia, about which either the trader who had carried it out or the *kārum* itself had appealed to the City. Then, somewhat later, the City decided to revoke its verdict, which meant that the official letter, by means of which it had been "published", was cancelled. The City did not leave it at that, however, but apparently considered it useful to unambiguously state what the legal situation was, declaring: "We have not fixed a (new) rule!". Without formal cancellation of the verdict one might have assumed that the rule had changed, which would be wrong: "The old rule (still) obtains." This rule apparently is the one inscribed on the stele, since both lines 11 and 16 use the same word, *awātum*, "words, stipulation, rule". Lines 13-15 mention this rule, stating: sale of gold among Assyrians is permitted. Since, however, the reference to "the words of the stele" only follows in line 16f., I would rather assume that what was actually written on the monument is contained in the next lines, 18-25. This would mean that the positive rule of lines 13-15 was only implied – and perhaps for that reason had to be stated clearly – by a law which consisted of an absolute prohibition ("whosoever..., anyone..."), sanctioned by a death penalty.[51] This law, forbidding trade in gold with all non-Assyrian inhabitants of Mesopotamia, is clearly protectionist. While this is not a complete surprise in view of what is known about trade policy, it strikes us by its uncompromising nature and heavy sanction. Indeed, Assur was determined to protect its commercial interests, as is now also

---

47 See *AOATT* 126f.

48 *Op.cit.* (see note 22) 260ff.

49 Transcription of lines 9-25: *aššumi hurāṣim iṣurtam* [10] *ulā nēṣur* [11] *awātum ša hurāṣim* [12] *pāniātumma* [13] *ahum ana ahim* [14] *ana šīmim* [15] *iddan* [16] *kīma awāt* [17] *naru'ā'im* [18] *mer'a Aššur šumšu* [19] *hurāṣam ana Akkidêm* [20] *Amurrêm* [21] *u Šubirêm* [22] *mamman* [23] *lā iddan* [24] *ša iddunu* [25] *ulā iballaṭ.*

50 See my analysis of this noun in "Old Assyrian *iṣurtum*, Akkadian *eṣērum* and Hittite GIŠ.ḪUR", in Th.P.J. van Hout and J. de Roos (eds.), *Studio Historiae Ardens. Ancient Near Eastern Studies Presented to Philo H.J. Houwink ten Cate* (Istanbul 1995) 311-332, esp. 321ff. [= pp. 225-243 in this volume].

51 The formulation is apodictive (*lā* with present tense), while the use of the indefinite pronouns *šumšu* and *mamman* lend it a general scope, as in public proclamations and decrees. [A death penalty is also stipulated in *Kültepe Tabletleri* VIa, 115, for the man who does not stick to the rule on appealing to the City-Assembly by pronouncing the «three words», see the Addendum at the end of the introduction to § I].

clear from the draft of a trade treaty with a small local ruler in southern Anatolia. The ruler not only promises to bar Babylonians from his territory, but also, if they get there, to hand them over to the Assyrians to be killed.[52]

As for the background of his letter, the original verdict, which remains unknown, may have forbidden a particular transaction in gold in Anatolia, whereby it was not shipped to Assur, as was usual.[53] **[1735]** On second thought, however, this may have been considered detrimental to the trade and to have conflicted with the written law that it could be freely traded among Assyrians, perhaps also to Anatolians and Syrians, as long as it did not get into the hands of other Mesopotamian traders. Hence, the verdict, which might be taken as a binding rule, a new law, had to be revoked.

B. The Legislative Procedure

The letter analyzed above[54] is also interesting because of the light its sheds on the legislative procedure. It distinguishes clearly between three different terms and perhaps stages in the decision making process. The first is a verdict (*dīnum*) by the City Assembly, a decision in a particular case with a specific impact. The next seems to be fixing a rule (*iṣurtam eṣārum*), which could imply that the *ad hoc* decision results in a rule with a more lasting and general effect. Then, the third stage seems to be a rule (*awātum*), which was or could be inscribed on a stele. The letter wants to make it clear that the second and third stages have not been reached. Old Assyrian letters and judicial documents mention many verdicts by the City Assembly, without, however, implying that these had or would acquire the status of a rule; they were concrete decisions settling conflicts or problems. That our letter deems it necessary to deny that a new rule had been fixed seems to indicate that the verdict in question was one of a more general nature, with wider implications. The verdict might come to serve as a normative precedent, which would then determine the freedom of action as to future transactions in gold in Anatolia. The city, however, wanted to avoid such a result.

Indeed, there are a few examples of verdicts which result in more general prohibitions or injunctions, as the one quoted above in note 22. Apparently, a verdict in a specific case, such as those concerning smuggling and the trade in Anatolian textiles, mentioned above, which did or could affect many traders and even the trade as such, might acquire the status of a binding rule. In both cases, the texts do not use the word "verdict", but *awātum*, "order, ukase". It is said to be "strong, binding" (*dannum*) and will overpower, "catch" (*kašādum*) whoever violates it.[55]

The term *awātum*, when used in the plural (lit. "words"), has various meanings in Akkadian. It can simply denote an order, an instruction. In the contexts we are interested in, however, when the **[1736]** reference is to a legal text inscribed on the stele, it can translate to "rule, stipulation", and this same meaning imposes itself in a few other texts as well. In paragraph II A I already mentioned the existence of a fixed rate of interest "in accordance with the rule (*awātum*) of the *kārum*," which supposes a decision with normative force. In note 25 I quoted a letter that reminds its addressee of the rule about collecting debts in Anatolia or Assur by asking him: "Don't you know the rule of the City?". A further, rather difficult example is in the letter KTS 11:26ff.: "Whoever withdraws for the

---

52 See Çeçen and Hecker, *op. cit.* (note 7).

53 Many texts speak of "gold for the caravan to the City", which in the light of this verdict may well refer to the rule or obligation to send all gold to Assur. In Assur the highly valued gold (eight times the value of silver) seems to have been hoarded. Whenever a caravan with a mixed load of silver and gold arrived in Assur, the gold was first converted into silver, which was the only "money" used to make purchases for equipping a new caravan. Gold hence did not enter the normal commercial circulation in Assur, apparently as a result of a clear policy as our letter shows.

54 See above note 49.

55 [See above, notes 45 and 46].

settlement will pay the debt of the colony in silver."[56] This rule has to do with the privilege that members of the *kārum* organization (who pay to it a substantial contribution, called *dātum*) do not have to pay single debts incurred, but can postpone payment until the periodic general settlement of accounts, when also book transfers could be made. It stipulates, as a normative ruling with important implications, that who does not lived up to the obligation this privilege entails incurs a heavy fine. A final example is found in the letter CCT 4, 27a, which deals with trade in copper. Some Assyrian traders used to buy copper of poor quality, which they then shipped to the city of Durhumit, the centre of the copper trade, in order to convert it there into "good" copper. The letter states in lines 26f.: "The rule of the *kārum* is: You shall not bring it into the city!" This probably was a decree meant to check or regulate the copper trade there.[56a]

It seems clear that such "words of the City" had a wide impact and general validity and hence can be defined as rules. This use of *awātum*, however, is not limited to the Old Assyrian period. In principle any "word" or "order" of a Mesopotamian king that had binding force for the future was a "rule". A very specific example of such rules are the decrees issued from time to time by kings of the Old Babylonian period, whereby certain debts and arrears were remitted in order to restore equity. The current name for such decrees is *ṣimdat šarrim*, "royal edict", but in a particular period and area (the kingdom of Larsa, under Rim-Sîn) the term *awāt šarrim* was also used.[57] Some of these decrees have come down to us in written form and it seems likely that also those of king Rim-Sîn were published in writing, although neither *ṣimdatum* nor *awātum* as such implies promulgation in written form.[57a] Similarly, it remains possible that the Old Assyrian rules designated as *awātum* had been written down on a tablet in order to make them known also in Anatolia or on a stele in the City as **[1737]** an act of publicity. We simply do not know whether engraving them on a stela required a separate decision – by what other institution than the City Assembly? – or whether, to use the terms of the letter discussed in the previous paragraph, "fixing a rule" already implied that it would be engraved on the stele.[58] If the latter were the case, we can understand the necessity of a very formal cancellation of the verdict, which otherwise would have become written law.

IV. THE NATURE OF OLD ASSYRIAN LAW

It is risky, with only a few short quotations and references, to speculate on the nature of Old Assyrian law, written on a stele we do not know. Moreover, our sources, commercial documents from Kanesh, may well offer a biased picture by referring only to stipulations affecting the trade. Provisions on other subjects so common in Mesopotamian laws, such as the family, agriculture and husbandry, bodily injury etc., when covered at all, had little chance of emerging in texts from Kanesh, although we do have a few contracts of

---

56 *i-na a-w[a-a]t a-lim*[ki] *ša a-[na]* [27] *ni-[kà]-sí i-ša-hu-ṭù-ni* [28] *hu-bu-lam ša kà-ri-im* KÙ. BABBAR[!] [29] *i-ša-qal* [I now follow the translation by J.G. Dercksen, *Old Assyrian Institutions* (Leiden 2004) 209, who restored KÙ.BABBAR and *i-ša-qal* (omitted in the copy) on the basis of collation. This translation leads to a different interpretation of the ukase of the City, which made me adapt my comment on it].

[56a See for this letter now J.G. Dercksen, *The Old Assyrian Copper Trade in Anatolia* (Istanbul 1996) 128 with note 401. He considers it a decree issued "in order to prevent a saturation of the local market with copper, or to avoid competition with Anatolian merchants on this point". He also notes that lines 30-31 of this letter show that Assyrian traders dodged this prohibition]

57 See for these decrees F.R. Kraus, *Königliche Verfügungen in altbabylonischer Zeit* (Leiden 1984) and p. 33ff. for the use of *awāt šarrim* alongside *ṣimdat šarrim*. The only reference to *awāt ālim*, "a ruling of the City", is in an unpublished early Old Babylonian record from the time of king Immerum of Sippar. It deals with the redemption of a field and house ordered by the king, *warki awāt ālim* (BM 97141 [published in K.R. Veenhof, "Redemption of Houses in Assur and Sippar", in: B. Böck *et al.* (eds.), *Munuscula Mesopotamica. Festschrift für Johannes Renger* (*AOAT* 267, Münster 1999) 599-516 = pp. 211-223 in this volume].

[57a See now K.R. Veenhof, The Relation Between Royal Decrees and 'Law Codes' in the Old Babylonian Period, *Jaarbericht Ex Oriente Lux* 35-36 (2001) 49-83 = pp. 297-328 in this volume].

58 In the article mentioned in note 50 I have tried to show that the words *iṣurtum* and *eṣārum*, notwithstanding their etymology ("to draw lines"), do not mean engraving a written text.

marriage, divorce, adoption and division of inheritance, and even a few verdicts dealing with such matters.[59]

A. Form

As to the form of the laws, the impression is one of short, concise provisions, similar to a number of verdicts, as the ones published in *EL* nos. 273ff. There is a marked difference with the frequently long, very detailed provisions of the Middle Assyrian Laws, which intend to cover a subject completely by mentioning details and variations. Our limited data make it impossible to establish whether particular subjects, for example liabilities and debts, were treated in a series of paragraphs, a "chapter". Such "chapters", as we know them from other law collections, seem to be the result of systematic, scholarly occupation with the law, which attempts to cover a subject by means of a representative and instructive selection of rules arranged according to redactional principles, drawing on tradition, precedent, theory and perhaps reforms. We note that the so-called "Statutes of the Kanesh Colony" (see note 6) show that fairly long and detailed regulations were not unknown. But we do not even know whether the various references to "the stele" are all to one single monument.

[1738] As of yet there is no clear proof of provisions of a casuistic nature, that is starting with a conditional sentence introduced by "if" (*šumma*), which are ubiquitous in Hammurabi's Laws. A conditional formulation is attested in a few verdicts (*e.g. EL* no. 283), usually representing the first stage of a lawsuit, when, due to the complexity of the issue and the unavailability of some data (witnesses and written proof could be in Assur or elsewhere in Anatolia) preliminary verdicts were inevitable.[60] The verdict quoted in note 22 uses conditional *šumma* twice, not as simple conditions, but to introduce two alternatives. This is also the case in the verdict quoted in Kt c/k 440:56-60 (unpubl., courtesy J.G. Dercksen): "The *kārum* passed the following verdict: A. son of K. shall go the city S. (and) in accordance with the tablet of Ṣ. (his creditor), if there is an agent who will pay the silver, he can leave, if there is none, he will be held (as pledge) by Ṣ." Most verdicts, however, are straightforward and apodictic (cf. *EL* nos. 273-76) and use the indicative in the present tense (negated in a prohibition) and this is also the case in the verdicts which refer to the stele or to a "rule of the City", quoted in notes 25, 33, 49, and 56. Also, it is important to note that the generalizing "whosoever" and "anybody" in the text quoted in note 49, which is also used in *EL* no. 273, resembles the style of a proclamation, not that of casuistic law.[61]

The subject of the action prescribed by the law is either a particular category of persons mentioned by name ("the creditors", note 34, "Assyrians", note 49) or is introduced by the relative pronoun "who" (*ša*), which can also be impersonal, followed by a passive verbal form (the rule quoted in note 25). This so-called "relative formulation" gives the provision a general validity and it has been associated with public proclamations.[62] The prohibition formulated in the law quoted in note 49 is followed by a sanction against who ignores or transgresses it, again in the relative formulation ("who does..."), as is the case in some verdicts with a general impact (*e.g. EL* no. 273). We also meet this feature in the rule stating that, whoever took assets of a dead trader shall return them: "Who does not return them shall be considered a thief".[63] The sanction of the law quoted in note 49 is the death penalty: "He shall not stay alive", which makes the breaking of this law a capital

---

59 *EL* nos. 275 and 276; KTS II no. 60.

60 *EL* speaks of "prozessführende und einstweilige Anordnungen" and see also *OACC* 328ff.

61 [Above (§ B.1) we observed that there is no convincing evidence that the conditional protasis of the verdict quoted in note 22, "If he has promised silver", was part of the rule quoted from the stele].

62 See R. Yaron, *The Laws of Eshnunna* (Jerusalem-Leiden 1988) 109f.

63 See above, note 28.

crime. This is a formulation attested in and outside legal texts,[64] whose meaning is not quite clear. It perhaps stresses the inescapability of the sanction, more than the factual "he shall be killed", which is common in the Laws of Hammurabi. The combination of a prohibition and a sanction for ignoring it (which gives "teeth" to the law), of the type: "He shall not ..., who does... shall...", is typical for the Old Babylonian royal decrees mentioned above (note 57). Ammi-ṣaduqa's edict,[65] § 4, which deals with the untimely collection of debts in violation of the royal decree, contains the following prohibition: "He shall not collect, who did collect shall give back, who does not give back shall die".[66] Style and content of this sanction are indeed very similar to the Old Assyrian law, even though the latter's purpose (commercial protectionism) is quite different.

B. Content

The data we have indicate that the laws deal with essential, and probably frequent issues and problems connected with the trade: when compound interest can be charged, how and where debts can be collected and investments recovered – presumably when a merchant had died – when and perhaps which compensation for losses incurred by a caravan is due, and which rules obtain for settling accounts with the *kārum* (if we may consider the rule quoted in note 56 as referring to a law). Only the law about the prohibition on the trade in gold is quite different. Although is was very important for the practice for the trade, it reflected the interests of the Assyrian "state" more than the wish and need to resolve juridical problems raised by the trade. The very fact that most of these "laws" are referred to or quoted in verdicts of the City Assembly shows that they were not traditional or learned provisions collected in a legal handbook, but legal rules of great practical importance, imposed with authority and applied by courts of law. It seems likely that they went back to earlier verdicts of the City Assembly, which somehow – automatically, if the verdict established an important rule of general validity, or later, when a verdict with the value of a precedent was raised to the status of law by a separate decision – had become rules of law. This would make them rather different from provisions in Old **[1740]** Babylonian laws, which seem to have incorporated not only precedents and earlier decrees, but also older legal traditions, scholarly paradigms and ideals of equity and righteousness, which were the king's responsibility. Instead, Old Assyrian law seems to reflect the needs and problems of contemporary trade. This link with reality must also be due to the identity of the lawgiver, not the king and his scholars, but the City Assembly, in which the merchant class itself was represented and of course vitally interested in passing verdicts and drafting rules for maintaining justice among its members. Hence, the rules were practical and sober, devoid of legal argument and scholarly refinement. The role of the City in this legislative process cannot fail to evoke comparison with the origin and function of law in the Greeks cities, but I cannot dwell on this aspect.

Not all juridical problems created by the sophisticated trade of course could be dealt with in the law, and many were resolved by verdicts of the courts of law in Assur and Kanesh. This situation made judicial procedure important, as these verdicts show, especially the provisional ones referred to in note 60. This also explains the value attached to testimony and proof, as is clear from many judicial records and depositions and from the phrase "when it is confirmed by witnesses", twice quoted as written on the stele.[67] The same concern is observable in the inscription of king Irishum (of which two copies were

64 See Yaron, *op.cit.*, 259f. (in the Laws of Eshnunna: "He shall die, he shall not stay alive"); see also ARM 2, 92:19 and ARM 5,72:5 for "not staying alive". [See now also *Kültepe Tabletleri* VIa, 115:45, quoted in the addendum to the introduction of § II].

65 Edited in Kraus *op. cit.* (see note 57), 170f. with the commentary on 201f.

66 Similarly, but shorter in § 6 of Ammi-ṣaduqa's edict. The key phrase, "who did collect shall give back", is actually quoted in the OB letter NBC 6311:17-18, edited by O. Tammuz, *RA* 90 (1006) 125.

67 See above notes 22 and 34.

found in Kanesh), which pays ample attention to testimony, oath and procedure, also by assigning an attorney to a plaintiff.[68] That a particular oath formula had been inscribed and perhaps prescribed on the (a) stele,[69] may reflect the same concern for procedure.

Unfortunately the references provide only limited information on the substance of law inscribed on the stele. While the verdict quoted in note 49 seems to quote a complete(?) law, those quoted in notes 22 and 34 at best give part of a ruling. This is, perhaps, as the text quoted in note 25 suggests, because such rules were supposed to be generally known, so that a simple reference or partial quotation would do. The reference told those concerned that the highest legal authority had concluded that the case in question came under a particular rule of law, which was known. Hence, the verdict itself could be very short. The reference to the stele may also have **[1741]** served to remind parties that the only option now was "to submit" (*šuka'unum*), as several people engaged in legal conflicts state they will do, when confronted with a tablet or verdict of the City and the ruler.

V. OLD ASSYRIAN AND OLD BABYLONIAN DATA COMPARED

A. Decrees and Laws

Here a comparison with a special category of Old Babylonian decrees is in order, not those of debt release, mentioned earlier,[70] but decrees (also called *ṣimdat šarrim*) that fix liabilities and penalties in connection with various contractual arrangements. These decrees themselves have not (yet) been discovered, but we know them thanks to usually short references in a variety of contracts, many of which have been discussed by Kraus [and later by the present writer].[71] They often use the words "in accordance with the decree of the king" (*kīma ṣimdat šarrim*) [and some simply state: "the royal decree" (scil. is applicable)], and occasionally a noun following *ṣimdat* designates the (trans)action to which the decree applies. The clause is frequent in contracts by means of which harvesters are hired in advance, with prepayment of part of their wages, where we read: "If they do not come (or: if a middleman does not supply them) according to the royal decree". We also meet it in slave sale contracts: "He (the seller) is responsible for claims in accordance with the royal decree". These references, though stipulating a liability, usually do not tell us what it consisted of and what compensation or penalty had been fixed. If a slave that had been sold was claimed, the seller probably had to vindicate the sale or supply a substitute. What was in store for the defaulting harvester is not immediately clear, but one could envisage providing a substitute, a fine or a compensation for the loss of the harvest. In connection with slave sale, however, we also have contracts where the liability of the seller is spelled out in combination with a reference to the royal decree. They state that the seller had to meet claims resulting from an investigation of the slave's legal status within three days, from the slave falling ill of epilepsy within one month, and from eviction by his former owner, with no time limit.[72]

These royal decrees served a practical purpose. They fix, with royal authority, liabilities, compensations and penalties for apparently frequent legal cases. By referring to them in contracts the parties, who must have known what the decree stipulated, were warned in advance what to expect if they defaulted, while the plaintiff was saved the trouble of a perhaps time consuming lawsuit (*e.g.* when the harvest was waiting on **[1742]**

---

68 See for the inscription, above, note 11, and for the attorney *OACC* 184ff.

69 See above, the introduction to § II.

70 See above, the end of § III, B.

71 F. R. Kraus, *Revue d'Assyriologie* 73 (1979) 51-62 and *Königliche Verfügungen* (see note 57) 8ff. [See now the article of the present writer mentioned in note 57a, to which the reader is referred for details and references to the texts. This study made me reconsider some points raised in the present article and resulted in some corrections and new formulations in what follows, which are not always marked as such].

72 See M. Stol, *Epilepsy in Babylonia* (Cuneiform Monographs 2, Groningen 1993) 133ff. [and now the article mentioned in footnote 57a, § 6, b, for more details].

the fields) and could realize his claim without problems.[73] The only task of the judges, if appealed to, was to ascertain that the complaint fell under the royal decree in question (which in such standard cases may have been self evident). And this, to all appearances, also was what the City Assembly in Assur did in cases where contracts or verdicts referred to "the words of the stele" (with an added condition of proof by testimony, because the cases were much more complicated).

While such legal rules became statutory law in early Assur, to which verdicts and letters refer as "the words of the law (stele)", Old Babylonian verdicts and contracts never do so, but they do refer to "royal decrees". We can distinguish two categories of references, a) those unknown from the law collections, and b) those whose subject matter is somehow reflected or incorporated in the laws. In addition law collections themselves contain a few references to such royal decrees.

To the first category belongs among others a decree on unfounded claims (*baqrū*). Such claims, especially those on property, are regularly forbidden in contracts of conveyance, which may also impose sanctions on. There is even a verdict that threatens a plaintiff with "the penalty for who raises a (groundless) claim", if he tries again, which suggests the existence of a generally known penalty for such a misdeed, most probably a monetary fine or perhaps (for recidivists?) a degrading, public corporal punishment[74]. It may have been rooted in customary law and (subsequently?) have been fixed by a royal decree, but it is not reflected in the law collections, which do not contain general rules on this subject. To the second category of decrees, whose subject matter is found in the law collections, belong the one on defaulting harvesters and the one dealing with slave sale. The former finds a very good parallel in § 9 the Laws of Eshnunna, and for the latter we may consult §§ 278-281 of the Laws of Hammurabi, which give rules on liability and guarantee in connection with the sale of a slave, which clearly link up with what slave sale contracts stipulate on such matters "in accordance with the royal decree".

A reference to a royal decree is found in § 58 of the Laws of Eshnunna, in the case of a man's son killed by the collapse of a wall of a house which had been neglected by its owner: "(It is) a capital case, (subject to) the royal decree".[75] This most probably does not mean that it is a case of "royal jurisdiction" (this is expressed in § 48 of the same laws by the words "it goes to the king"), but rather, in line with the basic meaning of *ṣimdatum*, that there was a decree, unknown to us, which dealt with the liability in case of homicide. Two references to "royal decrees" are found in the Laws of Hammurabi, in § 51 and § u. They deal with debtors unable to pay back in silver, who are allowed (§ 51) to do so in barley or sesame, "according to their market value, in accordance with the royal decree", and stipulate (§ u) that if the debtor has no silver, creditor shall accept barley and at an interest in barley at a rate of 20% (which is lower than the usual rate for barley and equals that for silver) "in accordance with the royal decree".[76] Both paragraphs probably refer to elements of a decree on various aspects of the payment of debts, meant to protect a weak debtor. While the paragraphs that contain these references themselves are not the "royal decree', they may incorporate elements of an existing, earlier decree and it

---

73 Kraus, *op. cit.* (note 71) 59: "ein Verfahren mit für die Parteien verbindlichem Urteil, das rechtskräftig und unmittelbar zu volziehen ist".

74 See for the evidence and its interpretation E. Dombradi, *Die Darstellung des Rechtsaustrags in den altbabylonischen Prozessurkunden*, I (Stuttgart 1996) 345ff., §§ 459-465 [and for the decree my article mentioned in note 57a, § 5, c; the text mentioning "the penalty for who raises a (groundless) claim" *(arān bāqirānim)* is VS 7, 152, from Hammurabi 12th year].

75 See for the text and its interpretation, Yaron, *Laws of Eshnunna* (see note 73) 121ff. and also S. Lafont, *Revue historique de droit français et étranger* 73 (1995) 500.

76 The text of § t is difficult and the reconstruction found in *LCMA* 97f., based on two damaged sources which offer variants, is not convincing. [I refer for details to my new restoration and interpretation of these laws in: K.R. Veenhof, The Interpretation of Paragraphs t and u of the Code of Hammurabi, in: Ş. Dönmez (ed.), *DUB.SAR É.DUB.BA.A. Studies Presented in Honour of Veysel Donbaz* (Istanbul 2010) 283-294 = pp. 285-296 in this volume].

is not impossible that more rulings in the laws are based on decrees. It is, however, not easy to identify such an "incorporation", because the ruling will have been recast in the traditional casuistic style that dominates law collections, which obscures its origin. It can in some cases be deduced from its subject matter and becomes likely if contemporary contracts reveal that it is akin to an issue covered by a decree, *e.g.* the one on guarantee in the case of slave sale or consignments. But, as pointed out in the study mentioned in note 57a, a decree can also be younger than the law collection, if the references to it are only found in contracts that are later than the laws and a decree thus appears to have been issued to supplement the law. Such new decrees must have met a practical need, because they provided the people involved in such transactions clarity about their rights and obligations and made the administration of justice easier.

B. Quotations from Decrees and Laws

This issue has some relevance, because one always has been struck by the fact that none of the thousands of contracts and especially verdicts known from the Old Babylonian period ever refers to or quotes Hammurabi's Laws, at least not *verbatim*. The fact that, as we have seen, Old Assyrian laws are quoted or referred to in official verdicts and letters makes this silence all the more remarkable. Various explanations have been given for this fact. Old Babylonian judges would not have been accustomed to refer to the laws and in general would not have argued for their sentences, at least not in verdicts and protocols of lawsuits. Moreover, Hammurabi's Laws would not have possessed the status of statutory law and hence would not have been referred to as authoritative and enforceable.[77]

The observations made above on the links between royal decrees and laws shows that the explanation is not as simple as that, because, as we have seen, several royal decrees are referred to and quoted in contemporary contracts and letters and some were apparently incorporated in or had precursors in law collections. The Old Assyrian evidence shows that it is too simple to explain the absence of explicit references to the law collections in Old Babylonian verdicts from judicial or contractual practice or principles, for verdicts of the City Assembly and the ruler of Assur did refer to and quoted "words written on the stele". It is more likely to explain it from the nature of these collections. Being a mixture of traditional lore, scholarly legal wisdom, royal ideology, exemplary verdicts and authoritative decrees, with a preference for rather specific and often difficult cases, the possibilities of using and referring to them in concrete cases must have been limited. Some royal rulings that were of practical importance for drawing up contractual agreements apparently were better known and more readily available in the form of specific royal decrees, which therefore were quoted and referred to. The absence of an updated or revised collection of laws by one of Hammurabi's successors also was a factor. In the later Old Babylonian period his learned collection was still copied (and studied) in the schools, but it seems that in the judicial practice royal decrees played a much more important role. Such decrees, which owed their existence to practical needs and probably to royal verdicts, make the best comparison with the rulings of Old Assyrian statutory law, inscribed on a stele, quoted in verdicts and letters, and presumably based on important decisions and verdicts of the City Assembly and the ruler. This origin, their close link with the practice of the trade and the needs of the society, and hence their applicability in concrete cases, easily explain their reflection in documents of legal practice such as verdicts, contracts and letters.

---

77 See for the discussion and the arguments R. Westbrook, *Zeitschrift für Assyriologie* 79 (1989) 201-22; W.F. Leemans, *Bibliotheca Orientalis* 48 (1991) 414-20; and J. Renger, in: H.J. Gehrke (ed.), *Rechtskodifizierung und soziale Normen im interkulturellen Vergleich* (Tübingen 1995) 27-58.

Trade and Politics in Ancient Assur Balancing of Public, Colonial and Entrepreneurial Interests*

1. Assur and its trade

Assur of the first centuries of the 2nd mill. B.C. was a well developed and prosperous city-state, located on the west bank of the Tigris, ca. 100 kms. south of Mosul. The city is built on a natural and well defensible eminence at the junction of two branches of the Tigris, "where the valley broadens to a bowl some 5 kms. in diameter, affording an expanse of alluvial land which can be profitably cultivated by irrigation".[1] It was strategically located, overlooking the Tigris, at a point where the valley road from the south, after skirting the foot of the western mountain range of the Jebel Makhlul,[2] turns back to the Tigris. Here caravan routes from east to west and south to north met. The area was easily accessible, both for Bedouins from the western steppe (via the Wadi Tarthar) and for people from the eastern foothills, who came to visit the ancient sanctuaries of the gods Assur and Ištar, to trade and barter, or with less peaceful intentions, attracted by the riches of the city. Archaeological remains and ancient texts[3] show that its rulers paid great attention to keeping the city's fortifications in good **[70]** shape and even the colonies in Anatolia had to contribute in the costs of the work on the city-wall.[4]

The old, triangular city, later known as "Inner City" (*libb'ālim*),[5] which rises ca. 40 m. above the alluvial plain, covered an area of ca. 40 hectares. Its build up during the Old Assyrian period is not well known, because the German excavations did not reach the residential quarters of the early periods. Of the upper city of before ca. 1800 B.C., its temples, palace, and the important "Stepgate", behind the Assur temple, only scanty architectural remains, mostly foundations, survive. What is usually called the "Ancient Palace" seems to date from the time of Šamšī-Adad I (ca. 1800 B.C).[6] The usually shown ground plan of the Assur temple seems to go back to Šamšī-Adad I, although it seems clear that the older temple, built a century and a half earlier, by Erišum I, "had basically the same form as it had from Šamšī-Adad I onwards, though its orientation was somewhat different."[7]

Irrigation agriculture in the nearby basin, rain-fed crops in good years, and husbandry (also in the western steppe) could supply what was needed for the city's subsistence, but

* Originally published in: C. Zaccagnini (ed.), Mercanti e politica nel mondo antico. Saggi di Storia Antica 21. Roma: «L'Erma» di Bretschneider, 2003. Additions to the original texts are references to new literature (see the bibliography at the end) and to recently published texts. Note in particular three general, informative books, which contain good bibliographies: Dercksen 2004, Larsen 2015 and Veenhof 2008.

1 D. Oates, *Studies in the Ancient History of Northern Iraq*, London 1968, p. 19.

2 The north-western continuation, on the right bank of the Tigris, of the Jebel Hamrin, which the ancient Assyrians themselves called Mount Abeḫ.

3 As revealed by a few original inscriptions (of Ilušuma and Erišum) and by several references in those of later builders mentioning work by early predecessors, see Larsen 1976, 34ff.

4 Contribution "imposed by the City", according to TC 1, 1, analysed by Larsen 1976, 163.

5 The southern "new city" was added later.

6 As shown by P.A. Miglius, "Untersuchungen zum Alten Palast in Assur" in *MDOG* 121 (1989), pp. 93-133, which confirms the conclusions reached earlier by J. Margueron. Of the still older palace, very little has been found.

7 See G. van Driel, *The Cult of Aššur*, Assen 1969, p. 9.

are unlikely to have been sufficient to generate the kind of surpluses which Babylonian cities could use for trade and barter. It is generally assumed that Assur's prosperity was due to its cultic importance, with its temples of Ištar and of Assur, originally presumably the local mountain god,[8] and to its strategic location and commercial role. The first is an assumption based on the conviction that important shrines by their cults, festivals, personnel, endowments and regional pilgrimage generate income, and it finds confirmation in the importance of the Assur temple in Old Assyrian society, also as recipient of many votive gifts and as investor in the trade. The second is based on the written **[71]** evidence on Old Assyrian trade discovered in the main Assyrian trading colony in Central Anatolia, in the lower town of ancient Kaniš.

As far as our evidence goes, of the articles traded only part of the woollen textiles were produced in the city, presumably by an efficient home industry, since there is no evidence at all for workshops of palace or temple. Tin was imported into Assur from Iran and many expensive woollen textiles from Babylonia. Both were bought by Assyrian traders who exported them en masse by donkey caravans to Anatolia, where they were sold directly or indirectly (via trade in copper and local wool) with profit for much silver (hundreds of kilograms each year) and less gold, which were the only articles shipped back to Assur. Silver invested in Assur via the Anatolian trade was converted into more silver, which as preferred means of payment and commercial exchange kept the flow of goods going and supplied the traders with the means for their business and for meeting their needs. Tin to all appearances was not imported into Assur by the Assyrians themselves, but brought there by foreign traders, presumably by Elamites from Iran.[9] Many woollen textiles were imported by what the texts call "Akkadians",[10] which means traders from Babylonia proper and presumably also from the Diyala region, the kingdom of Ešnunna. Babylonians probably also supplied the copper (originating from Oman and bought in Bahrain/Tilmun) which Assur needed but was not imported from Anatolia.[11] The great supply of silver and to some extent presumably also of gold (see § 4.3.3) available in Assur **[72]** must have attracted foreign traders and allowed the Assyrians to acquire rather easily what they needed for their city and for export to Anatolia.[12]

What Assur itself produced for the trade were locally made woollen textiles and the harness of the donkeys, while also the caravan donkeys themselves must have been raised and trained in the vicinity of the city.[13] Basically, however, Assur was not so much a producer city as a central place and port of trade, where caravans from south and east met and goods (merchandise and "money") changed hands under Assyrian supervision and with the use of their facilities. The trade links with Anatolia, which resulted in massive exports and imports, had turned the city into an important exchange market in

---

8 See W.G. Lambert, in *Iraq* 45 (9183) pp. 85ff and Veenhof, *Studies N. Özgüç*, p. 652 with n. 27 and pl. 124, fig. 3.

9 Its import in Assur is hardly ever mentioned in the thousands of trade texts, we only read that at times tin was not available, in short supply, or expected to arrive by caravan. Only the letters AKT 3, 73 and 74 (see below § 4.3.1) mention the (delayed) arrival of caravans with tin from the "country below".

10 According to the *locus classicus* VS 26, 17: 7ff.: "Since you left (the) Akkadians have not entered the city (of Assur), because their country is in revolt. When they arrive before the winter ... we will buy (Akkadian textiles) for you"; see Veenhof 1972, 98ff.

11 Understandable in view of its price in Anatolia (silver : copper = 60-100 : 1) and the cost of transport by donkey caravan to Assur (the value in silver of a donkey load of copper was only a little more than the price of the donkey plus the costs of the journey). In Babylonia "Persian Gulf copper" was cheaper (silver : copper, ca. 200-250 : 1) and could be shipped by boat, while sale prices in Assur were higher, ranging around 90-100 : 1 (see Dercksen 1996, 159).

12 The "caravan documents" always simply state that tin and textiles were bought for silver, but it is not clear whether or to what extent the "Kaniš traders" bought them directly from the foreign importers. Purchases were regularly made in "houses", apparently a kind of warehouses of Assyrian firms, but we have no evidence on how their owners acquired the merchandise. Anyhow, import of textiles and copper in Assur may have been a means of acquiring silver for Babylonians.

13 Since for the shipment of silver and gold back to Assur only few donkeys were needed, most of these expensive, trained animals (price ca. 20 shekels of silver) were sold in Anatolia, so that every new caravan needed new ones.

an international trading network,[14] where supply and demand met. Here the Assyrian traders could buy what they exported to Anatolia at a profitable rate of exchange for silver acquired 'cheaply' in Anatolia, which allowed net profits of at least fifty percent or more. It made Assur a rich and prosperous city.

Many people and institutions in Assur took part in and profited from the commerce, not only the traders and their families. The rulers and their sons (some of which were occasionally also active in Anatolia) also bought merchandise for export and sold it by means of their own agents, at times with the help of experienced traders.[15] The temples, which received many votive gifts in silver and gold, invested in the trade by entrusting at times **[73]** substantial amounts[16] to traders, who could manage them for several years before eventually settling accounts, which no doubt entailed a way of sharing profits. Some priests are involved in the business, occasionally perhaps even as wholesale dealers. One main administrator (*sangûm*) of a temple figures as year-eponym (no. 91) and hence as administrative head of the "City-house", and according to a letter purchases could be made in the house of a priest (*kumrum*) of the moon god.[17] Some kind of involvement of the temples is perhaps also implied by the fact that many daughters of successful traders, who received donations from their fathers[18] and were entitled to a full share in their inheritance, were priestesses.[19] Many other inhabitants of Assur had economic links with the trade, both as employees, transporters and messengers, and as craftsmen who produced and supplied what was needed for the caravans.

2. The institutional structures of ancient Assur

The institutional structures of Assur were rather different from those of contemporary Babylonia and the preceding Ur III empire. Three institutions dominate the political scene of ancient Assur: the ruler (*rubā'um*), the city (*ālum*), and the *līmum*, an **[74]** annually elected official who was the head of the "City-house" or "*līmum*-house", after whose turn of office records were dated, which has earned him the title "eponym". Larsen has provided the generally accepted picture of the power structure in Assur.[20]

The chief magistrate was the ruler, designated as ensi / *iššiakkum* on his official seal, the divinely appointed "steward" of the city-god Assur, for whom the title "king" was reserved. He was the *primus inter pares* (called *rubā'um*, "the big one") and "chief", "overseer" (*waklum*) of the community; Assyrian citizens refer to him as "my lord" (*bēlī*). In judicial, and presumably also other administrative matters, there was such a close cooperation between ruler and City that the two functioned as one institution.

---

14 See M.T. Larsen, "Commercial Networks in the Ancient Near East", in M. Rowlands et al. (eds.), *Centre and Periphery in the Ancient World*, Cambridge 1987, pp. 47-56.

15 The evidence is contained in private letters of the rulers, discussed in Larsen 1976, 132ff.; see for evidence on rulers and princes now Veenhof 2003, ch. 6, "The Rulers of Assur".

16 We do not know whether what the temples contributed – called *ikribū*; see for a full analysis J.G. Dercksen, "The Silver of the Gods. On Old Assyrian *ikribū*", in *ArAnat* 3 (1997), pp. 75-100 – was primarily capital or/and also merchandise, in particular textiles, perhaps even those produced in temple workshops, since we have no documents which record how *ikribū* were first entrusted to traders. One would not expect Assyrian temples to give silver to traders for buying merchandise in Assur; they may have supplied them indirectly via warehouses or with their own production, hence presumably textiles. *ikribū* were put at the disposal of traders for several years and when texts mention them we meet merchandise (textiles, tin and copper) as well as gold and silver, the latter usually to indicate their value or when they were shipped back to Assur as the proceeds from the sale of *ikribū*-merchandise.

17 See below n. 48.

18 The well known trader Pūšu-kēn in CCT 5, 43:29' calls his daughter's share of two minas of gold in a commercial enterprise "a donation (*iddinū*) to my daughter".

19 Designated as *ugbabtum* / nin.dingir. Their administrative relation with the temple remains unclear, since all evidence comes from private records, where we meet them as daughters involved in the fortunes of their fathers' households. [See for these women now C. Michel, « Les filles de marchands consacrées», in F. Briquel et al., (eds.), *Femmes, culture et société dans les civilisations méditerranéennes et proches-orientales de l'Antiquité*, Topoi Suppl. 10, pp. 145-163].

20 Larsen 1976, part II, pp.109ff. [and now also Dercksen 2004, and Larsen 2015, part II, "The Home Town"].

The City (Assembly) was the highest judicial authority, which functioned as court of law, but could also take "political" decisions, *e.g.* on the financial contribution the colonies in Anatolia had to make towards the costs of the fortification of the capital,[21] and decisions affecting the trade. The City Assembly could issue "orders" (*awatum*, "word", in the singular), and some "orders" and "verdicts" could acquire a more general validity to become "rulings" (*awātum*, in the plural), which in due course could be drafted and published as laws, written on a stele (*awāt naru'ā'im*).[22] The City exerted its power and influence within the colonial network by means of official, at time circulatory letters, addressed to "every single colony and trading station", which could contain verdicts and decisions, and by means of "Envoys of the City" (*šiprū ša ālim*), who were in particular involved in diplomatic contacts with Anatolian rulers and palaces. We know neither the identity nor the number of the members of the City Assembly, since it figures always as a collective. Presumably its members were the heads of the main families, if we may take the occasionally occurring "Elders" (*šībūtum*), who also pass verdicts, as a synonym. If not, we have to assume a bicameral system, with a large, general Assembly (*puḫrum*) and a smaller executive committee, "the Elders".

[75] We do not know what *līmum* means and the eponymic nature of the function, amply attested in dates, does not help us. Selection by casting lots suggest that it circulated among an unknown number of qualified citizens, probably, as Larsen suggests, as representatives of the main kinship groups in the city.[23] In slightly later texts from Mari the word occurs with the meaning "tribal lineage, clan",[24] and in the new Old Assyrian *līmum*-list we have examples of members of the same family serving as *līmum*, both fathers and sons and brothers, though always at several years distance.[25] The *līmum* was elected for one year as head of the "City-house" or "*līmum*-office", which must have been the main administrative and financial institution of the city. There is some evidence that it[26] was also involved in the trade, collected the export-tax and sold merchandise to "Kaniš traders", perhaps as a public warehouse,[27] managed for the City for periods of one year each by representatives of the main families. As such, it was to some extent comparable to the "houses" of private Assyrian merchants into which "Kaniš traders" would bring their silver to make purchases.

The power of the *līmum* is obvious from the measures he can take to enforce payment (taking pledges, hostages, sealing a debtor's house, selling its contents, and even the house itself) and the fear he can inspire.[28] It is revealing that such **[76]** administrative powers, which in Babylonia would rest with the palace, in Assur are vested in the *līmum*, an elected executive of and backed by the City Assembly, while a palace is completely absent in administrative matters.[29] This is the basis for Larsen's conclusion: "The year-

---

21 See TC 1, 1, and the analysis by Larsen 1976, 170.

22 See Veenhof 1995.

23 Larsen 1976, 371. The fact that once an eponym, presumably because he died early in his year of tenure, was succeeded by his brother, suggests that the function had been assigned to an individual as member of the family; see Veenhof 2003, ch. 5, § 5, [and now also Dercksen 2004, ch. 4].

24 See for published references and meaning J.-M. Durand, in *Studies Garelli*, p. 52f., n. b, and D.E. Fleming, in RA 92 (1998), p. 55f.

25 See Veenhof 2003, ch. 4, § 4.

26 It must have comprised several persons, because the verbal forms of which *līmum* is the subject occasionally are in the plural. There are also a few references to *līmū* with special tasks or areas of competence, e.g. the "barley-*līmum*", perhaps involved in its purchase, storage, and sale.

27 The evidence for its role is rather limited, because the reasons for "debts" owed to the "*līmum* house" are not normally stated, nor where traders bought merchandise for export. [The "City-house" is studied in detail in Dercksen 2004, Part.1, "The City Hall at Assur"].

28 Kt c/k 272: "Nobody is able to stop the *līmum*", in a case where the *līmum* intends to sell a trader's house in order to recover a debt, but is ready to grant still a few months' respite. See for some evidence, Veenhof 1999, esp. pp. 63f. and 80f.

29 There are only two references to a "slave of the palace", which could mean "belonging to the ruler's household".

eponymy may therefore be seen as a kind of counterbalance to the office of the king, and it presumably represented the interests of the main kinship groups among whom the office and its power rotated".[30] The close connection between the administrative role of the *līmum* and the trade is supported by the fact that the new eponym list shows that the office started during the reign of Erišum I (around the middle of the 20th century B.C.), under whom Assyrian trade on and penetration of Anatolia also seem to have started.

There was a close cooperation between City-Assembly and ruler in judicial and other matters. Plaintiffs appealed to "City and Lord" (in that order!) and this resulted in "verdicts and binding tablets of City and Lord", which were communicated to the colonies in official letters, written and sealed by the ruler, which open with the words: "The City (not "we"!) passed the following verdict...". There are only very few letters of the ruler on administrative matters where this is not the case. One deals with judicial procedures, which is perhaps explainable from his divine mandate to promote justice, which is also the topic of an inscription of Erišum.[31] Another, unpublished and heavily damaged (addressed to the "Envoys of the City and *kārum* Kaniš") deals with the problems a caravan had experienced in the city of Zalpa, mentions a decision (*nikištum*) which applies to "the citizens of Assur", and seems to deal (also?) with smuggling. But it is not impossible that such letters too reflect decisions of City Assembly.[31a]

With Larsen, we may assume that the ruler was also closely associated with the temple of the god Assur, whose chief steward he was; later he was given the title **[77]** SANGA, which designates him as its administrative head. The few surviving early royal inscriptions show that he not only built temples and walls and furthered the administration of justice, but probably also took measures to promote Assyrian trade (see below § 4.1). This would fit the ideology of the ruler as the god's steward on earth, appointed to serve the gods and to promote his subjects' welfare in maintaining justice, securing peace, and promoting prosperity.

One may consider this a biased picture, mainly based on predominantly private commercial documents from Anatolia, which, moreover, was an area beyond possible military intervention by Assur and its ruler. But many verdicts and letters found in Kaniš do originate from Assur and it is difficult to assume that autocratic royal activity only by accident is not reflected in the thousands of documents we have. Lack of or limited independent power of the ruler may have been due to his primarily religious and administrative role in conjunction with the City Assembly, and the absence of a strong palace organization, whose place may have been occupied by the City Assembly and the "City house".[32]

3. The city and its traders[32a]

Trade must have been as important for Assur as a whole as its traders were numerous and influential, and this is still clear from somewhat later texts from Mari, where nearly all references to Assyrians concern its traders and caravans.[33] It may be true that in Anatolia Assyrians could simply be designated as "trader',[34] this does not mean that

---

30 Larsen 1976, 371.

31 See for this inscription RIMA 1, p. 20f.

[31a See for all aspects of the jurisdiction in Assur now Th. K. Hertel, *Old Assyrian Legal Procedures. Law and Dispute in the Ancient Near East*, Leiden 2013].

32 In the ca. two hundred years younger treaty between Assur and the city-state of Šeḫna (Tell Leilan), in the Ḫabur-area, published by J. Eidem in *Studies Garelli*, pp. 184-207, the Assyrian party still is not Assur's ruler, but "the City of Assur and the citizens of Assur" (col. I: 26f.) or "the city of Assur and the *kārum*" (*scil.* of Assur in Šeḫna; col. III:4f.).

[32a See now also K.R. Veenhof, "Ancient Assur: The City, its Traders, and its Commercial Network,", *JESHO* 53 (21010) 39-82 = pp. 55-81 in this volume].

33 See the important observations by Charpin and Durand 1997, esp. p. 376f.; ARM XXVI 432 mentions no less than 300 Assyrian traders who are on their way.

34 E.g. in the contract kt n/k 141, where the divorced wife "may go where she prefers, either to a native (*nuā'um* = Anatolian) or to a trader (*tamkārum* = Assyrian)".

the situation was as simple in **[78]** Assur. The city comprised also other population and interest groups, such as the temples with their personnel, the craftsmen, the agricultural and husbandry sector, the military, and those working in the central administration, embodied in the "City office" or "*līmum*-bureau". Moreover, besides the numerous "Kaniš traders" and their families there probably were other merchants, *e.g.* those trading with Babylonia, Assur-based money-lenders or bankers, perhaps identical to the owners of the warehouses where the "Kaniš traders" bought the merchandise for the next caravan. And the interests of the Assyrian trading community in Anatolia, organized in a good dozen of "colonies" (called *kārum*) and roughly the same number of smaller "trading posts" (called *wabartum*), which enjoyed a fair measure of autonomy and were also very active in the inner Anatolian trade in wool, textiles and copper, were not necessarily identical to those of the mother-city.

3.1. The traders

The traders whose archives we have from Kaniš without any doubt were private entrepreneurs, active as Anatolian based "directors" or agents of family firms based in Assur. They worked with their own money and with that supplied by investors (family-members, rich citizens and fellow traders), who invested in the *tractator*'s capital (called "money bag", *naruqqum*).[35] Some temples too entrusted them with merchandise and/or also capital.[36] In addition, the traders also carried out all kinds of short term or *ad hoc* transactions, in commission, for partners, friends and relatives. The possible existence of a kind of licensed merchant-bankers ("intermédiaires agréés"), called *tamkārum*, whose duty it would have been to facilitate transactions by supplying credit, carrying out sales and perhaps even collecting claims, assumed by Garelli and questioned by me,[37] no longer needs to bother us, after **[79]** Garelli himself has revised his opinion.[38] In addition to the actual traders, travelling or working abroad (in my opinion the basic meaning of *tamkārum*), Assur also comprised a kind of "merchant-bankers" (perhaps including wealthy "Kaniš traders", who in old age had returned to Assur), who took part in the trade by investing (in "*naruqqum*-partnerships") and by granting commercial credit or loans. They may well have included the owners of the above mentioned (ware)houses, but we know little about them.[39]

To what extent were these various categories of business-men represented in the City Assembly and in a position to guard and further their interests? Without lists of members of the Assembly (the texts only refer to them collectively as "the City") we can only try to make some general observations. From the thousands of names occurring in the archival texts discovered in Kaniš it is clear that a substantial part of the population of the City was somehow involved in the trade on Anatolia. The main "Kaniš traders", more or less permanently based in Anatolia for many years (examples range from ten to more than thirty years), could not be members of the Assembly. They were the backbone of the colonial community, presumably the so-called "big" members of the *kārum* organization,

---

35 See for the resulting, highly important "*naruqqum*-contracts", which created long-term investment partnerships with a dozen or more "shareholders" and a capital of up to 15 kilograms of gold, M.T. Larsen, "*Naruqqu*-Verträge", in *RlA* 9/3-4 (1999), pp. 181-184 [and Larsen 2015, ch. 17, "Where Did he Money Come from?"].

36 See above, n. 16.

37 Veenhof 1999, 68.

38 P. Garelli, "Le problème du *tamkārum* à l'époque paléo-assyrienne", in *ArAnat* 3 (1997), pp. 125ff.: "J'avais considéré ces derniers comme des agents agréés, ce qui leur conférait un caractère officiel qu'ils n'avaient pas en réalité".

39 While those investing in a trader's *naruqqum*-capital are listed by name in the (few preserved) contracts, those extending commercial credit in other texts remain anonymous, since they only speak of "borrowing silver against interest at a merchant's house". The debt-notes resulting from such transactions of course stayed in Assur. The dozens of debt-notes where the creditor remains anonymous and only figures as *tamkārum* in general are not the result of such commercial loans, but of normal credit sales, where the creditor wishes to remain anonymous, also to make the transfer and collection of his debt by others easy.

which may have served as an executive committee.[40] Their collective interests (I ignore possible individual differences and conflicts of interests) must have been looked after by the *kārum* organization as a kind of chamber of commerce, which as such had contacts with the City Assembly. There are a few occurrences of a body called *nībum* (perhaps "the appointed one"), which **[80]** appears to be the representatives or spokesmen of the Kaniš colony in the capital. One famous letter tells how they pleaded with the Elders of Assur in order to prevent additional costs to be charged to the colonial administration,[41] but for the rest their composition and function remain unclear. In Assur senior relatives and business partners of prominent "Kaniš traders" must have been able to defend and promote the latter's interests in the City Assembly, presumably also the wholesale traders and merchant-bankers, whose business depended on the success of the 'Kaniš-trade'. Some of the "Kaniš traders" had links with the family of the ruler,[42] with a temple, or with the class of people selected to serve as *līmum*-eponyms. The many wealthy citizens of Assur who had made long-term investments (of usually between one and two kilograms of gold) in a *naruqqum*-partnership of a "Kaniš trader" must have been concerned to see his business thrive and profits come in, and hence might be expected not to ignore this in their capacity of members of the City-Assembly.

3.2. The *līmum*-eponyms

The discovery of the Old Assyrian list with the names and patronymics of ca. 130 *līmū* allows us to find out who these persons are, especially those serving during the ca. forty years

(between eponyms 75 and 125),[43] which are the period best documented by the archival records of Kaniš. Among them I can only identify a few traders known to have been living and active in Kaniš. The best example is Innāya, son of Amurrāya, recently studied by Michel,[44] who is attested for **[81]** a period of ca. 25 years. Fifteen years after his first appearance in the records he served as *līmum* in Assur, in the year 102. After that, he moved back to Kaniš, where he served as a week-eponym in the *kārum* administration between the years 104 and 108. A second example is Aššur-malik, son of Alāḫum, attested as week-eponym in Anatolia during the years 99 and 100, eighteen years after his first appearance in the sources, as *līmum* in Assur during the eponymy year 104.[45] There may be a few more examples of traders first working in or serving as week-eponym in Kaniš and later active in the administration of Assur. A small number of year-eponyms, before or after their year of tenure, also occur as witnesses, recipients of payments, occasionally also as investors or associated with large amounts of silver, activities which

40 See for the structure of the *kārum* organization, Larsen 1976, 283ff., ch. 3, "The Government of a Colony". [See also Dercksen 2004, Part 2, "The office of the Colony at Kanish", and Larsen 2015, ch. 12, "The Colonial System", and ch. 13, "The Government of a Colony"]

41 TC 1, 1, see Larsen 1976, 163.; an additional reference in kt a/k 95, whose writer warns against sending the *nībum* away. See also my article mentioned in n. 8, which presents the text of sealed bullae attached to packets sent by the *nībum* in Assur to Kaniš, which carry an impression of the official seal of the "City office" in Assur. Since we do not know the contents and purpose of these shipments, we remain ignorant of the link between the *nībum* and the "City office". [See for the *nībum* now Dercksen, 2004, ch. 4.2].

42 The trader Pūšu-kēn had commercial contacts with the rulers Ikūnum and Sargon, who asked him for help to collect debts from their trading agents.

43 The series of eponyms starts during the first year of Erišum I, ca. 1970 in the middle chronology. The best attested period of the trade starts halfway the reign of Sargon I (ca. 1900 B.C.) and lasts well into the reign of Naram-Suen, whose accession (during eponymy 102) took place in ca. 1870 B.C.

44 See Michel 1991, I: 225-247.

45 Since Aššur-malik is the most common Old Assyrian name, carried by at least 60 different persons, we can only use references which mention his father's name. Aššur-malik and Innāya serving as week-eponyms in the years 92-95 could be identical to our men.

clearly suggest involvement in the colonial trade or even a temporary stay in Anatolia.[46] The argument depends on the identity of the persons involved, which is difficult in the absence of patronyms and with very common names. We may also envisage a situation of senior members of families staying in Assur and serving as eponyms and younger ones active in Anatolia. These observations can be supplemented after the publication of more archives and by prosopographical studies, which with the help of the new eponym list can work out the periods of activity of individual traders.

The general impression is that on the whole only a limited number of year-eponyms at some time were active as colonial traders in Anatolia, but that more of them, especially in later years, in various ways may have participated in the trade and also visited or stayed in Anatolia. That two important "Kaniš **[82]** traders" in rapid succession (in years 102 and 104) did become heads of the "City office" reveals shared interests, administrative know-how and lack of antagonism between City and colonies.[47] On the other hand, a few year-eponyms are given professional designations, such as head of the temple administration (*sangûm*, nr. 91) and "boatman" (*malāḫum*, nr. 105), which shows that they were not professional traders (though also priests did partake in the trade).[48] The designation "the merchant" (*tamkārum*) of the late year-eponym Abu-šalim, son of Ili-ālum (nr. 128), presumably meant to be distinctive and suggests that this profession (by then?) was not normal for eponyms. Eponyms apparently were not normally recruited from the ranks of the important "Kaniš traders", but rather from Assur-based members of the main families, many of which, however, must have included "Kaniš traders" and other merchants. Still, on the assumption that the year-eponyms, as administrative heads of the "City-office", also played a role in the City Assembly, this body, however important trade was for the city as a whole, cannot simply have been a council of traders. It had to balance various interests.

4. Evidence of commercial policy

In this situation Assyrian trade politics should be differentiated for its goals and impact on the trade as a whole, on the Anatolian trade, and on the import trade which brought tin and textiles into the City. And when considering the Anatolian trade we can distinguish political decisions and measures of the City from those taken by the colonial authorities themselves, in the first place *kārum* Kaniš. While we cannot rule out an impact of the City on the activities of individual firms and traders, the "strong tablets" and verdicts of the City generally concern the administration **[83]** of justice in private conflicts (whereby the City and ruler can assign the plaintiff an attorney), not the implementation of a certain policy, unless one prefers to call a concern for honesty, justice and for fair accounting, and hence of smooth business, a political goal.

The evidence to be analysed below can be arranged in two ways, according to the sphere of impact of the policy – import or export trade in Assur, the Anatolian scene in general and specific areas, persons or products, and according to the policy makers – the City Assembly, the City-office, or the colonial administration. In what follows the latter arrangement is more obvious, but within it the substance of the measures taken provide a second organizing principle.

---

46 Ili-bāni son of Ikūnum (eponym 67) in TC 3, 187:7) is registered for 25 pounds of silver in what is called "Pūšu-kēn's lot"; Iddin-Aššur son of Kubidi (eponym 80) occurs in a list (KTS 2, 7:22f.) for an amount of nearly one talent of silver and as witness in Anatolia in I 722:9f. (was his house, mentioned in EL nr. 9, in Kaniš or in Assur?); Ili-ālum son of Sukkalia (eponym 111), according to KTS 2, 9:28ff., in a sealed contract acknowledged the receipt of 8 pounds of silver for 2 pounds of gold, apparently an investment in a commercial capital. See, moreover, the valuable observations in Larsen 1976, 207ff.

47 A potential *līmum* must have lived in Assur, since the election (by casting lots) at the end of the calendar year would have left too little time to inform him and for him to return to Assur to assume his office at the beginning of the new year in late autumn, before the Anatolian winter.

48 According to TC 3, 129:9'ff. a trader made purchases "in the house of the priest of Suen". Could the latter be identical to eponym 106, "Ennam-Suen, son of Šū-Aššur, the priest of Suen"?

4.1. Measures of Assyrian rulers

The vital importance of trade for the city must have implied a policy which tried to protect and promote it. We know nothing of the beginnings of Assyrian trade, which probably had early roots. The earliest written evidence for such a policy probably is contained in the inscription of king Ilušuma, written down only one or two generations after the demise of the centralistic Ur III state, an event which may have stimulated the now independent city and its ruler to stimulate or revive the trade. The part which concerns us here reads:[49]

> I established the *addurārum* of the Akkadians and their sons, I washed their copper, from the border of the marshes(?) and Ur and Nippur, Awal and Kismar, Dēr of the god Ištaran until the City (of Assur) I established their *addurārum*.

This inscription certainly cannot be interpreted as referring to a military campaign, but the difficult key word *addurārum*, which means a return to the original situation, freedom from obligations and servitude,[50] makes it not easy to establish its meaning. After a thorough analysis Larsen concludes that the **[84]** king must have "attempted to attract traders from the south to the market of Assur by giving them certain privileges".[51] The words "I washed their copper" anyhow must refer to the removal of an obstacle, either the cancellation of previous debts[52] ("to wash" is used in Old Assyrian texts for cancelling debts) or the abolition of taxes, and hence better access to the Assyrian market. This fits the fact that Assyrian copper must have been imported from the south and not from Anatolia (see note 11). Now that we know the location of Awal,[53] we can perceive an itinerary for caravans travelling to the south, following a route east of the Tigris, along the foot of the Djebel Hamrin, which crosses the Diyala near Awal and continues in southeasterly direction to Dēr (*Badreh*) and from there in southwesterly direction to Babylonia (Nippur) and beyond, to Ur and the shores of the Persian Gulf. From Dēr other caravans must have continued in southeasterly direction, to arrive at Susa in Elam, which probably was the route along which the tin, originating from Afghanistan, reached Babylonia and Assyria. Its southern part was more or less the same route as the one which in Achaemenid times went from Susa to Arbela.

Ilušuma's measure hence probably stimulated the import of both copper and Akkadian textiles, and indirectly perhaps also of tin (even though Susa and Elam are not mentioned), and so promoted Assur's role as central place and transit market in a commercial network linking south and north.

Further evidence of concern for Assur's commercial role is contained in an inscription of Ilušuma's son Erišum I, where we read:[54]

> When I undertook that work (on the temple of Assur), my city obeyed my orders and I established the *addurārum* of silver, gold, copper, tin, barley, and wool, down to bran and chaff.

The text follows the more traditional pattern of early second **[85]** millennium building inscriptions, with the topos of economic prosperity during the royal builder's reign. While this is usually demonstrated by quoting (too) favourable market prices,[55] Erišum prefers

---

49 RIMA 1, p. 18, lines 49-65.

50 See for *andurārum* most recently D. Charpin, "Les décrets royaux à l'époque paléo-babylonienne", *AfO* 34 (1987), pp. 36-44.

51 Larsen 1976, 63-84. There is an unpublished Old Assyrian text from Kaniš which uses *andurārum* to refer to the cancellation of debts by an Anatolian ruler.

52 Note that the text has "the Akkadians and their sons", hence a reference to more than one generation.

53 Tell Suleimeh, just west of the middle course of the Diyala, in the so-called "Hamrin Area".

54 See RIMA 1, p. 22f., lines 15-25.

55 See for these prices (which he calls "tariffs"), D.C. Snell, *Ledgers and Prices. Early Mesopotamian Merchant Accounts*, New Haven 1982, pp. 204-207.

to boast of free, untaxed and perhaps abundant circulation of all kinds goods. The link with the overland trade is constituted by the fact that this is the only time this topos includes references to *gold* and *tin*, which were so important for Assur.

4.2. Treaties and relations with Anatolian rulers[55a]

Whatever the success of these measures, given the limited size of the city-state (which did not include Ninive, 90 kms. to the north) and the distance between Assur and Anatolia (around 1000 kms.), the city was clearly unable to enforce or support its commercial penetration by military measures, not even to protect its caravans during most of the route leading there. Safe and regular trade hence was based on agreements, treaties (the texts call them "sworn oath", *mamītum*) with the various cities (city-states) passed by the caravans and in particular with those in Anatolia, where the Assyrians traders settled down. Such formal treaties were supplemented by goodwill gifts of various kinds offered to local rulers and chiefs, documented in the texts which list caravan expenses. The contents of the treaties with Anatolian rulers can be reconstructed on the basis of recurring features in caravan texts and in letters which report on swearing such oaths and on conflicts. The Assyrians apparently granted the Anatolian rulers:

1. import taxes (*nisḫātum*) amounting to five percent of the textiles and four pounds of tin per standard donkey-load of 130 pounds of tin;
2. a right of pre-emption of ten percent of the textiles, presumably first choice and at favourable prices.

In return the Anatolian rulers granted:

1. residence rights and protection in the commercial quarters (*kārum*) and trading stations (*wabartum*) of the Anatolian towns;
2. **[86]** extraterritorial rights, locally exercised by the administration of the colonies, which in political and judicial respect were extensions of the government of Assur;
3. protection of the caravans against robbery and brigandage, with compensation of losses and payment of blood money within a king's territory, presumably along the main roads.

This reconstruction is supplemented by the text kt n/k 794, found in a private archive, presumably the draft of an agreement under oath (in which the owner of the archive had been involved?), with a minor ruler of an unknown town in southern Anatolia, not far from Hahhum (the site of classical Samosate?), the nearest city with an Assyrian colony:[56]

> "In your country, neither rope nor peg,[57] no losses of an Assyrian shall occur. If they occur you shall search and return them to us. If bloodshed occurs in your country, you shall hand over to us the killers so that we can kill (them). You shall not let Akkadians come up (to you); if they come up to your land, you shall hand them over to us so that we can kill them. You shall not ask anything (extra) from us. Just like your father, from every caravan which goes up you shall receive 12 shekels of tin and from the one going down you will obtain ("eat, enjoy") 1 1/4 shekel of silver per donkey. You

[55a See for the treaties now Veenhof 2008, ch. 5].

56 Last edition by S. Çeçen-K. Hecker, in M. Dietrich-O. Loretz (eds.), *Vom Alten Orient zum Alten Testament. Festschrift W.von Soden*, Münster 1995, pp. 31-41 [See for the text now *Studies Larsen*, p. 250 note 8, and for its analysis Veenhof 2008, 186-187].

57 Meaning "not even (the loss of) a peg or rope". [The idea that their occurrence, after "in your country", refers to a territory demarcated by pegs and ropes (both were used for measuring fields in the Old Babylonian period, cf. the letter AbB 3, 55:22f.) has to be abandoned. In a new treaty, concluded with the city of Hahhum (see *Studies Larsen*, p. 257, lines 15-18, we read about the obligation to compensate "any loss that occurs, even of a rope and a peg, a stick or anything whatsoever"].

will not take anything extra. If there are hostilities and hence no caravans can come, one will send you from Ḫaḫḫum 5 pounds of tin... If we reject/violate the oath to you, our blood may be poured out like (the contents of this) cup!".

The figures make it clear that the text refers not to a trading centre but to a town passed en route. Hence the promise of very modest amounts of tin and silver per caravan passing and the compensation for loss of such income when no commercial traffic was possible,[58] no doubt to secure continuous safe passage. Important is the protectionist clause meant to prevent competition by Babylonian traders ("Akkadians"), which reveals the **[87]** Assyrian concern to monopolize the profitable tin trade. Since the town in question (in the neighbourhood of Ḫaḫḫum) must have been situated in the area where caravans crossed the Euphrates, the treaty stipulation probably meant to keep competitors out of the Anatolian core area.[59] The obligation of extraditing Babylonian rivals to the Assyrians to be killed is equally surprising by its ruthlessness as by revealing the determination of the Assyrian trade policy.

Several letters show that Anatolian rulers were eager to conclude or maintain such agreements, especially requests by new rulers of less important towns to renew such treaties, which had to be concluded with the authorities of the administrative capital of the Assyrian colonial network, *kārum* Kaniš, which these rulers referred to as "our fathers".[60] This reflects the importance of the profitable and vital trade (tin needed for the production of bronze), which both sides wished to safeguard and continue. The occasional conflicts we read about on the Assyrian side are usually caused by individual traders or caravans, which try to evade taxes by following by-roads and smuggling merchandise into Anatolian cities without paying import taxes. Anatolian rulers for their part occasionally acted high-handedly, by seizing traders or merchandise, but such conflicts were usually solved by negotiations, swearing oaths, presenting gifts or paying fines, ransom or compensation. Other problems were not related to the trade agreements, such as the fact that an Assyrian was apprehended with a letter written by an enemy of the king, in which he presumably asked for military assistance of another ruler.[61] Some **[88]** texts report on internal Anatolian political conflicts,[62] which were dangerous for

58 Starting from the standard price of tin in Anatolia, the five pounds of tin the ruler would receive equal his share from ca. 35 donkey loads.

59 There are other indications that the Euphrates served as a territorial limit; several slave sale contracts from Kaniš stipulate that the slaves cannot be sold (again) in that area, but only if they have been brought across the Euphrates or to people from Talḫad (in Northern Syria, perhaps within the western bend of the Euphrates) [See now K.R. Veenhof, in J.G. Dercksen (ed.), *Anatolia and the Jazira during the Old Assyrian Period*, Leiden 2008, pp. 18-21].

60 See for the edition and discussion of the older texts P. Garelli, *Les Assyriens en Cappadoce*, Paris 1963, part four, "Les relations politiques entre Assyriens et indigènes d'Anatolie", especially pp. 329ff. See for a new translation of these (and many other) Old Assyrian commercial texts CMK. [İ. Albayrak, in C. Michel (ed.), *Old Assyrian Studies in Memory of Paul Garelli*, Leiden 2008, pp. 111-115, publishes a new letter of an Anatolian ruler to *kārum* Kaniš, dealing with the death of an Assyrian trader, which starts with: "I am your son, you are my fathers!"].

61 Kt 93/k 145, published by C. Michel and P. Garelli, *WZKM* 86 (1996), pp. 277ff., and in an improved edition, on the basis of a duplicate found in another archive, by C. Günbattı in *Studies Veenhof*, pp. 151-160.

62 See for a serious political confrontation, M.T. Larsen, "A Revolt against Hattuša", in *JCS* 24 (1972), p. 100f., and for more general references to political upheaval, *CAD* S, p. 207, s.v. *seḫû*, and p. 237, s.v. *siḫītu*, "revolt".

Assyrian commercial traffic, or report that peace had been established, *e.g.* when two rival rulers had sworn a mutual oath.[63]

The text of a more than a century younger, unfortunately heavily damaged treaty between the ruler of the city-state of Šeḫna (Apum/Tell Leilan in the Ḫabur triangle) and the City of Assur (not its ruler!) confirms the picture of the Old Assyrian period.[64] Its purpose is to secure good relations between Šeḫna and the City of Assur and the local Assyrian merchant colony (*kārum*) there and protection and safe passage of Assyrian caravans. Texts from Mari reveal how in particular Assyrian caravans (*ellatum*) moving through Northern Mesopotamia within the framework of such regulations enjoy relatively safe passage, when their arrival had been formally announced (*tabrītum*). One text compares pastoral nomads to "a trader who travels between (areas in) war and peace".[65] Others show the risks traders might run into if they were used for or lent themselves to the transfer of vital information[66] or spying, a subject which recurs also later, *e.g.* in the Middle Assyrian Tukulti-Ninurta Epic (13th century B.C.).

The Old Assyrian policy of treaty agreements with Anatolian (and presumably also some North-Mesopotamian) rulers, initiated by *kārum* Kaniš and implemented with the assistance of the City, represented by its "Envoys" (*šiprū ša ālim*), appears to have worked well. Incidents and conflicts were not **[89]** numerous and were usually resolved, so that the Old Assyrian trade on Anatolia flourished for a period of more than a century, until ca. 1835 B.C. Its end, revealed by the destruction and abandonment of level II of *kārum* Kaniš, was the result of political upheaval and power struggle in Anatolia between rival rulers. There are no indications that developments in Northern Mesopotamia such as the growing military power of Ešnunna or Jamḫad/Aleppo caused its end, although it is clear that also Assur itself was not invulnerable.

4.3. Decisions of Assur's City Assembly affecting the Anatolian trade

Evidence for more specific Assyrian trade politics can be found in a few texts which acquaint us with decisions of the City Assembly of Assur. They consists of concrete verdicts (*dīnum*) in particular cases and of "orders, rulings" (*awātum*) of a more general nature and lasting impact, probably also resulting from decisions in specific affairs. Some of the latter could even take the form of a law, that is a binding rule enforced by a sanction, written (and hence 'published') on a stone monument, a stele (*naru'ā'um*). Some of them we know because a tablet with the ruling or verdict, in the form of an official letter sent by the ruler of Assur to the colony of Kaniš, has survived. Others are referred to or quoted in the private correspondence or in judicial records. I present the five most interesting examples.

---

63 KTS 2, nr. 40:27ff.: "There is peace in Burušḫattum, Ullama has now accepted the treaty (oath) from Burušḫattum". References to "peace" or "normal conditions" (*šulmum*) and its impact on the trade also occur in the letters VS, 26: 83:39ff., "When *šulmum* has been established and my goods in Kaniš will come down (after clearance) from the palace ...", and TC 3, 131:13'f.: "Within five days *šulmum* will be established [...]". [See more in general about such a situation K.R. Veenhof, "Old Assyrian Traders in War and Peace", in H. Neumann et al. (eds.), *Krieg und Frieden im Alten Vorderasien, CRRAI 52*, AOAT 401, Münster 2012, pp. 837-849, and more recently, G. Barjamovic, Th. Hertel, and M.T. Larsen, *Ups and Downs at Kanesh. Chronology, History and Society in the Old Assyrian Period*, Leiden 2012, ch. 2, "States, warfare and political centralization in Anatolia during the colony period"].

64 Published by Eidem, in *Studies Garelli*, pp. 185-207. [See now OBO 160/5, pp. 184-185].

65 Charpin and Durand 1997, p. 378 (A. 350+).

66 See the texts mentioned in n. 61. Note the role of the "overseer of the traders" described in the Old Babylonian letter AbB 8, 15, when the ruler of Ešnunna wishes to establish contact with Larsa for a joint military operation. The Mari letter A. 2776 shows that traders (and messengers) passing without asking permission could be put in jail.

4.3.1. Protection of the textile trade

The first example is a verdict of the City of Assur, quoted in the letter VS 26, 9, addressed to Pūšu-kēn in Kaniš by two colleagues in Assur, who write (lines 3ff.):[67]

> Here (in Assur) it has come to a lawsuit (*awātum ibbišiā*) concerning *saptinnu-* and *pirikannu*-textiles, woollen products, and many people have been fined. You too have been obliged to pay 10 [90] pounds of silver; you must pay one pound each year ... Please do not get involved in (the trade in) *saptinnu-* and *pirikannu*-textiles, don't buy them ... The ruling (*awātum*) of the City is severe!

The textiles involved were neither exported not imported into Assur, but were Anatolian fabrics which the Assyrians bought and sold in Anatolia with profit. *Pirikannu*-textiles in particular occur frequently and at times in large quantities[68] and Assyrian women probably also produced them.[69] The verdict had a general impact, since it resulted in fines for "*many* people". The penalty shows how serious this type of trade was taken and at the same time, according to the urgent advice given by the writers, made the measure effective. We have to conclude that this "colonial" commercial activity was considered detrimental to the trade in textiles imported from Assur.[70] Assyrian traders investing money and time in this kind of local trade may have been less involved and interested in the import trade. The verdict of the City-Assembly hence must be interpreted as a protectionist measure, in the interest of the Assyrian export and Assur-based traders, who wished to maintain the flow of woollen textiles from Assur into Anatolia. Their interests obviously were not identical to those of the colonial community, who tried "to make money" (*kaspam epāšum*) irrespective by which means.

The second and comparable example is found in two closely related letters, AKT 3 nrs. 73 and 74, written from Assur by Šalim-aḫum to his partner Pūšu-kēn and his son Dan-Aššur. Šalim-aḫum first reports that for an Anatolian shipment of forty **[91]** five pounds of silver he had purchased five donkey loads of tin and probably two of textiles, "in accordance with your instruction, before the verdict of the City" (*lama dīn ālim*, lines 9f.). The next shipment of thirty three pounds of silver, however, which has just arrived, could not be used according to their wishes, since):

> By verdict of the City one has to buy for one third (of it) tin. Buying tin, however, is impossible. There is no tin, because the tin caravan arriving from the land below (scil. to the south; *māt šapiltim*) is delayed (73:10ff.).

Should the caravan of the land below arrive, I will buy tin and textiles in accordance with the verdict of the City (74:8ff.).

---

67 Analysed in Veenhof 1972, 126f. and Larsen 1976, 172.

68 There are several occurrences of more than 50 *pirikannū*. CCT 5, 8b:8ff. mentions that a dead trader's house still contained 70 pieces, kt 89/k 421:4 a transport of 209 *pirikannū*. Although not expensive – prices range between one and three shekels apiece – a sum of 7 minas 43 shekels for *pirikannū* (POAT 26:11f.) implies a considerable turnover, although the profit on their trade, as stated in CCT 6, 14:48ff., was not always big. [See for these textiles now C. Michel and K.R. Veenhof, "The Textiles Traded by the Assyrians in Anatolia", in C. Michel and M.-L. Nosch (eds.), *Textile Terminologies in the Ancient Near East and Mediterranean from the Third to the First Millennium BC*, Oxford 2010, pp. 238-239. AKT 3, 19 mentions the sale of 300 *kutānu*-textiles (imported from Assur) and 300 *pirikannu*-textiles to an Anatolian palace]. These textiles often occur together with wool and this fits their occasional association with the towns of Mamma and Luḫusaddia (BIN 4, 78:16; TC 1, 43:3), which were centers of wool trade.

69 [E.g. Lamassutum, the wife of the Assyrian trader Elamma, who acquired amounts of wool for weaving, presumably with the aid of her five slave-girls, and records that she had given 9 *pirikannū* textiles to an agent to sell or exchange them ("for making purchases"); see AKT 8, ch. VIII,B].

70 In particular, as I have suggested in Veenhof 1972, 125, if locally made *pirikannū* could be worked into or serve as (cheaper?) substitutes of imported woollen *kutānu*-textiles.

Since this unique decision of the City speaks of "buying", "one third" does not refer to the number of donkey-loads, but to the amount of money (silver) spent on purchasing the two main articles for export to Anatolia, tin and textiles. The City ordered that henceforth of the silver shipped back from Anatolia and available in order to equip a new caravan, one third had to be spent on buying tin, and hence two-thirds on textiles. In this way the City wanted to influence the composition of the caravans, in other words the trader's decision how much tin and/or textiles he was going to export to Anatolia.

The main factors relevant for such decisions were supply, demand and profit. In Anatolia the availability and exchange value ("price") of silver, the demand for tin and textiles, and possibilities of selling mattered.[71] In Assur too, the availability and prices of both articles were important and at times decided whether and to what extent the orders received from Anatolia should or could be carried out. We read about situations were particular types of textiles were not available and it was decided to wait, or where tin was scarce and **[92]** expensive and hence (more) textiles were bought, or where an abundant supply of tin results in very favorable prices and hence the decision to buy much tin.[72] Thanks to the spread of the Assyrian commercial network over Anatolia, partnerships and representations, and a regular commercial mail both inside Anatolia and between Anatolia and Assur, information on the market situation was available and used. Moreover, traders apparently also wished to spread risks by serving both the metal and the textile market and not a few letters ask to buy for the silver sent to Assur "half tin, half textiles".[73] Finally, the sale of tin, presumably in the area of the copper mines, may have been easier, have required less travelling around, in addition may have offered the possibility of engaging in the Anatolian copper trade, using the transport capacity of the caravan donkeys who had discharged their tin loads.

In Assur one donkey-load of tin (standardized at 130 pounds) could be purchased for ca. 9 to 10 pounds of silver (price usually 1:14 to 1:15) and one ca. 25 woollen textiles for between 1 1/2 and 2 1/2 pounds of silver, depending the quality of the textiles (ca. 3 1/2 to 6 shekels apiece). In Anatolia tin was sold for silver at a rate of 6:1 to 7:1; normal textiles usually at 15 to 25 shekels of silver apiece. Taking into account all expenses (donkeys, travel, taxes and payments en route, costs of personnel, interest, etc.) the normal "net yield" of a donkey-load may have been around 16 pounds of silver for tin and roughly 5 to 6 pounds for textiles. More important was the net profit, that is how much additional silver an investment generated, because the backbone of the trade was that the exchange value of silver in Assur was about the double of that in Anatolia. A donkey load of tin ultimately may have provided a trader with roughly 5 to 7 pounds more silver than invested, one of textiles with roughly 3 to 4 pounds more. This means that in the end the amount of silver gained on a donkey-load of tin was bigger than on a donkey-load of textiles. This agrees which the observation, based on the "table of caravan texts" I drew up thirty years ago,[74] that in Assur on **[93]** the whole more silver was spent on buying tin than on purchasing textiles.

---

71 I limit myself to the essentials. The size of Assyrian imports could also affect demand and prices. We can read a warning that "there is much tin on the way" (from Assur to Anatolia), which entails the risk that its price drops or that the tin has to be kept in stock for some time, which means that it "stays hungry", does not generate silver. In some areas and periods (winter. harvest time, political upheaval) sales were difficult, and there were also indirect sales, when tin and textiles were first sold for copper and wool, which ultimately, by a second sale, were converted into silver. Such complications of course may also affect the net yield in silver, be it positively or negatively.

72 See for details Veenhof 1988.

73 Veenhof 1972, 80f.

74 *Ibid.*, pp. 70-76.

In this perspective the only reasonable explanation of the order of the City is to interpret it as a measure to limit the purchase of tin in favour of that of textiles.[75] Why? Tin by definition was not an Assyrian or even Mesopotamian product, but imported by foreign (Elamite?) traders. It reached Assur as a kind of central place, were it was bought in exchange for silver and gold and exported to Anatolia. Woollen textiles came from two sources. A presumably substantial part was imported from Babylonia, which had an almost industrial textile production. Another part was produced in Assur itself, to all appearances by a well developed home industry.[76] This is supported by later evidence from Mari, which reveals that for the pastoral Suḫu-nomads from the area of the Middle Euphrates and the Wadi Tharthar, Assur was the place where they would go with their herds to sell their wool.[77] The sale of Assyrian textiles to "Kaniš traders" hence must have been important for the Assyrian home industry and labour market, and that of "Akkadian" textiles for trading relations with Babylonia, which probably also supplied Assur with copper originating in Oman. This makes an order of the City Assembly to promote the purchase of textiles understandable, the more so when "Kaniš traders" may have preferred the trade in tin, perhaps also because it was vital and welcome to the Anatolian palaces, since it was indispensable for the production of copper. Note that according to the treaty quoted in § 4.2, the ruler involved would (wished to?) obtain only silver and tin, no textiles.

The order hence aims at protecting and promoting the textile trade in the interest of the domestic and commercial interests of the mother-city, at the expense of those of the "Kaniš traders". As such it is comparable to the first measure, discussed above, **[94]** which wants to protect trade in textiles imported from Assur against competition from local Anatolian products. Unfortunately, the information on these measures is contained in undated letters and we do not know the reasons for issuing them. They may have been emergency measures, in a particular situation, because trade in such local Anatolian textiles, especially *pirikannū*, is amply attested in our sources, apparently during many years. The measure, embodied in a verdict, hence the result of a lawsuit, suggests a concrete cause and dated validity, which are unknown to us.

4.3.2. Prevention of smuggling

The third example are two presumably related, but unfortunately heavily damaged letters, both addressed to the "Envoys of the City and *kārum* Kaniš". They deal with the use of the "narrow road" (*ḫarrān suqinnim*), hence smuggling inside Anatolia.[78] The first is addressed by the Colony of Zalpa (in Northern Syria) and reports about the arrival of a "tablet of the City" dealing with that issue. The second is written by the ruler of Assur, and describes the problems in Zalpa, where a caravan (*ellutum*) had been detained or was stuck for eight months. It mentions a "decision" (*nikištum*), valid from a particular day, which deals with "Assyrians" (DUMU *Aššur*) and the last lines mention the "narrow road". It seems plausible that the official letters of the City and the ruler contain an injunction to refrain from smuggling. Smuggling,[79] not without risks, but apparently possible and of

75 The delay of the tin caravan, mentioned in AKT 3, no. 73 and 74, is irrelevant for our issue, since the order of the City preceded this incident and it is stated that the order also applies to future purchases, when after the arrival of the tin caravan the supply is assured.

76 See Veenhof 1972, part two, "Textiles and wool". There is no evidence from Assur for large scale textile workshops, as documented for Babylonia and Mari.

77 Charpin and Durand 1997, pp. 377 and 387, text no. 4.

78 Chantre 11, discussed by Larsen 1976, 248f. with n. 3, and kt 91/k 100 (unpubl.). [Recent research identifies the "narrow road" with the one that links Timilkiya in the Elbistan Plain with Durhumit in the north, the area of the copper trade, and bypassed Kanesh, which consequently was unable to collect taxes and tolls. Its use, although not simply smuggling, was therefore disliked by he Anatolian authorities and also more risky. See G. Barjamovic, *A Historical Geography of Anatolia in the Old Assyrian Colony Period*, Copenhagen 2011, ch. 4.9, "The Narrow Track"].

79 Analysed in Veenhof 1972, chapters XIV-XVI. Since then, many additional references have become known. Note in particular CCT 6, 22a, which links up with BIN 4, 2 and TC 3, 13.

course profitable, was forbidden by treaty and infringements on that rule by individual caravans must have endangered the trade agreements and the position of the *kārum*. This explains official steps by the city and its concern is probably echoed by an order given by the authorities of the *kārum* to the trader Aššur-emūqī and his caravan (*ellutum*) phrased as a general ruling, enforced by a threat: "Nobody shall smuggle tin or textiles; the caravan that smuggles, the order of the **[95]** *kārum* will catch it!".[80] The same attitude of the *kārum* is voiced in the letter CTMMA 1, 72:28ff.: "Since the ruling of the *kārum* is firm, your (plan to) smuggle, you wrote us about, is not feasible, so we will not write you about your smuggling. It is entirely up to you, do not go by your colleagues. Beware!"

4.3.3. Limitations on the circulation of gold

The fourth example of "trade policy", which I have analysed a few years ago,[81] is very interesting. A letter by the ruler of Assur informs the authorities of *kārum* Kaniš about a recent decision of the City:

> "The tablet with the verdict of the City, which we sent you, that tablet is cancelled. We have not fixed any rule (*iṣurtum*) concerning gold. The earlier ruling (*awātum*) concerning gold still obtains: Assyrians can sell gold among each other but, in accordance with the words of the stele, no Assyrian whosoever shall give gold to an Akkadian, Amorite or Subaraean. Who does so shall not stay alive!"

An earlier verdict, whose contents are not detailed, which constitutes or would result in a new "fixed rule" (*iṣurtum*), is revoked and the colony is informed that the old ruling, inscribed and published on a stone monument, hence a rule of law, is still valid. It stipulates that sale of gold to non-Assyrian people (presumably traders) of greater Mesopotamia – Akkadians from Babylonia; Subaraeans, presumably the Hurrian speaking city-states east and north of Assur; and Amorites, the inhabitants of the land on both sides of the western bend of the Euphrates – is prohibited on penalty of death. Without information on the old ruling, the reasons for cancelling it, and the occasion and purpose of the new verdict, we can only speculate on what this means, taking into account what the Kültepe texts tell us about the role and use of gold.

The measure at least explains why the amounts of gold which **[96]** regularly arrived by caravan in Assur were never used to make purchases as (the much more abundant) silver was. Gold, at times designated as "gold for the caravan of the City" (*ša ḫarrān ālim*), was always first converted into or sold for silver, which then was used for equipping a new caravan or paying debts. We are never told where or to whom the gold was sold. It may have been to the temples, in particular that of the god Assur, which hoarded this prestige metal, since there is scattered evidence of gold in possession of temples,[82] or the City, which might have collected this bullion for storing wealth. In view of the amounts involved (many kilograms a year), however, I consider it more likely that the City needed the gold for buying particular goods from importers who preferred or insisted on payment in gold. This merchandise may well have been tin (possibly also lapis lazuli, which must have had the same origin), because the prohibition on selling gold to other traders does not include Elamites. Moreover, we know that a century later traders from Mari frequently paid gold for acquiring tin in Elam.[83] This fact in combination with the

---

80 Kt c/k 1055, published by K. Balkan in *Anatolian Studies Presented to Hans Gustav Güterbock on the Occasion of his 65th Birthday*, Istanbul 1974, p. 29 n. 2, lines 6ff. Note the use of *awātum* in the singular, "word", "order", versus its plural, "ruling", in VS 26, 9:25.

81 Veenhof 1995, 1732ff., on kt 79/k 101.

82 See J.G. Dercksen, "The Silver of the Gods. On Old Assyrian *ikribū*", in *ArAnat* 3 (1997) pp. 75-100, especially p. 86f. on the letter TC 3, 68, where a packet of gold, called *ikribū* of the god Assur, provided with a sealing which identifies its owner, is to be stored in a leather bag in the temple of Assur.

83 See F. Joannès, "L'Étain, de l'Élam à Mari", in L. De Meyer-H. Gasche (eds.), *Mésopotamie et Élam. Actes de la XXXVIème RAI, Gand 1989*, Ghent 1991, pp. 67-76, esp. p. 73.

prohibition of selling gold to the other population groups of greater Mesopotamia suggests that the Assyrian "law" on gold was mainly one of trade policy: a deliberate attempt to restrict access to gold, because it was vital for particular transactions in a particular leg of the international trade network of the time.

4.3.4. A measure to help indebted traders

The fifth example concerns a decision, reported in a letter, which aims at solving problems of indebted traders, who had been forced to sell their paternal houses.

> The god Assur has now done a favour to his City: a man whose house has been sold has to pay (only) half the price of his house to [97] move into it (again). For the remainder (of his debt) terms in three annual instalments have been set.

Referring to my recent analysis of this text,[84] I believe that the phrasing of the measure points at a problem of a more general nature, presumably in a period of economic crisis (caused by problems in Anatolia?). The Assyrian authorities, acting in the name of the god Assur, felt obliged to remedy the painful loss of the paternal or family property (presumably with the tombs of the ancestors under the floors) by indebted families in order to prevent social disruption. Redemption of the property is made easier by allowing payment in four instalments and stipulating that after the first one, of half the debt, the previous owners can get their property back. While this looks a measure of a primarily social nature, it also relates to the trade. The debtors, to judge from the size of their debts and the fact that the measure is reported in a letter found in the colony at Kaniš, were involved in the trade and two of the addressees (in Anatolia) in fact are the sons of the dead *pater familias*, who was a well-known "colonial" trader. The huge debts can only be explained from commercial failures and they were not simply cancelled, since debt cancellation in Mesopotamia was limited to consumptive debts and arrears to the state. Their extremely expensive houses in Assur (for which prices of up to fifteen pounds of silver were paid) were the most valuable assets of successful traders and hence almost the only ones of sufficient value to serve as security for commercial debts. Help for indebted and defaulting house owners hence also meant help for unlucky members of Assur's merchant class, to whom the City owed its prosperity.

The involvement of the City in matters relating to the trade is also noticeable in various decisions or rules (including laws), which aim at securing fair administrative procedures and the protection of the interests of individual traders in particular cases. They concern methods of accounting, compensation for losses of a joint caravan, correct liquidation of a dead trader's assets, the right to demand compound interest in particular **[98]** situations, and various forms of legal assistance, such as assigning them an attorney, when a first evaluation of their cases proved their complaints justified. Many of them, especially the judicial devices, imply the active cooperation of the colonial authorities.[85]

Finally, interference of the City in the practice of the Anatolian trade is evident in a few specific cases. One letter (TC 1, 18) mentions an "instruction (*têrtum*) of the City" (perhaps essentially a counsel based on knowledge of the local situation) to divide a caravan into three parts before entering Anatolia proper. A still unpublished letter from the trading station at Mamma mentions a letter of the City, which instructs the Assyrian authorities at Kuššara not to levy the customary *šaddu'utu*-tax from Assyrian caravans passing that city, because the funds are needed in Mamma to ransom Assyrians put in jail by the Anatolian authorities.[86]

---

84 K.R. Veenhof, in B. Böck et al. (eds.), *Munuscula Mesopotamica. Festschrift für J. Renger*. Münster 1999, pp. 599-616 [= pp. 211-223 in this volume].

85 See Veenhof 1995.

86 The letter Neşr 2, 34, discussed by J. Lewy in HUCA 33 (1962), p. 51 [and translated as *CMK* no. 58].

4.4. The role of the "City office"

As was mentioned in § 2, in Assur the "City office" (*bēt ālim*), also called the "*līmum* office" (*bēt līmim*), played an important commercial and administrative role. Our knowledge of this institution is unfortunately limited, based mainly on many short references in the private business letters; we lack its archives and even a single letter written by its head. Most references concern the at times substantial debts owed by traders to this institution. Part of them apparently represent arrears in the paying of the export tax (*waṣītum*), owed by every caravan leaving the city, at a rate of 1/120 part of the value of the load. The highest amount thus far attested as such is a debt of five pounds of silver, mentioned in TPK 1, 26:5, a text which also illustrates the serious consequences of not paying such debts in time.[87] The frequently much larger debts, however, must have another reason and may well be the price of merchandise sold by the "City office" on credit; thus far there is no evidence that it actually **[99]** gave out silver loans. We have some evidence that it sold textiles,[88] lapis lazuli, meteoric iron, and copper and an unpublished text actually designates a debt to it as "loan, trust" (*qīptum*), but in general our information is limited.[89]

Collecting the export tax must have implied checking the loads of the caravans leaving the city. It is reflected in the fact that the packets shipped to Anatolia are provided with "the seal of the City" and we actually have impressions of such an official seal (though from a slightly younger period of the Old Assyrian trade), which bears the inscription "Of divine Assur, of the excise, of the City office".[90] Such a check obviously allowed the City to discover whether its orders, such as the one on the relative quantities of tin and textiles to be exported (the second example in § 4.3.1) were carried out. This institution could influence the flow of goods to Anatolia even more directly if it indeed functioned as an (important) wholesale dealer or public warehouse, *e.g.* by limiting the sale of tin in accordance with the decision of the City just mentioned. We need more and better proof for this role, but it is clear that there was a link between certain activities of the "City office" and decisions or verdicts of the City (Assembly). In the case of the unpaid export tax, mentioned above, it is the City, not the "City office", which imposes the obligation to pay and the executive officials who put pressure on the debtor are "inspectors" (? *bērū*), not the *līmum*.[91] An unpublished letter which lists substantial debts to the "City office" at the end warns that "the orders of the City are severe" (*awāt ālim dannā*).

It is usually assumed that the "City office" also played an important role in the trade in lapis lazuli and meteoric iron. The **[100]** first, called *ḫusārum*,[92] occurs in the form of stones and lumps weighing between a few shekels and several pounds (once 15 kilograms). It was two to three times more expensive than silver. The second, called *amūtum* or *ašium*,[93] usually occurs in small amounts, never more than one pound and usually much less and, although extremely expensive (usually between 40 and 60 times the value of silver, and occasionally even much more), was much in demand. Larsen[94] assumed that the City office "held a monopoly on the trade in various luxury items",

---

87 Distraint and sale of the house of the debtor; other references mention how a debtor's house was sealed and valuable bronze objects were confiscated by the "City office".

88 TPAK 1, 143 mentions a shipment of three and a half pounds of silver to Assur "the price of textiles of the *līmum*-office".

89 TC 2, 20 surprises us by reporting that the *līmum*-official sold the investment (*šipkātum*) which a trader had made into another trader's capital. The *līmum* may have acquired it from a defaulting debtor, because the buyer states that he would not have done so "if it had not been (belonged to) our paternal house".

90 See Veenhof in *Studies N. Özgüç*, p. 651.

91 Friends of the debtor who prevented the sale of his house report: "We contracted a loan of 75 shekels of silver with a money-lender and paid the amount to the *bērū ša mišittim* and they brought it into the "City office" and we obtained a tablet of the City stating that ...". [See for the *bērū* now Dercksen 2004, ch. 4.5].

92 See now C. Michel, "Le lapis-lazuli des Assyriens au début du IIᵉ millénaire av. J.-C.", in *Studies Veenhof* pp. 341-360, an article which is my source for the following data and unpublished texts.

93 See for many references *CAD* A/II s.v. *amūtu* C and *aši'u*.

94 Larsen 1976, 198.

explicitly mentioning these two products, and Cécile Michel assumes that the trade in these goods was prohibited by the government of Assur, but the situation is not that clear. A general interdiction is excluded, because commercial texts actually mention payments to the City office for lapis lazuli. In kt 93/k 326 a trader writes: "The price of the lapis lazuli which your father acquired from the *laputtā'um*-officials of/in the "City office", you yourself have to pay". Some texts indeed record problems in connection with its acquisition and trade, but they probably refer to specific cases and situations. BIN 4, 91:17f. mentions for Assur "decisions in lawsuits" (plural!)[95] involving lapis lazuli, but there is no hint at what was at stake. It is by no means sure that we may compare this case with the verdict on trade in Anatolian textiles (discussed in § 4.3.1) or the prohibition of selling gold (§ 4.3.3). The issue might be a violation of the rules obtaining for its trade, or reflect a new or temporary measure. When the letter TC 2, 9:3ff. mentions that the City office does **[101]** not sell meteoric iron and lapis lazuli, for which the addressee had asked, rather than describing a general policy, it seems to refer to a special measure, or simply to the fact that its supply was temporarily exhausted ("do not sell" = "do not have them for sale"). This is actually suggested by the letter TC 2, 23:33ff., which speaks of an attempt to reserve it in case it arrives: "We will contractually bind (*kasā'um*) the *līmum* concerning the meteoric iron. If it becomes available we will acquire it in conformity with your instruction". These and other references also suggest that the situation as to lapis lazuli and meteoric iron was the same.

It is conceivable that the City kept a closer check on these precious, imported items, and therefore channelled or tried to channel their sale through the City office, which would go in the direction of a kind of import and sale monopoly in Assur. That Ikūnum, a ruler of Assur, according to KTS 1, 30, by means of his agent has shipped five pounds of extra fine lapis lazuli and eleven shekels of meteoric iron to Anatolia, in itself is no proof that *ex officio* he had easier access to these articles. Other traders too, as we have seen, could buy and own them.[96] CCT 4, 34c:13ff. simply asks to buy meteoric iron in case no textiles are available in Assur.[97] Anyhow, the City as such could and did not sell these products in Anatolia and this is the reason why we see them frequently in the hands of private traders. But it may have used its position in Assur to control its supplies and hence make a good profit on its sale.

The idea that trade in both articles and in particular in meteoric iron was forbidden in Anatolia[98] also lacks proof. Meteoric iron was not only acquired in Anatolia, as the file on an Assyrian partnership with a capital of 20 pounds of silver for buying it shows,[99] but also sold to local palaces and officials. That the latter may have been very keen on obtaining it and that this **[102]** may occasionally have resulted in moves to secure its acquisition is

---

95 In Assyrian *dīnū nakšū*, see Michel 1991, II, no. 7, who follows *CAD* N/1, p. 180, s.v. *nakāšu*, "to set aside". But in view of the evidence for a meaning "decision, prohibition" of Old Assyrian *nikištum* (see K. R. Veenhof in T.P.J. van Hout-J. de Roos (eds.), *Studio Historiae Ardens. Studies Presented to Philo P.H.J. Houwink ten Cate*, Istanbul 1995, p. 330 with n. 55 [= pp. 225-243 in this volume]; see for the verb also *MARI* 8, p. 388, g), our text means that the decision has been taken. The writers also report: "Our case has not yet been brought before the City Assembly, (and) when a verdict [will be/has been passed], we too will give back (the lapis lazuli?) – K.R.V.) and ...". It is by no means clear that the price of lapis lazuli sent to Assur according to Michel 1991, II, no. 46, was needed to pay the fine resulting from this verdict, and neither does TC 3, 49:36f. imply a lawsuit (see n. 100 on the meaning of *garā'um*).

96 See Michel, in *Studies Veenhof*, pp. 351f.

97 Kt 89/k 207 (courtesy Y. Kawasaki): "Send quickly silver to Assur, so that we can get hold of meteoric iron"; kt 89/k 231 reports on the sale of meteoric iron for silver and gold.

98 Larsen (1976, 245) includes the monopoly on their trade among the conditions Assyrian traders in Anatolia had agreed to by treaty.

99 Analysed by B. Landsberger, in *ArOr* 18,1/2 (1950) pp. 331-336. The fact, mentioned in the main source, ICK 1, 1:19f., that "the (local Anatolian) palace detains our father/boss" has nothing to do with this trading expedition.

a different matter.[100] ICK 1, 1:47 tells us that "the (local) place had contractually bound"[101] an Assyrian trader for a amount of eight shekels of meteoric iron. Both articles, just like all imported merchandise, in Anatolia were subject to taxation, presumably both by the Assyrian colonial administration and by the local palaces. One private and two official letters show that the Assyrian authorities collected both a tithe (*išrātum*) and a tax called *šaddu'utum* from Assyrians trading in meteoric iron,[102] which implies that this trade was legal and accepted. A protocol of a lawsuit before the *kārum*, EL 332:13ff., can mention among a trader's assets an amount of no less than "thirty-five pounds of silver, the price of (= earned by selling) meteoric iron and lapis lazuli". The request of a trader, in BIN 4, 45:16ff., to send meteoric iron "without the knowledge of the (Assyrian) *kārum*", is not made because its trade was forbidden or because he wished to avoid the heavy taxes, but to prevent the Assyrian authorities (they are meant by the words "mankind has become wicked"!) of laying their hands on it, because its sale to Anatolian officials is much more rewarding.[103] When, according to the letter ATHE 62, the trader Pūšu-kēn is put in jail by a local ruler and the writer warns to "leave the meteoric iron you are transporting behind in Timilkia, in a safe house", this is because he has been caught smuggling, hence trading without paying taxes due. Trade as such was allowed and possible in Anatolia, though there may have been certain constraints and occasional problems.

[103] *4.5. Decisions and rules of the colonial administration*

In Anatolia *kārum* Kaniš played a role in commercial politics. As the association of Assyrian traders it promoted their collective and if necessary individual interests, mainly in relation to the Anatolian palaces. Hence, on the one hand, its strong order to abstain from smuggling (see above § 4.3.2), addressed to a particular company, but phrased as a general injunction, and on the other hand two decisions which should help Assyrian traders who have problems with native debtors. The first, in the form of a normal verdict of the *kārum*, to which a sanction is added, stipulates a commercial boycott of a defaulting Anatolian official, the second, communicated in a private letter and called a "decision", is a general prohibition of selling goods to an anonymous native Anatolian:

> Nobody shall give (sell at credit) anything, whatsoever to the "Chief of the Stairway". Who does shall pay as much as the "Chief of the Stairway" owes to Ikūnum!" (EL 273)
>
> Here there is a decision of the *kārum*, to the effect that nobody shall sell anything to the native Anatolian (kt 91/k 297: 10-15).[104]

Such verdicts show how the Assyrian colonial society, devoid of military force, could protect its interests by economic means, such as a boycott. When applied to a high palace official – the "chief of the stairway" is attested as crown-prince and as second only to the local ruler – such measures become political instruments, which could only work thanks to Assyrian solidarity, hence the emphasis in both texts on "anybody" and "whatsoever".

---

100 Note especially BIN 4, 45:8ff., where two Anatolian commanders "are pressuring us, saying: 'Send a message if there is somewhere meteoric iron, so that I. and S. can collect it' ... but I did not give my word for the meteoric iron". The verb used, *garā'um* with personal accusative object, "to be hostile, to start a lawsuit", is used in Old Assyrian to describe the behaviour of "aggressive" buyers and sellers, and CCT 4, 4a:9: "I 'attacked' PN in GN, but since he could not pay silver I did not give him meteoric iron".

101 The same verb is used in TC 2, 23, mentioned above, where the *līmum* in Assur is "bound" to provide it when it becomes available.

102 VS 26, 12:7 (on an amount of 12 pounds of lapis lazuli) and kt 92/k 200 and 203, published by S. Çeçen in Belleten 61 (1997), pp. 223ff. [See now Veenhof in AKT 5, pp. 82-85].

103 "If you have in mind to send the meteoric iron, the *kārum* here must not know it; people have become wicked. They (two Anatolian generals) will bring silver and gold to pay cash for the meteoric iron! When you are clever, at least five pounds of silver will result for you!" (lines 16-24).

104 *annakam nikištam* (sic) *ša kārim ša kīma ana nu'ā'im mimma šīmim mamman la iddunu.*

Interference in a specific branch of the trade is documented for *kārum* Durḫumid, the centre of the copper trade, which had also fixed the rate of interest (on copper?).[105] A letter mentions a decree or order of this *kārum* which forbade the import into that city of poor copper in order to convert it there into fine copper.[106] **[104]** The measure must have had a commercial purpose, perhaps to prevent too large stocks of poor copper, which might harm the trade or would create problems in converting it into better copper.

As mentioned above (§ 4.2), *kārum* Kaniš, as the administrative headquarter of the Assyrian colonial society, together with the "Envoys of the City", took care of the diplomatic contacts and treaty agreements with the local Anatolian rulers, which could start off with contacts between a ruler and the local Assyrian establishment. The main tasks of the *kārum*, presumably detailed in the unfortunately very damaged "Statutes of the *kārum*",[107] were administrating the colonial society in Anatolia, organizing and facilitating the trade, and solving conflicts among its members. The first task also involved circulating and implementing decisions of the City Assembly in the colonial network and supervising the activities of the other colonies and trading stations, whose legal decisions it might cancel under circumstances (kt k/k 118, unpublished). There is no evidence of conflicts between the City of Assur and *kārum* Kaniš, which was subject to the authority of the City and took its verdicts and orders extremely serious. The only "incident" is the colony's delay in paying the silver it had to contribute to keeping the fortifications of Assur in good shape. It is reported in a letter of a still enigmatic body called *nībum*, which apparently represented the interests of the colonies in Assur. When the City threatened to send its own messenger to collect the silver – which would mean substantial added expenses – "they (the *nībum*) appealed to the Elders of the City" not to do so and they now admonish the *kārum* to collect the sum itself and to send it without delay. "If not, we shall take it here out of your own funds!". This important letter reveals how much is still unknown to us, since we have no idea of the composition and powers of the *nībum*, nor of the funds of the *kārum* in Assur, **[105]** where they were kept and how they were managed.

Activities directly linked with the trade were the organization of large scale commercial operations, to which individual members could subscribe by making funds or merchandise available; periodic (two or three times a year) general settlements of accounts (called "accounting of the *kārum*", in which the week-eponyms may have been involved), storage and credit facilities, and mediating the flow of certain goods and payments between the local palaces and (the members of) the *kārum*. Important in this respect was that the *kārum* (and not the City!) at some time had fixed the standard rate of interest on loans and credit at thirty percent per year, frequently referred to as "interest in accordance with the order/rule of the *kārum*" (*ṣibtum kīma awāt kārim*). In the frequent judicial activities the *kārum*, either plenary ("big and small") or by means of its committee, functioned as court of law, or supplied mediators and arbitrators to propose or implement legal solutions, to which the hundreds of judicial records bear eloquent testimony. Nearly all cases – the few exceptions have been mentioned above – concerned conflicts between various traders and firms. Securing justice, equity and solidarity within the Assyrian trading community abroad was important and might be called a political task, but not of the type discussed in this contribution.

---

105 Kt 91/k 390:8-9, on a debt of 50 pounds of copper interest has to be paid "in accordance with the ruling of the *kārum* Durḫumid" [probably a rate of 30% per year, see now AKT 8, 61, with comment, where also a reference is given for "the rate of *kārum* Timilkiya"].

106 See Dercksen 1996, 54, 4) and 155; he assumes that "to convert" refers to a commercial and not a metallurgical operation.

107 Analysed in Larsen 1976, part III, ch. 3, "The government of a Colony". We now know that the expression "man of the account" refers to a group of important members of the *kārum*, who, by paying substantial amounts of silver (called *dātum*) to the organization, earned among others the right to settle all kinds of payments due to the *kārum* not cash, but at the general settlement of accounts. [See now Dercksen 2004, ch. 11, "The Settlement of Accounts of the Kanish Colony"].

5. Markets and prices

Finally we have to ask whether there existed a policy which affected the prices of trade goods, which had an impact on supply and demand and ultimately on profit. While the examples quoted above show that the City tried to control and steer the trade in order to protect and stimulate its textile business and to restrict the free circulation of gold, there is no evidence of any regulation of the prices, exchange values or equivalencies of the main trade goods, neither a tariff, nor a legal ruling, nor even an *ad hoc* decision of the City Assembly or *kārum* Kaniš. None of the numerous so-called "caravan accounts", which specify the purchases made in Assur,[108] contains a reference to **[106]** it. The listing of the prices of barley, sesame oil and wool in a building inscription of king Šamšī-Adad I, from the later Old Assyrian period (ca. 1800 B.C.) is not a prescriptive tariff, but states how favourable the prices were at which these products "were bought on the market (*ina mahīrim*) of my city Assur". They proclaim the economic prosperity during the king's reign, but are idealistic, since real prices were much higher.[109] And, more important for our topic, they apply only to the three most common Mesopotamian subsistence products, not to the merchandise of Assyrian overland trade.

5.1. Markets

The texts frequently write on the prices of products (the caravan reports sent from Assur to Anatolia always contain information on the purchase prices in Assur) and their exchange values or equivalences. They use a rich variety of descriptive terms and expressions, with an at times modern, almost capitalistic flavour, which I have analysed long ago in my dissertation.[110] There are now many additional references, but the basic pattern has not changed: letters refer to unexpected and disappointing prices, usually conditioned by supply and demand, but occasionally by special circumstances (such as political unrest), which affect the possibilities of purchase or sale. In the absence of price regulation "the market" apparently was the determining factor. Some of these statements in letters use the word "market" (*maḫīrum*), most of which refer to Anatolia, but a few also to the City of Assur.

The question how to define "market" is a difficult and disputed one, ever since the publications by Polanyi on "marketless trading" in the ancient Near East.[111] The word "market" (*maḫīrum*) in Šamšī-Adad's inscription just quoted obviously refers to a market as a special place or facility, where (as shown **[107]** by the preposition "on", *ina*, with a locative meaning) one could buy goods. The opinion of Renger that "the existence of markets as real places would have to provide a word for such an institution",[112] is correct, but for the fact that *maḫīrum* is that very word, as several occurrences with a clearly local and spatial reference show: a ceremonial vessel and a statue are erected, and people meet each other or negotiate "on the *maḫīrum*", etc. This may be a secondary semantic

---

108 See for their nature and a representative selection, M.T. Larsen, *Old Assyrian Caravan Accounts*, Istanbul 1967.

109 See for the text and its interpretation, Veenhof 1972, 354f. For 1 shekel of silver one would have bought 500 liters of barley, 15 pounds of wool, and 20 liters of sesame oil, but in § 1 of the contemporary "Laws of Ešnunna" the prices are almost double!

110 Veenhof 1972, part 5, "Financial and Administrative Terminology".

111 K. Polanyi, "Marketless Trading in Hammurabi's Time", in Idem *et al.* (eds), *Trade and Market in Early Empires*, Glencoe 1957, pp. 12-26, and G. Dalton (ed.), *Primitive, Archaic, and Modern Economies. Essays of K. Polanyi*, Garden City 1968.

112 J. Renger, "On Economic Structures in Ancient Mesopotamia", in *OrNS* 63 (1994), p. 175. See for his philological arguments his observations in A. Archi (ed.), *Circulation of Goods in Non-Palatial Context in the Ancient Near East*, Roma 1984, pp. 76ff. It should be pointed out that Old Assyrian too knows the "market gate" (*bāb maḫīrim*), where purchases are made (kt 87/k 461:24), loans are contracted, and gold is collected (see the references in *CAD* M/1, p. 98). The words "of the market house" (*ša bēt maḫīrim*) qualify a large amount of checked and refined silver (RA 59 [1965], p. 173, no. 32:8), hence of a quality as demanded by and current, perhaps even gauged in the "market house" (in Old Babylonian too, most occurrences of "refined" and "sealed" silver are in commercial contexts).

development or result from an abbreviation of an original genitive compound, and of course it cannot be taken as its sole or principal meaning, but it cannot be denied for etymological or morphological reasons and contextual arguments simply demand it. On the other hand, the reference in Šamšī-Adad's inscription refers to trade and barter in local subsistence products and the situation as regards import and export products may or may not have been different. Hence the obligation to analyse references carefully, without preconceived ideas about the presence or absence of a market as a special locale and its function or workings, about which we indeed know rather little.[113]

For the dilemma tariffs and fixed prices or market prices due to supply and demand, a provision in the younger Edict of the Old Babylonian king Ammiṣaduqa presents a warning example. Its § 10 stipulates that merchants contracted by the palace to sell its surpluses, receive them in various cities "in the palace, according to the rate of exchange of the city (*kīma maḫīr ālim*)", that is current in the city where the deal takes place. Hence even for goods owned and disbursed by and in the palace itself no price is fixed, but the locally current exchange value of barley, dates, wool, etc. obtains.[114]

[108] 5.1.1. Markets in Anatolia

References to a market in Anatolia are more numerous and occur in connection with the purchase of slaves[115] and barley,[116] and as a place where traders could meet for business, to pay debts, or summon debtors.[117] There also existed an Anatolian title "head of the market" (*rabi maḫīrim*), now attested for four different persons, who figure as (*ex officio?*) witnesses to the sale of slaves,[118] houses, and pigs,[119] but they do not occur in connection with Assyrian import trade in Anatolia.

Most of the written evidence we have (in so-called "caravan reports") tells how Assyrian caravans upon arrival in an Anatolian town had to "go up" to the local palace, where the loads were inspected and taxes (excise, tithe) collected, after which the cleared goods could "go down" to be sold. But we have little information on the subsequent sales, part of which were carried out by travelling agents, whose debts, due dates and payments are recorded, but not how and where they sold their goods. Most tin probably was sold *en masse* in the copper mining areas, presumably directly to those exploiting the mines and involved in bronze production, perhaps the local palaces which may have controlled the metallurgical production, without interference of a market. Market sale of woollen textiles is conceivable, but the high prices (usually between fifteen and thirty shekels of silver) of these luxury products suggests a more restricted clientele of Anatolian traders and an élite which may not have been served primarily by barter on the market.

---

113 See for a broad survey, W. Röllig, "Der altmesopotamische Markt", *WO* 8 (1976), pp. 286-295. [See now also C. Michel, "Le commerce privé des Assyriens en Anatolie: un modèle du commerce archaïque selon K. Polanyi", in Ph. Clancier *et al.* (eds.), *Autour de Polanyi. Vocabulaires, theories et modalités des échanges*, Colloques de la Maison René-Ginouvès, Paris 2005, pp. 121-133, and Larsen 2015, ch. 21, "Economic Theory and Evidence"].

114 See for the text and its meaning, F.R. Kraus, *Königliche Verfügungen in altbabylonischer Zeit*, Leiden 1984, pp. 174f. and 226 ("zu lokalem Tagepreise").

115 Veenhof 1972, 390 no. 1, where the slave is "brought down from the market", comparable to kt j/k 288b:13, where a rebellious slave-girl will be "brought up to the market" (*ana ma-ḫi*ʾ*-re-e ušellūši*) to be sold. In kt 91/k 123:15 the buyer can sell the slave "on the market", in kt 87/k 287:10 (K. Hecker, *ArAnat* 3 [1997],p. 160f.) the seller of a slave is satisfied "on the market" (both *ina maḫīrim*).

116 Kt 89/k 241:35f (courtesy Y. Kawasaki), "since PN refuses to give us barley for our sustenance, we will buy it on the market" (*ina maḫīrim*).

117 Veenhof 1972, 392 nos. 6-7. [Kt c/k 108+:48-49 mentions that a trader "cried aloud on the market" (*rigmam immahīrim iddi*)].

118 See for the role of this official in the case of a fugitive debt-slave, B. Kienast, *Das altassyrische Kaufvertragsrecht*, Stuttgart 1984, p. 146, comments on no. 29.

119 The persons bearing this title are Wašuba (Veenhof 1972, 394), Aše'ed, Kalua, and Parwaliuman. One reference is in the legal record kt n/k 32, published by Donbaz, in *Aspects of Art*, p. 75f., no. 1, a text belonging to the later Old Assyrian period (*kārum* Kaniš level Ib). [We now know 9 persons with this title, see Veenhof 2008, 221-222; add there Ušnama, attested in Kt o/k 53:1 and 8].

[109] Still, several commercial letters which deal with the sale and purchase of tin, textiles, silver, gold and copper do mention the market in a general way, usually to report on problems, opportunities or special situations. Selling tin, textiles, or copper can be difficult when "there is no silver (and gold) on the market",[120] and we also read: "There was no 'payment' (*šīmum*) on the market; but today, as I hear, there is plenty of 'payment' on the market!",[121] where *šīmum* refers to the silver which Anatolians paid to buy Assyrian imports. The last example is instructive, as one of the much more numerous references which speak of the presence or absence of *šīmum* (in the singular or in the plural, which almost equals "trade") in Anatolia without mentioning the market, but may very well imply its existence. References which speak of the market as being "disturbed", "not well supplied", "deficient", "bound", "hit" etc.,[122] apparently refer to the process of "giving and receiving", barter, hence trade. But we should not *a priori* contrast them with and isolate them from references to the market as a locale or special facility. This might have some justification if the references were only to equivalencies or prices, that is the quantity of goods received in exchange for a standard unit of an accepted means of payment (such as one shekel of silver), which is the original meaning of *maḫīrum*.[123] But the word is also used when there is no trade at all, no supply or demand, a situation which can also be described by the words "there is no silver *on* the market".

[110] Hence the role of the market as a special locale or facility might be more important than the few occurrences of the word itself suggest. This could imply that the distinction, preferred by some, between barter of subsistence goods on a local market(-place) and trade in imported and bulk goods in a marketless, institutional setting is only a relative one, governed less by principles than by practical considerations such as the nature, value and purpose of the goods traded. The strategic importance of imported tin explains the dominant role of the palace, apart from the fact that the specialized craft of bronze making hardly qualified this expensive metal for barter on a local market.

5.1.2. The market of Assur

While the existence of a market in *Assur* is beyond doubt, its role in the import and overland trade is unclear and was probably limited. Again, the "caravan reports" only list export goods bought and at what prices; whether or not on a market for their readers was obvious and irrelevant. We only hear a little more in case of delays or problems, due to the fact that caravans or traders bringing tin and textiles to Assur have not arrived or are delayed. A few times we hear that "Kaniš traders", upon arrival in Assur "brought the silver into" the "houses" of certain (wholesale?) traders to make their purchases. Only one letter mentions the market in connection with the export of textiles: a trader bought a ready-made "heavy textile" on the market, because the special type of wool from which it had to be made was not available in Assur,[124] so that he could not have one made, as requested by his Anatolian addressee. Buying textiles on the market obviously was an alternative to producing them from wool bought in Assur. This reference concerns a special, presumably expensive type of textile, which is not rare and indeed produced by

---

120 CCT 4, 34c:8f. and kt n/k 1689:6ff., which adds that the writer expects to be able "to buy gold within ten days".

121 TC 3, 111:15ff., Veenhof 1972, 391 no. 4. Alternative translations of *šīmum* are the concrete "bullion, money" and the more dynamic "sale transactions, trade", but the latter is better reserved for its plural *šīmū*. In Ka 435 (*Anatolica* 12 [1985], p. 132 no. 1) a textile is sold "on the market" for copper.

122 See the references discussed in Veenhof 1972, 382ff.; "disturbed" also in I 598:8. A recently published letter, V. Donbaz, *Cuneiform Texts in the Sadberk Hanım Museum*, Istanbul 1999, no. 17:11ff., reports that "here the prices/sales of textiles are hit, the market of Kaniš is deficient/not well supplied (with silver which allows the Anatolians to buy them), so that textiles of better quality remain unsold" (*annakam ana ṣubātē šīmū maḫṣū ana maḫīrim ša Kaniš batiq ṣubātū qabliūtum ibaššiū*).

123 Grammatically *maḫīrum* is a noun derived from the verbal adjective *maḫrum*, "received", with a concrete meaning, "that which is received" (scil. in exchange for something).

124 See for the text *CAD* Š/III, p. 342 s.v. *šurbuītu*.

Assyrian women for export, but usually occurs in single pieces or small numbers.[125] But something similar is written in a letter sent **[111]** from Anatolia to a woman in Assur: "If you cannot manage to make fine textiles, as I hear they are plenty for sale over there (= in Assur), buy and send them to me".[126] This reference speaks in more general terms and shows that this fact was common knowledge in Anatolia. Even more importantly, it deals with a situation very similar to that of the previous letter, but without using the word "market". This again implies that many texts which simple speak of "being for sale", "being available / absent" (*ibaššiu / laššû*) in Assur, may imply market sale as well a purchase in the "houses" of wholesale traders. Lack of detailed information must make us cautious in claiming the one or the other as the dominant mode of purchase. The market may have been more than an alternative to home production only; it may also have served "Kaniš traders" alongside warehouses and wholesale dealers.

In connection with tin we lack such references; we only hear about its presence or absence and about prices in Assur, and only once its temporary absence is explained by the delay of the caravans which bring it (from Elam?) to Assur. Since all tin was imported, its sale may have been controlled more easily and channeled through warehouses, both private ones and that of the "City office". The more so if part of the imported tin was paid for in gold, which private "Kaniš traders" were not allowed to use for making purchases in Assur (§ 4.3.3). Still, without information on how and where "Kaniš traders" bought their goods caution is necessary and the role of the market remains unclear.

5.2. Prices

The "market" as the place where or mode in which goods were sold, bought or exchanged implies the existence of mutually accepted equivalencies between quantities of different goods (actually the basic meaning of *maḫīrum*), which in turn are unthinkable without standards of quality to which the equivalencies apply. All kinds of goods hence can be qualified as "of the market" (*ša maḫīrim*), both in a general way, hence "marketable", **[112]** and more specifically as "of the *maḫīrum* of city X", hence meeting a specific local norm.[127] While such qualifications seem to refer in the first place to quality (perhaps also shape), presumably the standard quality required for and current in the overland trade, they may also relate to the price currently paid there. This is an important aspect in Old Assyrian trade, since there is ample evidence for both general and local price fluctuations (best attested for tin) and because the commercial or exchange value of the various articles of trade was much different in Assur and Anatolia, a difference which in effect was the basis of the success of Old Assyrian trade. It is difficult to distinguish these two meanings in less explicit contexts and in fact both may well go together. The simple request of BIN 6, 262:11'f., "buy pure tin *maḫīr* the city", probably refers to the quality, as the use of the adjective "pure" suggests.[128] But when in TPAK 1, 191 a debtor has the choice between sending his creditor in Assur 20 shekels of silver or paying him in Anatolia "tin *maḫīr* of the city", he probably means the quantity of tin normally obtainable for that amount of silver in Assur. And indeed, a settlement of accounts (I 521:5ff.) states that a claim of one pound of silver can be settled by deducting from the merchandise owed "tin *maḫīrum* of the city", and adds how much that is: fourteen pounds. This is possible because traders knew what the "normal" or standard price of tin in Assur was: between 14 to 15 shekels of tin for 1 shekel of silver. When the contract kt c/k 459 (unpubl.) stipulates that a trader will weigh out in Anatolia, in the city Burušḫattum, for each pound of silver

---

125 See Veenhof 1972, 183, c).

126 *Ibidem*, p. 104, TC 3, 17:29-33.

127 Tin (etc.) *maḫīr ālim* can be compared with simple *ša maḫīrim* (used of gold in EL 137:3 and kt a/k 424:2) The basic meaning of *mahīrum*, "what is received (in exchange for something else)" suggest the reference to the standard amount obtainable on the basis of the normal equivalency. But *mahīr ālim* secondarily also applies to the quality, to what is given in exchange on the market, hence "marketable".

128 The latter probably was the case when in *RA* 59 (1965), p. 173, no. 32:7, 10 pounds of silver are qualified as "of the market house" (*bēt maḫīrim*).

no less than seventeen pounds of tin, the text specifies that this is "the *maḫīrum* of the city". The debtor in Anatolia had received two pounds of silver and promised to pay the tin he had been able to buy for it (at a very favourable price indeed) in Assur. In Anatolia, because of the large area, with different supplies **[113]** of goods and different "markets", such a reference could be specified by a geographical name. In kt 91/k 181 a trader who has ceded a claim of copper and silver to a colleague, if the latter does not collect it, will pay him "copper (of) the *maḫīrum* of Durḫumid", the city which was the main copper market and where, hence, supply and demand formed the price.[129] This is also reflected by the expression "as the *maḫīrum* stands" (*maḫīr izzazzu*), used in kt 91/k 401:8 for tin in Anatolia and in RSM 1922/243:17 of copper and silver.[130]

Prices current in Old Assyrian trade were those which had established themselves in the course of time and were accepted by both parties as "normal" and "fair". The *locus classicus* TC 1, 11:9ff. puts it as follows: "For the two pounds of silver you sent me, since the price of Akkadian textiles has been "affected" (*lapit*), I will not (buy and) send them to you. If the price of Akkadian textiles does not become normal again (*ešārum*) within ten days, I will buy and send you tin instead" (cf. TC 2, 7:21). The reason for such an apparently short-time price fluctuation are changes in supply, as a related letter shows (VS 26, 17:4ff.): "As for the price (or: purchase) of Akkadian textiles, about which you wrote, since you left no Akkadians have arrived in the City (of Assur); their country is in turmoil, but if they arrive before the winter I will make a profitable purchase for you". Lack of import affects the Assyrian market, there is no supply and prices rise; clever traders wait or switch to other products. Such variations in supply and demand affect the possibilities of trading and the prices. A famous letter (CCT 4, 10a) reports that in Anatolia the "market is disturbed", because the people have left the city, which means that "silver is hard to get/expensive (*kaspū dannū*) and prices/sales bad", so that the **[114]** transaction yields less than expected (*šīmū batqū*). Similar effects occur when there is a blockade or suspension of commercial traffic (*sukurtum*, see *CAD* S s.v.), or when the season interferes: no trade during the winter and in harvest time, when the Anatolians are so occupied by the work on the fields that "purchases/trade comes to a standstill" (*šīmū kassū*, BIN 4, 39:7ff.).

The effects of these situations can be easily observed by comparing the results of transactions or figures in accounts, for which I may refer to an earlier analysis.[131] Price differences can be in the range of twenty-five to fifty percent. The price or rate of exchange at which tin was sold for silver in Anatolia was ideally 6:1, but it might go down (from the Assyrian perspective) to as far as eight and (rarely) even nine or ten to one. Even bigger differences are attested for woollen textiles, where, however, clear differences in quality also play a role.[132] The absence of "fixed prices" is clear from "caravan accounts" which contain information on prices and market, and from detailed reports on individual transactions. An unpublished letter (kt 89/ k 252; courtesy Y. Kawasaki) reports that a local Anatolian palace, which wishes to obtain textiles stored in an Assyrian's house, presses him to fix their price (*šīmšina ēṣir*), so that the deal can be concluded. In another

---

129 The current price is also referred by expressions such as "as one sells", or "as is being sold". See also ATHE 38:6ff.: "When S. arrived, tin was being sold at a rate of 9 or 10 pounds (of copper for) each (mina of tin)".

130 Similar references omit the word *maḫīrum* and use only the verb "to stand" (*izizzum*). This may refer to the equivalency or price, as in "tin is expensive here, it stands at 14 shekels per (shekel of silver) and even lower" (BIN 6, 59:rev.13'ff., *annukū ... 14* GÍN.TA *u šapliš izzaz*), also used with *ana*, "one donkey stand at 50 minas (of copper)" (KTS 1, 55a:25-26, *1* ANŠE *ana 50 mana ... izzaz*), or introduced by the comparative *kīma*, "settle accounts (on the basis of) how tin 'stands' for silver" (CCT 4, 40a:17f., *kīma annukū ana kaspim izzazzu*). But "to stand" alone may also refer to the supply, the availability on the market, as in "silver is hard to obtain here..., but since gold 'stands' (is available) as price (to be paid by the Anatolians), we will 'make' gold for you" (KTS 18:24-28, *ana šīmim hurāṣum izzaz*).

131 Veenhof 1988.

132 The most expensive textiles were sold for 45 shekels of silver apiece.

case (ATHE 32) a clever trader reports that the local Anatolian palace has sold "lots of copper" for silver to traders from the North-Syrian city of Ebla, at a favourable exchange rate of 140:1. "Within ten days its stock of copper will be finished, then I will buy silver [by selling his copper] and send it to you", obviously in an attempt to exploit the price changes caused by the palace's abundance of silver and its lack of copper for his own profit. In TC 2, 18 a trader reports that in the city of Burušḫattum "copper has been hit", which apparently means little or no trade and low prices. This situation makes him decide not to hire wagons for hauling this metal there, but to wait for his own caravan donkeys, no doubt in order to save costs and presumably in the hope that in the meantime the copper market will improve.

[115] Prices called "normal" and considered "fair" are a general feature of antiquity and do not imply the existence of tariffs and equivalencies fixed in agreements (though both may reflect them). Prices in Assur hence are comparable to those attested elsewhere in Mesopotamia around these times. While in Assur in the 19th century B.C. tin usually could be bought at a rate of 14 to 15 (with variations from 12 1/2 to 17) shekels of tin for one shekel of silver, in Mari, a good century later, the purchase price of tin fluctuated between 11 and 10 shekels for one shekel of silver, which is ca. thirty percent more expensive. At least two factors explain the difference. The first is the distance from the supplier of tin in the east, in both cases presumably Elam,[133] which is shorter for Assur than for Mari, and higher transport costs apparently affected the price. The second are intermediaries, central places and taxes or tolls, which are unavoidable in relay trade to connect the different stages of a commercial network. While Assur probably acquired tin directly from caravans arriving from Elam, Mari most of the time had to buy it from Mesopotamian suppliers, presumably in Ešnunna or Sippar, which meant a higher price. The analysis by Joannès[134] has shown that the prices in Mari were lower (going down to 13-15:1) during the two years when Mari had established direct diplomatic and commercial contacts with Elam (see also § 4.3.3, above). A possible third factor was the exchange value of silver, the generally accepted means of (indirect) payment – always in abundant supply in Assur and presumably less so in Babylonia – and gold, which in 18th century Babylonia and Mari was cheaper than in Assur a century earlier.[135] Price differences may increase or decrease due to indirect exchange. In an Old Babylonian letter from around 1800 B.C. (TIM 1, 20:20ff.) we hear of a trader with a capital of about six pounds of gold, which he first sold for silver at a rate of 5,5:1, to sell the silver subsequently for tin at a rate of 16:1. The favourable price of the tin is somewhat balanced by the low price (at least according to Old **[116]** Assyrian standards) of the gold, which in Assyria was worth about eight times as much as silver.

Price differences immediately affected the profit of the trade, which was vital to maintain the expensive and labour intensive caravan and colonial system. For that reason information on the Assyrian "market" was regularly sent to Anatolia, also by separate mail, so that the traders knew in advance the quantities and prices of the merchandise on its way and could decide on how and where to sell it. The same happened inside Anatolia, where the Assyrian trading network of about thirty-five colonies and trading stations made it possible to watch the markets and take decisions on the basis of local observations and oral or written reports from elsewhere. Their efficient communication and transport system allowed the Assyrian traders to evade or reduce market problems and at times even to exploit regional differences. Merchandise could be kept in store, waiting for better times, or sent to where the market was in better shape, but one could also resort

---

133 See for the origin of the tin and the route along which it arrived in Mesopotamia and Assur, above § 4.1 and 4.3.1 on AKT 3, 73-74, which mention its arrival with caravans coming from the "country below" (*māt šapiltim*; also in KTS 41a:7).

134 Joannès, in "l'Étain" (see note 83).

135 In Babylonia and Mari one shekel of gold equaled between 5,5 and 3 shekels of silver, in Assur normally 8 shekels. See for the role of gold in Assur, § 4.3.3.

to indirect exchange by selling tin and textiles for wool or copper, which were converted into silver or gold elsewhere. All problems of course could not be avoided, especially not when traders were trapped by political or military problems, when they needed silver without delay to pay their interest bearing debts, or when they had to meet deadlines in order to be able to ship their silver and gold to Assur with the next caravan or before the winter made traffic impossible. But the overall pattern is one of considerable skill, flexibility and resourcefulness in a market dominated by supply and demand, by regional differences, and not by fixed prices and regulated equivalencies.

6. Conclusion

We may conclude that there is good evidence for various forms of "trade policy" in ancient Assur. Its early rulers seem to have inaugurated a policy of attracting foreign, especially Babylonian and probably also Elamite traders to the city, in order to strengthen its position as strategic market, central place and transit town in the international commercial network of the time. The facilities obtained by the Assyrians in Anatolia were based on treaties ("sworn oaths"), which involved both the City, via its Envoys, and *kārum* Kaniš. They stipulated and balanced the **[117]** rights and duties of Anatolian rulers and Assyrian traders for their mutual benefit in a way which secured a century of uninterrupted, profitable and expanding trade. Both the City of Assur and the administration of the colonies tried to prevent Assyrians from infringing on these agreements by smuggling. It could also counsel or direct traders how to proceed with their caravans, presumably in times of trouble. Sworn agreements also secured a safe and unhindered passage through parts of Northern Mesopotamia.

These agreements contained stipulations on the tariffs of import tax and preemption, but not on prices, equivalencies or quantities of the goods traded. The trade, also with Anatolian rulers, was basically governed by supply, demand and barter, which started from traditional, accepted equivalencies. Both parties were free in what they wished to sell and buy, but we cannot exclude that in particular cases, especially when luxury products such as meteoric iron and lapis lazuli were involved, Anatolian pressure and diplomatic considerations played a role.

The City of Assur probably also stimulated the trade by securing the import of textiles and of tin, for the acquisition of which gold may have been used and in which the "City office" may have played a role. But we have almost no information on these imports, we know nothing of trade agreements with either Elamites or Babylonians, and it is unclear which facilities (if any) the latter had in Assur. The City seemed to have lacked a special commercial quarter (*kārum*) where foreign traders could settle and work. Assur tried to prevent competition by Babylonians, a purpose served by making arrangements with local Anatolian rulers to bar Babylonian caravans from their territory and perhaps also by the prohibition of selling them gold. Assur tried to promote and protect the export and sale of Assyrian woollen textiles, both by forbidding and penalizing the trade in local Anatolian textile products and by limiting (in a particular situation/period?) the amount of tin "Kaniš traders" could buy and take along to Anatolia. The City office offered export goods for sale, also lapis lazuli and meteoric iron, which may have enabled it to control the amounts of these precious products available for export. The City apparently had empowered this institution, and supported it by special verdicts, to collect arrears and debts from "Kaniš traders", but on the other hand the City also took measures to help indebted and bankrupt traders to redeem their **[118]** family houses, thereby preventing social disruption.

Inside Anatolia the colonial administration carried out a policy of keeping friends with the various rulers and palace aristocracies by making, renewing and upholding sworn agreements, by special gifts, by mediating the solution of problems between rulers and individual traders and by assisting local Assyrian trading stations in such matters. But it also filed formal complaints and negotiated with the rulers, especially when caravans had been robbed and people killed, and defaulting Anatolian dignitaries and traders could be hit by an Assyrian boycott. By means of orders it could steer or interfere in the trade, as the case of the unwanted accumulation of cheap, unrefined copper in Durḫumid shows. The *kārum* organization, based in Kaniš, was strict in collecting the taxes and fees due from Assyrian traders, an income which was needed for maintaining central facilities, administrative services, and taking care of diplomatic contacts both with Anatolian rulers and the authorities in Assur. It advanced fair trade by imposing a standard rate of interest (thirty percent per year) among Assyrians, by the administration of justice, by taking care of well regulated general settlements of accounts, and by channeling the transfer of goods and payments (especially copper) between the local palace and members of the *kārum*. As the colonial branch of the government of Assur, which represented and administered the corporation of Assyrian traders in Anatolia, it efficiently played both a commercial and a political role.

Bibliography

Charpin, D., and Durand J.-M. 1997. Aššur avant l'Assyrie", *MARI* 8, 367-391.

Dercksen, J.G. 1996. *The Old Assyrian Copper Trade in Anatolia*, Leiden.

–. 2004. *Old Assyrian Institutions*, Leiden.

Larsen, M.T. 1976. *The Old Assyrian City-State and its Colonies*, Mesopotamia 4, Copenhagen.

–. 2015. *Ancient Kanesh. A Merchant Colony in Bronze Age Anatolia*, Cambridge.

Michel, C. 1991. *Innāya dans les tablettes paléo-assyriennes*, I-II, Paris 1991.

Veenhof, K.R. 1972. *Aspects of Old Assyrian Trade and its Terminology*, Leiden.

–. 1988. "Price and Trade. The Old Assyrian Evidence", *AoF* 15, 243-263.

–. 1995. "'In Accordance with the Words of the Stele'. Evidence for Old Assyrian Legislation", *Chicago-Kent Law Journal* 70/4, 1717-1744 [= pp. 109-127 in this volume].

–. 1999. "Silver and Credit in Old Assyrian Trade", in J.G. Dercksen (ed.), *Trade and Finance in Ancient Mesopotamia*, Leiden 1999, 55-83 [= pp. 159-184 in this volume].

–. 2003. *The Old Assyrian List of Year Eponyms from Karum Kanish and its Chonological Implications*, Ankara 2003.

–. 2008. "The Old Assyrian Period", in M. Wäfler (ed.), *Mesopotamia. The Old Assyrian Period. Annäherungen* 5, OBO 160/5, Fribourg-Göttingen 2008, Teil 1, pp. 13-264.

Silver and Credit in Old Assyrian Trade

1. Introduction

Silver played a vital role in Old Assyrian trade. Its acquisition was the main goal of the traders whose caravans imported tin and woollen textiles into Anatolia in order to convert them, directly or indirectly, into silver,[2] which was invariably shipped back to Assur. There, after the necessary payments had been made (expenses, taxes, debts, interest, dividend), much of what remained was again used for commercial purposes, either directly, by contributing to or equipping a new caravan, or indirectly, by investing it in a firm or issuing a loan to a trader. Silver, thus, was not only the goal of the trade, it was also its motor and lubricant which kept the system going. As generally accepted and easily shipped means of payment and as valuta of account it facilitated commercial transactions, also in indirect exchange and by book transfer. Most importantly, it played a key-role in all kind of credit transactions (commercial credit, straight loans, investments) which dominated the trading system. Much silver, moreover, entered Assyrian society, both on a public level, in the form of payments for facilities, taxes, fines and institutional profit, and in the private sphere, as dividend, interest, profit, commission, wages (for personnel), and as payment to those who supplied caravans with donkeys, harnesses, and food. Traders and their families, moreover, used it to buy (expensive) houses and the necessities of life, such as barley, oil, and wool.

Gold too was exported from Anatolia to Assur, though on a more modest scale, but it played a peculiar role. Gold which arrived in Assur[3] was normally converted into silver, which then was used for payments and purchases. It is never mentioned who bought the gold, but thanks to a letter by the ruler of the City to the colony in Kanish we know that there existed a law (inscribed on a stele) which prohibited the sale of gold to non-Assyrians (the text speaks of people, presumably traders, from Akkad, Amurru, and Subartu) on penalty of death.[4] On the other hand, gold was the preferred valuta in which standard investments or shares (called *šipkātum)* in a trader's "sack capital" (*naruqqum*) **[56]** were rated. But it is clear that actual payments for obtaining such shares were made in silver.[5] Whoever may have acquired the gold which arrived in Assur (we may suspect institutional hoarding), its role in the actual trade must have been limited and we may ignore it here.

The following remarks do not deal with investments, the capital of the traders and firms, partnerships etc (key words: *naruqqum*, *šipkātum*, *ebuṭṭū*, *bulātum*, *ummeānum*,

* Originally published in J. G. Dercksen (ed.), Trade and Finance in Ancient Mesopotamia. Proceedings of the First MOS Symposium (Leiden 1997). MOS Studies 1. PIHANS 84. Istanbul: Nederlands Historisch-Archaeologisch Instituut, 1999, pp. 55-83.

1 Footnote lapsed.

2 The texts use the expression *luqūtam ana kaspim ta"urum*, "to turn merchandise into silver".

3 In Anatolia one used the designation *ḫurāṣum ša ḫarrān ālim*, "gold for the journey to Assur", possibly meaning "gold to be shipped to Assur", perhaps in order to distinguish it from gold used locally. See for the role of gold, Veenhof 1972, 381f. [and now also Dercksen 2004, ch. 5,3 and 4].

4 See for the text and its interpretation Veenhof 1995a, 1733ff.

5 See for *naruqqum*, Larsen 1977 and *RlA* 9 (1999) *s.v. naruqqum* [and now also Larsen 2015, 220-227]. Collation of the one known *naruqqum*-contract Kay 313, preserved in the museum at Kayseri (Larsen 1977, 125 n. 16), has shown that the first line which is preserved contains the word *šipkātum*.

tappūtum, etc.), which are discussed in Dercksen 1999. My focus is the role of silver in the actual trade and especially in commercial credit of various kinds, which means features such as loans, debts, advances, consignment, agency, and special arrangements for paying debts or their deferment. And this of course requires a serious look at the persons involved in such operations, especially the ubiquitous *tamkārum*, whose role still is a matter of disagreement.

Before doing so a few essential features of the trade, which condition the role of the silver and those who handle it, have to be mentioned.

a. The long-distance trade, carried out by regular donkey caravans and operating through a system of trading stations spread out over a large part of Anatolia, required considerable investments in transport, communications, local facilities, and personnel. It was feasible and profitable thanks to the differences between the exchange value of the goods traded in Assur and Anatolia. Silver, rich in supply in Anatolia, once shipped to Assur allowed the Assyrians to buy there tin and textiles, which in Anatolia could again be sold for two (tin) to four times (textiles) as much silver as they had cost in Assur.

b. The overland trade required caravan journeys of ca. six weeks between Assur and Kanish and was impossible during the ca. four months of the Anatolian winter. This made time precious and timing important. If purchases and sales could be carried out without delay two journeys *vice versa* within one year might just be possible. Reduction of transaction time meant reduced costs and offered the possibility of additional profit. In achieving this, silver as a highly valued, generally accepted, and easily transported type of money played a key role. This may also account for the high official ("according to the ruling of the *kārum*") rate of interest of 30 per cent per year (during the preceding Ur III period and in roughly contemporary Babylonia the annual rate of interest usually was only 20 per cent) and explains that silver was always in demand and constantly changed hands.

c. The continuous presence of Assyrian traders in Anatolia, in a network of ca. 30 trading stations [*wabartum*] and "colonies" [*kārum*] substantially enlarged commercial possibilities. More and different markets could be reached, storage in reaction to seasonal fluctuations in demand and supply or to political disturbances became possible, and medium and long term credit (up to 12 months; *ana ūmē qurbūtim/patiūtim*) could be granted, both to Assyrian agents (*tamkārum*) and to local traders and palaces. Trade could also be carried out by indirect exchange (tin or textiles > copper > silver, or > wool > silver) over a wider area and between different markets, either for reasons of Anatolian supply or in order to increase profits.[6] But this development also entailed additional costs and risks and required new legal procedures and rules for the conversion of goods, the transfer of **[57]** payments among a bigger number of participants, and periodic accounting. Giving credit frequently was unavoidable due to the market situation (local palaces usually did not pay cash) or was preferred in order to obtain better prices and to serve more markets by means of selling agents traveling around with merchandise given on credit (called *qīptum*). Credit sale, however, meant deferred payment and the possibility of problems with insolvent, overdue or unwilling debtors and agents, which explains the many references in letters to outstanding claims (*bābtum*) resulting from "leaving behind" (*ezābum*) merchandise.[7] Payments not infrequently had to be enforced from both Assyrians and local customers by the threat of fines (default interest) or by means of formal summonses and lawsuits. Anatolian palaces, rulers and dignitaries at times had to be induced by

6 See for this type of exchange, in which copper played a prominent role, Dercksen 1996, 149f.

7 See Veenhof 1972, 419ff. with n. 537, and Skaist 1994, 46ff ., 186ff.

gifts and bribes to meet their obligations. All these complications, of course, added to the costs and resulted in more correspondence and more administration, as the archives show.

2. Commercial Credit and Straight Loans

In the framework of the trade commercial credit was granted in different situations and for various reasons. We meet it in connection with the purchase of merchandise in Assur, with its sale in Anatolia, and in a variety of situations in both areas, where need for credit arose. Commercial loans were granted both to people at the bottom of the commercial hierarchy and to rich merchants, not only in order to enable them to carry out more trade and to make more profit, but also because, to quote a phrase of Goitein (used to describe the situation during the early medieval trade in the Mediterranean), which fully applies to the Old Assyrian situation, "owing to the principle of having one's capital working all the time and other circumstances even well-to-do persons were not rarely short of cash".[8]

a. Commercial Credit

A first form of credit were interest-free advances to relatives and close business associates, to which the sources refer with phrases such as "I paid for you out of my own funds" (*ina raminia ašqulakkum*), "let your silver be withdrawn from your disposal for a few months" (*kaspum libbe'elka*),[9] or when there is mention of "favors" (*gimillum*), usually granted in such conditions. These "favors" often consisted in making merchandise available at favorable conditions, buying it quickly at a good price, or sending the silver which the merchandise would yield to Assur as soon as possible, even before the sale was completed. Such "favors" apparently could imply specific agreements on quantities, prices and terms and we have texts which speak of "the rest of the favor" still due.[10] In (the second page of) a letter,[11] a trader offers his addressee to **[58]** send silver to pay for the investments he made for him, but adds: "Do me a favor (*scil.* by advancing the silver), and if you cannot advance it, charge me interest as brothers pay to each other". In KKS 29 the favor asked by a trader who calls himself "a man of favors", to stress the mutuality of the concept, consists of quickly buying tin and textiles and shipping the silver to Assur. The writer of KKS 12 mentions two alternatives, either paying interest for 2½ months or granting (lit. "to become indebted to me for") a favor (*gimillam liḫḫiblam*). In KTS 1 22b a trader asks for help to carry out a quick sale of his *ḫusārum*-stone (lapis lazuli), suggesting that the addressee might pay for it immediately, out of his own funds, and he concludes with: "For the silver which you will send me from your own funds I will owe you a favor (*gimillam laḫḫiblakkum*". Many such requests occur in the correspondence of business partners and close associates, *e.g.* that between Pūšu-kēn and Šalim-aḫum, where the latter in particular is always anxious to speed up transactions in order to obtain silver as soon as possible. In one of his letters[12] Šalimaḫum writes:

---

8 Goitein 1967, 252.

9 See for this expression Veenhof 1972, 409ff.

10 In the unpublished letter Kt n/k 1654 (courtesy of S. Çeçen) we read: "Let him give (to P.) 70 minas of tin ... of the favor I owe to E. and let him (P.) give him (for it) 10 minas of silver, not later than in spring. Approach him (E.) in connection with the rest of the favor he is entitled to and say: 'Do not force the gentleman to pay directly from the (yield of) his *naruqqum*-capital. Let him send you favors (plural!) from the City (of Assur), so that he may do you a favor'". Apparently E. is asked to be kind enough to supply him with merchandise from Assur, which he can sell in Anatolia, so that he will be able to pay the favor due to E. with the silver he had earned. This becomes clear from the related letter Kt n/k 1346:18ff., where we also learn that the size of the original favor was 30 minas of silver.

11 The Burton-letter, published by R.D. Biggs in E. Leichty *et al.* (eds.), *A Scientific Humanist. Studies in Memory of Abraham Sachs* (Philadelphia 1988), 33ff.

12 Published by D.O. Edzard and K. Hecker in *MDOG* 102 (1970), 86f.

"If you agree, send me, as soon as you hear my letter, 13 1/3 minas of silver and I will make available twice as much (*šitta qātēn laddi*). Then I will make the purchases you will write me and send them to you (even) while the merchandise which belongs to us jointly is still on its way up (to Anatolia). When D. (the transporter, a son of the writer) arrives there, you can take your silver from the first sales you make and one can bring me my silver here (later)".

This type of informal credit is quite common in early trade, also in the Geniza documents studied by Goitein, and we leave it with these general remarks.

For the sale of the merchandise in Anatolia various methods were used. Part of it was usually kept by the manager in Kanish (or elsewhere) who was the destination of the caravan, probably because he intended to sell some of it himself. Part was sold to the local palaces, usually at credit,[13] part was entrusted to employees of the firm, at times the transporters who had accompanied the caravan and who also had to sell their own textiles.[14] A substantial part usually was entrusted to selling agents (called *tamkārum*), who must have sold it elsewhere in Anatolia, but since their sales apparently were mostly cash, we have very little evidence on their activities. This last option meant, as the texts say, that lots of merchandise (frequently including transport donkeys) were "given to" (*tadānum ana*), "laid/given upon" (*nadā'um/tadānum iṣṣēr*) or "entrusted to" (*qiāpum* with double accusative) such agents; the different terms at times are used in one and the **[59]** same document.[15] The various options are nicely described in Aššur-iddin's letter POAT 5, which deals with the sale of a load of tin and textiles which has arrived in Kanish. The writer first cancels an earlier instruction to "give" the load to I. (apparently an employee and transporter of the firm), because "he has (already) 'taken' much tin from his (previous) transport" (line 29 speaks of "20 minas of earlier silver owed by him"). The better textiles and the tin now must be handed over or sent to A. (one of the addressees of the letter and hence also an employee or partner of the writer), who has to ship them to "wherever any silver can be earned for me". If A. has already left on a trip, the merchandise has to entrusted to ("laid upon") a reliable agent for a specified credit term (*ana ūmē*) and a few months longer do not matter, if only the agent is reliable![16]

The merchandise such agents received hence could be called *qīptum*, which implies, as is the case in Old Babylonian,[17] that they were middlemen who sold the goods to the real customers and had to pay back in due time to their owners who had granted them credit. As was the case with Old Babylonian *qīptum*-loans, no interest was charged, but the due date of the credit was fixed and the price agreed upon obviously depended to some extent on the length of the credit term. Such credit transactions yielded promissory notes, the most frequent type of Old Assyrian contract, which simply state that a particular person has a debt claim on (*iṣṣēr ... išu*) another person for a sum of silver to be paid not later than a particular date, on penalty of default interest, among Assyrians usually a rate of 30 per cent per year. Occasionally such contracts mention a guarantor, rarely a pledge (see below).[18] Contrary to Rosen, I am convinced that the bulk of these contracts does reflect

---

13 See for the behaviour of the local Anatolian palaces as buyer of merchandise, Dercksen 1996, 165ff. and my observations on the type of debt-note called *iṣurtum* in Veenhof 1995b, especially 321ff.

14 Textiles they usually bought in Assur with the silver of the interest-free loan (normally 25 to 30 shekels of silver, called *be'ūlātum),* which was made available to them there in remuneration of their work with the caravan; see Veenhof 1972, 86f., with notes 130f.

15 *E.g.* in Kt n/k 528 (courtesy of C. Günbattı), which summarizes various such transactions with the words: "In all we entrusted (*niqīp*) two talents minus one mina of silver".

16 The letter has a virtual duplicate in BIN 4 53 and also links up with CCT 4 2b, both of which help to improve its reading and understanding as offered in POAT. [These letters have now been edited in Larsen 2002, nos 2 and 19].

17 See Skaist 1994, 41ff., for Old Babylonian ŠU.LÁ = *qīptum.*

18 See for such contracts EL 12-103, where they figure as *Verpflichtungsscheine,* and Rosen 1977, who edited such contracts published after 1935.

commercial credit, but this is not so easy to prove because the documents almost never state the reason and background of such debt claims. Among the few exceptions are EL 88, a debt-note for "51 shekels of silver, price of three *kutānu*textiles", and ICK 1 102, a quittance for "two minas of silver, price of two donkeys and two *kutānu*-textiles".[19] When the debt claims recorded are large amounts of silver or copper a commercial background has to be assumed. But many of the contracts which record relatively small debts of up to one mina of silver, may also reflect credit sale of merchandise, in particular textiles. In the trade documented by the Cairo Geniza it was as true as in Old Assyrian times, to quote again Goitein,[20] that "the wholesale textile merchants often sold single pieces too. The reason for this was the relatively high value of each piece" (good textiles were sold in Anatolia for prices ranging from 10 to 45 shekels of silver apiece, usually 20 to 30 shekels). Of course, various other commercial transactions and liabilities could also result in such promissory notes, which were also drawn up in consequence of settlements of accounts to record remaining debt claims.[21]

[60] Proof that the bare facts mentioned in such contracts do reflect commercial credit granted to selling agents may be derived from some letters, called "caravan accounts, group 2" in Larsen 1967, of which the letter BIN 4 61 (Larsen type 3:11) is a good example. It tells us that upon arrival of a caravan with tin and textiles some merchandise was "given" to those working for the sender (lines 42ff.), some was sold to the local palace (44ff.), and some was entrusted to the caravan-leader as interest bearing-loan (49-69). The bulk, however, was entrusted to two persons (*illibbi* PN *tadin*) acting as selling agents, who were to pay for it fixed sums of silver (in all 68 minas) after 45, 47, and 50 weeks (lines 26-42a). Promissory notes for similar amounts of silver and similar credit terms are not rare and the letter quoted explicitly states that the credit agreement resulted in written contracts, whose dates (month III) are mentioned in the caravan account. Many more letters refer to such claims recorded in "valid deeds" (*ṭuppum harmum*), sealed by the debtor, with a fixed due date, but actual contracts which mention more facts than the name of creditor and debtor, the amount of silver to be paid and the due date are rare. An exception, already quoted in Larsen 1967, 162f., is ICK 1 162: "31 minas of tin (and) six *kutānu*-textiles, (part of) our trust (*ša qīptini*), N. has carried to Ḫattum. He shall not yield tin or textiles (to somebody).[22] For this merchandise he will pay eight minas and 10 shekels of silver within 37 weeks, (reckoned) from the week of S. and D. (sealed by two witnesses)".

The persons who were granted such commercial credit were not working for a fee or a share in the profit, as a Babylonian commercial agent (*šamallā'um*)[23] might, nor was interest charged for the credit received (as could be the case in Old Babylonian, see the Laws of Hammurabi, paragraph 100). They were only liable for paying the amount of silver stated in the promissory note at the due date mentioned. They would sell the goods

---

19 It is no accident that these two contracts are the only ones dealing with the sale of imported goods to figure in Kienast 1984 (as nrs. 33 and 35).

20 Goitein 1967, 150.

21 Old Assyrian promissory notes almost never use the so-called ŠU BA.AN.TI / *ilqe*-formula, which usually identifies the claim as resulting from a straight loan. The standard formula "creditor has a claim of ... on debtor" (*iṣṣēr* ... *išu*), which does not reveal the background of the transaction, may refer to a straight loan, to commercial credit (*qīptum*), to claims resulting from partial payments and settlements of accounts, and to taxes, fees, and profits still due. The very frequent description of amounts of silver (or merchandise) as *ina libbi* PN, "(still) owed by PN", is equally vague and may refer to all kind of transactions and liabilities. Only interest free loans supplied to personnel contracted to serve as transporters are clearly recognizable, because the loan is designated as *be'ūlātum*, "working capital" (lit. "put at their free disposal", *ana be'ālim*) and their recipient is said "to be held by the silver (received)" (*išti kaspim uktāl*, an expression also used of personal pledges). See for *be'ūlātum*, Kienast 1989 and Veenhof 1994.

22 Assyrian *waššurum*, "to release, to yield", which means credit sale which results in an outstanding claim (*bābtum*) and deferred payment

23 The term occurs in Old Assyrian, but is rare; see *CAD* Š/1, 291, 1a.

during the term granted at the best possible prices and what they earned over the amount due was their own profit, from which they had to live and to cover their expenses. The at times long credit terms must have allowed them to do more than just sell their merchandise and I assume that in the meantime they may have used the silver acquired for additional transactions in the hope of maximizing their earnings before their due dates[24] (see also below, the remarks on the impact of default interest).

[61] The use of these selling agents allowed merchants to supply more customers and markets and saved them the time and trouble of acting themselves as travelling salesmen in deals with local inhabitants and institutions and to face problems such as deferred payments, payment in other valuta than silver or gold (copper, wool), and various risks and delays due to political or military problems, season (no trade during harvest time), or climate (no trade during winter). In return for fixed and guaranteed sums of silver they must have sacrificed part of the profit and accepted delays in the recovery of the silver. We note that letters frequently raise the issue of the conditions of credit granted, notably the alternatives of cash sale (*ana itaṭlim*), short-term (*ana ūmē qurbūtim*) or long-term (*ana ūmē patiūtim*) credit. "Let your report reach me concerning my merchandise, whether you have entrusted it to an agent for a particular period, or whether you have sold it cash" (Kt 87/k 347: llff., courtesy of K. Hecker). Medium and long-term credit must have allowed better prices. In BIN 4 61, those for the terms of almost one year (45-50 weeks) were one shekel of silver for seven shekels of tin and 30 shekels of silver per textile, which is very favorable. The selling agent of the contract ICK 1 162, quoted in the previous paragraph, would have been able to pay the silver due, if he managed to sell his tin at a rate of one shekel of silver for six shekels of tin (yield: five minas and 10 shekels) and his textiles at 30 shekels apiece (yield: three minas). Hence an even higher price for the tin, notwithstanding the fact that he had about three months less time to realize his sales. The mere existence of this contract shows that such conditions could be met and that there still must have been a margin allowing the agent to earn something for himself. Unfortunately, we are mostly unable to relate such prices to the realities of supply and demand (time, place, specific conditions) and the relations between those granting credit (*e.g.* the anonymous "we" in ICK 1 162) and the selling agents. But there is no doubt that "market factors" were at work, as the letter TC 3 49 shows, where cash sale was impossible and "silver was difficult to obtain/expensive" (*kaspū dannū*). The selling agent eventually found agreed to a credit term of four weeks and it does not surprise that the prices were rather low, in particular that of only 13½ shekels of silver per *kutānu*-textile, which is 55 per cent less than the price in BIN 4 61 and ICK 1 162. But, as will be seen below, there were also cases where indebted and defaulting agents had to accept hard conditions in order to survive.

Equally important must have been at what time of the year credit was granted, because it mattered much whether payment could be expected well before the winter, so that the silver could be sent to Assur in time and people there could arrange to have the next caravan ready for departure in early spring, as soon as "the roads became open". In BIN 4 61, the contracts with the selling agents were drawn up in the third month, that is in early spring, which left them lots of time for selling their goods. The remainder of the merchandise was "given" to an employee of the firm only in the eleventh month, shortly before the winter, and he had to pay only one shekel of silver for eight shekels of tin and 20 shekels of silver per *kutānu*-textile, hence resp. 15 and 33% less, but he was charged interest.

---

24 Something similar must have been the case with some Old Babylonian trading agents in Larsa. In TCL 10 125, an agent (in Ešnunna?) receives a consignment of silver for delivery in Larsa, within six or eight months, and in TCL 10 20 the term for delivery of the silver in Susa is five months (see for the texts Leemans 1960, chapter 3). These agents may not have received cash silver, but rather merchandise for which they had to weigh out in due time, in the cities mentioned, silver, presumably less than what they could have earned by selling their goods.

Cash sale, which made it possible to ship the silver to Assur "with the next caravan", in order to equip a new caravan or to pay debts whose "interest is mounting", was of course the most attractive option and at times friends were asked the "favour" (*gimillum*) of paying cash for merchandise from their own funds (see above). Not rare are instructions of the type "They must sell tin and textiles cash, not grant credit, nor yield **[62]** them. They shall not yield tin and textiles until the silver arrives".[25] We find them in several letters sent by Šalim-aḫum to Pūšu-kēn, but cash sale frequently was impossible. What was meant by "to yield"[26] is not very clear, because it is a general term for giving up possession of something, also used for giving back debt-notes after the debt has been paid. It presumably means real credit sale, not to agents but to customers who will pay later, hence a transaction also described as "leaving behind" (*ezābum*) merchandise, which creates "outstanding claims" (*bābtum*), a frequent topic of Old Assyrian business letters.[27] Other, more careful and patient traders insist on the quality of the selling agent who should be "reliable as you yourself",[28] so that there will be no reason for fear. In such cases they even are ready to grant longer credit,[29] but there were other options too. The writer of the letter POAT 22, Imdīlum, asks his correspondent to sell tin and textiles cash, but "if this is impossible, let my tin remain under seal", hence be kept in store for the time being. At times a compromise was inevitable, as in the unpublished letter Kt n/k 524:44ff. (courtesy of C. Günbattı): "Of all the merchandise which has been cleared you must entrust (*nadā'um iṣṣēr*) half at long-term and half at short-term credit to reliable selling agents with fixed terms. Do not attach too much importance to a few months, if only your agents are reliable!". Frequent emphasis on the reliability of the agent is rooted in the experience that *tamkārums* regularly exceed their terms and delay payments, when they get into financial problems or may prove to be "unwise" (*lā tašīmtum*). This creates serious problems for the merchant in question, who has to meet his own due dates for satisfying financiers and authorities in Assur, as we learn from Pūšu-kēn's letter BIN 4 32, discussed in Dercksen 1999.[30] How merchants tried to deal with defaulting agents will be discussed in paragraph 4.

b. Straight Loans

There are dozens of references which show that all kind of traders were able to "obtain silver at interest" (*kaspam ana ṣibtim laqā'um*) in Assur. Frequently this happened "at a merchant's house" (*bēt tamkārim*), at times in considerable quantities, ranging from a few to 30 minas of silver. This shows that there was a lot of silver available in the city and that its owners apparently were ready to use it not only for (longterm) investments in the capital (*naruqqum*) of a trader, but also to extend straight loans at interest to businessmen in need of money. The silver borrowed frequently served to acquire or increase funds necessary for buying merchandise for export to Anatolia. Some examples are: TC 3 26:7: "We borrowed silver in accordance with your instruction and now we will buy textiles"; BIN 6 117:15ff.: "When we bought tin we borrowed four **[63]** minas of silver at interest; let the interest on the silver not get (too) much!"; TC 128: 10f.: "S. and M. brought us 8 ½ minas of silver and in accordance with your instruction we (also) borrowed silver at a merchant's house and made purchases for you"; TC 2 11:19ff.: "Since tin was expensive, we did not call at a merchant's house and did not buy it, we only sent you what we bought with your own silver"; TC 3 73:28ff.: "(For) the tin I sent him I had borrowed silver at

---

25 *Ana itaṭlim liddinū lā iqippū lā uššurū adi kaspum errubu annakam u ṣubāti lā uššurū*; variant: *lā uṣṣiū*, "they (the goods) shall not leave (before ...)".

26 *Waššurum*, see above n. 22.

27 See for these terms the literature quoted in n. 7.

28 *Lū kēn kīma qaqqidika.*

29 "Do not attach too much value to a few months" (*warham ištēn u šina lā tušēqarā* or *tabe''elā*), cf. Veenhof 1972, 443f.

30 Lines 17ff.: "Among the selling agents on whom I depend there are two or three unwise ones, so that I have lost much silver, but it is not expedient to reveal their names to you".

a merchant's house; the interest is mounting, I am worried"; TC 3 36:30ff.: "Your wrote me: 'I will send you the eight minas of silver later'. Since the caravan [is delayed?], we borrowed 7 ½ minas [+ x shekels] of silver as equivalent of the (delayed) eight minas of silver"; AnOr 6 2 rev.:5'ff.: "We borrowed five minas (of silver) at a merchant's house and we (ourselves) added six minas of silver. We paid it for (buying) the textiles for wrapping which E. had brought for you, until the silver shipped by H. had arrived".

All examples mention the borrowing of silver and the question arises whether loans granted or credit received "at a merchant's house" could not also consist of merchandise (hence tin and textiles), perhaps rated in and in due time to be paid in silver. In the unpublished text Kt m/k 92:14f. (courtesy of K. Hecker), which uses the designation *qīptum*, we read: "We fully paid in silver (*kaspam nušabbi*) for all *qīptum*-loans we contracted at a/various merchant's house(s)",[31] but there is no proof that *qīptum* here refers to merchandise. CCT 4 32b:15 states: "For the merchandise (*luqūtum*) which we contracted (as a loan; verb *šasā'um*) at a merchant's house, you only sent us the capital sum (*šīmat kaspim*); because we also had to add interest and had to refine the silver (you sent), the merchant still has a claim on us of one mina and 22 1/3 shekels of silver and he retained our promissory note. (To pay it) we borrowed the silver at interest and interest accrues since the eleventh month". Here the loan or credit received could be the merchandise mentioned, but it is certainly not impossible to understand the words "the merchandise which we contracted (as loan)" as an abbreviation of "the merchandise for (the purchase of which) we contracted (a loan)". Without better proof the question has to remain open.

Loans were also taken out to meet financial liabilities, both debts to the City-office (for which people were dunned by the *līmum*-official, who could seal the house of a debtor and eventually even sell it) and to private creditors. I offer just a few illustrative examples. According to Kt n/k 515 and related texts,[32] D., who was guarantor for M., "called at a merchant's house to borrow eight minas of silver and paid it for your debt to the City-office". In TPAK 1 26:17ff., *bēru*-officials (inspectors?) in Assur seized a family's house for debts to the City, whereupon "we called at a merchant's house for 75 shekels of silver, your share, and paid it to the *bērū*, who brought it to the City-office". Private debts are a reason for borrowing money, *e.g.* in BIN 6 74: 6-15, where I. writes to E.: "You wrote me as follows: 'Let your report reach me about how much silver you took at interest and inform me.' As soon as I heard this tablet, I wrote you in my letter 'For the 30 minas of silver which you owe me I borrowed refined silver at an interest of 5/6 shekel (per mina per month)'". This also happens in ATHE 28: 17-25: "In addition to the 18 minas of silver which you brought me, I borrowed for you 13 minas of refined silver at an interest of 20 per cent per year. They sealed our contract and then we paid 31 **[64]** minas of refined silver, your debt to P.". In a letter in the Trinity Museum of Archaeology (San Antonio; unpublished), the addressee is asked to collect a claim which P. has on E. and he is ordered: "If he (= E.) refuses to settle the silver account and does not yield the merchandise, borrow eight minas of silver at interest and let P. establish his claim on it".[32a]

Silver and at times copper were also borrowed for the purchase of usually expensive houses in Assur.[33] The writer of the letter VS 26 8 tells the addressee: "We borrowed at interest the silver which we owe to A. and paid him. We also borrowed six talents of copper, being the price of the house. Send silver lest the interest becomes a problem for you (*imarraṣakkum*)" (lines 9-18). And in TTC 6:12ff., a letter addressed to Pūšu-kēn, we read: "Ša. and Šu., without (consulting) us, bought the house for you for 16 minas of silver and now they have written to you: 'We borrowed the silver at interest'. But we did not

---

31 The verb is in the iterative Gtn-stem and *bēt tamkārim*, with the regens in the construct state, may also be a plural.

32 See the analysis in Veenhof 1995a, 1723f.

[32a See K. Balkan, *Orientalia* 36 (1967) 396, note 2, c)]

33 See also Michel 1996, 295f.

borrow any silver at interest for you, Ša. paid 10 minas of silver as price for the house out of his own money". [34]

Borrowing silver for such purposes apparently was an established practice and one never reads that this was difficult or impossible. Silver was available and its owners were ready to extend loans, not only friendly advances or soft, interest-free loans to relatives and close associates, on whose help one might rely "when one had to be saved" (*ana ūm eṭārim*), but also business loans at the attractive rate of interest of 30 per cent per year, at times also cheaper. We have references both to people taking out such loans and to those granting them and to how they recorded them in valid debt-notes. The writer of Kt n/k 486 (unpublished, courtesy C. Günbattı) gives the following instruction: "As for the 30 minas of silver I wrote you about, let E. give 20 minas of silver and you yourself give 10 minas, send it to me (in Assur) and take the interest from me when I arrive". In AKT 3 64:7-12, a debt of more than 11 minas of silver had to be paid to I. The debtors sent one mina of gold and two minas of silver and add: "As for the remainder, borrow at interest whatever you need and pay the debt we owe to I.". The writer of TC 3 31 asks his addressees "to deposit silver as his share at the *kārum*-office and to take it from the silver you have obtained from my outstanding claims. If you have not obtained it from [my] outstanding claims, borrow it at interest" (lines 29-33). Some texts show that traders used the possibility of lending out silver which would not be used for making purchases in the near future, in order to make it productive.[35] BIN 6 25:15ff. "You wrote me: 'B. has paid us silver and it lies idle here (*nadi*)'. The silver must not lie idle (*la nadi*)! If I. needs it, let him take it, but if not, lend it out (*tadānum*) at interest!" Very instructive is Šu-Suen's letter VS 26 69:

> E. brought 20 minas of silver under your seals and the son of K. brought you 10 minas. Was it my instruction to have the silver sent in order to let it lie idle? Please, my brothers, if one needs silver in the *kārum*-office, unpack the silver and loan it at [65] interest. If you cannot give it to the *kārum*-office, loan it at interest to a trader reliable as you yourselves, who need not be feared![36]

Another example is VS 26 67:7ff.:

> "You wrote me as follows: 'We acquired the silver of A., but since the terms of your selling agents were almost due (*ūmū tamkārīka qurbū*), we loaned it at interest, thinking: we will send all the silver (later) with Š.' Payment by my agents, however, has been delayed (*ūmū tamkārīa ana warkišunu ittūrūnim*), therefore send the silver of A. with K. and do not (wait until you can also) send the silver of my agents."[36a]

In the letter I 637, in reaction to a request to buy tin in order to earn ("make") silver, the writer answers: "There is no tin for sale here, but there is silver for sale and you must send as much silver as can be put out at interest" (*ana ṣibtim alākum*). Revealing is the text of the last will *RA* 60 (1966), 143:26ff., where two ladies receive as their share in an inheritance the usufruct of a capital of five minas of silver (which eventually will be divided between two brothers), which is put out at interest: "From the remainder (of the assets) they will put out at interest five minas of silver and she and her mother will have

---

34 See for this letter C. Michel, *RA* 80 (1986), 110f. The letter written by Ša. and Šu. must have been very similar to TC 2 11, where Aššur-bānī and Ša. inform Pūšu-kēn about their purchase of the house in question for 16 minas of silver. [See for such sales and purchases now K.R. Veenhof, "Houses in the Ancient City of Assur", in B.S. Düring *et al.* (eds.), *Correlates of Complexity. Essays in Archaeology and Assyriology Dedicated to Diederik J.W. Meijer in Honour of his 65th Birthday* (PIHANS 116, Leiden 2011) 220-228].

35 Silver not used, not invested in the trade for making purchases and profit, could be said "to be(come) hungry", see Veenhof 1987, 62ff.

36 See the edition of this letter in Michel 1991, 230f. no. 169; I take lines 6f. as an ironical question.

[36a See Michel 1991, II, no. 78.]

its usufruct (*ekkalā*)". In TC 3 29: 10ff. a trader, being asked for silver, answers: "the silver has been put out at interest, I need its interest".

All this suggests that there was indeed a constant circulation of silver in Assur and in this flow we can distinguish various "streams". In the *first* place the vast amounts of silver which arrive from Anatolia, the bulk of which was regularly used by "Kanish traders" to buy merchandise for caravans leaving for Anatolia. Most of this silver was paid to the "houses" of merchants, and presumably also to the "City-office" (*bēt ālim*), which acted as a kind of wholesale dealers. The latter in turn must have used a large part of this silver to buy tin and textiles from the traders (from Elam(?) and Babylonia) who imported these goods into Assur. This is the *second* stream, which left Assur. In the *third* place there was the stream of silver made available to those who traded on Anatolia, either as long-term investment (*na-ruqqum*, *ebuṭṭū*, etc.) or by granting credit and straight loans to those in need of cash. The first and third streams to a considerable extent must have consisted of the same silver, earned by "Kanish traders" and reinvested in the trade by Assur-based merchants. We have to assume that investments, commercial credit, and short-term loans of some size – apart from what moved between close relatives and business partners – were granted by persons grown rich from the trade. This group of people probably comprised men of means who had always stayed in Assur and successful, presumably older merchants who had returned there from Anatolia and may have become wholesale dealers who granted credit and used their capital also as financiers and money-lenders. Both may have functioned as a kind of merchant-bankers, who could supply the silver needed by the traders. If this is correct, we may perhaps distinguish two kinds of merchants. On the one hand those directly involved in the actual trade on Anatolia, frequently on the move or staying abroad and constantly in need of silver for their transactions and hence pressing their debtors and selling agents for prompt payment. On the other hand those, presumably older and richer, who lived in Assur as wholesale dealers, investors, and merchant-bankers. They enjoyed the 30 per cent interest received on credit and loans and hence perhaps were more patient with their debtors as long as the latter did not default on interest, while they could supplement their earnings as money-lenders by the dividends and profits which their investments yielded.

[66] The references to borrowing silver (and occasionally also copper), including those which add "at a merchant's house", however, are not restricted to Assur. The same happened in Anatolia, especially in Kanish, as the following examples show. In EL 254 the representatives of the debtor Š. authorize the son of his creditor "to borrow silver at a merchant's house at interest", promising that they would pay him back capital plus interest from the assets of the debtor. According to TPAK 1 6:8ff., "We called at a merchant's house for two talents of copper and paid it to our father's creditor", and also in Kt e/k 67 somebody "borrows copper at interest" in order to be able to pay the installment of his debt to his creditor. In I 612 the writer states: "I borrowed 8 ¼ shekels of silver at a merchant's house and paid it to the Anatolian for our mother's debt". TC 3 67: 10ff. mentions that the trader Enlil-bānī in Kanish "had been booked in a merchant's house as guarantor for K.", who must have borrowed silver there, and Kt m/k 122:24ff. (courtesy of K. Hecker) mentions "silver for settling accounts, at a rate of three shekels per mina, at a merchant's house, paid in the name of K.". Other examples of silver borrowed in Anatolia are TC 2 39:2lff. (3 ½ minas) and BIN 6 33 (10 minas), while the writer of CCT 4 8b:16ff., who intends "to sell tin before there is too much tin here" (which will affect the price), "will borrow tin for a value of 10 minas of silver at a merchant's house". We also have about a dozen debt-notes, which authorize the creditor "to enter a merchant's house and to borrow silver at interest for (at the expense of) the debtor" if the latter fails to pay back in time (published examples: EL 87 and 185; ICK 2 95 and 147; AKT 1 34; TPAK 1 169), most of which seem to refer to transactions in Anatolia. Finally it should be mentioned here that the expression "to enter a merchant's house in order to borrow (take) silver (at interest)" has a perfect parallel on the Anatolian scene, where the word "merchant (which in Anatolia may also have the meaning "Assyrian trader") is replaced by "native

Anatolian" (*nu'ā'um*).[37] It shows that for people in need of cash also Anatolian merchants or money-lenders were available. The only published occurrence is in AKT 2 53:20-24: "Make S. pay the silver and if he refuses to pay, say to him: 'I will borrow it at interest in the house of an Anatolian'".

c. Borrowing at a bēt tamkārim

In many cases loans are referred to simply by the words "to borrow (take) silver at interest" (*kaspam ana ṣibtim laqā'um*), without any indication of where and from whom the silver was borrowed. But more frequently (in a few dozen cases) it is stated that silver is borrowed "at a merchant's house" (*bēt tamkārim*; henceforth *b. t.*). The majority are in letters, which give instructions about or report on such loans, but there are also about 10 occurrences in promissory notes, which stipulate that, if the debtor defaults the creditor will "take" the silver due "at a merchant's house". While promissory notes are always formulated objectively, in the third person ("the creditor has a claim of x silver on the debtor"), the clause authorizing the creditor to borrow is always in the first person singular. We meet it in various formulations:

[67] 1) "I will enter and take (the) silver at a merchant's house" (*errabma b. t. kaspam alaqqe*), EL 87:11ff.;185:12ff.; Kt a/k 604:10f.;

2) "I will enter and take silver in a merchant's house" (*errabma ina b. t. kaspam alaqqe*), I 475:17ff.;

3) "I will enter a merchant's house and take silver" (*ana b. t. errabma kaspam alaqqe*), ICK 2 147:19'ff. (*nerrabma*, with two creditors, who borrow "the silver and the interest on it"); TPAK 1 169:7'f. (in a letter);

4) "I will take silver at a merchant's house" (*kaspam b. t. alaqqe*, without *errab*), AKT 1 34:15ff.; ICK 2 95:8f.

Interest is mentioned in various ways. I 475 writes "I will take silver at interest" (*ana ṣibtim*), followed by "and he shall compensate (*mallu'um*) the interest". TPAK 1 169:10'f. adds "and you will be responsible to me for (*ana* ... *tazzazzam*) the silver and the interest on it". Some contracts do not speak only of "taking silver", but state that the loan is *ana bitiqtim*, "(to make up) for what is missing" (AKT 1 34:15f.; EL 185:13f.; Kt a/k 604: 11f.), or add that "he (the debtor) shall compensate what is missing" (*bitiqtam šūtma umalla*; AKT 1 34:18f.; Kt a/k 604:14f .; ICK 2 95:10, with plural *bitqātim*). In some cases we have *alaqqešum* (EL 87:13; AKT 1 34:17; Kt a/k 604:13; in letters also *alaqqe'akkum*), where the pronominal dative suffix refers to the debtor "for whom/at whose expense" the silver is borrowed.

The occurrences in promissory notes are the only ones where the verb "to enter" is used to describe the action of the creditor;[38] it never occurs in letters. I would link this with the fact that it is only in these contracts that the creditor speaks in the first person ("I will enter and take ...") and assume that they reveal the full wording (*verba solemnia*) of a formulaic expression by means of which the creditor publicly states his right to

---

37 Kt f/k 101:22f. distinguishes a person's debtors in *nu'ā'ū* and *tamkārū*. In the divorce settlement Kt n/k 1414:7ff. (Sever 1992) the divorced wife is allowed "to go either to a *nu'ā'um* or to a *tamkārum*, whatever she prefers", and the letter Kt k/k 47:9ff. asks for the purchase of two slave boys (*ṣuhārū*), "either of *tamkārums* or of citizens of Kanish".

38 Earlier (see *e.g.* EL 87 with commentary) the debtor was considered to be the subject of the verb "to enter" and the clause was interpreted as stating that he would "enter the house of the creditor (*tamkārum*)", presumably in antichretic debt bondage. The occurrence of the plural *nerrab*, "we will enter", in ICK 2 147:19', followed by *kaspam nilaqqe*, "we will borrow the silver", shows that it actually was the creditor who took out the loan.

indemnify himself at the expense of the defaulting debtor. Letters and other non-legal documents omit the formulaic "I will enter and", without changing the meaning.

There are actually two variants when the expression is used without the verb "to enter". One uses the verb "to take/to borrow" (*laqā'um*), the other the verb "to call (at)" (*šasā'um*, *e.g.* CCT 4 32b:4f.; KTS 1 9a:5; TC 1 28:7; TC 2 11:20; TPAK 1 6:11f.; 26:17f.; *CAD* Š/3, 159f., 6 translates: "to ask a creditor for, to contract for a loan"). The use of the latter verb perhaps indicates a public and formal act, since borrowing at the expense of somebody else cannot be done privately, but requires witnesses and probably evidence of the claim on which the action is based. Compare also the Old Babylonian expression *bīt* (in Old Babylonian Susa also *bāb*) PN *šasûm*, "to call at a person's house/gate to demand (something from him)", which also has a formal ring.[39] But *laqā'um* and *šasā'um* are used as synonyms in our expression, as the alternation between the two in EL 309, tablet and case (both with personal dative suffix) shows.

[68] Equally remarkable in the expression is the regular mention of "the house" of the merchant as the place where one borrows silver, also in the dozens of occurrences which omit the verb "to enter". This mention of "the house of the merchant" as the place where one borrows is also (but rarely) attested in Old Babylonian. In ARMT 13 17 rev. 2', it occurs together with the verb "to enter", when a heavily fined man states "I will en[ter] the house of a merchant and will borrow [silver]".[40] In AbB 9 64:10f. a man intends "to borrow (take) silver in a merchant's house" in order to buy an ox (cf. AbB 13 53:13). But one may also omit "the house" and use simply (*kaspam*) *itti tamkārim leqûm* (AbB 12 88:25, for buying barley; perhaps also AbB 13 4:7), which parallels in Old Assyrian *kaspam išti tamkārim laqā'um* (CCT 4 49a:17f.), which is very rare. The use of *erābum* in the full expression shows that *bētum* is a physical entity, not "firm, household", but "house". The substantial loans we are dealing with were not negotiated on the market, but in a merchant's office and the expression evokes the picture of a person in need of silver calling at and entering a merchant-banker's office, where the latter works, keeps his bullion (in a strong room or safe) and draws up and keeps his records.

How we understand *bēt tamkārim* depends on the interpretation of *tamkārum*. Garelli described him as a kind of merchant-banker, whose role or perhaps duty it was to facilitate commercial transactions of other merchants by granting credit and also by taking care of the sale of merchandise on the basis of his knowledge of the market. The many debt-notes with *tamkārum* as creditor would reflect his role as *intermédiaire agréé*, because they would allow merchants who granted credit to travelling traders to transfer their claims to such a *tamkārum*, who then could pay off their debts or carry out purchases for them.[41] In a later study he draws the picture of the well-known merchant Pūšu-kēn as such a *tamkārum*.[42] In his first analysis he also quotes TC 1 28:6f., where he translates *kaspam bēt tamkārim laqā'um* with "prélever de l'argent dans la maison du *tamkārum*" (in this letter for making purchases in Assur) and this indicates that in his opinion it was indeed the house of such an intermediary where one usually borrowed silver. Garelli's use of the article ("du *tamkārum*"), while probably not meant to indicate that there was only one such figure, nevertheless suggests a specific function held by a few persons generally known and recognized as such, which hence could remain anonymous.

It is difficult to find conclusive evidence for this view and in my opinion none of the texts discussed by Garelli supports it. We certainly know that not all people designated as *tamkārum* had the same status, job, or background. The term is frequently used to designate the selling agents who acquired merchandise on credit, at times it is the designation of important managers or *tractatores*, presumably the heads of the

39 See the discussion in Kraus 1984, 301f.

40 See the improved rendering of this text in *MARI* 1 (1982), 149f.

41 Garelli 1963, 237f.

42 Garelli 1977 [Later Garelli has revised his interpretation, see his "Le problème du *tamkārum* à l'époque paléo-assyrienne", *Archivum Anatolicum* 3 (1998) 125-130].

Anatolian branches of the firms and prominent ("big") members of Kanish (probably also known as "*dātum*-payers" or "men with an account" in the *kārum*-office), at times it designates the owners of silver or merchandise who wish to remain anonymous. The noun, in my opinion, is less a professional designation than a term indicating a person's activity or function in a particular context.[43] This ambiguity makes it difficult to prove and risky to **[69]** assume that the *tamkārums* in whose houses one could borrow silver represented a special class, with a specific function. A translation "a merchant's house" hence is fully acceptable. It implies that there were several (perhaps many) merchants who were ready and perhaps in the habit of loaning silver. And in fact, such "houses" do not occur only in Assur, but also in Anatolia. Moreover, that Assyrians, as pointed out above (3b, end), could "borrow silver at a native's house" (*bēt nu'ā'im*), indicates that rich Anatolian merchants were ready to loan silver in a similar way, and there is no evidence that the Anatolian kingdoms too had special *intermédiares agréés* to facilitate the trade. Just as in the trade documented by the Geniza material, successful merchants not only regularly granted commercial credit in natura, but could also supply straight loans for commercial purposes.

Perhaps we may go one step further and suggest that wealthy merchants who did not (no longer?) travel used their capital more and more for financing the trade, either as investors, or by granting commercial credit (especially if they were also owners of warehouses), or by straight loans, satisfied with the dividends, profits, fees and interest they were entitled to (usually 30 per cent per year, but 20 per cent in ATHE 28:20 and 16 2/3 per cent in BIN 6 74:14). They were willing and able to provide cash silver, at times as short-term loan, when traders were temporarily short of funds or wanted to carry out purchases or to leave on a caravan journey before the silver due from Anatolia had arrived. Just as there were other merchants who, when the silver from Anatolia could not yet be used for the trade, tried to put it out at interest, because they hated to see it "lie idle" (see above, 2b). Such practices help to explain that a list of a dead merchant's assets mentions not only "silver under seals which he has left behind, silver of his which he has deposited somewhere, and tablets of his with outstanding claims", but also "silver which he has loaned at interest to somebody (*lu kaspam ana ṣibtim ana mamman iddin*), either in Ḫattum or in Burušḫattum".[44] The rare Old Babylonian references to (houses of) merchants where one may borrow silver (for making purchases) must reflect a similar situation. There is no reason to assume, with W.F. Leemans, a more public or at least communal character of such a *bīt tamkārim*.[45]

3. Special Arrangements

Besides straight silver loans to traders and credit granted to selling agents (which resulted in debt-notes simply mentioning a silver debt), there were various other forms of commercial credit, whereby silver or merchandise were entrusted to relatives and business associates on special conditions. As an example I quote KTH 24 (= EL 109, analyzed in Larsen 1967, 24), which concerns a certain Dadaja (= D.):

> The 15 minas of refined silver, excise added and transport fee paid for, which $S._1$ made D. bring to the City, to the address of P., E., and I., for making purchases – the **[70]** silver from here (Kanish) and the merchandise from there (Assur) will cross the country in the name of *tamkārum*. When the merchandise will come up from the

43 See the remarks in Veenhof 1997, 351-364 on the use of the term, the role of the *tamkārum*, and his frequent anonymity. [But I have to add now that a recently deciphered text, Kt 92/k 206: 11 and 30, mentions a year-eponym identified not only by the name of his father, but also by the designation *tamkārum*: "Abu-šalim, *tamkārum*, son of Ilī-ālum"; see now AKT 5 (2010) no. 46, he was eponym in ca. 1845 BC (middle chronology)].

44 P. Garelli, *RA* 59 (1965), 152 no. 23: 45ff.

45 In his *The Old Babylonian Merchant* (SD 3, Leiden 1950), 89f., where he refers for his interpretation to the meaning of *bēt tamkārim* in Old Assyrian!

City, if he wants (it), D. can take the merchandise and pay 22 ½ minas of silver. If he does not want (it), *tamkārum* will take the merchandise and he will hand over to D. the tablet which A.$_1$, A.$_2$, and L. have sealed. Witnessed by S.$_2$, A.$_3$, and A.$_1$.

This is neither a straight loan nor credit granted to a selling agent, nor a standard partnership (which implies sharing profit and losses). D. also seems to be more than a normal transporter (*kaṣṣārum*) – who works within the framework of a service contract and brings silver to Assur and merchandise back to Kanish, – since he has the option of buying the merchandise upon arrival in Kanish. Moreover, the last clause shows that there was a previous written contract (recording a liability of his), which will be "yielded" (*waššurum*) to him if he does not take the merchandise but leaves it to *tamkārum*. The latter must be identified with S.$_1$, the owner of the silver, in whose name and at whose cost silver and merchandise are shipped, but who wants to remain anonymous. As the discussion by Larsen shows (1967, 24 with 179f.), it is not easy to discover what is behind this contract. The most likely solution, in my opinion, is that D. is "used" by S.$_1$ to get a lot of merchandise from Assur to Kanish, because D. owes him a debt (recorded in the tablet he eventually will get back). The "value" of the work to be done by D. is fixed at 7 ½ minas of silver and if he yields the goods brought from Assur to his creditor, his debt to the same amount (cf. the debt recorded in two documents edited in Larsen 1967, 22f.) will be cancelled. The alternative is to pay 22 ½ minas of silver (the silver given him plus the added value once the goods are in Kanish) to his creditor and to keep the merchandise. He is assumed to be able to sell them in Anatolia with a profit of even more than 50 per cent, which will allow him to pay his creditor (he would have signed a promissory note for the 22 ½ minas of silver, or perhaps more depending the length of his credit term) and also to earn something for himself.

Was this a normal arrangement or something special? The limited number of such agreements suggests the latter and the fact that the conditions laid down for D. are not unfavorable, is indicative of a form of help rather than an ultimatum by his creditor.

From time to time Old Assyrian traders of course did run into financial problems, due to losses during caravan trips, political unrest in Anatolia (resulting in the breaking down of communications, *sukurtum*), delayed payments (by agents and by local palaces), defaulting debtors, or actions (such as smuggling) which earned them at times heavy fines (in Assur) or imprisonment and payment of ransom (in Anatolia). All these misfortunes could result in mounting debts and interest, but it remains a guess how frequent and serious such problems were, since most of our evidence bears on individual cases reported in letters which are difficult to date. The well-known trader Pūšu-kēn obviously ran into serious financial problems in his earlier years, as described in the famous letter BIN 4 32.[46] And when he had died, his daughter wrote, in a letter in Prague (I 680), that "the complete fortune of our father has been spent" (*emūq abini kulušu ittagmar*), even though that clearly was too pessimistic an assessment, since Pūšu-kēn's children do inherit shares in the various investments he had made.

Mutual help among partners and relatives, supplemented by straight loans, could help to overcome temporary cash problems, as pointed out above. When problems got **[71]** very serious special measures might be taken, because the commercial debts usually were so big that the traditional Mesopotamian security devices such as pledging, selling property, and debt slavery must have been utterly insufficient; only the forced sale of expensive houses in Assur might have helped. Since nobody would really profit from a bankruptcy, it may have been up to the creditors to try to solve such crises, in particular if the person in problems was a relative, a close business associate, or an employee, whose ruin would have both economic and social effects (for traders their "reputation", *šumu*, was very important and "coming to shame in the city-gate" was dreadful). The obvious

46 See Garelli 1963, 233f., and Dercksen 1999. [The letter is also discussed in Larsen 2015, 225].

solution was to offer the debtor a chance to recover (*balāṭum*) by granting him a special loan or credit while exploiting the only asset he still had to offer, his energy and skill. The person (boss, creditor, guarantor, etc.) who helped the debtor of course wanted to make sure that the loan given or the merchandise entrusted to the debtor would not be seized by other creditors and would be put to good use in Assur, through the purchase of merchandise which could be sold in Anatolia with a nice profit. In some cases, it seems, the debtor was not even granted a loan, but is simply exploited as transporter or agent for his creditor, so that his condition was not unlike that of an person working for his creditor as antichretic pledge.

A first example of such a special arrangement concerns Kukkulānum (henceforth K.) in his relation with Enlil-bānī (henceforth E.), as described in EL 108 (published as VS 26 102), TC 3 67, and CCT 3 27a. All three texts were edited and discussed in Larsen 1967, 8ff., as his "standard texts" (the contract type 1:1, and the letters type 2:1 and type 3:1), on the assumption that all three indeed refer to the same transaction. K. travels to Assur with 30 minas of silver, entrusted to him for transport (type 1:1:5), secured by his own and E.'s seals (type 2: 1:6f.), but also called "E.'s silver" (type 1:1:7). E. had formally established his claim on or title to this silver ("E.'s hand has been laid on it", *qātam šakānum ina*, type 2:1:13f.), and the same has to be done in Assur by E.'s representatives (the addressees of the letter type 2:1) with the merchandise bought there, publicly (type 1:2:26f. specifies "in the city-gate"). In Assur the purchase of tin and textiles has to be closely supervised by E.'s representatives, who have to assist K. (type 2: 1:15f.), so that the purchase is one which guarantees profit, allows him "to recover" (*šīmum ša balāṭisu*, a term typical for such situations).[47] E. advised them to use half of the silver for buying tin and half for buying textiles, apparently in order to spread the risk (type 2:1:17f.).[48] When the caravan with tin and textiles arrives in Kanish, E. will take the merchandise (type 1:1:13ff.; one of the alternatives mentioned in EL 109, quoted above). The special arrangement which allows E. to control every stage of the transaction and to secure a profitable purchase, must be explained from the fact that E. "has been inscribed here (in Kanish) in a merchant's house as K.'s guarantor: (type 2:1:10ff.; *qātāt* K. *allipit*). Apparently K. had been forced to borrow a substantial amount of silver from a merchant-banker and E. had been ready to guarantee for him, which implies a fairly close relationship between the two. E. may have been the head of the firm for which K. was working and/or E. already may have had a debt claim on K. (in type 3:1:35, K. calls E. *tamkārum*). As guarantor E. would have to pay for K. if he defaulted,[49] hence E.'s **[72]** concern to use the loan the loan optimally, also for his own benefit. The "caravan account" (text type 3:1, sent from Assur) reveals that K. brings back an amount of textiles and tin, which could be sold in Anatolia for at least 50 or 60 minas of silver, presumably more than enough to pay back the loan from the merchant-banker.

However, if the contract type 1:1 bears on this same transaction, E. would have taken the merchandise upon arrival in Kanish and then it remains unclear what benefit K. would have derived from his caravan journey. If the 30 minas of silver really was the amount borrowed by K. from a merchant-banker, it is strange that E. fully controls the transaction and is entitled to take the merchandise upon arrival in Kanish. In my view, the only solution which explains all the facts is that E., as guarantor, already had been forced to pay for K. and that the amount of 30 minas of silver was actually made available to K. by E. in order to allow him to recover. Type 1:1 then shows that K. was only "used" as transporter in order to allow E. to make a profit from selling merchandise brought from Assur by K. How K. would have had to pay his own debts (which had forced him to take out the loan) remains unclear. He did not have the favourable option offered Dadāja in EL 109.

47 See for this terminology, Veenhof 1987, 56ff.

48 For unknown reasons, much more silver is used for buying tin, even though it was expensive, than for textiles.

49 As will be shown below, the distinction between a guarantor and a co-debtor was not very big.

Since the interpretation of the relationship between E. and K. is difficult and hypothetical, I offer a few other examples of “special arrangements”. The second is POAT 2, which records an arrangement between I. and his creditor A. It reads [see now Larsen 2002, no. 142]:

> [1] A. will give to I. 10 minas of refined silver for one year. I. will add the excise and transport fee, and [7] for the silver which A. will give to I. a debt-note of I. for an amount of 29 minas of silver will be drawn up, [11] stating that the silver will travel twice to the City and that A. (then) will take his 29 minas of silver. [15] If there is more, I. will take it, if there is too little, I. will supplement it. 18 From month IV, eponymy-year of PN. [20] The valid debt-notes in Kanish, Durḫumit, or Kunanamit, or those in the possession of D. – all these earlier bonds recording debts of I. are herewith cancelled. (Before three witnesses).

The last lines show that this agreement (still to be carried out, since all the verbs are in the future tense) results from a settlement of accounts between A. and I. Its purpose is to enable I., by means of a caravan trip to Assur, to earn an amount of silver which has to be paid to A., apparently his creditor, enough to pay for his old debts and to return the new loan of 10 minas. This makes it highly likely that this new loan was granted for this very purpose and the rather harsh conditions – almost tripling the amount borrowed by two trips Kanish-Assur and *vice versa* within one year,[50] – suggest that I. was in serious problems and had little choice. The operations would be successful if I. managed to realize a net profit of ca. 75 per cent per trip,[51] which means a gross profit of ca. 100 per cent, minus travel expenses of ca. 10 per cent per trip, exit and import fees, dead capital invested in donkeys and loans to personnel, etc. Note that I. does not have to hand over to A. the merchandise brought from Assur (as K. has to E. in the previous case and as is one of the options of Dadāja in EL 109), but simply an amount of silver. This means that he is supposed to sell himself the merchandise brought twice from Assur, and that all **[73]** within one year. The agreement is dated to the fourth month, which means early spring, so that I. would have had at least eight months available, ca. six months for traveling twice to Assur and back (ca. six weeks per trip), plus two months for selling the loads in Anatolia. This may have allowed him to succeed, but it is a tight schedule and the agreement is realistic enough to consider both a deficit and a surplus.

There are a few other texts which inform us about the possibilities of multiplying a sum of silver by caravan trips Assur-Kanish and *vice versa.* In the unpublished contract Cole 1, a person who receives 31 3/4 minas of silver agrees to pay back 42 1/3 minas or 50 per cent more to his creditor “after the merchandise has come up from the City and has been converted into silver”. EL 216 assumes that a trader who is given 30 minas of silver is able to pay back the double (*i.e.* one talent) if “the silver travels twice to the City”.[52] These arrangements are much more realistic and favorable than the one of POAT 2, which

50 EL 109, analyzed above, starts from a profit of only 50 per cent per trip.

51 The curious amount of 29 minas may reflect the amount of the previous debts plus interest or be equal to three times the loan minus certain fees and costs.

52 Travelling twice to the City is also mentioned in ATHE 64:18ff. but without exact figures. I also mention the contract published recently as AKT 3 28, where an anonymous creditor (*tamkārum*) “gives” to the scribe A. the huge amount of 92 minas of silver, to be shipped to Assur for making purchases. The creditor is entitled to take the merchandise which A. will bring up from Assur, if he likes it. If not, A. has to pay him the double, “[three talents and] four minas of silver”. The second alternative implies that A. would be able to make a net profit of at least 100 per cent on the sale of the merchandise in Anatolia. Damage of the text (line 22) robs us of information on the amount of time granted him to achieve this, but the contract is dated to the eighth month, which may have left him just enough time to ship the merchandise to Anatolia before the winter. The fact that A., if his creditor decides to take the merchandise, was left with empty hands and apparently without reward for his caravan trip, may indicate that A. as a defaulting debtor was “exploited” by his creditor, as was Kukkulānum in EL 108.

can only be compared with ICK 2 262, where one-third mina has to become one mina "when he comes up from the City", but here the amount of silver is very small indeed.

My third example is in BIN 4 224, a letter written by Iddin-Suen (I.) to the creditors (*bēl kaspim*) of Aššur-bēl-malkim (A.), which deals with the debts of the latter. It reads:

> [7] 30 minas of silver A. owes to you (plur.) and he also owes me 30 minas of silver, for which I have his valid bond. According to your proposal, you would make available (*nadā'um*, "deposit") the capital put at his disposal (*būlātišu*) and the silver which you yourselves hold back (*ka'ulum*), [14] and send that silver to the City, so that goods bought (*šiāmātum*) would come up (to Anatolia) and you then could satisfy yourselves (*tuštabbā*) with your silver and I would take what remains. [19] A. is now bringing you 11 minas of silver under my seal and you must (now) give back his capital which you hold back. Seal all this silver together and send it to Š. and your representatives (in Assur), [25] and let A., assisted by your representatives, carry out a purchase which is profitable for him (*šīmam ša balāṭišu*) and let the merchandise come up and be converted into silver and then satisfy yourselves with your silver and I will take what remains. [34] If you do not put this silver and his capital which you hold back under seal and send it to the City, you must divide with me (what is available) on the basis of our respective claims in silver (*ana ba'abāt kaspini*).

Without entering into the details of this complicated arrangement, we can state that A. was a debtor both of I. and of a group of creditors. Both had agreed to make capital available to A., which would allow him to make a caravan trip to Assur and back, in the **[74]** hope that the proceeds of this trip would allow them to get back their silver. I. is rather modest in proposing that they would first take their claim, whereas he would be satisfied with what remains. The amount of silver to be made available to A. by the creditor apparently is a capital to which A. is somehow entitled without owning it, "capital put at his disposal" (*būlātišu*), but which they (because he is a defaulting debtor?) "hold back". *i.e.* thus far have not made available to him (lines 12f. mention "his capital *and* the silver which you hold back", line 21 has "his capital which you hold back"). The last line of the letter, which is a plea to the creditors to live up to their earlier promise, states that if this arrangement cannot be carried out, the creditor and the writer will have to divide A.'s assets in proportion to their claims and to be satisfied with what is now available.

This document is interesting because it shows that different creditors cooperated to reach an agreement on supplying a defaulting debtor with a loan, a special arrangement for granting commercial credit, which aims at recovering their capital.

4. Collection and Payment of Debts

A system based on regular commercial credit and deferred payments, supplemented by straight loans, could only thrive if financial liabilities were taken seriously (the "ethics" of the trade), could be enforced, and if there existed good procedures for collecting payments. This was particularly urgent in a system of overland trade, based on at times complicated contractual (which is not identical to written) relationships, where those involved could not always be personally present on due dates at places agreed, while at the same time the caravan system required good timing.

Collection of payments due in general seems to have worked fairly well, otherwise the trade could not have been so successful. On the other hand, in many letters and judicial records (of private summonses and formal trials) collecting payments, dunning overdue or defaulting debtors, and solving disagreements on such liabilities are important and frequent issues. The imperatives "seize him and make him pay" (*ṣabassuma šašqilšu*) abound in the correspondence and concern in particular the many, at times elusive selling agents (called *tamkārum*), who had acquired lots of merchandise on credit (for which they sealed promissory notes rated in silver) and regularly exceeded their terms (*ūmē šētuqum*). The occasional insistence on "reliable ones, trustworthy as you yourself, for which you don't have to be afraid" and the existence of many memorandums listing overdue commercial debts from various years, also point to problems. Some may have been due to special circumstances – *e.g.* interruption of commercial traffic (*sukurtum*, "blockade"; political turmoil) or the sudden death of an active trader, which always meant delays and complications – but they are not the main causes of financial problems of merchants.

It is difficult to estimate how serious and frequent such payment problems were. The written sources which mention them in many cases owe their existence to them and transactions finished smoothly do not leave such written traces. The briskness of the trade and the large number of participants must have meant many hundreds of individual transactions each year, so that a few dozen problem cases should not surprise us. More serious difficulties, moreover, could easily result in small files (of up to 10 documents) of letters and records, all dealing with one particular case, which may yield a somewhat biased picture. The number of surviving promissory notes reflecting loans or credit **[75]** granted to selling agents and other business associates – perhaps around 300 – cannot simply be interpreted as evidence of unfinished transactions and unpaid debts. Normally returned and "killed" upon payment, such bonds might also be preserved, since without the sealed envelope (which turned them into a "valid deed", *ṭuppum ḫarmum*) they lacked legal force.[53] The numbers of records of old debts found in the regularly excavated archives (as far as we can see at present) is not alarmingly big. Moreover, however much traders strove for written evidence of financial liabilities, there were always also oral transactions, conducted before witnesses and among close relatives or associates, which might have caused part of the problems reflected in the documentation, especially if a trader died and claims could only be honored if "proved by witnesses" (*ina šībēšu ikūan*), as stipulated in Old Assyrian law.

Financial claims were protected by various means, including those known from slightly earlier (Ur III period) and contemporary Babylonia, such as (default) interest or fines, surety by collateral, and guarantors. But the Old Assyrians also developed new devices for easily and quickly collecting payments due.

a. *Interest and Default Interest*[53a]

The "official" rate of interest, between Assyrians normally 30 per cent per year (occasionally lower, *e.g.* between friends, or higher for loans contracted by bad debtors), "in accordance with the ruling of the *kārum*", was rather high compared with Babylonia (20 per cent per year). Many documents mention high amounts of silver due as interest, which must be the result of debts left unpaid for many years, other complain about or warn of "interest which mounts" (*ima''id*) or "becomes a problem" (*imarraṣ*). There are not a few cases where debtors at first only can pay back part of a debt or only the capital sum (*šīmtum*), at times in installments, and only get their promissory note back later, after the final installment (*tašbītum*) or the interest has been paid. The rather high rate of interest (which I would like to explain from the commercial value of the silver in the overland trade) may have had a dual effect. On the one hand it offered the creditor an attractive compensation if the debtor defaulted, the same one wealthy merchants received on straight silver loans. This may explain why some promissory notes do not stipulate a due date and why we meet many overdue debts listed in memorandums. Merchant-bankers, active as financiers and granting credit or loans, apparently were ready to settle for this interest. But this probably was much less the case with active traders, who needed the silver for their commercial activities, which aimed at much higher profits, though at the expense of more investments, work, trouble, and risks. On the other hand, a debtor or selling agent should not be too afraid of this rate of interest when he defaulted. The frequently rather long credit terms (many between 6 and 12 months) granted to selling

53 See for this issue also Veenhof 1987, 46ff. and Michel 1995, 19ff.

[53a See for interest in OA, K.R. Veenhof, "Zins, Altassyrisch", in RlA 15, 313-315, Berlin 2017.]

agents must have allowed them not only to sell the merchandise acquired on credit with profit, but also to use the silver earned in the mean time for additional transactions in order to increase their profit, before they had to pay back their creditors. Such additional profit may have balanced default interest and could explain the occurrence of many delayed payments and old debts.

[76] b. *Pledges*

Protection of claims by pledges (*šapartum*, *erubbatum*) was not widespread. Most occurrences (household goods, slaves, houses) are in loans to native Anatolians (which are regularly charged higher interest), but they are much less common with commercial loans or credit granted to Assyrians.[54] They do occur, a few times also for substantial debts, possibly in cases where payment already had been deferred or loans were novated and the creditor required added surety, but not frequently enough to warrant C. Michel's statement that "houses frequently served as surety for the creditor".[55] According to the letter KTS 2 9, a claim of 49 pounds of silver is secured by a pledge (*erubbātum*) of two (usually expensive) houses in Assur.[56] Gold serves as a pledge in CCT 4 29b // BIN 4 4 // AnOr 6 19, where a claim of 25 pounds of silver is protected by a pledge of 10 pounds of gold and a guarantor has to provide additional surety, which is remarkable since the value of the gold (usually eight times the value of silver, hence equal to ca. 80 pounds of silver) is already the multiple of the claim. In Kt 87/k 119 (courtesy K. Hecker) nearly one mina of gold serves as a pledge (*šapartum*) for a debt. Pledges also occur for small commercial debts. In VS 26 60:14ff., an amount of tin was given (offered?) as pledge for a debt of nearly one talent of copper (value ca. half a mina of silver), and in KTS 1 13b:28 an unspecified amount of tin secured a debt of only 15 shekels of silver.

Noteworthy is the fact that at times also promissory notes served as pledges. In the Neukirch-tablet lines 5ff., there is mention of "a valid bond for 20 minas of wool!, being P.'s debt, pledged to the creditor (*erubbāt tamkārim*), which A. is bringing you".[57] In VS 26 1, A. reports:

> I owed K. 24 talents and 10 minas of good copper and my representatives have satisfied K. in Ullama with that copper, obtained my debt-note and left it in deposit (*ana nabšêm*) with I. Today I. refused to yield my tablet, saying "They deposited it with me as pledge", although it was not as pledge that they deposited it!

EL 320:14ff. and CCT 3 42b:6ff. show that a pledged tablet (bond) might be used to recover money owed to the one who had obtained it. In the former the documents pledged (called *iṣurātum*) most likely recorded liabilities of an Anatolian palace to pay copper to the *kārum*, which the *kārum* for whatever reason had ceded to B. The latter in turn had left them behind for (or ceded them to) I. and now wants to know whether I. had used them to collect copper in B.'s name.[58] In the second text too, the possibility is considered that the creditor has used the records pledged to collect silver.[59] This shows that pledged bonds could be more than hypothecary pledges, since their owner might use them to **[77]**

---

54 An example is EL 169, where household utensils serve as pledge for half a mina of silver due as interest. See for an earlier survey, with emphasis on the legal aspects, Kienast 1975-76. [See for OA pledges now Veenhof 2001, 125-142].

55 Michel 1996, 298.

56 Lines 6-9: A tablet of 49 minas of silver *ša* A.$_{1}$, the *gubabtu*-priestess, his sister, and A.$_{2}$, his brother *ša šina bētān erubbātūni*; see for this letter Michel 1995, 25f. Note also TPAK 1 194, where a house is pledged for a debt of little more than two minas of silver.

57 Quoted EL I, 231 note d.

58 See for this document my remarks in Veenhof 1995b, 325.

59 "Today I hear that he has deposited the bond as pledge. Inform me how much silver he has collected where (from the person with whom) he has deposited the bond" (lines 5-10).

collect the assets they embodied.[60] He might do this either for himself or in the name of the original creditor, in order to balance the money collected in this way with the debts due to him from their original owner. A creditor quite naturally felt cheated when, as was the case in Kt r/k 17:6-9, he received as security tablets which were no longer valid (*ṭuppū ukkušūtim*). How and under which condition pledged tablets could be converted into money is a difficult question and I may refer to my observations in Veenhof 1997, 356ff. I also call attention to the arrangement worked out in EL 104, where A. leaves/cedes (*ezābum*) to I. two bonds with debt claims on B. and U. for in all to 7 ½ minas of silver. I. pays him their value ("equivalent", *meḫrātum*) in silver, 7 ½ minas of silver, and henceforth B. and U. are debtors of I., liable for the payment of interest, which A., their original creditor, guarantees.

c. *Guarantors*

Guarantors are more frequent in commercial debt-notes of Assyrians than pledges, but by no means a standard feature. I have noted ca. 15 cases, usually a simple mention at the end of the contract: "PN is guarantor" (*qātātum*).[61] Also persons designated as *šazzuztum*, a general term meaning "representative" (lit. the person who is made to "stand in" for somebody, who is designated and empowered to act for him),[62] hence frequently "agent", can act as guarantors. In the letter AKT 3 83:8-16, E. writes: "The one mina and half a shekel of silver, which A. owes to the *kārum* and for which I am 'stand-in' (*šazzuztu anākuma*), I indeed paid that silver out of my own funds". While references to guarantors in contracts are usually short and laconic ("PN is guarantor"), we know more about them from letters and judicial records, when debtors were asked or forced to supply them[63] or problems arose about the settlement of accounts between debtors and guarantors. In a number of cases the guarantor (*bēl qātātim*) is made responsible for the presence of the debtor at the time and place of payment *(Gestellungsbürgschaft)*. Such contracts speak of the guarantor's duty of "bringing the man (usually a debtor, who is about to leave on a business trip) back".[64] More frequent are cases where being a guarantor implied the liability of paying for the defaulting debtor. In such cases the guarantor's right of regress on the debtor is at stake, together with the question of the **[78]** whereabouts of the debt-note, which the original creditor should hand over to the guarantor who paid him instead of the debtor.[65] Regress by the guarantor on the debtor could be the substance of a verdict by the City, which could authorize him (especially if he had been forced to take out a loan in order to be able to meet his liability) to charge the debtor "interest and interest on interest", due to the guarantor as new creditor and to the merchant who had provided

---

60 This is probably also the case in the Neukirch-tablet (see note 57), since the writer goes on to say that the wool (recorded as debt in the pledged debt-note) should be given to a trader for transport.

61 See for references EL II, 123ff. and CAD Q, 170, 3a; see also CTMMA 1, 84:16f.; KKS 13 (debt of 10 minas of silver); JCS 14 (1960), 1 no. 1:1-4; *ibidem*, 10 no. 5:5-10. [See now for guaranty in OA, it forms and terminology, Veenhof 2001,104-125].

62 The noun occurs together with the verb "to stand", both in the basic stem (*šazzuzti* PN *izzaz*) and with the causative stem (*šazzuztam ušazzaz*); see for references CAD Š/2, 245f. Note that in the two connected documents mentioned below, in footnote 65, the one states that the son-in-law "stands in for the debt" (*ana ḫubullim izzaz*) of his father-in-law, while the other designates him as "guarantor" (*qātātum*).

63 The expression is *ana ša qātātim tadānum*, with personal accusative object. *E.g.* KTS 1 38c: 12: "If they refuse to pay, hold them by the hem of their garments and make them provide guarantors until I arrive" (*a-ša qātātim adi allakanni itaddināšunu*). From the point of view of the guarantor the action can be described as "let oneself be booked/inscribed as somebody's guarantor" (*qātāt* PN *litaptum/nalputum*, with the verb both in the reflexive Gt- and in the N-stem).[See now Veenhof 2001, 104-106]

64 In Akkadian *awīlam ta''urum*; see for references P. Garelli, in *Studies Erica Reiner* (AOS 67, Connecticut 1987), 111f. and VS 26 37 [and now Veenhof 2001, 109-112, "Gestellungsbürgschaft"].

65 See *e.g.* EL 325-326, BIN 6, 215; JCS 14, 10 no. 5. A nice example, involving a man and his son-in-law, is to be found in two interrelated documents excavated in 1991, published in my article 'Two Marriage Documents from Kültepe', *Archivum Anatolicum* 3 (Emin Bilgiç Memorial Volume, Ankara 1998), 357ff.

the loan. He may also be authorized "to look for (*še'ā'um*) silver of the debtor, wherever it proves to be/turns up".[66]

In Kanish, as we have seen above (§ 2d), Enlil-bānī "had been booked as guarantor of Kukkulanum (*qātāt* K. *nalputum*) in "a merchant's house" (TC 3 67:10), where K. must have taken out a loan of 30 pounds of silver in order to meet his cash problems. This supports the idea that in most (?) cases guarantors were only asked for if a debtor was (already) in financial problems, which can also explain the not infrequent combination of a guarantor and a pledge (TC 3 232; BIN 4 4 and parallel texts, see above under b, "Pledges"). In CCT 5 8a, Aḫaḫa reminds her brothers (sons of Pūšu-kēn) of their liability, since "they had been booked as guarantors for their (by now dead) father for an amount of 30 pounds of silver". Several times we meet persons "booked as guarantor" for debts owed by somebody to the City-office in Assur, which the *līmu*-official is collecting.[67] In EL 332, a man is guarantor for the debt of a business partner of no less than 50 minas of silver.

Being guarantor, as wisdom texts stress, is risky because of the inescapable obligation of paying for the debtor, even if a loan has to be contracted for that purpose. The writer of BIN 6 27:16ff. even fears that it might tum him into a (debt)slave (*ana wardūtim erābum*), which explains why usually only relatives or close business associates were ready to act as such, *e.g.* the sons of Pūšu-kēn for their father in CCT 5 8a, a sister and a son as guarantors in EL 215:4 and 227:33, 45, and Enlil-bānī for his employee(?) Kukkulānum. Guarantors also tried to protect themselves against the risks they took. The unpublished contract Kt 92/k 173 stipulates that, if A.'s debt of 11 minas of silver, for which B. and C. have been recorded as his guarantors, "is collected at the expense of B. and C., A.'s house in Assur is a pledge for the silver". The obligation of subsidiary payment and the already existing close association between guarantor and debtor may explain why in the same transactions persons can be designated both as guarantor and as co-debtor,[68] an association which can also be formalized by the clause of subsidiary liability for the debt, literally "the silver is contractually bound on the person ('head') of the one who is solvent and present".[69] But this did not mean that debtor and guarantor were identical and exchangeable. The contract Kt 91/k 135 explicitly states, after mentioning that S. is D.'s guarantor and that there is subsidiary liability for the debt, "S. **[79]** did not receive anything, D. shall pay it". D. hence is the original debtor, who received the tin owed and accordingly has to weigh it out, while S.'s liability is subsidiary.[70] Plurality of guarantors is not rare and if one of them pays accounts have to be settled with the others and later with the debtor, which may create complications resulting in records.

As an example of the complications caused by guarantee, which also shows how small the differences between the status of guarantor, co-debtor, and partner were and how flexible Old Assyrian traders could be, I quote from the letter TC 3 110. It was written by Ennam-Aššur to Aššur-ennam and concerns copper borrowed by the former (D. = debtor) from the son of A. (C. = creditor) whereby Aššur-ennam acted as guarantor (G.) D. states:

> We (D. and G.) borrowed one talent of copper from C., whereby you acted as G. Later you came back on the transaction, saying: "I will give you a tablet with my seal for the copper and the interests (plural!) on it, stating that the debt is our debt and not that of you (alone)". In the presence of two sons of financiers (acting as witnesses) you gave (were to give?) me that tablet with your seal, but you changed your mind and

66 One may used the verb *bašā'um*, "to be", or *buārum*, "to turn up, to prove to be". See Veenhof 1995a, 1723ff. for a well documented case.

67 See the case discussed in Veenhof 1995a, 1723f.

68 See for examples EL 331 // 332 and the remarks in EL II, 124 and Veenhof 1983-84, 20 n. 19. Additional examples are Kt 91/k 131 and 135.

69 *Kaspum ina qaqqad šalmišunu u kēnišunu rakis*; examples are BIN 6 238; Kt k/k 44:44f.; and Kt 87/k 293: 30. The reservation still made in EL II, 124 hence is not necessary.

70 *S. mimma lā ilqe D. išaqqalšu.*

(*tassiḫirma u*) wrote a tablet for one talent of copper, stating that I (D.) would enjoy half of the profit and would be responsible for half of the losses. I (D. speaks again) have satisfied you with the copper and you gave me my tablet. I asked you also for the (original) tablet of C., with my seals, and you said: "What does it concern you?" A tablet with my seals to which you are not entitled you shall not keep! You have been satisfied with the copper, therefore give the tablet of C. with my seals to my father. Do not keep it!

The final lines imply that G., by paying for D. to C., had obtained the original promissory note of D., which the latter wants back now that he has fully paid G. Having paid for D., G. had become his creditor and was entitled to get the copper back from him, but he decided to make himself co-debtor, which means that D. only owes him half a talent of copper. The purpose must have been to maintain some kind of relationship with D., by creating a common fund, which could be used for commercial purposes, even though D.'s share consisted only of the copper granted him as credit by G. The next step of G. was to define their relationship more clearly as a kind of (unequal) partnership, in which profits and losses would be shared. D.'s contribution, at least as long as he had not paid back G., most probably would be to manage the capital and do the actual trading (just like the manager or tractator of a *naruqqum*-enterprise, to whom similar stipulations on profits and losses applied), while G., as financier, would be rewarded with his share in the profits and probably also with interest on the capital which he had advanced to D. Moreover, D., when successful could use his share in the profits to pay back his creditor G., which in fact might well be the main reason why the latter opted for a partnership.

d. *Measures against Defaulting Debtors*

Defaulting debtors were warned, privately summoned (before witnesses, which could yield a valid record of the summons), or sued in a formal trial, especially if the **[80]** summons failed. Another possibility was to seize property, frequently slaves, of the debtor as security or pledge, for which one uses the verb *katā'um*.[71] An example is TC 3 60:10ff.:

When you lived in Kanish and S. was living in your presence, you failed to seize him and make him pay the silver. Now you are running around in the countryside (Anatolia) over a distance of 10 double hours (in order to seize him). Does he not have a slave-girl and a slave in Kanish? Take his slave-girl and his slave as surety and (so) obtain the silver!

Another measure was to seal a debtor's house, thus denying him access to his property (merchandise) and archives, a measure which probably had to be authorized by the judicial authorities. "The City has passed the following verdict: A. shall take x silver from whatever B. owns. He (A.) has indeed sealed our house once and twice" (YBC 13089:8-11, unpublished). The next step could be the sale of the debtor's property, as described in the letter AKT 3 87:35-59:

Ḫ. and S., by order of the City, have to pay (to the writer of this letter) 22 minas of silver from whatever they own. [38] They are jointly liable for this silver. Here [40] Ḫ. has not given me anything! Seize him and make him pay the 22 minas of silver! If he refuses to pay, [43] in accordance with the verdict of the City, sell all he owns for silver and take the silver! (...) [49] I paid three minas and half a shekel of silver to the Anatolian in the name of A., [51] in the sixth month, during the eponymy of [52] Kapatia. By virtue of a verdict of the City I am entitled to take from all he owns, from the stock

71 With as internal object *kutu'ātum*, see for references CAD K *s.v.* [see now Veenhof 2001, 154-155, "3. Distraint"].

(in the *kārum*), while calling for 20 per cent (interest), the silver [54] and the interest on it (to be reckoned) from the day I paid the silver. [56] Make him pay the silver and the interest on it. (If not) [57] I have a tablet of the City, sell all he owns and give him notice!

The same measure was applied in Assur by officials of the City to people indebted to the City-office. They could confiscate merchandise, take and sell household goods (especially valuable bronze objects) and even sell the house itself. In TPAK 1 26, it is reported that *bērum*-officials ("inspectors"?) of the City, because of fiscal debts to the City-office, seize a family's house in order to force its four members to pay each 75 shekels of silver (in all five pounds) and even threaten to sell it, whereupon the writer of the letter takes out a loan with a merchant to pay the debt. In TPAK 1 46, we read (rather differently from the editors, who misunderstood parts of this letter): "Our father's stocks (*išittum*) and houses have been entrusted (*paqqudā*; to the creditor or a guarantor?) for silver". Because it was not sufficient, the writer's own house, together with the household goods (*utuptum*!) of him and his wife were sold. From this document we also gather that such sales of houses by defaulting debtors at times (in periods of economic crisis?) were considered a social problem and that measures were taken to counter them. After the lines quoted we read to our surprise: "Assur has now taken mercy on his city: a **[81]** man whose house has been sold can again enter it when he pays half of its price, and for the rest (of the price) terms in three (annual?) installments haven been set".[72]

e. *Collection of Payment for Creditors*

The Old Assyrian merchants used and developed a few additional procedures to help the creditor get back his silver without delay, irrespective of where creditor or debtor stayed. Many debts were collected by representatives, partners (it was one of the possibilities granted by a formal partnership, as we learn from its dissolution as recorded in ATHE 24), and employees. In the absence of the original promissory note (which might be deposited elsewhere and which one did not like to send overland) this could be achieved by means of copies made available to a partner, agent, or employee who was asked to collect the silver, at times with a written authorization. It was apparently assumed that the debtor, confronted with the exact data on his debt and with the names of the witnesses to the transaction, would not refuse to meet his liability, also because he incurred the risk of having to pay default interest. When paying in such situations, he would normally receive a formal quittance (a *ṭuppum ša šabā'ē*, "a tablet of satisfaction", sealed by the one who received the payment), which in due time he could exchange for the original bond,[73] whereupon both tablets could be cancelled ("die").

f. *Payment Contracts*[73a]

At times, however, a debtor would refuse to pay, because he wanted to be shown the original debt-note, because he had already paid (elsewhere or to somebody else), because he contested the claim as such, or for other reasons. To prevent a deadlock one could then "take a contract against" (*tarkistam laqā'um ana*) the party which refused to comply, either the debtor who refused to pay or the creditor who pressed his disputed claim. Such a contract basically consisted of a formal promise, before witnesses and usually recorded in a tablet sealed by the one making the promise, of an extra payment if the refusal or claim in due time could be formally refuted by testimony or written evidence. The fine usually was paying two or three times the amount disputed or twice the normal amount of interest for the unpaid debt. A clear example is EL 182 (published as VS 26 98): "R., representing Z., seized five shekels of silver of S. Should he (Z.) not have a claim on

---

72 Read in lines 22f. *Aššur ennān ālišu ilteqe awīlum ša* .... Elsewhere I will offer a full analysis of this text and the unique legal measure it describes [see for this text now Veenhof 1999, 599-607].

73 See for evidence Veenhof 1983-84, 13f.

[73a See for these contracts now Hertel 2013, 252-266, "Binding contracts – *rakkusum* and *tarkistum*".]

S., then R. shall pay 10 shekels of silver to S.; witnessed by P. and I.". Persons confronted with the choice between paying or giving up their claim and signing such a contract, of course would give in unless they were very sure of being right and able to prove it. In TC 3 263, S. claims 13 pounds of copper from A., who however tells him that a certain Q. had already paid back for him to I. (apparently a friend or agent of S). "If Q. confirms him (A.'s statement), S. will pay the triple (*šušalšum*) to A., without resorting to legal trial or fight". The writer of the letter CCT 4 5b requests: "Seize P. and make him pay the gold, it is mine. (...) I have here his valid promissory note. If he protests, take a contract **[82]** against him and make him pay the gold". According to *RA* 59 (1965), 31f. no. 11:11ff., Q. owes to P. one pound of silver and P. tries to enforce his claim, even though the silver already would have been collected for P. by A. and I. "If Q. produces A. and I. (as witnesses), P. will pay to Q. as capital sum (*šīmtum*; this term may have been chosen to leave the matter of additional interest open) two minas of silver". In TC 3 251, where a creditor seizes silver from D., we read: "Should D. prove not to owe him silver, he will add three shekels of silver per mina per month since (...)" (no doubt apart from the obligation to return the capital), which means twice the normal rate of interest of 30 per cent per year).

Such contracts by their heavy sanction prevented unfounded demands and refusals, hence delay of payment and so contributed to the circulation of silver. They could build on a stipulation already attested during the preceding Ur III period, that debtors who failed to pay in time, at times after a summons followed by a promise, would pay double.[74] The Old Assyrian traders adapted this device, which during the Ur III period only protected the interests of the creditor and used it to solve payment problems in the interests of both creditors and debtors. A later adaptation is found in the Laws of Hammurabi, paragraphs 106-108, where the trading agent who denies his liability has to pay three times the capital, but the financier and creditor who denies payment by the agent, six times, an (idealistic?) attempt to balance justice with the goal of protecting the weaker party.

g. *Borrowing by Creditors*

A last device to help the creditor was a clause in the promissory note which authorized him, if the debtor defaulted, "to borrow for him" (*laqā'um* with personal dative suffix) the sum owed "at a merchant's house", where "for him" means for the debtor and at his expense. See for full data and an analysis above, under 2c. It was an efficient and fast method of self-help, which could avoid the problems and loss of time which the use of pledges, guarantors, summonses, and lawsuits would entail. The occasional use of the verb "to call" (*šasā'um*), instead of "to take/borrow" (*laqā'um*), suggests a formal, public act, as one would expect when one takes out a loan at the expense of somebody else. There is no evidence that the debtor had to repay the merchant-moneylender, the loan plus the interest to be paid on it remained the liability of the creditor, but he would charge it to his debtor, in addition to the interest he was anyhow entitled to since payment was overdue. This explains the clause "and he (the debtor) shall supplement the interest". The promise, in EL 309, that the creditor is allowed "to borrow silver at a merchant's house at an interest of three shekels per mina per month" (which is twice the normal rate), perhaps refers to the double interest due to the creditor or is a fine for a broken promise (see for this feature above, under 4f). The solution was similar to the one offered to guarantors who had to take out a loan in order to be able to pay for a debtor (see above, 4c). The presence of the "*bēt tamkārim* clause" in the debt-note itself allowed creditors to act quickly on the basis of a contractual right, without having to resort to "lawsuit and fight" *(balum dīnim balum ṣaltim išaqqal*, TC 3 263:24). If it is no accident that the amounts of silver owed in such cases are not very big, **[83]** the device will have been introduced to avoid time-consuming and expensive procedures when only minor debts were at stake.

74 See H. Limet, *OrNS* 38 (1976), 520-32 and Neumann 1992, 171f.

5. Promissory Notes to tamkārum and "Bearer Cheques"

A last device to be mentioned here are promissory notes which do not mention the creditor by name, but refer to him as *tamkārum*, "the merchant/creditor". In a few cases such notes at the end add the phrase "the bearer of this tablet is *tamkārum*" *(wābil ṭuppim šūt tamkārum)*. This clause suggests the possibility of a transfer of debt-notes and of ceding claims, which would make it a precursor of later "bearer cheques". It is a very interesting procedure for facilitating the flow of money and especially the collection of debts, when creditor and/or debtor were in different places (which must have happened frequently in a community of overland traders) or perhaps even before the due date. I have recently discussed it and instead of repeating my conclusions I refer the reader to this publication.[75] I may add that in general the size of the debts owed to "the merchant/creditor", and especially those of the rather few debt-notes mentioning that "the bearer of the tablet is the creditor", again are not very big, which is confirmed by two new examples. In Kt 92/k: 202 the debt is (only) 12 minas of copper (equivalent to seven or eight shekels of silver) and in TPAK 1 120a (which uses the phrase "who holds the tablet", *muka''il ṭuppim*) half a mina of silver, owed by two debtors.[76] This suggests that this device may have been developed in the interest of creditors, for easily collecting small debts or settling accounts by transferring bonds instead of cash money (see the remarks on EL 104 at the end of paragraph 4b).

Bibliography

Dercksen, J.G. 1996. *The Old Assyrian Copper Trade in Anatolia*, PIHANS 75, Istanbul.

–. 1999. "On the Financing of Old Assyrian Merchants", in J.G. Dercksen (ed.), *Trade and Finance in Ancient Mesopotamia. Proceedings of the First MOS Symposiun*, MOS Studies 1, PIHANS 84, Leiden, 85-99.

[–. 2004. *Old Assyrian Institutions*. PIHANS 98, Leiden].

Garelli, P. 1963. *Les Assyriens en Cappadoce*, Paris.

–. 1977. "Marchands et *tamkārū* assyriens en Cappadoce", *Iraq* 39, 99-107.

Goitein, S.D. 1967. *A Mediterranan Society, I. Economic Foundations*, Berkeley.

[Hertel, Th. K. 2013. *Old Assyrian Legal Practices. Law and Dispute in the Ancient Near East.* OAAS 6. PIHANS 123. Leiden].

Kienast, B. 1975-76. "Bemerkungen zum altassyrischen Pfandrecht", *WO* 8, 218-227.

–. 1984. *Das altassyrische Kaufvertragsrecht*. FAOS Beiheft 1. Stuttgart.

–. 1989. "The Old Assyrian *beʾūlātum*", *JCS* 41, 87-95.

Kraus, F.R. 1984. *Königliche Verfügungen in altbabylonischer Zeit*, SD 11, Leiden.

Larsen, M.T. 1967. *Old Assyrian Caravan Procedures*. PIHANS 22. Istanbul.

–. 1977. "Partnerships in the Old Assyrian Trade", *Iraq* 39, 119-145.

[–. 2002. *The Aššur-nādā Archive*, Old Assyrian Archives 1, PIHANS 96, Leiden 2002].

[–. 2015. *Ancient Kanesh. A Merchant Colony in Bronze Age Anatolia*, Cambridge].

Leemans, W.F. 1960. *Foreign Trade in the Old Babylonian Period*, SD 6, Leiden.

Michel, C. 1991. *Innāya dans les tablettes paléo-assyriennes*. Paris.

–. 1995. "Validité et durée de vie des contrats et reconnaissances de dettes paléo-assyriennes", *RA* 89, 15-27.

–. 1996. "Propriétés immobiliaires dans les tablettes paléo-assyriennes", in K.R. Veenhof (ed.), *Houses and Households in Ancient Mesopotamia* (= CRRAI 40), PIHANS 78, Istanbul, 285-300.

Neumann, H. 1992. "Zur privaten Geschäftstätigkeit in Nippur in der Ur III-Zeit", in M. deJong Ellis (ed.), *Nippur at the Centennial* (= CRRAI 35), Philadelphia, 161-176.

75 Veenhof 1997, 351ff.

76 The contract was drawn up to state that henceforth only one of the debtors was liable for it; when it was claimed from the other he had to "clear" him (read *ú-ba-áb*[!]*-šu* in line 22). [The rare designation *muka''il ṭuppim* is now also attested in AKT 4, 26:11 (*muka''il*) and Kt 91/k 195:27 (*mu-ki-il*$_5$, mistake?)].

Rosen, B.L. 1977. *Studies in Old Assyrian Loan Contracts*, unpublished dissertation Brandeis University, UM no. 77-22.827.

Sever, H. 1992. "Eine neue Ehescheidungsurkunde", in H. Otten *et al.* (eds.), *Hittite and Other Anatolian and Near Eastern Studies in Honour of Sedat Alp*, Ankara, 483-486.

Skaist, A. 1994. *The Old Babylonian Loan Contract. Its History and Geography*, Ramat Gan.

Veenhof, K.R. 1972. *Aspects of Old Assyrian Trade and its Terminology*, SD 10, Leiden.

–. 1983-84. "Observations on Old Assyrian Memorandums", *JEOL* 28, 10-23.

–. 1987. "'Dying Tablets' and 'Hungry Silver'. Elements of Figurative Language in Akkadian Commercial Terminology", in M. Mindlin, M.J. Geller, and J.E. Wansborough (eds), *Figurative Language in the Ancient Near East*, London, 41-75.

–. 1994. "Miete. C. Altassyrisch", *RlA* 8, 181-184.

–. 1995a. "'In Accordance with the Words of the Stele': Evidence for Old Assyrian Legislation", *Chicago-Kent Law Review* 70/4, 1717-44 [= pp. 109-127 in this volume].

–. 1995b. "Old Assyrian *iṣurtum*, Akkadian *eṣērum* and Hittite GIŠ.ḪUR", in Th.P.J. van den Hout and J. de Roos (eds), *Studio Historiae Ardens. Ancient Near Eastern Studies Presented to Philo H.J. Houwink ten Cate*, Istanbul, 311-332 [= pp. 225-243 in this volume].

–. 1997. "'Modern' Features in Old Assyrian Trade", *JESHO* 40, 336-66.

–. 1999. "Redemption of Houses in Assur and Sippar", in B. Böck *et al.* (eds), *Munuscula Mesopotamica, Festschrift für Johannes Renger*, AOAT 267, Münster, 599-616 [= pp. 211-223 in this volume].

[–. 2001. "The Old Assyrian Period", in R. Westbrook and R. Jasnow (eds.), *Security for Debt in Ancient Near Eastern Law*, Culture and History of the Ancient Near East 9, Leiden-Boston, 93-159].

Old Assyrian and Ancient Anatolian Evidence for the Care of the Elderly*

I. Assyrian Evidence
1. Adoption
2. Excursus: The care of the elderly in Emar
2.1. *wabālum* 'to support'
2.2. *palāḫum* 'to serve'
2.3. purpose: care in old age
3. Inheritance
3.1. marriage contracts and last wills
3.2. women's rights
3.3. kt 91/k 389, an inheritance division
II. Anatolian evidence
1. Textual sources
2. Group 1, texts A-F: brotherhood in a common household
2.1. a sample, text E = kt 89/k 370
2.2. comments and comparison
2.3. interpretation
3. Group 2, texts G-H: divisions among brothers

The evidence presented here derives from tablets written in the Old Assyrian script and language discovered not in the city of Assur itself (which has yielded very few documents from this period), but in the lower town of the ancient Anatolian city of Kanesh. Most tablets belong to the archives of Old Assyrian traders who lived and worked there in the 19th century B.C. and the data on social institutions and legal customs found in their letters, contracts and judicial records do reflect Old Assyrian customary law. A much smaller number of tablets belonged to native Anatolian inhabitants of Kanesh, probably mostly business men, who also lived in the commercial district of the city.[1] Their records were **[120]** also written in Old Assyrian, the only written language available there and then, either by Assyrian or by local scribes who had somehow mastered the cuneiform script and Assyrian language.[2] The legal substance of these documents must reflect native Anatolian legal custom, but we should be aware of the fact that it is preserved in Assyrian linguistic garb. The question arises whether the Assyrian language was a completely neutral vehicle of communication or may have influenced the formulation and even substance of the records. Much depends on our assessment of the competence of

* Originally published in M. Stol and S. P. Vleeming (eds), The Care of the Elderly in the Ancient Near East. Studies in the Culture and History of the Ancient Near East, vol. 14. Leiden/Boston/Köln: Brill, 119-60.

1 See for a summary description of Kanesh and its commercial district, K. R. Veenhof, "Kanesh: an Assyrian Colony in Anatolia", in Jack M. Sasson (ed.), *Civilizations of the Ancient Near East* (New York 1995) vol. II, 859-871.

2 Although we do not know the latter by name, we can occasionally identify them as non-Assyrian on the basis of the typical orthographical and grammatical mistakes they make, in dealing with tenses, case endings and pronominal suffixes.

these scribes, of their ability of adequately rendering Anatolian terms and concepts in Assyrian.[3] A careful reading of the records in question will have to answer that question.

My presentation hence falls into two parts, dealing with the Assyrian and the Anatolian evidence respectively.

[121] I. ASSYRIAN EVIDENCE

Assyrian data on care of the elderly are scarce, because our main source, the archives of the traders living in Kanesh, primarily deals with commercial matters. Information on family life and its legal aspects is limited and accidental, as it depends on the personal circumstances of the traders. Some enjoyed a family life in Kanesh, having brought their Assyrian wife along or having married there an Assyrian or Anatolian girl, some (in addition) got involved in legal fights with relatives in Assur. Both circumstances could result in the presence in their archives of records which may contain data we are interested in.[3a]

In most cases no special contractual provisions seem to have been necessary to ensure the care of the elderly. Assyrian traders, as heads of households, could count on being cared for by their children, in some cases perhaps also by a younger or secondary wife, or by other relatives, as demanded by custom and family ethics and made possible by their generally rather strong financial position, which would even have enabled them to recruit paid services. Consequently, no specific type of contract for securing or enforcing such care has been discovered. That the elderly were traditionally being cared for within the family probably was also the reason why some traders eventually returned home, to Assur, also in order to be buried with their ancestors, although this was not a general rule. There are several examples of traders who died in Anatolia, perhaps because they refused to return home or, more likely, because death came suddenly and they died "in harness"; the well known trader Pushu-ken is an example.[4] In several letters, especially those exchanged with wives, the issue of returning home in order to "see the face of Assur" and/or their relatives is raised, but usually we cannot make out whether the reference is to one of the regular visits to Assur or to a final return. There are examples of traders returning to Assur for good, leaving the business in the hands of a brother or son, as was the case with Imdilum, whose brother Ennu-Belum and son Puzur-Ishtar henceforth **[122]** led the Anatolian branch of the firm.[5] But there are also examples of senior traders always staying in Assur and leaving the business in Kanesh to a trusted son, *e.g.* Iddin-

3 In K. R. Veenhof, "An Ancient Anatolian Money-Lender. His Loans, Securities and Debt-Slaves", in: B. Hruška and G. Komoróczy (eds.), *Festschrift Lubor Matouš*, vol. II (Budapest 1978) 305 note 26, discussing records concerning debts, pledges, and guaranty, I observed: "One gets the impression that at times native Anatolian deeds show an accumulation of security clauses, borrowed from the Assyrians, but perhaps not always properly understood and inserted, and hence to be used with care in a reconstruction of customary law." See also my remarks in H.J. Nissen and J. Renger (eds.), *Mesopotamien und seine Nachbarn (=Berliner Beiträge zum Vorderen Orient* 1/1, Berlin 1982) 152f.

[3a See for evidence on Old Assyrian family life, both social and legal aspects, my contribution "Families of Old Assyrian Traders", in: L. Marti (ed.), *Compte Rendu de la 55ième Rencontre Assyriologique Internationale, Paris 2009* (Winona Lake 2014) 341-371.]

4 There are many references in the letters to traders who died "unfortunately" (*lā libbi ilim*). At times many people died at the same time, probably due to epidemics, cf. the references collected by S. Çeçen, "*Mutanu* in den Kültepe-Texten", *Archivum Anatolicum* 1 (Ankara 1995) 43-72.

5 See for Imdi-ilum, M. T. Larsen, "Your Money or Your Life! A Portrait of an Assyrian Businessman", in: J. N. Postgate a.o. (eds.), *Societies and Languages of the Ancient Near East. Studies in Honour of I. M. Diakonoff* (Warminster 1982) 214-245, esp. 226 with note 60. Some of the letters written by Imdi-ilum are archive copies of letters sent by him from Kanesh (cf. *VAS* 26, 17 ad no.4), others were sent from Assur to Kanesh after he had returned home.

Assur and his son Assur-nada (whose children remained in Assur to be raised there by his father),[6] a situation which led to a lively correspondence between father and son.[7]

However lively such correspondences, they do not reveal to us how old the traders were at the various stages of their career, such as the move to Kanesh, the return to Assur, or their death, and the question remains how to define "old" or "elderly". In general we may assume that a trader needed experience (gained *e.g.* by serving on the caravans travelling between Assur and Anatolia) before he was entrusted (by older members of the family firm and by investors) with the care of the Anatolian branch of a firm, which means that he was probably at least twenty to twenty-five years old. That the sons of several traders apparently were old and experienced enough to take over from their fathers, implies that the latter by that time were at least in their forties. Better data can be extracted from a study of the archives of such traders, in particular from the numerous debt-notes in which they figure (as creditors or debtors), dated by Assyrian year eponymies. Even though the exact sequence of all eponymies has not yet been secured, the number of different eponymies during which a trader is attested yields at least a minimal length of his activity in Kanesh. From such studies[8] we know *e.g.* that the trader **[123]** Enlil-bani worked in Kanesh for at least fifteen years, Alahum and Pushu-ken for at least twenty years, Imdi-ilum at least twenty-five years, and Elamma, whose archive was excavated in 1991, for more than thirty years. Several traders hence will have been at least fifty years old before they died in Kanesh or returned home.

1. Adoption

While there are a few Anatolian deeds of adoption[9] and there are references to adoption in some Assyrian texts, thus far not a single Assyrian adoption contract has been found in the archives in Kanesh. Such contracts, which must have existed, presumably were kept in the family archives in Assur, which remain to be excavated. Fortunately, we have one such document, though perhaps one or two generations younger than the bulk of the "Kültepe texts", which comes from Assyria but turned up on the antiques market and in due time was donated to the Allard Pierson Museum in Amsterdam. For our purpose I only present its essentials and refer the reader to the full publication.[10] An Assyrian couple manumits and apparently adopts (the verbal description of adoption is missing, but the opening sentence states that the manumitted boy (now) "is the son of P.") a slave boy (*ṣuḫārum*), who now has to support and respect them as long as they live. After their death he will acquire *(laqā'um)* a field (of ca. 6,5 ha) and one ox. Both parties will be punished if they deny or breach the contract, the father gets a heavy fine, the son will be sold (again) into slavery. The probably childless couple (no other child is mentioned nor is

6 See *CCT* 3, 6b: 24-33 (letter sent by the father to the son): "I raised your son, but he said: 'You are not my father', whereupon he left; I also raised your daughters, but they said: 'You are not our father'. On the third day they left and departed for you and now I want to know what you have to tell me."

7 See for them M. T. Larsen, *The Old Assyrian City-State and its Colonies* (*Mesopotamia* 4, Copenhagen 1976) 97ff.

8 The chronology of several archives and the length of the careers of several traders have been studied by G. Kryszat in his dissertation of 1995, *Studien und Materialien zur Chronologie der Kaufmannsarchive aus der Schicht II des Karum Kanis* (defended in Munster in 1995) [**Add.** It was eventually published in 2004, under the title *Zur Chronologie der Kaufmannsarchive aus der Schicht 2 des Kārum Kaneš* (*OAAS* 2, Leiden 2004). In this publication Kryszat could use the data of the Old Assyrian Eponym List, which I had discovered in 1998. This allows a much better insight in the chronology of the lives of the traders and their families, for which one can now consult G. Barjamovic, Th. Hertel, and M. Trolle Larsen, *Ups and Downs at Kanesh. Chronology, History and Society in the Old Assyrian Period* (*OAAS* 5, Leiden 2012), especially in Ch.3, Social History].

9 *EL* nos. 7 and 8. [**Add.** See for a new study of the OA adoption contracts my "Some Old Assyrian and Old Babylonian Adoption Contracts", in: G. Suurmeijer (ed.), Proceedings of a Workshop held in the University of Ghent (ms. completed in 2012). It contains (new) editions of *EL* nos. 7 and 8, Kt 89/k 379 and Kt n/k 2100].

10 See K. R. Veenhof, "A deed of Manumission and Adoption from the Later Old Assyrian Period", in: *Zikir Šumim* (Festschrift for F.R. Kraus, Leiden 1983, 359-381 [= pp. 245-265 in this volume].

the subsequent birth of a natural son considered)[11] through this legal act acquires a child with the obligations and duties of a son. The support and respect demanded must have been the condition for acquiring or inheriting the property, even though the formulation is not conditional (by means of *summa*, "if") and the clause of acquiring the inheritance is not even logically (by means of an enclitic **[124]** *-ma*, "and then/so", after the verb *ippuš)* connected to the one mentioning the son's duties.[12]

The contract reveals its Assyrian character by the use of the verb *wabālum* in the iterative or I/3 stem (instead of *našûm* in the same stem, current in Babylonia) for "to support, to sustain", a "northern feature", also attested in Middle Assyrian deeds, in Alalach (level IV, 15th century B.C.)[13] and in Emar. It combines this verb with *palāḫum*, "to fear, respect", used all over Mesopotamia (also in Babylonia, Susa, Nuzi, and Emar) in such contexts.[14] *Wabālum* I/3 refers primarily to material support and physical care,[15] while *palāḫum*, basically "to fear", has a broader connotation, referring to "respect, obedience" and to the action this implies, "to serve, to work for". This broad meaning clearly applies when it is the only verb used to describe the duties of a child or servant vis-à-vis its parent or master, as in the Middle Babylonian contract BE 14 40:11ff. and in many contracts from Emar.

While *wabālum/našûm* I/3 is factual and does not necessarily imply subordination, *palāḫum* usually does. It is used for the care and cult of the family gods and the dead ancestors (both in Nuzi and in Emar, in contracts of adoption and inheritance)[16] and designates the proper attitude towards an older person with authority, of sons vis-à-vis their **[125]** mother (*CT* 8 34b: 17ff.), of relatives (brothers, nephews) towards a lady as whose heirs they hope to qualify (*CT* 4 lb:19ff.). But it is also used to describe the relation between partners in a marriage (Middle Assyrian, *KAJ* 7:12f. and *TIM* 4 45:7ff.). *Wabālum* I/3, however, is also used in situations of inequality, to define the duties of younger persons, occasionally also clearly of lower status. Hence there is a factual overlap between the two, and we may consider them synonyms, as also the rather neat distribution of both verbs over two different scribal traditions at Emar shows (see below 1.2). Moreover, the semantic field of "support, care, respect" is fairly broad, as occasional alternatives or variants in Old Babylonian deeds show: *kubbutum*, "to honour"; *libbam ṭubbum*, "to give pleasure, to satisfy"; *râmum*, "to love"; *ina pîm šemûm*, "to obey".[17] Therefore, when in our text both verbs are used, rather than stressing the difference between them a synthetic meaning, almost a hendiadys is called for, "to support with due respect".

The childless couple in our Old Assyrian contract by adopting a slave and offering him the prospect of becoming their heir secured his care and service during their old age. But the duties of a child did not stop at the death of its parents. They also included the duty of

11 As was the case in the Middle Assyrian deed of adoption *KAJ* 7 rev.

12 See for *šumma* in such clauses *AlT* no.16:13ff. and *CT* 2, 35 (=*VAB* 5, 13A):9ff., and for a connecting *-ma* *CT* 6, 26a:15ff. In contracts from Emar the condition is expressed by a *šumma* clause or by a clause introduced by *kīme* (*ipallaḫ*), "when (he shows respect)", see *AulOrS* 1 no. 5:18f. and *Emar 6.3* nos. 69:7, 93:6, 112:9. In no.181:10f. a special clause is inserted: "whoever does not support ..."; no syntactical connection in 177:20'f.

13 *AlT* no.16:5,14,19. The verb occurs also in the Amarna Letter *EA* no.161, from Amurru, lines 27f.: "H. will come to meet me and take care of me like a father and a mother" (*uttanabbal(an)ni kīma ummi kīma abi*).

14 See *Zikir šumim* p. 376ff.

15 *AHw* 1452b, s.v. II, 1, c, also refers to ZA 66 (1977) 212: 24 (Wilcke's edition of the MAss. last will *KAJ* 9), but here the widow is subject of the verb (parallel to *ka''ulum*, "to hold, keep, sustain"), which should have the meaning "to manage, take care of (property)", meaning 2 of *AHw* ("verwalten").

16 See for Nuzi *SCCNH* 1 (1981) 386 no.6: 31 ("whoever among my daughters holds my fields and houses [and] lives in my house shall revere my gods and the spirits [of] my [ancestors]"); see in general K. Deller, *ibidem*, 73ff. See for Emar *AulOrS* 1 75: 16' (other texts use *nabûm* / *nubbûm*, "to invoke", cf. *RA* 77, 13ff. no.1:8 and no.2:1lf. and *AulOr* 5, 1987, 233 no.13:6f., or *kunnûm*, *ibidem* 238 no.16:26f.). See also the reference in note 32.

17 See also the observations by J. C. Greenfield in *AfO Beiheft* 19 (*CRRAI* 28, Wien 1982) 309ff., who stresses more the practical side of sustaining, serving, looking after the needs of.

mourning (*bakûm*, *bikītum*) and burying (*qebērum*, *quburum*) them and of performing the customary funerary rites after their burial (*kispum*, "funerary offerings"; *zakārum*, "to name, invoke"; *paqādum*, "to care for, sustain"; *mē naqûm*, "to libate water"), such as also a father would perform for his dead son.[18] As an Old Babylonian contract from Susa (*MDP* 23 285: 14-16) states, the daughter adopted as heir "shall provide me with food as long as I am alive and perform the funeral rites (*kispa takassap*) when I am dead". Mourning and burial are not mentioned in the extant Old Babylonian adoption contracts, but they certainly were in the mind of the adoptive parents, as the writer of *AbB* 9 228:24-28 shows: "And I raised one young boy, thinking: He may grow up so that he can bury me (*ana qebēria lirbia*)"; but now he is forced to sell him due to an uncompromising creditor. Mourning and burial are frequently mentioned in deeds **[126]** of adoption from Nuzi,[19] while a rare Middle Babylonian deed of adoption (of a girl) is the only one to stipulate the duty of "libating water for her (her mother) when she dies" (*BE* 14 40:13ff.).

While we have no Old Assyrian deeds of adoption to prove this, there are a few references in texts dealing with complications in connection with the division of an inheritance, which mention expenses made for the tomb/burial (*quburum*) and the mourning (*bikītum*). The archive of the trader Elamma, excavated in 1991 and assigned to me for publication, contains records dealing with the death and inheritance of the lady Ishtarlamassi, first married to an Assyrian and subsequently to the Anatolian Lulu. Having assigned, on her deathbed, in the presence of her sister and other witnesses, amounts of silver to her sons, their shares subsequently have to be reduced by 27 shekels of silver, to be refunded to her Anatolian husband, who had paid for the costs of the mourning and burial. The sons seem to have been grown up and thus must have been the children of Ishtar-lamassi's first and Assyrian husband, who had died long ago (one record states that she had been married to her second husband for ten years). That the second husband (with whom she appears not to have had children) is refunded the costs of mourning and burying her at the expense of the shares of her sons, shows that this was typically the duty of the children. But the situation with a second, Anatolian husband, is complicated and it seems wise to wait for more evidence before drawing too firm conclusions from this interesting file.[20]

The excavations of *kārum* Kanesh have revealed that it was customary to bury the dead under the floors of the houses. This arrangement made it quite natural to combine the ownership of a house with the care for the burial and funerary rites of the dead parents.[21]

---

18 See W.H. van Soldt, *AbB* 13,21:5ff., for a son presumed dead (note the use of the iterative stem of *kasāpum*).

19 See for examples *CAD* B 37,3,a, and Q 202,a.

20 It comprises in the main the texts Kt 91/k 369, 413, 423, 425, 441, and 443. [**Add.** I have since studied them in the article «The Death and Burial of Ištar-lamassī in *kārum* Kanesh», in: R.J. van der Spek (ed.), *Studies in Ancient Near Eastern World View and Society Presented to Marten Stol on the Occasion of his 65th Birthday* (Bethesda 2008, 97-119). The records are edited in my book *The Archive of Elamma, son of Iddin-Suen, and his Family, AKT 8* (Ankara, in the press), Ch. X]. Also some texts from the archive Kt m/k contain references to the payment of considerable expenses incurred for the burial or tomb (*quburum*) of a father, again in the context of a fight about the division of the inheritance (courtesy K. Hecker). [Expenses for tombs are also mentioned in AKT 6, 251:6-7; TPAK 1, 212:1-3; Kt c/k 54:8-9; and n/k 204:27-28. AKT 6, 273:33'-35' mentions the erection of a building (*bētum*) "in front of the grave where our father is buried"].

21 We have no Old Assyrian references to the *kispum* ceremony, but it seems very likely that Old Assyrian customs in this respect were not much different from those in Babylonia or Mari. Respect for the (spirits of the) dead (*eṭemmū*) anyhow is well attested. Note the passage *KTK* 18:7ff. *urram aḫium mamman kaspam 1 šiqil iddanniātima bēt abini u eṭemmē ukāl*, "tomorrow, will any outsider give me even one single shekel of silver so that I can sustain our paternal home and the spirits of the dead?". The importance of the spirits of the ancestors is also borne out by the occurrence of an oath "by Aššur, Amurrum and the spirits of my ancestors" (*eṭammū ša abbē'a)* by a father whose son accuses him of cheating (kt 91/k 139:26f.). See also *BIN* 4, 96:19f. and 6, 59:8f. (quoted in H. Hirsch, *Untersuchungen zur altassyrischen Religion (=AfO Beiheft* 13/4, Osnabrück 1972) 71 sub IIIA), and *AKT* 1,14:12f.: *ilum lū idē u eṭammū lū idi'ū*. [See now also C. Michel, "Les Assyriens et les esprits de leur morts" in: C. Michel (ed.), *Old Assyrian Studies in Memory of Paul Garelli* (OAAS 4, Leiden 2009) 181-197, and K.R. Veenhof, "Old Assyrian Families ..." (above note 3a), § 6.3.1].

The excavations **[127]** have also revealed that it was customary to adorn the persons buried with jewelry and pieces of precious metal,[22] and together with the costs of making a cist grave, of the grave goods added, and of the funerary rites accompanying a burial this must have added up to considerable expenses. It does not surprise that such costs were taken into account when the inheritance of the person buried was divided and that the heir who became the new owner of the house had to assume special responsibilities in this respect, even more if it was customary to bury husband and wife in the same house. Unfortunately, the archaeological record, also in the absence of written material in the tombs, is not helpful in identifying the persons buried. When owners of houses and archives can be identified and analysis of skeletal remains offers some insight into the gender and age of the persons buried, tentative correlations perhaps can be made in support of these suggestions.

2. Excursus: palāḫum, wabālum and the care of the elderly in Emar[23]

Both verbs occur frequently in the new family law documents from Emar, but unlike their use in Assyria, *palāḫum* (more than 30 times) and *wabālum* I/3 (a dozen times) never occur together in one and the same **[128]** contract. Since we know that these texts from Emar originate from two different scribal schools or traditions, designated as "Syrian" (or "Syro-Mesopotamian") and "Syro-Hittite" respectively,[24] the choice of verb could reflect this distinction. And in fact *all* occurrences of *palāḫum* are in documents of the "Syro-Hittite" type (E. nos. 5, 16, 30-32, 69, 86, 93, 112, 117, 177, 201, 213; A. nos. 28, 39-42, 45-46, 71-75, 78; *AulOr* 5 234f. no. 14; *SMEA* 30 207ff., nos. 7-9; *Iraq* 54 87 no. 1). The occurrences of *wabālum* I/3, on the other hand, are almost all in texts of the "Syrian"; type (E. nos. 15, 156, 176; A. nos. 48, 50, 69; *RA* 77 11f. no. 1; *Iraq* 54 93f. no. 2, 103f. no. 6; *AulOr* 5 235f. no. 15; *ASJ* 16,231f.).

There are only two exceptions to this pattern: A. no. 77 and E. no. 181, both of the "Syro-Hittite" type, use *wabālum* I/3. In the former a widow stipulates that her sister U. shall support her as long as she lives (*adi balṭāku ittanabbalanni*), while making her son and daughter U.'s children. The latter is a man's last will by means of which he divides his property among his three sons, stipulating that they have to support Mrs. A., whom he designates as "their father-and-mother" (A. *abašunu u ummašunu littanabbalu*!), to all appearances his wife and future widow, who after his death will take the position of *paterfamilias*.[25]

This pattern of distribution, notwithstanding the two exceptions, strongly suggests that the verbs are synonyms used in different scribal traditions and this is confirmed

22 See Tahsin Özgüç, *Kültepe-Kaniş. New Researches at the Trading Center of the Ancient Near East* (Ankara 1986) 23ff., who notes that "much of the jewelry came from the burials of women." The single Old Assyrian grave discovered during the excavations of Assur (grave 20) contained a rich variety of golden objects, four diadems ("apparently produced as funerary ornaments on the occasion of the burial"), a variety of beads, ear rings and other rings; see now P.O. Harper a.o., *Discoveries at Ashur on the Tigris. Assyrian Origins. Antiquities in the Vorderasiatisches Museum, Berlin* (Metropolitan Museum of Art, New York 1995) 44f. Textual evidence for such expenses may be derived from a statement by a woman in an unpublished Old Assyrian letter to her husband(?), where she reproaches him for not sending her silver from Kanesh, kt a/k 478: 10: "Don't you hear that there is famine in the City? When I die from hunger you will bury me with silver!" (*inūmi ina bubūtim amūtu* [13] *ina kaspim taqabbiranni*).

23 In what follows E. is an abbreviation for D. Arnaud *Emar 6.3*, and A. for idem, *AulOrS* 1.

24 See for the evidence *AulOrS* 1, 9f. and C. Wilcke, "AḪ, die "Brüder" von Emar. Untersuchungen zur Schreibtradition am Euphratknie", *AulOr* 10 (1992) 115-150.

25 The appointment of a woman (usually the testator's wife, but occasionally also his daughter) as "father-and-mother of the house", explicitly recorded in several contracts, is only implied here.

by the new texts published in *TVE*.[26] This is also suggested by the evidence from Nuzi, were *palāḫum* is fre quent[27] and *wabālum* is not used. This conclusion becomes fully **[129]** acceptable if the legal and social context in which both verbs are used proves to be similar or identical.

2.1. *wabālum*, "to support"

The use of *wabālum* to describe the duty of natural children[28] towards their mother is attested in E. 15, 156, 181, A. 50, *Iraq* 54 no. 6, and *AulOr* 5 no. 15. In three of these texts (E. 15, A. 50, *Iraq* 54 no. 6) the mother (who will become a widow) had been made "father-and-mother of the house" (cf. *ASJ* 16 231f., where she is made "father" only).[28a] In E. 176, where the eldest son is designated as heir, a daughter has "to support" her mother, but she is allowed to present a slave-girl as substitute to perform this duty. In A. 69 the widow and her daughter will share the house with the second son and the daughter has "to support" her mother on penalty of loosing her personal ornaments. In *ASJ* 16 23lff. (a last will) it is the duty of a man's (natural?) son vis-à-vis his father's wife who is made "his father" while he becomes her son.

In A. 48 the obligation is imposed on a son adopted by a widow, an adoption which secures her care during old age and at the same time is a reward (it includes the possession of the house and the house gods) for the person adopted, who had already "supported" the lady during a period of emergency. In A. 77, as mentioned above, a man adopts his younger sister for this purpose, while making her "mother" of his children. Finally, in *RA* 77 11f. no. 1, a daughter made "woman-and-man" (hence full heir, with the obligation of taking care of the cult of the house gods and the ancestors), will be "supported" by her father's three sons, perhaps grandsons, since she is designated as their mother (or is she made their mother by means of this contract?).

In *TVE,* in texts of the Syrian type, the duty of support rests on natural sons (37) and daughters (15:14; in both cases towards their mother), **[130]** and on a natural and/or adopted son (28 and 30; towards their parents). In nos. 30:26ff. and 37:26ff. actual support is a condition for inheriting.

According to some texts the duty of "support" may devolve on other members of the family or relatives, not mentioned by name, when those normally responsible for it are not available or have failed to do what they should. In *Iraq* 54 no. 2 a man and his family have left (the city) and his property will fall to any surviving relative (*ina nīšēia*) who turns up, but if his wife and daughter are still alive (and return?) they will enjoy its usufruct (*akālum*) and "whoever supports them" (*ša ittanabbalšunu*) will receive their possessions. In A. 50 the widow, made "father-and-mother" and head of the household (*kīma qaqqadia ana bītia aškunši*), if her children fail to live up to their duty will give her property "to whoever among the descendants of my (= her husband's) father will support

---

26 In *TVE wabālum* I/3 occurs in nos. 15, 28, 30, 37, and 94 (=*AulOr* 5, 237f. no.16), all of Syrian type, while *palāḫum* occurs in nos. 6, 10, 13, 25, 26, 63, 66, 85, and 88, all of Syro-Hittite type (the restoration of *palāḫum* in no.87, of Syrian type, hence must be wrong). Note the I/3 form of *palāḫum* in no. 85:23, *ittanapallaḫši,* instead of *iptanallaḫši,* patterned after the I/3 of *wabālum.* A limited measure of "overlap" of scribal traditions cannot be excluded with scribes working in one and the same town. Wilcke (see note 24) 125 already pointed out that there probably are examples of two generations of scribes, father and son, belonging to different "schools".

27 See for the evidence S. Stohlman, *Real Adoption at Nuzi* (Dissertation Brandeis Univ. 1971, Univ . Microfilms 72-18.000), ch. II; J. Breneman, *Nuzi Marriage Tablets* (Dissertation Brandeis Univ. 1971, UM 71-30.118) ch. vii; and J.S. Paradise, *Nuzi Inheritance Practices* (Dissertation Brandeis Univ. 1972 UM 72-25.644) 32, comment on line 11.

28 It is not always easy to distinguish natural and adopted children. I assume that children are natural if they are simply referred to as "my son/daughter" without mention of adoption and if there is no final clause which considers the possibility of terminating the relationship (by means of the statement "you are not my son/father", etc.). Occasionally children could also mean grandchildren.

[28a That a husband in his testament makes his widowed wife "father and mother of his house/estate" is now already attested in an Old Assyrian contract, see C. Michel, *RA* 94 (2000) 1-10.]

her" (*ina* NUMUN.MEŠ *abia ašar ittanabbalši*), and the same provision is found in *TVE* no. 15:27ff. In A. 69, similarly, the mother and widow will give her possessions to the one among her sons who supports her (*ina libbi mārīši*[!] *ša ittanabbaluši*). These clauses show that the prospect of inheriting was used as a means of securing support from a potential heir, as was the case in some Old Babylonian contracts (*e.g. CT* 4 1b).

2.2. *palāḫum*, "to serve"

The duty of *palāḫum*, according to the contracts from Emar, may rest on both natural and adopted children, slaves, and indebted persons who have entered the household of a *paterfamilias*. Natural sons and daughters have to "respect and serve" both parents in A. 28, and their (widowed) mother in E. 93, A. 41 and in E. 112, A. 45, 71 and *SMEA* 30 207f. no. 8, where the husband makes his wife "father-and-mother of the house". Adopted sons have this duty towards their mother in E. 5a (1-10), E. 69, A. 75 (the subject of line 1' is singular), and *AulOr* 5 no. 14; in the last three cases the adopted son also marries his mother's daughter. In A. 74 a daughter appointed as "son" by her father adopts a son who has to "serve" his mother. Adopted sons contractually obliged to "serve" their father occur in E. 5b (11-16), 30, *Iraq* 54 no. 1, and also in A. 72, 73 and 78, where the adoptee married his father's daughter (in the last case after having paid his father's debts, as did the adoptee for his mother in A. 74). In E. 32 adoptive daughters have to serve their **[131]** mother, and in E. 31 their eldest sister, made "father-and-mother" by her father.

Palāḫum used to describe the obligation of slaves is rare. In E. 177:20'ff. (beginning damaged) a man stipulates that the son of his slave girl shall serve his wife. In the second part of A. 41 (lines 30ff.) a man gives his slave as son (*ana marutti...attadinšu*) to his wife and eldest son to "serve" them as long as they live. Both slaves, after their death of their master, will gain their freedom, hence their status and "service" were different from those to be rendered by ordinary slaves and on a par with that of adopted children towards their adoptive parents.

There are a number of contracts involving persons who because of unpaid debts have been forced to enter their creditor's household for perhaps antichretic debt service (the creditor designates them as "my man/retainer", *awīluttī*). The creditor by contract cancels his debt (*ḫulluqum*), several times adopts him as son and makes him to marry his daughter (without the usual payment of a *terḫatum*), and stipulates that he shall henceforth "serve" his master/father (and the latter's wife) until their death. Having faithfully served he is allowed to leave the household after the death of his master/father, with his family and to go "where he wishes". Although several times adopted as sons, they do not qualify as heirs and the inheritance seems to be reserved for the natural sons of the former creditor. The best examples of this arrangement are A. 39 (the sons of the creditor are mentioned in the broken line 25') and A. 40. In E. 16 and 117 no adoption is recorded, nor is the wife of the retainer (which his master gives him in E. 16, but which he had already married before entering his creditor's household in E. 117) identified as the daughter of the creditor. Comparable is A. 74, where a daughter, made his son by her father, left behind after the death of her brothers "without son or (somebody else) who will serve me" (DUMU.NITA NU.TUKU *u ša ipallaḫanni jānu*, line 5), adopts a man in debts to "serve" her, but he is also made her heir.[29] Related is *SMEA* 30 210f. no. 9, where a man, also stating that "he has no son and heir [or (somebody else) who will serve **[132]** me]",[30] makes a man with his family "enter his house" in order to serve him and his mother; but we learn that the man had

29 In E. 211, I do not follow Arnaud who reads in line 1 *ana* LÚ-*ut-tú-šú īpuš*, "I made him my man", but prefer to read with Durand in his review *ana ma-ra-šu*, because the spelling and the expression would be abnormal and the person adopted becomes a prospective heir, which is not the case with the other retainers adopted.

30 From lines 17ff. we learn that this happened after his eldest(?) daughter whom he had given a particular status (text broken) and had made his heir, had left [him] and had not "served" him.

also paid his debts (20 shekels of silver and 20 measures of barley) and had sustained his two daughters during a year of famine.

In four other contracts where a man adopts a son and marries him to his daughter to secure his service (A. 43, 46, 72, 75), Arnaud assumes a similar background of antichretic service,[31] because the adoptee, if he wishes to terminate the relationship and leave his father's household has to pay a substantial fine (30 to 60 shekels of silver). There are, however, basic differences between the contracts of this group and the group explicitly dealing with indebted retainers. In the latter the retainer (who does not become an heir, even when he has been adopted), if he wishes to leave pays a fine which regularly amounts to the double of his original debt and looses his wife (given him by his father without payment) and children. In two texts of the former group both partners to the adoption agreement have to pay the same fine for terminating it and the adoptive son, with his wife, is regularly appointed as (co)heir. In A. 43 (where the scribe has mistakenly omitted a verbal form of *palāḫum* in line 6) and A. 72 both pay 60 shekels, in A. 43 the adoptee looses his wife (and children), but in A. 72 he is allowed to take her along if he still pays the *terḫatum*, set at 30 shekels. In A. 46 the adoptive parents are fined 80 shekels, the adoptive son only 30 for no clear reason; in A. 75 (beginning broken) the adoptive son, if he wishes to divorce (*muššurum*) his wife (the daughter of the widow who had adopted him), has to depart alone, is fined 60 shekels and looses his wife. In this group the fines imposed are basically penalties for breaking the contract, in the other group this penalty is added to and the equivalent of the original debt, which again becomes due. It is understandable that, if the adoptive son wants to leave with his family, an amount is added to or included in the fine as payment for the wife acquired without paying a *terḫatum*. He had obtained her "free" in exchange for the service he had agreed to render.[32] In **[133]** *SMEA* 30 210f. no. 9, mentioned above, the person entering the household of the man he will serve (and whose debts he had paid) is compensated by receiving the latter's two daughters, apparently without further payment, as wives for his sons and by the fact that these married couples in due time will inherit the property (this must be the gist of the difficult and broken lines 13-16).

As for the texts of the Syro-Hittite type in *TVE*, in nos. 10:1-4 and 13:1-6 the absence of "anybody who will serve me" is the reason for adopting a son "in order to serve me (and to pay my creditors)". In nos. 25, 41, and 88(?), adopted sons married to the adopter's daughters, will inherit "when (*kīme*) they serve" their fathers/parents. The adoptive son, married to a slave-girl of the adopter in no. 26, and (after his debts have been cancelled) to the adopter's daughter in no. 63, if they have served their parents well, in due time both will be free to leave with their wives and children. In no. 66 a manumitted slave (with his family), having served his master well will become a free member of the *marijannu* class, and in no. 85 whosoever has served a *qadištu*, made heir by her father, will inherit from her. That "serving" (*palāḫum*) is a condition for becoming an heir or free is also stipulated in nos. 10:5ff., 13:7ff., 25:6ff., and 26:7ff.

This short survey shows that there is a basic agreement between the use of *wabālum* I/3 in the "Syrian" texts and *palāḫum* in the "SyroHittite" ones. The element of subordination, "respect", "service", probably inherent to the second verb, matches its use in contractual relations rooted in inequality and difference of status, especially that between a slave and his master or between a (former) debt servant and his creditor and/or adoptive father. Debts are cancelled in exchange for lifelong service, made attractive by a rise in status through adoption and a marriage to the master's or father's daughter. The verb *wabālum* is not attested in such relationships. We may also note that *wabālum* is more frequent

31 *AulOrS* 1, 19.

32 Compare the Middle Assyrian contract *VAS* 19 37, edited by J.N. Postgate, *Iraq* 41 (1979) 93f. (which he compares with the arrangement between Laban and Jacob in Genesis 29), where the retainer (not adopted as son) binds himself to serve ten years in the household of a man, who gives him his daughter as wife, after which he is allowed to leave with his wife.

in relations between parents and their natural children or other close relatives, while *palāḫum* occurs more often in connection with adoption. Still, both verbs are used of adoptive children and in situations **[134]** where women (mothers, widows) are made "father-and-mother of the house" and the hierarchical relations hence must be similar. In Nuzi too *palāḫum* is frequent in situations where a woman is granted "fatherhood" (*ēpišat abuttim*). On the other hand, E. 213: 11ff. uses *palāḫum* of the care and support expected from a widow's brothers-in-law, where subordination is unlikely. All in all these nuances and partly statistical differences are not sufficient to claim different meanings and to deny synonymy. After all, the Old Assyrian contract which uses both verbs and triggered this discussion deals with a manumitted and adopted slave boy, who is made heir, hence also a blend of subordination and equality.

2.3. Purpose: care in old age

In all these contracts, notwithstanding their variety, the main concern was to secure care in old age. This could be done by contractually binding (*rakāsum*) somebody to provide lifelong service (slaves and debt servants, who would earn their freedom at the death of their master or creditor), but perhaps even better by making such a person a full and free member of the household. By adoption and marriage and by granting such persons inheritance rights one could also make sure that the family would continue to exist and that the respect and care would continue after death. For the heir received the duty, usually connected with the possession of the principal house, to extend *palāḫum* to the family gods and the dead ancestors, as A. 75:12'ff. clearly state: "And if my daughter K. dies, A. my (adopted) son shall under no circumstances leave my house (*lū lā uṣṣi*), because he has to care for my gods and my dead (ancestors)!".[33] Even the continued respect and support by natural children could be earned or secured in this way, by making the person to be cared for the main heir and the inheritance rights of the children dependent on their **[135]** proper behaviour towards him. A. 69 (which uses *wabālum*) shows that a widow could give her personal possessions (*mimmêši*!) to the son who supported her (*ina libbi mārīši*! *ša ittanabbaluši*, lines 32f.), as the (unmarried) *qadištu* could in *TVE* 85:22ff.

That service was the core and aim of the arrangement is also clear from E. 16:8-12, where the former debtor, even when he somehow manages to pay the remainder of his original debt,[34] is not allowed to stop "serving", and from the fact that his intention to terminate the agreement is not expressed by "I will leave you", but by "I will no longer serve you!" (line 18). Similarly, in *SMEA* 30 210f. no. 9:19f., the daughter who has left her father is simply said not to have served him. The considerations expressed in A. 74 and *SMEA* 30 no. 9 ("I have no son to serve me..."), quoted above, now also attested in *TVE* 10:lf., show that the basic concern of the person acting was to acquire a substitute for a son, who would naturally support and serve his parents until their death. The same concern is expressed in A. 78:2ff., where a father explains his decision to adopt a son by mentioning that his sons have left him(?) and have not served him, so that he now has

33 See also *TVE* 85:14, where a man's daughter, a *qadištu*, given male and female status and made his heir, has to serve (*palāḫum*) "my gods and my dead ancestors" (*ilānija u eṭemmēja*). See for the cult of domestic gods and ancestors at Emar, K. van der Toom, in: K.R.Veenhof (ed.), *Houses and Households in Ancient Mesopotamia. Papers Read at the 40e Rencontre Assyriologique Internationale (Leiden 1993)* (Istanbul 1996) 74f. [and Wayne T. Pitard, "Care of the Dead at Emar", and Brian B. Schmidt, "The Gods and the Dead of the Domestic Cult at Emar", in: Mark W. Chavalas (ed.), *Emar: The History, Religion, and Culture of a Syrian Town in the Late Bronze Age* (Bethesda 1996) 123-140 and 141-163; new references are in *TVE* 23:16ff. and 30:5ff., where the verb *nabbu'um* is used with "the gods and the dead" as object].

34 When the contract was drawn up he had been acquitted 20 shekels of his debt of 41 shekels. If he wants to leave he has to pay 61 shekels, twice the amount acquitted plus the remainder of the debt. The line mentioning the payment of the remainder of the debt (10) is difficult: "if in the future silver becomes available to B as ransom(? silver *ana B i-paa-da-šu;* see the remarks by Durand, *RA* 83, 174) to be given (or: he shall give it) to his creditor, after (having paid) the silver, B. shall (continue to) serve them as long as they live."

nobody to serve him.[35] The widow speaking in E. 213:10ff. has an even more dramatic story to tell to argue for the necessity of marrying her only daughter and heir off to a husband who becomes his wife's co-heir: "And now, after my husband's death, I am poor (*muškēnāku*) and I have made debts (20 shekels of silver and 30 *parisu* of barley) and there is no one among my brothers-in-law who will care for me (*palāḫum*)". One can hardly expect a brother-in-law to act as servant of his brother's widow, but she obviously hoped he would support and help her, also by paying her debts, no **[136]** doubt in exchange for a title to her house, which she assigns to her son-in-law. By contract and in-marriage of her son-in-law she tries to secure the care and support to which a parent is entitled from his children. Failure to do so is a breach of contract and amounts to cutting the bond with the family. The culprit hence forfeits his status of (adopted) child and heir and is forced to leave the house and he has "to place his garment on the stool and can go where he wishes".[36] His behaviour is shameful and deserves public denouncement: the widowed wife, made "father-and-mother of the house" by her husband in *Iraq* 54 103 no. 6:15f., in that case has to "strike his cheek and to throw him into the street" (*lettašu lū tamḫaṣ ana sūqi lū taṣlišu*). The same humiliating disinheritance is in store for the son of the testator in *ASJ* 16 231f., should he repudiate his mother, who had been made "father" in his father's last will: "she must strike his cheek and drive him out of the door" (*lētašu lu tamḫaṣma u ina babi lū tukaššidaššu*).[37]

3. Inheritance

Care for the elderly could also be secured by means of a disposition or last will, *šimtum* in Assyrian (usually in the expression *šimtam šiāmum* or *šimti bētim šiāmum*), by means of which a person fixed the division of the property he would leave behind. Such last wills, unknown from Babylonia but well attested in Assyria (also during the Middle Assyrian period) and in peripheral areas (Susa, Nuzi, Emar, Alalaḫ, and Ugarit),[38] could serve two purposes.[39] They could assign (additional) property to those members of the family that might not receive a (sufficient) share in the inheritance, if the division were to take place among the heirs following legal custom, *ab intestato.* And they could impose special **[137]** obligations (conditions) on (some of) the heirs, such as taking care of the surviving parent. The head of the household hence might use a last will to secure the future of his wife who was to survive him, if by custom she would not count as heir.

3.1. Marriage contracts and last wills

Contracts recording the itemized division of an inheritance among heirs, well known from Babylonia and our main source for the reconstruction the law of succession there,[40] are not known from ancient Assyria. This makes it difficult to know what the legal custom was and which elements in last wills hence were meant to adapt or go beyond it. In general we note that in the Old Assyrian commercial society women enjoyed more freedom and

---

35 The verbal form at the end of line 2 is read tentatively *um-ḫír-ru-ni-ni* by Arnaud ("m'ont affronté"); I would rather expect a form *umtešširuninni*, "they have left me", also used in *SMEA* 30 no. 9:19. A different verb to describe the estrangement is used in E. 201:29, with prepositional *ultu pānia* (see for an attempt Durand *RA* 84, 84), perhaps *nazāmum* praet. I/3 or simply *waṣûm*?

36 Passim in texts from Emar, e.g. A. 42: *ana bītia gabbi mimmmūia ul iraššī ṣubātšī*! *ina litti liškunma ašar libbišī*! *lillik,* but also used in Ugarit, cf. *CAD* L s.v. *littu* B, a.

37 See for this contract and for the meaning and legal implications of this treatment now Martha Roth, "Mesopotamian Legal Tradition", *Chicago-Kent Law Review* 71 (1995) 13-39, esp. 32ff., where the occurrence in *Iraq* 54 103 no. 6 can be added. See now also *TVE* 15:22ff., for the same treatment of two daughters who fail to support (*wabālum*, I/3) their mother.

38 See for references *CAD* Š/1, 363, 3,b (add Ugarit: *Ugaritica* V, 10 no. 7 = RS 17.36:3) and Š/3, 18, 4,a (the reference cited as 4,b also refers to a last will).

39 Von Soden, "Ein altassyrisches Testament", *WO* 8 (1976) 211, argued that making a last will was not necessary when the testator did not wish to favor a particular heir.

40 See for Babylonia, Kraus, SD 9, 94ff., § 2, and for local variation § 5 (note that a double share for the eldest son is also attested at Eshnunna, see *TIM* 4, 50:6ff.).

more independence, also in economic respect. They owned private property, derived i.a. from the sale of textiles which they produced, we see them taking out and extending loans, and buying and selling slaves in their one name. Marriage contracts indicate that wife and husband to a large extent enjoyed equal rights. While, traditionally, only the husband figured as subject of the verb "to marry" (*aḫāzum*), a married wife too had the possibility of successfully instituting a divorce. Both in marriage contracts which consider a possible divorce and in actual divorce records fines and payments are the same for husband and wife.[41] The wife normally seems to receive a divorce settlement (*ēzibtum*) and does not forfeit her possessions. And there even exists a last will of a woman, the widow of an Assyrian husband subsequently married to an Anatolian (Kt 91/k 453). Moreover, a long record from the same archive (Kt 91/k 421) lists the property (valuable objects, silver, debt claims, textiles, slaves and slave-girls) left behind (*ezābum*) in Kanesh by Lamassatum, widow of the trader Elamma. These possessions have to be "brought to the City (of Assur), where my daughter, the priestess, and my sons will act in accordance with the dispositions made for them".[42] The reference to *šīmātum*, "dispositions", implies that the lady in question had made her last will, which this record seems to quote when speaking in the first **[138]** person singular of "silver under my seals" (line 3), (which) "I gave" (line 19), and "my daughter and my sons" (lines 36f.), even though the essential statement, "she left behind" (line 28) uses the third person. We do not know whether Lamassatum had also inherited some of her property from her husband who had died a few years earlier, because we lack the last will of Elamma and Kt 91/k 421 does not mention property inherited from him (*warkat Elamma*). We have a contract concerning the division of some property of Elamma between his four children, but Lamassatum does not figure in it. It reflects a later stage in the division of Elamma' s inheritance, when two heirs yield their share in a debt claim in silver in exchange for the ownership of a (the?) house in Assur. Lamassatum, who seems to have stayed in Kanesh (presumably living in Elamma's house there), need not have been involved, if by then she was still alive. Anyhow, these data do not allow us to answer the question whether an Old Assyrian wife (widow) by custom would inherit part of her husband's property.

3.2. Women's rights

In Babylonia, according to the Laws of Hammurabi (§ 171f.), a widow with grown-up children had the right to continue to reside in her husband's house, sustained by her sons, while enjoying the usufruct of her dowry. If her husband had not made her a gift, she was entitled to one share in her husband's property. A young widow with little children (CH § 177), even if she remarried, following a decision of the judges could keep the usufruct of her husband's estate to raise the children, who in due time would inherit his estate.[43]

In ancient Assyria the absence of regular divisions of inheritance in combination with the frequent references to "last wills" seems to indicate that disposition by last will was the normal procedure. That a trader had died "without having made his disposition", as a letter reports,[44] indicates that that was unusual. Several judicial documents dealing

---

41 See now R. Rems, "Eine Kleinigkeit zum altassyrischen Eherecht", *WZKM* 86 (*Festschrift für Hans Hirsch*, Wien 1996) 355-367.

42 Kt 91/k 421: 32ff: *ana ālim*[ki] *ubbulūma ammala šīmātisunu eppuš[ū]*.[See for this text and Kt 91/k 453 now *AKT 8*, 164 and 179, and for the Old Assyrian inheritance customs and last wills K.R. Veenhof, "Last Wills and Inheritance of Old Assyrian Traders, with four records from the Archive of Elamma", in: K. Abraham – J. Fleischmann (eds.), *Looking at the Ancient Near East and the Bible through the Same Eyes. A Tribute to Aaron Skaist* (Bethesda 2012) 169-202].

43 See Kraus, SD 9 § 6. In the unpublished Old Babylonian record BM 96956 the shares of three young children are specified (as *CH* § 177 prescribes), and the mother/widow herself receives one cow and amounts of barley and emmer wheat. More than fifty years later, apparently after the death of the mother, the house is divided among the children (BM 96990).

44 *BIN* 6, 2:3-5: *Elalī mēt šimtušu ulā išīm*, "Elali is dead, he did not make his disposition".

with the **[139]** division of an inheritance refer to a "last will" which we do not know,[45] a few times said "to be in Assur". Such last wills were of great value and were treated accordingly.[46] They seem to have been at the basis of various judicial proceedings[47] and we also have several narrative reports on how persons made final decisions (without the term *šimtum* being used) "on their deathbed/ before their death".[48] Moreover, what interests us here, there is good evidence that such last wills were also used as a means of taking care of women, in particular the widow and the daughter who as a priestess remained unmarried, as the following texts reveal.

In the last will known as "*Tablette Thierry*"[49] the family relations are complicated. I prefer Wilcke's reconstruction according to which the testator's father had married twice (not uncommon among Old Assyrian traders) and the lady Šāt-Adad, mentioned first in the will, is the testator's **[140]** half-sister (from a different mother).[50] The testator, Adad-bāni, apparently unmarried and hence without sons and heirs, gives his half-sister the house in Kanesh, which he may have inherited from his father and which she may have to share with his brothers and full sisters.[51] In addition, her brothers will put out at interest from the testator's assets 5 minas of silver for the benefit of Šat-Adad and her mother ("they will eat it, have its usufruct", line 29). Moreover, "the ladies" will receive two shares of all the testator leaves behind. Finally (lines 43ff., broken) the brothers will give her (Šat-Adad) something else, and she will be the owner of a slave-girl.

The main concern of the testator apparently is to take care of his half sister and her mother (his step-mother) who seem to live together. Both get a full share, on a par with her brothers, a substantial annual allowance (90 shekels of silver annually according to the current rate of interest of 30% a year) plus a house and a slave-girl. We note that the testator's assets include property which had accrued to him as inheritance (*warkatum*) of "our mother" (line 13f., *i.e.* his father's first wife, the mother of his brothers and their (half-) sisters), which may imply that earlier on she had inherited property from his late father, presumably by means of the latter's last will in which he may have secured her material well-being. What his own half-sister and her mother receive from him (the house, silver, bronze objects, furniture, slaves) in due time will be left behind (*warkat awīlātim*, line 38f.) to his brothers, who are made responsible for the payment of certain debts (lines 50ff.).

---

45 E.g. *TCL* 14, 21:11: the heirs (and creditors?) of Šu-Nunu "shall divide (his estate) in accordance with the dispositions made for them" (*ammala šīmātišunu izuzzū*). It is possible that, if a last will did not exist, judges or arbitrators were called in to carry out a fair division. In *EL* no. 244, dealing with the inheritance of Pushu-ken, we read that "the five men committee has made a disposition for us (for two sons of Pushu-ken) behind the temple of Assur"; but it is also possible that the *šimtum* mentioned here was a specific decision meant to resolve a conflict which had arisen notwithstanding the fact that Pushu-ken had made a last will.

46 Cf. W.C. Gwaltney, *The Pennsylvania Old Assyrian Texts* (Cincinnati 1983) no.19:28-35: "The tablet with the last will of A. is in Hurama with Š., son of E. Write that one brings that tablet to you, but wrap the tablet in reed (*ṭuppam ina qanu'ē lawwiā*) and be kind enough to entrust it to a reliable trader to bring it to me."

47 E.g. in *EL* no. 9 (*KTK* 103) and in Kt m/k 69 reverse (readable from the photo published in B. Hrouda (ed.), *Der Alte Orient. Geschichte und Kultur des Alten Vorderasien*, Gütersloh [1991] 87) lines 30' *(šīmāt abini ina ālim)*. Here a conflict between two brothers will be resolved by negotiations on the basis of their father's last will in Assur (lines 14'ff.: "let us listen to our father's last will and then negotiate in the City in accordance with his last will", *šīmāt abini lū nišmema ammala šīmāt abini ina ālim lu nētuwu*).

48 *TCL* 19, 76:5ff. reports that a trader "on his deathbed" *(ina bāb muātisu)* gave 30 minas of silver to a friend to hand it over, in due time, to his sons, without the knowledge of his principals; *CCT* 5, 9b:16ff. tells us how a trader "on his deathbed" talked about the contents of his storeroom and handed over his cylinder seal to a friend; and Kt 91/k 423 reports how a lady "on her deathbed" (*ina bāb mu-wa-tim*), in the presence of witnesses, opened her strongbox and divided the silver it contained among her children, a division which agrees with part of her last will, Kt 91/k 453, which may have been written somewhat earlier. [These last two texts have now been edited in *AKT 8*, 179-180].

49 P. Garelli, *RA* 60 (1966) 131-8, with C. Wilcke, "Assyrische Testamente", *ZA* 66 (1976) 204-8.

50 Garelli makes her the testator's wife, and "her brothers" would figure as heirs because the couple (due to the early death of the testator?) apparently was still childless.

51 The clauses which follow, partly broken, are not clear. I doubt whether *ú-ša-ba* in line 8 is to be read *ušabba*, "he shall satisfy"; perhaps we have to read in 7f.: *išt[ēniš] uššabā*, "they will (continue to) live together"(cf. the clause in *EL* no. 7:7f.).

In *ICK 1, 12,* analysed by von Soden,[52] the testator's first concern is for his daughter Ahatum, who is a *gubabtum*-priestess[53] and hence had to stay unmarried and live independently. She receives a number of itemized records with considerable debt claims in tin, copper and silver, one **[141]** single share in the testator's remaining assets (consisting of debt claims in Anatolia and in Assur), an annual allowance of 6 minas of copper from each of her two brothers, in addition to "breast pieces" as offering gifts. His wife, Lamassi, receives [the house] in Kanesh and a tablet with a debt claim of 1 ½ mina of silver, which may have just allowed her to live her own life.

In the damaged tablet *BIN 6, 222* Amur-Ishtar grants his wife, also called Lamassi and designated as *qadištum*, "hierodule", "his house in Kanesh, together with the slave-girls and all the [...]". The text also says something about the duties of the sons and we can still read: "and she will chase out of the house that one among my sons who does not [...]", a clause which aims at enforcing respect for and care of their mother by a heavy sanction. Finally the text stipulates what will happen with Lamassi's property after her death (lines 11'f.: *warkat L.*).

In Kt *91/k 453,* the last will of the lady Ishtar-lamassī, widow of an Assyrian, mentioned above, her daughter who is a *gubabtum*-priestess receives a share (silver and gold and her cylinder seal) alongside her brothers.

3.3. Kt 91/k 389, an inheritance division

A final example of care of the elderly in the framework hereditary arrangements is kt 91/k 389, in which two sons divide their father's estate, but where no mention is made of his last will. This contract, according to the text on the unopened envelope, reads as follows:

KIŠIB *Ni-mar-Ištar* DUMU *Ba-lá*		Seal of Nimar-Ištar, son of Bala.
seal A		seal A
KISIB *En-um-A-šur* DUMU		Seal of Ennum-Aššur, son of
I-dí-Sú-in KIŠIB *En-um-A-šur*		Idi-Suen. Seal of Ennum-Aššur
DUMU *E-lá-ma*		son of Elamma.
seal B		seal B
[I-dí-Išta]r ù ^{d}NIN.ŠUBUR-*ba-ni*		[Iddin-Išta]r and Ilabrat-bani
[i-mì]-ig-ru-ma	e.	reached this agreement:
seal B		seal B
seal C		seal C
É*tù ša Kà-ni-iš*		The house in Kanesh and
ù u-ṭù-up-tum ša I-dí-Ištar		the household goods are of Iddin-Ištar,
^{d}NIN.ŠUBUR-*ba-ni lá ṭá-ḫu a-na*		Ilabrat-bani has no title (to them).
ḫu-bu-ul a-bi-šu-nu ki-la-la-šu-nu-ma		Both together are responsible for their
i-za-zu ana qú-bu-ur Pu-zu-ur		father's debt. For the burial of Puzur,
[142] *um-mi-šu-nu*		their mother,
seal D		seal D
a-na gam-ri-im ù ḫu-bu-ul		for expenses and for the debt of
Pu-zu-ur um-mi-šu-nu		their mother Puzur
seal A		seal A
I-dí-Ištar-ma i-za-az		Idi-Ištar alone is responsible.
i-nu-mì ša i-na a-l[im^{ki}*]*	l.e.	When the property in the C[ity]
i-za-ku-ú-ni É*tù*		will be cleared, the house
ša Kà-ni-iš lá i-ša-ku-nu		in Kanesh shall not be included.

52 Von Soden (note 39) 212ff., cf. Wilcke (note 49) 202f.

53 It is the Assyrian equivalent of the Sumerogram NIN.DINGIR. Many prominent traders had daughters which served as *gubabtum*-priestesses, which did not prevent them from being actively engaged in the family business.

This contract [see now *AKT 8*, 297] records the division of an inheritance by two sons some time after their father's death. Together they will be responsible for his debts, but the eldest son (he is mentioned first) will inherit the house in Kanesh with its belongings (*uṭuptum*)[54] and assume responsibility for the tomb (*qubūrum*), expenses and debts of their mother. He receives the biggest share, but on the condition that he takes care of his mother in every respect, as long as she lives. As mentioned above, I assume that the combination of inheriting the house and having to care for his mother is not accidental and reflects the customary duties of the (eldest) son. We do not know whether this arrangement was based on their father's last will, which is not referred to, but it was apparently carried out after their father's death, when the brothers wished to terminate the situation of a common, undivided household (*aḫḫū lā zīzū*), stopped "living together" (*ištēnis wašābum*), and had to agree on their individual rights and duties. It was at any rate not long after their father's death, since his debts are mentioned (line 10) and the contract still looks ahead at a final settlement of the inheritance in Assur (lines 16ff.). We know from many texts that when a trader died all (evidence of) his assets and debts had to be **[143]** collected in Assur, where a final settlement between heirs, debtors and creditors had to be worked out on the basis of the trader's last will.[55] Our contract refers to this procedure by means of the verb *zakā'um*, "to become clear(ed), to settle accounts", and the verb *šakānum*, "to deposit, to submit (for accounting)".[56] The clause must mean that the house in Kanesh together with its contents, given to the elder brother, is considered an extra share (*elītum*), as compensation for his taking care of their mother, and shall not be included in the assets to be divided in Assur.

The eldest son's care for his mother, summarized in a few words, is comprehensive: she is probably allowed to reside in her late husband's house which he has inherited, he has to pay for her (daily) expenses, for her debts (presumably those she had contracted before her husband's death), and has to give her a proper burial.[57]

Additional evidence for the importance of a house for an elderly person as a place to live in probably can be found in the contract Kt a/k 1255 (see note 54), where a certain Ikuppia buys a house which a woman (Gamu[ ]) "will inhabit as long as [she] lives; nobody will chase her away, as long as she lives the house is hers" (lines 11-17). The contract secures the woman the right to live in Ikuppia's house until her death. She may have been a relative of the buyer, who put the house at her disposal or, perhaps more likely, of the seller who stipulated that she could continue to live in the house after its sale. Anyhow, she seems to have been an unmarried and probably elderly woman who obtained a house to live in or was not forced to move when it was sold. Something similar is stipulated in the contract H.K. 1005-5534, a copy of which I owe to the kindness of Veysel Donbaz. It deals with a woman called Musa, identified as the wife of the Assyrian I. and hence probably his widow. The witnessed contract stipulates that "she **[144]**

---

54 I cannot accept J. Hengstl's interpretation of this word as "Guthaben, Kapital", "zumindest auch die Aussenstände" (*ZA* 82, 1992, 215ff.). The close association between this word and *bētum*, "house" ("the house and its/the *u.*"), also in CCT 5,8a: 15f. (read: "the house in Assur and its *u.*") and kt a/k 1255 (S. Bayram and K.R. Veenhof, *JEOL* 32, 1991-2, 98 no.5: the house alongside the chair(s), the table and the *u.*), where "house" means the building and not the family or the firm, supports a meaning "household goods, belongings", perhaps to be distinguished from the furniture proper on the basis of kt a/k 1255. The affluence of the households (which owned a.o. many bronze and copper objects) implies that *u.* could be valuable. A meaning "capital, assets" is excluded by the enumeration of *CCT* 5,14b:2f., where *u.* is mentioned alongside gold, silver, tin, copper, slave-girls, slaves, textiles, a cauldron, bronze, and bonds, which leaves no room for an additional word for "capital" or the like.

55 See for such arrangements the observations by J.G. Dercksen, *BiOr* 49 (1992) 794, C. Michel, "Le décès d'un contractant", *RA* 86 (1992) 113-119, and my remarks in *Chicago-Kent Law Review* 70/4 (1995) 1724ff.

56 Probably an abbreviation for *ina nikkassi šakānum*, "to submit at the accounting", cf. K. R. Veenhof, *Aspects of Old Assyrian Trade and its Terminology (SD* 10 Leiden 1972) 434f.

57 The presence of this record in the archives of Elamma requires an explanation beyond he fact that one of his sons, Ennum-Aššur, is among its three witnesses. The main persons probably were related to Elamma's family.

will live in the house belonging to A., son of P. (not her husband or son), as long as she lives, in the same house belonging to A. she will ..., A. and his sons shall not chase her away".[58] The verbal form of line 8, left untranslated, can only be derived from *šabārum*, "to break", most probably as present tense of the passive (*taššabbir*), but its meaning is difficult because "to be broken" is thus far is not attested with human beings as subject. There is no evidence for considering it a euphemism for "to die", but it might perhaps be translated by "to become disabled", "to break down" and be taken to refer to the physical problems of old age leading to death. For this meaning I can only refer to a text from Nuzi (*JEN* 335:19, see *CAD* Š/2, 250, 5), where a cow "fell down", "was broken" and "died", but the context suggests that the animal actually broke its legs. The statement in our text, following the stipulation that the woman will inhabit the house as long as she lives, is likely to look ahead at the end of her life. In a legal contract a clause that she is allowed to get old or die in the house in question, seems superfluous, because this is implied in the right to inhabit it "as long as she lives". One would rather expect a clause on what will happen to her "in the same house" after her death and that can only be the right to be buried there. In Old Assyrian this would be expressed by *taqqabbir*, a form similar enough to *taššabbir* to consider the possibility of a mistake of the ancient scribe, also in view of the observations made in § 1.[59]

The Old Assyrian evidence is still limited, but important both for its substance and because it derives from last wills, which offer a testator the possibility of imposing a division of his assets which takes into account both his preferences and the personal circumstances of those who need to be cared for. There is no doubt that our information on such arrangements will increase, even though many last wills must have been kept in the city of Assur, where they are still inaccessible. But more last wills (or copies of them) will turn up in the archives **[145]** excavated in Kanesh,[60] together with letters and judicial records, to inform us about last dispositions of testators and disagreements between heirs.

II. ANATOLIAN EVIDENCE

1. Textual sources

We have a small number of Anatolian family law contracts dealing with matters of brotherhood and inheritance which we may divide into two groups. Those of *group 1* formulate rules for the way in which parents and children, the latter designated as "brothers" (*atḫu*), will live together or can terminate such a situation. Some contain clauses which are important for our subject and most also envisage the possibility of the death of one or both parents or one of the brothers and this entails stipulations on the division of the inheritance. A few other contracts, *group 2*, record the actual division of the property between brothers and they also contain clauses on how to deal with the parents. Both groups seems to originate from level Ib of *kārum* Kanesh, which means that they are some generations younger than the bulk of the "Kültepe texts" discussed above under 1.3.

Group 1 consists of six contracts (A-F), group 2 of two (H-G), but in the following survey I also list and use texts I-K, contracts dealing with division of property, separation and other arrangements between brothers, which provide additional information. Most of the texts have been published, but not those belonging the the Kt f/k group, excavated in 1953 (F-H), which are known to me from transliterations left behind by Landsberger.

---

58 *ina bēti ša A.* [4] *mer'a P. adi* [5] *balṭatni* [6] *tuššab ina bētim* [7] *ša A.-ma* [8] *ta-ša-bi$_4$-ir A.* [9] *u mer'ūšu lā iṭarrudūši* [Now edited by V. Donbaz, *Cuneiform Texts in the Sadberk Hanim Museum* (Istanbul 1999) as no. 28, whose reading of the line 9 has to be corrected: l. 13 is to be read *ú-lá tù-ra-áb*, "nor shall she pledge (the property)", with a D-stem of *erābum*].

59 The sign for *qá* more or less equals that for *ša* minus its final vertical wedge. A similar passive form of *qabārum*, "to bury", is found in *Laws of Eshnunna* § 60, see *CAD* Q 203b, 6).

60 Kt 91/k 396 [= AKT 8, 118] is an unpublished last will of Iddin-Aššur, son of Ilī-dan, according to the short text written on its unopened envelope, sealed by three witnesses (identified as *bēl šīmātia*) and the testator himself.

They will be published in due time in the dissertation of Mrs. Leyla Umur, who allowed me to study her provisional manuscript. For that reason I will limit my use of them to a few essential quotations, which are of direct importance for our subject.[60a] Several of these texts are badly written and/or damaged and due to their specific subject matter the reading of several lines is uncertain or impossible. Thanks to collations carried out in Ankara and a comparative analysis the reading and **[146]** interpretation of some of them in Donbaz 1989 and 1993 could be improved, but the reader is referred to his editions and comments, elements of which are used in my analysis which, due to the focus of this contribution, can only be selective. A full edition of the whole corpus of Anatolian family law documents, including those dealing with marriage and slave sale, with a prosopographical analysis, remains highly desirable.

The texts used in the following analysis are:

A. L. Matouš-M. Matoušová, *Kappadokische Keilschrifttafeln mit Siegeln* (Prag 1984) no. 57, republished by L. Matouš in: H. A. Hoffner – G. M. Beckman (eds.), *Kanišśuwar. A Tribute to Hans G. Güterbock on his Seventy-fifth Birthday, May 27, 1983*, Assyriological Studies 23 (Chicago, 1986) 141-150. See also Donbaz 1993, 142, note 47; I owe a few collations to K. Hecker.
B. *TCL* 4, 62, treated by J. Lewy in *AHDO* 2 (1938) 103 note 2; damaged, collated by M. T. Larsen ("horrible script").
C. Kt e/k 167, transliteration Donbaz 1993, 141 note 46 with pl. 28, 3; damaged, collated.
D. Kt 89/k 369, edition Donbaz 1993, 143f. with pl. 29,1; collated.
E. Kt 89/k 370, edition Donbaz 1993, 140f. with pl. 28,2; collated [see *Studies Larsen* 170].
F. Kt f/k 59, unpublished.
G. Kt f/k 96, unpublished.
H. Kt f/k 61, unpublished.
I. Kt 89/k 383, edition in Donbaz 1993, 134f.; collated [see *Studies Larsen*, 170f.].
J. Kt 89/k 365, edition in Donbaz 1993, 133f. with pl. 26, 1; collated [see *Studies Larsen* 169].
K. Kt r/k 15, V. Donbaz 1989, 78f.; collated [see *Studies Larsen* 167f.].

2. Group 1, texts A-F: brotherhood in a common household

Since it is impossible and not necessary for our purpose to give full transliterations and translations of all the sources mentioned above, I present one of them in full and add a commentary which quotes and discusses parallels and deviations in the other contracts. I have selected text E as sample, because it contains a clause which is important for our subject.

2.1. A sample, text E = kt 89/k 370

After the mention of the presence of the seal impressions of three persons we read:

[147] [5] *Tù-ud-ḫa-li-*[a] [6] *u* A-(stamp seal)-*na-na* (stamp seal) *a-b[u-um]* [7] *um-mu-um Zu-ru* [8] *A-ta- ta ú I-na-ar* [9] *3 at-ḫu-ú be-tám* [10] *pu-ḫu-ur uš-bu* [11] *a-be-tim is-té-en*$_6$ [12] *ú-kà-šu-ú ú šu-ma ma-ma-an* [13] *i-b[a-r]i-[šu-nu] i-ṣé-er* [14] *a-bi*$_4$*-im ummì-im* [15] *i-ša-lá mì-ma* [rev. 16] *ú-pá-za-ar 10 ma-na* KÙ.BABBAR [17] *i-ša-qal šu-ma A-na-na* [18] *um-*(stamp seal)*-ma-šu-nu i-mu-a-at* [19] *u 3 at-ḫu-ú* (stamp seal) [20] *Tù-ud-ḫa-li-a* <*a*>*-bu-šu-nu* [21] *i-na-ṣú-ru ú šu-ma* [22] *Tù-ud-ḫa-li-a i-mu-at* [23] *3 at-ḫu-ú A-na-na um-ma-š[u-n]u* [24] *i-na-ṣú-ru i-nu-mì* [25] *a-bu-um um-mu-um* [26] *i-mu-tù-ni 3 at-ḫu-[ú]* [27] *i-zu-uz-zu* [x x x] [28] *ša ur-d[im*? x x x] [29] *be-tám* [x x x] [30] *zi-tám [ša*?*]* [31] *a-bi-šu* [DUMU-*ú-šu*(?)*]* [33] *i-da-g[al ú-nu-ša-am ú]* [33] *ar-ḫa-lam ša na-ṣí-ir* [34] *a-lim ú-kà-lu i-qá-at Zu-zu* [365] *ru-ba-im Ištar-ib-ra* GAL *sí-mì-il*$_5$*-tí*

[60a Leyla Umur has since left the field and it is my responsibility to see to the eventual publication of these texts, all of which I studied together with her. I therefore take the freedom to present here, in a few additions, more quotes from the records to be discussed in what follows].

"Tudḫalia and Anana are father (and) mother, Zuru, Atata and Inar (are) three brothers. [9b] They are dwelling together in one single house. [11] For (this) single household they will make profit. [12b] If anyone among them does harm to (his) father (and) mother or hides anything, he shall pay 10 minas of silver. [17b] If Anana, their mother, dies, the three brothers shall take care of their father Tudḫalia. [21b] And if Tudḫalia dies, the three brothers shall take care of their mother Anana. [24b] When father (and) mother (both) have died the three brothers will divide (the inheritance) ... [30] the house... [31] the share [of] his father [his son?] will own. [323b] The *unuššu*-service and the *arḫalum* of the Protector of the City they will hold (together). [34b] Authorized by Zuzu, the ruler, and by Ishtaribra, Chief of the Stairway.

2.2. Comments and comparison

Starting from the sequence of text E, the following elements and clauses can be distinguished in texts A-F:

1 (5-9). A statement of status: "A (and B) are father (and) mother, C, D, etc. are brothers". "Brothers" translates *atḫū* (B:3!, C:9, D:4, F:2) and their number varies between two and four. While A:6, with two brothers, writes "C ... and D, his brother" (*aḫušu*), G:2 and H:2, also with two brothers, write *a-ta-ḫu*. Note that none of the contracts states: "(They are) sons of A (and) B", but sonship is implied by the use of the term "father (and) mother".

2 (9-10). "They are dwelling together in one single house" (A:6f., C:9f. *[uš-bu]*, D:5, E:9f.). This primarily refers to the brothers, who have to stay together, but it may include the parents in whose house they apparently live. The stative *ušbū* (also in the deed of adoption *EL* no. 7:7f.) links this clause with **1**, as part of the statement of status, the legal basis for the following stipulations. In B:4, *bētam ušēšibšunu*, "he (the father) made them dwell in a (single) house", refers to what had happened **[148]** before, of which the stative *ušbū* is the result. However, in *EL* no. 7:7f. where an adopted girl and the (natural) son of her adoptive parents to whom she is to be married[61] *bētam ištēniš ušbū*, and in C: rev.2'f. where we read "if they prefer so *p[u-ḫu-ur]* [3'] *uš-bu*", the statives most probably are mistakes for the future tense *uššubū*. This tense is also used in F:4: "C (and) D are brothers, as long as their father (and) mother live they will dwell together" (C D [2] *athū adi abušunu* [3] *u ummašunu balṭūni* [4] *ištēniš uššubū*). Even though the structure of text F is different, doubt remains whether *ušbū* in our contracts is really meant as a descriptive stative and might not also be a mistake for a future tense, which would be understandable, since the stative is typical for Akkadian and absent in the substrate language of the writers. But without compelling evidence to the contrary and with four occurrences in texts that write a rather good Akkadian, I feel not entitled to change the text. It is known that a newly created legal situation may be rendered in the relevant contract by means of a statement of status, regularly in the form of a nominal phrase (in the case of adoption by "A. (herewith) is the son of B."), but also by means of a stative when a nominal phrase is impossible.

B:5-6 has an additional clause, connected with "he made them dwell in a (single) house" by means of *-ma*, which reads: "He (the father) gave them 4? donkeys?, 2 oxen, 15 sheep as marriage (gift)" (*mutum u aššutum*), probably on the occasion of their marriage or in order to enable them to marry.

3 (11-12a). "They will make profit for (the benefit of) the single house". The reading *ukaššû*, confirmed by collation in A:8 and B:7 (broken in C:l 1and D:5), a form derived from the verb *kaššu'um* (cf. its derivative *takšītum*), reveals that the households probably were engaged in commercial activities, which frequently went hand in hand with partnerships.[62] B:7b-8a adds a broken clause which I do not understand.

61 Reading at the end of line 6 *e-ḫ[u-uz]*, cf. Donbaz 1993, 138, note 37.

62 Cf. for Old Assyrian *ICK* 1, 83 + 2, 60 and for Old Babylonian *VAS* 8, 71, see *CAD* K s.v. *kašû* B.

4 (12b-17a). "If anyone among them does harm to (his) father (and) mother or hides something, he shall pay 10 minas of silver". A heavy fine (the same fine in I:20f. and J:21f., where the death penalty is added) has to protect the parents against harm or financial injury[63] and to prevent **[149]** the dodging of the stipulations of **3** by keeping earnings for oneself. Both clauses occur also in A:9-11 (read in line 11 *ú-pá-zár*!) and D:6-8, however, not as simple prohibitions, but as conditional phrases: "If anyone is rebellious, hides, they will sell him..." (in A: 12 *i-dí-nu-š*[u] is a mistake for *iddunūšu*). The insubordination clause with *šalā'um* must also be read in B:9-10a and is missing in C due to damage. A:8-11 adds: "(If) he demands a (his) share (in the property)" (*zittam išassi*), as does D:8. Claiming one's share means asking for a division of the inheritance, which would break up the single household. The clauses strongly remind one of those attested in the later "brotherhood contracts" from Nuzi where the brothers are forbidden "to mention a share/division" (*šumi zittim qabûm*), to "acquire personal property" (*sikiltam rašûm*), and also have to dwell together (*wašābum itti*).[64] The Old Assyrian clauses in our contracts seem to be their forerunners. D:9 adds another prohibition, "to take his wife (to live) aside/outside" (*aššassu a-b/patti iṣabbat*), probably in order to leave the paternal house to start a household of his own. One may compare the deed of adoption *EL* no. 7:9ff.: "If they do not like it (dwelling together), they (the parents) will make them dwell outside/separately" (*b/pattam ušeššubūšunu*), that is the married couple will be allowed to start its own household. In *EL* no. 8: 16f. the adopted son is forbidden "to turn his neck aside/elsewhere",[65] which must have a similar meaning.

B: 10b-14 has additional, broken clauses: *aḫum ana aḫim ul*[ā...] 12 *Perua ša-ni-am*? [...] 13 *i-ṣa-ba*!*-a*[*t*]? *i-re-ší-šu-nu-ma* 14 *i-dí-nu ša aššātišunu a*-[...], which are difficult to restore and understand. Line 12 may mention the possibility or prohibition of taking another **[150]** [brother?], line 14 seems to be a clause dealing with the ownership of personal possessions "the gifts(?) of their wives".[66]

---

63 The verb *šalā'um*, attested only in Old Assyrian, as the examples quoted in *CAD* Š/1 241a show, always refers to economic harm and financial injury (also in *CCT* 5, 1a: 20, where the incriminated slave is holding back silver, which he refuses to pay, see lines 8-15). In *KTS* 1b:26ff. a woman intends to travel to Kanesh in order to "protect" the house(hold) of her husband and son, "lest anyone tries to harm your paternal household" (*bēt abikunu*). We cannot exclude that the verb had a wider meaning than these references in commercial letters suggest, but in the context of the brotherhood contracts the economic, financial background seems clear in view of the proximity of *kaššu'um*, "to make profit" and *pazzurum*, "to hide (profit)".

64 See G. Dosch, "Gesellschaftsformen im Königreich Arraphe (*aḫḫutu*) (II)", in *SCCNH* 5 (1995) 3-20. Such texts may also state that "here is no (distinction between) older and younger among them", that they will jointly perform service duties (*ilku* and *dikūtu*), and that possessions are "merged" (*šummuḫum*).

65 Reading with *CAD* K 447a *kišassu ana b/pattim ipannu*.

66 The noun *i-dí-nu*, thus far unknown, occurs six times in Old Assyrian family law contracts:

a) text B:14 *i-dí-nu ša aššātisunu a[-...]*, "the *i.* of their wives...";

b) text C:10': "If one of the brothers dies his sons will own (*dagālum*) his share, his wife her *i.* (*[i-dí-ni]- ša*)";

c) text D:19: "His sons [will own] his share, his wife her *i.* (*i-dí-[ni-ša]*)";

d) text I:10: "S., his eldest son, received as share everything which is in the house. His share 10 and his *i.* (*i-dí-ni-šu*) he took out of the house" (*uštēṣi ištu bētim*);

e) kt j/k 625:15f. (divorce; Donbaz 1989, 84f.): 13 6 1/2 shekels of silver, her divorce settlement 15 *[ú] i-dí- ni(m)-ša* "he gave her";

f) *Tablettes paléo-assyriennes de Kültepe*, 1 (1997) no. 159: N. *amassu* 2 K. *i-dí-nu-šu* 3 *ša* N. 4 N. *ana* 5 *šīmim iddin*, "N. sold his slave-girl K., (who was) a gift to him".

[Addendum:

[g) Kt 75/k 44 (fragment of a last will, courtesy C. Michel):11'-14'*: qaqqad ummika* 12' *lū taṣṣur 6 ṣubātū* 13' *damqūtum watrūtum 2 ṣubātū ahamma* 14' *ša i-dí-ni* (is *lū taṣṣur* a mistake for *lū tanaṣṣar*?);

h) CCT 5, 43:29:29: 2 minas of gold (a share in a joint-stock fund) *i-dí-nu ša Waqqurtim mer'itia.*

i) Kt 88/k 651 (*Archivum Anatolicum* 2 [1996] 19-20]: «What have you decided concerning our sister (who will be married off), what will we give her as her marriage gift?» (10 *mīnam i-dí<<na>>-ni-ša niddaššim*)].

Texts a)-c) and e) suggest something typical for women, but in d) and f) it belongs to a man. It must denote a personal "gift", and one could parse the noun as *iddinū* (*iprisū*-formation of *t/nadānum*).

5. (17b-24a). The obligation to care jointly for the surviving parent does not occur in the other contracts, which immediately move on to the situation where both parents are dead (B after having considered the consequences of the death of the oldest brother). We will consider the implications of this difference later. For "caring for" our text uses the verb *naṣārum*, "to protect", "to take good care of", which is unique in such a context. It is used with fields, houses and animals as objects, and in Codex Hammurapi § 177 its object is the estate of a dead father, to be "protected" for his children by his remarried widow and her husband. In Old Assyrian, *KTS* lb:27f. provides a parallel, where a woman in Assur writes to her son that she intends to travel to Kanesh "in order to take care of the house(hold) of your father and of you".

D:20-22a has a stipulation about what happens when the father (Galidi) dies, but the text is damaged and I cannot reconstruct what his sons will do in that case (DUMU-*ú-šu* x[x x x] [22] [x] y *ZU-ú*). Donbaz's *ṣú-ḫa-ri-šu* (end of 21) is not on the tablet and *y* in line 22 looks more like a damaged SI = *ší*, hence perhaps rather *[ú-š]é-ṣú-ú*, "they will take out",[67] than *[i-z]u-zu-ú*, "they will divide", though the latter **[151]** makes better sense. The next lines enumerate what property "they will give to [their] mother Buza, whereupon she leaves (the house)" ([25b] *ana Buza ummi*[*šunu*] [26] [i]-*du-nu-ma tu-ṣí*) "1! slave-girl, 1 ox, 10 [sheep?], a *šaršarranu*-container with oil, 4 minas of wool, 10 *panniru*, 10 *umṣú*, [x] *ukāpu* and 1! *kutinnu*-jar". This share in the property is apparently meant to allow her to live independently as a widow.

6 (25b-27). When both parents are dead the brothers will divide the property and the single household will be broken up (*parāsum*, cf. I: 11 [; see also *Studies Larsen* 143]). Most contracts deal with this situation, but they show that there are two options. Dwelling together may continue by agreement, "if the brothers like/prefer it", but separation follows "when they do not like/prefer it" (*šumma ṭābū*; in F:2f. *šumma ṭābšunūti*; in the deed of adoption *EL* no. 7:9f.: *šumma lā iṭiabšunūti*). A: 13ff. read: "When both parents die..." (*inūmi*... [14] *kilallāšunu* ... [15] *šu-ma! at-ḫu! ṭ[á-bu]*, cf. D:l2), B:l7 and F:5 have "After they have died" (*ištu...imuttūni*), and C:rev.2' can be restored accordingly, see Donbaz's transliteration. The division has to be in equal parts, *mitḫa/iris izuzzū*, as in Nuzi, but in B:l9ff. the older (natural?) son receives a double share, the younger a single one. It consists of "the house (and) whatever is present" (*bētam (u) mimma ibaššiu*, A:l7f., B:l8f., C:4', D:13f.; F:9 only has *mimma [ibaššiu]*).[68]

7 (28-32). Damaged lines with stipulations about the details of the division, probably in case one of the brothers dies and "[his son will own] the share of his father". What happens with the house (line 29) remains unclear. I will not analyze here what the other contracts stipulate for this eventuality in partly broken passages.[69]

[152] 8 (32b-34). A clause about the performance of service duties (*unuššum*) and *arḫalum*, probably its material compensation, see also I:33ff. and J:36. This feature cannot be discussed here.[70]

---

67 Anatolian contracts frequently write long final vowels at the end of plural verbal forms, also in strong verbs, but text D generally follows Assyrian writing conventions (*i-zu-zu* in line 32) and only has long vowels in masculine plural nouns in the nominative (*at-ḫu-ú*).

68 Read in B: *bētam mimma* [19] *ibaššiu 2! qá-ta-tim* [20] Š. *[ilaqqe] 1? qá-tám* P. [22] *ilaqqe*!].

69 Some of the readings in the edition can be improved: A:30: x DUMU-*ú?-šu idaggulu*, 34: *inūmi at[ḫū] izuzzūnim*; B:15f.: *aššassu zi-tù-<šu> talaqqe*; C: 20: *[z]i-tù-šu* DUMU*ú-šu* [21] *[i]-da-gal-lu a-ša-sú* [22] *[i-dí-ni]-ša idaggal* (for *tadaggal)*, see note 66; D:32 beginning: not "his sons", but presumably a verbal form ending with *-ma* followed by *izuzzū*; next follows the share for Aduwa, "their youngest brother", *aḫušunu ṣaḫrum!* (TUR), who also receives something [34] *[iṣṣēr zi]-tí-šu utram*, "extra, on top of his share" (because he still has to marry?); [35]: [x x x *t]ù bu la im-ZI-ma*, obscure.

70 Donbaz 1993, 148f. deals with *arḫalum*, but there remain questions. [See now J.G. Dercksen in *Studies Larsen*, 140-147].

9. (34b-35). The well known authorization of the contract by the local ruler and his second man, cf. A:36-38 (same pair), D:37f. and H:35f.

2.3. Interpretation

The contracts of group 1 deal with "brothers dwelling together", in community of property, a legal institution known from various periods and areas of the Ancient Near East, recently analysed by R. Westbrook,[71] and for Nuzi by G. Dosch,[72] both of whom also point out correspondences with an early Roman legal institution called *ercto non cito*, "undivided ownership".

"Brotherhood", as analysed by Westbrook, can be of two types: a) between natural brothers who stay together after the death of the *pater familias*, postponing the division of the inheritance and maintaining one single household; and b) between persons who are no natural coheirs but whose "brotherhood" is established by *adoptio in fratrem*, which creates a partnership with community of property.[73] Since in the contracts of group 1 the parents are still alive and there is also no mention of brothers adopting each other they represent neither type a) nor type b). Since there is no explicit mention of adoption of the brothers by the married couples (called "father, mother") and they are not called their "sons", we have to ask what is at stake here. Do the contracts fix the relations between parents and their natural sons or are the brothers (in part?) adopted sons? And, if yes, is previous adoption merely implied or was it realized at the very time these contracts were drawn up?

The initial statements fix the status of the parents and of the brothers (in relation to each other, hence *atḫū*) and the situation of living together in one house. In text B:4 (see above under 2) the father is said "to have **[153]** made them dwell together in the house", most probably at the time he gave them property in connection with their marriage. This indicates that it was the father who proposed/ imposed the contract, probably to prevent his grown-up sons from leaving the family household to start a family of their own elsewhere (in Akkadian *bētam epēšum*). In fact, the second person mentioned in the enumeration of the brothers, on account of her name (Jataligga) most probably was a woman, to all appearances the wife of the first brother.[74] The same is probably the case in A:5 which enumerates "Wali, his wife, Kunuwan, his brother", where the wife of the first brother remains anonymous.[75] That the younger brother will receive something extra (a slave) when they divide the inheritance probably is because he still has to acquire a wife for which he needs extra money. Text D:9 supports this view (see above under 4), forbidding any brother "to demand his share (and) to take his wife (to live) separately". In F the eldest son also seems to be married, for it is stipulated that when the brothers inherit the property after their parents' death, they will set aside (*nadā'um*) an amount of silver in order to enable the younger to acquire a wife. This was probably also the reason why the youngest brother in D:32ff. would receive extra items on top of his share (see note 69). That he is the only one to receive them could imply that his brothers had already married.

---

71 R. Westbrook, *Property and the Family in Biblical Law* (JSOT Suppl. 113, Sheffield 1991) 118-141, ch. 6, "Undivided Inheritance".

72 *Op. cit.* (see note 64).

73 Westbrook 127 adduces evidence from Old Babylonian Susa, i.a. *MDP* 28 no. 425, where he translates (lines 8-13): "should P. acquire property or silver, I. will be able to divide it" (and *vice versa*). The second verbal form, written *i-za-az-sum*, is better taken as *izzassum* (*izzaz+šum*), meaning "it is (also) at his disposal, it belongs (also) to him".

74 Lines 16f. mention the rights of "his wife" after the death of the first brother, her husband.

75 Lines 20f. read: "When Wali (and) his wife dies" (verb in the singular, since they are considered a single legal entity?); lines 22f. probably have to be restored to read: "(after his death) [his sons] will own", which also suggests a marriage.

While the authority of the *paterfamilias* may have prevented a division of the inheritance during his lifetime,[76] that grown-up married sons left the family house to start their own household may have been fairly normal, also in ancient Anatolia. Hence a specific type of contract which (by agreement?) obliged them to continue dwelling together and to share all property, also that newly acquired through commerce, would be understandable. The Anatolian adoption contract *EL* no. 7 (see above under 2.2 ad 2) supports this conclusion. The young couple, consisting of the adopted girl and the son to whom she is married, "if they like it, will live **[154]** together (with the parents) in the house, if they do not like it, they (the parents) will make them (allow them to) live separately". For grown-up, married children dwelling in the same house with the parents was a matter of free will, by agreement, but the agreement could be terminated, as could contracts of brotherhood and partnership.[77]

The brothers' status of sons is not explicitly mentioned in our contracts, probably because it was a matter of fact and because the focus, understandably, was on the brotherhood between them that they would have to stay together and live in partnership (*atḫū*). The status of the "father (and) mother" is also stressed, because it was the natural basis of the brotherhood, secured their authority over the household and implied filial duties on the part of the sons/brothers. Moreover, the parents in a way were also partners in the household, since they shared the house and probably also the property with the sons/brothers, who were forbidden to claim their individual shares in it as long as the parents were alive.

Sharing all property, clearly expressed in brotherhood contracts from Susa, Nuzi and Ugarit, is also mentioned in the Anatolian adoption contract *EL* no. 8, which resembles our contracts also in other respects. The adoptive son, Š., is obliged "to bring every *k/qilb/pum* he acquires anywhere to his father's house" and is forbidden "to hide anything from him", and the community of property is laid down by the phrase "whatever they own, be it little or much, belongs to the three of them".[78] The duties of a single, adopted son, made heir, are similar to those of the brothers in our contracts, and this son too is forbidden "to turn his neck elsewhere". The complication of our contracts is that there are several brothers and that the obligations also (or primarily?) apply to their mutual relationship, hence the use of *atḫū*.

Still, this parallel also raises the question whether the contracts of group 1 could not deal with adopted children. That they do not mention adoption as such is not decisive. Adoption could be expressed verbally, as in *EL* no. 7:2f. and kt 89/k 379 (Donbaz 1993, 137):6ff. (*ana mer'ūtim laqā'um*), but also by means of a statement of (newly **[155]** acquired) status, as in *EL* no. 8:lf.: "H. and$^{!}$ ^{f}N., Š. is his$^{!}$ son" (Š. *me-ra-šu*), in which case the parents are not identified as "father (and) mother".[78a] Our contracts may imply adoption by a double statement of status, of "father (and) mother" and of "(each other's) brothers".

The term *atḫū*, unfortunately, is not helpful in deciding the issue, since it is used both of natural and adopted brothers, and also of partners in business. The latter is the case in contracts from Susa (*MDP* 24 332:4 and 28 425:2) and probably also in the Old Assyrian letter *BIN* 6 16:5f.: "If you are my brother (*aḫī*), we are truly each other's brothers!" (*atḫuāni*).[79] For § 38 of the Laws of Eshnunna ("If one among *atḫū* intends to sell his share") commentators hesitate between "undivided brothers" and business partners. Partners are very likely in the Old Babylonian letters *AbB* 10 188:10' and 11 150:23, but in *AbB* 12 9 *atḫū* seems to be used for natural brothers: four *atḫū* have sold a slave belonging

---

76 Cf. Westbrook (note 71) 121 with note 2: rare and aberrant in ancient Mesopotamia.

77 See also Westbrook (note 71) 128.

78 Lines 3-5: *šumma Š.* KI-*il*$_5$-BA-*am mimma* <*a*>*-a-kam ikaššuduni ana bet Ḫ. ubbal*; the word describing his acquisition is unknown. Lines 10f.: *eṣṣunu u māssunu ša 3-šunūti*.

[78a This is also the case in a new Anatolian adoption contract, Kt n/k 2100, which starts with: Š. W. *u* I. *mer'ūšu*, "As for Š., W. and I. are his sons", and continues with a stipulation on what happens when "they leave Š." (*šumma* Š. *ēzibū*).]

79 In the Old Assyrian business letters traders regularly address friends and partners as "my brother".

to their (dead) father's estate and a fifth one, the eldest son, succeeds in acquiring his share in the yield. If this is correct, it also indicates that the number of brothers in our contracts (between two and four) is no argument pro or contra adoption. The three surviving Anatolian adoption contracts also cannot decide the issue. *EL* no. 7 has been discussed above and kt 89/k 379 (Donbaz 1993, 137) is damaged and atypical, since it seems to record the cancellation of an adoption. *EL* no. 8 is the most elaborate one and some clauses have been quoted above because of their similarity with our brotherhood contracts. That an adoptive son could be obliged to live under the same stipulations as agreed upon in "brotherhood contracts" is not really surprising, since the aim of the latter is to lay down rules for the cohabitation of sons-and-brothers both among themselves and with their (natural or adopted) parents. But there are also differences. Even though the adoptive son of *EL* no. 8 had received property (lines 15f., a fortified house, *dunnum*) and had been made heir, his father retains the right to sell him if he becomes poor,[80] not surprising since we know from Anatolian slave sales that parents did sell their children in such emergencies. The father's right to do so may have been explicitly recorded because, a few lines before, community of **[156]** property between parents and son had been laid down. The father must have wished to reserve this right for a case of emergency, as a last resort. Whatever the explanation, it seems likely that in "brotherhood contracts" there simply was no room for such a clause since they focussed at equality and partnership, irrespective of whether the brothers were natural or adopted sons.[81]

Whatever the status of the "brothers", natural or (also) adopted sons of the couple identified as "father (and) mother", it seems clear that the purpose of these contracts was to ensure the continuation of the single, common household at the time when (some of) the sons had become grown-up, were about to marry and might start their own family and household. Apparently, a special "brotherhood contract" was necessary to prevent the dissolution of the household at this stage. Its clauses suggest that the motives for such a decision were primarily of an economic nature and may have been conditioned by the commercial activities (*kaššu'um*) of the families in question. Whatever its benefits for all participants, it is clear that the parents (who probably took the initiative to realize it) profited from it in a special way. Since it dealt with married sons, the parents must have been in their middle age and the arrangement would have been a good insurance against the problems of old age. The sons, linked by brotherhood, were not to leave the household, were not to accumulate private capital, and were not allowed to ask for their shares in the common property. The aging parents would be assured of the continuing support of their sons by sharing the family house, the property and the earnings of the household.

Most contracts only deal with the situation arising after the death of both parents, when the continuation or dissolution of the common household is a matter of preference, of free choice (element 6). But E, our sample text (Kt 89/k 370), considers the more probable case of one parent surviving the other and in that case the three sons together will take care of the surviving parent. The death of the father (Tudhalia) apparently does not allow the brothers to divide the common property, since according to lines 24ff. this has to wait for the death of both parents. **[157]** Text D, which first envisages the possibility of the death of both parents (simultaneously?), later on (lines 20ff., see above element 5) has clauses about what will happen at the death of each of them separately. The damaged lines 21f. probably stipulate that when the father dies his sons will somehow divide the property, while the surviving widow, Buza, will receive a substantial gift whereupon she will (have to) leave the house, apparently to live on her own. Two other texts, A:19 and F:10, only mention the death of both parents, followed by a dissolution of the household and division of the property if the brothers prefer so.

---

80 Lines 18f.: *šumma* H. *ilappin* Š. *ana šīmim iddiššu* (mistake for *iddaššu*).

81 Note, for comparison, the clause of solidarity between husband and wife, in poverty and prosperity, in the Anatolian marriage contract quoted *CAD* L 81 s.v. *lapānu*, 1, a.

This difference between the contracts seems to indicate that there was no standard rule how to act when one of the parents died. The fate of the surviving mother probably was better in text E than in text D. In both cases she was taken care of, but while in E she could continue to live in the family house as a full member of the household, in D she was expected to take care of herself, in her own house, using the property given to her, which included a slave-girl to serve her. We cannot consider the treatment of the widow in text D simply a legal way of getting rid of her, so that the sons and heirs can acquire the house and the (remaining) property for themselves, since the contract was drawn up when the father and mother were still alive. It seems more likely to assume the underlying notion that, differently from text F, the death of the father or *paterfamilias* would lead to a division of the property followed by a setting up of separate households, which raised the problem of the fate of the widow. The solution was not to entrust her to the care of one of the sons (who in that case perhaps would inherit the family house, as in the Assyrian contract Kt 91/k 389; see above 1.3), but to make her economically independent by giving her a fair share of the property, which would allow her to live alone and independently. Various contractual solutions apparently were possible in such situations, probably conditioned by social and economic factors which remain unknown to us, as also the contracts to be discussed in the next paragraph show.

3. Group 2, texts G-H: divisions among brothers

Above we noted that text F stipulates (see under 1.2, elements 2 and 6) that two brothers (*a-t[a-ḫu]*), Šu. and Ša., shall live together (with their parents) in one household as long as their father and mother are alive. To our surprise, however, text G, from the same archive and dealing with **[158]** the same two brothers, records the division of the household and property, apparently during their parents' lifetime. This is clear from the stipulation that the youngest brother, Ša. (he is always mentioned in the second place and was still unmarried in text F), acquires as his share not only the house, two slave-girls and the debt, but also "mother and father" (mentioned in the first place and in that order).[82] Anatolian contracts are undated, but it seems likely that text G is the later one, which then implies a change or cancellation of contract F. It may have been at the request of the sons, in particular of the eldest one who leaves the house to start a separate household, and (also) because of the old age of the parents and in particular of the father, which may have prevented him to function as *paterfamilias* and as an active member of the household. Such a development must have made a change of the contract, by mutual consent, possible. The division worked out anyhow takes the obligation to take care of the aging parents serious, thus honoring what probably was one of the motives for the creation of a brotherhood and common household. We note again that the acquisition of the house and its contents is linked with the duty of caring for the parents, who will continue to live there. We do not know whether the younger son, Ša., had married in the time elapsed between the two contracts; if not, his mother (mentioned first in line 4!) may have continued to care for the household, which included the perhaps aging father (mentioned in the second place). The eldest son leaves the house, after having taken his share, an amount of silver and a (his) bed.

Something similar happens in text H, from the same archive, but dealing with different persons. It records the division of a paternal estate (*bēt abišunu*) between three brothers (*ataḫū*). The second brother acquires an amount of silver, barley, "their father, their mother, the house" (lines 6f.).[82a] Since no related brotherhood contract is

82 [The beginning of text F reads: *Šu. Ša.* [2] *athū adi abušunu* [3] *u ummašunu balṭūni* [4] *ištêniš uššubū* [5] *ištu abušunu u umm[a]šnu* [6] *imuttūni šumma* [7] *ṭābšunūti ištêniš* [8] *uššubu šumma la ṭābšunūti* [9] *mimma išûni* [10] *kilallānma [izuz]zū* ... Text G reads: [*Šu.] u [Š]a. a-t[a-hu]* [3] *[me-e]r-ú Šak.* [4] *izuzzū ummam* [5] *abam bētam* [6] *2 amāti u hubul[lam]* [8] *Ša. ilqe*].

[82a The beginning of text H reads: H. Š. [2] *u* T. *a-ta-hu-ú* [3] É *a-bi-<šu>-nu izuzzūma* [4] Š. *1 mana kaspam* [5] *10 naruq uṭṭatam* [6] *abušunu u ummašunu* [7] *bētam* <<Š.>> [8] *ilqe*].

(thus far) known, we do not know whether text H also implies the change of an older contract. Anyhow, the solution is similar to that of text G, and in fact also to that of the Assyrian contract Kt 91/k 389, analyzed above. There the division (with the elder brother inheriting the house, its contents, and the obligation to take care of and bury his widowed mother) was reached "by **[159]** agreement" (*magārum*, N stem) and something similar may have triggered the dissolution of the household in the Anatolian contracts G and H too. But in all cases the agreement reached included the obligation of one of the brothers/heirs to take care of the (surviving) parent(s), for which he was compensated by acquiring something in addition to his regular share, usually the paternal house and its contents (*uṭuptum*).

A division is also recorded in *EL* no. 10 (= *TC* 2 73), to which we can add *TC* 3 215 (a fragment of its envelope),[83] where "Labarša, Lamassī and Šuppišamnuman divided, whereupon Labarša left the house". The persons mentioned, though not identified as "children of PN"[84] or designated as "brothers" (*atḫū*), to all appearances divided an inheritance, probably a paternal estate, presumably when the eldest brother (the one mentioned first) decided to leave the common household. Text K (Kt r/k 15 [see Dercksen, in *Studies Larsen* 167-8]), is a division worked out between two couples. Together they apparently formed one household, since the second couple, after receiving an amount of goods from the first, leaves the house (lines 7f.: *ištu bētē ip-ru-šu*[sic]*-šu-nu*), but it seems to be a temporary measure. Those leaving are for a period of five years free from a certain service duty and have no claim on its material benefits *(arḫalum, unuššum*), but after that period both husbands will again perform it (lines 17f.: *kilallān eppušū*). We do not know the background of this contract, but we note that the two husbands are designated as "brothers" (*atḫū*). We cannot exclude the possibility that their brotherhood was a continuation of a situation created by their parents, along the lines of texts A-E, whereby the service duty, incumbent on the single household, was inherited by both of them jointly. Similar questions arise in connection with the contracts of texts I and J, where also the division and acquisition (*laqā'um*) of property is recorded, followed by a separation (*parāsum*), and where also the issue of service duties is at stake. But we know too little of their background and of the social conditions of ancient Anatolia to indulge in speculations. Since none of these contracts deals with the fate of the parents they fall outside the scope of this contribution.

[160] Even though the issue of the care of the elderly in texts F and G is treated in a way similar to that of the Old Assyrian contract Kt 91/k 389 (but note that in the latter the father has died and that both brothers share the debts of their mother), this is hardly sufficient to suggest that the contractual arrangements in these Anatolian contracts are of Assyrian inspiration. They cannot be separated from and are rooted in the same social structure as the Anatolian "brotherhood contracts". The latter are indeed written in Assyrian (many by non-Assyrian scribes, as their typical mistakes show) and by consequence use Assyrian terminology. It is of course possible to discover similarities in the legal customs governing the dissolution of a household and the division of the property in different ancient societies. But the complete absence of comparable Assyrian contracts concerning "undivided brothers" living with their parents in one and the same household, and the original features and consistent basic structure of the relevant Anatolian contracts warrant the conclusion that they reflect native customary law. One should admire the scribes who were able to render original elements of Anatolian customary law into reasonably good Assyrian and to write these interesting contracts.

83 See for this document also Donbaz 1989, 89.

84 The presence of a woman with an Assyrian name (Lamassī, "my angel") between two Anatolians in an otherwise purely Anatolian record is surprising. Was she the Assyrian widow of a dead brother whose share she had inherited, or was the name Lamassī also used for an Anatolian girl?

Bibliography

Donbaz, V. 1989. Some Remarkable Contracts of 1-B Period Kültepe Tablets I, in: K. Emre *et al.* (eds.), *Anatolia and the Ancient Near East. Studies in Honor of Tahsin Özgüç*, Ankara, 75-89 with pls. 15-18.

–. 1993. Some Remarkable Contracts from 1- B Period Kültepe Tablets II, in: M. J. Mellink *et al.* (eds.), *Aspects of Art and Iconography: Anatolia and its Neighbours. Studies in Honor of Nimet Özgüç*, Ankara, 130-154 with pls. 26-29.

Redemption of Houses in Assur and Sippar*

1. "The favor of Assur"

One of the Old Assyrian letters excavated in *kārum* Kanish during the campaign of 1990 and published as no. 46 in the edition by Cecile Michel and Paul Garelli,[1] contains new and unique information about a legal decision taken in the city of Assur. For that reason it deserves special attention, the more so since the editors have misunderstood the crucial l. 22. I start with a new translation, which incorporates changes in the transliteration and translation of some other passages, which will be argued for below. In the absence of a cuneiform copy, my observations are based on the transliteration by the editors, but I venture a few emendations (in lines 11 and 16) which yield a better sense and are close to the reading of the cuneiform signs the editors saw on the tablet.[2] I also assume that nothing is missing at the beginning of the indented l. 15.

1.1. The text: TPK no. 46

> "<Speak> to Ilī-nādā, Aššur-nādā, Dan-Assur, Aššuriš-tikal and Išm(e)Aššur, and in particular to Aššuriš-tikal and Išme-Aššur, thus Puzur-Ištar:
> '[5] You must have heard from various sides that since three years the stocks of your (plur.) father's household and our houses have been handed over for silver. [9] Since this was not enough, also the house I myself had acquired [11] and the household goods (*ú-ṭù-up*$^{!}$*-tum*), both mine and those belonging to my wife, have been sold for silver, which has been paid for your father's debt. [15] But you^{plur}, instead of sending (16 end: *šé-bu-lim*$^{!}$) the silver you still owe, of assisting (*qātam ṣabātum*) your paternal house and of (thus) saving the spirits of your ancestors, [20] you do nothing but send me here reports on your fights! [22] Divine Aššur has now done a favor to his City (*Aššur* **[600]** *ennān ālišu* [23] *ilteqe)*: A man whose house has been sold has to pay (only) half [25] of the price of his house to (be allowed to) move into it (again). For the remainder (of his debt) terms in three instalments (*šalšišu*) have been set. [29] Since outsiders have moved to harm$^{?}$ (*ana ša"urim*) our paternal house, [31] I entered a merchant's house and called for (a loan of) 5 minas of silver and weighed it out as payment for the house and [35] now we have (again) moved into the house! [36] As for the payment for the new house, make every mina of silver you can available[3] and send me the silver. Talk to my representatives <and let me know> their answer."

* Originally published in B. Böck, E. Cancik-Kirschbaum, and Th. Richter (eds), Munuscula Mesopotamica, Festschrift für Johannes Renger. AOAT 267. Münster: Ugarit-Verlag, 1999, pp. 599-616.

1 *Tablettes paléo-assyriennes de Kultepe*, 1 (*Kt 90/k*), (Paris 1997); henceforth *TPK*.

2 My proposals (reading UB for KAM in l. 11, and LI-IM for DÍ+SA-DÍ$^{?}$ in l. 16) can be checked by converting the signs back into cuneiform.

3 One expects the construction *ša nadā'im id'āma*, "deposit what you can/must", which suggests that IH-*da-ma (i'dāma)* is a mistake for *id'āma*. The alternative is to read *ša na-da[im id-a]* and take the following *i'-da-ma* as the beginning of a new sentence, linked with the following imperative *šēbilānim*.

1.2. Notes on the text

8. While it is clear that in OAss. there was hardly any difference between the singular *bētum* and the plural *bētū*[4] the meaning and use of the plural *bētātum* is not easily established. The occurrence of the two plurals, *bētū* and *bētātum*, is registered in the grammars, but without mention of a possible difference in meaning. Does *bētātum* refer to several different houses (comparable to the individualizing mascul. plural on -*ānu*), or has it been lexicalized, perhaps meaning "a large house, a mansion"? I have noted the following occurrences of this plural (henceforth *b.*):

a) TPK 46:8: "Our *b.* have been handed over for silver" (*bētātuni ana kaspim paqqudā*), that is, *b.* that are the common property of the writer and his two brothers as heirs of their father and are distinguished from the house privately owned by the writer, mentioned in lines 10f. The use of the D-stem of the stative fits well with a noun in the plural, but does not show whether it is a grammatical or a semantic plural. Does "the price of the *b.*" in l. 38 refer to the silver necessary to redeem only the *b.* of l. 8f. or also the various houses, including that owned by the writer and sold according to lines 10-13?

b) CCT 5, lb:9: The local Anatolian palace (in Kanish) is after the Assyrian Š., who hence is unable to leave, "and also our *b.* have been sealed" *(u ni'ā'ātum bētātuni kannukā)*. Does the writer mean "the house of our firm" or several houses, including those of colleagues? The use of the D-stem of the stative again does not help.

[601] *c) BIN* 6, 119:20: "Why do you (plur.) keep storing straw and wood in [my?] house (É [*x* (*x*)]? Don't you own houses of yourselves?" (É$^{ta-ti-ku-nu}$-*ú la tadaggalā*). Since this is a letter to five persons, who do not belong to one single family, the reference must be to several different "houses".

d) BIN 6, 195:24': The addressees are asked to approach the *kārum* authorities for a settlement of the writer's debts and to say: "His investors have appropriated his *b.*, his ready goods, and whatever he owns and have left the man empty-handed" (É$^{ta-ti-šu}$ *šalissu u mimma išū ummeānūšu ittablū awīlam eriššišu uštazzizū*). The context suggests a single house, owned by the indebted trader in question.

e) Kt e/k 270: 15: "Tomorrow they (the creditors) might take away our *b.* even *(-ma)* for the interest!" (*urram ana ṣibtimma* ^{15}*bé-ta-tí-ni litbulū).* The plural may refer to the houses of the speakers, but also to that of members of one family, hence one single house.

f) TPK no. 26:6: Because of a debt of 5 minas of silver which our father owes to the city-office "the inspectors have seized our *b.* (^{6} É$^{ta-ti-ni}$ *iṣbutū)* and the City has imposed on us the 75 shekels of silver, which all four of us have been ordered to pay" (l. 8: *ša ša-qá-*<*lam*> *qabiānini).* The writer has paid the amount due by three of them, but not that due by Šu-Hubur, "whose house (*bēssu*, singular, l. 13) the inspectors (still) hold". Different houses are meant, also because only two of the men fined are brothers.

g) CCT 5, 8a: A letter of Ahaha, daughter of Pušuken in Assur, which deals with the problems caused by the debts of her by now dead father. Addressing her brothers she speaks of *bé-ta-ku-nu* (nom., l. 9), of the price of É$^{ta-ku-nu}$ (l. 12), and of *išitti* É$^{ta-ku-nu}$, "the

4 See the list of occurrences in S. Bayram and K.R. Veenhof, "Unpublished Kültepe Texts on Real Estate", *JEOL* 32 (1991/92) 88f.

stocks of your *b.*" (l. 11). All three forms are grammatically unacceptable as singulars (they should be **bētkunu* and **bētikunu),* hence it is tempting to interpret them as *bētātu/ikunu.*

No simple conclusion is possible. The use of statives of the D-stem in texts a) and b) frequently a mark of plurality[5] is semantically not decisive, because the word is grammatically plural. In some cases the context shows that several different houses are meant (texts c and f), in others (especially text d) a single house is rather likely. The situation in text g is similar to that of our letter, since is also deals with the debts of a dead father, for which his sons are responsible,[6] and in both *bētātum* could refer to the family house in Assur jointly owned by the children. In that case *bētāum* might be used as a *pluralis extensionis,* to designate a large mansion, which in Assur could be **[602]** very expensive (up to 16 minas of silver),[7] although we have little information on sizes.[8] The alternative is to assume that the father in our text (Hinnaya), as a successful trader who liked to invest in real estate, had acquired several houses, as was the case with Pusuken (Ahaha's letter quoted above as text g, mentions the sale of two other houses, one of Ukida and a *bēt nakīrim).* The lack of information on Hinnaya's family makes it impossible to decide the issue.

9. The stocks and house(s) have been "entrusted for silver",[9] but it is not mentioned how and to whom. There is no question of an outright sale (as happened with the house of l. 10f.) and *paqādum* does not mean transfer of property rights. The normal OAss. vocabulary for pledging (*erubbātum, ana šapartim nadā'um*) is not used,[10] but the result cannot have been much different, since not only the house, hence the building (which could be used or leased out by the creditor), but also its "treasures, stocks" (*išittum,* also in *CCT* 5, 8a: 10), presumably items such as barley, oil, copper and bronze objects, are mentioned. Perhaps "entrusted for silver" means that the property after three years was still in the hands of the creditors or moneylenders, authorized to sell it, but that the actual sale had not yet taken place.

10. OAss uses *qātum* plus possessive suffix as emphatic personal subject of a verbal form, "my own hands, I myself ..." (etc.), see for examples *CAD Ṣ* 13a, 3'.

11-13. *Uṭuptum*, "household goods, movable property", fits well alongside *bētum,* which refers to the building itself.[11] The same combination, in a similar context, is attested in *CCT* 5, 8a: 15ff., where we read about "the house in Assur and its household goods [which serve as security?] for the 30 minas (of silver) for which you have been booked as guarantor" (É *Aššur ú uṭuptušu* [17][x x x] *ana 30 mana* [18][*š*]*a qātātišu* [19][*n*]*alputātini).* To pay for the debts of the family everything was sold and this general sale is **[603]** reflected in the verbal form of l. 13, *i-ta-dí-nu* = *ittaddinu,* a praeterite of the Ntn-stem (not yet recorded in the grammars).

---

5 See N.J.C. Kouwenberg, *Gemination in the Akkadian Verb* (Assen, 1997) 141.

6 See, e.g., *ICK* 1, 11:26f., *CCT* 5, 8b:24ff., and Kt 91/k 389:9ff.

7 See for data on OAss houses C. Michel, "Propriétés immobilières dans les tablettes paléoassyriennes", in K.R. Veenhof (ed.), *Houses and Households in Ancient Mesopotamia* (Istanbul, 1996) 285-300 [and now K.R. Veenhof, "Houses in the Ancient City of Assur", in: B.S. Düring *et al.* (eds.), *Correlates of Complexity. Essays in Archaeology and Assyriology dedicated to Diederik J.W. Meijer* (Leiden: NINO, 2011) 211-232].

8 The one of 16 minas measured 3 *šubtum,* perhaps ca. 110 m^2, which is smaller than the "grandes résidences" from the OB period at Larsa, with a surface area of up to 500 m^2; see Y. Calvet, "Maisons privés paléo-babyloniennes à Larsa", in *Houses and Households* (see previous note) 197-209.

9 *Paqqudā*, a D stative, with plural subject, also in KTH 18:34, 38; VS 26, 47:14'; *RA* 59 (1965) 151 no. 23:23.

10 See C. Michel, in: *Houses and Households* (see note 7), 298, 3.3 [and now K.R. Veenhof in: R. Westbrook and R. Jasnow (eds.), *Security for Debt in Ancient Near Eastern Law* (Leiden-Boston, 2001) 126-131].

11 See for the meaning of *uṭuptum* my remarks in M. Stol/S.P. Vleming (eds.), *The Care of the Eldery in the Ancient Near East* (Leiden 1997), 142 note 54; J. and H. Lewy, "Old Assyrian *subrum*", *HUCA* 38 (1967), 9 note 42 translate "chattels".

15. The construction *kīma* + infinitive, "instead of ...", not recorded in the grammars, is not uncommon in OAss., see *TC* 3, 60:25, *BIN* 6, 219: 10f., *TC* 1, 29:13f., and *TC* 3, 90:32f., reflected in the verbal form of l. 13, *i-ta-dí-nu* = *ittaddinu,* a praeterite of the Ntn-stem (not yet recorded in the grammars). *Ša libbi* + poss. suff. means a liability, hence silver the addressees owe and have to send to Assur.

17. See for *qātam ṣabātum,* "to help, assist", in OAss, *CAD Q* 31b, 2' (*CCT* 4 14b:9), my remarks in *Akkadica* 94-95 (1995) 35, and TPAK 1, 156b, where a man has to support (*qāssa iṣabbat*) the woman who redeemed him.

19. I read two plurals, *eṭammē ša abbēkunu,* since all references to *eṭa/emmum* in OAss are in the plural and hence refer to "the ancestral spirits" (also Kt 91/k 139:26f., an oath by Aššur, Amurrum and *eṭemmū ša abbē'a*). The expression may be a metaphor for "to save the family (estate)", but I prefer a more concrete interpretation, since the family house is the place where the ancestors are buried, a notion which may explain the expression "I uphold the paternal house and the (ancestral) spirits" *(bēt abini u eṭemmē ukāl),* in *KTK* 18:8f. Preventing the sale or financing the redemption of the paternal house hence amounts to "saving" the ancestral spirits.

22. *Ennānum,* "favour, grace" (from the verb *enānum*)[12] is well known in OAss in the plural, *ennānātum,* in concrete it usually means extension of payment asked from the Assyrian authorities in Anatolia or Assur (see *CAD* E 169b s.v, [and now also J.G. Dercksen, *Old Assyrian Institutions*, Leiden 2004, 251ff.]. The singular with the verb *laqā'um* is also attested in I 662:24'- 28' (*ennāniki la ilqe'ū/laqe*), I 668:24-26 (*ennān ṣuhārika la talaqqe ennānia liqi*; both courtesy K. Hecker), [Kt h/k 40:22 *(e-na-ni-ša-ma la talqe)*], and Kt 91/k 173:9) *ūmam ennānika alqe*). The mention of both Aššsur and *ālišu* makes it clear that the former is the god Aššur (written without divine determinative).

25f. The words *ana šalšišu ūmū šaknū*, lit. "triple terms have been set", obviously mean that the remainder, the other half of the sale price of the house, has to be paid in three (annual) instalments, a mode of payment also attested in some debt-notes; cf. *EL* no. 49 (after 2 weeks, 13 weeks and 8 months) and no. 69. See for an arrangement to pay a large debt in three instalments (the background could be similar to that of our text, since it concerns the debt of a father paid by his son), *ICK* 2, 133:4-10: "I settled the affair of my father in the City, with the following result: [6] You have to pay (now) in the *kārum* 30 minas of silver and for 36 minas [of silver] [8] terms have been set for you (*ūmūka šaknūnikkum*). You have to pay every two years 12 minas, [10] so that you will have made full payment (*tašbītum*) **[604]** in six years".[13]

29-31. The word order of this sentence is abnormal, with foregrounded *ana bēt abini,* (which depends on *izzizū)* and repeated *ana*, but we may interpret it as **ahiūtum ana bēt abini ša-ú-ri-im izzizū. Ša''urum* must be an inf. of a D-stem verb, but its meaning is difficult. Candidates are *ša'ārum*, "to be victorious", *ša'ārum* (in Mari in the form *i-ša-i-ra-*

12 See for occurrences *CAD* E s.v. *enēnum* C, "to grant a favor"; a new reference in Kt n/k 203: 16ff. (courtesy S. Bayram): "(When the *kārum* had imposed a fine of 16 minas of silver) we showed them mercy for 8 minas of silver (*8 mana kaspim nēnunšunūtima*), so that you had to pay only 8 minas of silver" [an example of the Dtn-stem in AKT 6, 806:25, *išti kārim ú-ta-na-na-an*, "I keep imploring the *kārum*"].

13 See for *tašbītum*, "full payment", "final instalment", K. Balkan's review of *ICK* 2, in *OLZ* 60 (1965) 153 and TTC 6 (C. Michel, "Réédition des trente tablettes 'cappadociennes' de G. Contenau", *RA* 80 [1986] 109f.), which deals with the purchase of a house for 16 minas of silver, 10 minas of which were supplied by Š.: "Take care to send the silver of Š. and send me 6 minas of silver as final payment" (*tašbītam*).

kum, which Durand tentatively explains as denominated from *šārum*, "wind"),[14] perhaps **šu''urum*, "to make dirty", or even *šâru*, attested in in the D-stem in ElAmarna letters, where it glosses "to slander, accuse" *(CAD* Š/2, 140). Since the first *ša'ārum* and a West-Semitic verb are unlikely in ancient Assyria, a denominative verb is preferable, which must mean something negative, as the writer warns his addressees that "outsiders" are about to do it to the family estate; perhaps something like "to harm, to degrade".

1.3. Interpretation

The letter informs us about the financial problems of a family in Assur, caused by debts left behind by the father upon his death (see lines 18f.). The writer first tells his addressees, in Anatolia, what has happened thus far (lines 6-14), how houses and goods had to be handed over and sold to pay for the debts, and then criticizes them for their irresponsible behaviour (lines 15-21). Next he reports about an unexpected opportunity, due to "the favour of Aššur", of getting the houses sold back (lines 22-28). This requires a cash payment of half of the sale price of the house, for which purpose the writer took out a loan. Finally he urges his correspondents to make every possible mina of silver available and to send it to Assur, since he wants to pay back the silver he had borrowed.

The writer, Puzur-Ištar, son of Hinnāya, apparently is the father of one of the two owners of the archive discovered in 1990, Šumi-abiya, as pointed out in *TPK* p. 20f. The five addressees are not simply "ses collègues", but consist of two groups. The two main addressees (whose names hence are repeated in l. 4) seem to be brothers of Puzur-Ištar, who share the responsibility for the debts of their dead father (Hinnāya). This is suggested by the contents of the **[605]** letter itself and by the fact that both. Aššuriš-tikal and Išme-Aššur, are attested as son of Hinnāya; see for the former *KTS* 2, 27:28, *POAT* 37:2, Kt 87/k 258:1, Kt 91/k 495:15, and for the latter Kt 91/k 127:20, I 609:8, and an unpublished tablet in the possession of Mr. Struwe, l. 4f. (witness). The three other addressees, mentioned first, most probably are the writer's representatives, who are informed of the problems and their possible solution, no doubt to monitor the reaction of Puzur-Ištar's brothers. In the (incomplete) last line of the letter they are explicitly asked to inform the writer about the reaction of his brothers. The words missing most probably can be restored from the fragment of the envelope of a letter, published as *TPK* no. 75, where we read: "Report back^plur.^ the answer they will give you^plur.^, whether it is yes or no", that is the answer to his urgent request to collect and send the silver he needs (lines 37f.).

The writer alternates between "*our* houses", "the house of *our* father" (lines 8 and 29) and "the house / the debt / the spirit of *your* (plur.) father" (lines 7, 13f., 17-19), and moreover distinguishes between "*our* houses" (l. 8) and "the house *I myself* acquired" (l. 10). I assume that he speaks of "the house of *your* father" to stress that his brothers, though in Anatolia, as sons and heirs are equally involved in the fate of the family estate and should not saddle him alone with the problems in Assur. However, since all three are sons and heirs, he may also speak of "*our* houses", which are handed over for silver (l. 8f.) and "our family" which is threatened (l. 29). The family house must have been the one left behind by the father, now the joint property the three sons, where also their father or ancestors were buried (hence the statement in lines 18f.), now in the hands of others. There also seems to be a distinction between *bētum* and *bētātu* on the one hand, which refer to the building (lines 8, 10, 25f., 34-36, 38), and *bēt abim* plus possessive suffix, which means the estate and property of the family, left behind by the dead father. It comprised stores (*išittum*) and needs support in order to survive (lines 17f.), because outsiders threaten it (l. 29). Apart from the houses left behind by the father, the writer himself had acquired a house of his own, as successful traders in Assur liked to do, perhaps upon his marriage (hence the reference to the goods "belonging to me and to my wife"), which he

14 J.-M. Durand, "L'empereur d'Elam et ses vassaux", in: H. Gasche *et al.* (eds.), *Cinquante-deux reflexions sur le Proche-Orient Ancien offertes en hommage à Léon de Meyer* (Leuven, 1994) 21f. See for *še'ērum, ibid.* 22, c., and note also *šahārum* (*CAD* Š/1, 81), equated with *hamāṭu* and *u'ulu.*

had had to sell together with its contents (lines 10-13). I assume that this is the "new(ly acquired) house" mentioned in l. 36.

That debts, both current ones and those left behind by dead traders, could cause many problems is abundantly clear from the OAss correspondence. Creditors could put constraints on debtors and force them to pay or to provide securities. This could also be achieved with the help of the cityassembly (*ālum*), which in particular situations could authorize them to **[606]** appropriate a debtor's assets wherever they might be or turn up.[15] This entitled them not only to seize a debtor's merchandise or silver circulating in the trade, but also to lay claim to a debtor's house and its inventory. Such actions could start by sealing the house in order to enforce payment by denying the debtor access to and use of his possessions. An example is found in the unpublished letter YBC 13089 (courtesy M.T. Larsen), a letter from Tariš-mātum and Bēlatum to Pūšu-kēn, in which they write: "A., son of K., went to the City and the City Assembly passed the following verdict: '[7] A., son of K. will take 11 minas of silver from whatever A. owns. [9] He has tried to seal our house several times (*adi mala u šinišu bētni iknuk*). [13] Of the 11 minas, 5 minas of silver, belonging to U. are available. [16] We will borrow 6 minas at interest so that we can pay K.'s son the 11 minas of silver". The next step, in the absence of guarantors or the possibility of obtaining a special loan, would be the sale of the house, either by the creditor, if he had obtained authorization to do so, or by the debtor himself, if he somehow still was in control of his property. Since OAss commercial debts amount to many minas of silver, it does not surprise that the expensive houses (with their valuable contents) frequently were the only assets valuable enough to be used for settling debts. The real estate in Assur left behind by a rich trader, recorded in Kt 91/k 347:4-5 consists of "a plot of land of 10 *šubtum,* (and) a house in good repair" (*10 šubātim qaqqirē bētam epšam),* representing a substantial value. That such assets were used for settling debts is clear from letter of Ahaha *CCT* 5, 8a, quoted above as text g) in the note on l. 8.

The creditors could be of two kinds, either private Assyrians who had granted credit, extended loans or invested (*ummeānū,* who owned shares in a trader's business capital, (*naruqqum),* or the authorities, usually the (office of) the *līmum,* also called the "city-office" (*bēt ālim*). The *līmum* apparently could take measures similar to those to which a private creditor might resort. In Kt c/k 266:3f. we read about the sealing of a debtor's house by a *līmum,* with the consequence that "I (the owner) am unable to touch anything" (*liptamma la alappat*). A good example of the problems caused by debts to the authorities is contained in the letters *TPK* nos. 26 and 27 (see already above, note on l. 8, text f), where official "inspectors" (*bērū)* seize several houses to enforce a payment. Three of the four debtors paid, whereupon the seizure must have been lifted, but the inspectors still "hold" (*ka''ulum,* l. 13) the house of the fourth one, which they "have offered for sale" *(aššīmim ukallimūma,* l. 15).[16] I will not discuss the data on the debts to the *līmum* and the city-office and the measures to which they may lead, since this will be the subject of a **[607]** forthcoming publication by J.G. Dercksen [*Old Assyrian Institutions*, Ch. 3, "The Debt-Policy of the City Hall", see above the note on l. 22]. The pressure put on debtors by private creditors is also amply documented and an example is contained in text c, quoted above in the note on l. 8, where a trader's *ummeānū* have taken away (*tabālum*) his house, ready goods *(šaliṭṭum)* and "everything he owns", leaving him behind naked.

1.4. Redemption of property sold

The measure taken by (the city of) Assur, which enables debtors to recover the houses they had been forced to sell for their debts, may be compared with a class of Old Babylonian royal decrees (*ṣimdat šarrim*) published and analysed by F.R. Kraus.[17] These

15 See the example discussed by the present writer in "'In Accordance with the Words of the Stele': Evidence for Old Assyrian Legislation", *Chicago-Kent Law Review* 70/4 (1995), 1723f. [= pp. 109-127 in this volume]

16 The use of *kallumum,* "to show", instead of the more usual *ana šīmim ka''ulum,* suggests a public auction.

17 F.R. Kraus, *Königliche Verfügungen in altbabylonischer Zeit* (SD XI, Leiden, 1984).

decrees, called *mīšarum*, "equity", or *andurārum*, "return to the previous / original status", not only meant the remission of consumptive debts, but also the repair of the negative consequences, such as loss of property, for debtors "who had become weak" (Laws of Eshnunna §39). The extant text of the decrees only mentions the effects on the person or family of the debtor, such as being sold into slavery, entering debt bondage *kiššatum*) or becoming pledges (*manzazānum*).[18] They regain their freedom, return home. A variety of records, however, analysed by Kraus in his chapters three to five, leaves no doubt that also the forced sale of real property[19] by such debtors was cancelled. Some are records of lawsuits and contracts, which reveal or imply that houses, building plots, fields and gardens, sold by the debtor, were claimed by or given back to their original owners "on the basis/because of (*ina, ana, aššum*) the royal decree". Others, deeds of sale of such properties, state that the sale had been concluded "after/later than" (EGIR, *warki, warkat, ištu* + verb) the royal decree and hence (the decrees were only retroactive) was not affected by such a cancellation.[20]

A few official letters from the royal Babylonian chancery clearly mention or describe these effects of the measure. *AbB* 4, 56:9-11 (time of Hammurabi): "A royal decree (is in force), as you know (this means for) fields: what has been bought has to be given back" (*eqlum šīmātum turrā).* In *AbB* 4, 69 (same time) a claim is refuted because (l. 38) "purchases have been cancelled" (*šīmātum šūlā).* From an appeal to king Samsuiluna, *AbB* 7, 153:8f. we learn that in Sippar, the judges "read the deeds of sale of fields, **[608]** houses, and gardens" and cancelled those which "had become invalid by the decree" *(ina mīšarim waṣiā).* This is also attested outside Babylonia. Several deeds of sale of houses, fields and gardens from the kingdom of Hana also state they will not be affected by such a measure, which apparently would cancel them.[21] From Mari we have a letter which tells us that a similar royal measure taken by the king of Aleppo also meant that "houses had been given back".[22] And the existence of such measures at Mari is implied by the contract *ARM* 8, 6, which states that a field acquired will not return to its owner by means of an *andurāru*-measure.[23]

Such royal decrees, however, as shown by Kraus (p. 72), did not imply that property sold was automatically returned to the original owner. Who considered himself their beneficiary had to claim the property from its present owner and this usually required legal investigation or action. The administrative handling of many such claims might, on occasion, call for special measures, such as the convening of a court of law in Sippar in order to inspect the written evidence for such claims (*AbB* 7, 153). When the claims were honoured, the present owner might simply return the property or, if he wished to retain it (he might have improved it in the mean time), [24] offer something in exchange or formally buy it (again).[25] Prices paid to keep such property might differ from the original price, since the first sale was a forced one, to pay off debts fallen due. The market value paid by an outsider in a free sale must have differed from that paid to an impoverished owner (Laws of Eshnunna §§38-39).[26]

---

18 *Ibidem*, 180f., §20.

19 Rarely also the sale of a temple prebend, see *ibid.* 49f., on *UET* 5, 263.

20 Once, in *CT* 8, 35b, this statement is found in the deed of sale of a slave and an ox, which suggests that the royal measures could have implications also for such forced sales by debtors.

21 F.R. Kraus, *Königliche Verfügungen*, 99f., with O. Rouault, *Terqa Final Reports No. 1 – L 'Archive de Puzurum* (*BiMes* 16, Malibu, 1984), TFR 1.1:17, 1.3:22, and 1.6:22 (the measure is called *uddu/andu/addarārum*).

22 D. Charpin, "Les décrets royaux a l'époque paléo-babylonienne, à propos d'un ouvrage récent", *AfO* 34 (1987) 41, note 39, l. 20.

23 See Idem, "L'*andurârum* a Mari", *MARI* 6 (1988) 264f., for an improved interpretation. The silver value of the field is called the "complete ransom" paid for a number of people by the person who acquires it.

24 See for an example, F.R. Kraus, *Königliche Verfügungen*, 47f., on L R-S 17.

25 An example is YOS 14, 146:l0ff.: property *ina ṣimdat šarrim ibbaqirma itūrma išām.*

26 See R. Westbrook, *Property and the Family in Biblical Law* (JSOT Suppl. Series 113, Sheffield, 1991) 90 and 101.

Whatever had been the case in the, past – an outright sale or a transaction whereby the property, already pledged, had been acquired by the creditor – the original owner received his property back without payment. And this is a basic difference with the measure described in our Old Assyrian letter, where the previous owners had to buy it back. This is not surprising, because the decrees by Babylonian kings were meant to help people who "had become weak" and indebted due to consumptive loans, not to repair the negative **[609]** effects of commercial and speculative loans (as defined in § 8 of Ammi-ṣaduqa's decree). The debts that, as their size alone shows, no doubt were of a commercial nature, had forced the family of Hinnāya to sell its houses. Their cancellation by an official decree (on the assumption that the Babylonian *mīšarum* institution was known in Assur)[27] hence is not to be expected. The "favour of Assur" apparently made it possible to redeem the property at favourable conditions and allowed the original owner to reoccupy his house after a first payment of fifty per cent of the price. I assume that "the price of his house" (l. 25) means the price originally paid by the present owner, in line with the observations by Westbrook (see note 26). Perhaps the measure did not only concern the condition of redemption, but redemption as such, if it was restricted by a time limit beyond which it may have been possible only for a higher price (perhaps the market price) and if the present owner was willing.[28] The short statement in our letter does not allow us to decide these issues.

We note, finally, that the measure is called a favour bestowed by the god Aššur on his city, although we have assumed that, in actual fact, it was a decision taken by the main legislative body, the city-assembly, in conjunction with the ruler. See for this aspect below, § 2.4.

2. Redemption by Order of the King and Decree of the City

Redemption (*paṭārum* / du$_8$) of real property by the seller or his relatives is well attested in the Old Babylonian period and probably was a generally accepted right when a "paternal estate" (*ša bīt abišu* / é ad.da.ni) was as stake. Paragraph 39 of the Laws of Eshnunna (reflected in the rules found in Leviticus 25:25 and 47) suggests that this right applied if the sale had taken place because the owner "had become weak". While the role of the king in issuing decrees cancelling such sales and making the property return to its original owner *(andurārum)* is well known, that of a city, comparable to what happened in Assur according to *TPK* 1 no. 46, thus far unknown, is attested in a new early Old Babylonian deed of sale from Sippar.[29]

[610] *2.1. The text BM 97141*

3 IKU A.ŠÀ *i-na* A.GÀR *Na-hi-iš-/tim*	"A 3 *iku* field in the polder Nahištum
DA *a-ta-pí-im*	alongside the irrigation ditch
ša Maš-ni-te-el	of Mašnitêl
ù DA DUMU.MUNUS *Ra-bi-im*	and next to the daughter of Rabûm,
KI *Da-di-i-a*	from Dadiya,
Aš-di-i-a	Ašdiya
ù ^{d}EN.ZU-*re-me-ni* DUMU.A.NI	and his son Sîn-remenni
^{pd}IŠKUR-*ra-bí* DUMU *E-tel*-KA-/^{d}EN.ZU	Adad-rabi, son of Etel-pī-Sîn,
iš-tu A.ŠÀ *ù* É	after Immerum had ordered

27 We lack evidence from native Assyrian texts to prove this. The references to the ruler who "washes away debts", found in K. Balkan, "Cancellation of Debts in Cappadocian Tablets from Kültepe" (in: K. Bittel *et al.* (eds.), *Anatolian Studies Presented to Hans Gustav Güterbock on the Occasion of his 65th Birthday*, Istanbul, 1974, 29-42) occur in native Anatolian debt-notes. If they are of Assyrian inspiration we may have to postulate a similar institution in ancient Assur.

28 This was the case in a number of Anatolian slave sales, for which I may refer to my observations on the conditions of redemption in B. Hruška and G. Komoróczy (eds.), *Festschrift Lubor Matous* II (Budapest, 1978) 297f.

29 Published by kind permission of the Trustees of the British Museum.

	Im-me-ru-um pa-ṭà-ra-am	the redemption of fields and houses,
	iq-bu-ú wa-ar-ki a-wa-at / a-li-im	after the decree of the city,
	IN.ŠI.ŠÁM	bought.
	ŠÁM.TIL.LA.NI.ŠÈ	As his full payment
	KÙ.BABBAR IN.NA.AN.LÁ	he weighed out silver.
	$^{[giš]}$GAN.NA ÍB.TA.BAL	It has been moved across the pestle,
rev.	INIM.BI AL.TIL	the transaction is completed.
	U$_4$.KÚR LÚ.LÚ.[RA]	[That] in the future they will not
	NU.MU.UN.GI$_4$.GI$_4$.DAM	come back against each other
	MU ^{d}UTU *ù Im-me-ru-um*	they have sworn with an oath
	IN.PÀ.DÉ.EŠ	by Šamaš and Immerum.
	e-zi-ib KA DUB-*šu*	Apart from what is stated in his
	ša 6 IKU A.ŠÀ	contract about the 6-*iku* field,
	ša a-na Nu-ru-ub-tim	which he had given to
	NU.BAR *id-di-nu*	the *kulmašītum* Nurubtum.
	IGI ^{d}IŠKUR-*ra-bi*	In the presence of Adad-rabi,
	IGI *I-pí-iq-Nu-nu*	of Ipiq-Nūnu,
	IGI *I-din-*^{d}UTU	of Iddin-Šamaš,
	IGI *Ma-nu-um*	of Manum,
	IGI *E*$^{?}$*-te-i-a*	of Etēya,
	IGI ^{d}EN.ZU-*i-din-nam*	of Sîn-idinnam,
	IGI ^{d}EN.ZU-*e-ri-ba-am*	of Sîn-erîbam,
	IGI *Ib-ni-*^{d}IŠKUR	of Ibni-Adad,
l.e.	IGI *A-pil-ki-nu-úo*	f Apil-kīnū.”

[611] *2.2. Notes on the text*

1-3. While the name of the polder is well known from Sippar, that of the irrigation ditch (named after the man who dug or owned it) is new, but this type of name is not uncommon; see, e.g., the indexes of L. Dekiere, *Old Babylonian Real Estate Documents* (= *OBRED*) vols. 1 (Ghent, 1994) 269, and 5 (1996) 314.

5-7. It seems likely that the three sellers are husband, wife and son. Note that in lines 5 (less clear), 6 and 9 *i-a* is written with two separate signs.

21-25. *OBRED* 6 no. 924 (undated):1-7 records the “donation of a field of 9 *iku,* in the polder Nahištum, bordering on the field of Rabîm’s daughter and on the irrigation ditch, by Nurubtum, daughter of Dadiya, to her[!] daughter Naramti, *nadītum* of Šamaš”.

2.3. Interpretation

Lines 9-11 mention a legal measure dealing with the redemption of property which had been sold,[30] no doubt as a way of meeting a debt liability. The words “after the king had ordered the redemption” and “after the decree of the city” state that the present sale took place after and hence was not affected by the legal measure in question, which, as usual, was only retroactive.[31] By inserting them the buyer protected himself against the risk of loosing the field, which is even more understandable in our deed of sale, since it is not

30 Perhaps even pledged, since *paṭārum* may refer, also in OB, to the release of pledged property, e.g. in *JCS* 14 (1960) 26 no. 54 = *YOS* 14 no. 35, and IM 54685:13 (Tell Harmal), a use better known from Middle Assyrian texts. In Nuzi royal measures designated as *šūdūtu* or *andurāru* also affected real property mortgaged or sold for debts, cf. M. Müller, “Sozial- und wirtschaftspolitische Rechtserlasse im Lande Arrapḫa”, in: H. Klengel (ed.), *Beitrage zur sozialen Struktur des alten Vorderasiens* (Berlin, 1971) 56f. See in general for such measures and their background, M. Weinfeld, *Social Justice in Ancient Israel and in the Ancient Near East* (Jerusalem/Minneapolis, 1995), 75ff.

31 F.R. Kraus, *Königliche Verfügungen,* 112, I, b: “mit einem oder höchstens zwei kurzen Satzen lakonisch erwähnt in … ‘Sicherstellungen’ der Urkunden”.

dated. *Awātum*, "word, order, decree", is also used in some records from Larsa (instead of the more usual *ṣimdatum* or *ṣimdat šarrim)* to refer to royal measures of king Rim-Sin.[32] It has a parallel in Old Assyrian, where *awātum* is used for orders and decrees both of the city-assembly in Assur and of *kārum* Kanish.[33]

The royal measure dealt with "the redemption of fields and houses", hence real property in general, just like other OB royal measures which imply **[612]** the cancellation of forced sales of various types of real estate, both in a city (É, É.DÙ.A, É.KI.GAL, É.KISLAH) and in the countryside (gardens, fields).[34] But this short reference, like many similar ones to "the royal decree" (*ṣimdat šarrim*) in OB documents, does not tell us what exactly its contents and aims were and we lack the text of a relevant royal decree to inform us.

Our text mentions both "the order of the king" and "the decree of the city" and I assume that both refer to the same measure, which had been taken in the recent past.[35] This is remarkable, for "a decree of the city" does not occur in Kraus's comprehensive survey of such measures. Our contract hence is the only one to reveal that also the city in which the measure was issued played an active part in realizing it. It should, however, not come as a great surprise, because it is in Sippar that we would expect this in the first place, in view of the prominent role the city *(ālum)* played in administrative and judiciary procedures and in the oath, which is regularly sworn there by the god, the king and the city of Sippar. In this respect Sippar is comparable to Assur, also a city whose assembly of elders played an important role in the administration of justice.

We do not know which were the specific roles of king and city in early Sippar, but the situation at Assur may provide an analogy, where the city assembly, presumably headed by the local ruler as its main executive officer, passed verdicts, issued decrees, and presumably drafted laws.[36] In this special case, a measure to restore equity, the ruler as the steward of the local god (in Assur the city-god was king, the ruler his *iššiakkum)* may have had the "ideological initiative",[37] which had a long tradition in Mesopotamia, since the days of Uru'inimgina. The presumed royal initiative in Assur must have resulted in a formal decree, passed or homologated by the cityassembly. Something similar may have been the case in early Sippar. The formulation of our contract, which mentions the king's order (*qabûm*) first, may support this view, which would imply that the "decree" (*awātum*) of the city was perhaps more concerned with its administration and implementation. It is interesting that this form of "cooperation" is attested in what were real city-states, where the administrative realms of ruler and city-assembly coincided and their authority merged. This was true both of early Assur and of early Sippar under Immerum, before it was integrated into the territorial state created by Sumula'el of Babylon. That the reference to a joint action of king and city is only attested in such an early contract and never in the much more numerous **[613]** ones of the "classical" OB period, could suggest that by then a change had taken place. In territorial states such as Larsa and Babylon the powerful kings appear to have taken the sole responsibility for such actions, while the role of the city-assembly and its "elders" was much reduced, essentially to the administration of justice on the local level.

The use of the expression "the favour of Assur" should be noted, because neither verb nor noun is attested in such contexts in contemporary Babylonia. But the verb occurs in Old Babylonian Susa, where it qualifies certain acts of the ruler (the *šukkalum* of Elam) versus his subjects, *e.g.* in *MDP* 23, 282:5, where "in his favour he returned" fields to one

---

32 See *ibid.* 35f.; note *YOS* 8, 139:5f., EGIR INIM LUGAL (= *warki awāt šarrim*).

33 See my remarks quoted in note 15.

34 See *AbB* 7, 153, mentioned above in § 1.4.

35 Both *ištu* + verb and *warki* + noun occur in references to other royal measures, e.g. one of Sumula'el of Babylon, a contemporary of Immerum, see F.R. Kraus, *Königliche Verfügungen*, 50ff., S-1-E 2/3 and S-L-E 7.

36 See the article quoted in note 15, p. 1732-1741.

37 The "ideology" is also responsible for the fact that such decrees are issued soon after a king's accession to the throne or his conquest of a city, see D. Charpin, *AfO* 34 (1987) 40b.

of his servants, although he had bought them at the full price.[38] While the expression "to bestow a favour upon" is well attested in OAss (see above, § 1.2, note on l. 22), we do not know whether it was used in the official proclamation of the decree or was a reflection of the way the measure was experienced by its beneficiaries. Anyhow, our two documents from Assur and Sippar together mention all three powers instrumental in restoring equity, the city-god, the ruler and the city-assembly.

2.4. Redemption by decree?

A final problem remains, because redemption of family property (called É AD.DA or *bīt abim*), sold in economic distress, seems to have been a traditional right, attested in many OB records. If this is true, a joint measure of king and city is only explainable if the implementation and/or modalities of this right had become a problem, but our contract does not reveal what these problems were. Since the written laws hardly pay attention to this issue (an exception is Laws of Eshnunna §39), we have to reconstruct it from a variety of practice documents (contracts, judicial records, some letters), which is not easy, as also Westbrook's analysis of the "price factor in the redemption of land" has shown.[39] The wording of the measure in our text, "redemption of houses and fields", points to a general problem, perhaps as the result of an economic crisis which had forced many citizens to sell family property. In the absence of evidence we can only mention a few possible problems.

The first one is the price to be paid. Redemption of paternal property at the original sale price (which in such cases of forced sale must have been below the market price), according to Westbrook "the most likely possibility", must have been vital to allow (former) debtors to exercise that right. Laws of Eshnunna §39 grants the impoverished seller the right of **[614]** redemption if the buyer (presumably his creditor) wants to sell his property. But what if he did not or could not redeem it? This law suggests that re-sale by the first buyer made a difference and the question is whether (as Westbrook, *op. cit.* 101 assumes) the second buyer indeed could be forced to sell it to the original owner at the original price.[40] In general one may assume that such buyers of real estate, (under)sold by debtors, tried to secure their new property, also by making redemption, within the limits of customary law, less easy. In the case reported in the letter from Assur, redemption is made possible through a measure which allows payment in four instalments in combination with the right to re-occupy the paternal house after the first one of half the sale price. Although there is a difference between the substantial commercial debts of the traders in Assur and the much smaller, frequently consumptive ones for which real property was pledged or sold in Babylonia, it is not impossible that the measure taken in early Sippar also meant to facilitate redemption, perhaps by means of a payment agreement. The redeemer in the Assur text was able to take advantage of the new measure by taking out a loan to pay the first instalment. This contrasts with a stipulation in an Old Babylonian contract from Khafaǧe, which allows redemption only if the buyer "acquires silver of his own", not by means of somebody else.[41] A royal measure to neutralize such obstacles is conceivable.

---

38 *Īnunma eqlāti ... utīršum*, see *CAD E* 164 s.v. *enēnu* C, for more occurrences.

39 See note 26, and note my critical observations in notes 40 and 44 below.

40 In the case of *BE 6/2*, 38 and 64 (R. Westbrook, *Property and the family*, 93f.) we do not know the price paid in at the original sale (stage A), but the redemption price paid in stage C (sixteen years later) is not only higher, but the property may also have lost in value: the "built house" (É.DÙ.A) of stage B, sold for 3 shekels, has become an empty lot (É.KISLAH) in stage C. The laws dealing with redemption of slaves at the original price, Cod. Ham. §§119 and 281, adduced by Westbrook, both refer to redemption from the first buyer.

41 R. Harris, "The Archive of the Sin Temple in Khafajah", *JCS* 9 (1955) 96 no. 82, with R. Westbrook, *Property and the family*, 112 note 2. The clause, not surprisingly, seems to be intended to protect the new owner, who may have acquired the field cheaply.

The second one are the limits of the right of redemption. Was there a time limit, were second or even later buyers still obliged to grant redemption, and which relatives of the original owner and seller were still entitled to execute the right? Data on a time limit are very rare, but some OAss slave sale contracts (see note 28) stipulate that redemption of the person sold into debt-slavery, at the original price, is only possible during a relatively short period of time. Something similar cannot *a priori* be ruled out for real property. A contract from Tell Harmal (see note 30) stipulates that a field pledged for a small silver loan has to be redeemed in a particular month. This may have to do with the annual pattern of cultivation, but we cannot exclude the possibility that, if it was not redeemed by then, the ownership of the pledged field would pass to the creditor.[42] In the letter from Assur the redeemer quickly **[615]** borrows silver to redeem the house, because "outsiders" are ready to take advantage of the situation, which may also hint at a time limit.

The rules obtaining for a second and later buyer, unfortunately not mentioned in Laws of Eshnunna §39, are not easily established. The few redemption contracts where the seller is neither the original buyer nor (as far as we can observe) a relative of him,[43] still use the verb "to redeem", describe the property as (part of) a "paternal estate", and may mention the earlier sale. This could be an indication that the sale was not purely consensual but coercive, but it is clear that the mention of these facts in the contract was in the interest of the redeemer, probably to protect his ownership of the paternal property thus acquired also against other members of the family. There are in fact some records where redemption of property sold leads to problems within the family, such as the record of a trial *CT* 45,3. It deals with a paternal house, inherited by three children, one of which sells his share "for the full price". It is later redeemed by a daughter (with her husband) from a brother of the seller, but subsequently claimed by her aunt, the sister of the original owner.[44] Hence, I feel not certain about the the obligations of the second buyer and Westbrook is careful enough to state that "it is more reasonable to suppose that the owner could force the first or second buyer to resell him at the original price".

Those using the right of redemption are the original owner and seller,[45] his sons,[46] and presumably daughters, and other relatives.[47] But without information on the sale price and not certain about the consensual or coercive nature of the transaction, it is difficult to establish which relatives could exercise the right, for how many years, and whether it was linked to the status of heir of the original seller. The wish to get back family property at times may have been strong enough to redeem it also at a normal, full price in a consensual transaction. More prosopographical data in the context of an **[616]** archival study and a full analysis of the existing redemption documents, promised by Charpin (his article mentioned in note 44, p. 212 note 5) may provide more answers.

[Addendum:
A. Godderis, *Economy and Society in Northern Babylonia in the Early Old Babylonian Period (ca. 2000-1800 BC)*, (*OLA* 109, Leuven, 2002) 331, notes that *awāt ālim*, "an order / decree of the city", also occurs in text 27 in L. de Meyer (ed.), *Tell ed-Dēr* II (Ghent, 1978)

---

42 See for this type of arrangement, *ibid*, 109f.

43 *BE* 6/2 38 and 62, see i*bid*. 93f.; L. Dekiere, *Old Babylonian Real Estate Documents* (OBRED), part 6 (Ghent, 1994) no. 868.

44 The analysis by R. Westbrook, *Property and the Family*, 113f., has to be corrected on the basis of the new, closely related contract *OBRED* 1 no. 41. The new interpretation also does not allow Westbrook's assumption of a second sale, therefore there is no question of a first sale at a discount and a later one "for its full value". See for other complications within one family, D. Charpin, in his analysis of *Documents cunéiformes de Strasbourg* (= *DCS*; Paris, 1981) no. 97 in "Contribution à la redécouverte de Maškan-Šapir", in: *Cinquante-deux reflexions* ... (see note 14) 209ff.

45 One of the sellers in *BE* 6/2, 45 + *ARN* 116.

46 *DCS* no. 97, *OBRED* 6 no. 868, and the text edited by W. Farber in *ZA* 74 (1984) 71-75.

47 In *CT* 45, 3 the daughter of the brother of the seller; in *CT* 3, 13 the brother of the woman who originally bought it; in *CT* 45, 62 a grandson of the original owner, acting *kīma bīt abišu*; in *ARN* 117 perhaps a sister or daughter of the seller.

165. It is a contract for a small silver loan, with interest in barley, dated to the reign of Ammi-ṣura (a predecessor of Immerum). Silver and interest in barley are to be measured out (env. 4', *i-m[a-da-ad]*) at harvest time. Then follows, before the date, in her reading: *a-na a-wa-at* [10] *a-li-im ú-la i-zu-zu*, which would mean "by order of the city they shall not divide". This is enigmatic (who are "they" and one would expect *ina awāt*) and excluded by env. 5', which has *ú*-x(B[A]?-[x (x)], but I have no proposal for its reading. See for silver debts with interest rated in barley – usually 60 sila per shekel, *i.e.* 20%, the normal rate of interest of silver – my observations in Ş. Dönmez (ed.), *DUB.SAR É.DUB.BA.A. Studies Presented in Honour of Veysel Donbaz* (Istanbul, 2010) [= pp. 285-296 in this volume], § 3.2., "The payment of mixed loans and CH § t".].

Old Assyrian *Iṣurtum*, Akkadian *Eṣērum* and Hittite GIŠ.ḪUR*

Written documents play a vital role in Old Assyrian trade and no other corpus of texts probably contains so many references to them as the so-called Kültepe texts. Letters were essential for communication between Assur and Anatolia and inside Anatolia between the various trading stations. Contracts and judicial records of every kind recorded and validated a variety of legal transactions of which they served as written evidence, also in lawsuits. Many lists, notes and memorandums enabled the traders to keep track of their goods and transactions, especially lists of outstanding claims which were used for collecting debts and for the periodic settling of accounts (*nikkassū*) arranged by the organization of the traders, the *kārum*.

The terminology reflects this state of affairs. The use of the all-embracing word *ṭuppum* "(inscribed clay) tablet", is ubiquitous, often with a reference to it being sealed – i.e . encased in a clay envelope on which the seals are impressed – which lends its legal, evidentiary force (*ṭuppum ḫarmum*, with or without added *ša kunukkim*). A variety of genitival adjuncts helps to specify the nature, contents or function of a tablet: *ša šībē*, "of witnesses", a recorded testimony or deposition validated by seal impressions; *ša naruqqim*, "of a money bag", a record of a capital investment in a firm; *ša šabā'ē*, "of satisfaction", a quittance issued when the original debt-note could not be returned to the debtor upon payment; *ša mamītim*, "of an oath" sworn in the "gate of the god" in the context of a lawsuit; *ša šiamātim*, "of purchases", a letter specifying purchases made and expenses paid for equipping a caravan in Assur; *ša be'ūlātim*, "of a working capital", recording an interest free loan granted to caravan personnel instead of a fixed wage in exchange for their service; etc. Duplicates (*meḫrum*) of tablets occur time and again, written as archive copies, for sharing essential information with partners and associates, or drawn up for reasons of security, when valuable original deeds had to be sent overland. Other frequently mentioned types of documents are *našpertum*, "document sent (overland)", often under seals and with the legal force of an authorized statement or order,[1] and *taḫsistum*, "memorandum", in particular lists of outstanding debts without legal force but as **[312]** aid to memory.[2] Rare and less well defined are *dannutum*, "strong, valid document", probably not a specific type of text but a designation stressing its binding and final character,[3] and *nudu'um*, "booking", derived from the use of the verb *nadā'um*, "to

1 See M.T. Larsen, in: M. Gibson and R.D. Biggs (eds.), *Seals and Sealing in the Ancient Near East (Bibl. Mes.* 6, Malibu 1977), 97f., with *CAD* N s.v.

2 See K.R. Veenhof, Observations on Old Assyrian memorandums ..., *JEOL* 28 (1983-4) 10-23.

3 See *CAD* D, 90, 8 and 91a, 2, with *JNES* 16 (1957) 164: 35ff. and M.T. Larsen and E. Møller, *Festschrift Garelli* (Paris 1991) 229 no. 2:14 (*ana mala dannitišu*). See for its character the expression *ṭuppum ša dannātim* (BIN 6, 162:4') and the use of *dannum* and the verb *dannunum* used of tablets, both binding orders and records containing valid testimonies. See for the Middle Assyrian occurrences and meaning J.N. Postgate, *AoF* 13 (1986), 17f. and for Neo-Assyrian also *SAAB* 5 (1991) 85f. no. 38. [See for these terms my article Some Contributions to the Old Assyrian Lexicon, to appear in *Orientalia* in 2016, § 5].

* Originally published in: Th. P. J. van den Hout and J. de Roos (eds), Studio Historiae Ardens. Ancient Near Eastern Studies Presented to Philo H. J. Houwink ten Cate, Istanbul: Nederlands Historisch-Archaeologisch Instituut, 1995, 311-332.

note down", especially in the expression *taḫsistam nadā'um*, "to draw up a note", "to put to writing", as aid to memory.[4]

Less frequent and still rather enigmatic is *iṣurtum*, of which some twenty occurrences are known to me. In EL no. 320: 14 Julius Lewy translated "Aufzeichnungen" and in footnote h) he argued for his translation by referring to CCT 1, 37b:2f. (below no. 4), where the word is the direct object of the verb *eṣārum*, "to draw", assuming that the OA term is a dialectical variant of the well-known *uṣurtum*, "drawing", attested in Assyrian and Babylonian in most other periods.

The occurrence of records called "drawing" during the Old Assyrian period in Anatolia (roughly the 19th century B.C.) soon caught the attention of Hittitologists, not surprising since the Boğazköy tablets had acquainted them with the existence of a type of document designated by the sumerogram GIŠ.ḪUR, which in Akkadian has the equivalent *uṣurtum*, "drawing", probably the same word as *iṣurtum*. Among the Hittites the word was used to refer to a type of "wooden tablets", presumably a wooden writing board coated with wax. H.G. Güterbock was the first to refer to OA *iṣurtum* in his discussion of GIŠ.ḪUR and "wooden tablets". While for the latter he hesitated between the meanings "record", "list" and "catalogue", OA *iṣurtum*, in his opinion, could only be a kind of record ("Urkunde").[5] B. Landsberger,[6] in 1948, believed that *iṣurtam eṣārum* was used for the drawing up of a debt-note or quittance, not in cuneiform writing, but as a "prägrafische Urkundenform", whose nature, however, he did not define. H.Th. Bossert deduced from the occurrence of *iṣurtam eṣārum* in the framework of commercial contacts between Assyrians and native, Anatolian palaces "dass die einheimische anatolische Bevölkerung ihre Schriftstücke in Bilderschrift anfertigte, also wirklich "eine Zeichnung zeichnete", denn um diese Zeit müssen die einzelne Zeichen der hethitischen Hieroglyphenschrift noch in grosseren **[313]** Ausmasse erkennbare Bilder gewesen sein".[7] His ideas may have influenced Julius Lewy, who observed in 1954[8] that OA *iṣurtum* referred to "documents relating to goods sold by Assyrians to non-Assyrian princes and their servants, thus strongly suggesting that *iṣurtum* was used as a technical term for "*records written in a foreign language and script*" (italics mine, K.R.V.). But Lewy did not try to identify these nor did he suggest they were Hittite hieroglyphs, although this would have been the most likely identification given the time and place of their occurrence. Bossert's conviction, that the so-called Hittite hieroglyphs represented the older "genuine Hittite" script (based on his belief that the "real Hittites" were the ones using that script) and that the introduction of cuneiform only came later, was soon refuted by H.G. Güterbock, who also argued that the oldest evidence for the existence of the hieroglyphic script was not really earlier than the middle of the second mill. B.C.[9]

In 1964 H. Otten conceded: "das früheste Vorkommen der Hieroglyphen, wohl mit symbolhaften Charakter, schon zur Zeit der altassyrischen Handelsniederlassungen, scheint unbestreitbar", but he too did not refer to OA *iṣurtum* nor did he speak of the hieroglyphic script.[10] Subsequently many Hittitologists have dealt with the Hittite "wooden

---

4 See *CAD* N s.v. with Adana 237B (Donbaz, *AfO* 31 (1984) 23f.): 48 (plural); cf. for *taḫsistam nadā'um* i.a. CCT 5, 17c: 8ff.

5 In *Festschrift P. Koschaker* (Leiden 1939), 35f. His reference to *uṣurtum* (GIŠ.ḪUR) in UM 2/2 no. 81:33 (MBab.), also found in *AHw* 1440 a s.v. 3), is better ignored, since the reading most probably has to be GIŠ.KÍN, to be equated with *kiškanû*, a type of tree and wood, cf. also *NABU* 1987 no. 2.

6 *Sam'al* I (Ankara 1948), 107f.

7 *BiOr* 9 (1952) 172f.; cf. his contributions in *WO* 1 (1952) 480ff. and in *Minoica. Festschrift J. Sundwall* (1958) 67ff.

8 *HUCA* 25 (1954) 196 with note 108.

9 *OLZ* 1956 Sp. 513ff.

10 H. Otten, Schrift, Sprache und Literatur der Hethiter 14, in: G. Walser (ed.), *Neuere Hethiterforschung*, Historia, Einzelschriften – Heft 7 (Wiesbaden 1964), 11-22.

tablets", GIŠ.ḪUR, their shape, nature, function and implications,[11] recently also using a few occurrences outside the Boğazköy corpus, in texts from Ugarit and Emar.[12] The present writer, notwithstanding the references kindly supplied by J. de Roos, also on the problems of identification of other types of Hittite administrative records,[13] does not feel competent to enter this discussion, which is better left to specialists,[14] who now can draw on the admirable summary and analysis by D. Symington.[15] It is also **[314]** not necessary, since in these recent discussions OA *iṣurtum* no longer plays a role. Short remarks by some Old Assyrian specialists[16] may have convinced Hittitologists that this word, notwithstanding Lewy's statement quoted above, is not a document drawn (up) in Hittite hieroglyphs, hence is not relevant for the meaning of GIŠ.ḪUR. Moreover, the more recent consensus[17] that, even when isolated symbols incorporated in the hieroglyphic script may have occurred earlier, the script as such, as a fully developed system, is not attested before the end of the 16th century B.C. (hence at least three hundred years later than the occurrences of *iṣurtum)* may have discouraged them of considering a possible link.

But the question what exactly an *iṣurtum* is, also found in *AHw* ("von einheimischen Fürsten (nichtassyrisch?) ausgestellte Urkunde"),[18] still has to be answered. The last clear answer was given by Balkan in 1965,[19] who stated on the basis of ten occurrences, that *iṣurtam eṣārum* means "das Herstellen einer speziell für die einheimische Bevölkerung in Bilderschrift gezeichnete (hölzerne) Schuldurkunde", a statement that revived the ideas of Landsberger, Bossert and Lewy. This conviction should give Hittitologists cause for concern, the more so since both Garelli and Laroche[20] have shown that the bulk of the population of Anatolia in Old Assyrian times was already "Neshite", *i.e.* culturally and linguistically the direct ancestors of the Hittites. Since also students of Old Assyrian trade are still not certain what an *iṣurtum* is, a fresh investigation seems useful. It might be of interest to the jubilarian too, who in the Netherlands embodies the scholarly interest in the cultural history of Anatolia.

The verb *eṣērum*

Iṣurtum is derived from *eṣērum*, which means "to draw, to make a drawing". The references quoted in *CAD E* s.v. show that this can be done by means of paint, paste or flour upon the ground, on walls and other surfaces, but also by simply drawing lines in the soil, the clay

---

11 Bossert's views were accepted by J. Friedrich, *HW* 274: GIŠ.ḪUR is "Holztafel (Urkunde) mit hethitischer Hieroglyphenschrift", but in his *Geschichte der Schrift* (1966) 63, he did not repeat this identification, merely stating that this type of script "kann ein selbständiges Produkt des alten Kleinasien sein, das neben (oder sogar vor?) der aus der Fremde importierten Keilschrift in vielleicht zunächst primitiver Gestalt erfunden wurde".

12 Cf. D. Arnaud, *Hethitica* 8 (1987) 13f. with note 43; in *Emar* VI no. 261:20f. we meet a dub.sar.giš living in Šatappi. See for Ugarit, PRU VI no. 19 (*ṭuppa ša iškuri*, a wax coated tablet, to serve as quittance); RSO VII no. 7: 23 and no. 8: 22, both letters of the king of Karkemish. [See for wax coated tablets, *ṭuppum ša iskūrim*, attested in Old Assyrian texts now K.R. Veenhof, *The Archive of Kuliya, son of Ali-abum, Kültepe Tabletleri* 5 (Ankara 2010) 11:21-22, with the comment].

13 Such as *dušdumi-*, *lalami*, and *parzaki-*.

14 See, most recently, the observations by Ph.H.J. Houwink ten Cate, *BiOr* 51 (1994) 235f. on the nature and contents of wooden tablets in connection with the discovery of deposits of royal bullae at Boğazköy. [See now a new study by W. Waal in *AoF* 39 (2012) 287-315, mentioned in the Addendum to this article].

15 Late Bronze Age Writing Boards and their Uses. Textual Evidence from Anatolia and Syria, *AnSt* 41 (1991) 111-123, with pls. xvii-xix.

16 B. Kienast, *ATHE* (1960) ad no.12:1 ("Urkunde" not "Aufzeichnung", with a reference to Landsberger quoted above note 6), and P. Garelli, *AC* 227 note 1, *RHA* XVlll/66 39:14, and *RA* 59 46f. ad MAH 19613:2, where he always translates *iṣurtum* with "relevé".

17 Cf. E. Laroche in *RlA* 4, 399, §5, 2, and J.D. Hawkins, Writing in Anatolia: Imported and Indigenous Systems, *World Archaeology* 17/3 (1986) 363-76, esp. 371.

18 *AHw* 391b s.v. 2, with reference to J. Lewy (as quoted in note 8 above).

19 *OLZ* 1965 Sp. 157f. ad ICK 2, 292.

20 E. Laroche, *NH* 364, and P. Garelli, *AC* 133ff., notably 150 and 167: "Les Assyriens se sont établis dans un milieu hétérogène, mais où les éléments hittitisants prédominent."

(of a tablet), the wax of a writing-board. But it can also be done by engraving on metal or stone. It may even refer to the making of reliefs in stone and metal, such as the war scenes on **[315]** sculptured stone slabs in Assyrian palaces or the bronze plaques picturing Ishtar while she is driving a lion.[21] It is also used for describing the reliefs on boundary stones, depicting the "seats", symbols, weapons and "images" of the gods.[22]

The verb is common in extispicy texts to designate various grooves and linear marks observed by diviners on the intestines, both the "standard features" (the "presence", *manzāzum*; the "path", *padānum*; the "yoke", *nīrum*)[23] and some "fortuitous marks",[24] such as the "split" (*piṭrum*), the "foot" (*šēpum*), and the "cross" (*pillurtum*). They may appear as straight (*išāriš*), curved (like a *gamlum*), long, short or crossed (*parkiš*) lines. "Drawings" are also observed in the sky and identified as stars and features related to the halo.[25]

Since OA *iṣurtum* must be some kind of inscribed document, the question arises whether the meaning "to draw" could have developed into "to write", and that at a fairly early moment in view of the date of OA *iṣurtum*. It is known that in extispicy some marks or grooves, belonging to the "fortuitous marks", already in the Old Babylonian period were considered so similar to certain cuneiform signs that they were actually given their names. There is a mark called *kakkum*, not primarily because it looks like a weapon (the meaning of the Akkadian word *kakkum*), but because it exhibits the typical shape of the cuneiform sign KAK (in the shape of the capital V turned 90 degrees to the left). Other signs or sign names used in this way are AŠ, BAD, PAP, LÁ, DINGIR, ḪAL and IDIM.[26] In describing them, however, the texts never state that such a sign/mark is "drawn" (*eṣir*), let alone "written" (*šaṭir*), but simply state its presence (*ibašši, šakin*). Lieberman is probably right in assuming that it was the similarity of some of them with cuneiform signs which gave rise to the idea that the gods Shamash and Adad wrote their message or verdict on the liver, and not the idea of or belief in divine writing which led to the recognition of cuneiform signs on the surface of **[316]** the liver.[27] The idea of linking "drawing" and "writing" might have arisen much earlier, from the technique of "drawing" the earliest pictographs on tablets. But the technique of writing in the Old Babylonian period – impressing the tip or edge of a stylus in the wet clay, for which the verbs *lapātum, šaṭarum* and *maḫāṣum* are used – apparently was considered different from that of making a drawing, drawing lines in clay.

There are even a few (late) references which actually contrast writing and drawing. Sennacherib in OIP 2, 140:9 distinguishes the god Assur, whose image (*ṣalmum*) is drawn (*eṣir*) on a gate, from other gods "not drawn" but "whose names (only) are written down".

---

21 Cf. *CAD* Ṣ 84b, b), 4', 1 and Winckler, *Sargon* pl. 48:18

22 *MDP* 2 pl. 23 VII:34, and cf. *ZA* 65 (1975) 58:76ff., with some variation, though in both texts pictorial representations (for which the verbs *uddûm* or *bašāmum, kullumum* and *uṣṣurum* are used) are distinguished from verbal renderings ("whose names are mentioned", with *zakārum*). See also U. Seidl, *BaMitt.* 4 (1968) 113f. [S. Paulus, *Die babylonischen Kudurru-Inschriften von der kassitischen bis zur frühneubabylonischen Zeit* (AOAT 51, Münster 2014) 62, writes "*uṣurtu* "(Ritz)zeichnung" kann sich wohl auf alle Arten der Darstellung beziehen und schliesst damit auch die zoomorphen Symbole ein"]

23 According to J.W. Meyer, *Untersuchungen zu den Tonlebermodellen aus dem Alten Orient* (*AOAT* 39; Neukirchen 1987) 69f., 81f., these "normal drawings" (*uṣurātu kajjanātu*) usually are impressions on the surface of the liver made by neighboring organs.

24 They are anomalous and refer to changes in the parts of the liver which are the result of diseases, worms etc. Cf. J.W. Meyer, op. cit. 72f., and U. Jeyes, *Old Babylonian Extispicy* (Leiden 1989) 180 note 7.

25 Cf. *CAD E* 348a, a, 1', end and see also *SAA* VIII (1992) nos. 19 rev:6f., 55:4, 124:6 and 530:4. In no. 19 "stars should be drawn on an Akkadian writing-board (*le'u*) of the king". See for actual drawings E. Weidner, *Gestirndarstellungen auf babylonischen Tontafeln* (Wien 1967).

26 See S.J. Lieberman, in: M. de Jong Ellis (ed.), *Essays on the Ancient Near East in Memory of Jacob Joel Finkelstein* (Hamden 1977) 147-154.

27 Ibidem 150 note 43.

And the Lamashtu text LKU 33 rev.:19 mentions a tablet to be written (*šaṭārum*), on which also a crescent and a sun-disc are to be drawn (*eṣērum*).[28]

Occasionally the verb has the meaning "to notch, to score". The demon Lamashtu counts the days of the pregnant women by "scoring" them on a wall.[29] And Utnapishtim's wife used the same device to convince Gilgamesh that he had slept through seven days (Gilgamesh XI:212). This seems to be the nearest approach to a meaning "to register, to book", conceived as a simple, primitive bookkeeping system.

uṣurtum and giš.ḫur

A development "drawing" > "writing" also cannot be argued for from the meaning of the noun *uṣurtum* and its Sumerian counterpart giš.ḫur, borrowed into Akkadian as *gišḫurrum*. The primary meaning is "drawing", "ground plan". According to Gudea Cyl. A V:2ff. the king in his dream saw a hero holding a lapis lazuli plaque (*le'um*) with the "drawing" of the temple to be built, possibly its ground plan, as shown on Gudea's statue B (AO 2, "l'architecte au plan"). The hero is identified in VI:5ff. as the god Nin.dub, "who put on it the drawing of the house" (é.a giš.ḫur.ba im.mi.sè.sè.ge). Giš.ḫur is interpreted by D.O. Edzard as "holz einritzen",[30] referring to the action itself and to its result: the drawing/engraving of or the engraved wood(en board). The term **[317]** is very frequent in literary texts with the meaning "plan, regulation", referring to divine or meta-divine plans or rules, frequently also rites of temples and cults, once "drawn" and hence fixed, which are at the basis of phenomena and ritual acts and determine how they should be and should function.[31] They must not be changed, turned over or be forsaken (kúr, bal, ḫalam), but be maintained and kept in correct state (si.sá). The use of giš.ḫur seems to stress the notion that such rules have been drawn, fixed from old and hence cannot be changed. There is, again, no reference to writing, but rather to a design, a ground plan, a pattern laid down. The terminology is that of an architect, surveyor or accountant rather than that of a scribe. Hendursanga is the "accountant" (ŠITA$_5$.DÙ) of Nindar, "for whom Nanše made the stick and staff grow for (drawing?) the giš.ḫur".[32] According to Šulgi Hymn C:46, the king was trained in "counting and accounting the giš.ḫur of the land", and this can be connected with the statement that Lipit-Ishtar was granted both the art of writing (with a golden stylus on a (clay) tablet, dub) and the art of surveying, "the measuring rod (lustrous) like lapis lazuli, the *ašlum*-cubit and the wooden tablet (*le'um*), which bestows wisdom".[33] Surveying implied calculations and drawing a ground plan on a writing board, the giš.ḫur of Gudea.

The same is true of Akkadian *uṣurtum*, originally "drawing, design" (ARMT 18, 12:20; *AbB* 5, 229 :5', an oath sworn in the temple court *ina* GIŠ.ḪUR-*tim* / *uṣurtim*; cf. *uṣurāt qātim* in *MSL* 9, 69:28), but more frequently metaphorically "plan, regulation, rule". Such

28 According to LKA 137:16 "seven gods should be drawn upon the ground" *(iṣir ina qaqqari)*, which *CAD E* 347a, 1' renders by "draw seven (names of) gods ...", an interpretation accepted by W. Horowitz and V. Hurowitz in *JANESCU* 21 (1922) 103f. with note 32, though they mention S. Paul's view, that actually divine symbols were drawn. Line 4 on the rev. of the text presents the names of the seven gods to be drawn in vertical position with irregular interspace. This layout, though writing the names, is clearly intended to show the position of the drawings upon the ground and does not mean that cuneiform signs should be written on the soil. Images or symbols have to be drawn.

29 LKU 33: 15' // KAR 239 I:4', where *eṣērum* D is used in parallelism with *manû*, "to count".

30 *ZA* 62 (1962) 8.

31 See the analysis in G. Farber-F1ügge, *Der Mythos "Inanna und Enid"* ... (Rome 1973) 18lff.

32 In *Festschrift S.N. Kramer* (*AOAT* 25; Neukirchen-Vluyn 1976) 144:15ff.

33 See for the texts and their interpretation A. Sjöberg, *Festschrift T. Jacobsen* (*AS* 20; Chicago 1975) 173ff. Note that Šulgi Hymn B: 45 also mentions a lapis lazuli tablet, cf. Gudea Cyl. A V:3. In Šulgi B: 161 the verb giš.ḫur is used in connection with music, for the tuning of the lyre (Th. Krispijn, *Akkadica* 70 (1990) 1, with commentary: "Ich habe die Schemata . . . aufgestellt") . See for the verb also *TCS* 3 (1969) 176:5', "the temple which sketches the outlines of heaven and earth".

uṣurātum rest in the hand of Marduk[34] and according to a bilingual text from Ugarit it is by the god Ea that the *uṣurātum* are drawn (parallel: *ḫimmātum*), "regulations" which, like those of heaven and earth, cannot be changed (CT 17, 34:5f.). The best known examples of *uṣurātum* produced by a human being are to be found in Hammurapi's Code. In his epilogue he tries to secure the survival of and regard for his stela and its wise verdicts by means of prayers, blessings and curses: his words should not be distorted, his verdicts not be rejected (*šussukum*) or blotted out (*pussusum*), his *uṣurātum* not be changed/discarded (*nukkurum*) nor his written name erased **[318]** (*pašāṭum*; col. xlix:2ff.). In col. xl:92 and xli:74 he also uses *šussukum* with *uṣurātum* as object, and *CAD* N/2, 19,5a translates "removes what I engraved/my reliefs". The various verbs used for describing the harm to be done to monuments and inscriptions in OB show a measure of free variation and overlap in meaning, but neither *nukkurum* nor *šussukum* demand an inscription, a written text as object. They primarily refer to the (inscribed) object itself. As a rule only *pussusum* and *pašāṭum* are used when the erasing, the blotting out of an inscription is meant. The *CAD* could be right in taking *uṣurātum* as "what I engraved", which could mean both the relief at the top of the stela and the engraved text. One could adduce the bilingual inscription of Šulgi, no doubt originally also engraved on a stone monument, TIM 9, 35:13: *ša uṣurāt narēja ašar uṣṣaru upaššaṭu*, where exceptionally the verb *pašāṭum* D is used, which suggests an inscription, a written text, as object. Still, it remains possible that Hammurapi was not primarily referring to the signs he had engraved, but metaphorically to the rules and regulations which his stela embodied. We need more proof before we can posit a meaning "(lapidary) inscription" for *uṣurtum*.

Specific uses of *eṣērum* in Old Babylonian

In some OB letters and administrative texts we meet *eṣērum* with a meaning which cannot simply be "to draw". Twice the verb is used with a fine or punishment as object. In *BaMi* 2 (1963) 79f., W 20472/102:22f. a man, charged with the task of guarding prisoners, is made responsible to the king. For any prisoner which escapes *aran mutim ina ramanišu i-ṣi-ir*. And in *AbB* 1, 14:26 people guilty of having instituted unfounded claims against a woman[35] for her inheritance, "in conformity with the tablet of the (royal) decree, because they have claimed what is not theirs ([25] *šērtam* [26] *i-ṣi-ru-šu-nu-ši-im*)".

Falkenstein translates in the first text "zieht sich selbst die Todesstrafe zu", which is more or less what the text means, but his derivation of the verbal form from *zêrum*, "to hate" > "to disregard", is not acceptable. With Kraus and von Soden[36] we have to take the verb as *eṣērum*. Von Soden proposes "(Strafe) verhängen", which he adds as a fifth meaning of *eṣērum* G.[37] Kraus translates **[319]** "hat sich selbst die Todesstrafe eintatowiert", referring to *AbB* 1, 14:25f., adding "bildlich gebraucht". Such a figurative use of the verb is not impossible, especially in view of the added *ina ramanišu* and it evokes the scene of a culprit who is not simply branded, but in whose skin words revealing his crime are "engraved" as a tattoo. Such a custom is indeed attested in *ana ittišu*, with a fugitive

---

34 F.N. al-Rawi, *RA* 86 (1992) 79:11. I see no reason to parse the plural of *uṣurtum* in OB, with F. Reschid and C. Wilcke (*ZA* 65, 1975, 62), as *uṣṣurātum*. The indeed "irregular" plural is also attested with *nukurtum* – *nukurātum* and I assume the insertion of an epenthetic vowel to resolve the cluster VCV*rtum*. It may not be a coincidence that the alternation between *u* and *i* as first vowels is also attested in *ni/ukurtum*.

35 The wronged party is a *nadītum*, with the name Ibbi-Šamaš, cf. O.R. Gurney, *WZKM* 77 (1987) 197f.

36 See *BiOr* 22 (1965) 290a, *ad loc.*, and *AHw* 1554b. *CAD* Š/2 324, 2, a writes *i-ṢI-ru* and translates "exacted a penalty" in *AbB* 1, 14.

37 As a D-stem of this verb *AHw* 1498a, s.v. *w/muṣṣuru(m)*, refers to CT 48, 10:15, a text edited by Kümmel in *AfO* 25, 79. In front of a series of witnesses lady H [25] *rittam issuḫ* [26] *u šībūša ú-wa-ṣi-ru*. Assuming that *rittam nasāḫum* is a symbolic gesture, presumably marking the end of some link or involvement, the role of the witnesses must have been to certify this fact, which should be what the verb (*w*)*uṣṣurum* must mean, "to establish, ascertain". The document CT 48, 10 is probably the concrete result of this action: it is recorded, fixed, on a tablet. The form *uwanṣir* in *AEM* 1/2, 437:28, perhaps from the same verb, could mean "to establish, to inform, to warn". [**Add.**: *CAD* U s.v. *uṣṣuru* A, now gives as its meaning "to be attentive", referring to *AbB* 11, 108:31 and *TIM* 4, 5:7].

slave, but the verb used here is not *eṣērum* but *naqārum*.[38] Therefore, I prefer another interpretation, which derives support from the use of the verb to denote the result of an administrative action, whereby certain data are "drawn", *i.e.* "fixed, determined".

In *AbB* 3, 38 the addressee is blamed for having spent much more barley than the ration (ŠUKU) assigned for three months, which was 6 kor. The writer adds: DUMU.É.DUB.BA [28] ŠUKU *e-ṣi-ra-ku-um*, "the administrator has "drawn" the ration for you", and warns him that he will have to answer for his waste. He has with him a tablet with the figures of what was available to him (SAG.NÍG.GA-*ka našiāku*) and wants to meet him to settle accounts. Lines 27f. mean either that the ration had been "fixed" for him – hence he knew he was spending too much – or that the amount actually spent had been "drawn", "booked" – hence there was no way of denying his waste. The continuation makes me favor the second interpretation, but it is anyhow clear that *eṣērum* means "to fix, to book": the figures were known, "black upon white". The same meaning fits well for the two occurrences dealing with a fine or punishment: by their deeds the culprits have passed their own verdict, fixed their own predictable penalty. In *BaMi* 2:69 the penalty for negligence is stated in advance, in the very order to guard the prisoners; in *AbB* 1, 14 a standard punishment apparently is meted out "in accordance with the text of the (royal) decree" (*ana pī ṣimdatim*), which had already fixed the penalty for the presumably not infrequent cases of unfounded claims.[39]

"Drawing", whether by means of actual drawings, by notching, by marking something in a list or ledger, or by booking it on a tablet yields clear data, tangible evidence that cannot be disputed. At times it is impossible to decide which method was used. In *AbB* 3, 12:10 the writer is asked "to draw the **[320]** area/surface (*qaqqarum*) on his tablet".[40] Does the writer expect a clear description with exact data and figures of the garden plot in question or a ground plan with added figures?[41]

An even more specific use of *eṣērum* is attested in the unpublished legal document YBC 11041, made available to me by M. Stol. The record deals with a large amount of barley, the delivery of which had been assigned ("given") to a military unit in Babylonia in the year Samsu-iluna 12. Since it had not been duly delivered (line 7: MU.TÚM *lā iršû*), when the accounts were settled, four years later, the old sealed record "was drawn" (*kanīkum labirum in-ne-ṣi-ir-ma*, 1.9), whereupon those responsible for the delivery "issued a (new) sealed record" (*kanīkam īzibū*, l.15), which acknowledged their duty to pay the barley to the palace, when it would issue them a call ([16] *ūm ekallum išassūšunūšim* [17] *še'am ekallam ippalū*).[41a] The context leaves no doubt that "drawing" here means "to strike, to scratch out", apparently by drawing lines over the tablet, a practice actually attested for the OB period. In *MARI* 3 (1984) 258f., D. Charpin observed that small account tablets were marked by drawing red stripes over their full length, to indicate that they had been filed and digested and could be discarded, apparently without being "broken".

---

38 See *ana ittišu* II, iv:14. The words "a runaway, seize him" are to be "engraved" in his face, on his forehead. Cf. *CAD* N/l 332, d) for a similar use of *naqārum* in *AbB* 2, 46:21 and 3, 22:9, both times with *ṣalmum*, "picture"', as object, and ibid. 4, for examples with the D-stem (i.a. a figure in metal). The verb is also used for the scratching of a bird in the soil and the hollowing out of a bowl by a stonecutter, and also has the notion of mutilation, scarification (Middle Assyrian Laws). But note the occurrence of *uṣṣuru*, "marked", said of a slave in *Cambyses* 290:3 (ref. M. Stol).

39 See F.R. Kraus, *SD* 11 (1984) 9, 5 for this letter and a possible relation to CH § 179. Claiming without title earns the plaintiff a penalty also in *AbB* 4, 67:16ff. Cf. CT 8, 24b:4-8 and 47, 63:49 (cases of *ragāmum*) and *AbB* 6, 6:23ff. (*dabābum*).[See for such a decree K.R. Veenhof, The Relation between Royal Decrees and 'Law Codes', *JEOL* 35-36 (2001) 49-83, § 5, e, "Decree on groundless claims" = pp. 297-328 in this volume].

40 See for this letter and the closely related TIM *2*/*AbB* 8, 152, R. Frankena, *SLB* 4 (1968) 133 *ad loc.*

41 Cf. *AbB* 3, 11:38ff. and *AbB* 2, 90, where in view of a problem with fields (to be) assigned to service-men, the writer has consulted "the tablet of allotments to (service-men now) dead" and has booked in a list (*mudasû*) where they hold fields and their plots/surfaces (*qaqqarātum*, 1.19-23), probably by noting the *ugārum*, the neighbours, and the size.

[41a This record has now been published by M. Stol in *Anatolica* 41 (2015) 23-31, with remarks on *eṣērum* in note 10].

An even better example is CT 6,6, a judicial record, stating that when a field was sold the old title deeds (*ṭuppāt ummātim u serdē*), to be handed over to the new owner, could not be found. It states that the sellers will search for them and that they belong to the new owner when they turn up. By drawing a large X over both sides of the tablet it was "crossed out", invalidated, "wohl weil die vermissten Urkunden wieder auftauchten".[42] Another tablet "crossed out" is CT 45, 46 (Ad 6), which records a large sum of silver, "the remainder of an *ilkum* obligation", to be delivered to the palace by the overseer of the traders in Sippar, when it is asked for (lines 15-20). The tablet may have been "crossed out" for reasons similar to those mentioned in YBS 11041. The tablets in question were not destroyed ("broken"), presumably because one wished to keep them as archival records but they had to be cancelled in another way.

Finally there is the statement in the letter *AbB* 1 142:26ff.: "Two sealed records [27] of 10 shekels of silver of B. [28] *e-ṣi-ra-am-ma uštābilakkum,* [29] give (them) to him [30] and his sealed record (of) 1 1/3 shekel of silver ... [32] let him collect (it)". Kraus translates: "Zwei Quittungen ... habe ich gesiegelt und schicke ich dir hiermit", a translation which seems to assume that "to draw" can be used for applying a seal to a tablet, perhaps because of the pictorial nature of **[321]** the scene engraved on the seal. But on wonders why *kanākum* was not used or why the verb was not simply omitted since *kanīkum* implies sealing. Were the two tablets shipped in a sealed bag? It seems better to understand this text in the light of YBS 11041 and CT 6, 6. This means that *kanīkum* is not a quittance, as proof of payment, but the original sealed debt-note, which the creditor has to return to the debtor upon payment. Since the debtor lived elsewhere they had to be sent overland and this entailed the risk that they might fall into other people's hands. Before sending them off they were "crossed out", invalidated. The debtor, having received them, would destroy or discard them (this could be the reason why so few crossed out tablets have come to light). The creditor himself was not allowed to do that, since the debt-note was considered the tablet of the debtor, he had sealed it and he was entitled to receive it back upon payment, as we know from numerous OA examples.

eṣārum and *iṣurtum* in Old Assyrian

The last discussed meaning of *eṣērum* in OB is very specific and rare, but the one first mentioned, where "to draw" acquires the meaning "to decide, to fix", also by booking something, perhaps comparable to our "to put down in black and white", may help us to understand the OA occurrences. I present them in groups, in a sequential numbering.

In support of Balkan's opinion, quoted above, that *iṣurtum* (henceforth *i.*) was a debt-note drawn up for native Anatolians, several texts can be adduced.

No. 1, CCT 1, 33b: 1-10, lists various items, "all owed by the Anatolian Tarmana".[43] It starts with: "8 minas 21 ¾ shekels of [2] silver of his *i.* (*ša iṣurtišu*), [3-4] the price of *kusītum*-textiles", followed by some silver paid for copper, an amount of wheat and one fattened ox (the text continues by listing claims on three other Anatolians (the last one the *alaḫḫinnum*). It is closely linked to

no. 2, ATHE 12. "(As for) the *i.* of Tarmana, [2] to the amount of 8 minas 21 ¾ shekels [3] of silver with the interest on it, [4] it has mounted up to 12 minas". Next it is mentioned that

42 C. Wilcke, in *Zikir šumim, Festschrift Kraus* (1982) 467.

43 Tarmana figures as customer and supplier in records and letters of B(uzāzu) and P(uzurAššur), to which our texts nos. 1-3 belong. In BIN 6, 62:26f. B. tells P. that Tarmana should not be without goods; he has to be granted whatever he asks. In KTS 32:6 he delivers an ox (cf. no. 1:8f.), in CCT 3, 48b:7 he supplies grain, payments of silver by him are recorded in KTS 29a:6 and TC 3, 16:3ff. (interest). B. is asked to collect silver from him in TC 3, 13:19f., VS 26, 136:11 mentions the sale of a textile to his wife, and 124:11ff. lists a claim on him for grain, flour and oil. Cf. also TuM I, 27a:3.

this is claimed by "me" (Buzāzu) and Puzur-Aššur. The structure of no.1 is comparable to that of

no. 3, *RHA* XVIII/66, 39. After listing in lines 1-12 claims on a certain Dudu and Nakiaḫšu, lines 13-22 record debts due from (*išti*) the ruler of Tišima. This listing starts with: " [13] 6 minas 3 shekels of silver [14] of his *i.*" (*ša iṣurtišu*), **[322]** followed by items given to him, promised by him, or due from him. Nakiaḫšu (lines 7 and 12) recurs in text

no. 4, CCT 1, 37b. "15 shekels of silver [2-3] I gave him on the day he drew (up) for me an/ the *i.*" (*iṣurtam e-ṣí-ra-ni*). The text continues by listing silver and textiles owed by him *(illibbišu)*, items paid to the man of Mamma, metals taken by a blacksmith, and two expensive textiles "which I gave to him". The "him" is identified in the last line (16): "memorandum (*tahsista*) of/about Nakiaḫšu". An *i.* alongside a memorandum (*taḫsistum*) also occurs in

no. 5, Kt n/k 126 (courtesy S. Bayram). Its heavily damaged obv. lists claims, to all appearances in copper [in all more than 25 talents] on native Anatolians, concluding with: "all this they will pay in springtime" (1-18). The rev. adds: "Separately, 65 minas, [20] one *i.*, [21] one talent, a second [22-3] *i.*, due from T. [24] In the memorandum [25] of outstanding claims [26] which [27] I. left behind [28] it is not written" (*1 GÚ 5 mana aḫamma* [20] *ištēt iṣurtam* [21] *šanītum 1* GÚ [22] *iṣurtum* [23] *išti* T. [24] *ina taḫsistim* [25] *ša bābtim* [26] *ša* I. [27] *ezibu* [28] *ulā lapit*). Two additional claims, not entered in the memorandum, are substantiated by mentioning the existence of *i.*s in which they are recorded.

No. 6, KTS 57c (duplicate of *RA* 59 [1965] 47f., MAH 19613, no. 21). "4 minas 13 ½ shekels of silver [2-3] of the previous *i.* of /concerning small wares". The note continues by listing additional, new deliveries made to Dalaš (8), a smith (10) and Tamišed, all of which result in claims.

No. 7, ICK 2, 296. "170 minas (of copper) [2] of the *i.* which you drew (up) for me" (*ša iṣurtim ša jāti te-ṣú-ra-ni*), followed by other items which "you took" (3b-6) and [7-8] "20 minas (of copper which) have not been entered in/added to the *i.*" (*ana iṣurtim lā ṭaḫḫūni*).[44] Summary: "In all 300[+x] minas of copper due from (*išti*) Alāhum". [A memo in the 1st person singular, and we do not know to whom the words are addressed, but see Dercksen[44a]] We may compare the unpublished text (courtesy J.G. Dercksen):

No. 8, kt a/k 488b (cf. Balkan, *OLZ* 1965, 157). A letter written by an Assyrian to the *alaḫḫinnum* of the town of Ninašša: "2 *kutānum*-textiles, a ruler's wear (*lubūš rubā'im*), and 12 shekels of *ḫusārum* I gave to your escort (*radium*), which you sent along with my transport and he brought it to you. [10] And over there my partner has entered it in his *i.* (*ana iṣurtišu uṭaḫḫi*). Here I took the price of the textiles and of my *ḫusārum* from the silver of my partner. [19] Give him his silver over there!".

These texts, personal memorandums without legal force (cf. 4:16), list debts due from and deliveries made to various Anatolians. They distinguish between older, existing claims, already recorded in an *i.*, and later deliveries, at times specified with their value in silver, apparently not yet entered in an *i.* Note that no. 6:3 speaks of a "previous *i.*" and that no.7 distinguishes items for which an *i.* had been drawn (up) from those "not (yet) entered in an

44 Cf. Balkan, OLZ 1965, 158, who quotes the unpubl. text K/t b/k 36: *ana iṣurtim* [5] *lā ṭaḫḫū*.

[44a J.G. Dercksen, *The Old Assyrian Copper Trade in Anatolia* (Istanbul 1996) 167-8, "written by an Assyrian for another Assyrian". He assumed that the *i.* was a special account on which credits owed by the palace were recorded and that "such a tablet (an *iṣurtum* – K.R.V.) was apparently kept in the *kārum* office, and a merchant was credited on it for the copper owed him by the palace".]

i." The verb used **[323]** here, *ṭaḫḫu'um ana*,[45] is known as a bookkeeping term and its exact translation depends on our idea about the writing material used. If an *i.* was a wax-coated writing-board, one could enter new items in an existing *i.*, but if it was a clay tablet, one would have to draw up a new *i.* for every new item. The data of such individual *i.*s in due time could be digested in a "memorandum" (*taḫsistum*), as mentioned in no. 4, and no. 5 distinguishes data about individual claims booked in a memorandum from those not (yet) booked, but for which individual *i.*s are available as proof. No. 7 speaks of "entering in an/the *i.*", which could mean the drawing (up) of a (new) *i.*, but no.8 speaks of entering something "in his *i.*", which might suggest an existing *i.*, to which data were added.

An *i.*, as is clear from nos. 4:3 and 7:3 (both with personal dative after the verb), was drawn (up) for the creditor. But "his *i.*", according to Old Assyrian parlance, refers to the debtor. His seal (in the case of clay tablets) was impressed on the debt-note and when he paid his debt he received *his* tablet back in order to "kill" it.[46] The fact that some texts simply speak of "an *i.* of x. silver" is also in accordance with Old Assyrian custom. For merchandise sold on credit or given on consignment the recipient had to seal a valid bond (*ṭuppum ḫarmum*), which as a rule only mentioned the amount of silver due, the term of payment and the rate of default interest, but not the merchandise taken. The way our texts speak of or perhaps quote *i.*s suggests that they were functionally similar to debt-notes. This is confirmed by no. 2, where there is question of interest on a debt recorded in an *i.*, apparently on fixed terms (rate, date), which allows the writer to calculate how much interest in the meantime has accrued (more than 40 percent of the capital). No. 8 seems to present a problem. It informs the Anatolian ruler, to whom this letter was addressed by his Assyrian creditor, that his debt had been entered by the latter's partner "in his *i.*" (not: "in *your i.*"). But note that the writer of the letter[47] had already indemnified himself by taking the price of the goods, his claim, from his partner's silver (14 f.), whereupon the latter had booked it "in his *i.*". Now the Anatolian recipient and debtor is asked to refund the partner, who seems to have lived in the same place as the Anatolian ("there", lines 10, 19), which explains the complications. But we have to retain that the Assyrian partner kept an *i.* of his claims. Who "drew (up) the *i.* for me", **[324]** in no. 7, is not clear; not necessarily the Assyrian debtor, mentioned in the summary, since it uses the third person.

A clear link between *i.* and Anatolians is also attested in a few texts where an *i.* is a document issued by a local palace, which has bought Assyrian merchandise on credit. In principle the situation is not different from that in the first set of references, where private Anatolians appear, since some of the latter may have acted for a palace. I quote three new texts:

No. 9, VS 26, 146. A memorandum on the acquisition of merchandise by a local palace. First 62 textiles are "taken" in the temple of the weather god (É ᵈIŠKUR) by the "head of the storage" (*rabi ḫuršātim*, lines l-8a , next some tin and 2 donkeys. "All this the palace bought, [15] its (price in) silver is owed by the palace. [17] I have an *i.* of the textiles, but not one of the tin" (verb: *ka''ulum*).

No. 10, VS 26, 56. Sueija reports to have been forced by a local *kārum* to bring all his textiles up to the palace, where he must "reach an agreement" *(išti ekallim mitgar*, 18f.). He has brought them up, "but the palace has not yet given me an *i.*" He now wants to go

45 See for *ṭahhu'um ana*, "to add to an account", expressions like *kaspam ana nikkassī ana qāt* PN *ṭaḫḫu'um*, KTS 4a, :7f., 14; BIN 4, 42:39f. (to add to an existing debt), BIN 6, 183:24 (to "add" gold to somebody's tablet), *TTAED* 4 (1940) 12 no. 2:12-15 (*ana ša ṭuppišu) [*see now *CAD* Ṭ, 80, 4, a, for more references]. Cf. in OB TCL 10, 96:8-13 and YOS 8, 154:16f. (*ana ṭuppim*).

46 See my remarks in E. Mindlin *et al.* (eds), *Figurative Language in the Ancient Near East* (London, 1987) 46ff.

47 The sender, Irišum, son of Amur-Šamaš, was a business associate, perhaps even partner of Adad-ṣululī, whose archives are registered under kt a/k. Since this letter was found in a sealed envelope in Adad-ṣululī's house, it may have been an archive copy or duplicate, passed on to Irišum's partner to inform him about his request to the *alaḫḫinnum* to pay back to Adad-ṣululī.

to the palace together with the representatives of the *kārum*, in order "to remind (it) personally (of his claim)" (*raminī luḫassis*), so that the palace will speak/negotiate (*dabābum*, 28) with him.

No. 11, [K. Hecker *et al.*, *Kappadokische Keilschrifttafeln aus den Sammlungen der Karlsuniversität Prag* (Prag 1998)] I 507. Two Assyrians report that "until now the copper has not yet become freely available for me (*izku'am*). Ask $Š_1$ over there how much copper (there is) in the palace, either belonging/owed to you or to D. Seize $Š_2$ and let him make available to you (all) the copper in accordance with the *i.* he left to him" ([20] *ammala* $Š_2$ [21] *iṣurtam* [22] *ēzibušunni* [23] *[ṣ]abassuma* URUDU [24] *lūballiṭakkum*).

The situation in nos. 9 and 10 is clear. The palace has bought merchandise without paying cash and has issued/should issue an *i.* to its creditor/supplier. Such an *i.* is not simply a list of goods taken (the merchants themselves certainly kept such lists), but an acknowledgement of its debt, hence a legal document and presumably sealed. It must have stated how much and presumably also when it would pay. In no. 10 the owner of the merchandise is still waiting for such a document and that it is more than just a receipt can be gathered from the fact that he is told by the *kārum* "to reach an agreement with the palace". When reporting that he complied he does not mention the agreement and its absence probably explains why no *i.* has yet been issued to him. Because the palace is contractually entitled to levy fixed taxes and preempt part of the textiles, the agreement hence must have concerned the purchase of additional goods, most likely textiles, the price of which had to be negotiated on the basis of their quality. Suejja intends to discuss the matter personally with the palace.

The background of no. 11 is similar, but since OA does not know *ezābum* in the meaning "to issue a (legal) document", lines 2lf. must mean that the *i.*, previously issued by the palace, has been left to/with $Š_2$ when the (main) writer of the letter had to depart. Since $Š_2$ has failed to collect the copper on the basis of the *i.* and has not notified its owners, he has to be seized by the addressee in order to force him to make the copper available (*balluṭum*). The text mentions **[325]** that two traders are entitled to receive their share of the copper in the palace and this could mean that they had taken part in a collective transaction organized by the *kārum.*

The *kārum* also plays a role in the difficult text

no. 12, EL 320 + CCT 6, 17a (a perfect join, which yields a complete record). Buzāzu states that, when he had to leave, he had left to Il-wedāku *i.*s, which *kārum* Wahšušana had put at his disposal as pledges (*šapartum*), and he wants to know whether I. has used them to collect copper in his name. We cannot go into details,[48] but it is clear that possession of an *i.* made collection of a claim possible. We may assume that the *i.*s here embody claims by the *karum* on the palace, which it had, for unknown reason, ceded to B. An alternative interpretation is that the *kārum* had acted as court-of-law and had assigned somebody else's *i.*s (perhaps entitling him to a share in a transaction as assumed for no. 11) to B., his creditor, as security. This latter interpretation is supported by EL no. 316, where the assumption is that I. has collected claims of B., among them amounts of copper from two native Anatolians. The Anatolians in question could have issued these *i.*'s to an Assyrian trader (perhaps Šu-Ištar), who had had to yield them to B.

48 Read in lines 13f.: *[ina] Wahšušana šazzuzti* [14] *ušāzizka u iṣurātim* [15] *ša kārum W.* [16] *ana šapartim iddianni* [17] *ēzibakkum ina erīm šuāti* [18] *kīma jāti mimma talqe.* See for the transactions and the background of this text also MP 1 (*RA* 60[1966] 12lf.) and EL no. 321, according to which Šū-Ištar was a debtor of Buzāzu, while Puzur-Aššur – whose death is at the basis of our lawsuit – had been his guarantor. The *i.*s, being Š.'s bonds, might have been given as pledges first to P. (his guarantor) and after the latter's death to B., whose claim on Š. was finally settled by the agreement recorded in EL no 321. It entailed that B. ultimately would "release" (*waššurum*) "his tablets to Š.", which could mean the release of the bonds handed over as security (cf. EL II p. 53).

The *Kārum* is also involved in

no. 13, Kt c/k 459:12-17 (cf. Balkan, *OLZ* 1965, 158 [and Dercksen, *Copper* – see note 44a – 167]). In this memorandum we read: "(for) 216 minas (of copper) (recorded) in the first/ previous tablet, the big *i.* (*ina ṭuppim* [14] *panîm ina iṣurtim* [15] *rabītim*), I will collect 45½ shekels of silver in the *kārum* office".

> [Addition: Balkan in quoting this text restored <*ina*> *iṣurtim*, without giving a translation; Dercksen, *Copper* 167, note 524, using his quotation, omitted *ina* and translated "booked on the first tablet, the large *iṣurtum*". In his own transcription, based on study of the tablet itself, he now reads *i-na iṣurtim*, but even so his interpretation as apposition is still the most likely one. The only alternative is to split the sentence: "216 minas (of copper are booked) on the first tablet; from the big *i.* I will collect 45 ½ shekels of silver in the *kārum* office", but this is less likely.]

The interpretation remains difficult, but it is clear that the amount of silver the writer will collect for the 218 minas of copper he had sold or was entitled to, applies a rate of exchange of ca. 1 shekel of silver for ca. 28½ shekels of copper, which is entirely acceptable. The mention of the "big *i.*" may have served to make its identification easy, but why for a modest claim of copper a big *i.* was needed. The *i.* may have contained a list of assets of which only the first one written on the tablet (excerpted in the *i.*?) mattered here. In that case a comparison with the few occurrences of "big tablets" (BIN 6, 156:7; KUG 18:7f.; VS 26, 46:4f.) may be in order, since they invariably refer to bookkeeping in the *kārum*-office, which played an important role in the copper trade. Not very clear is

no. 14, kt n/k 516:12 (courtesy C. Günbattı). Its writer, Lā-qēp, accuses Nab-Suen of having taken silver belonging to "our father" without having sent him any silver "to save his life": "Fine, you did not take anything of what is (recorded) in the *i.* (*ina ša i-ṣur-tim*)!"

I.'s recording claims that could be collected are mentioned in

[326] no. 15, CTMMA I no. 84. Lines 32-38 of this protocol, which lists the contents of an archive of which a trader was robbed, mention: "One tablet (stating) that I. and A. have been paid in full the 35 talents of good copper being the price of the *i.*s (*ša šīm iṣurātim)* ... [35] One tablet (stating) that I. and A. gave me 30 talents of good copper of the *i.*s and that I. will (now) be responsible for the debt of 30 talents of good copper which I_2. owes to the *alaḫḫinnum* of Dašušu". The first tablet is a quittance, either for the purchase price paid for some *i.*s (Larsen's translation) or for the amount of copper recorded in them as the price to be paid by an (Anatolian) debtor who had bought Assyrian import goods at credit in exchange for copper, an interpretation I favor because the text writes *ša šīm* and not simply *šīm*. The second is a legal document whereby S. assumed responsibility for (*izizzum ana*) paying a debt in copper to an *alaḫḫinnum*, after I. and A. had paid him the amount in question that was recorded in some *i.*s. Perhaps the two transactions recorded in these tablets were complimentary and part of a general settlement of accounts (an attorney was involved according to lines 34f.). Whatever the details, the specified list of records missing only speaks of "tablets" (*ṭuppū*) and it is therefore remarkable that the summary in lines 58ff. states: "*ṭuppū'a iṣurātū'a lū taḫsisātū'a* of much copper, all this under seals in two coffers" and hence includes *i.*s. The settlement of lines 32ff. implies that *i.*s changed hands and they may have ended up in the coffers in question, but the list of lines 10-47 does not mention them. Judging from the use of *lū* in OA in enumerations (see my *AOATT* 18 note 35), the Assyrian phrase quoted does not mean three categories, "tablets, as well as *i.*s and memorandums", but probably two, "tablets, both *i.*s and memorandums". The general category "(clay) tablets", to which all records listed in lines 10-47 belong, then is distinguished in two groups: legal documents as proof of claims designates as *i.*s, and memorandums without legal force, but serving as aids to memory. This would mean that *i.*s are clay tablets of a specific kind, a conclusion which can also be drawn from text no. 13, lines 13-15, *ina ṭuppim panīm ina iṣurtim rabītim*, where *i.* seems to be in apposition to *ṭuppum*. It is possible, but not certain that the term was used here because among the tablets missing there was quite a number of promissory notes recording debts in copper.

I also note that in both occurrences in text 15 *i.* occurs in the plural. The transactions recorded apparently referred to a number of claims in copper, each of them booked in a separate *i.* For administrative purposes and when accounts were settled, a number of separately registered claims could be booked on one single record and it is possible that the "big *i.*" mentioned in text no. 13 meant such a record.

In almost all examples quoted an *i.* must be a legal document made out to an Assyrian supplier or creditor by an Anatolian person or palace, in which the latter acknowledges a debt and, at least in some cases, promises to pay at a certain date on the penalty of default interest. Only in no. 6 we do not know who **[327]** wrote the *i.* for the creditor and in no. 7 an Assyrian trader entered a payment due "in his *i.*". As a legal document an *i.* must have been sealed by the debtor who accepted the liability recorded. But if that is true, why did they not simply designate such debt-notes or bonds as *ṭuppum ḫarmum* (*ša kunukkišu*)? This becomes a serious question in

no. 16, ICK 1, 13. In this letter by Assur-mālik to five persons, among whom two Anatolians, we read: "[5] 12½ minas of silver and 100 bags of barley Happuala, the shepherd of the queen, owes me. [8] I have his valid tablet with his seal *(ṭuppušu ḫarmam ša kunukkišu).* [10] Since 4 years it is accumulating interest for his account according to the word (rule) of Kanish. [12] Please, my fathers, my lords, [14] try as best as you can to make him pay the capital, silver and barley, [16] and charge him the interest on silver and barley [19] and make him pay in annual installments (*šattišamma*). [20] Please ... take care to collect my capital of silver and barley [24] and draw up his *i.* (*iṣurtušu eṣrā*) for the interest on the silver and the barley". Why a *ṭuppum ḫarmum* for the capital loan and an *i.* for the contract recording the accumulated interest? Could the latter, notwithstanding the functional similarity have been a record of a native type, perhaps a tablet with a native Anatolian seal impression and not encased in a sealed envelope? But sealed tablets do not occur during level II of the *kārum* and only start to appear during the younger level Ib. The alternative, a wooden writing board (comparable to the Hittite GIŠ.ḪUR), is also unlikely. It might have disintegrated without a trace, but since *i.*s must have been sealed, one should have found the sealed clay bullae once attached to them, as was the case in Hattuša, according to the convincing explanation for the discovery of hoards of bullae with royal seals.[49] But this has not been the case in *kārum* Kanish; the bullae discovered in many houses seem to have served transport and storage of merchandise, silver and clay tablets.[50] Moreover, as we have seen, the native hieroglyphic script, as a fully developed writing system that would be required to draw up records of the *i.*-type, only came into existence much later. In the absence of any other native Anatolian candidate, a clay tablet, inscribed in cuneiform, is the only possible candidate for a record listing a debt, a date and /or term of payment, an interest clause and the names of the debtor and creditor.

Our difficulty in identifying such *i.*s among the clay tablets excavated may simply be due to the fact that it was not really different from a *ṭuppum ḫarmum.* There is, as far as I know, not a single debt-note with an Anatolian palace as debtor. But no. 9 shows that the palace acted through its officials: the *rabi ḫuršātim* "takes" textiles, but later it is stated that they were actually bought by the palace, which owed their price in silver.

---

49 See the reference mentioned in note 14, above, and see also P. Neve, *Hattuša, Stadt der Götter und Tempel* (Mainz 1993) 55.

50 See my remarks on such bullae in *Fs N. Özgüç*, 645ff.

[*Addition*: This is also the case in an additional source, a tablet in the possession of Mr. Struwe (which I copied long ago), in which a palace, its official and *i.* occur: **No. 16a**. It deals with problems between three traders about the sale of meteoric iron (*amūtu*) for copper to an Anatolian palace official or palace. Its lines 12-22 report the decision reached before *kārum* Kanish: "As for the meteoric iron of M., which was sold to the *rabi sikkātim*-official, whether copper [16] has come forth (for it) and is in Š.'s house,[17] or (there is) an *iṣurtu*, or (part of the) copper is still due from the palace, while (another part of the) copper has come forth from the palace – the three of them, Š., E. and M., [21] shall convert it into silver that will go to Kanish, where they will negotiate on the basis of their tablets and valid deeds" (*lū* URUDU [16] *uṣ'am* : É *Šu-Ištar* [17] *ibašši* : *lu i-ṣú-ur-tum* [18] *lu* URUDU : *ina* É.GAL-*lim* [19] *aḫḫur lū* URUDU *ina* [20] É.GAL-*lim ú-ṣí-am* : *3-šunu* [21] *ana kaspim utarrūma* [22] *kaspum ana Kaneš* [23] *illakma* : Š. [24] E. *u* M. [25] *ana ṭuppēšunu u dannātišunu* [26] *etawwū*). For the iron sold to the *rabi sikkātim* copper is expected to come forth from the palace. The text seems to consider three possibilities: a) (all) copper has come forth and is now in the house of Š., b) (this is not the case, but) there is an *i.*, and c) only part of the copper has been delivered, while the rest is still due. The existence of an *i.* means that the liability of the palace to pay has been officially recorded, but no payment had yet been made.]

Hence debt-notes sealed by Anatolians may well be the *i.*s we are looking for, although it is **[328]** remarkable that the number of contracts recording debts/credits in copper, granted by Assyrians to Anatolians is small. Garelli *AC* p. 384 lists only two small amounts and p. 389f. only one large amount. Since there was much trade in copper and certainly not all payments were cash, we have to assume that the nature of these transactions or the way they were administered was different. Trade in copper in most cases was bulk trade in a product mined in Anatolia, which perhaps made it less suited for transactions with private Anatolians. On the Assyrian side, there is clear evidence for active involvement of the *kārum* organization, even though Garelli's statement (*AC* p. 294.4, cf. p. 176, 1, a) "le commerce du cuivre faisait l'object d'un contrôle strict de l'office des marchands qui centralisait des achats et le produit des ventes" goes too far. Anyhow, this may have resulted in many indirect transactions in copper between the *kārum*s and the palaces, in which individual traders could take a share and the administration of which probably was kept in the *kārum* office (cf. the role of the *kārum* in text no. 12 [and see now Dercksen, *Copper*, ch. 5, 2-4]). *I.*s dealing with copper hence may (also) have been issued by or kept by that office and text no. 13 may reflect that situation.[51] This may also be the case in text

no. 17, Kt u/k 2 (photo in T. Özgüç, *Kültepe-Kaniş* II, 1986, pl. 60, 2; collated). This letter by Ah-šalim in lines 20-30 states: "If the affair of I. has been settled (or: set down for trial? *awātum ittaškan*), you and A_1. must retort (or: raise it again, *ta''erā*). And B. and A_2. ... have knowledge (of the facts). [27] Let them open their mouths there, before the *kārum* (and declare) that one has made a deduction from my *i.*s."[52] The plaintiff considers himself the victim of an administrative measure (penalty?), whereby his claim, recorded on an *i.*, probably kept in the *kārum*, was reduced.

These observations suggest that the designation *i.* was used for a clay tablet recording a claim, a debt or an acknowledgement, in order to stress that it was a particular type of tablet.

An occurrence of *i.* in a different context and with a different meaning is attested in

---

51 [See for the role of the *kārum* organization in the copper trade Dercksen, *Copper Trade* (above note 44a), especially ch. 5.4, "The transfer of copper from the palace to the *kārum*-office".]

52 The verb, *ṣaḫḫurum*, is typical for administrative operations, whereby accounts are settled, taxes paid, not by cash payment but by balancing assets and debts.

no. 18, Kt 79/k 101 (H. Sever, *DTCFD* 34, 1990, 260-3). The beginning of this letter by the ruler (*waklum*) of Assur to *kārum* Kanish reads as follows: "The tablet [5] with the verdict of the City (of Assur), [6] which concerned the sale of gold, [7] which we sent you – [8] that tablet is invalid (cancelled; *akkuš*). [9] Concerning gold we 'have not "drawn" an *i.*' (*iṣurtam* [10] *ulā né-ṣú-ur*). The rules (*awātum*) for gold are (still) [12] the previous (*paniātum*) ones." The text then spells them out: gold may be sold between Assyrians, but not, "according to the stipulation of the stela" (*kīma awāt naru'āim*, 16f.), to Akkadians, Amorites or Subaraeans, under penalty of death.

[329] I interpret this fascinating incident as follows. The City of Assur, the highest judicial authority, presumably at the request of a trader or *kārum* Kanish (where the case must have started), had passed a verdict which forbade or approved the sale of gold by an Assyrian to a nonAssyrian in a particular case. *Kārum* Kanish had been informed about this verdict by an official letter. Soon, however, the authorities in Assur realized that their verdict was liable to misunderstanding, since it could be interpreted as a change of a hitherto valid regulation, "published" by being carved on a stela. By means of our letter the *kārum* was informed that the verdict was revoked and that the previous regulation was still valid. In order to exclude any doubts the letter added: "We have not made an *i.* concerning gold". This must mean: "We did not draw up/decide on/ draft a (new) rule" and the verb *eṣārum* is used with a meaning akin to that deduced for some OB references quoted above. The *i.* is the result of taking a decision, fixing a rule.

The reference to the stela is intriguing, since it was an official stone monument, on which the text of regulations were engraved (cf. the words of Hammurapi and Šulgi about their *uṣurātum* embodied in stelae). But I doubt whether this aspect is responsible for the use of this noun and verb in our text. The focus is on the fact that no new regulation has been fixed, irrespective of where it was inscribed and how it was "published". The words in question can be interpreted as "we never really intended to change the rules", or as "the cancellation of the verdict means that no new rule has been fixed". The move seems understandable if the verdict – as some verdicts were – was formulated in a rather general way. Such a permission to sell gold would undermine the regulation of the stela, since gold could not be sold to Akkadians, Amorites and Subaraeans, hence to Mesopotamian people/traders. But a generally formulated prohibition would harm the trading activities in Anatolia, where in particular cases gold might have to be sold to Anatolians. The Anatolian trade was not to suffer, but the Assyrian monopoly on the trade in gold inside Mesopotamia was maintained; all gold had to be concentrated in the city of Assur.[53]

In this text the medium of writing and the language were irrelevant; what mattered was the decision taken. It is understandable that in the context of the Assyrian trade, where bookkeeping and recording, especially of liabilities, played such an important role and was so useful, in practice *i.* in many cases may have come to denote a record, a bond. But the element of deciding is not absent. In commenting on text no. 10 we observed that the **[330]** absence of an agreement with the palace, apparently on the number and the price of the textiles to be bought, explained the absence of an *i.* fixing the liability.

The use of *eṣārum* with the meaning "to decide, to fix", is attested a few more times in Old Assyrian:

No. 19, Kt 89/k 252 (courtesy Y. Kawasaki). The letter informs I. that the palace needs textiles which are stored with Z. and that he had told the writer of the letter that the palace keeps pressing him and that the ruler had told him: [13] "Fix their price (*šīmšina*

53 The frequent expression "gold for the journey to the City" (*ḫurāṣum ša ḫarrān ālim*) now acquires a new dimension. The fact that all gold acquired in Anatolia was shipped to Assur was not just the goal of the traders, it was a commercial policy of the city-state, even embodied in a regulation carved in a stela. This also explains why, whenever gold arrived from Anatolia, it was not used to buy merchandise for a next caravan, but was first converted into silver, which was used as "money" for making purchases.

e-ṣir-ma), so that I can take them. But since I. has not (yet) fixed their price (*e-ṣí-ru-ni*), I refused to give them. Write to him, that he may fix their price for me (*le-ṣí-ra-ma*) and we may give them" (15-21).

No. 20, [K. Hecker *et al.*, see above, no. 11] Prag I 439. A verdict of *Kārum* Kanish stipulates that I. and E. shall take three impartial traders to inspect (*amārum*) a lot of disputed textiles and "they will fix their price" (*šīmšunu e-ṣí-ru-ma*, 22), whereupon I. and E. will take them.

No. 21, C 43 (Collection Holzmeister, transliteration by Landsberger). Atata writes to Innāja: [3] "Even when your instruction does not come to me, [5] for you, what I wrote to you concerning your copper of good quality, I will fix (it) for you!".[54] I assume that the writer means he will stick to what he had promised on the price and quantity of copper. He uses *eṣārum* to assure that his promise will be fixed in writing, so that simple *eṣārum* may have the meaning of "to draw up an *iṣurtum*", to put down "in black and white". The same meaning of the verb is attested in the OB record YOS 5, 186:8, which lists capital goods delivered to merchants in Larsa (by the palace) consisting of sesame, wool and sheep, of which it is said: *ša adīni* KAR.BI *lā*[!] *eṣ-ru*, "whose exchange value has not yet been fixed". The same fact is registered in the comparable text YOS 5, 153:4 (referring to sesame and wool) by means of the words KAR.BI NU.GAR.

The idea of deciding, fixing something is also present in

no. 22, CCT 4, la: 7ff. [see now M.. Larsen, *OAA* 1 no. 13]. As in other letters, Aššur-idī urges his son to "heed the words of the god(s)" and to stick to his promise. He warns him: *ana nikištim* [8] *ša ilum i-ṣí-ra-ku-ni* [9] *lā tatu'ar.* Thus far the meaning of *nikištum*, the object of *eṣārum*, was not very clear,[55] but a new reference suggests that it is something like a warning, a prohibition as the result of a decision. In Kt 91/k 297 [= *Kültepe Tabletleri* VIII, 266, and see note 55] the writer states that certain textiles and an amount of oil have not been sold and are still in stock. Lines 10ff. explain why: "Here, by *nikištum* of the *kārum*, nobody shall **[331]** sell anything to the Anatolian". The *kārum* apparently had issued a prohibition of commercial dealings with an Anatolian, presumably because he had refused to meet his obligations vis-à-vis the Assyrians. We know other cases where the *kārum* authorities issued such prohibitions, which could be made known by a letter or as verdict.[56] Something similar must have been the case here and the use of the verb *eṣārum* with *nikištum* as object in our text indicates that the god had made it (painfully?) clear to Aššur-nādā (in comparable cases we read about relatives being visited by demons and evil spirits or being plagued by illness)[57] that a limit had been reached. The god had made known his will, issued a strong warning.

---

54 [3] *u šumma ana jāti* [4] *tērtaka lā illakam* [5] *ana kuātima* [6] *ša adi* URUDU-*i-ka* SIG_5 [7] *ašpurakkunni le-ṣú-ra-kum.*

55 The letters where *nikištum* occurs were discussed by H. Hirsch in *UAR*[2] 1, § 1 and in Nachträge 5f. Derivation from *nakāsum* seems excluded, but the meaning of *nkš* is not quite clear. Hirsch proposes "etwa Abgabe-verpflichtung", echoed in *CAD* N/2, 222f. "contribution(?)". The new reference in Kt 91/k 297 does not support these interpretations. It reads: [10] *annakam ni-ki-iš-tám* [11] *ša kārim* [12] *ša kīma ana* [13] *nuā'im mimma* [14] *šīmim mamman* [15] *lā iddunu. Nikištam* seems to be an adverbial accusative, while *ša kīma* introduces the contents of the decision, as it is used after terms for written documents, orders, etc., "Here there is a decision of the kārum, to the effect that nobody shall sell anything to the Anatolian". [**Add.** AKT 3, 102:16 mentions a *nikištum ša ellitim*, "a decision about the caravan"; Kt 87/k 387:34, a *nikištum* about *kutānu*-textiles, which leads to an appeal to the *kārum* to contact the *rabi sikkitim*; and Kt h/k 18 mentions big expenses incurred by a trader due to the *nikišātum* of the palace and the blood-money"].

56 Cf. the order of the *kārum* communicated by letter in kt c/k 1055 and the *kārum* verdict edited as EL 273. See for both texts Larsen, *OACC* 263 and 327.

57 Cf. MAH 19612 (*RA* 59, 1965, 165f., no. 28), KTS 24 and 25. See my discussion of these texts in K.R. Veenhof (ed.), *Schrijvend Verleden* (Leiden/Zutphen 1983) 86ff.

The examples quoted reveal the semantic range of the verb, "to draw, to make a drawing, to design, to fix, to decide". Perhaps one may even add "to shape, to fashion", if our verb is indeed attested in the expression *duram i-*ZI*-ir*, twice used in OA royal inscriptions, both in the first and in the third pers. sing.[58] *AHw* 252b, 4 lists them under "gestalten", together with the first line of Etana, *ālam iṣirū*, but *CAD* E 349a, which translates with "to construct", has doubts. One could translate "to design", but the rulers in question no doubt also meant the realization of their building projects.[59] Another problem of the verb is the remarkable variation of the stem vowel. We have a preterit with *-i-* (texts nos. 4, 19 and 21; cf. the imperative *eṣir* in no. 19:13) and with *-u-* (texts nos. 18 and 20). I cannot explain it – perhaps free variation or conditioned by the final stem consonant *-r* – but it does not affect the meaning of the verb.

Summing up, we may conclude that an *i.* was a clay tablet in the nature of a valid legal document written in cuneiform, which recorded a liability of the same kind as a promissory note called *ṭuppum ḫarmum*. Most *i.*s were records of liabilities by Anatolians or Anatolian palaces, but in rare cases they were also said to be drawn up by Assyrians. It embodies the obligation or promise to pay a certain amount of money/goods (frequently copper), which presupposes a commercial decision. But such a decision was never a matter of one party only and every commercial transaction implied such decisions, whereby both parties agreed (*namgurum*) on the conditions, both quantities and prices, because there were no fixed prices. In no. 19 the Assyrian trader had to fix the price of his textiles which the palace wished to buy, and in nos. 20 and 21 prices were **[332]** decided upon and fixed between Assyrians. Therefore I am reluctant to explain the use of *i.* from the fact that it implied a decision. I would rather assume that its use reflects the importance attached to the fact that the seller/creditor finally got into his hands a valid bond, recording the amount he was entitled to in writing, secured by the debtor's seal. But this does not explain why the term was used by preference in describing dealings in copper with Anatolians. The fact that Anatolians usually made use of stamp seals hardly can have made the difference. And if *i.* was preferred because it was a convenient one-word equivalent of the rather cumbrous *ṭuppum ḫarmum ša kunuk* ..., it would not have been so rare in purely Assyrian commercial contexts. It is unsatisfactory that we cannot identify even one single *i.* among the bonds sealed by native Anatolians, but perhaps more references within a well defined archival context will allow such identifications in the future. And a better knowledge of the still imperfectly understood administrative procedures of the *kārum* office, whose discovery remains a serious desideratum, may turn out to be helpful. With so many thousands of texts still unpublished and with the excavations of *kārum* Kanish bringing to light hundreds of new texts every year, there is no reason to be pessimistic about the possibility of solving old and new riddles of the Kültepe texts and the techniques of Old Assyrian trade.

Addendum:

The meaning of *iṣurtum* (in what follows *i.*) was recently discussed anew in an important article by Willemijn Waal, "Writing in Anatolia: The Origins of the Anatolian Hieroglyphs and the Introductions of the Cuneiform Script", *AoF* 39 (2012) 287-315. In footnote 13 she lists some additional references for *i.* (of which MAH 19613, as I mentioned, is a duplicate of my text 6).

Her conclusion that *i.*, "occurs only in commercial contacts between the Assyrians and Anatolians ... mostly concerns an official document made out to an Assyrian supplier or

58 See for the text and context *RIMA* 1 17:28 and 23:40.

59 The root *jṣr* is well attested in West-Semitic, where it means "to shape, to fashion". In the Old Testament it is used *i.a.* for the work of the potter and for the creation of man. B. Otzen, in *ThWAT* III (1981) 830, adduces Akkadian *eṣērum*, but obscures the semantic facts by giving "formen" as its first meaning. His mention of the noun *ēṣirum*, "potter" is a mistake, since it is only attested as "seal cutter, carver of reliefs" (*CAD* E 350).

creditor by an Anatolian person or the palace, in which the latter acknowledges a debt" more or less agrees with mine. While *i.*'s are found in Assyrian archives and Assyrian traders can speak of "my *i.*'s", they usually seem to mean" *i.*'s made out to me" or in my possession. Waal stresses that *i.* "does not appear to be attested in purely Assyrian contexts", which must mean written by Assyrians and made out to fellow Assyrians for recording liabilities. I raised the question whether Assyrians too could produce an *i.* above in connection with Kt a/k 488b, my text no. 8, which Waal mentions in her footnote 15, correctly observing that "here an Anatolian official is involved as well". In this letter an Assyrian writes to an Anatolian ruler: "My partner has entered (the silver due from you) in *his i.*," (*ana iṣurtišu uṭahhi*), and not "in *your i.*". Had the Assyrian partner done this himself or is the expression short for "had seen to it that it was entered (by the ruler) in an *i.* for my partner"? And is this also the case in ICK 1, 13 (my text no 16, presented and discussed by Waal on p. 294f.)? But why does the instruction given there to obtain an *i.* for the interest owed by the Anatolian not read "make him (the Anatolian) draw up his *i.*" (**iṣurtušu šēṣirā*; or "let him give you his *i.*"), but uses an imperative of the basic stem, with Assyrians as subject, "draw up his *i.*" (*iṣurtušu eṣrā*)? Is this again short for "see to it that his *i.* is drawn up", or did the Assyrians produce an *i.*, which the Anatolian debtor only had to seal to acknowledge his debt? I considered this possible and therefore suggested that an *i.* was a specific type of sealed cuneiform tablet (*ṭuppum harmum*), because I believed, on the authority of H.G. Güterbock in particular, that in Old Assyrian times the hieroglyphic script was not yet available.

Waal states (291f.) stresses that *eṣērum* and *uṣurtum* in Babylonian basically mean "to draw, to make a drawing" and metaphorically "to make a plan, a regulation", but never refer to writing. She finds this back in OA *uṣurtam eṣārum* meaning "to draw up/ decide on a rule" as "used in strictly Assyrian context", in Kt 79/k 101 (my text no. 18), referring to deciding on/fixing a regulation by the City-Assembly, and in a new text, AKT 6, 231:11, where *iṣurātim eṣṣurum*, used in connection with a last will, would mean "to draw up plans", referring to the shares assigned to the individual heirs (therefore the plural). To explain the fact that verb + noun (*iṣurtam eṣārum*) refer to writing "exclusively in Anatolian context" (p. 292),[60] Waal makes the interesting proposal that it was a loan translation of Hittite/Luwian *gulzattar* GUL-s-, which uses a verb that means "to write" on wood, stone or metal and never on clay. In the absence of Hittite/Luwian texts from this early period it is difficult to prove this, but the Assyrians may have picked it up in oral contacts with their Anatolian customers and used the expression for a way of recording for which their own terminology (they use *lapātum*, rarely *šaṭārum*, for "to write") was not well-suited. If so, it would be another proof of the Assyrian linguistic creativity in coining the terminology needed to describe their commercial activities (see my contribution to Mindlin *et al.*, above note 46).

In my discussion I mentioned in passing the possibility that *i.* was an inscribed wax-coated tablet, and this has now gained some probability, because such a tablet has recently turned up in Old Assyrian sources. Waal believes that *i.* refers to another type of document, because the wax-coated tablet was called *ṭuppum ša iškurim* in Assyrian. But this argument in my opinion is not convincing, as a closer look at the thus far two occurrences shows. The first is in a letter written to Kuliya in Kanesh by his wife in Assur: "All I gave him for A. has been registered in a wax tablet (*ina ṭuppim* [22] *ša i-is-ku-ri-im lapput*; see K.R. Veenhof, *AKT* 5 [Ankara 2010] no. 11:22, with comment). The second is in M.T. Larsen's AKT 6b, 468, an inventory of what seems to be a private chapel, which included among the god's possessions (lines 12-13) *1 ṭuppum ša is-ku-ri-im*. Because of its

60 The contrast she makes between "to write" and "to fix, decide" in my opinion is too strict. For in both texts *i. eṣārum* results in and thus also refers to a written text, a decision or ruling of the City of Assur, sent to Kanesh in an official letter (and subsequently revoked) and testamentary disposition, in Old Assyrian written in record sealed by the testator, his witnesses and testamentary executors, which carefully fixes the shares of each heir (their *uṣurātum*) as we know from preserved ones.

specific Anatolian connection and meaning, it is unlikely that *i.* was used in Assur, where a wax tablet, already attested during the Ur III period, had its "Mesopotamian" name. This also applies to the "wax tablet" in the chapel in Kanesh, which also would not be named *i.* One wonders what a wax-coated tablet, hardly a valuable object (although it could of coarse be made of precious wood or even be inlaid), does in a god's chapel. In the list it is preceded by *1 nikkassū,* which, as indicated by the editor with a reference to *CAD* N/II 229, 4, is known as an emblem of the god Šamaš. In Larsa Šamaš's (large) *nikkassū* were "set up" in his temple (TCL 10, 4:28) or "came down" from it (TCL 11, 173:4), alongside his double axe and his "(weighing) stone", or his weapon, during judicial procedures, when important financial settlements had to be made concerning family property. I suggest that *nikkassū* (probably an object used for calculating and accounting) and *ṭuppum ša iskūrim* were symbols of the god who would see to it that in his presence accounts were settled in a honest and fair way.

This means that *iṣurtum* after all may have been a wax tablet, used by Anatolian officials to record a debt acknowledgment and handed over to their Assyrian creditors. Whether such tablets were inscribed in hieroglyphs is a different question and depends on how well developed this script was in Old Assyrian times. I feel unable to pass a judgment, but it must be clear that, if an *i.* in Old Assyrian refers to a tablet (wax-coated or not) inscribed in hieroglyphs, the script must have been suited to produce detailed records. In the case of ICK 1, 13 (above text no. 16), *e.g.*, it must have stated the amounts of silver and barley owed by Happuala (presumably to be paid for what he had bought), how much interest on both had accrued in four years and how much he now had to pay "each year" (*šattišamma*), either because he was allowed to pay in installments (which then should be mentioned, with their length) or as default interest, which requires the mention of the date when the liability (had) started. In addition, of course, the names of the debtor and the creditor and those of the witnesses had to be mentioned and one wonders how an Assyrian name was rendered.

We must also assume that if an *iṣurtum* was inscribed in hieroglyphs the Assyrian creditor was somehow able to read it (or learn its contents with the help of a translator), to be sure that his claims were properly recorded. And if so, he could also have produced one, as some texts suggest, probably with the help of an Anatolian scribe. Moreover, such a tablet, essentially a type of debt-note, must have been sealed to give it legal validity and the question is how this was done. One of my arguments against considering *i.* a wooden tablet was the complete absence of sealed bullae, originally attached to it (by means of strings), as known from discoveries at Hattuša. It is countered by Waal's observation (p. 308-9) that sealing need not have been done in this way, while she also questions (with Mora) whether the bullae found at Hattuša had been attached to writing boards. But she fails to indicate how *i.*'s then were provided with their essential sealings and here the alternative of a wax coated tablet might provide an explanation. If the Anatolian stamp seals had been impressed in the wax of the tablets, they would have perished together with the tablet itself. We have to consider these questions, if we wish to solve a fascinating puzzle of the ancient Anatolian scribal culture.

A Deed of Manumission and Adoption from the Later Old Assyrian Period*

Its Writing, Language, and Contents in Comparative Perspective

The publication of the text APM 9220[1] in a volume in honor of my teacher hardly needs justification. The document belongs to the poorly represented category of deeds from Assyria during the reign of Šamšī-Adad I (ca. 1800 B.C.[2]) and shows interesting and original features, among others the combining of Assyrian and Babylonian elements of linguistic, administrative, and legal nature. The text therefore should present some interest to the philologist and the legal historian. In a way it links two bodies of texts and fields within Assyriology which happen to reflect our respective main interests, and I trust that Professor Kraus, who guided and stimulated my studies in both of them, will share my pleasure in reading this new text.

THE TEXT (fig. 1)

^{1} ^{p}*E-tel*-KA-^{d}MAR.TU ^{2} DUMU *Pu-ḫa-nu* ^{pd}UTU-GAL ^{3} *ṣú-ḫa-ar-šu pu-us-sú* ^{4} *ú-li-il*$^{!}$ *a-di E-tel*-KA-^{d}[MAR.T]U ^{5} *a-bu-šu ù* ^{mi}*A-ḫa-tu-a* ^{6} *um-ma-šu ba-al-ṭú-ni* ^{7} *it-ta-na-bal-šu-nu-ma* ^{8} *ša pa-la-ḫi-šu-nu i-pu-uš* ^{9} *i+na ur-ki-ti E-tel*-KA-^{d}M[AR.T]U ^{10} *a-bi-šu ù* ^{mi}*A-ḫa-tu-ạ* ^{11} *um-mi-šu 18* GÁN A.ŠA-*lim* ^{12} *i+na* A.GÀR *A-ba-ba-at* ^{13} *1* GUD *i-lá-aq-qé* ^{14} *šum-ma E-tel*-KA-^{d}MAR.TU ^{15} *i-ba-qir-šu 2 ma-na* KÙ.BABBAR ^{16} Ì.LÁ.E *ù šum-ma* ^{d}UTU-GAL ^{17} *i-ir-ti E-tel*-KA-^{d}MAR.TU ^{18} *ù* ^{mí}*A-ḫa-tu-a* ^{19} *i-ra-ḫi-iṣ-ma* (rev.) ^{20} *it-ta-la-ak* ^{21} *i+na* KAR *in-na-ma-ru* ^{22} *a-na* KÙ.BABBAR *in-na-di-in* ^{23} MU ^{d}*A-šur* ^{d}IM ^{24} *ù* ^{d}UTU-*ši*-^{d}IM LU[G]AL ^{25} *ma-ma-an la i-ba-qir*

---

^{26} IGI *Ta-ri-ba-tu[m* DUM]U *Zu-ú-a* ^{27} IGI *Sú-sí-na*-[t]*um* [DU]MU *Te-x-x* ^{28} IGI *E-tel*-KA-^{d}*Ạ-šur* DU[MU] *x [x x x (x)]* ^{29} IGI *Ku-nu-ni-i-zi-x* [x x] ^{30} IGI *Be-lu-ba-ni* DUB.SAR ^{31} IGI *A-pa-pa* DUMU XXX-*ta-a-/a*[r] ^{32} I[T]U *ša ke-na-ti li-mu* ^{33} ^{p}*Iš-me*-^{d}*Da-gan* ^{34} DUMU ^{d}UTU-*ši*-^{d}IM

---

first seal: [N]A_4 *ša Ku-nu-ni-e-x* [ ]

---

1 I am grateful to Professor J. M. Hemelrijk, director of the Allard Pierson Museum, Amsterdam, for his permission to publish the text in this volume, and to my colleague, Professor Houwink ten Cate, for bringing this important tablet to my attention, several years ago.

2 Unfortunately this assignment can only be a provisional, though in my opinion highly probable one, because the Assyrian King list records twice a sequence Šamši-Adad – Išme-Dagan, respectively as kings nos. 39 and 40 and as kings nos. 57 and 58. The latter pair, father and son according to the figures of the King list, must have reigned some 20 years around 1600 B.C. (Middle Chronology). The complete lack of documents from that period – even though it would make our text even more interesting – does not favor this dating. In favor of my assignment I can only point to the negative fact that nothing in orthography, phonology, or morphology of the text seems to require a later dating. Paleographic features cannot be used as an argument. [**Add.** The publication, in 2008, of an OA eponym list that covers the period until ca. 1720 BC, shows that the "eponymy of Išme-Dagan, son of Šamšī-Adad" must be the later one and that our text consequently dates from around 1600 BC].

* Originally published in: G. van Driel et al. (eds), Zikir šumim. Assyriological Studies Presented to F. R. Kraus on the Occasion of his Seventieth Birthday, Leiden, 1982, pp. 359-85.

Fig. 1. APM 9220. From left to right and from top to bottom: obverse, right side, left side with seal impressions, reverse with traces of seal impression at the bottom; upper edge, lower edge with traces of seal impression (two or three figures and a moon crescent), and drawing of the seal impression on the left side. Photographs: Staff.

second seal: [NA$_4$ *š]a* [*Sú-sí-na-tu*][*m*]

third seal: N[A$_4$ *š]a A-pa-pa*

Translation

Etel-pī-Amurrum, son of Puḫānu, manumitted his servant Šamaš-rabi. As long as Etel-pī-Amurrum, his father, and Aḫatu'a, his mother, live he will support them and take good care to obey them. After (the death of) Etel-pī-Amurrum, his father, and Aḫatu'a, his mother, he will receive 18 *iku* of land in the agricultural district of Ababat (and) 1 ox. If Etel-pī-Amurrum reclaims him (as slave) he will pay 2 minas of silver. If Šamaš-rabi repudiates Etel-pī-Amurrum and Aḫatu'a and departs, he may be sold for silver in the commercial district of any town where he is spotted. The oath to Aššur, to Adad, and to king Šamšī-Adad (was sworn); none of them will raise claims.

(names of six witnesses, among which the scribe Bēlu-bāni)
Month: *ša kenāti(m)*, eponymy: Išmē-Dagan son of Šamšī-Adad.

COMPARATIVE MATERIAL

The text, as mentioned above, contains Assyrian as well as Babylonian elements, both in linguistic features and in legal and administrative formulary. A comparison with similar and/or contemporaneous Assyrian and Babylonian documents is desirable in order to bring out its characteristics.

The Assyrian background of the text, as indicated by oath formula and dating, calls for a comparison with Assyrian texts from the beginning of the 2nd millennium B.C. The Old Assyrian texts discovered in *kārum* Kaniš level II, the bulk of the Old Assyrian material, while providing valuable contrasting features, do not offer good parallels. The reasons are that our text is a legal document of a type which is not represented among the predominantly commercial texts from Kültepe and moreover dates from after the floruit of the first and well documented phase of Old Assyrian trade, which came to an end during the reign of Puzur-Aššur II, presumably some time around 1840 B.C. (Middle Chronology). We have to extend our comparison to the slightly later texts available: the few documents from *kārum* Kaniš level I B (a period considered to include the time of ŠamšīAdad's reign) of which transliterations and quotations are available in publications by Balkan, OA texts from Boğazköy and Alişar, and a few isolated texts from the same or a somewhat later period, such as the text published by Gelb and Sollberger[3] (called "later Old Assyrian"), and the isolated marriage contract TIM 4,45, believed to date from before the earliest Middle Assyrian documents and at times qualified as "early Middle Assyrian".[4] We may

---

3 JNES 16 (1957), 173 f., in their article "The first legal document from the later Old Assyrian period". Since the *līmum* is unknown from other sources and no king is mentioned the text has to be dated by circumstantial evidence. The editors arrive at the convincing conclusion that the document is only "a few generations younger than the standard Old Assyrian documents" (p. 175a), which means the beginning of the 18th century B.C. Cf. J. Lewy, *Analecta Biblica* 12 (1959), 226.

4 Qualified as Middle Assyrian in CAD M/2, 319b, *mutūtu*; similarly AHw 8i 3a, *palāḫu(m)* 4, b; Landsberger, *Symbolae M. David* (1965), 105 ad 91, calls it "early Middle Assyrian". The text has been studied by Saporetti in OrAnt 7 (1968), 181 ff ., where he collected evidence indicating a date before the bulk of the MA documents, perhaps the 15th century B.C. Because the text of this document is important for our comparison we add a transliteration, following Saporetti, with one exception (line 8): ^{p}MU-*lib-ši* DUMU DINGIR-*šu-na-ṣir* [2] *ù* ^{mí}*Be-el-ti-a-bi-ša* DUMU.MÍ$^{!}$ [*A]p-pa-[je-e]* [3] *i-na mi-ig-ra-ti-šu-nu* [4] *mu-tu-ut-<ta> ù aš-šu-ut-ta* [5] *id-bu-bu* ^{p}MU-*lib-ši mu-sà* [6] *ù* ^{mí}*Be-el-ti-a-bi-ša aš-ša-sú* [7] *i-na* A.ŠÀ *ù* ŠÀ-*bi a-[lim]* [8] *pa-la-ḫa ša a-ḫu-a-[ḫa]* [9] *i-pu-šu* [10] *šum-ma* MU-*lib-ši la aš-[š]a-ti-mi* [11] *i-qa-áb-bi ½ ma-n[a* K]Ù.BABBAR [12] Ì.LÁ.E [13] *ù šum-ma* ^{mí}*Be-el-ti-a-[b]i-ša* [14] *la mu-ti-mi ta-q[a-á]b-bi* [15] *½ ma-[na* KÙ.BABBA]R [16] *ta-ša-qa-al* (open space) [17] IGI *Ap-pa-je-e* [18] DUMU *A-ta-na-aḫ* [19] IGI *A-[p]il-[K]u-be* [20] DUMU *A-bi*$_4$-KAM-*iš* [21] IGI *A-a-bì-šu* [22] DUMU ÌR-*a-bi*$_4$ [23] IGI ÌR-^{d}*Še-ru-a* [24] DUMU *Bur*-^{d}IM [25] IGI *Uš-šu-rum* DUB.SAR [26] ITU NIN.É.GAL-*lim* [27] *li-mu* ÌR-^{d}*Še-ru-ja*. The reading of the end of line 8 fits better into the available space, and *palāḫum* requires an accusative rather than *ana*.

add to this category a "tablet of unusual type from Tell Asmar", published by Gelb,[5] which contains a large number of typical Old Assyrian traits.

Other texts from the period around 1800 B.C. and originating from Assyria or politically or geographically related areas, such as the Mari texts sent from Assur by Šamšī-Adad or his son Išme-Dagan, the documents from Šušarra, and the texts from Tell al-Rimah do not provide much help. Those originating from Assyria provide clear evidence of the changes in scribal practice and perhaps linguistic situation brought about by Šamšī-Adad, who introduced standard Old Babylonian in his monumental inscriptions[6] and in his royal administration. His and his son's letters discovered at Mari show no genuine "Assyrian" features of orthography, phonology, or morphology.[7] The same holds good for the texts from Šušarra as far as they are known from Læssøe's provisional publications,[8] and for the texts from Tell al-Rimah, including those actually sent there from the city of Assur.[9] None of these deserve the qualification "later Old Assyrian"; they are accordingly not helpful in tracing the gradual infiltration of the Babylonian language and scribal tradition into ancient Assyria.

A comparison with standard Old Babylonian material serves to reveal how many genuinely Assyrian features our text still preserves. Comparing it to other Old Babylonian texts – very early ones or those from so-called "peripheral areas", that preserve certain traits no longer in evidence in standard OB – seems useful because our text takes an intermediate position between Babylonian and Assyrian.

A group of very early OB documents might be adduced showing linguistic features which, as has been repeatedly noted, have parallels in OA. The most important of these features are: the use of the syllabograms GA for *kà*, TI for *dì*, SI for *ṣí/é*, and LAL for *lá*; the single writing of geminated consonants; the use of short forms of *ina* and *ana* (with assimilation of the final *-n*); the preservation of original */a/*, which had become */e/*

5 A tablet of unusual type from Tell Asmar, in JNES 1 (1942), 219 ff., pl. vi. The parallels to OA bear not only on orthography, phonology, and morphology, but also on such features as the graphic form of the signs, rulings between the lines, and the use of a word dividing wedge. Gelb suggests the possibility that we have to assume, beside the main Old Assyrian dialect, "small regions, each with its own local peculiarities in writing and language" (p. 224). One of the local varieties may be represented by the OA texts from Gasur (HSS 10 nos. 223-227; cf. the analysis by J. Lewy, JAOS 58 (1938), 456ff). Note that one of the characteristics of the Tell Asmar tablet, the writing of the name of the moon-god as *Sí-in*, also found at Gasur (HSS 10, 224: 8), is now attested three more times in OA texts from Kültepe *kārum* II; see Balkan, *Observations* (1955), 69 note 24.

6 Gelb, OIP 27, 42 note 1.

7 See Gelb's cautious statement in *Language* 33 (1957), 199: "(c) letters coming from Assyria, which may reflect influences of the Old Assyrian dialect". Neither he, nor Finet, whose grammar he is reviewing, could point out examples proving such Assyrian influence. The Mari syllabary, moreover, does not comprise typically OA syllabograms.

8 See for these texts the provisional remarks by J. Læssøe, *The Shemshara Tablets* (1959), 91 note 6. The "Assyrian" features noted with some reserve are concentrated in three letters, SH 812, 822, and 827, all from the same scribe. "Assyrian" features probably are the use of the syllabograms ME = *mi*, BE = *pè* (SH 812: 55), and EL = il_5, and the use of the short, assimilated form of the preposition *ina* (a feature, however, also found in the Diyala texts and elsewhere in OB). The subjunctive ending *-nu* (SH 812:6) is unlike Assyrian *-(u)ni*, and the spelling *ma-ra-šu* ("his son") shows an *a*-vowel in the first syllable, which is exceptional in OA (see Gelb, OIP 27, 22 f.). The fact that the very scribe of these texts spelled king Šamšī-Adad's name *Sa-am-si-*ᵈIM does not point to an Assyrian scribal tradition (see Læssøe, op. cit., 72 note 58). The letters, in fact, do not seem to originate from Assur.

9 The texts from Tell Rimah, dating to roughly our period, show no traces of Assyrian influence, even though that city is not too far from Aššur. The use of a number of "exceptional" syllabograms, listed by Mrs Dalley, *The Old Babylonian texts from Tell al Rimah* (1976), p. 37, is rightly not claimed as such. But her claim, on the same page, that the three letters nos. 120-122, sent by Iltani's sister from Aššur, would contain "distinct characteristics that may be attributed to the current dialect of Aššur" is not convincing. I cannot detect any typically Assyrian trait in either orthography, phonology, or morphology. There is only contextual evidence supporting an Assyrian origin, like the mention of the god Aššur in no. 122:4 (where the reading DINGIR *Ka*?*-ni*?*-iš*ᵏⁱ is impossible) and the occurrence of ᵘʳᵘ*kigamlum* (121:16, 21), which thus far was known only from OA.

in standard OB in particular phonetic contexts; and the use of the personal pronoun *šūt* and the negative particle *ula*.[10]

Some of these features have even been considered as betraying some measure of Old Assyrian influence.[11] This interpretation, however, is not convincing, because the texts in question contain other features too, which differ from standard OB as well as from OA writing conventions and morphology.[12] A partial, selective OA influence is rather unlikely, as all features seem to be part of one scribal tradition.

Moreover, there are indications, collected by Larsen,[13] that some of the typical OA writing conventions (notably the preference for certain syllabograms) are themselves the result of a gradual development. Typical OA syllabograms like DÍ = *dí, tí*, LAL = *lá*, and also ÁB = *áb* start replacing older TI = *tì, dì*, LA = *la*, and AB = *ab* in Assyrian royal inscriptions only towards the end of the 20th century B.C., too late to have influenced the writers of the early OB texts mentioned above.[14]

We might better explain the similarities noted by assuming the existence of an older, shared scribal tradition, basically the one current during the Ur III period for writing Akkadian,[15] though we cannot exclude regional differences (*e.g.* between North and South) even that early. The political and hence administrative fragmentation after ca. 2000 B.C. paved the way for increasing differentiation, observable in certain regions, dialects, or groups of texts. The very early OB texts, mentioned above, are one separate group, well attested at Ešnunna and called "archaic OB" by R. Whiting in his forthcoming edition of early OB letters from that city.[16] Old Assyrian was another development, becoming standardized during the second half of the 20th century B.C. The texts from Mari belonging

10 See for a listing of the relevant texts and an analysis of features J. Goodnick-Westenholz, JNES 33 (1974) p. 411 (review of Kraus, AbB 5) and A. Westenholz, BiOr 35 (1978; publ. 1980) 163f. with notes 25 f.

11 Westenholz, op. cit., note 25, in connection with PBS 1/2, 1 + PBS 7, 1, PBS 5, 156, and AbB 5, 156.

12 Such as the use of the syllabograms TU for *tu*, MI for *mi*, TI for *di* and GI for *qì*, plene-writings like *mi-i-ma, na-a-dì*, and a subjunctive ending *-na*.

13 M. T. Larsen, *The Old Assyrian City State and its Colonies* (1976), 144 with note 109. Ilušuma only uses AB; ÁB appears for the first time with Irišum in the copy of his inscription found in Kültepe, line 22; the word is broken in the parallel AOB 1, V, 12: 10.

14 Westenholz, op. cit. note 48, notes that Sarriqum's inscription from Aššur (KAH II:2) is not written in Old Akkadian but in Babylonian and shows no Assyrian features. This is correct, but we should note that the distinctive OA features make their written appearance only ca. 100 years later. There is no feature in Šalimaḫum's inscription (AOB 1, III, 1), neither in orthography nor in language, which makes it OA (note the use of *i-pu-uš* and *i-ri-iš-su-ma*, "he asked from him", against OA *e-ri-šuma* (*erišsuma*) e.g. in TC 3, 53:25). Ilušuma's inscription (ZA 43, 115) shows some OA features in orthography and phonology, but they are basically those shared by OA with "archaic OB" (see for the use of the dual pers. pron. in this text R. M. Whiting, JNES 31 (1972), 331 f.). The various copies of the inscription show a hesitation as to the use of the 1st or 3rd person and the choice of the prefix vowel: *i-zi-ir-ma/ e-zi-ir-ma*, line 26, and *a-zu-uz/ i-zu-uz*, line 29. The main copy, however, followed by Weidner, has *i-zi-ir-ma ... a-zu-uz*, which means an *i*-prefix for the 1st pers. sing.; all copies, moreover, write *i-pu-uš* in line 22, a writing still attested in some of Irišum's texts.

15 See for reasons for considering the Akkadian of the Ur III-period a separate dialect, with its own writing conventions, Westenholz, op. cit. note 24.

16 I am grateful to Dr. Whiting for allowing me to read the part containing the linguistic analysis. [**Add.** See now R.M. Whiting, *Old Babylonian Letters from Tell Asmar* (AS 22, Chicago 19870), esp. its Introduction, pp. 5-22, parts 6-8, on writing and language. Note the statement on pp. 17-18, "Although most of the features that characterize archaic Old Babylonian are also found in Old Assyrian, there is no need to consider these features as "Assyrianisms" since almost all of them can be traced back to Old Akkadian"].

to the so-called *Šakkanakku*-period (20th century B.C.) exhibit still another set of scribal conventions and dialect traits.[17]

WRITING AND GRAMMAR

In what follows we use the following abbreviations for the various texts: U(r): Akkadian texts from Ur III; Š: Mari texts from the *šakkanakku* period; OA : standard Old Assyrian; G(eneva): text mentioned in note 3; D(iyala): text mentioned in note 5; T: TIM 4, 45, mentioned in note 4; A : APM 9220, published here.

Paleography

The absence of paleographic studies of OB sign forms analysing temporal and/or regional differences limits the scope of our comparison. In general our text is fairly similar to G: both deviate from OA in the omission of the word-dividing wedge and in avoiding slanting wedges and upward slanting lines; A lacks rulings between the lines, a feature shared by G and OA. While a number of sign-forms are also very similar in G and A, and both alternate freely between UD and EREN in writing the name of Šamaš, there are a number of differences, tabulated below and compared to OA (which is practically identical to D, in other respects as well, see note 5).[18]

It is not easy to draw chronological conclusions from the differences between G and A – both apparently younger than OA – but a comparison between the forms of ḪI, GU (cf. BU in G:42), and AḪ suggests an earlier date for G. The absence of any information about the origin of both texts, and the fact that G can hardly be older than A, which dates from Šamsī-Adad's reign, forces us to account for the differences by assuming either scribal idiosyncracy or rather a certain conservatism on the part of G's scribal school, and/or Babylonian influence on A, which is also evident in writing and language, as will be shown below. A comparison with T, which uses sign-forms in the Babylonian tradition, shows that this text must be somewhat younger: T has the same form of ŠÀ as A, but its MU with only four "Winkelhaken", its ÌR with a single unbroken vertical, its ITU with two horizontals and a broken vertical, and its form of AḪ in line 18 are revealing. A comparison between A and texts from Kültepe IB is hardly possible in the absence of cuneiform copies, and we can only use Anum-ḫirbi's letter, assuming that it has been written by an Assyrian scribe. This text shows some sign-forms deviating from standard OA, such as ÙḪ, IG, UB, and LAM, but a comparison remains problematic. The clearest differences between standard OA forms and those occurring in later texts from the I B period (primarily represented by the OA texts from Boğazköy) are found in the signs ŠÙR, LAM, and EL, but none of these signs occurs in A.[19] The forms of KÙ.BABBAR (15,

17 See H. Limet, *Textes administratifs de l'époque des šakkanakku*, ARM 19 (1976), with his study "Observations sur la grammaire des anciennes tablettes de Mari", in *Syria* 2 (1975), 37-52, and the important review by Westenholz, mentioned in note 10. There are strong reasons for keeping the inscriptions on the Mari liver models – notwithstanding correspondences in writing and language – apart from the *šakkanakku*-texts; as pointed out by Gelb, RA 50 (1956), 3 and Westenholz, op. cit. note 9, they do not constitute a uniform body of texts, combining material and scribal traditions from various sources. This applies also to their contents, as shown by D. Snell in his "The Mari livers and the omen tradition", JANES 6 (1974), 117-123. As noted by Westenholz, the inscriptions of the rulers of Mari from this period show almost no local peculiarities, a fact which links up with the observations made in note 14.

18 OA sign forms, of course, show some measure of variation, perhaps in consequence of a gradual evolution over the years, certainly related to the quality of the scribe: professional, at times "conservative" hands can be distinguished from more cursive ones, and careful writing from coarse writing, probably by the merchants themselves with only a basic training in cuneiform (see also Larsen, *The Old Assyrian City-State*, 304 f.).

19 See for the more cursive LAM, *Anum-ḫirbi* line 30 and KBo 9 no. 6: 5.8; for EL *Anum-ḫirbi* line 17 and KBo 9 no. 6:21; and for ŠÙR KBo 9 no. 5:34 (in this more cursive form of ŠÙR the small horizontal wedge, normally drawn in the middle of three "Winkelhaken" in the central part of the sign – see e.g. BIN 6 1:1 – has disappeared; an intermediate stage is perhaps represented by G, where this wedge has moved to the right, so that the sign now ends with two horizontals, see lines 14, 18). Note in the texts from Boğazköy also the cursive forms of KAM (KBo 9 nos. 5:27 and 27:r.9') and NAM (no. 5:34).

OA
G
A
OA
G
A
52 ITU
70 NA
75 NU
101 SUR
142 I
151 LUGAL
206 DU
298 AL
335 DA
391 ḪI
381 UD
384 ŠÀ
401 ḪAR
468 KÙ.B.
559 GU
589 ḪA

			U	Š	OA	G	A	T	OB
1	AŠ	aš	+	-	(-)	0	0	+	+
192	ÁŠ	áš	+	+	+	0	0	-	+
93	AB	ab/p	+	+	+	-	0	+	+
244	ÁB	áb/p	+	-	+	+	0	+	-
4	BA	pá	+	+	+	+	-	-	-
153	PA	pa	+	-	(-)	-	+	+	+
42	BE	be	+	+	+	+	+	+	+
42	BE	bi_4	-	-	+	+	-	-	-
140	BI	bi, pí	+	+	+	-	+	+	+
122	NE	bí	+	-	(-)	-	-	-	(+)
223	WA	pi	+	-	-	-	0	0	+
191	DA	da, ṭa	+	+	+	+	+	0	+
102	TA	ta	+	-	+	0	+	+	+
266	DI	di, ṭi	+	0	-	-	+	0	+
270	TIN	dí, tí	(+)	(-)	+	+	-	0	-
46	TI	dì, ti	+	+	+	-	+	+	+
218	TE	te	+	+	-	-	0	0	+
135	DU	tù, ṭù	+	-	+	+	-	-	+
135	DU	du	+	-	+	+	0	0	+
30	TU	tu, ṭú	+	+	(-)	-	+	+	+
27	LA	la	+	-	+	-	+	+	+
277	LAL	lá	+	+	+	+	+	-	-
306	EL	il_5	(-)	-	+	0	-	0	(+)
306	EL	el	+	+	+	0	0	0	+
134	IL	il	+	+	-	0	+	0	+
287	ME	mì	+	+	+	+	-	-	-
248	MI	mi	+	-	-	-	+	+	+
170	GA	qá	+	+	+	+	0	-	+
170	GA	kà	+	+	+	+	0	0	(-)
15	KA	ka	(-)	-	-	-	0	0	+
36	QA	šál	+	+	+	0	0	0	-
36	QA	qa	-	-	-	-	0	+	+
316	ZA	sà, ṣa, za	+	+	+	+	0	+	+
76	SA	sa	+	-	(+)	-	0	0	+
266	DI	sá	+	+	+	0	-	0	-
202	ŠA	ša	+	(-)	+	+	+	+	+
85	SI	si/e	-	+	-	-	0	0	+
85	SI	ší/é	+	+	+	+	-	-	-
59	ZI	sí/é	+	+	+	+	+	0	+
261	LIM	ši	+	(+)	(-)	(-)	+	+	+
212	ŠE	še	+	-	(-)	-	0	+	+

A comparison between sets of representative syllabograms of, from left to right, Ur III Akk. (MAD II, 47ff.; = U), Mari *šakkanakku*-period (ARM 19, 152ff. with Westenholz, BiOr. 35, 161 f.; = Š), standard Old Assyrian (OA), later Old Assyrian texts from G(eneva), A(msterdam) and (in) T(IM 4), and standard Old Babylonian. The numbers refer to *Syllabar*^{3} and are also used in MAD II and ARM 19. The meaning of the symbols used in the chart is:

+ attested in full use;

(+) attested, but used only in special positions and on a limited scale (*e.g.* NE = bí in the address of letters);

- not attested and apparently no used, as the syllable is rendered by another syllabogram;

(-) not used except in very few, rare occasions (statistically rare, as the OA values mentioned below in note 28, or limited to a particular position, as OA LIM = *ši* only in ^{d}UTU-*ši*);

0 no evidence, mostly because of the limitations of the text corpus; the syllable in question is not written with another syllabogram.

See for details the syllabaries mentioned, and the remarks in notes 20, 24, 26, and 28. The facts mentioned in the last column present a simplified picture, as the various OB conventions (von Soden-Röllig, *Syllabar*^{3}, xxxix: 2, a-k) have not been distinguished.

22) and the ligature I + NA (with the "full" NA; 9, 12, 21; similar ligatures in Old Hittite texts, see Balkan, *Schenkungs-Urkunde ... Inandik* (1973), 71 and 96) deserve attention, and eventually may provide a clue. A, like G, uses the younger form of AN (two horizontals crossed by one vertical) which is rare in standard OA (attested *e.g.* in ATHE 3: 18).

[*Addendum.* That text A, as noted in the addendum to footnote 2, dates from around 1600 BC and thus most probably is younger than G, calls for a revision of some of the conclusions reached here and this affects also the position of A in the comparative survey of the syllabary. Its implications cannot be worked out here, but the comparison shows that G is either older or represents an older scribal tradition, since it does not use the signs PA, TI, TU and MI, attested in A; see also the Corrigenda and addenda at the end of this article].

Syllabary

In matters of syllabary the position of our text is much clearer. As the comparative table on the preceding page shows – a representative selection of syllabograms chosen for illustrating continuity and diversification – the syllabary of A, almost identical to that of T, is basically that of standard OB. A number of syllabograms are of course not represented in the limited number of words of A and T, but the blanks in the chart should not bother us. Both texts have only one clear deviation from the OB column: LAL for *lá* in A, and ÁB for *áb* in T. Both must be considered vanishing traces of the Old Assyrian scribal practice, which is still fully alive in G, even though this text most probably dates from about the same time as A.[20] In fact the syllabary of G is even more "purely" OA than OA itself. In all cases where OA has a redundancy, offering an option between two syllabograms with equal phonetic values – AB/ÁB, DA/TA, LA/LAL, SÁ/ZA, IŠ/EŠ, TIN/TI – G always uses only the one which is statistically dominant in OA as it took shape during the 20th century B.C. (see note 13).

The presence of some options in OA shows that even this simplified syllabary carries along some historical ballast, going back to the Ur III syllabary still basically in use in the oldest OA royal inscriptions. The standard OA syllabary favored signs like AB, LA, TIN, EL, BE (= bi_4), ME, GA, ZA, and DU, and the fact that they are all simpler and smaller than their "rivals" is certainly not accidental.[21] The redundancy in the group used for rendering the sibilants is smaller than it appears to be: SA for /sa/ is rare, DI = *sá* is not too frequent, and there is a preference for ZA = *sà*, a syllabogram which at the same time is the only one used for /ṣa/ and /za/. IGI with the value /*ši*/ is only used in the combination ᵈUTU-*ši*, while ŠE is extremely rare, though it is used as a logogram in ŠE = *uṭṭatum*, "grain", and ŠE-*um*, "barley".[22]

---

20 [This fits the fact that we now know that A is a much younger text, perhaps even somewhat younger than G, see the Addendum above]. The syllabary of the late OA text discovered by Kocher (JNES 16, 175b) is almost identical to that of G: note ME.EŠ for personal plur. (also in G), IŠ = *mil*, and ŠE = *še* (both in PNs), and the occasional use of the "Personenkeil" (not in G). The text accordingly shows somewhat more Babylonian influence than G, but far less than A. I am most grateful to Dr. Köcher for allowing to mention these facts on the basis of a provisional transliteration available in the material for the CAD. [This text is VAT 19864, for which I refer to the Corrigenda and Addenda at the end of this article]. Another late OA text which should be mentioned here is the inscription of Puzur-Sîn (Landsberger, JCS 8, 32 f.). This text, while using a number of typically OA syllabograms (ME = *mi*, DU = *tù*, SI = *ší*, TIN = *dí*), also knows Babylonian or at least not OA ones (KA = *ka*, QA = *qa*, MI = *mi*, PA = *pa*, TE = *te*(?), AS = *aš*). While the text constantly writes mimation correctly, occasional writings of geminated consonants and the use of IA = *ia* in *pa-ni-ia* (IV, 7) also indicate southern influence and/or a somewhat later date (cf. Landsberger, *op. cit.*, note 6).

21 The OA preference for short signs links up with the use of less space consuming ways in the writing of numerals: OA has special signs for 1/4 and 1/6 and frequently writes numerals which are 2, 1 or ½ unit smaller than the next round figure as "x minus y", e.g. 59 = *60* LA *1* (where "1" nicely fits into the open space created by the vertical and horizontal of the LÁ-sign).

22 Von Soden and Rollig, *Syllabar*³, no. 212, do not mention ŠE = *še*, which is attested in BIN 6 125:19 (*še-še-ra-ma*). TE is not attested, a fact which favours the reading *Ḫu-up!-ša-lim* in AS 16, pl. 15 (OA votive sword).

Š also reduced the redundancies of U, but with different preferences, as shown by the non-occurrence or rejection of TA, ÁB, DU, EL, and TIN. It is difficult to say whether this was an innovative tendency or the effect of older, regional writing conventions, independent of Ur III.[23] If we accept the modifications proposed by Westenholz,[24] the redundancies in Š become few indeed (such as RU = *ri* and URU = *rí*). Further peculiarities are the (imperfect) devices – notably the use of syllabograms like U, É and MÁ – for rendering "weak consonants", as discussed by Limet and Westenholz; the use of such devices in OA cannot be established.[25] In general one may say that both Š and OA streamlined the copious Ur III syllabary, but in different ways. OA also developed a few special syllabograms, like KIB = tur_4 and the frequent use of BE for bi_4; Š preserved more of the variety of Ur III syllabograms, in particular of the CVC-type, and in general makes a slightly more archaic impression;[26] note that it uses neither TA nor ŠA.

In analyzing and comparing syllabaries we should be conscious of the fact that every scribe with reasonable training knew many more syllabograms than he normally used. The study of basic Sumerian logograms and of the frequently archaic and/or logographic names of gods, places, months, and persons provided him with a repertoire which he would not normally use in the syllabic spelling of his own dialect. But there was nothing to prevent him from occasionally using such less common signs. Rare OA syllabograms like TU = *tu*, GUR = *kúr*, ḪAL = *ḫal*, LÀL = *làl*, LUM = *lum*, É = *é*, ÚR = *úr*, ṢI = *ṣi*, MAḪ = *maḫ*, and NI = *zal* are all attested once or twice in names, but statistics make it perfectly clear that they did not belong to the standard OA syllabary. We have to take this factor into account when evaluating the syllabary of Š, where (apart from the lexical problems) the number of syllabograms based on personal names is rather large and accounts for a number of entries in the list.[27] Note that in G, using the purest possible OA syllabary, two remarkable deviations are due to occurrences in names (*Ri-ši-ia* with exceptional LIM = *ši* and IA = *ja*, and ᵈAG = ᵈ*Nabium* (lines 39, 44)), perhaps of Babylonians with their names written according to the Babylonian tradition (even though the scribe, using ᵈAG in his own name, produced a purely OA text!). Note in T the remarkable alternation between the writings *Še-ru-a* and *Še-ru-ja* (lines 23 and 27).

Rare syllabic values are occasionally used outside names as well, for reasons hard to establish, though lack of space on the edges of tablets no doubt sometimes was one; note the number of rare OB syllabograms used by the scribe who produced the liver model CT 6 pl. 1 ff., and who had to squeeze his omens within the narrow limits of his squares. OA scribes in rare cases used syllabograms like AŠ, BE = *bat,* IL, PA, KIR, KUR = gur_{16}, U, LÁL = la_5, ÌR = *ir*, KIŠ = *kis*, and the pseudo-syllabogram KA in NÍG.KA-*sú* = *nikkassū*.[28]

---

23 See I.J. Gelb, "Thoughts about Ibla", in *Syro-Mesopotamian Studies* I, 1 (1977), esp. p. 13 ff., for the existence of an ancient "Kish tradition", which reached Mari in an early stage and provides links with writing conventions also used at Ebla, but which differs from those at home in early Sumerian Southern Mesopotamia.

24 Op. cit. (note 10) p. 163, where he proposes to eliminate the syllabograms SA, ŠA, SU_4 and SU (?); only LIM = *ši* provides a doublet alongside SI = *ší*; DI = *sá* is used for /ša/ and /śa/.

25 See Hecker, *Grammatik* §22 esp. sub c and d.

26 There are, however, doubts about some of the values listed in Limet's syllabary, especially in cases where one could assume a logogram with phonetic complement instead of two syllabograms; cf. a case like his no. 248: MI = *ṣíl* in MI-*lá*, interpreted as *Ṣíl-lá*, but perhaps rather MI^lá as long as *ṣíl* is not attested in other combinations. Note that no. 298: SAL = *šál* should be omitted; the sign according to the copy of text no. 267 is QA, already listed as *šál* under no. 36.

27 The same question can be asked concerning the Ur III syllabary as registered in MAD II. Only a substantial increase of textual material will make it possible to distinguish rare and isolated syllabograms from "standard" ones, as in OA.

28 See for evidence Von Soden-Rollig, *Syllabar*³. BE = *bat* is attested in G:1; KIŠ = *kis* in c/k 440:52 (*ra-kis*); ZUR = *ṣár* (no. 255, Syllabar³, Nachträge) also in TC 3, 276:11; ICK 2, 107b:5: *iš*-DI, is a hybrid form, mixing up *iš-tí* and KI!. Note exceptional LÚ in L 29-561 (HUCA 39 (1968), 17): L.E. 53: *a-lá* LÚ *taškunanni*, where lack of space on the edge caused the use of LÚ.

Orthography and grammar

In matters of orthography the following features may be noted. Geminated consonants are regularly written in non-verbal forms: *šum-ma* (14), *um-ma(mi)-šu* (6, 11), *pu-us-sú* (3), but note *ma-ma-an* (25). In verbal forms the reduplication of the middle consonant marking the present tense is not rendered (eight cases, lines 7, 8, 15, 19-22, 25), with the exception of the writing *i-lá-aq-qé* (13). But geminated consonants serving as indicators of verbal stems other than G – only *ú-li-il* (4) is an exception – are duly written twice: *it-ta-na-bal* (Gtn, 7), *it-ta-la-ak* (Gt, 20), *in-na-ma-ru* and *in-na-di-in* (N, 21-22). This looks like a conscious effort to reduce ambiguities (the duratives and the praet. D have additional markers allowing identification). Note that G (JNES 16, 1 74b) and the text mentioned in note 20 (*an-ni-im*, line 16; *šar-ra-nim*, line 27) both have two cases of geminated consonants expressed in writing, but that in G *ù-ša-be-ú* (tablet, 24) alternates with *ù-ša-áb-be-ú* (env., 24).

Evidence as to mimation is difficult to evaluate. Where mimation is written (lines 11, 26, 27, and with seal no. 2) it is with a CVC-sign. This is also the way T writes mimation in lines 25, 26, while its lines 4 and 27 show clear omission of mimation. A omits it in the PN *Be-lu-ba-ni* (30) and twice in line 32: *ki-na-ti* and *li-mu.* Balkan, *Observations* 42 with note 9, observes that in texts from Kültepe I B there is a "beginning of the omission of the rigid mimation rules of the Old Assyrian dialect". G has five cases where mimation is omitted alongside eight cases where it is written, and Gelb, OIP 27, 19 f., notes the same feature for the OA texts from Alişar. The texts from Boğazköy, on the other hand, regularly write mimation, as does the text mentioned in note 20 (6 times). Garelli[29] has rightly questioned some of the facts and in particular their use for chronological purposes, pointing out that occasional omission of mimation is already attested in texts from level II of Kültepe, and that the evidence from level I B has to be used with caution, the omission probably being (also) due to the activity of less well trained scribes, perhaps of Anatolian extraction. This does not mean that the observation that "rigid mimation rules" apply in the texts from level II is not correct, but it calls attention to the role of the scribe. We may assume that mimation was being dropped increasingly by Old Assyrian speakers and the question is only to what extent and how soon this was being reflected in writing. As in comparable cases[30] we must assume that mimation, even after its disappearance, was still being written by various scribes with various degrees of consistency, dependent on their professional conservatism, age, and schooling, and in some words and in some combinations (with CVC-syllabograms) longer than in others. We may note that texts from Kültepe I B and Boğazköy consistently write *li-mu-um* and preserve mimation in the names of months; G and the text quoted in note 20 also write *li-mu-um*, while A and all texts from Mari during the period of Assyrian domination write *li-mu.* A writes the month name *ša ki-na-ti*, a feature also attested twice in texts from Alişar (OIP 27 nos. 18B:10' and 29:3'). It is difficult to draw chronological conclusions from these facts, although it is clear that general omission of mimation asks for a later date.[31]

We further note the following scribal features in A: *A-ḫa-tu-a* and not *A-ḫa-tu-ia* (5),[32] and *urkīti* for *warkīti* (9), following the OA conventions. Deviations from these conventions

---

29 *Les Assyriens en Cappadoce* (1963), 53 ff.

30 E.g. in the transition from Old Aramaic to Imperial Aramaic. We witness differences between the orthography of the professional scribes of official documents (from Elephantine) and that of private writers of personal letters, as the Hermopolis Papyri (see Porten-Greenfield, ZAW 80 (1968), 219 ff.). The phoneme /ḏ/ rendered by the grapheme *z* in Old Aramaic, started to be written with *d* following an evolution in pronunciation (6th century B.C.). Very common, frequently written words like the pronouns *znh, z'*, and *zy*, continue to be written according to the traditional orthography for quite some time. The (mis)use of such differences in writing, e.g. for dating the Aramaic parts of the Old Testament, is a warning example.

31 This rule should not be reversed. The Puzur-Sîn inscription (see note 20), younger than most of the texts discussed here, consistently writes mimation. Note that the writing *áb šar-ra-nim* in the text quoted in note 20, seems to be a mistake or hypercorrection; the common OA form of the month name, *ab šarrāni*, is normally considered a plural.

32 See for this feature JNES 16 (1957), 174a, C. Saporetti, OrAnt 7 (1968), 182 f., and *Onomastica Medio-Assira* II (1970), 91, 1 F.

are: no "vowel harmony" (6, 21; observed in G, but equally abandoned in T); three times a "Personenkeil" (1, 2, 33; not in G, occasionally in the text of note 20); the verbal form *išaqqal* rendered by the logogram Ì.LÁ.E, and the use of logograms not attested in OA: MU instead of *nīš*, KAR for *kà-ar*, NA_4 instead of KIŠIB,[33] ITU instead of ITU.KAM,[34] and the use of A.GÀR and A.ŠÀ not attested in OA.[35]

Grammatical features to be qualified as Assyrian are: the subjunctive (*adi*) *balṭuni* (6), the object suffix in *ittanabbalšunuma* (7), and the negative particle *la* (25). Babylonian features on the other hand are: *ippuš* (8; not *eppaš*) and *innaddin* (22; not *innaddan*). Similar traits betray the Assyrian background of T: the prefix *ta* for verbal forms 3rd pers. fem. sing. (*taqabbi*, 14; *tašaqqal*, 16).[36] The presence of such features shows that essentials of Assyrian morphology could be preserved in texts which are strongly "Babylonianized" in matters of syllabary and orthography.

A is sealed, a feature not attested for OA tablets from Kültepe level II, but not uncommon for tablets from level I B, where, however, it may be an Anatolian innovation. The tablet G, though provided with a sealed envelope, also bears seals on the left edge, but it lacks inscriptions accompanying anepigraphic seals, attested on A. This feature is known from OB, especially from Middle and Northern Babylonia, as numerous examples from Sippar (and occasionally Nippur) attest; the inscriptions are in smaller signs, as is the case in A, and consist of the name of the seal owner, which may be preceded by KIŠIB. In text A the names are preceded by NA_4.[37]

VOCABULARY AND FORMULARY

The terminology of A confirms its mixed character; alongside well known OB terms we meet words and clauses which reflect an Assyrian background: they contrast with contemporary OB terminology and recur in Middle Assyrian texts. We can make the following observations.

Manumission

The clause stating the manumission uses the Babylonian terminology. It has an exact parallel in CT 4, 42:5 (*pussu ullil*, in a deed of adoption and manumission), and its Sumerian counterpart (sag.ki.ni in.dadag) is attested in BE 6/2, 8:6 (VAB 5 no. 23) and PBS 8/2, 137:5. Most OB texts use this *terminus technicus* for manumission in its abbreviated form: *ullulum* alone.[38] By contrast, Assyrian documents never use *ullulum* but have *zakku'um*,

33 The reading of the inscriptions accompanying the seal impression as NA_4 *ša PN* is tentative; *ša* seems fairly clear with no. 2, and the sign preceding the traces of *ša* with no. 3 cannot be KIŠIB.

34 The same feature in G, T, the text mentioned in note 20, and in texts from Mari.

35 This may be accidental, due to the nature of the texts which do not deal with landed property. Note, however , that OA regularly uses GÁN for *eqlum*, while A uses GÁN, alongside A.ŠÀ, as a surface measure. The writing A.ŠÀ-*lim* provides no clues for date or origin, as stated recently by R. Frankena, SLB 4 (1978), 18 ad 8. The use of more logograms is anyhow typical for later OA texts, cf. ḪA.LA in G, 9 and MEŠ in G, A, T, and the text mentioned in note 20.

36 Another typically Assyrian trait in T is the spelling of the abstract formation as *aššutta*. The text mentioned in note 20 betrays its Assyrian origin also by the subjunctive ending *-uni* (4) and by the use of the negative particle *la* (21).

37 According to CAD K 546, b, 1', NA_4 alone is restricted to Nuzi, where it seems to be an abbreviation of the also attested NA_4.KISIB. NA_4 *ša PN*, if correct, would be unique, not being recorded in CAD K loc. cit. See for the OB practices in this respect J. Renger in McG. Gibson and R. D. Biggs (eds.) *Seals and Sealing in the Ancient Near East* (Bibl. Mes. 6; Malibu 1977), 76 and 82, notes 21 f. (rare examples from the Diyala region [19th century B.C.], not attested at Ešnunna).

38 See for references CAD E 82, *elēlu* 2, d; add now Szlechter TJDB pl. x (MAH 15.954):5 (*ullilši*) and CT 48, 33:16' (GEME IR *ul ullal ana kaspim ul inaddin*; stipulation concerning inheritance gift by a father to his daughter, who is a Šamaš *nadītu*). See for *pūtam ullulum* Kraus, *Edikt*, 202 ad (10), and for its interpretation as referring to a symbolic unction Veenhof, BiOr 23 (1966), 310b.

notably KAJ 7:8 (*ina amuttiša uzakkiši*; a slave girl married off). Texts from Ugarit also prefer *zakûm* in such cases, cf. in particular RS 16.267 and 8.208, edited in PRU III p. 110.[39]

The clause of lines l-4a describes an action which has taken place, using the normal word order: subject, object, verb. Many OB deeds of manumission start in a different way, with a nominal sentence which has declarative force: "B is the son of A", followed by "A manumitted him". This formulary is well attested for Babylonian contracts from the north (Sippar, Dilbat: VAB 5 nos. 23-27, Szlechter TJDB no. 2).[40] Our text has a different formulary, comparable to the following deeds from Nippur (nos. 1-3) and Larsa (? no. 4):

1. BE 6/2, 8: *A* (former owner) *B* geme.ni.im ama.ar.gi$_4$.ni in.gar sag.ki.ni in.dadag;
2. PBS 8/2, 137: (kišib.nam.sik[il.la.ni]) *B* sag.geme *A* (former owner) ama.ar.gi$_4$.ni in.gar sag.ki.ni in.dadag;
3. TIM 4, 15: *B* ÌR *A* (former owner) *abbuttašu ugallimma*;
4. BIN 2, 76: *B* ÌR *A* (former owner) *ina maḫar Šamaš addurāršu iškun pūtam elletam iddiššum.*[41]

In these texts "A has manumitted (removed the slave-mark of) B, his slave (girl)" is the only translation possible. Where the deeds of manumission, mentioned above, have two sentences – a nominal sentence in which A is the rectum in a genitive compound, and a verbal sentence of which he is the subject – our texts try to combine them into one. The transformation, however, is somewhat strained: our text *e.g.* does not read *A pūt B ṣuḫarišu ullil*, but adds *ṣuḫāršu* as an appositive to the object. In 1), where the word order is comparable to that of our text, the object is followed by the appositive geme.ni.im, which has the copula; in 2)-4) the word order, with the former slave in initial position, is that of the initial nominal sentence mentioned above. Nevertheless, we can only translate them as one verbal sentence, as is also shown by the fact that, in contradistinction to the deeds from the north, the former owner is mentioned only once, while a change of subject is unlikely.

This new formulary is not a scribal whim, or simply an attempt to streamline the formulary. The omission of the sentence "B is the son of A", a sentence with declarative force, is for a special reason: in none of the texts 1)-4) was the former slave adopted as son or daughter by the person who manumitted him. In 1) the slave girl paid to obtain her freedom, and the text only mentions that a deed of manumission was drawn up, as was the case in 2). In 4) the manumitted slave has to perform service and corvé duties like the sons of his former owner (*ilkam u ḫarrānam mala marē A illak*!), but he is not adopted and there is no provision about an inheritance; the text only states that he will no longer be called "slave". In 3), finally, the slave is adopted, but not by his former owner, but by the latter's married son.

One deed of manumission from Nippur does start with a nominal sentence, stating the former status of the slave-girl manumitted:

---

39 See for references CAD Z, *zakû* 5, a (p. 29), and for the use of the basic stem ibid. p. 27, 2, a. Add now PRU 6, 45:28. Note that OA knows the counterpart of Bab. *pūtam ullulum* in *pūtkunu lu zakku'at* in TC 2, 21:25. [The verb *zakku'um* is also used metaphorically, used for clearing, freeing of claims, e.g. *pūt bēt abika zakki*, Kt 93/143b:44, with as variant the verb *ebābum* in the D-stem, AKT 6, 236:16-17, *pūt abini u bēt abini e-bi-ba*, cf. *pūtkunu e-bi-ba* in AKT 3, 56:29]. See for a unique use of *nummurum*, "to make shining, clear", PRU 3, p. 82:18, with CAD N/l, 217b, 6.

40 A similar nominal phrase is attested at the beginning of a number of deeds of adoption (e.g. BAP nos. 96 and 97; CT 2, 40a; CT 45, 16; TIM 4, 14; UET 5, 89 and 98; ARM 8 no. 1). David, *Adoption* 45 f., observes that this type of formulary is preferred for cases where the parents or owners of the adoptee are not mentioned, and hence are not available and no partners in the contract.

41 ARN no. 62, also a deed of manumission, is too broken to be of use here, see ARN p. 104, Ni. 9277; a payment (ransom ?) is mentioned, followed by stipulations about support on an annual base. Another deed of manumission is YOS 14 no. 42 (JCS 14, 30, no. 64): ^{f}*B* GEME *A* (former owner) *ana* ^{d}UTU *ellet*, "B, the slave-girl of A, has been manumitted before (so rather than: "to"; see BiOr 23 (1966), 310) Šamaš" (case: KIŠIB ^{f}B *ana* ^{d}UTU *ellet*).

5. ARN no. 7 : *B* sag.g[eme] ^{2} geme *A* ^{3} *ù* C dam.a.ni ^{4} *A* lugal.a.ni ^{5} *ù* C dam.a.ni ^{6} ama.ar. gi$_{4}$.a.ni ^{7} in.gar.re.eš ^{8} en.na *A ù* C ^{9} na.an.ga.ti.la.aš ^{10} igi.ni.ne.šè ì.gub.bu, "B, the slave-girl, is a slave of A and of C, his wife; A, her owner, and C, his wife, have manumitted her. As long as A and C live she will be under their orders".

The meaning of the initial sentence here is not obvious and the repeated sag geme ... geme reveals problems with the formulary.

It seems likely that the scribes were developing a special formulary for manumission not followed by adoption.[42] While the scribe of text 5 only changed words but left the structure intact, the scribes of texts 1-4 tried, with more or less success, to adapt the formulary. Our text follows their example, being closest to no. 1, which also is the least strained. Nevertheless, the manumitted slave to all appearances *was* adopted as son in our text, as implied by the use of the words "his father/mother" and by the fact that he will acquire in due time (part of) their property. The use by the scribe of our text of a formulary adapted for manumission without adoption was not compensated by inserting a clause which specifically mentioned the adoption, as was the case in VAB 5 no. 29. That both manumission and adoption could be stated clearly, even in the absence of the initial nominal sentence "B is the son of A", is proved by the scribe of a new deed, probably from Larsa (Ḫ. 40):

6. RA 69, 131 (BM 13922): *B* MU.NI *A u* C *abbuttašu ugallibu* NAM.DUMU.NI.ŠÈ IN.GAR NAM.IBILA.NI.ŠÈ IN.GAR, "A and C (former owners) removed the slave mark of the (slave) named B; he installed him as his son, he installed him as his heir".

Support and obedience

As is the case in many Babylonian deeds of manumission (VAB 5 nos. 23-25, 27, 29; Szlechter TJDB no. 2) and in some deeds of adoption (CT 45, 16; UET 5, 91; IM 63308 (JCS 27, 135): 8),[43] the clause about manumission/adoption is immediately followed by the mention of the obligation to support the new adoptive parents for life.[43a] Our text expresses this by the Gtn of *wabālum*, a typical Assyrian feature; the verb is also used in MA deeds (KAJ 1:9; 9:24) and is missing from Babylonian texts, which prefer *našûm* Gtn with the same meaning, in deeds both of manumission and adoption.[44] It is noteworthy that outside Mesopotamia proper, in Alalakh, *wabālum* Gtn is used, which indicates influence from

42 No . 5 mentions the obligation of the person manumitted "to stay before, to remain at the order of" his former owner. This does not imply adoption, but it is a clause by means of which the latter secures himself of the services of his former slave during his old age. Such services could eventually be rewarded by inheritance rights, after the death of the former owner, as is clear from an unpublished OB deed of manumission from Nippur (3 N-T 845:8-11; courtesy M. Civil): u$_{4}$.til.l[a.n]i.šè ì.gub.bu ba.úš.a.ta ibila *PN*. The expression igi ... šè gub, also attested in TIM 4, 27: 13 (en.na *PN* ama.ne.ne al.ti.la.šè igi.ni.šè ì.gub$^{!}$.bu$^{!}$) and UET 5, 99:3' (cf. igi ... gub, used of a slave in MAD 4, 153: II, 8, rather than igi ... túm proposed in ZA 63, 224 ad. loc.) may be compared with Akkadian *maḫar* PN *wašābum* attested in CT 47, 58:22 f. (if the adoptee declares: "I am leaving, *ina maḫriki ul uššab*"), MDP 24, 379: 19f. (*māru ša palāḫša ippušu maḫriša uššab*), and the texts quoted in CAD A/2, 401 a. Kienast ((*Gesellschaftsklassen* ..., = CRRAI 18, 101) interprets a case like our no. 5 as "Freilassung auf Todesfall".

43 See for a new deed of "emancipatory adoption" M. de J. Ellis, JCS 27 (1975), 130-151, who also discusses some of the issues raised in this article.

43a The clause in UET 5, 98:4 is not clear to me. In ARM 8, 1 the statement of sonship (without explicit mention of the act of adoption) is followed by a phrase establishing solidarity between adoptee and adopter: they will share weal and woe; a similar statement would be recorded in IM 63244 according to M. de J. Ellis, JCS 27 (1975), 133.

44 Also in the Diyala region (see the article mentioned in note 43). Note the alternation in VS 8, 109:18 between *našû*, Gtn (case) and *epērum* (tablet); UET 5, 91, 9 uses the concrete *akālum*, Š.

Assyria or Northern Mesopotamia.[45] The inter-dialectal distribution of these two verbs is also attested in the pair OA *wābil ṭuppim* – OB *nāši ṭuppim.*

The adopted son's obligation to support his parents in our text is connected by means of *-ma* with the one expressed by the verb *palāḫum.*[46] Clauses mentioning *palāḫum* are attested in some OB deeds. In two cases the clause is recorded in connection with adoption:

1. CT 2, 35:5 ff. (VAB 5 no. 13A): *adi PN balṭat PN_2* (adoptee) *PN ipallaḫ ukabbassi šumma pa-al-ḫi-ša* (sic) < *ipuš* > *bītum ... ša PN_2;*
2. CT 45, 11:30 f. *adi PN balṭat PN_2* (adoptee) *ipallaḫši.*
   Two further occurrences are in acts recording gifts to women:
3. CT 4, 1b:19 ff. (VAB 5 no. 208): *ina aḫḫēša ana ša ra-mu* (for: *irammû* ?) *u ipallaḫuši aplūssa inaddin;*
4. 4) CT 8, 34b : 17 ff. (VAB 5 no. 202): *ina marē PN* (her husband) *ana ša ipallaḫuši u libbaša uṭabbu* <*aplūssa*> *inaddin.*

The restricted number of attestations indicates that a *palāḫum* clause did not belong to the standard formulary of the OB deeds of adoption and/or manumission. In nos. 1, 3, and 4 *palāḫum* etc. is made a condition for receiving an inheritance, and that may well have been the case in no. 2 too.

The clause has a similar function in some deeds from OB Susa: *maruša ša* <<*ša*>> *palāḫša ippušu maḫriša uššab* (will inherit from the woman receiving a gift from her husband) MDP 24, 379: l 9ff. ; *aplum ša la ipalla*[*ḫu*]*šima ina* É.DÙ.[A] *ūl šū*[*ḫuz*] (similar case) MDP 28, 402: 10ff. ; a donation by a woman to a son (?) qualified as *rā'imiša u pāliḫiša* is recorded in MDP 28, 400: 9 ff.[47]

A clause mentioning *palāḫum* is regularly attested in MA legal documents, both in deeds of adoption, such as:[48]

1. KAJ 1:8ff.: *adi balṭuni ipallaḫ*[*šu*]*nu ittanabbalšunu* A.ŠÀ *ù* ŠÀ *ālim ša palāḫišunu eppaš* (subject: adopted son);
2. KAJ 4:9f.: A.[ŠÀ *ù*] ŠÀ URU *ša* [*palāḫi*]*šu ep*[*paš*] (subject: adopted son);
3. KAJ 6:11f.: A.ŠÀ *ù libba āla* (sic) *ipallaḫšu* ... (17ff.) *šumma A B la ipallaḫ* ...,
4. and in marriage deeds, such as:
5. KAJ 7:12f.: *adi balṭu* A.ŠÀ *ù* Š[À-*b]i* URU *palāḫ aḫa'iš eppu*[šu];
6. TIN 4, 45:7ff.: *ina* A.ŠÀ *ù* ŠÀ-*bi ā*[*lim*] *palāḫa ša aḫua*[*ḫa*] *ippušu.*

The clause is further frequently attested in legal texts from Nuzi, both in deeds of real) adoption and in marriage deeds, but in the latter as a rule only when there existed a special relation between the person who is the object of *palāḫum* and the person whose

---

45 *Alalakh Texts* no. 16 (15th century B.C.): 2 ff. : *PN PN_2 ana abušu ipuš adi*! << *bal* >> *balṭat it-ta-na-bal-šu* ... (13f.) *šumma PN_2 abušu it-ta-na-bal-šu* ... (18f.) *šumma abušu ūl it-ta-na-bal-šu.* This reference should be added to CAD A/ 1, 23b, c), where we have three quotations which show that this use of *wabālum,* Gtn was also known to the scribes of the Amarna letters. [**Add.** See for the use of *wabālum* Gtn and *palāhum* in texts from Emar, K.R. Veenhof, "Old Assyrian and Anatolian Evidence", in M. Stol and S.P. Vleeming (eds.), *The Care of the Elderly in the Ancient Near East* (Leiden-Boston 1998), Excursus, pp. 127-136 = pp. 185-210 in this volume, where it was pointed out that both verbs never occur together in the same contract. *Palāḫum* is used in documents of the so-called Syro-Hittite type and *wabālum* I/3 in those of the so-called Syrian type, which suggests that they were almost synonyms].

46 I assume that the construction *ša* + inf. + *epēšum* (not mentioned in Buccellati's study on infinitives with *ša,* JSS 17 (1972), 1 ff.) lends special emphasis to the activity mentioned: "to do everything possible in order to ...", "to take good care to ..."; see my remarks in *Aspects of Old Assyrian Trade and its Terminology* (1972), 319 note 440, where one should add as e) *ali* +inf. gen.: *ali šalāmika [u ša]lām luqūtija epušma,* VS 26, 83:r.16' f.; *ali balāṭija epša,* CCT 2, 34:23.

47 See also MDP 28, 399:13 f., in a unique context.

48 That the clause is not used in KAJ 2 and 3 could be connected with the fact that these deeds record the adoption of girls.

obligation it was: the bride was a (manumitted) slave girl, the bridegroom an adopted son of his father-in-law, who had given him his daughter in marriage, etc. There is in Nuzi no parallel to the MA clause requiring mutual respect from both partners in a marriage (above nos. 4 and 5).[49]

The close correspondence with the MA examples – the combination *palāḫum* + *itabbulum*, and the use of a construction *ša* +inf. + *epāšum* – suggests considering this particular clause an Assyrian or at least "northern" feature, now attested already in the later OA period. This latter fact helps to explain how similar clauses came in vogue in Nuzi (15th century B.C.) and also in Babylonia proper, where it is attested in one of the rare MB deeds of adoption, BE 14, 40: 12 f.: *adi* ᶠ*PN balṭu* ᶠPN_2 (the adoptee) *ipallaḫši*.[50]

The meaning of *palāḫum* is not immediately clear. Arguing from the Nuzi texts Stohlmann defines the meaning as "to perform obligations, to serve", pointing out that the verb is attested not only in deeds of adoption, but also in a *tidennūtu*contract (JEN 304) and in "slave-texts" like HSS 5, 59, where the slave-girl A, donated to a woman B, *adi B balṭu u A ipallaḫšu*. At times the basic support clause would be replaced by *palāḫum*, showing that this verb could and did comprise also the notion of "to support, sustain".[51] Eichler,[52] arguing along the same lines, observes moreover that *palāḫum* is used in the so-called *ḫapīru* documents (*e.g.* JEN 456: 15), where a meaning "to serve" is inescapable. [See above, the addition to note 45, on *palāhum* and *wabālum* I/3 as synonyms in the Emar texts].

That the support clause is almost always present while *palāḫum* is at times omitted in deeds of adoption (*e.g.* in JEN 569, 577, 595; HSS 13, 490; Gadd, RA 23, no. 51) does not suggest that they be equated. The concrete support clause was apparently deemed more essential, and one might argue that supporting one's parents was an act of *palāḫum*. There is no evidence for Stohlmann's suggestion that the *palāḫum* clause had any (historical) priority, in particular in view of the fact that our text juxtaposes *palāḫum* and *itabbulum* at a fairly early date, nor that *palāḫum* was subsequently replaced by verbs expressing more concrete action.

Considering the verbs used in conjunction with *palāḫum* in OB texts as quoted *above* – *kubbutum*, "to honour"; *libbam ṭubbum*, "to please, meet one's demands"; *râmum*, "to show affection" ; *wašābum maḫar*, "to be at somebody's orders" -, and the fact that the verb is used for describing the desired mutual behaviour of husband and wife (who are treated as equals in some OA and MA marriage contracts), we arrive not at a meaning "to support, sustain",[53] but rather at one "to obey, to respect". The fact that the Nuzi text HSS 5, 7 :21 contrasts the required *palāḫum* with *ina pī ša PN la išemmê*, "does not obey PN", supports this interpretation.[54] That obedience, to be shown through deeds, in a relation of

---

49 See for textual evidence and discussions S. C. Stohlman, *Real Adoption at Nuzi* (diss. 1972, UM 72.1800) and J. M. Breneman, *Nuzi Marriage Tablets* (diss. 1971, UM 71.30118).

50 The origins of the legal formulary used by the scribes of the OB texts from Susa is a difficult issue. The clauses quoted above could go back to OB examples, but influence from the North (by way of Ešnunna ?) cannot be excluded. See for an interesting example of agreement between MA and OB Susa clauses Deller and Saporetti, OrAnt 9 (1970), 44 on *ṭuppum ana ḫipi* (*ḫapi* in VS 19,38:10) *nadât*, and in general on the problem Y. Muffs, *Studies in the Aramaic Legal Papyri from Elephantine* (1969), 15 note 3 (with Add. on p. 195), 90 ff. and 100 note 4.

51 Stohlman refers to JEN 410 and Gadd nos. 9 and 36. But note that JEN 410 uses the Hurrianized expression *erweššašu našû*, which most probably means "to support", that Gadd no. 7 is damaged and incomplete (HSS 19: 101, e.g., contains a support-clause following the obligation to take care of the burial!), and that Gadd no. 36 is an atypical text.

52 B. L. Eichler, *Indenture at Nuzi* (YNER 5; 1973), 115, a. That HSS 9, 22: 13 replaces *palāḫum* by *nadānum* is not correct; read *adi A [balṭu] u B* [ŠE.BA *u* TÚG.BA] *inandinaššu u [ipallaḫšu] enūma* ... The *enūma-clause* does not start immediately after *inandinaššu* (it is not normally introduced by the *u* of the apodosis, though there are some exceptions) and there is room for *[ipallaḫšu]*.

53 Eichler's contention that *ipallaḫši* in HSS 19, 11:22 f. is glossed by NINDA.MEŠ *ušakkalši u* TÚG *ultabbaš* is begging the question; rather we have *palāḫum* followed by a specified support clause.

54 This clause is regularly used in inheritance texts (*ṭuppi šīmti*) from Nuzi, when a guardian is appointed (*ana abbuti epēšum*) over the (junior) heirs; the latter have "to obey" her and are penalized for *ana pīša la šemûm*. See J. Paradise, *Nuzi Inheritance Practices* (diss. 1972; UM 72.25644), 216 f.

inequality – slave/master, client/retainer, junior heir/guardian, (adopted) son/ father – has the implication of "service" is beyond question, and *palāḫum* is used in relations implying servitude (KAJ 159:5; later *e.g.* in Iraq 16, 35, ND 2094: 6 and ADD 76: 6).[55] But this does not mean that "to serve" is to be preferred over "to obey" in all cases.[56]

Property

The stipulation about what will happen after the death of both the adoptive parents[57] is introduced by *ina urkīti* PN. While the form *urkīti* is Assyrian, the combination as such is unusual. MA deeds use *ina urkīti*, "later, afterwards", alone, without following genitive, while OB deeds prefer *warki*/EGIR *PN*, without the preposition, which is only found in later texts, i.a. at Nuzi as the references in CAD A/2 s.v. *arki* (prep.) and *arkītu* show. *Ina urkīti* PN looks like a blend of Assyrian and Babylonian idioms.[58] The stipulation itself states that the adoptive son "acquires" (*leqûm*) a field and an ox, no doubt originally the property of his adoptive parents. As the verb *leqûm* is regularly used (in OA, OB, and MA) for describing that an heir acquires his share, we may consider its use here an indication that the adoptive son inherited from his parents' estate. The wording is, however, very laconic and does not inform us about his hereditary position. There is no mention of others heirs – the fact that what he will acquire is exactly fixed suggests that he received only part of the estate, and that consequently there were other heirs – and the acquisition of his share is apparently unconditional.

Claims

The stipulations about possible violations of the contract in our text are again rather original, both in content and in wording. OB deeds of manumission regularly state that the person manumitted is henceforth free from any claims on his person (*mamman mimma elišu ūl išû*)[59] and forbid the heirs of the former owner – his relatives and in the first place

---

55 See also J.N. Postgate, *Fifty Neo-Assyrian Legal Documents* (1976) §§ 3.7,2 and 8,2 on *palāḫum* used of pledged persons and debtors.

56 The stipulation in UET 5, 88:8 ff.: *adi balṭu PN$_2$ u kirīšu* (case adds: *kī wardišu*) *ippeš*, is in my opinion not a standard description of what *palāḫum* means and the deed is an atypical one (PN "given" to PN$_2$ *ana tablittim*).

57 Our text mentions both parents in lines 4-11, but the father alone in 1 ff. (manumission) and 14 f. (vindication). Cf. CT 4, 50a, where the wife is only mentioned in the first line.

58 OA uses *warki/urki* + gen. or *warkītam/urkītam*. Szlechter, TJDB no. 2:9, TIM 4, 50:10, and IM 63303:8 have *ulliš*, "ultimately".

59 This clause also in BE 6/1, 17:26 f., where the person adopted actually is a former slave, and in Sumerian in UET 5, 191:17 (ugu former slave níg.na.me nu.tuku.uš). The clause frequently follows the support clause, several times linked to it by the connective *-ma* (VAB 5 nos. 25:10; 27:10; IM 63303:8; CT 8, 29a:7), which favours an interpretation as the apodosis to a conditional protasis, as Schorr translates ("Wenn ... unterhalten wird, wird ... niemand ..."). He and others apparently assume that the person manumitted only enjoyed a conditional, limited freedom as long as his former owner and adoptive father stayed alive. Kienast (*Gesellschaftsklassen* ..., = CRRAI 18 (1972), 101 f.) rightly points out that this kind of "Ankindungsfreilassung" assures the person manumitted complete freedom, notwithstanding the fact that he has certain obligations to fulfill (alimentation) and is now subjected to the authority of the *pater familias*, just like natural children (he refers to VAB 5 no. 23:23 ff.; something similar must be implied in the unpubl. BM 82504: 6, quoted CAD A/2, 56a, b, 1': *itti marī awīli imnušī*). The situation must be similar in our OA deed: the manumission grants the slave *de jure* complete freedom, even though his obligations of support and obedience/service *de facto* impose certain limitations. See also note 42 above on 3 N-T 845 and the remarks on *palāḫum* in OB deeds.

his natural children – to raise claims on him (*ragāmum*, inim gá.gá, rarely *baqārum*).[60] Our text differs, considering only the possibility that the former owner himself reclaims his slave, the most far reaching breach of contract, not envisaged in the OB deeds which only consider a possible repudiation of the manumitted and adopted son.[61] That our text does not mention this possibility may be due to the fact that adoption is not explicitly recorded.

The claim by the former owner is punished with a heavy fine: 2 minas of silver. As has been noted,[62] such fines, though they do occur, are rather uncommon in deeds from (northern) Babylonia, while they are attested in deeds from Ešnunna, Mari, Ḫana and Susa. Without attempting an analysis of the pattern of occurrences of such fines – particularly frequent in deeds of adoption, and occasionally linked with severe corporal punishments (as an alternative?), especially in the Diyala region and in some cases in OB Susa, see note 64 -, we can at least distinguish two different types.

1. Heavy fines of 2-10 minas of silver, in no relation to the values at stake and strong deterrents rather than contractual punishments, are attested in Ḫana (10 minas, payment to the palace), Ešnunna (5 minas and less), Mari (10 minas and less, payment (always? ARM 8 nos. 12 and 19, case) to the palace), Susa (10 minas), and occasionally in Babylonia proper. The fines occur in clauses at the very end of the deed, in close connection with the oath formula, and they issue a general prohibition of any claim – the preferred expression is *bāqir ibaqqaru*, glossed by *ša ina birišunu ibbalkit* in the Ḫana text *Syria* 37, 206:19 f.; cf. TIM 4, 39:7 – which is qualified as a sacrilege or a capital crime.[63] Examples are YOS 14, 42 (JCS 14, 30 no. 64): fine of 5 minas, deed of manumission; TIM 4, 50:18 ff.: fine of 5 minas, deed of adoption or legitimation; ARM 8, 1:27 ff.: fine of 3⅓ minas, deed of adoption. TIM 5, 4:17 ff.: fine of 2 minas, to be paid to the king, deed of adoption.[64] Compare also CT 47, 68 case: 16 ff.: fine of 3 minas in a deed of donation, a contract conceptually akin to a deed of manu mission.[65]

60 *ragāmum* occurs in VAB 5 nos. 27 and 29, and in Szlechter, TJDB no. 2:13; its Sumerian equivalent inim gá.gá in VAB 5 no. 28 and ARN 7:18. *Baqārum* is attested in connection with manumission/adoption in the formula *bāqir ibaqqaru* in Waterman, Bus. Doc. no. 54:9 and YOS 14, 42:4, and in the complex formulation of IM 63303:20 ff. (JCS 27 (1975), 135). BIN 2, 76:11 has a straightforward "they/one shall not call him slave (ÌR *lā iqabbûšu*!; cf. ÌR-*ni lā iqabbû* in RA 70, 47:18 and in Sumerian in UET 5, 191:24 f.: ìr é.ad.da.me nu.mu.na.an.du$_{11}$.uš). Those who might be tempted to raise claims for the former slave are qualified as "children, male and female" (VAB 5 no. 25), "children, heirs" (ibid. no. 28). Szlechter, TJDB no. 2 mentions "brothers and relatives" (*aḫḫū u nišūtum*), YOS 14, 42:5 "his brothers and sons" (case adds: and daughters), scil. of the former owner. Such relatives, uncles and cousins are also recorded in VAB 5 no. 27: 15 ff., while ibid. no. 32 exceptionally mentions a possible claim by the adoptive parents themselves (who had married off the manumitted and adopted slave-girl) and their children. This shows, in my opinion, that vindication and claims concern the former slaves themselves, whose new status is contested. This of course implies property rights acquired by their new status, which M. de J. Ellis, JCS 27 (1975), 146 ff., makes the main issue of the *baqārum* clause in the deeds of adoption discussed by her. But since adoption normally grants the adoptee right of succession, contesting their status as sons or daughters must be the main issue. Such a vindication, if successful, not only would rob them of their share in the inheritance but add them to the property to be divided.

61 See David, *Adoption*, 85 f., where the manumitted and adopted slave, when repudiated by his parents, earns his freedom (24 f.: *ana ramanišu ittallak*). This seems, surprisingly, to be also the case with the manumitted and adopted slave who repudiates his adoptive mother in CT 45, 101:28 ff.: he leaves after a small payment.

62 Boyer, ARMT 8, 167, §13 ff.

63 Cf. A . Marzal, CBQ 33 (1971), 344 ff. ARM 8 no. 1:28 ff. e.g. speaks of *asak* DN_1 *u* DN_2 RN_1 *u* RN_2 *akālum*, and of *dīn napištim*; YOS 14, 42:6 f. has: *nīš DN u RN īkul*. [See for these matters now D. Charpin, Amendes et châtiments prévus dans les contrats paléo-babyloniens, in: J.-M. Durand *et al.* (eds.), *La faute et sa punition dans les sociétés orientales* (Leuven 2012) 1-22].

64 Corporal punishments are prescribed in addition to heavy fines: *lišānam nakāsum*/*lapātum*/*šalāpum* in Ešnunna, *rittam u lišānam nakāsum* in Susa (MDP 23, 121: r.10, e.a.), and *qaqqadam kupram emmam kapārum* in Ḫana.

65 In Waterman, Bus. Doc. no. 54 *bāqir ibaqqarušu* MU ᵈUTU ᵈ*Marduk u Ḫammurabi* is not followed by a fine, as in the comparable TIM 4, 50:18 ff. Note the variant *rāgim iraggamu* in YOS 14, 74:21 f., also attested in CT 4, 13b:10 (contract about the fee of a wet-nurse; fine ⅓ mina of silver), in texts from the Diyala (JCS 26 (1974), 133 ff., texts A, B, D, and E), and in ARM 8, 5:8 (sale of field; fine 1 mina).

These final prohibitions are normally not the only ones; the normal punishments for the breach of an adoption contract – loss of property for the adoptive parents; sale as slave for the adoptive son – are regularly mentioned in the body of the deed. Only YOS 14 no. 42 is an exception, as the *baqārum* clause is the only one present; its subjects accordingly are specified as the brother and sons (the case adds: and daughters) of the former owner.

2. Much smaller fines, stipulated for specific breaches of contract by the parties involved, ranging from ⅓ to 1 mina of silver. TIM 4, 13 and 14 impose a fine of ⅓ mina on adoptive father and adopted son (who also lose income from offices), and the same fine for the adoptive father in TIM 4, 15 (the adoptive son is sold as a slave). In a similar case, BE 6/2, 57 has a fine of ½ mina for the father, while TIM 5, 2 and 3 stipulate fines of 1 mina for the adoptive parents; in all these cases the rebellious son is sold as a slave. Szlechter TJDB no. 2, finally, fines the relatives of the former owner (*aḫḫū u nišūtum*) with 1 mina of silver if they raise claims (*ragāmum*).

It is, again, difficult to decide to which category our text belongs. The amount of the fine and the use of *baqārum* strongly remind us of type 1). But the fact that a specific action by a party mentioned by name is involved, while the rebellious son is sold as slave, suggests a connection with 2), also supported by the fact that our text adds a general prohibition against raising claims – without, however, using the *bāqir ibaqqaru* formula; but *mamman la ibaqqir* in line 25 is very similar in function – affirmed by an oath.

Repudiation

While the possible misbehavior of the adopted son – repudiation of his parents – and its punishment – being sold as slave – are identical to what almost all OB deeds of adoption stipulate, the wording of our text is original. Instead of having the son pronounce the standard formulaic words "you are not my father/mother"[66] our text describes what the son does, using the expression *irti PN raḫāṣum+atlukum. Irtam raḫāṣum* was not previously known among the various idiomatic expressions containing *irtum*,[67] but its meaning is fairly clear. While *irtam ne'ûm* means to stop somebody in a course of action, *irtam raḫāṣum* should mean "to push away, cast off, repudiate", being a synonym of *irtam sakāpum/ maḫāṣum*, referring to a powerful gesture with emotional overtones, just like its idiomatic Dutch equivalent "iemand voor de borst stoten".[68]

The rather static Babylonian formulary is replaced in our text by a more realistic description of what happens: the rebellious son of course does not wait for his stipulated punishment, but makes off and has to be located and apprehended before he can actually be sold as a slave. The natural place where a fugitive fleeing to another town may be discovered is the *kārum* or harbor district (in a wider sense: commercial district, in particular in Assyria, where traveling by boat was not usual). The expression *ina kār*

66 Also in the "Sumerian family laws", YOS 1 no. 28, IV:19 ff. There are some exceptions: CT 8, 49b: 17 f. describes what the adoptive son does as *libbam šumruṣum*, and Szlechter, TJDB no. 2: 18 f. uses *qullulum* (!). Cf. BE 6/1, 17:23, where *dullam mullûm* is what the adoptive parents might do to their adoptive son.

67 *Irtum* is attested with *ne'ûm, parākum* (also CCT 6, 17b:20), *tarāṣum, sakāpum, maḫāṣum* (see CAD I/J 185, 3', a'), and with *turrum* (Kraus AbB 7, 157 no. 186, a). [CAD R s.v. *rahāṣu* A registers no additional examples].

68 See for *sakāpum* and its Sumerian equivalents, meaning "wegstossen", the semantically related verb *darāsum* (Sum. zà.kin.di/e) and their possible relation to *raḫāṣum*, Sjoberg, OrNS 39 (1970), 87ff. (note that AHw 942 s.v. reads the equation in Antagal N II :14 as gìr.ság = *raḫāṣum ša e-d[e?-e]*). *Raḫāṣum* has a meaning "to trample down" (cf. CCT 4, 1a, 4: *kīma šēp Adad rāpidim bētī raḫiṣ*, "my house is trampled down as if Adad himself had overrun it"), as stated by Landsberger, JNES 8 (1949) 249[8] – perhaps the lexically attested gìr.su.gi_4.gi_4 = *raḫāṣu ša amēli* (AHw loc. cit.) ? – but it seems to refer to an action with the feet rather than to one with the arms. Conceptually and semantically related is the Sumerian loanword *gabaraḫḫu* = gaba.raḫ, "rebellion, strife".

innammaru is known from OB sources in clauses referring to the payment of private or commercial debts, and is attested in OB Susa, Babylonia proper, and Mari.[69] Texts from Susa and VS 9, 84 use the expression *ina kār innammaru ana nāš ṭuppišu išaqqal*, ARM 8, 78 *ina kārim ša innammaru ša pī ṭuppim annîm*, and TIM 3, 135 only *ina kār innammaru.* All texts suppose a situation where the debtor is away from home or traveling around (in particular the texts from Susa, dealing with a commercial society), and debt notes are transferable. It seems likely that the expression is of Babylon origin, as *kārū* are not attested in Assyria proper.[70] Our text suggests, if we take it literally, that the fugitive ex-son, recognized and seized, may be sold as a slave on the spot.[71]

Oath

The presence in an Assyrian deed of an oath formula in close connection with the prohibition of any claim is noteworthy.[72] Although the swearing of oaths was of course known in the Old Assyrian society – witnesses had to testify under oath "before the dagger-sword of Aššur", and in the course of a lawsuit a party could make an appeal to the higher legal authorities in the city of Assur with the formula *ša nīš ālim u bēlija ka'ilā*[73] – I know of no OA deeds or contracts containing an oath sealing the promise to renounce any future claims. There are some examples where people promise under oath (*nīš ālim itmû*) that they will not go back on (*tuārum ana*) agreements made or persons involved, but such documents most probably are not regular contracts but records of statements made before witnesses in the course of a lawsuit.[74] The other, later Old Assyrian deeds referred to in this article (texts G and T and the deeds mentioned in note 20, a marriage contract and two deeds of sale) do not contain an oath. This makes it likely that the oath in our text is due to Babylonian influence, the more so as it uses MU instead of the invariable OA *nīš* (always written syllabically).

The oath is sworn to the gods Aššur and Adad, and to the king. The mention of the two gods is hardly surprising: both are mentioned in the curse formulae of the OA inscriptions of Irišum (AOB 1, V, 10:29 f., *Belleten* 14 pl. 24, line 26 [see now RIMA 1, p. 21 l. 50 and p. 37, lines 29f.] in both cases followed by Bēlum, "my god"). Beside Aššur and Ištar, mentioned in the royal inscriptions, Adad was the most prominent god, whose temple was built by Irišum and Ikunum, [75] and his importance as Assyrian "Wettergott"

69 See the texts quoted in CAD A/2, 24b, b, 1'; ARM 8, 78: 24 cited in CAD K 233, 2 bottom; and TIM 3, 135:7. CAD K loc. cit., mentions an OB text where a debt was actually settled by people meeting in the *kārum* (of Nippur), and something similar is foreseen in YOS 14, 158:18 ff.: *PN ina ālim ša immarušunūti itti šalmim kaspam ileqqe*.

70 The concept *kārum* was of course well known in Assyria , and a phrase as *alī innammuru išaqqal* (ATHE 34: 22) shows that the expression could have been familiar in Assyria, although it is not attested in OA in the particular form discussed here. [**Add.** See for the various ways one expresses in OA that the debtor has to pay where the creditor meets or spots him (*alī emmurušu, alī innammuru* and *alī ninnammuru*) the remarks in K.R. Veenhof, *Kültepe Tabletleri* V (Ankara 2010), comment on text 44: 13'ff.].

71 Sale abroad or at least to foreigners of rebellious adoptive children is provided in *Tell Sifr* 13:14 ff. and UET 5, 97:19 ff., Sutûm, Yaḫmutum and Elam being mentioned by name. [See also my note NABU 2015/12]

72 The prohibition of raising claims in our text is – in the absence of a subjunctive – not syntactically dependent on the oath, but the logical connection cannot be doubted.

73 See for the OA oath Hirsch, UAR 68f. with Add. p. 27, and note the existence of special records of declarations under oath, beginning with the invocation "Listen, god(dess) of the oath", ibid. 39b and Add. p. 82 [See now R. Westbrook (ed.), *A History of Ancient Near Eastern Law* (HdO section I, vol. 72/1, Leiden Boston 2003) 445-6, § 3.3.3, under "Litigation"].

74 See EL nos. 6 and 9, and cf. the statement in no. 332: 35 ff. [**Add.** In none of the deeds of sale of slaves and houses studied in B. Kienast, *Das altassyrische Kaufvertragsrecht* (FAOS Beiheft 1, Stuttgart 1984), is the "Verzichtklausel" (ch. IV.2; either apodictic, *ula iturrū*, or conditional, *šumma iturrū / ša iturru*, with a fine as apodosis) secured by an oath].

75 AOB 1 V nos. 9, 10; VI no. 1 [see now RIMA 1, pp. 37ff., nos. 14-16 and p. 41f. no. 1]. The importance of Adad may also be deduced from the fact that he is one of the few gods (the others are Aššur and Sîn) called LUGAL / *šarrum*, "king" in PNs. Note in connection with Adad the late 3rd millennium seal found on the tell of Kültepe (Balkan, *Anum-Ḫirbi*, fig. 12): *A-bu-a-hi* / ^{d}IM / DINGIR-*su* / *ra-e*$^{!}$-*im* / AN.ŠIR.KI.

was stressed by Šamšī-Adad's erection of a temple for Anum-Adad, which associated him with the supreme sky god from the South.

Dating

The dating, by means of a *līmum* eponym following the Assyrian practice, provides us with an important piece of information. Not only is this particular *līmum* a new one – adding to the slowly growing number of *līmū* from the later Old Assyrian period[76] – but it is unique in so far as it shows that king Šamšī-Adad made his eldest son and future successor *līmum*. The recent study by Larsen of the institution of the *līmum* came to the following conclusion: "... the Old Assyrian year-eponymy was an important element in the political structure of the city-state. It represented the interests of the major families and even functioned as a kind of counterbalance against the powers of the king".[77] The *līmum* was chosen in a ceremony which involved the casting of lots. By making his son *līmum* ŠamšīAdad – called "a man of foreign extraction, not of the 'flesh of the City of Aššur'" in Puzur-Sîn's inscription – seriously encroached on an institution which had among others to counterbalance the royal powers, and he must have manipulated the (religious?) ceremony of casting lots in order to arrive at the desired result. By doing so he anticipated what was to become a Assyrian royal practice towards the end of the 14th century B.C., when Assyrian kings themselves started to hold the year-eponymy during the beginning of their reigns.[78]

This new *līmum* is but another piece of evidence showing the serious impact of Šamšī-Adad's usurpation of the throne of Aššur, to be added to the facts already known, such as the introduction of the Babylonian language for his inscriptions and administration, the appointment of a royal *wakil tamkārī* supervising the traders, the promotion of the cult of Enlil, and – according to Puzur-Sîn – the building of his palace after the destruction and removal of a temple. New textual material from Aššur would probably provide still more evidence for his break with certain Assyrian traditions and the influx of Babylonian scribal practices, which was probably also responsible for the particular characteristics of our text.

SOME CORRIGENDA AND ADDENDA

Some addenda are given in the text and mainly in the footnotes to correct some statements, especially because it turned out that APM 9220 is ca. 175 years younger than I had assumed (see above, footnote 2). This new date anyhow removes my accusation that Šamšī-Adad I had manipulated the selection of the *līmum* in favor of his son and successor.

Updating an article written 35 years ago is not well possible. There is much new literature on adoption and on the formulary of adoption contracts and a short overview is found in R. Westbrook (ed.), *A History of Ancient Near Eastern Law*, Handbuch der Orientalistik, section I, vol. 72/1 (Leiden-Boston 2003) 391-393, and see also G. Suurmeijer, ""He took him as his son". Adoption in Old Babylonian Sippar", *RA* 104 (2010) 9-40 (with bibliography), which includes the edition of six new adoption contracts (from the Belgian excavations at Tell ed-Dēr). For some new OA adoption contracts I refer to my article "Some Old Assyrian and Old Babylonian Adoption Contracts", in: G. Suurmeijer (ed.), Proceedings of a Workshop held in the University of Gent, written four years ago, but still unpublished. I note that APM 9220 does not contain a clause on the consequences of a

---

76 I intend to present a survey and analysis of all known later OA *līmū* in a forthcoming article [published as The Chronology of *Kārum* Kanish. Some New Observations, written in 1988, finally published in the CRRAI 34 (of Istanbul 1987), Ankara 1998, 421-450].

77 M. T. Larsen, *The Old Assyrian City-State*, 217.

78 *Ibidem*, 220f. [It is now clear that Šamšī-Adad, the father of the *līmum* Išme-Dagan in our text, was Šamšī-Adad II, no. 57 of the King List (see RlA 7 [1981] p. 107), of around 1600 B.C. But he remains the first king known to have made his son and successor *līmum*].

possible later birth of a natural son for the hereditary status of the adoptive son; perhaps the couple was too old to consider this eventuality.

We now also have two more "late Old Assyrian" texts to complement and in some aspects correct the comparative picture drawn above. They are:

1. VAT 19864, published as KAM 10 (*WVDOG* 130) no.1, belonging to the Middle Assyrian archive designated as M 9 and dated to the (otherwise unknown) eponymy of Aššur-bāni, son of Išme-Dagan; see already above, footnote 20. After V. Donbaz's preliminary transcription in *Akkadica* 42 (185) 9 note 6, based on the "Grabungsphoto", it was recently edited by J.J. de Ridder in *NABU* 2015/38, who also pointed out some features of spelling and orthography, which deviate from standard OA and betray Babylonian influence. As for the formulary, I note that there is no oath to secure the contract, which is standard in Babylonia and also occurs in APM 9220. De Ridder notes the first occurrence in an OA sale contract of a disclaimer clause beginning with *ištu ūmim annîm*, "from this day onwards" (l. 15), later also used in contracts from Nuzi and Ugarit. This expression is now also attested in the OA treaty with the magnates of Hahhum, *ištu ūmim annîm adi balṭātununi* (IV:23', cf. C. Günbattı, *Studies Larsen* [Leiden 2004] 259), and is known from OB treaties from Mari and Tell Leilan. Its OB equivalent in disclaimer clauses is *ana warkiat ūmē* (Sum. u_4.kúr.šè), but we have also the rare Sumerian combination in a judicial record, u_4.da.ta (inim ...ì.til) ... .u_4.kúr.šè (nu ...bal) in UET 5, 198:27 (cf. F.R. Kraus, *WdO* 2 (1954-59) 132. In ARM 8, 8:6 we have the unique u_4.1.e (collated) ... nu gi. The Old-Hittite deed of donation, published by K. Balkan, *Eine Schenkungsurkunde aus der althethitischen Zeit, gefunden in İnandık 1966* (Ankara 1973), in line 15 starts the disclaimer clause with *urram šēram*, "in the future", also attested in a Hittite royal decree and a treaty. It is from known from OB letters and now also from an OA judicial record (AKT VII-a, 108:17-19) and is (rarely) used contracts, in Mari (ARM 8, 67:6, about guaranty), Alalakh and Emar (see *CAD* Š/II, 334, c).

2. A tablet without envelope in the Yavuz Tatış collection at Izmir (inv. no. 1439), made known in transliteration only by V. Donbaz in *NABU* 2001/56. It is a contract about the sale of real estate from the eponymy of Warad-Šerua (ÌR-*Šé-ru-a*), son of Aššur-bāni (see Donbaz's remarks in 2001/55 on the eponymic dating and the prosopography), written by the scribe Nabium-qarrād (dPA-UR.SAG), who also wrote the text in Geneva (see above note 3), which figures as G in my comparative lists.

Still unpublished is VAT 19865 = Ass. 14446dz. It is, as Ms. E. Fritzsche kindly told me in a letter of Aug. 2010, the first tablet on the third row of tablets shown on the 'Grabungsphoto' Ass 4159 (where VAT 19864 = Ass 1446ay is the first tablet on the second row). She also stated that of the 13 tablets shown on the photo this tablet and 19864 "deutlich älter sind". O. Pedersen, *Archives and Libraries in the City of Assur*, I (Uppsala 1985) lists it on p. 99, no. 122 as *Ass. 14446dz, where the added asterisk denotes "faulty or questionable number". And indeed, its identification with VAT 8795 = KAJ 3, edited in M. David, *Die Adoption* (1927) 103, is wrong. This interesting "late Old Assyrian tablet", a contract about adoption, dedication and donation, dated to the eponymy of Uššurum, which I could study in Berlin in 1991, certainly deserves publication.

The publication of VAT 19864 allows some additional observations on the comparative lists published above under "paleography" and "syllabary", for which I can also use good photos and a copy made by H. Freydank in 1995, which differs not only in 'style', but also in some details from the one published as KAM 10 no. 1.

The *syllabary* is almost "pure" OA, with as only exception, in personal names only, the use of ŠE (in *Še-le-bu*) and perhaps ŠI (in GA-ŠI-WA-RI), but the meaning of this perhaps Hurrian name (ending in *-atal*) is not clear and ŠI could stand for *lim*. Not attested in OA is IŠ = *mil*, perhaps absent in because names with *-gāmil/igmil* as predicate are not attested in OA. Mimation is indicated, apart from Šelebu, and – as observed by De Ridder –

there are two cases where a doubled consonant is written: in *an-ni-im* (l. 16) and in the month-name *Áb-šar-ra-nim*, whose ending also deviates from normal OA Abšarrāni. Note further that in l. 19 *hubullūšunu* must be short – not a mistake by omission, which would have yielded *hubullišunu* – for *bēl hubullišunu*, "their creditors", the presence of a "Personenkeil" before Uzua at the beginning of a line (as in G) – but not before Eddin-Aššur in l. 18! – and the writing of the determinative for the plural as MEŠ, and not as ME+EŠ, as has been claimed, see above note 20.

As for the paleography, noteworthy sign forms (not all signs are represented) are:

EN:  (13, 20); HAR:  (9); HI:  (4, 6); IG:  12;
IŠTAR:  (9); ITU:  (27); KÙ.BABBAR:  (10); RU:  (21);
LUGAL:  (24); ŠAR:  (27); ŠÙR:  (3ff.); ZI:  (13, 20).

These scribal features – even when allowing for some variations in the paleography due to the specific "hand" of the scribe – clearly show that VAT 19864 is closer to G than to A; note especially the forms of HI, HAR and KÙ.BABBAR. It also shows almost no Babylonian influence, which is not surprising considering its presumably earlier date (although its exact date is unknown).

Before Hammurabi of Babylon Law and the Laws in Early Mesopotamia*

1. Introduction

Since Mesopotamia, the cradle of the civilizations of Sumerians and Babylonians, has yielded the oldest legal sources known today, one might expect them to figure prominently in the study of "early law". But what is "old" or even "oldest" in chronological terms is not necessarily "early" in the sense of reflecting the very beginnings, the first stages of law, as described in the programme of this symposium. The chronological notion implied by the use of "early" is less an absolute one, translatable into data of world history, than an internal and relative one, used to characterize a stage in the development of law in a particular society, irrespective of its absolute date.

This does not mean, of course, that the oldest law and legal documents are without interest for the study of early law. Its data may help to define it, also by casting historical light on its development and the processes which lead to the emergence of the first legal records. This is particularly true of ancient Mesopotamia, where developments, starting soon after 3000 B.C., can be followed over many centuries, down to the stage of full grown law and formal legislation. But we have to realize that Mesopotamian civilization, notwithstanding the survival of some of its elements, including legal traditions, in neighbouring and later cultures, is a completely dead one. In the absence of a continuous oral tradition, written documents, recorded in cuneiform writing, are our only source of knowledge. Consequently, the study of "early" law has to be based on the careful analysis of the oldest legal records, their emergence, nature and function within the framework of what we now about the society; of their structure, subject matter, formulary and terminology; and of their gradual evolution, spread and coverage, also in relation to other sources relevant for legal history, such as official inscriptions, legislative texts, and documents from the school.

Records imply the availability of a script, which was invented in Mesopotamia shortly before 3000 B.C., to serve the bureaucratic and managerial needs of a rapidly expanding, sophisticated, urbanizing culture in a densely populated country. But this invention and the subsequent appearance of the first legal documents do not coincide with the birth, the very beginning of law. Attempts to maintain a social order and to regulate important events by rules for securing fair transactions, upholding justice, and arbitrating conflicts must have preceded the use of writing, when unwritten customary law based on wisdom, experience and oral tradition ruled. Moreover, however rich and varied, the written documentation, not surprisingly, is less abundant and informative for the early phases in which we are interested here. Not only because the oldest strata of important ruins which might yield early records are generally less accessible, but also because the use of writing for other than bureaucratic **[138]** purposes was a gradual process. Apart from a few welcome exceptions, the slowly growing stream of legal documents only begins around the middle of the third millennium B.C. Moreover, the oldest texts, notably the so-called "archaic *kudurrus*" (see below), still offer many problems of interpretation.

* Originally published in: F. J. M. Feldbrugge (ed.), The Law's Beginnings (proceedings of a symposium held in Leiden, May 2002), Nijhoff, Leiden 2003, 137-159.

My title mentions king Hammurabi of Babylon (*ca.* 1792-1750 B.C.), in the first place because his name is linked with the largest and most impressive collection of ancient Mesopotamian laws, the so-called "Codex Hammurabi", which became known to legal historians one hundred years ago.[1] But he is also mentioned because his times and in general the so-called Old Babylonian period (*ca.* 2000-1600 B.C.) for which he stands, may serve as a lower chronological boundary and as a frame of reference. By the end of the third millennium B.C. the stage of early law was certainly past. This does not imply that the development of law and legal insights came to an end, but means that my observations on "early law" will focus on the third millennium B.C.

It is not easy to fix the time when in a particular culture "early law" started and when it reached the phase of fully developed law. Its origins are usually badly recorded and difficult to capture, certainly for a dead culture, and its end depends to some extent on our definitions and the availability of adequate documentation. For coming to grips with early Mesopotamian law it is helpful to look back from the Old Babylonian (and the contemporary Old Assyrian) period, because by that time and already at the end of the third millennium B.C. (the Third Dynasty of Ur, which covers the 21st century B.C.), by common agreement, law was fully developed. The juridification of the social order and the ways of solving conflicts was well established by then and professionally, at times extensively, recorded, both in collections of laws and royal decrees and in a great variety of legal records. The latter comprised both private contracts dealing with a great variety of transactions and liabilities[2] and documents from the administration of justice issued by courts of law (which consist of local judges, but at times also comprised "judges of the king"), such as formal judgments, records of court proceedings and various depositions.[3] Moreover, we have ample evidence that by then the education of professional scribes in the schools paid **[139]** serious attention to law and legal phraseology and used selections of legal rulings, model contracts, and records of exemplary verdicts as teaching tools.[4] This must have resulted in increased knowledge of the law and a growing standardization of

---

1 *Editio princeps* by V. Scheil, in *Textes élamities-sémitiques, deuxième série*, Mémoires de la Délégation en Perse, t. 4, Paris 1902). The impressive stele with the text (now in the Louvre, in Paris, see fig. 5) was discovered in 1901 by the French excavators of the Elamite capital Susa, where it had been taken as spoil of war by an Elamite king in the 12th century B.C., some six hundred years after it had been erected in Babylon.

2 See for the Ur III period *e.g.* P. Steinkeller, *Sale Documents of the Ur-III-Period*, Stuttgart 1989, and H. Lutzmann, *Die Neusumerischen Schuldurkunden* I , Heidelberg 1976. For the Old Babylonian period the sample collected in M. Schorr, *Urkunden des Altbabylonischen Zivil- und Prozessrecht*, Leipzig 1913, and special investigations, such as G. Mauer, *Das Formular der altbabylonischen Bodenpachtverträge*, München 1980 (dissertation, Selbstverlag); R. Westbrook, *Old Babylonian Marriage Law*, Horn 1988; A. Skaist, *The Old Babylonian Loan Contract*, Ramat Gan 1994; and R. Westbrook & R. Jasnow, *Security for Debt in Ancient Near Eastern Law*, Leiden 2001, 63-160 (the Old Babylonian and Old Assyrian periods).

3 See for the Ur III period, A. Falkenstein, *Die neusumerischen Gerechtsurkunden* I-III, München 1956-1957, and for Old Babylonian data, E. Dombradi, *Die Darstellung des Rechtsaustrags in den altbabylonischen Prozessurkunden*, I-II, Freiburger Altorientalische Studien 20/1-2, Stuttgart 1996. A recent selection of judicial records of all periods translated into French is now available in F. Joannès (ed.), *Rendre la juistice en Mésopotamie. Archives judiciaires du Proche-Orient ancien (IIIe/Ier millénaires avant J.-C.)*, Saint-Denis 2000.

4 There is no comprehensive study of scribal education in general and of training in legal matters in particular. An important tool was a (partially preserved) handbook on seven tablets (with *ca.* 1600 lines of writing), which acquaints the scribe with the bilingual (Sumerian and Akkadian) terminology for drawing up all kinds of contracts and judgments (in Babylonian fashion named *ana ittišu* after its opening line), edited by B. Landsberger, *Die Serie ana ittišu, Materialien zum Sumerischen Lexikon. Vokabulare und Formularbücher* 1, Roma 1937. Only a few model contracts and court records have been published thus far. A short survey of the latter, as far as known, is offered by M.T. Roth in *Journal of the American Oriental Society* 103, 1983, 279ff. Elsewhere she has published three texts used in the schools, a collection of "Laws About Rented Oxen", a "Sumerian Laws Exercise Tablet", and a "Sumerian Laws Handbook of Forms", see M. T. Roth, *Law Collections from Mesopotamia and Asia Minor, Writings from the Ancient ...*

the legal terminology and the formulary of contracts and judicial records,[5] though it did not mean that in Hammurabi's empire all regional and local differences in terminology and substance of law had by then disappeared.

Hammurabi's time makes a good frame of reference also because his extensive collection of laws is usually considered the culmination of early Mesopotamian legislative activity.[6] In Mesopotamia itself his laws must have had a lasting influence, since they were copied and studied through the centuries, down to the middle of the first millennium B.C.[7] From the time of his dynasty, moreover, we have evidence concerning a substantial number of royal decrees, issued to maintain or restore "equity" for the benefit of weak and indebted citizens or to supplement the laws by adapting and specifying rules for contractual liabilities and penalties.[8] Finally, the abundance and variety of contracts and judicial records from the Old Babylonian period allow a comparison between the laws and regulations and current legal practice. This comparison, in conjunction with some of Hammurabi's programmatic statements in the prologue and epilogue of his laws, is important for the question of the nature of the laws and the motives for recording them in writing, an issue which is relevant for the study of "early law", if only because it may be considered to mark the end of that phase.

[140] 2. The relevant cuneiform sources

2.1. Survey of the sources

Written documents in early Mesopotamia, *ca.* 3200-1600 B.C.

ca. 3200-3000	Late Uruk Period, levels IV-III
	earliest administrative documents, school texts and kudurrus
ca. 2900-2550	Early Dynastic Period I-II
	administrative texts, ancient kudurrus
ca. 2650	*earliest royal inscription*
ca. 2600-2500	Early Dynastic Period IIIa
ca. 2500-2350	Early Dynastic Period IIIb
	royal inscriptions, administrative archives, ancient kudurrus, earliest contracts
ca. 2500	Texts from Shuruppak:

...*World* 6, Atlanta 1995, 40-54. [**Add.** Additional "model contracts" have been published by W.W. Hallo, "A Model Court Case Concerning Inheritance", in: T. Abusch (ed.) *Riches Hidden in Secret Places. Ancient Near Eastern Studies in Memory of Thorkild Jacobsen*, Winona Lake 2002, 141-154, and by J. Klein & T. M. Sharlach, "A Collection of Model Court Cases from Old Babylonian Nippur", *Zeitschrift für Assyriologie* 97 (2007) 1-25. New evidence from the Old Babylonian Period on the use of law collections in the scribal education, also outside Babylonia, is now available in W. Horowitz *et al.*, "Hazor 18: Fragments of a Cuneiform Law Collection from Hazor", *Israel Exploration Journal* 62 (2012) 158-176].

5 The same holds true of the contemporary Old Assyrian period (*ca.* 2000-1750 B.C.), where our knowledge of legal history is based primarily on the extensive archives of Old Assyrian traders, which comprise a wide range of contracts and judicial documents and also evidence of legislation. See for the latter K.R. Veenhof, "'In Accordance with the Words of the Stele': Evidence for Old Assyrian Legislation", *Chicago-Kent Law Review* 70/4, 1995, 1717-1744 [= pp. 109-127 in this volume].

6 A subsequent culmination was the so-called "Middle Assyrian Laws", collected and recorded during the 12th century B.C. on a series of (originally presumably four or five) very large tablets, each with *ca.* 800 lines of writing and dealing with specific subjects. Of this series one complete and one rather damaged tablet and a series of fragments are preserved. See for this and all other collections of laws from Mesopotamia and their bibliography Roth, *Law Collections* (note 4).

7 See for this feature, M.T. Roth, "Mesopotamian Legal Traditions and the Laws of Hammurabi", *Chicago-Kent Law Review* 71, 1995, 13-37, esp. 19-21.

8 See for the royal decrees aimed at restoring equity, F. R. Kraus, *Königliche Verfügungen in altbabylonischer Zeit*, Leiden 1984, and for decrees on other legal issues, K.R. Veenhof, "The Relation Between Royal Decrees and 'Law Codes' of the Old Babylonian Period", *Jaarbericht Ex Oriente Lux* 35-36, 1997-2000, 49-83 [= pp. 297-328 in this volume].

ca. 2500-2375	First Dynasty of Lagash
	administrative archives, contracts, royal inscriptions
ca. 2430	Enmetena
ca. 2400	Uruinimgina
ca. 2350-2200	Old Akkadian Empire
	increasing variety of contracts, earliest judicial records
ca. 2110-2000	Third Dynasty of Ur III
	administrative archives, contracts, judicial records, legislation
ca. 2100	*Laws of Urnamma*
ca. 2000-1600	Old Babylonian Period
	contracts, judicial records, school texts, legislation, royal decrees
ca. 1930	*Laws of Lipit-Ishtar* (Isin)
ca. 1800	*Laws of Eshnunna*
ca. 1760	*Laws of Hammurabi*
ca. 1740	*decree of Samsuiluna of Babylon*
ca. 1650	*decree of Ammiṣaduqa of Babylon*

A short survey of the main sources from the third millennium B.C. is necessary, because their nature, relative frequency, first appearance, availability or absence play a role in what follows. In general we may distinguish four different types of written sources:

(a) Contracts, that is records of completed legal transactions of various kinds. The oldest, from the very beginning of the third millennium B.C., are a small number of inscriptions on stone (some are named after their first owner or the city where they were kept), frequently difficult to read and to understand and occasionally provided with a pictorial relief, which probably document some kind of transfer of land (figs. 1 and 2). Assyriologists call them "ancient *kudurrus*" (*kudurru* is the term much later used for sculptured and inscribed "boundary stones" which record land grants and **[141]** similar donations) and they are accessible in a recent edition, with full comparative analysis, in two impressive volumes, published in 1991.[9] They were perhaps (only a few stem from official excavations) deposited in temples, presumably not because the land (originally) belonged to that institution, but out of the wish to place these **[142]** records, made of stone in order to secure their durability, under divine protection. Around 2500 B.C. they are followed by the oldest recognizable contracts, at first in part still on stone, but soon mainly on clay tablets, which record that fields and houses (a little later also slaves) had been acquired from their owners by individuals against payment (in silver or copper), in the presence of witnesses.[10] The largest group of tablets comprises nearly fifty contracts excavated in the ancient city of Shuruppak (the name of the modern ruin is *Tell Fara*, in middle Babylonia, which is responsible for the designation "Fara texts"), which have received much attention in recent years.[11] Some sizable documents (on stone and clay) are not the primary records of transfer, but (excerpted) compilations of a series of such transactions by the same buyer. Most are deeds of sale, but there is also some evidence of exchange,

9 I.J. Gelb, P. Steinkeller & R.M. Whiting, *Earliest Lands Tenure Systems in the Near East: Ancient Kudurrus*, I, text, II, plates, Oriental Institute Publications 104, Chicago 1991, henceforth *ELTS*. Note also the extensive review article by C. Wilcke, "Neue Rechtsurkunden der Altsumerischen Zeit", *Zeitschrift für Assyriologie* 86, 1996, 1-67.

10 The most important editions of these early legal documents are D.O. Ezard, *Sumerische Rechtsurkunden des III. Jahrtausend aus der Zeit vor der III. Dynastie von Ur*, München 1968 (several of which are re-edited in *ELTS*, see previous note), supplemented by J. Krecher, "Neue Sumerische Rechtsurkunden des 3. Jahrtausend", *Zeitschrift für Assyriologie* 63, 1974, 145-271 (edition of 27 new records).

11 Note G. Visicato, *The Bureaucracy of Šuruppak*, Münster 1995; G. Viscato & A. Westenholz, "Some Unpublished Sale Contracts from Fara", in: *Studies in Memory of Luigi Cagni*, vol. 2, Naples 2000, 1107-1133, and H.P. Martin *e.a.*, *The Fara Tablets in the University of Pennsylvania Museum of Archaeology and Anthropology*, Bethesda 2001.

Fig. 1. "Blau plaque", *ca.* 3000 B.C., greenish stone, *ca.* 16 x 7 cm. Possibly recording the conveyance of a field, with a representation of the seller (left figure) holding an object with may symbolize the transfer of the property (*ELTS* no. 11).

Fig. 2. "Hoffman-tablet", *ca.* 3000 B.C., inscribed black stone, *ca.* 9 x 9 cm. Records the acquisition of in all ca. 350 hectares (left column, top: 5 x 10 bùr + 5 x 1 bùr = 55 bùr of 6.5 hectare each; the sum of the figures in the other two columns) against payment (*ELTS* no. 1).

donation and perhaps of acquisition of pledged real estate. In the 24th century B.C., along with these records of conveyance of real estate (among which still some very big stone documents),[12] the first records of liabilities resulting from debt and guaranty appear, together with records on hereditary divisions and, again somewhat later, on transactions relating to marriage and a variety of other subjects.

(b) The earliest *judicial records* stem from the 24th century B.C., from the Old Akkadian Period. They are court judgements in conflicts of various nature, dealing with debts, disputed sales, fugitive slaves, compensation for damage, an unproved accusation, a broken marriage promise, etc. In addition, short narrative records of proceedings, separate depositions by witnesses, and records of statements under oath and of the application of the water ordeal (a form of divine judgment) appear for the first time.[13] Certain documents, recording a series of cases dealt with by the same judge or dated to the same period, apparently served as memoranda preserved in a judicial archive, to be available for future reference, presumably if the same or similar cases came up again.

12 The largest and most famous is the so-called "Obelisk of Manishtushu" (an Old Akkadian king), which records on no less than 24 columns of writing, the acquisition by the king of eight parcels of land, in all *ca.* 3420 hectares, each from several sellers of the same kinship group. Edited and analysed in *ELTS* I, 116-140, no. 40.

13 Many are found in Edzard, *Sumerische Rechtsurkunden* (note 10).

They probably are the precursors of a few large archives of short records of "concluded cases", "final verdicts" (in Sumerian di.til.la), known from the period of the Third Dynasty of Ur (21st century B.C.).[14]
[*Addendum*. An overview of the "law" of the Early Dynastic and Sargonic Periods, in which the various sources are discussed, § 2.1 addendum to a), and J.G. Dercksen, Old Assyrian Institutions is given by C. Wilcke, in: R. Westbrook (ed.), *A History of Ancien Near Eastern Law*, Handbuch der Orientalistik, section I, vol. 72/1 (Leiden-Boston 2003)141-181].

[143] *(c)* The first *official inscription* in which a king records his concern with justice dates to from *ca.* 2425 B.C. Enmetena of the state of Lagash, is the first ruler of whom measures for the benefit of impoverished, indebted and exploited (sold into debt-slavery) citizens are mentioned:

> He cancelled obligations for Lagash, having mother restored to child and child restored to mother. He cancelled obligations regarding interest-bearing grain loans.[15]

His second successor, called Urukagina or Uruinimgina, is better known for what are called his "Reform Edicts", a long, fascinating, difficult and highly ideological text, in which he claims to have abolished a number of current evil practices and restored the conventions of former times, presented as the traditional values of the ancient temple community. As such he mentions – among others – the economic power of the palace over property (land and animals) of the temples and the abuse of power and exploitation of common citizens by officials and mighty men.

> From the citizens of Lagash he wiped out the imprisonment caused by sitting in debts… Uruinimgina solemnly promised Ningirsu (the city-god of his capital) that he would not subjugate the waif and the widow to the powerful.[16]

By these measures – certainly also meant to strengthen his position as usurper of the throne and less reformist than he would like his readers to believe – this ruler gained himself the reputation of the first "social reformer".

(d) The first truly *legislative text* finally appears around 2100 B.C., the so-called "Laws of Urnamma", the founder of the empire of Ur III, an early forerunner of Hammurabi's code. In a long prologue he boasts of what he has accomplished for the security and prosperity of his land and of his measures in the interest of the citizens. Among those measures he mentions putting an end to the exploitation by superiors, liberation from slavery under foreign domination, standardization of weights and measures, and protection of the weak and poor:

> The orphan is not delivered to the rich man, the widow not to the mighty. The man of one shekel [of silver] is not delivered to the man of one pound, the man of one sheep not to the man of one ox.

---

14 The basic edition (to which dozens of new records can now be added) still is Falkenstein, *Neusumerische Gerichtsurkunden* (note 3).

15 See J.S. Cooper, *Presargonic Inscriptions, Sumerian and Akkadian Royal Inscriptions* I, New Haven 1986, 58, La 5.4, col. IV. The expression "to restore/return to the mother", in Sumerian *amargi*, soon became the technical term for restoring the original, good situation, in Akkadian *andurārum*, which is usually, but not quite accurately, translated as "freedom".

16 Latest translation in H. Steible, *Die altsumerischen Bau- und Weihinschriften, Freiburger Altorientalische Studien* 5, Wiesbaden 1982, 288ff. Ukg. 4-5. See for a recent evaluation, P. Steinkeller, "Land-Tenure Conditions in Third Millennium Babylonia", in M. Hudson & B.A. Levine (eds.), *Urbanization and Land Ownership in the Ancient Near East*, Cambridge MA 1999, 298.

[144] After a concluding sentence, "I made evil, violence, and the cry for justice disappear", there follow the laws, introduced by "At that time: (¶1) If a man kills, that man will be killed", etc.[17]

2.2. Nature and background of the sources

Using written sources of Mesopotamian law, especially those from the early periods, we have to realize a few things. The first is that their availability depends on "the luck of the spade", since every document has been excavated, professionally or not, and that they are usable only after decipherment and publication. Their availability and spread are therefore capricious, conditioned by such factors as the preference of excavators, the political climate (excavation permits; the inaccessibility of Iraq since 1990 has resulted in a massive increase of archaeological work in Syria) and the choices and chances of epigraphists. Many records still lay inaccessible or unstudied in public and private collections. Most written documents from the early periods, *i.e.* of most of the third millennium B.C., originate from the area south of Baghdad, the region of the early Sumerian city-states. Early legal documents from other areas are rare and also those from the Sumerian core area before ca. 2500 B.C. are limited in number. Disregarding archaeological factors, this is mainly due to the fact that the recording of legal transactions in writing, apart from some exceptions, apparently only started around 2500 B.C. and remained selective during the following centuries. Filling this gap by retroprojection from later periods is risky. Notwithstanding the power of (legal) traditions, there was evolution, due to social and political developments, changes in the form and substance of law, and progressive juridification and growing professionalism of administrators and scribes. Moreover, regional differences, the legacy of the system of independent Sumerian city-states which dominated the so-called Early Dynastic period (*ca.* 2900-2400 B.C.), persisted to some extent, even into the second millennium B.C. Finally, we have to live with the fact that Mesopotamian scholarship, which certainly included law, did not produce legal treatises or juridical literature. The only written sources the Babylonian schools produced and used were lexical lists (such as the series *ana ittišu*, see note 4) and model texts. Instruction and explanation of legal texts and matters apparently were an oral business, which we cannot recover. Even though schools and scribes kept and used earlier documents (*e.g.* precursors of Hammurabi's Laws), there is no evidence of a historical or comparative interest, such as attested with the Hittites, where later editions of their laws record (for some revised provisions) how it had been before. Our knowledge of early Mesopotamian law and its development has to be derived from numerous practice documents with only some help from a few rather late legislative texts, whose status as valid, binding law is still disputed.

[145] *2.3. Observations on the sources*

What is recorded in the earliest texts is not the beginning of law. Growing prosperity, population increase and urbanization shortly before 3000 B.C. in southern Mesopotamia led to the invention of writing as an instrument for managerial and administrative purposes, both as external memory and as a device for checking transactions and storage.[18] This was the culmination of a development of several centuries, during what Assyriologists call the "Late Uruk Period" (ca. 3500-3000 B.C.), a period in which law

---

17 See for this (incompletely preserved) corpus of laws, Roth, *Law Collections* (note 4), 13-22, and for a recent new edition C. Wilcke, "Der Kodex Urnamma (CU): Versuch einer Rekonstruktion", in T. Abusch (ed.), *Riches Hidden in Secret Places. Ancient Near Eastern Studies in Memory of Thorkild Jacobsen*, Winona Lake 2002, 291-333 [and now, by the same, "Gesetze in sumerischer Sprache" in: N.V. Koslova *et al.* (eds.), *Studies in Sumerian language and literature*: *Festschrift für Joachim Krecher*, Babel und Bibel 8, 2015].

18 See for this use of the script the fascinating book by H.J. Nissen, P. Damerow & R.K. Englund, *Frühe Schrift und Techniken der Wirtschaftsverwaltung im alten Vorderen Orient. Informationsspeicherung und -verarbeitung vor 5000 Jahren*, Berlin 1990.

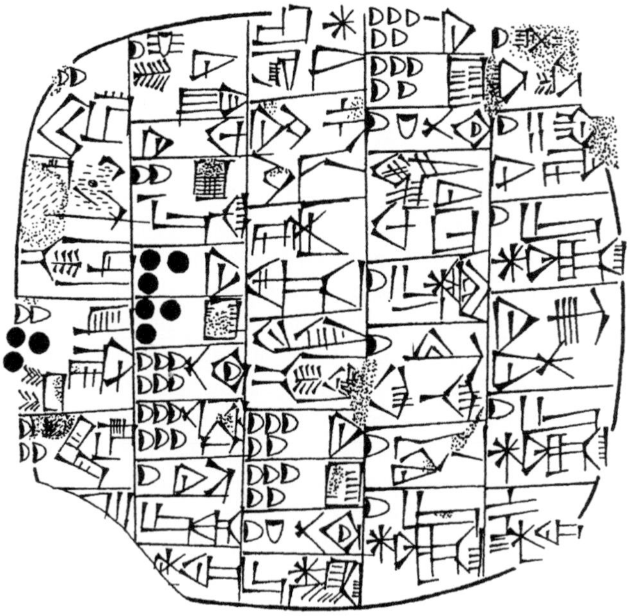

Fig. 3. Clay tablet recording the sale of a field, *ca.* 10 x 10 cm, Shuruppak, *ca.* 2500 B.C., obverse (M.P. Martin *et al.* (note 11), p. 79 no. 97).

cannot have been absent and must have developed, but a prehistoric phase about which we have no information.

Our knowledge of the next period, the so-called Early Dynastic Period (ca. 2900-2400 B.C.) is limited. The number of documents from the first centuries is small and the interpretation of the oldest ones fraught with difficulties. It is only from ca. 2500 B.C. onwards that we have groups of intelligible legal documents, with a recognizable structure and formulary. But, however important, they deal with a very small range of subjects: the transfer of fields and houses, and somewhat later also of slaves. It takes another century before the variety of subjects increases and judicial records make their first appearance. But during this half millennium Mesopotamian society, as we know from the oldest administrative documents and from the list of professions and titles used in the earliest schools, was already complex and stratified. Temples, and somewhat later also palaces, had considerable bureaucratic and administrative expertise at their disposal. Many legal transactions must have taken place, rules must have been applied, adapted or developed to meet the needs of this developing society, but they escape us when not recorded in writing. To be honest, we must admit that Mesopotamia during the first half of the third millennium B.C., from the point of view of legal history is to a large extent still *terra incognita*. Recording the outcome of judicial procedures in writing, as mentioned above, only started slowly during the 24th century B.C. and was at first apparently restricted to specific cases, presumably conditioned by the status of the parties or the nature of the goods at stake. Such records primarily served evidentiary purposes and reflect the wish to obtain written, durable proof (which would outlast human memory) of rights acquired or vindicated by the winner of the case, in whose archive such records are usually found. But some records may have been kept in the archive of the judge(s) for future reference. Although a few of these early documents mention sanctions for breach of contract, written proof of penal law is still missing, since verdicts were only rarely written down.

The earliest legal texts, as mentioned above, are records of the transfer of real estate, fields and houses.[19] They may contains dozens of lines of writing (fig. 3), most of which list the names of the seller(s) and buyer(s), their relatives and neighbours, and the witnesses

---

19 See the editions listed in notes 9 and 10.

to the transaction. But of course also the essential data of the item sold, its location and measures, and the payments made, which usually consisted of a **[146]** number of different transfers. First comes the purchase price proper (in copper or silver), next an "additional payment", presumably a compensation for what had been invested in the property, and finally a "gift" or "allotment", usually consisting of *naturalia*, such as articles of food, oil, clothes, and wool. The latter are meant for the seller(s), his relatives and relations, called "witnesses", but most probably to be identified as a kind of "secondary sellers", who had certain links with the property and its seller(s) and had to be compensated when (part of) a family property was alienated. Next there appear three, occasionally four "professionals", in house sales a "master house surveyor" and a "street herald", in field sales a "field scribe" and a "manager of the arable land" (called engar.uš), in whose stead a few times a "field recorder" and a "field assessor" occur.[20] Finally there follow a group of (real) witnesses, who receive nothing, and a date.

3. Reasons for the appearance of the oldest legal records

3.1. Buyers, scribal expertise and evidentiary purposes

The earliest documents record economically and socially important transactions in real estate and somewhat later in persons. The fields sold (especially in the oldest records at times vast areas of land) frequently were family property, which was surrendered to others or perhaps parcelled up; the persons sold were or became slaves. **[147]** The always individual buyers, as far as they can be identified, frequently were wealthy persons, belonging to the local elites, such as governors, temple officials, functionaries of the palace, also scribes and traders, men but occasionally also women.[21] The just mentioned professionals may have functioned as "neutral participants", presumably also in order to serve as publicity witnesses.

A variety of factors may explain the existence of such texts. Apart from the importance of the transaction and the status of the buyer, the new owner of the property, also the availability of scribal expertise must have played a role. The big temple households had practised from the very beginning a system of book-keeping for the registration of goods and persons passing through their administrative channels. It is hardly surprising that this bureaucratic expertise was in due time also used for the recording of important transactions with legal implications, presumably first and primarily by and for persons who belonged to or had links with these institutions and hence access to scribal expertise. This link and stimulus are also indicated by the fact that the earliest legal records do not yet use transactional verbs. They register, like book-keeping records, only facts: the location, size (and name) of the field, the name of the seller, the price paid, the name of the persons who receive (lit "consume") the price, the witnesses, the actions of the professionals and what they received. The oldest deeds of sale are therefore, from a formal point of view, a kind of administrative documents, memoranda; verbs which describe the transactions and sealings only appear somewhat later. But the testimony of the parties and witnesses mentioned is able to "activate" these documents, whose mere existence probably already inspired trust in the facts recorded. Such a document, in particular if it was made of valuable stone, provided the person who had acquired the property with detailed and durable evidence of his title.

---

20 See the for their occurrences and functions *ELTS* I, 237f.

21 See for a survey of the prosopography, Martin *et al.*, *The Fara Tablets* (note 11) 118f., who conclude: "we infer that in Fara the possibility of participating in purchase contracts was limited to a small circle of people. The occurrence in the sale contracts of officials who are mentioned in various capacities in the institutional hierarchy indicate that these elite families also wielded political power".

3.2 Public interest and the role of the government

That certain "professionals" played a role in many sale transactions has been interpreted as proof of public interest, of the wish of the authorities to check and register them. Some of the officials, apart from their specific tasks (such as surveying the property, weighing out the price, or writing the official record), may also have served as publicity witnesses. The implications of their presence, however, are not very clear. If they indeed were in the service of, or represented a public institution – in Shuruppak both "the palace" and "the city", which comprised also the temples, are attested as such – the fact remains that, as recorded in the contract, they were paid by the buyer. This could mean that they acted at his request, but it is perhaps possible that he had to pay for the services of persons he was obliged to engage, as is still the case today with public notaries. Anyhow, their expertise guaranteed the quality of **[148]** the transaction and the resulting record, which must have been in the interest of the buyer as the new owner. One may assume that the "master house surveyor" and the "(field) scribe" were "clearly responsible for the surveying, and probably also for the registration, of real estate" (*ELTS* I, 237),[22] but, unfortunately, nothing is known about obligatory registration and deposition of such records and the (admittedly rather meagre) evidence on their find spots does not point to a central, public depository. The fact that many buyers belonged to the urban elite, presumably with links with the temple and the palace, may indicate a connection between these public institutions with their scribal expertise and the existence of these early records. But we lack good evidence for attributing their existence to stimuli by these authorities or a growing involvement of the government in legal transactions.

What is clear, however, is that such real estate transactions were made public. To quote *ELTS* (I, 237): "We can assume, therefore, that, in the context of sales, the 'street herald', and similarly the 'chief herald', was responsible for the publicity of concluded transactions, more specifically transactions which involved estate located within the city limits, *i.e.* houses." A "(town) herald" with the same function also occurs in a slightly younger house sale contract from Lagash. The task of the herald or town crier was to drive into the wall of the house sold a wooden peg, which passed through a hole in the cone shaped clay record (see fig. 4), and to "apply its (*i.e.* of the transaction) oil on the side". This publicity act may have served to ceremonially finalize the transaction and was probably accompanied (never mentioned in the records, but suggested by the name of the official in question) by a public announcement of the transfer. Such duties of a "town crier" are known from various cultures, especially in an analphabetic environment and in the absence of other publication media. In the ancient city of Assur, around 1200 B.C., a law still prescribed that the intended purchase of a house within the city or of a field in its commons had to be publicly announced by the town herald three times within one month. Only after three city officials had made a deposition about it and confirmed that no rightful claimant had presented himself, the sale was considered valid and final.[23]

Driving a peg or nail into the foundations of a building was a very old custom in Mesopotamia, especially when kings dedicated a temple, which symbolized that the soil and building were formally transferred and had become the property of the god who lived there.[24]

The originally uninscribed pegs were soon provided with an inscription, later also fixed into or combined with an a inscribed tablet. It does not surprise that the earliest recording of the sale and transfer of houses uses the same symbolism. But it is equally interesting that while the "foundation pegs" of temples remained invisible in their foundations, the "peg-records" of house sales were publicly applied and remained visible,

---

22 This is also assumed for scribes qualified as "field surveyors", which occur in slightly younger field sales from Lagash, see *ELTS* I, 238 under 7.11.2.

23 See for this law, Roth, *Law Collections* (note 4) 177, MAL B ¶ 6.

24 See for this custom, R.S. Ellis, *Foundation Deposits in Ancient Mesopotamia, Yale Near Eastern Researches* 2, New Haven 1968, esp. ch. 3, "Peg Deposits".

Fig. 4. Cone shaped, sealed (on the middle of bottom) clay record of the sale of a house on a wooden peg, to be driven into the wall of the house sold. Girsu-Lagash, *ca*. 2400 B.C. Photocredits: photo © RMN-Grand Palais (musée du Louvre) / Mathieu Rabeau.

together with the clay cone with the details of the property and the transfer. One might compare them with the Greek *horoi*, inscribed slabs of stone **[149]** which originally served to mark off the boundaries of agricultural property, but later were also used to identify it (and in due time also houses) as legally unencumbered (mortgaged or pledged). Finley calls it "a very crude way of achieving some of the purposes of the modern register of titles and deeds".[25] Similarly, while the action of the "town herald" in early Sumerian cities reveals a clear interest of the authorities in who owned houses and fields in and around their city and who therefore lived in the city, his very action and the use of peg-plus-inscribed-cone do not support the idea of a public registration of records, because the peg ritual rather looks like its archaic precursor. But this publicity act, patterned after the inscribed foundation deposits of temples, may have stimulated the recording in writing of the transfer, which was necessary to reveal data which a peg alone could not communicate or preserve for posterity.

[150] 4. The development of legal documentation

4.1. The evolution of the legal record

Even though these records are not the very beginning of law, they do document early law. While, as pointed out above, the oldest contracts still reflect patterns of institutional book-keeping practices, they soon develop their own character and formulary, to go beyond the purely administrative desiderata. Apart from carefully recording all the facts and actions, some of the oldest records already include short "final clauses". They concern the liability of the seller for undisputed ownership by the buyer and stipulate sanctions if a third party "retains" the item sold, *i.e.* is able to assert prior rights to it at the expense of the buyer.[26]

That the earliest records belong to the phase of "early law" is borne out by the mention of various details of the transaction and of formal or symbolic actions which accompanied it, such as the surveying of the property, the weighing out of the purchase price, the application of the peg with the clay record, the libation of water, etc. The careful enumeration of all persons who were involved and the handing over of *naturalia* as gifts to all those who had some relation with the property and the main seller – what we call

25 M. I. Finley, *Economy and Society in Ancient Greece*, Penguin Books, Harmondsworth 1983, 63f..

26 See Krecher, "Neue Rechtsurkunden" (note 10) 188ff., "Die Erklärung des Verkaufers zur Haftung", and *ELTS* I, 247f., 7.12.7.1, "dù-clause". In such a case the seller has to pay double compensation or offer something valuable in exchange. In house sales the fraudulent seller suffers an exemplary punishment, meant as a deterrent: the wooden peg, to which the cone shaped clay deed of sale was attached, was now driven into his mouth, obviously because he had lied (which may imply that he had declared at the transfer that the property was indeed his and was unencumbered).

the "secondary sellers", *i.e.* relatives and various categories of neighbours, designated as "the brothers of the land who live there" and neighbouring farmers – means that they were paid or compensated for relinquishing their rights and approving the transaction. But (part of) goods were at the same time used for and consumed by them during a ceremonial meal, which the buyer arranged for the seller and his companions. In this way he created a relation of guest-friendship, a bond which made the transfer of essential (family) property possible. The clothes and oil, as suggested by Wilcke, were perhaps meant to cloth the party of the sellers anew and to anoint them in a rite of passage.[27] All this shows that these records were meant to be a faithful reflection of what happened, of what was ancient customary law and qualifies them as evidence of "early law".

That these documents, notwithstanding a basic similarity, exhibit a fair measure of variation in terminology,[28] is most probably evidence of local variation and perhaps also of some individual scribal idiosyncracy. But, whatever the variation, no written record can, or intends to, give a complete report of what happened at such an occasion. And indeed, the early specimens already make a selection, because the solemn words, which no doubt were spoken on such occasions, are not reported and **[151]** there is a concentration on facts and actions. This selection is the beginning of a gradual evolution of the written record, characterized by a concentration on what from the legal point of view is essential and leads to a simplification of the narrative account. The various categories gradually develop their own format, style and terminology and get more standardized. Many of the details and the ceremonial or symbolic actions, mentioned above, gradually disappear from the formulary, though this does not necessarily mean that they no longer took place, as is clear from the fact that some may turn up later in "unusual" or "provincial" documents.[29] The result, already reached towards the end of the third millennium B.C., is a record in the form of a short, objective, narrative account in the third person, in deeds of sale usually formulated with the buyer as subject (*ex latere emptoris*). It reports a dated transaction which has taken place, the correctness of which is acknowledged by witnesses who impress their seals on the (envelope) of the cuneiform tablet.

4.2. The role of the scribal craft

This whole process is inconceivable without the professional scribe, who was responsible for the document and who, according to the early records, was paid for his work. The evolution of the documents he produced bears witness to two complementary trends: a gradual simplification and standardization of the narrative report of the transaction and an increase in the number and variety of so-called "final clauses". The latter reflect the wish to provide buyers, creditors, lessors, depositors, etc. with better and more sophisticated securities, also by stipulating fines and compensations for breach of

---

27 See Wilcke, "Neue Rechtsurkunden" (note 9) 16f., and for similar symbolic actions accompanying legal transactions, E. Cassin, "Symboles de cession immobilière dans l'ancien droit mésopotamien", *Année sociologique* 1952, 107ff., and M. Malul, *Studies in Mesopotamian Legal Symbolism*, Neukirchen-Vluyn 1988.

28 See the survey by Wilcke, "Neue Rechtsurkunden" (note 9), 37ff., "Zu den Formularen", and *ELTS* I, chapters 6 and 7.

29 An "archaic" sale from the city of Mari, perhaps from the 19th century B.C., still mentions six "surveyors who drove in the pegs" (to stake out the field sold) and reports that seller and buyer "ate bread, drank beer, and anointed each other in the house of the buyer" (see J.-M. Durand, *MARI* 1, 1982, 79ff). In slave sales, the ceremonial "bringing across the wooden staff/pestle" of the person sold is still mentioned during the Old Babylonian period and the manumission of slaves was still accompanied (effectuated?) by anointing their foreheads, which explains why the verb "to purify" (the forehead) acquired the meaning "to manumit". That certain symbolic actions were continued in later times is clear from some court records, where witnesses, interrogated whether a transaction really had taken place, may mention such actions as proof, even though they are not included in the standard formulary of a contract (*e.g.* the ceremonial cutting of the hems of the garments of groom and bride, knotted together at the marriage ceremony, and cut on divorce). [**Add.** See also my remarks on "the cutting of the *hāmum*", which accompanied the sale of a slave in an Old Assyrian contract, in: G.J. Selz (ed.), *Festschrift für Burkhart Kienast*, Alter Orient und Altest Testament 274, Münster 2003, 699-705].

contract, stipulations which should prevent or restrict the number of legal disputes or at least make their solution easier. Such adaptations of the written contracts, of course, were not simply scribal inventions, but must reflect the experience of litigation, whereby lessons of judicial practice and precedents were translated into new stipulations and "final clauses". This may also have been the case with the "law collections", which have a clear preference for difficult cases and potential conflicts, as it certainly was with the more realistic, separate decrees and regulations of the later Old Babylonian period.[30] All these legal sources document a link between judicial practice and scribal expertise, a combination of the experience and insights of the qualified judges and administrators of the courts of law with the know-how **[151]** of scribes trained in Babylonian schools in the handling of legal terminology and concepts. This development is clear proof of progressive juridification, which had reached maturity by the end of the third millennium B.C., when we are clearly beyond the phase of "early law".

The link between scribal education and the production of legal records is already probable for ancient Shuruppak, which yielded impressive evidence of early scribal training around 2500 B.C.[31] The large corpus of "school texts" discovered in that city, however, – and this is also true of comparable finds in other cities – did not contain legal texts nor a precursor of the later "legal vocabulary" (*ana ittišu*, see note 4). This is not surprising, because the early scribe was primarily trained in writing and reading the difficult cuneiform script, also by acquainting himself with a number of literary compositions in his native Sumerian language. Having done that, the reading and writing of contemporary legal records cannot have presented serious problems, because at this early stage there was still hardly question of a professional legal jargon. All this changed after *ca.* 2000 B.C., when the Sumerian language had to give way to the Semitic Akkadian as spoken language, but traditional texts, like legal records, continued to use also Sumerian terminology which had established itself.[32] The Semitic Babylonian scribe now had to be trained in the dead Sumerian language, which entailed the study of the professional terminology and of instructive sample texts. We assume that this training in writing and reading Sumerian texts was accompanied by oral comments and instruction, also in elementary legal matters, but we have no written proof of this.

5. Early law and legislation

Judicial experience in combination with scribal expertise in due time might also lead to legislation, at least if those wielding power or invested with authority wished to do so for practical or ideological motives. Legislation requires not only authority and wisdom, but usually also sources from which the law-giver (and his professional scribes) can draw. Judgments as precedents and contract law, both of which may include sanctions and penalties, are the most obvious sources as manifestations and applications of unwritten customary law, familiar to judges, wise men and to those who were regularly involved in legal transactions. In Mesopotamia, as we have seen above, written contracts only became available *ca.* 2500 B.C. and were at first limited to conveyances; other types of contracts and judicial records only started to appear a good century later, at first in small numbers. Written records from which a potential law-giver could draw were therefore at first rather rare, limited in scope and hardly an adequate source of inspiration for legislation, in the sense of codification of prevailing customary law. But even if they could be used and supplemented by oral common law and judgments, there must have been a

---

30 See Veenhof, "Royal Decrees" (note 8), and in general for "final clauses" during the Old Babylonian period, particularly rich in conveyances of property, M. San Nicoló, *Die Schlussklauseln der altbabylonischen Kauf- und Tauschverträge*, 2nd edition, München 1974.

31 See for the role of the early scribes in Mesopotamian civilization, G. Visicato, *The Power and the Writing. The Early Scribes of Mesopotamia*, Bethesda 2000.

32 The status of Sumerian may be compared with that of Latin as the language of traditional scholarship in the Middle Ages.

good reason for legislation, **[153]** certainly when this happened for the first time. Both factors may help to explain why there is no trace of legislation in early Mesopotamia before the end of the third millennium, even though common law must have been well developed by 3000 B.C.

5.1. The role of the city (assembly)

If we look for power, authority and judicial experience as a condition for legislation, there are two candidates in early Mesopotamia: the ruler or king and "the city", that is the city assembly. The city assembly was either a plenary body consisting of (all?) free citizens or, more likely, a council which comprised the city elders, *i.e.* the heads of families and senior and influential citizens. Originally, in a city-state, this assembly may have functioned as an instrument of civil administration, but we know very little of its composition, authority and tasks, although "city elders" occur in various ancient sources. Some rulers mention the city assembly as a platform for deliberation, but we have no formal descriptions nor texts issued by it, and when the evidence becomes clearer (after 2000 B.C.), it serves almost exclusively as a local court of law. Regularly involved in litigation, judicial deliberation and in passing judgments (excerpts of some of which may have been kept in a judicial archive), such a city assembly must have been a mine of judicial wisdom and experience and a possible source of legislation. But while there are a few indications that it took decisions, legislation by a city assembly is not attested for early Mesopotamia or later Babylonia.

Only for Assur (early second millennium B.C.) do we have evidence of an important role of its city assembly (actually simply called "the city") as the highest administrative body and court of law. It operated in conjunction with the ruler, who did not bear the title of king (the city god was the real king, as whose steward the ruler was regarded), and who seems to have served as its chairman and main executive officer, although in official letters and judgments he is always mentioned after the city ("The city and the ruler passed the following judgment ...").[33] The well documented judicial activity of this city also resulted in legislation, in the form of binding regulations engraved (= published) on a stone stele which we do not know, but to which judgments and letters refer.[34] The regulations fixed by Assyrian legislation apparently were considered necessary in order to cope with recurrent legal problems arising within the framework of Assur's sophisticated commercial activities. As such they are evidence of legal evolution and juridification in the context of international trade, but their date and substance set them apart from "early law",[35] while also this example of legislation by a city (assembly) is thus far unique.

[154] *5.2. The role of the king*

In the city-states of Early Dynastic Sumer power and authority were increasingly vested in the local ruler, considered the appointee and regent of the main god of the city. After *ca.* 2500 B.C. we occasionally meet kings of larger territorial states, and still later even a kind of emperors, such as the (eventually deified) kings of the powerful Old Akkadian Empire (24th-23rd centuries B.C.) and the Third Dynasty of Ur (21st century B.C.).[36]

33 See for the political institutions of ancient Assur and the roles of city and ruler, M.T. Larsen, *The Old Assyrian City-State and its Colonies*, Copenhagen 1976, 109- 191. [**Add.** See now also K.R. Veenhof, in Westbrook (above § 2.1, addendum to a), 434-437, and Th.K. Hertel, *Old Assyrian Legal Practices*, Leiden 2013, ch. 3 and 4].

34 See K.R. Veenhof, "Old Assyrian Legislation" (note 5).

35 There is some older evidence for regulating trade by means of treaties, but Assur provides the earliest evidence for laws dealing with commercial activities and trade. The need for such laws arose in the period after *ca.* 2000 B.C., when trade became more and more an entrepreneurial activity of private merchants, working with funds of the state and private investors. In Babylonia proper Hammurabi's Laws are the first to deal with trade and commercial credit, as a true reflection of the social reality.

36 The designation "emperor" is suggested by the enormous power and almost superhuman status of some these rulers of large, centralizes empires, who were extolled in royal hymns, deified in iconography and cult and by whom oaths were sworn.

Perhaps surprisingly, none of these early rulers is known for legislation, which makes it first appearance only with Urnamma, the founder of the last mentioned dynasty of Ur, towards the end of the third millennium. This is not because these ancient rulers were not concerned with justice. They were considered supreme judges and had the god-given task of caring for the well-being of their – actually their gods' – subjects, also by maintaining justice and equity, but for many centuries this duty did not lead to legislative activity.

Apparently, early royal involvement in legal matters was of old of two kinds. First the less spectacular administration of justice by the king as supreme judge, which must have been rather natural in a small city-state with a hierarchical administrative structure. In territorial empires the administration of justice basically remained a regional or local affair, with local judges and courts, but presumably (the written evidence is rather meagre) with the possibility of appeal to the king, by whom oaths were sworn. This role of the king as supreme judge is not a prominent feature in early royal inscriptions, which usually only speak in general terms of his concern for justice. Moreover, statements that he "established justice in the land" refer primarily to actions which concern the second kind of involvement, to be mentioned in the next paragraph. An exception is the inscription of Irishum, an early ruler of Assur (20th century B.C.), which dwells on judicial procedure, the curses which will befall those who give false testimony, and the help which the ruler would offer *bona fide* plaintiffs by granting them the authorization to hire an attorney.[37]

In the second place the king, appointed by the gods to take care of his subjects, felt particularly responsible for maintaining equity, *i.e.* preventing abuse and exploitation of which the ordinary citizens would become the victim. This duty implied preventing abuse of power by officials of the state and powerful citizens, and was epitomized in statements (quoted above, in § 2.1, c and d) that the king wished to protect the widow and orphan, the poor and weak against the mighty, to establish (which apparently meant to restore) equity by redressing what was unfair and bringing back the good situation of the past. Because proclaiming the king's will and efforts to meet this sacred duty obviously had an ideological and propagandistic value and served his legitimation, it became a favorite topic of royal **[155]** hymns and public inscriptions. Such statements were no hollow phrases and resulted in specific measures and decrees, proclaimed with some ceremonial and recorded in the king's year-names. While some them may have had a somewhat more lasting effect (abolition of prerogatives and curbing of the power of officials, reduction of service duties and taxes), many, and in the course of time more and more, were essentially *ad hoc* measures with only retroactive effect, such as the cancellation of existing consumptive debts and of arrears payable to the state, the liberation of debt-slaves, and the restoration of property of defaulting debtors that has been pledged or sold to meet debt liabilities.

This is quite different from legislation in the sense of creating a collection of laws, which was a rather late royal initiative. The first collection which deserves that name is the one of king Urnamma, the founder and first king of the powerful empire of Ur III (*ca.* 2100 B.C.), already mentioned above (§ 2.1. d). Its late appearance and contents indicate that it was the result of a long development and may be considered to mark the end of the period of early law. Urnamma's innovative example proved to be inspiring and during the next centuries at least three kings emulated it: Lipit-Ishtar, a king of the dynasty of Isin (*ca.* 1930 B.C.), which followed that of Ur III and was very keen on proving itself its worthy successor, which purpose also Isin's collection of laws may have served; a king (Dadusha?) of the state of Eshnunna (*ca.* 1800 B.C.), who produced a small corpus of nearly 60 provisions, and Hammurabi of Babylon (*ca.* 1760 B.C.), the first two producing laws in Sumerian, the latter two in the Semitic Akkadian.

37 See for Irishum and his inscription, Larsen, *Old Assyrian City-State* (note 33), 56ff. and 184. The attention paid to the administration of justice is probably due to the fact that this inscription was placed in a monumental structure, called "the Step Gate", where the court of law convened in the presence of (the statues of) the "seven divine judges", which are enumerated in the inscription.

The question what these law collections really are is still being discussed, but it is clear, if only from the selective treatment of legal issues, that they were not a codification in the sense that all earlier written or oral law was brought together and codified for public use in a systematic and positive form, covering all legal phenomena. Nor did it mean that all pre-code law was repealed an replaced by a new comprehensive code. In a recent study M.T. Roth [38] is inclined to assume a process of reorganization and systematization of existing law (which could result in what has been called a "perpetual index codification"), but hesitates to do so because of the lack of convincing evidence. And again, this does not fit the rather selective treatment of the law, the application of which is attested by contemporary contractual stipulations. While it is true that these legislative texts do not reveal how the law-givers worked and are silent on their sources, it is clear that the collection used earlier law compilations, precedents in the form of actual royal pronouncements,[39] and expanded what was supplied by tradition or precedent by means of extrapolation and variation. But the law-givers must also have made new regulations (which of course could have been based on existing contractual law or separate royal decrees), which were required by social and economic developments, such as (in Hammurabi's collection of laws) provisions on servants of the crown who held palace land, on issues connected with trade, commercial borrowing, credit and partnerships, and on the status and rights of a class of well to do religious women (called *nadītum*), who had to remain unmarried and **[156]** were forbidden to bear children. Finally, we may discern a number of laws which clearly had the goal of protecting and helping those who were weak and vulnerable, either by their status or due to economic problems or natural disasters. This last category of laws, which fits the explicit goal of protecting the week, formulated in the epilogue, obviously links up with the substance of the royal decrees, which aim at "restoring justice", mentioned above. Experience with such measures and an awareness of their limited effects may have led to making of legal rulings with a lasting effect, the implementation of which, however, is not well documented.

Still, the legislative process as such, which for Hammurabi's law collection to all appearances must have included "a deliberate collecting, revising, and responding to prior law" (Roth), for lack of hard evidence remains basically unknown. And this is even more the case with the earliest collection, that of Urnamma, more than 300 years older. While his legislative activity, as the programmatic statements in the prologue of his laws (see § 2.1. d) show, clearly stands in the old tradition of the king's duty of maintaining equity and protecting the poor and weak, he did not have any legislative predecessors, as far as we know. We also know very little about the schools (perhaps we should say school and state chancery) of his times as a possible source or instrument of legal recording. But he certainly could have drawn on the by then well developed common law incorporated in written contracts, while also his own judicial activity, especially in his capital Ur, must have supplied judgments as precedents, perhaps available in a judicial archive, which is attested for other cities (provincial capitals) whose governors functioned as highest judges.[40]

In his case the fact that he was the energetic and successful founder of a new, centralized empire, which again (as had already been the case during the hey-day of the Old Akkadian empire) incorporated the originally independent city-states, with their legal traditions, may have provided an added stimulus. His legislation would serve the wish to prove himself the right and righteous king, by establishing and publishing a

---

38 M.T. Roth, "The Law Collection of King Hammurabi: Toward an Understanding of Codification and Text", in Ed. Lévy (ed.), *La Codification des lois dans l'Antiquité*, Paris 2000, 9-31. [**Add.** A nice example of the use of an older collection is that § 61 of Hammurabi's collection is a literal translation of Lipit-Ishtar's § 8, where one has to read with ms C šà ha.la.ba.ni.šè in.na.an.sum.mu = *ana libbi zittišu išakkanūšum*, "they shall include it in his share". See for the issue of the use of "earlier legal material" also R. Yaron, "'Enquire now about Hammurabi, Ruler of Babylon'", *Tijdschrift voor Rechtsgeschiedenis* 59 (1991) 222-238, esp. 225-226, where he contrasts *antiquum ius* with "what Hammurabi and/or his expert staff offer us of their own".]

39 Which had to be abstracted and reformulated as casuistic rules to fit the format and style of the laws.

40 See Falkenstein, *Gerichtsurkunden* (note 3).

collection of legal rules which henceforth would obtain in his entire empire. If this was the case, his example may have inspired Hammurabi, who published his collection of laws rather late in his reign, at a time (as the enumeration in the prologue of all the cities he then ruled proves) when he had finally established his sovereignty over the whole of Sumer and Akkad. It is not impossible that the words in his epilogue (col. xlvii: 70ff.) that this collection of laws was published "in order to render judgments of the land and to make decisions of the land", by "land" meant the whole of the realm which the king then governed, which might suggest a link between political success and legislation. On the other hand, as mentioned above, this obviously does not mean that Hammurabi's legislative activity made all differences in law disappear. In the realm of family law, for instance, common law concerning marriage and divorce or the share in the inheritance of the eldest son had not become uniform.[41]. And if absence of uniformity in combination with local/regional **[157]** variation is considered typical for early law, then even the Old Babylonian period still exhibits traits of that phase.

This lack of uniformity, finally, is related to the difficult question of the status and legal force of these early royal law collections, which is still a matter of controversy. The law collections themselves nowhere explicitly state that the rules they contain will henceforth be binding and valid and will have to be applied by judges and courts. As pointed out above (§ 2.1. d), from a formal point of view the text is not prescriptive, but descriptive. After mentioning the accomplishments of Urnamma, the laws are introduced by "At that time", followed by the first ruling, an example which is copied in Hammurabi's collection. The rules are therefore not imposed, but stated to be in force, applied, which obviously fits the ideological goal of the text, which has to prove that during its reign justice and righteousness did indeed prevail. Two categories of persons are directly addressed in the epilogue of Hammurabi's laws: a) (col. xlviii: 59ff.) future kings, who are warned not to abolish or change anything and to respect the inscribed stele, and b) (col. xlviii: 3ff.) people who consider themselves wronged. The latter are invited to listen to what the text says, followed by "let my stele reveal to him his lawsuit, so that he sees his case/judgment and he may calm his (troubled) heart" and praise the king for what he did. There is therefore no order or invitation to the judges and the courts to apply these laws, which would be necessary if they were to be effective. And it has also repeatedly been observed that none of the hundreds of verdicts and judicial records of this period explicitly refer to or quote a law from this collection. Several scholars therefore deny the collection's legal force and its character of a binding law promulgated by the king, and stress its primarily scholarly, literary character and its mainly persuasive and moral authority, based on the respect for the king and his wisdom.[42] On the other hand, it is possible, as Roth suggests,[43] that the wronged citizen, who was to derive relief from reading the stele, was the victim of the judicial system and feels that he had wrongly lost his case in court. In that case Hammurabi's invitation to him would amount to an indirect appeal and warning to the judges to apply Hammurabi's just rulings.

The much earlier "Codex Urnamma", of course, could be appreciated in the same way. But its latest editor, Wilcke, considers it a collection of laws "die 'an diesem Tage'

---

41 It was either a double share, or a single one plus 10 percent, or simply one share, perhaps with first choice. See for these differences, F.R. Kraus in J. Brugman e.a., *Essays on Oriental Laws of Succession, Studia et Documenta ad Iura Orientis Antiqui Pertinentia* IX, Leiden 1969, 11f, to which we can now add that a double share is also attested for Eshnunna. See also below, note 44.

42 There is an ongoing discussion of these issues, which is beyond the scope of this contribution. But see, *e.g.* R. Westbrook, *i.a.* in "Cuneiform Law Codes and the Origins of Legislation", *Zeitschrift für Assyriologie* 79 (1989) 201-222, and "Codex Hammurabi and the Ends of the Earth", in L. Milano *et al.* (eds.), *Landscapes, Frontiers and Horizons in the Ancient Near East* III, Padova 2000, 101-106; Roth, "Law Collection" (note 38) 21ff., "The effect and effectiveness of the text"; S. Lafont, "Les actes législatifs des rois mésopotamiens" in S. Dauchy *et al.* (eds.), *Auctoritates. Xenia R.C. van Caneghem Oblata, Iuris Scripta Historica* XIII, Bruxelles 1997, 3-27; and also the remarks in Veenhof, "Royal Decrees" (note 8) 78-82.

43 "The Law Collection" (note 38) 20f.

Gültigkeit erhielten und zweifellos auch behalten sollten". He links this dating with the ceremonial dedication of the law stele (with sacrifices in the whole country), which would be its official, dated promulgation (hence his use of "codex"). He assumes that the same was the case with the "Codex Hammurabi", which also introduces the laws proper by "At that time". That the words immediately following this collection, "the righteous judgments which Hammurabi ... established ..." **[158]** (xlvii: 1ff.), are the only ones to speak of the king in the third person, he takes as proof that the whole complex beginning with "At that time" and ending with "which Hammurabi established", are quoted from a different official inscription that would have commemorated the actual promulgation of the laws, apparently a number of years before the erection of the well known law stele.[44]

However that may be, irrespective of our judgment on the formal validity and binding force of the law collections, they are clearly the culmination of a long development and gradual evolution of unwritten law. It becomes tangible for us in the earliest records of conveyance, in the course of the centuries followed by more and more formal ones and by an ever increasing variety of written contracts and judicial records. They imply a growing and gradually more sophisticated expertise both of legal specialists and professional writers, which lead to a gradual increase of written records, both for private persons, institutions and presumably also courts of law. This process was stimulated by the need to meet the demands of a society which was becoming more complex, in particular because alongside and at times at the expense of the "large institutions", private citizens with their property, public and private liabilities, personnel, entrepreneurial activities and public offices had become more prominent. For evidentiary reasons they wished to have their transactions, rights and the outcome of their legal disputes duly recorded in writing. This social evolution, probably in combination with the effects of a diminishing institutional protection, growing economic problems and exploitation, also due to the effects of political conflicts and natural disasters, called for more legal intervention. This presented a challenge to rulers who had the duty of maintaining justice and equity and to protect the poor. The need to make people "follow the right course" and to meet socio-economic problems by "restoring equity" led to the promulgation of both more traditional collections of legal rulings and more specific "decrees of equity". And the latter, which continued the old tradition of royal measures to redress wrongs, probably also paved the way for formulating laws of equity (which may have incorporated elements of earlier decrees) with a more lasting effect. This legislative activity has been triggered or stimulated in some cases (Urnamma, Hammurabi) by the creation of new territorial states, which meant a challenge to their kings, who probably were aware of local differences in law and keen to win over or reassure their new subjects by demonstrating their concern for justice and equity.

The knowledge accumulated, in oral or written form, in royal and local courts of law, in combination with the juridical expertise of professional writers of legal records and of scholars attached to the chancery[45] or schools, by the end of the third millennium B.C., if not earlier, was clearly sufficient for compiling substantial and **[159]** well-organized law collections. Unfortunately, the scholars and scribes, without whom the kings would have been unable to accomplish this task, and consequently also their education and how they went to work, remain unknown, since they did not describe their work, and their personalities are overshadowed by the royal law-givers in whose service they worked and whose reputation they had to promote.

---

44 Wilcke, "Kodex Urnamma" (note 17) 298f. In note 26 he also connects the legislative activity of Hammurabi and Urnamma with the desire to promote unity of law in their newly established territorial states (irrespective of the question whether or to what extent they succeeded in doing so).

45 This is especially clear from the letters emanating from the chancery of King Hammurabi, many of which deal with legal issues, in particular those of sorting out, after his conquest of southern Babylonia, problems with the allotment and redistribution of land and the offices, status and holdings of old and new servants of the crown. More than 200 of such letters are available in translation in the series F.R. Kraus (ed.), *Altbabylonische Briefe in Umschrift und Übersetzung*, vols. 2, 4, 9, 11, and 13, Leiden 1966-1994.

The Interpretation of Paragraphs t and u of the Code of Hammurabi*

1. Introduction

My old friend Veysel Donbaz's interest is focused on Assyria's written heritage, on Neo-, Middle and in particular Old Assyrian records. But he occasionally also ventures outside this area, when a collection he could publish contains also texts from other periods or areas, such as the one of the Sadberk Hanım Museum, or when, as curator of the tablet collection of the Istanbul Museum, he is asked to study specific tablets. For F. R. Kraus he prepared the cuneiform copy of Ni. 632, the tablet with the text of the Edict of king Ammi-ṣaduqa of Babylon, and to the joint publication, together with H. Sauren, of "Ni 2553 + 2565, a missing link of the Hammurabi Law-Code", he contributed the cuneiform copy (Donbaz/Sauren 1991). This large, damaged tablet helps to fill the lacuna in the text of the Louvre stele with 'Hammurabi's Code', due to the Elamite king who had seven columns, with in all ca. 500 lines of text, chiseled away to make room for his own triumphal inscription, which, however, was never written there. The loss of these columns, between what modern editors have numbered § 65 and §100 (I follow the numbering in Roth 1995) is particularly annoying for those interested in economic and commercial matters, which the CH is the first "law collection" to treat in considerable detail. The missing columns, after having continued the topic described by Petschow (1965:155f.) as "ausservertragliche unerlaubte Handlungen gegenüber Feldeigentümern" and comparable stipulations concerning houses, deals in particular with debt liabilities and the various ways in which a *tamkārum*, "merchant, creditor", can be satisfied.

The Nippur tablet in Istanbul and another OB tablet from Nippur, preserved in Philadelphia (CBS 15284; Poebel 1914: pl. 39-40, no. 93) are the only ones to cover what are now numbered §§ s-w, which deal in particular with the payment and rates of interest of debts. The existence of the tablet in Istanbul was already known to Driver and Miles on the basis of a provisional copy by Mrs. H. Kızılyay[1] and it was later examined by J.J. Finkelstein, who presented evidence for its Late Old Babylonian date, confirmed by its colophon with a (broken) year-name of Ammi-ṣaduqa, and suggested that it was the second tablet of a series that must have contained the whole CH.[2]

The latest edition of CH in Roth 1995 of course uses these tablets for its reconstruction of §§ t-w, but their reading still offers problems due to the damage of the tablets (whose texts are also not completely identical), while also the interpretation of these paragraphs raises questions. I therefore asked Veysel Donbaz many years ago to collate the tablet, to find out whether some readings I favored were possible. He reacted to my questions in 1998 in a letter to which he was kind enough to add a new copy of ms. **t**, col. III, lines 31-45 that cover §§ s-u. I made use of what he sent me when I studied the phrase *kīma ṣimdat*

* Originally published in S. Dönmez (ed.), Studies Presented to Veysel Donbaz (Istanbul: Zerobooks, 2010), 283-294.

1 Driver and Miles 1952: II, 1, note 3, mentions "variants taken from Mme Bozkurt's copy ... checked on a visit to Istanbul in 1951", but no variants from this tablet are listed or used for the paragraphs treated in this article, called L and M by them.

2 Finkelstein 1967: footnotes 2 and 6, and his Addenda on p. 48.

šarrim, "in accordance with the royal decree", that occurs **[284]** in § u of the Code, and mentioned my intention to deal with these paragraphs more in detail elsewhere (Veenhof 2001: 75f. [= pp. 297-328 in this volume]). This contribution, with includes Donbaz' new copy of §§ s-u, finally realizes that intention and his Festschrift seems an appropriate place to do so. In what follows the ms Poebel 1914, no. 93 is designated as **S**, and Ni 2553+2565 as **t**, in line with the sigla listed in Roth 1995, 252f.

The subject of these paragraphs are complications in the payment of debts rated in silver and/or barley and their implications for the rates of interest to be charged. Paragraph **u** states that a debtor, unable to pay back silver, is allowed to pay barley and deals with the consequences of this change for the rate of interest. Paragraph **t** in Roth's reading is almost a tariff that fixes the rates of interest for debts in silver and barley, somewhat comparable to LE §§ 20-21. Almost, because the first line of § **t** speaks of "giving grain and/or silver as an interest-bearing loan" and seems to stipulate for both the same interest, 33⅓ %, the one current for barley, which is puzzling. This is matched by the surprising and in fact contradictory statement in § **u** that, if a debtor has no silver, his creditor shall take "grain and silver". It shows that these stipulations require a new analysis, for which the new copy made by Donbaz is helpful. I first present my reading of the texts of the paragraphs, followed by some text-critical remarks and observations on the problems they present, and then turn to their interpretation.

2. The text of paragraphs t and u of CH

§ **t** can been reconstructed from mss. **S** I:5'-12' and **t** III:35-40:

S 5'-6'	[*šu*]*m*-[*m*]*a* DA[M.GÀR x (x)] KÙ.BABBAR-*am* / *ạ-na* UR$_5$-RA [*id-d*]*i-in*
t 35-36	*šum-ma* DAM.GÀR ŠE-*am ù* K[Ù.BABBAR] / *a-na hu-bu-ul-li* [*id-di-in*]
S 7'-8'	*a-na 1* GUR-Ẹ *0,*[*1.0*] ŠE MÁŠ / *i-le-*[*e*]*q-qé*
t 37	*a-na 1* ŠE.GUR *0,1.0* ŠE-*am* MÁŠ *ị-*[*le-eq-qé*]
S 9'	*šum-ma* KÙ.BABBAR *a-na* UR$_5$.R[A *i*]*d-di-in*
t 38	*šum-ma* <KÙ.BABBAR> *a-na hu-bu-ul-li id-di-i*[*n*]
S 10'-12'	*a-na 1* GÍN KÙ.BABBAR-*im* / IGI.*6*.GÁL *6* ŠE MÁŠ-*ạm* / *i-le-eq-qé*
t 39-40	*a-na 1* GÍN KÙ.BABBAR IGI.*6*.GÁL[!] *ù 6* ŠE KÙ.BABBAR / MÁŠ *i-le-eq-qé*

"If a merchant/creditor has given barley and/or (*u*) silver as interest-bearing loan, he will collect as interest 60 silas of barley per gur; if he has given silver as interest-bearing loan, he will collect 36 corns (of silver) per shekel of silver".

The lines of **S** are shorter than those in **t**, where their ends are broken, but their length is shown by **t**:41 in Donbaz' new copy. Differences that cause no problems of interpretation are in the writing of *hubullum* as logogram in **S**:6' and syllabically in **t**:36, without mimation, and of *ana 1* GUR.E in **S**:7' alongside *ana 1* ŠE.GUR in **t**:37. Ms. **S** adds phonetic complements to KÙ.BABBAR (5', 10') and even to MÁŠ (11'), while **t**:35 writes ŠE-*am* and adds KÙ.BABBAR in line 39, which it omits, no doubt by mistake, in line 38.

The main problem are the first lines. Assuming that the texts of both manuscripts basically agree, I have restored K[Ù.BABBAR] at the end of **t**:35 (where the head of the final vertical still visible could be the beginning of KÙ)[3] and [ŠE *ù*] in the gap in **S**:5', although there is little room for it between DA[M.GÀR] and KÙ.BABBAR.[4] If this is correct, the question is what is meant by "loaning barley *u* silver", for we expect the first half of the paragraph to deal with a barley loan, since its second half treats a silver loan. A clue is provided by the rate of interest **[285]** mentioned in **S**:7'//**t**:37. Since in **t** *0,1.0* ŠE is clear and there is in **S**:7' no room

3 In the other occurrences of the sign Ù in ms. **t**, it ends with one vertical wedge.

4 Restoring simply DA[M.GÀR] KÙ.BABBAR-*am* conflicts with **t**, would not mention a barley loan, and duplicate the beginning of the second part of this paragraph.

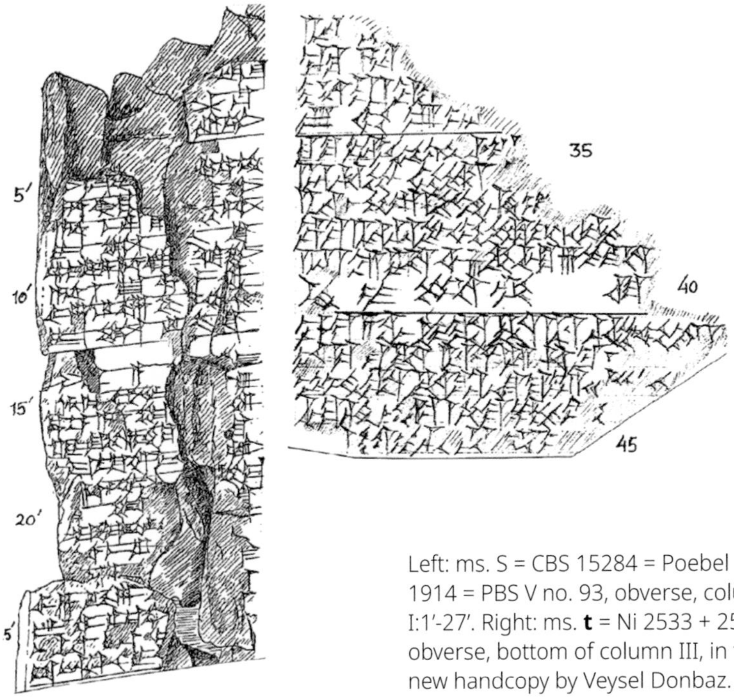

Left: ms. S = CBS 15284 = Poebel 1914 = PBS V no. 93, obverse, column I:1′-27′. Right: ms. **t** = Ni 2533 + 2565, obverse, bottom of column III, in the new handcopy by Veysel Donbaz.

for adding *4* (BÁN) between the single vertical and ŠE, the interest is 60 silas (= 1/5 gur), which equals 20%, on the basis of the standard equation *1* GUR ŠE = 1 shekel of silver. This is the usual rate for silver, cf. the first part of LE § 18A. The reading *0,1.4* ŠE (= 100 silas = 1/3 gur) = 33⅓ %, the normal rate of interest for barley, also stipulated in the second part of LE § 18A and advocated by Leemans 1950: 18ff.,[5] followed Skaist 1994: 105, and Roth 1995: 97, is impossible. The "silver rate" of 20%, expressed in barley, is a clue for understanding this paragraph. Driver and Miles's proposal to consider "silver" in S:5' a mistake for "barley" is unacceptable, not primarily because their reading turns this paragraph into a simple listing of the standard rates of interest for loans of barley and silver (comparable to LE § 18A), but because the new reading of the interest rate as 60 silas of barley per gur[6] would be strange for a simple barley loan. We need "silver" to explain its presence.

§ **u** can been reconstructed from mss. **S** I:14'-27' and **t** III:41-45:[7]

S 14'-15'	[*š*]*um*-[*m*]*a a-w*[*i-l*]*um* / [*š*]*a hu-bu-ul-la*[*m ir-š*]*u-ú*
t 41-42a	*šum-ma a-wi-lum ša* KÙ.BABBAR *a-na hu-bu-ul-li* / *il?-qú-ú?*
S 16'-17'	KÙ.BABBAR *a-na tu-*[*ur-ri*]*-im* / [*l*]*a i-šu* ŠE*-a-am-ma* [*i*]*-šu*
[286] t 42b-43a	KÙ.BABBAR *a-na tu-ur-ri la*$^{!}$ [*i-šu*] / ŠE*-am ša* KÙ.BABBAR *i?-šu?*
S 18'-19'a	[*k*]*i-ma ṣi-im-d*[*a-at*] LUGAL / [DAM.GÀR] *a-na* MÁŠ.BI *1* [GUR-E]
t 43b-44a	*ki-ma ṣi-i*[*m-d*]*a-*[*at* LUGAL DAM.GÀR ŠE] / *ù* MÁŠ *1* GUR.E$^{!}$
S 19b'-21'	[*0,1.0*] ŠE*-ma* / *ị-le-*[*eq-q*]*é* / [*šu*]*m-ma* DAM.GÀR MÁŠ [UR$_{5}$-R]A$^{?}$
t 44b-45	*0,1.0* ŠE*-ma i-le*$^{!}$*-*[*e*]*q-*[*qé*] / [*šum-m*]*a* DAM.GÀR MÁ[Š] *hu-*[*b*]*u-u*[*l-li*]
S 22'-23'	[*e*]*-li 1* GUR.[E *0,1.0* Š]E / [*ù e-l*]*i* KÙ.[BABBAR *1* GÍN.Ẹ
S 24'-25'	IGI.*6*.GÁL *6* ŠE [KÙ.BABBA]R$^{!}$ / *ú-wa-at-te-*[*er-ma*]
S 26'-27'	*il-qé ị-*[*n*]*a m*[*i-im-ma*] / *ša id-di-nu i-t*[*e-el-li*]

5 He was followed by Driver and Miles 1952: I, 173; Kraus 1979: 61, f; and by Borger 2006: I, 21.

6 Rejected by Driver and Miles 1952: I, 173, because this rate, readable in Poebel's copy, "would imply an innovation in the law."

7 As the photo and copy in Donbaz and Sauren 1991 show, nothing remains of the beginning of col. IV of ms. **t**.

"If a man who has contracted an interest-bearing loan has no silver with which to repay it, but does have barley (**t**: to the value of the silver), in accordance with the royal decree the creditor shall take (**t**: barley and) as interest still only 60 silas per gur. If the creditor takes as interest on his loan more than 60 silas per gur of barley or more than 36 barley corns per shekel of silver, he will forfeit whatever he has given."

> A few emendations in are necessary to make the texts agree and meaningful. At the beginning of **t**:42, on the basis of Donbaz' copy and because **t** adds the object *kaspam*, I have preferred *ilqû* over *iršû*, used in **S**:15', but there is no material difference between the two readings. LA at the end of **t**:42 is necessary and *išû* in *še'am ša kaspim išû* is the only reading that makes sense; *še'am ša kaspišu* (used in CH § 49) is excluded by the copy and *ša kaspiša* is impossible and ungrammatical; the nice *še'am+ma* of **S**:17', "but (has) barley", also given by Borger, cannot be reconciled with the copy of **t**. The verb *ileqqe* (**S**:20'//**t**:44b) requires *tamkārum* as new subject (thus far the debtor was the subject) and he can and must be accommodated at the beginning of **S**:19', but **t**:44 begins with a clear Ù, which suggests restoring ŠE at the end of line 43 and the required DAM.GÀR (unless the scribe omitted it by mistake) can only be accommodated before ŠE on the assumption that line 43 continued on the edge. The logogram at the end of **S**:21' is read (as in **S**:6') because the final vertical wedge excludes [*hu-bu-ul-li*]*m*, for which there is also little room. The reading [ŠE] / *ù* in **t**:43-44 makes explicit, as implied by the earlier statement that, if the debtor has not silver the creditor has to collect both his capital and the interest on it in barley. The convincing reading *e-li* in **S**:22' and 23' (supported by the traces in Poebel's copy) was already proposed in Driver and Miles 1952 and fits the use of *watārum* (D-stem and Š-stem), cf. *CAD* A/II, 490,2' and 491,4,b,1'. I do not understand why Roth and Borger did not accept it.

Read thus the paragraph becomes consistent. The contradiction in Roth's rendering "if a man ... does not have silver with which to pay, he (the merchant) shall take grain and silver", and the surprising qualification of the interest as "annual rate" (the tentative reading of MU.ŠÈ as *ana šattim*, based on Donbaz' earlier copy) disappear. The purpose of the paragraph, even though its first phrase does not explicitly say that it concerns a silver loan, apparently is to make sure that the creditor, obliged to accept from his debtor payment in barley instead of silver, sticks to the lower rate of 20%, normal for a silver debt, here expressed in barley (60 silas per 1 gur), because it is paid in barley. The obligation imposed on the creditor is "given teeth" by stipulating that if he takes more he will forfeit "everything he gave", that is his original claim. Mentioning the obligatory rate of 20% both in barley and in silver (36 barley corns per shekels) may be due to the fact that the original debt-note recording a silver debt would have stated it in silver. That it was added to extend the law and make it a general prohibition against overcharging interest, applicable also to silver debts paid in silver, is unlikely, because such debt-notes normally fixed the interest due at 20%.

[287] 3. Interpretation

*3.1. CH § **u** and the change of the valuta of a loan*

In my article of 2001 I dealt with § **u**, because it refers to a "royal decree" *(ṣimdat šarrim)*. Since such references, when they occur in contracts, always precede and introduce a royal ruling, the one in § **u** must have fixed the rate of interest at 20% for this particular situation. One could formulate it more generally as: Permission to repay an original silver debt in barley by a debtor in problems does not allow the creditor to charge him the higher rate of interest current for barley. The same issue seems to be at stake in CH § **51**: "If he (the debtor) has no silver to repay, he will give to the creditor <grain or> sesame according to their rates of exchange (*ana mahīrātišunu*) for the value of (*ša*) the silver with its interest that he had borrowed from the creditor, in conformity with the text of the royal decree."[8] But there is a difference, because § **u,** which has the creditor as subject, focuses on *the rate of interest*, while § **51**, with the debtor as subject, states the right to repay in a different commodity and focuses on *the rate of conversion* to be applied in such as case. But, as stated in footnote 8, the position in the sentence and the meaning of *ana pī ṣimdat* leave some doubt about what the decree actually ruled.

When a debtor could not pay back his debt in silver three questions were at stake:

a. When and under what conditions could he pay back his debt in barley?
b. What consequences would this have for the rate of interest?
c. By what exchange rate was the silver of the debt converted into barley?

a) A decree that provided the legal basis for *a)* seems essential, because not all creditors will have liked and accepted the change of valuta. If a creditor was a merchant who preferred silver, he himself would have to convert the barley or sesame into silver, while at harvest time their exchange value was probably less attractive. A legal ruling therefore must have been required to force him to accept it and this could be reflected by the wording of § **u**, where we could translate the present tense *ileqqe* by "(the creditor) shall collect". While a creditor, as the stronger party, might have changed the valuta under certain circumstances,[9] a debtor most probably could not do so without his creditor's permission, unless a loan from the start had been rated in two valutas (a special type of the so-called "mixed loans") and allowed a choice between them (see below, § 3.2). Accordingly, paying a silver debt in barley or sesame, mentioned in CH § **51**, most probably was based on a royal measure of the '*mēšarum* type', meant to help debtors in problems and its mention in this paragraph refers to it. This fits the context of this paragraph, since §§ 47-50 are all meant to give a weak debtor (a small farmer or tenant) some legal protection and help. Such a decree, however, is not known as a separate text, nor does any loan contract contain a reference to it of the type "he shall repay... according to the royal decree".

Kraus 1979: 61f. tried to solve this problem by assuming that the references to the royal decree in §§ **51** and **u** actually mean "nach der vorliegenden königlichen Bestimmung". The law according to him would refer to its own stipulation as a "royal decree", with the term originally coined for "eine königliche Sondermassregel",[10] **[288]** as was the case in § 4 of the Edict of Ammi-ṣaduqa. It stipulated that a creditor, who has collected a debt that had been cancelled by this very decree, shall give back what he took, followed by "who does not give back *ana ṣimdat šarrim* will die". This is indeed an internal reference, but this is not the case in §§ **51** and **u**. A meaning "nach der vorliegenden Bestimmung" does not work in § **51**, where the royal measure seems to bear on paying back in another valuta and especially on the conversion of barley and sesame into silver "according to their rates of exchange". But this is only a short reference to the measure and too general to be its

8 My translation follows the word order of the Akkadian text to show the position in the sentence of *ana pī ṣimdat šarrim*, which is rare compared with *kīma ṣimdat šarrim* used in § **u**. In Veenhof 2001: 75 note 120, I tried to distinguish the two by suggesting that, while "*kīma* ... seems to refer to a standard, a norm to be applied, *ana pī* may focus more on the details of a stipulation ..., which have to be implemented". That the scribe made a mistake by omitting *še'am ulu* is clear from § 52.

9 According to LE § 20 he could convert the barley he had loaned into silver, presumably when the contract was drawn up; the sequence *iddinma – uštepīl* expresses the order of the actions, but does not imply that much time had elapsed between them (the translation "wants to convert it into barley" in *CAD* Š/III, 332, 1, b, is not necessary). Unfortunately the words between *še'am* and *iddin* are damaged and not understood. One would expect *ana hubullim* (as interest bearing debt), as in CH § **t**, but the traces do not allow this and what is preserved looks like *ana mala* x x x, which could express the reason for doing so or the norm for the conversion.

10 As pointed out in Veenhof 2001: 74ff., it is very likely that some originally separate royal decrees were in due time incorporated into royal law compilations, and I mentioned LE §§ 9, 18A en 20-21 as likely candidates. Though probably slightly reformulated, they retain the material substance of the original decree.

text itself, since these "rates of exchanges" are not specified (also not elsewhere in CH), also not by writing in § **51** "according to the current rates" (*mahīrāt illakā*). Moreover, the subject matter of §§ **51** and **u**, though related, is not the same. While both state or imply the right to pay back in another valuta, § **u** clearly deals with the consequences of a change of the valuta of the debt for the rate of interest, while § **51** focuses on the rate of the conversion itself.

b) A decree that (only) fixed the exchange values (*mahīrātum*) of silver, barley and perhaps sesame. This was an essential aspect of the stipulation, explicitly mentioned in § **51**, and Driver/Miles 1952: I, 147, assume a "rate of exchange for grain and silver set forth by the ordinances of the king." Such a list or tariff, attested in LE §§ 1ff., is missing in CH, but it might have existed separately and the particular wording of § 51, with *ana pī* instead of *kīma ṣimdat šarrim*, might imply its existence (see footnote 8). San Nicolò 1974: 219 takes it as "dass vom König festgesetzte Umrechungsverhältnis zwischen Silber under den wichtigsten vertretbaren Naturalien des damaligen Verkehrs". Such a decree would not only have created clarity, but would also have offered protection, *e.g.* against the so-called "verhüllte Fruchtwucher", in cases of barley loans disguised as silver loans, where barley, rated in silver when it was scarce, had to be paid back after the harvest, at the by then "the current rate of exchange" (*mahīrat illaku*), which was cheaper. But again, such a separate edict is not known nor referred to in contracts.

c) A decree that according to § **u** dealt with the interest on debts paid back in a different valuta, *in casu* one stipulating that the rate recorded in a contract for the original valuta of the debt would not be affected by this change. In § **u** this provision is in the interest of the debtor, who pays the lower original interest on silver and if this was the goal of the decree, it may have been one of the *mēšarum* type, meant to help debtors who had taken out consumptive loans. The question is how to relate this to the roughly contemporary LE § 20, which states that a creditor, who for some reason or in some way converts an original barley debt into one in silver, at harvest time will nevertheless collect the normal interest on barley, 33⅓ %. This looks similar CH § **u**, in that in both cases the original valuta and hence rate of interest of the loan remains unaffected by the change of the valuta in which the debt is paid back. But while § **u** seems to be in the interest of the debtor, LE § 20, on the surface, seems to favor the creditor, but the neutral *ileqqe*, "he collects", obscures what is actually meant: is he still *allowed* to or *has* he to do so?

> LE § 20 is one of a small "chapter" dealing with the payment of debts and their interest. It starts with § 18A, which lays down the normal, generally attested rates: 20% for debts in silver and 33⅓ % for those in barley.[11] The next three paragraphs offer problems of interpretation, due to damage and lexical problems (see above note 15), but by taking them as an interrelated triplet they become somewhat clearer: § 21 deals with a debt that right away, from the outset (*ana panišu*) was rated in silver, § 20 with one originally in barley and then converted into silver, and § 19 with a silver loan given "against its corresponding commodity(?)" (Roth), presumably one that has to or can be paid in another valuta (barley), at the threshing floor.

We cannot exclude that the goal or circumstances of the change of valuta in LE § 20, hidden in the unclear words before *iddin*, stated that it was a special case, in the interest or with the consent of the debtor, or that commercial motives favoring silver were at play. Anyhow, this uncertainty makes it impossible to consider it simply the opposite of CH § **u** and it also rather daring to consider the "royal decree" referred to in the

11 See for the position and meaning of this paragraph Yaron 1988: 33f. and 235f.; Otto 1992 again connects § 18 with § 18A, but has not convinced me. Note that this paragraph does not explicitly mention silver and barley debts, but implies them by writing about interest "per 1 shekel" (of silver) and "per 1 gur" (of barley).

Babylonian CH § **u** as correcting a practice harming a debtor attested in a legal ruling issued in the realm of Eshnunna.

[289] The different focus of the legal rulings and the unlikelihood of the existence of several royal decrees dealing with various aspects of the change of the valuta of a debt, in my opinion suggest the existence of one more comprehensive royal decree that dealt with all three interrelated elements (a-c) mentioned above. Considering the various issues at stake it must have been rather detailed (although it remains uncertain whether it actually listed the exchange values or equivalencies of the commodities involved), and the various paragraphs of the law collection could simply refer to it, without quoting it more *in extenso*. It is a pity that its text remains unknown, but it is not surprising that we do not find references to it in loan contracts, because it is unlikely that such contracts would consider the apparently not very frequent eventuality of a desired or forced change of the valuta in which was paid.

3.2. The payment of mixed loans and CH § t

This formulation of the rate of interest in § **t** (and **u**), as "60 silas per gur of barley" is fairly rare but, as Skaist 1994: 109f. observes, this rate, though always specified as "60 silas of barley *per shekel of silver*", has forerunners in the Ur III period[12] and occurs in some early OB silver loan contracts from the Diyala region, Sippar-Amnānum, Kisurra, and elsewhere (TIM 3, 136; OECT 13, 281). It not only surprises to find interest on a silver loan specified as an amount of barley, but also that there is a variation in the verb of the payment clause. Several use LÁ/*šaqālum*, ["to weigh out, typical for the payment of silver], which suggests that the formula only fixes the rate of interest at 20% and does not imply payment in barley.[13] Others use the general verb SUM/*nadānum*, "to give", which can cover payment of silver or barley, in particular when it is used without object, "to be given back" (at due date), [14] and there is even a case where ÁG/*madādum*, "to measure out", typical for barley, is used: YOS 14, 54: *3* GÍN KÙ.BABBAR / *1* GÍN *0,1.0* ŠE.TA / MÁŠ.BI *ú-ṣa-ab* / KI E. / R. / ŠU.BA.AN.TI / *a-na* MAŠ.KÁN-*ni-i*[*m*] / Ì. ÁG. E, "3 shekels of silver – per shekel he will add 60 silas of barley as interest – from E. R. has received; he will measure (it) out by threshing time." [15] Such features raise the question of the nature and purpose of such loans, which is not easy to answer because the texts are laconic and we do not know their background.

Silver loans to be repaid in barley occur more often and were discussed by Edzard 1970: 30ff. in his excursus on "Silberdarlehen mit Rückzahlung von Gerste". The majority of the contracts he lists (including texts 3-5 of his volume) ask payment (usually at the time of harvesting or threshing) "at the (by then) current rate of exchange" (the so-called "Kursklausel"), but several others (including text 2 of his volume) omit this clause.[16] Edzard saw two possible explanations: "Entweder Zahlungserleichterung für den Schuldner, der nach der Ernte (= Rückzahlungstermin) Korn leichter beschaffen konnte als Silber; oder

---

12 See Lutzmann 1976: 50, with note 126; the formulation is: *1* gín kù.babbar (once: *1* gín.a) *0,1.0* še si-ge$_4$-dam. Skaist 1994: 110 also compares the rate of *1* GÍN *0,0.3* ŠE.TA, "30 silas of barley per 1 shekel", attested in a few early OB contracts, which amounts to an interest of 10% only.

13 Kienast 1978: nos. 3, 47; OECT 13, 281; perhaps TIM 3, 136, and the examples from the Ur III period, see the previous note.

14 In Kienast 1978: nos. 20 and 33, both without object, and in Sulaiman 1979: 134, no. 69:1ff., 12 GÍN KÙ.BABBAR / MÁŠ *1* GÍN *0,1,0* ŠE.TA / *uṣṣab* ...[8] *ana maškannim / kaspam ù ṣibassu / inaddin*, where the object is silver.

15 Another example could be *Tell ed-Dēr* II, 165, no. 27, where the payment clause in line 8 is damaged, but the traces suggest *i-ma-da-/ad*; unclear is *ibidem* no. 24. Exceptional is *RA* 73 (1979) 123, no. 50, where this rate of interest is stipulated for a loan of 1 gur of barley, to be "given" (SUM) at harvest time.

16 See for other contracts that stipulate payment of barley for a loan of silver: *RA* 73 (1979) 127f. no 55 (12 shekels of silver, verb SUM), no. 57 (2 shekels of silver, *qīptu*-loan, verb ÁG); *RA* 85 (1991) 17 no. 6 (*qīptum*, verb ÁG). But note *RA* 72 (1978) 120 no. 7, a loan of 1 shekel of silver, where the tablet has ŠE *ù* MÁŠ.BI Ì.ÁG.E, but the envelope replaces ŠE by KÙ, and *ibidem* 128 no. 15, a loan of oil to be paid back by measuring out barley.

der Gläubiger war selbst daran interessiert zum Rückzahlungstermin Korn statt Silber zu erhalten". He even considered the possibility that this construction was in the interest of both parties, which in several cases could have been the reason for not mentioning interest.[17]

[290] Others believe that the debtor may have actually received barley and that his debt was rated in silver, because this allowed the creditor to collect after the harvest, when it was cheap, more barley than he had loaned, namely the amount equivalent to the sum of silver at the by then "current rate of exchange" (*mahīr(at) illaku*).[18] This would make the contracts with the "Kursklausel" disguised barley loans collected with "verhüllte Fruchtwucher". Edzard is not ready to accept this for lack of good evidence and declares himself unable to define the nature of such "loans", which may cover different realities and be due to various interests of the parties. If a loan of silver is to be repaid in barley the mention of a rate of exchange is necessary, also when the aim is not "verhüllte Fruchtwucher".

Since many of the loans analyzed by Edzard are without interest[19] and none stipulates a 20% interest in barley, they are different from the ones mentioned at the beginning of this paragraph. Kienast (1978: 60, § 82), who accepted the idea that this interest formula implied that the capital too had to be paid back in barley (as is obvious in YOS 14, 54, quoted above), says nothing about the question whether the debtor had actually received silver or barley, nor does Skaist (1994: 109ff.). This is an issue that is also at stake with the so-called "mixed loans", normally consisting of amounts of silver and barley, and again Kienast (1978: 64) does not raise the question what the debtor had actually received. Such "mixed loans" were also investigated by Edzard 1970: 45ff., Exkurs, as a comment on his texts 18 and 19, which exemplify two different types. In no. 18 both silver and barley are borrowed, each at its own (normal) rate of interest and payment of both – expressed by the two verbs LÁ and ÁG – shall take place "on the threshing floor". But in no. 19, where the debt consists of 2,4,2 gur of barley, at 33⅓ % of interest, and 4 5/6 shekels of silver, at "the interest of Shamash" (which equals the current rate of 20%), the payment clause mentions only barley, to be measured out (ÁG) at harvest time at the current rate of exchange" (*mahīr illaku*). Edzard's list contains 35 contracts comparable to his no. 18, which state that both items have to paid back, each with its own rate of interest, mostly using the two verbs, ÁG and LÁ, but occasionally also SUM = *nadānum*, "to give", applicable to both items.[20] But in 10 contracts and in his no. 19 only one commodity has to be paid back, in most cases barley (in 5 contracts "with its interest"), twice (where silver and barley or sesame are owed) apparently silver.[21] Edzard is inclined to consider those of the latter group, where only barley is paid back, "normal loans" without "verhüllte Fruchtwucher", but admits that it remains unclear why only barley had to be paid and also why in some "mixed loans" (BIN 7, 83; VS 13, 59; UET 5, 389) the amount of silver in comparison with the amount of barley is very small indeed.

Long ago, when dealing with some Old Assyrian "mixed loans", I attempted to find evidence for the fact that in some of them, also during the OB period, the debtor in fact only received one commodity and that the silver and barley mentioned could represent alternative ratings of the same debt.[22] As far as I know nobody has reacted to this proposal

---

17 He believes that the absence of interest also allows an interpretation as "Lieferungskauf" (see for this type of "loans", Skaist 1994: 63ff.), whereby the "debtor" accepts silver for which in due time he will deliver other goods to the "creditor". But the contracts we are discussing do not state that the silver is borrowed *ana* (ŠÁM), "for (the purchase of)" other goods, the formulation typical for this type of transaction.

18 See Edzard 1970: 32.

19 Most are qualified as ŠU.LÁ (=*qīptum*), one demands "the interest of Shamash", one "the normal interest," and one 25% (*1* GÍN IGI.*4*.GÁL, see Skaist 1994: 114).

20 That different items are involved is clear from PBS 8/2, 143, where the debt consists of 4 gur of barley, interest-bearing, and ⅓ gur of barley plus ½ shekel of silver (qualified as "purchase price"), the latter two not interest-bearing.

21 In *RA* 54 (1960) 25ff., nos. 31 and 34. Add no. 30, with a debt of 1 shekel of silver, 4/5 gur of barley, at an interest of *0,1.0* ŠE[!] per gur and a payment clause that uses the verb LÁ.

22 In Veenhof 1978: 301 with note 14.

and I therefore repeat it here shortly. I observed that in a number of mixed loans from Tell Harmal and elsewhere, published Simmons 1959-60, the amounts of barley and silver were fairly equal in value, fluctuating around the regular or ideal equivalency of 1 shekel of silver = 1 gur of barley.[23] And this may also the case in Edzard 1970: no. 19, with 2 gur 260 silas of barey and 4 5/6 shekels of silver, if barley was expensive when it was borrowed (the contract is not dated). Even more striking is his text no. 18, where 10 1/6 shekels of silver and 10 gur 160 silas of barley are very close to the normal equivalency of 1 shekel of silver =1 gur of barley and **[291]** seem to be alternative ratings of one and the same debt. That the text stipulates payment of both, each with its own rate of interest, does not necessarily refute this interpretation, because it may have been inserted to make clear that payment in the commodity chosen had to be accompanied by its appropriate rate of interest, both of which are accordingly mentioned. Stating the value of the loan at the outset both in silver and in barley made a clause requiring repayment "at the (by then) current rate of exchange" superfluous. Such a clause would only be necessary and effective in so-called disguised silver loans, where only the silver value of the barley borrowed was registered as owed and one had to know how much barley had to be repaid.

That the two commodities mentioned at the beginning of so-called "mixed loans" are always listed asyndetically,[24] makes it possible to consider one the equivalent of the other, especially when they are more or less equal in value, as suggested for Edzard 1970: nos. 18 and 19. The same is true for Kienast 1978: no. 55, with a debt described as "1 gur of barley, 1 shekel of silver", both at an interest of 20%, defined as 60 silas of barley per 1 gur / 1 shekel (there is no payment clause!). Another example is Sigrist 1990: nos. 11 and 12, where the loan consists of "1,1.1 gur of barley, 1 shekel of silver", to be paid back each with its (appropriate) interest at harvest time (month III). That the payment clause has only the verb ÁG and that the values of the silver (1 shekel) and barley (ca. 1¼ gur) are comparable suggests a barley loan rated in silver and to be paid back in barley. An Old Assyrian debt-note supports this view, TCL 21, 219B, where we read: "4 ½ minas of tin, 25 shekels of refined silver, A has as debt claim on B." After stating the default interest of 20%, the text ends with: "Wherever I will see him I will take (collect) my silver". Here he creditor had sold (given in commission) to the debtor an amount of tin, for which he would pay him back in due time silver (as the last line states), but the text at the outset mentions how much he would pay, how much his debt in silver was, and this is done by juxtaposing both commodities asyndetically, which we could render by "x tin which (is worth = has to yield) y silver".[25] Even though the background and purpose of many OB mixed loans may be different, it shows that an asyndetic listing of amounts of both commodities can be interpreted as expressing an equivalency.

In this connection I call attention to four loans from the Diyala region, whose payment clause contains a unique stipulation, which in my opinion only makes sense if it considers and allows payment in silver or in barley:

Ahmad 1964: no. 39: *5* GÍN KÙ.BABBAR [2] *1* GÍN-*um 0,1.0* ŠE.TA [3] *ṣibtam uṣṣab* ... [8] *ina maškannim* [9] *kaspam ù pa-ni-šu* [10] *inaddin;*
Ahmad 1964: no. 44: *1 ma-na* KÙ.BABBAR [2] *1* GÍN *0,1.0* ŠE *uṣṣab* ... [7] *ana* MU.DU ŠE [8] *kaspam ù pa-ni-šu* [9] *inaddin;*

23 It seemed possible for some OA mixed loans, considering the prices in silver obtaining there for grain, see Veenhof 1978: 286f.

24 Also in Old Assyrian; the only exception I know is a loan between native Anatolians, CCT 1, 10b+11a (= *EL* no. 15): 5f., where the debt is: "15 shekels of silver *ù* three bags of grain" (both to be paid at harvest time).

25 The amounts mentioned imply a price of 12 shekels of tin for 1 shekel of silver, actually attested as retail price in Assur.

Tell Asmar 30.328: [x] *ma-na 4* GÍN KÙ.BABBAR [2] *1* GÍN GUR[!?] *0,1.0* ŠE [3] MÁŠ.BI *ú-ṣa-ab*, received by the debtors, [9] *ina* ITU *Magrātim* [10] KÙ.BABBAR *ù pa-ni-šu* [11] *i-na-di-nu*.[26]
IM 63171/1:[27] *1/3 mana kaspam* / *1* GÍN-*um 0,1.0* ŠE MÁŠ *uṣṣab* / KI Mu. / son of Ma. / I. son of A. / ŠU.BA.AN.TI / *ina maškannim* / *kaspam ù pa-ni-šu* / *utâr*.

[292] *CAD P* (see note 26) suggests that *panū* (taken as plural) is "a type of payment",[28] but I believe that it means "its counterpart", "its equivalent" (the suffix *-šu* refers to the preceding silver). This meaning, although I cannot adduce a parallel, fits the general notion of the noun ("what faces it") and is supported by the use of the non-specific verbs *nadānum*, "to give", and *turrum*, "to give back", which can be used with both commodities as object. Compare the use of the reciprocal Gt-stem of *naṭālum*, "to look at", used in OB to express that items "face / match each other", that is are of equal value.[29] The payment clause in these contracts thus can be translated as: "On the threshing floor / at the time of bringing in the barley / in month III he / they will give (back) the silver or its counterpart".

These contracts are similar to the ones mentioned in the beginning of this paragraph, to which Skaist drew attention, all with a silver debt and an interest of 20%, specified as 60 silas of barley per shekel of silver. This rate must have been obligatory, since the debt was stated to be in silver, but the description of the interest as an amount of barley per shekel of silver, and not as "36 barley corns of silver", normal for silver debts, shows that payment in barley was considered or obligatory. This is made explicit in the Diyala contracts by mentioning the handing over at the due date of "the silver or its counterpart" (*kaspam u panišu*), where *u* must mean "or" and not "and", because the debt was not a mixed one, but in silver only. This clause is remarkable, because other silver loans that state or imply payment in barley (Edzard 1970: 31f.) never offer the choice of paying in one of the two valutas, they all require "measuring out" barley. But Edzard 1970: no. 18 too, mentioned above, seems to offer this choice, if I am right in considering it one single debt, specified as an amount of silver and one of barley that are equal in value.

Three questions arise: a) Who could choose the commodity to be paid back? b) Which rate of exchange would apply if payment was in barley? And c), the most difficult one, did the debtor actually receive silver or was it barley whose value in silver was registered as his debt?

The answer to a) is not clear,[30] but it seems unlikely that in a normal silver or barley loan the valuta could be changed without mutual agreement and in § 3.1 I therefore suggested that a royal decree should have made clear when this was possible. In this paragraph I also suggested that such a royal decree could contain rules about the conversion of the valuta, mentioned in CH § **51**, but we do not know in which way. We cannot deduce the conversion rate from the interest clause in § **u**, based on the equation 1 shekel of silver = 300 silas of barley, because its only purpose was to prevent that payment

---

26 Partially quoted in *CAD* P, 96, top left. I am grateful to Martha Roth and Ed Stratford for providing me with a transliteration of the text and permission to quote it. The contract is dated to the reign of king Belakum of Eshnunna (ca. 1840 BC). The interest clause in line 2 looks like a conflation of *1* GÍN and *1* GUR, with or without locative ending, but since the latter is very rare, GUR is perhaps a scribal mistake for the locative ending *-um* or -E.

27 Sulaiman1978: 136 no. 73, a contract from Tell Harmal, dated to the reign of king Ammi-dušur. It contrasts with *ibidem* no. 69, with the same creditor, where 12 shekels of silver are borrowed also at an interest of 60 silas of barley per shekel of silver and payable on the threshing floor, but now simply in silver (although the verb used is not *šaqālum* but *nadānum*). What could be the reason for the difference in the payment clause is a question more difficult to answer when one also compares *ibidem* nos. 70-72, also silver loans payable in silver on the threshing floor, but now with "the interest of Shamash".

28 *CAD loc.cit.* also quotes § 21 of LE, "If a man gives (loans) silver *ana pa-ni-šu*", but this prepositional expression is different, see above under § 3.1, with footnote 16.

29 See for examples *CAD* N/II, 127, 8, a, "to be equal in value", used of a pledge that matches the value of a debt and of what partners contribute to a common fund, and see also 8, c, *mīlu u šamû ittaṭṭalū*, "the (amount of water of) the flooding and the rain will match each other".

30 See also the observation on LE § 20 in the previous paragraph.

in barley would make the creditor charge the debtor a higher interest than originally due for the silver. How much barley would be paid in the four debt-notes from the Diyala region must be implied in the words *u panišu*, "or its counterpart/ equivalent", which may refer to the current rate of exchange or perhaps to list of equivalencies, as the one in LE § 1. As for c), as mentioned above, it is difficult to prove that the debtor did not receive silver but barley, but I still consider it rather likely in several cases, because it is not obvious why in some cases (such as Kienast 1978: no. 55 and Edzard 1970: no. 19) debts would consist of small and more or less equivalent amounts of barley and silver, both at the same rate of interest, specified for both in barley, and at times also payable at the same time, the end of the harvest. They do not appear among the loans listed in Edzard 1970: 31f., and represent a special type, drafted in this way to allow payment in both valutas, or representing barley loans disguised as silver loans.

If we use these observations for understanding CH § **t**, the most likely solution in my opinion is that the words "If a creditor/merchant gives barley and/(*u*) or silver as interest-bearing loan" mean a contract where barley (mentioned first, as in Kienast 1978: no. 55 and Ezdard 1970: no. 19) was loaned, but the debt-note stated or also **[293]** stated its value in silver. The copula *u* then reveals a loan of barley with its equivalency in silver, where the silver is clearly secondary and therefore the interest is specified as an amount of barley "per gur of barley". Since the rating in silver most probably was the choice of the creditor he has to stick to it and its rate of interest, and when the double rating allowed payment in both commodities (as in the four contracts from the Diyala area) he is forbidden, when he collect barley, to claim also the higher interest on it. Stating the obligatory interest as obtaining "per 1 gur of barley" and not "per 1 shekel of silver" (used in most debt-notes), must be to stress that payment in barley does not change the rate of interest. Only when the first part of § **t** deals with was is basically a barley loan do we get a good contrast with its second half, which deals with a silver loan, with an interest rate specified in silver.

This interpretation also makes a good transition to § **u**, were the main issue is the same: no change in the interest rate at the disadvantage of a weak debtor. Here the debt was originally only in silver and when the debtor, nevertheless, thanks to a royal decree, is allowed to pay in barley, the original valuta of the debt decides on the rate of interest: 60 silas of barley per 1 gur of barley, not "per 1 shekel of silver", stated in this way because payment is in barley. Payment and interest are in the same valuta, but in this case the latter does not affect the rate of interest.[31]

Bibliography

Ahmad, A.K.A. 1964. *Old Babylonian Loan Contracts in the Iraq Museum from Tell al-Dhiba'i and Tell Harmal*, dissertation University of Baghdad.

Borger, R. 2006. *Babylonisch-assyrische Lesestücke* I-III, 3rd ed. Roma.

Donbaz, V., and Sauren, H. 1991. "Ni 2553 +2565, A Missing Link of the Hammurabi Law-Code", *Orientalia Lovaniensia Periodica* 22: 5-28.

Driver, G.R., and Miles, J.C. 1952. *The Babylonian Laws* I-II. Oxford.

Edzard, D.O. 1970. *Altbabylonische Rechts- un Wirtschaftsurkunden aus Tell ed-Dēr im Iraq Museum, Baghdad*, Bayer. Akad. der Wiss., Abh. Phil.-Hist. Klasse, Heft 72. München.

Finkelstein, J.J. 1967. A Late Old Babylonian Copy of the Laws of Hammurabi, *Journal of Cuneiform Studies* 21: 39-48.

Kienast, B. 1978. *Die altbabylonischen Briefe und Urkunden aus Kisurra* I-II, Freiburger Altorientalische Studien 2. Wiesbaden.

Kraus, F.R. 1979. Akkadische Wörter und Ausdrücke, XII, *Revue d'Assyriologie* 73: 51-62.

31 I do not comment of CH § **s**, which, as Roth 1995: 97 shows, also presents many problems. The new copy by Donbaz in **t**:32f. suggests: *šum-ma a-na* [x x x] / *it-ta?-ba-a*[*l-šu*] (the last two signs suggested by what remains in **S**:3'), which refutes the reading *itarrakaššu*, proposed by Roth.

Leemans, W.F. 1950. The Rate of Interest in Old Babylonian Times, *Revue international des droits de l'antiquité*, 3ème série, tome V: 7-34.
Lutzman, H. 1976. *Die Neusumerischen Schuldurkunden*, I. Selbstverlag, Heidelberg.
Otto, E. 1992. Der reduzierte Brautpreis. Ehe- und Zinsrecht in den Paragraphen 18 und 18a des Kodex Ešnunna, *Zeitschrift der Savigny-Stiftung für Rechtsgeschichte* 109: 475-8.
Petschow, H. 1965.Zur Systematik und Gesetzestechnik im Codex Hammurabi, *Zeitschrift für Assyriologie* 57: 146-172.
Poebel, A. 1914. *Historical and Grammatical Texts*. Publications of the Babylonian Section of the University Museum of the University of Pennsylvania, V. Philadelphia.
Roth, M.T. 1995. *Law Collections from Mesopotamia and Asia Minor*, SBL Writings of the Ancient World Series 6. Atlanta.
San Nicolò, M. 1974. *Die Schlussklauseln der altbabylonischen Kauf- und Tauschverträge*, 2nd ed. edited by H. Petschow. München.
Sigrist, M. 1990. *Old Babylonian Account Texts in the Horn Archeological Museum*. Andrew University Cuneiform Texts, IV. Berrien Springs.
Simmons, J.C. 1959-60. Early Old Babylonian Tablets from Ḫarmal and Elsewhere, *Journal of Cuneiform Studies* 13 (1959) 105-119 and 14 (1960) 23-32.
Skaist, A. 1994. *The Old Babylonian Loan Contract*. Ramat Gan.
Sulaiman, A. 1979. Harvest Documents and Loan Contracts from the Old Babylonian Period, *Sumer* 34: 130-138.
Veenhof, K.R. 1978. An Ancient Anatolian Money-Lender. His Loans, Securities and Debt-Slaves", in: B. Hruška and G. Komoróczy (eds.), *Festschrift Lubor Matouš* II. Budapest: 279-311.
–. 2001. The Relation Between Royal Decrees and 'Law Codes' in the Old Babylonian Period", *Jaarbericht Ex Oriente Lux* 35-36: 49-83 [= pp. 297-328 in this volume].
Yaron, R. 1988. *The Laws of Eshnunna*, 2nd ed., Jerusalem-Leiden.

The Relation between Royal Decrees and 'Law Codes' of the Old Babylonian Period*

The publication of *Ein Edict des Königs Ammiṣaduqa of Babylon* (Kraus 1958) for the first time gave assyriologists and legal historians a good idea of the nature and implications of a particular type of Old Babylonian royal decree. Its aim was to "restore equity" (*mīšarum*) by the cancellation of certain private, consumptive debts and by remitting arrears of various servants of the crown, in order to "strengthen the tributaries (of the crown)"[1] and to bring relief to debt-ridden subjects. While native sources call it simply "royal decree" (*ṣimdat šarrim*), scholarly literature frequently uses the designation '*mīšarum*-act', in order to distinguish it from a different type of royal decrees, treated below in § 2.[2]

Its publication inevitably raised the question of the relation between such royal decrees (*ṣimdat šarrim*) and the so-called 'law codes' of the Old Babylonian period,[3] which in turn led to a renewed discussion of the nature of the latter, inaugurated by Kraus's lecture "Ein zentrales Problem des altmesopotamischen Rechtes: was ist der Codex Hammurabi?" (Kraus 1960), a discussion which continues until this day.[4] As regards the relation between 'law codes' and royal decrees, two facts in particular were noted. The first was that some Old Babylonian kings, known for their 'law codes', in their inscriptions and year-names also boast of having "restored equity" (*mīšaram šakānum*; nig.si.sá gar), the very expression which describes the essence and purpose of the '*mīšarum*-acts'. The second is that although these royal acts consist mainly of stipulations designed to effect economic adjustments for the instant and hence only have retroactive legal force,[5] they may also contain a few rulings of a more general and lasting nature,[6] which, as noted by Kraus (1958, 184f.) are not introduced by the programmatic statement "because the king has restored equity". Kraus (1984, 241f.) also pointed out that the expression *mīšaram šakānum* originally did not only refer to such adjustments for the instant. Some royal inscriptions refer to decrees which "teilweise den Charakter von Reformen besessen hätten" and obviously were meant to have a lasting **[50]** validity. The latter are therefore similar to and might have been incorporated in 'law collections', which contain normative rulings with unlimited validity.

---

1 A quote from a famous letter of king Samsu-iluna, which accompanied a decree issued on the occasion of his accession to the throne, *TCL* 17, 76, see Kraus 1958, 225f. [now edited as AbB 14, 130].

2 Kraus 1984, 113f. designates *mīšarum*-acts as 'Rechtsakte, Typus IIa'.

3 In what follows I use LE for the 'laws of Eshnunna', LH for the 'laws of Hammurabi' (both quoted according to the paragraph numbering in Roth 1995) and EA for the edict of Ammi-ṣaduqa, quoted according to the second edition in Kraus 1984, 168ff.

4 Kraus 1984, 114f. abandoned his earlier views on their legal force and validity. See for differing views on this issue W.F. Leemans, *BiOr* 48 (1991) 417ff., R. Westbrook, *RB* 92 (1985) 247ff. and *ZA* 79 (1989) 201ff., and Lafont 1997.

5 Contracts hence may take pains to mention that the transaction recorded had taken place "after the royal decree" and thus was not effected by it.

6 E.g. those dealing with fraudulent creditors and the misuse of administrative power by state officials in EA §§ 18 and § 22.

* Originally published in Jaarbericht Ex Oriente Lux 35-36 (1997-2000) 49-83.

These observations raise several questions. What evidence do we have for this latter type of royal decrees, their substance and function? Do the 'law collections' we have from the Old Babylonian period, LE (*ca.* 1800 B.C.) and LH (*ca.* 1760 B.C.), contain the substance of earlier royal decrees? If so, can we detect them and if not, why not? What does it mean that we have no 'law codes' from the later Old Babylonian period, but only (references to) royal decrees and what were therefore their roles and impact? Trying to find answers I treat the following issues:

1. 'Law codes' and '*mīšarum*-decrees'
2. A second type of royal decrees
3. The origin of decrees of the second type
4. References to and identification of decrees
5. Decrees whose subject matter is not found in the 'laws'
    a. Decree on revolting adoptive sons
    b. Decree on a defaulting ox drivers
    c. Decree on absentee 'field managers'
    d. Decree on the division of the harvest
    e. Decree on groundless claims
6. Decrees whose subject matter is found in the 'laws'
    a. Decree on defaulting harvest laborers
    b. Decree on liabilities in connection with slave sale
    c. Decree on consignment (*šēbultum*)
    d. Decree on the return of a dowry
    e. Decree on the recovery of missing goods (*hulqum*)
7. Decrees referred to in the text of the 'laws'
    a. Decree on homicide
    b. Decree on paying debts in different valuta
    c. More decrees incorporated in law collections?
8. The impact of 'laws' and decrees
    a. Nature and use of 'laws' and decrees
    b. Old Assyrian laws and Babylonian royal decrees
    c. Petitions and appeals to the king of Babylon.

1. 'Law codes' and '*mīšarum*-decrees'

The relation between the two was discussed by Finkelstein soon after the publication of EA.[7] He admits "that the 'law-codes' are not the evidence for the *mīšarum*-acts of the kings who issued them", and that there is a distance between the latter and the 'laws',[8] because "none of the so-called 'law codes' contains any provisions which constitute the primary ingredient of a *mīšarum*, namely acts remitting certain financial obligations just for the limited time of effectiveness". But on the other hand he states that "there is nevertheless some basis for assuming a degree of relationship between *mīšarum*-act and 'law' promulgation, which consists precisely of those sections of the Ammi-ṣaduqa edict which purport to effect **[51]** 'reforms' that are to have permanent effect". Evidence for such a relationship he finds in the first part (§§ 1-21) of LE, on the basis of the form-critical argument that "many of its provisions are set out in the "apodictic" style (considered typical for a royal decree – K.R.V.), rather than the "casuistic or tukumbi/

7 Finkelstein 1961, 100ff.

8 Also chronologically, because *mīšarum*-acts in his opinion were usually declared at the beginning of a king's rule (and hence are mentioned in the name of his first or second year), while LE (to judge from the broken year-name) and LH are from the later years of the kings who issued them (cf. note 10). [See on the 'rythm' of the OB '*mīšarum*-acts', Charpin 2000, 202f.]

šumma formulation" (typical for 'law codes' as scholarly works – K.R.V.).[9] He considers it "probable that LE to a large extent is to be related – although less directly than Ed. Am – to a *mīšarum*-act" and that "the extant text was definitely written some time after such a *mīšarum*".[10] But he also finds rulings in LH, which "seem to have been intended as economic reforms of a permanent nature", which "may well have formed part of the original *mīšarum* complex of enactments, either in the form in which they are preserved in the 'code' or in paraphrase".[11]

Jean Bottéro shares this view and also mentions the possibility that LH, "en tant précisement que traduisant, à sa façon, la volonté et l'autorité du souverain, ait pu être regardé comme un recueil de ces décisions". He adduces a terminological argument, pointing to a late Old Babylonian copy of LH on a cuneiform tablet, which in its colophon calls LH *ṣimdāt šarrim*, 'royal decrees', the very name normally used for the '*mīšarum*-acts'. "Sanctionnées par l'autorité royale, ces *dînâtu*-sentences[12] puvaient donc, au moins avec du recul, être tenues pour des façons de *ṣimdâtu*-décisions".[13]

The idea of *mīšarum*-rulings later incorporated in 'law codes' and the concrete suggestion by Finkelstein on LE thus far have not been followed up in detail. R. Yaron, in his edition of LE,[14] after analyzing the forms, substance and possible 'settings in life' of the various sections, concludes that they had basically two sources: *a)* the activity of the ruler, resulting in decrees of one kind or another, reflecting statute law, and *b)* litigation and precedents, based on common law. To the first group, which includes "directly regulatory provisions" (such as those on prices and hire), he assigns rulings primarily on the basis of substance and formulation. As "substance" he also counts the occurrence of a reference to a 'royal decree' in the text of a law (§ 58). Relevant for "formulation" is whether a ruling contains a combination of equivalents, which suggests the possibility of reformulation of an existing decree for inclusion in the laws. But a clear link with a royal edict is only suggested for § 19,[15] on the basis of formal and material arguments. It exhibits the so-called "relative formulation" ("a man who...", *awīlum ša*), considered typical for a proclamation, the terminology (*šuddunum*, 'to collect' a debt) typical for '*mīšarum*-acts' (such as EA),[16] but also the reformulation required for inclusion in the laws. The latter implies that a past case ("A man who gave...") becomes a general rule for the future ("A man who gives...") and that the presumably originally negative **[52]** provision of the apodosis ("He shall not...") becomes positive, with addition of a date for meeting the obligation ("He shall pay not later than..."). Such features make it a prescriptive ruling and distinguish it from the traditional casuistic ones, which start from something which has taken place ("If", followed by a past tense) and may reflect both royal jurisdiction (as precedent) and scholarship. Yaron concludes "that LE 19 may have been "lifted" out of an early edict providing ... for the absolution of certain debts". But elsewhere, in the comments on individual rulings and sections, and also in the paragraph on *ṣimdat šarrim* (pp. 121-125), the possibility of underlying royal decrees is not further explored. Not even in the comments on § 9 (p. 252), although there is evidence from the realm of Eshnunna for a royal decree on its subject matter, the failure of a contracted harvester to perform (see below, § 6,a).

---

9 The *šumma*-sections in LE § 1-21 "usually deal with delicts arising out of activity touched upon in a regulatory way in a preceding section", as is the case with *šumma*-sections of EA.

10 Finkelstein argues that some date-formulae of kings of Eshnunna contain evidence for *mīšarum*-acts, while the broken date formula which introduces the text of LE does not refer to one and hence must be later.

11 As such he mentions §§ L-100 and 215-277.

12 The name Hammurabi himself (rev. xxiv:1-2) gave to his 'codex', see Kraus 1960, 284ff.

13 Bottéro 1987, 219.

14 Yaron 1988, 106-113.

15 Yaron's translation: "A man, who gives for its equivalent, at?/from? the threshing floor will collect" (Roth 1995: "A man who lends against its corresponding commodity(?)..").

16 The non-occurrence of *šuddunum* in the 'laws' (Yaron 1988, 111) in my opinion is accidental, because the comparable verb *esērum*, 'to press for payment', is used in CH § a. Moreover, the 'laws' deal with what the main actors, debtor and creditor, (fail to) do (*nadānum, šaqālum, apālum, leqûm*), not with the use of a collecting agent by the creditor.

The reason for this failure seems to be too much attention for the more spectacular and thanks to Kraus's editions well known and periodic type of royal '*mīšarum*-act', which aims at restoring "equity" (*mīšarum*) and the original situation (*andurārum*). They are meant by many of the references to a 'royal decree' (*ṣimdat šarrim*) in practice documents, which usually state in one way or the other that the transaction recorded was concluded "after the royal decree" (Kraus calls this the "Sicherstellungsvermerk") and hence is not affected by it. Several, found in judicial records, mention that legal action was undertaken "on the basis/because (*ina / aššum*) of the royal decree" by people who considered themselves its beneficiaries. For these royal acts not only cancelled debts and ordered the return of dependents of the defaulting debtors which have come into the power of creditors as pledge, security, or debt-slave (Kraus's 'Rechtsakt' type II,1). They also secured the return of real property lost by forced sale (Kraus's type II,2), a fact not mentioned in the text of the decrees we know, but clear from judicial records dealing with this issue.[17] But this did not happen automatically and required legal action by those who had lost it, which resulted in judicial records which refer to or imply the existence of a '*mīšarum*-act'. These royal decrees obviously had force of law in economic life[18] and Finkelstein contrasts them with the so-called "law codes" (Kraus's 'Rechtsakt' type III), which he considers "representatives of a literary genre, of the retrospective type" (p. 101).

The Sumerian equivalent of *mīšaram šakānum*, níg.si.sá gar, which occurs already in the 'Laws of Ur-Nammu' (*ca.* 2100 B.C.), basically means royal intervention in prevailing law and administrative legal practices, in order to do away with abuses. Such measures could have a wide scope, probably also relating to compulsory service, taxes, the power of government officials, and the use of correct weights and measures. But their main focus, which earned them the designation "restoring equity", was redressing what was considered unjust. As such they served a dual goal, helping those whose rights had been violated (in Babylonian *hablum*) by those with power (be they private individuals or state officials), and protecting the poor and weak, especially in situations of economic distress, against those who are strong and apply the merciless debt-laws. Helping the weak might be done by carrying out changes in the administration of justice and in common law, as applied by courts and judges, which seems to **[53]** have been the goal of some of the rulings contained in LH.[19] But, judging from the references in year names and practice documents, the focus of royal measures for helping the weak in due time seems to have shifted more and more to cancelling debts and remitting obligations. Such measures, ceremoniously announced by "the lifting of the golden torch" and described as "breaking/throwing away sealed bonds/debts" and "restoring freedom", were welcomed by the population and used by rulers to promote their image of righteous kings and to win the favor of their subjects, *i.a.* at their accession to the throne and their conquest of a city.[20] This explains their popularity and the interest they have generated among historians.

2. A second type of royal decrees

This interest, however, is also responsible for the fact that a second type of royal decrees (*ṣimdat šarrim*) has received much less attention. They contain legal rulings of a more traditional nature, by means of which a king lays down liabilities in connection with certain transactions and especially penalties and compensations for various types of

17 See for the evidence for this type of measure, his 'Rechtsakte' type II,2, Kraus 1984, 38-50 (three such measures of Rim-Sin of Larsa), 58f. (by Hammurabi), 69ff. (by Samsu-iluna). Also D. Charpin, *Le clergé d'Ur au siècle d'Hammurabi* (Genève/Paris 1986) 70ff., idem, *RA* 83 (1989) 106f., and Veenhof 1999, 607f.

18 Lafont 1997, 3ff. distinguishes them from "legislative texts in a technical sense" (such as law codes, etc.), because their duration and subject matter are more restricted.

19 E.g. §§ 47f., 117.

20 See for the terminology, Kraus 1984, ch. 7, and Charpin 1987, together with his observations in *NABU* 1992/76 [and now also Charpin 2000].

breach of contract or other violations of the law.[21] While their subject matter indeed seems to be restricted to one issue or legal problem, there are no indications that their validity was restricted in time (let alone was only retroactive), so that they are a special type of sources of normative, positive law. These decrees themselves, though apparently available in writing, have not (yet) been discovered, but we know of them thanks to usually short references in a variety of contracts, most of which have been discussed by Kraus.[22] Practice documents usually refer to them either by a factual statement of the type "he is responsible for ... in accordance with the decree of the king" (*kīma ṣimdat šarrim*) or, after mentioning the possibility of a breach of contract, by means of the same three words used as a verbless clause: "if he/who does (not) ...: in accordance with the decree of the king", or simply *ṣimdat šarrim*, "the decree of the king", scil. is applicable or comes into operation. Occasionally, we have *ṣimdatum* in the construct state (with a grammatically conditioned omission of *šarrim*), followed by a noun in the genitive, which identifies the (trans)action to which to decree applies, *e.g. ṣimdat šūbultim*, "the decree concerning consignment".[23]

The short formula is frequent in contracts by means of which harvesters are hired in advance, with prepayment of part of their wages, where we read: "They will come, if they do not come: (in accordance with) the royal decree". It also occurs regularly in the guaranty **[54]** clause of slave sale contracts: "He (the seller) is responsible for claims in accordance with the royal decree". Such references state a fixed contractual liability of general validity, but they usually do not tell us what it consisted of, what compensation or penalty had to be paid in case of breach of contract. A few contracts suggest that the penalty for the defaulting harvester was a fine (see below § 6.a). In connection with slave sale we also have contracts where the liabilities of the seller are spelled out: he has to guarantee the new owner the undisputed ownership and physical integrity of the slave bought (see below § 6.b). Other references of this type in contracts concern ox drivers, hired with their animals (*inītum*), who fail to turn up in time or let their oxen stay idle (§ 5.b) and an adoptive son who rejects his father (see below § 5.a). Some letters contain similar references, *e.g.* on absentee 'field managers' (*iššiakkum duppurum*, below § 5.c), on the division of the harvest between tenant and field owner, on depriving them of what they are entitled to (*mikis eqlim, habālum*; below § 5.d), and on groundless property claims (*baqrū*; below § 5.e). But most references in letters are of a more general nature and concern the administration of justice in cases dealing with the return of a dowry (*AbB* 9, 25), of goods given in safe deposit (*maṣṣartum, AbB* 13, 27), the compensation of damage or deprivation (*habālum, hibiltum, AbB* 2, 19; 10, 161; 12, 194; 13, 176), the defense of property rights on real estate bought (*AbB* 6, 142), a creditor's denial of having been paid his claim (*JCS* 11, 106 no.1), the detention of a free citizen as slave (*AbB* 6, 80), the violation of the interests of the owner of a field in which he has invested work (*AbB* 3, 86), or which he had rented for cultivation (*JCS* 23, p.29 no. 1), the return of or compensation for missing goods (*hulqum, ABIM* 33), and reduction of the amount of barley a man is entitled to (*AbB* 11, 183), etc.

---

21 Kraus 1979, 58f. suggests that *ṣimdatum* ("königliche Massregel") originally may have designated specific measures aimed at restoring equity and only later (towards the end of Hammurabi's reign?), when such measures had developed into more comprehensive decrees (designated as "restoring *mīšarum*"), became available to designate a regulation or procedure in the administration of justice ("königliches Gerichtsverfahren"), occasionally even one of legal nature, a meaning fully acknowledged in Kraus 1984, 8ff. I assume a shift in focus of a word which according to its etymology and in practice may designate various types measures, also a pact or treaty between kings (see now also *ARM* 26/2, 404:22).

22 Kraus 1979, supplemented by 1984, 8-12.

23 Comparable to the headings over groups of laws of Hammurabi's Code, found in two OB manuscripts (see *JCS* 21 [1967] 42ff.), which use the logogram DI.DAB$_5$.BA = *ṣimdatum*, "regulations", e.g. in *ṣimdāt nipūtim*, "regulations on seizure, distress" (§ 113ff.). Kraus 1979, 53f. believes that these glosses reflect training in Sumerian in the Old Babylonian school.

Addressees of such letters may be asked or ordered to solve conflicts, redress wrongs and punish culprits by administering justice (the expressions used are *dīnam šūhuzum/ qabûm*) "in accordance with the (royal) regulation". Several of them are administrative officials, local authorities (mayors and city-elders), judges, and persons like Sin-idinnam, the governor of the Larsa province. Hammurabi usually first tells him that he has been informed or appealed to by people who consider themselves wronged and next instructs Sin-idinnam to handle their cases and administer justice *kīma ṣimdatim*.[24] Some letters allow us to see what the issue was, others are too damaged or too vague to know what exactly is at stake.

Not all letters and judicial records containing such phrases, however, refer to this type of regulation. Royal '*mīšarum*-acts', by means of which debts are cancelled, as mentioned above in § 1, may also lead to legal action by their beneficiaries *kīma ṣimdat šarrim*, in order to get back the property they had been forced to sell (see the summary in Kraus 1984: 114, 2). Such acts are also implied by the official letters *AbB* 4, 38 and 69, and referred to in *AbB* 4, 56 (Lu-Ninurta to Šamaš-hazir) and an unpublished letter from Hammurabi to Sin-iddinam.[25] While *AbB* 4, 56:9 simply states that "a/the decree is in force (*ba'lat*), as you know", in the second letter Hammurabi instructs his governor in the case of a complaint about a garden bought but vindicated, to have the plaintiff obtain a verdict "in accordance with the decree" (*dīnam kīma ṣimdatim šūhissu*, 15f.).

[55] At times it is not immediately obvious to which type of decree a reference is and what "in accordance with the *ṣimdatum*" in such official letters actually means. Eva Dombradi,[26] in her discussion of the expression *dīnam šūhuzum*, deals with two letters, *AbB* 2, 19 and *TCL* 1, 2 (comparable to *AbB* 4, 59 [now edited as *AbB* 14, 2]), in which Hammurabi instructs Sin-idinnam to do this "in accordance with the *ṣimdatum*". She rejects Driver and Miles's idea that Hammurabi means "to pass a judgment according to the ordinances" and assumes (with Lautner) that the expression refers only to accepting a case for trial, hence to judicial procedure. She supports this idea by referring to the expression *ina ṣimdat šarrim baqārum*, "entsprechend der königlichen Verordnung Rechte geltend machen", as attested in *VAS* 7, 7 and *YOS* 14, 146. But this view requires two corrections. The first is that while the last two references, analyzed in Kraus 1984, 54ff., do refer to a royal '*mīšarum*-act', which prompts defaulting debtors to start a lawsuit in order to reclaim property they had been forced to sell, *AbB* 2, 19 and *TCL* 1, 2. They are similar to Hammurabi's other letters to Sin-idinnam, listed in note 24, whose subject matter has no relation to a '*mīšarum*-decree'. Moreover, the use of the preposition *ina*, "by means, on the basis of", rather than *kīma*, "in accordance with", suggests that the reference is to the substance of the decree rather than to procedure.

These letters show that we have to assume the existence of a number of specific royal regulations, which would allow Sin-iddinam and other officials or judges to decide not so much whether a case was to be accepted for trial, but what verdict they had to pass for the plaintiff[27] and which penalty to impose on the culprit in order to solve a conflict or redress a wrong. Such decrees hence contained rulings on the substance of administrative or

---

24 See *AbB* 2, 19; 10, 161(?); 13, 27. 38. 47 and 48; *TCL* 1, 2 [= *AbB* 14, 2]. Note also *AbB* 9, 6 by Marduk-mušallim to Sin-iddinam; 9, 25 by the judges of Babylon to Muhaddûm; and 11, 183 by Muhaddûm, which speak of "the regulation of my/our lord". [**Add.**: In *AbB* 14, 184 Sîn-iddinam writes to the judges of Adab(?): "Evaluate the affair of N. and provide [her] with a verdict in accordance with the decree of my lord" (*dīnam kīma ṣimdat bēlia šūhizānim*)].

25 Ermitage MA 9649, communicated in Kraus 1984, 61.

26 Dombradi 1996, II, note 2065. In general she pays little attention to the information on judicial procedure in Old Babylonian letters and to Kraus's relevant observations. References to *ṣimdat šarrim* (left blank in the index, vol. II, 365!) occur only in notes 2065, 2161 and 2341.

27 Note the use of the expression *dīnam qabûm* with personal dative suffix in *AbB* 1, 120:13'; 7, 135:12' (in Babylon); 13, 176:13 (in Babylon); and *JCS* 23 (1969) 29 no. 1:31. Hammurabi('s chancery) does not use *dīnam qabûm*, but only *dīnam šūhuzum*, with personal accusative suffix, and the king never writes "in accordance with my *ṣimdatum*", although his servants may speak of "the *ṣimdatum* of my/our lord" (see note 24).

penal law. References in letters also show that such decrees apparently were available in written, perhaps even in "published" form. In *AbB* 1, 14 the authorities of Sippar report to have fixed(!)[28] the punishment of a group of people "on the basis of the text of the tablet with the decree" (*ana pī ṭuppi ṣimdatim*, lines 19-26). In *AbB* 11, 101:24f., a letter addressed to some officials,[29] the decree is said "to be available with" the addressee (*kīma ṣimdati ša mahrika ibaššû*), and *ABIM* 33:12ff.[30] states that such a decree is "in the hands of" the mayor and city-elders to whom the letter is addressed (*kīma ṣimdatim ša ina qātikunu ibaššû*).

[*Addendum*: In *AbB* 11, 159:20ff., the authorities of Isin instruct the judges of Nippur, "investigate their case and *dīn ina qātikunu ibaššû šūhizāšunūti*", which Stol renders by "conduct a trial for them as is within your power". In my opinion this means rendering a verdict based on a written source available to them. This reference evokes comparison with *AbB* 11, 78:11f., "May my lord render a final decision (*ligmur*) about his adversary *kīma dīnim ša mahar bēlia ibaššû*", where Stol translates "in accordance with the legal practices obtaining with my lord".]

Unfortunately, as far as I am aware, no tablets containing the text of such a decree has been identified, unless the rescript of king Samsu-iluna, discussed in the next paragraph, though not called *ṣimdatum*, qualifies as such.

Such royal decrees apparently served a practical purpose. Most seem to fix, with royal authority, liabilities, compensations and penalties for apparently not uncommon misdeeds, including breach of contract. By referring to them in contracts, the parties, who most **[56]** probably were familiar with the substance of the decree, were warned in advance what to expect in case of breach of contract. And the plaintiff was saved the trouble of a perhaps time consuming lawsuit, *e.g.* against defaulting harvesters, while the ripe harvest was waiting on the fields. As stated by Kraus, such decrees guarantee "ein Verfahren mit für Parteien verbindlichem Urteil, das rechtskräftig und unmittelbar zu vollziehen ist".[31] The only task of the judges, when appealed to, was to ascertain that the wrong fell under the provision of the royal decree, which in standard cases, such as that of a defaulting harvester, must have been self evident.

The best known examples, not surprisingly, concern rather frequent and important issues, such as hiring laborers, buying slaves, vindication and claims where conflicts and breach of contract (deliberate or due to force majeure) were not rare and judicial action was predictable. Here a clear and binding rule, imposed by royal authority, which guaranteed fast reparation, must have been welcome both to plaintiffs and judges, as an improvement over common law, which may have led to time consuming legal fights. For others, such as the one on the rebellious adoptive so (see § 5a), this is not obvious. Known from one single reference only, it suggests that we have to reckon with the existence of still others, not yet documented.

All in all we have to assume quite a number of such decrees or regulations, which must have played an important role in the administration of justice. This raises the question whether we can detect links between these regulations, as far as the context of the references in contracts and letters allow us to understand their nature and contents, and rulings contained in more or less contemporary law collections. This applies in particular to LH, because most relevant contracts and letters originate from the realm governed by Hammurabi and his successors.

---

28 See for the meaning of *eṣērum*, "to fix", my remarks in T.P.J. van Hout – J. de Roos (eds.), *Studio Historiae Ardens... .Studies Presented to Ph.H.J. Houwink ten Cate* (Istanbul 1995) 318 [= pp. 225-243 in this volume].

29 The subject matter of the appeal is unique: a man complaining about the fact that the woman living in his quarters, who has been in his service(?) for twenty years, has left him to enter another man's house.

30 Deals with loss of property suffered by a woman living as tenant in a house.

31 Kraus 1979, 59.

3. The origin of decrees of the second type

While it is clear that the '*mīšarum*-decrees' were frequently issued at special times (*e.g.* by a new king at his accession to the throne), in a ceremonial way ("raising the golden torch"), also to promote the ruler's image as righteous king and to gain favour with the subjects, we know little about the second type of decrees. If, as is likely, they were somehow based on precedent, how did they acquire the status of *ṣimdat šarrim*? A serious possibility is that some were rescripts,[32] that is rulings in the form of a written answer to a question concerning a legal problem submitted to the king, which by its authority, style, terminology, or subject matter acquired a more general validity and applicability. An example is the by now well-known decision of king Samsu-iluna on two different problems concerning the maintenance and the property of an important class of women (called *nadītum*), dedicated to the sun-god of Sippar.[33] It was in the form of a royal letter addressed to the authorities of Sippar, written in reaction to information and complaints[34] submitted to the king by certain officials(?) in Sippar.[35] The answer of the king indeed offers more than a verdict in a concrete case. It uses a general **[57]** formulation ("a *nadītum* who..."), which creates a basic rule, applicable in other cases too. The answer to the second problem, moreover, widens the case by dealing not only with monetary debts (as the complaint did), but also with service-duties (*ilkum*).[36]

The ruling on the first problem (the maintenance of the *nadītums*), is presented in the style of a letter, as a royal order, "I ordered" (*aqbi*, in ms. A lines 17 and 23),[37] with the king quoting his own decision. The second ruling, which deals with attempts to use assets of a *nadītum* to pay for her father's debts, is more 'law-like' in omitting the "I ordered". It consists of two(?) relative sentences ("The *nadītum* who...", followed by "Creditors who..."), and ends by invoking a curse ("that man is a foe of Šamaš!") against who violates the ruling. This recalls the style of a royal decree, comparable to those known from Mari[38] and to clauses in early contracts from Sippar, where the violator is declared "an evildoer/enemy (*lemun*) of Šamaš".[39]

We know this letter thanks to (the remains of) four tablets with its text, most of which are one or two generations younger than the original, while (at least) two of them in their colophon are identified as copies of Samsu-iluna's letter, kept (lit. "placed") in two different places, one in the Cloister, the other probably in the Šamaš temple.

---

32 According to Lafont 1997, 5, a rescript is "édicté par le roi à partir d'une question de droit dont il est saisi". She classifies it as the third category of normative royal acts, alongside law codes and '*mīšarum*-decrees'.

33 Published and analysed in Janssen 1991.

34 The verb is *lummudum*, also current in Hammurabi's official letters. It shows that they were written in reaction to information received in the form of an appeal or a complaint by a subject.

35 The identity of the senders is unknown due to a break in all three sources available; the traces in *CT* 52, 111:3' allow [UGULA LUKU][R [d]]UTU.MEŠ, "the overseers of the *nadītums* (in Sippar)".

36 See the analysis in Lafont 1994, 97ff. and 1997, especially 24f. [**Add.**: And also M. T. Roth, in: Ed. Lévy (ed.), *La codification des lois dans l'antiquité* (Paris, 2000) 23-27 (but I do not follow her in distinguishing in the king's letter twice between a 'previous pronouncement' (lines 16-17 and 43-47) and a 'current resolution' (lines 18-23 and 48-50). I see an alternation between a prohibition (*lā šurubša aqbi* and [*ul iṣṣabbat*]) and an order and condemnation (*šūrubša aqbi* and *ajābu ša* [d]*Šamaš*)].

37 The first royal directive is translated in the *editio princeps* as "If a *nadītum* ... is not taken care of", because it takes the stative *lā ṣuddud* of line 16 (see note 11) as a descriptive, almost conditional sentence. But this is impossible with a feminine subject and we have to read *la ṣú-ud-du-tam* (accusative of the verbal adjective fem.), "not taken care of". The king's order basically is an apodictic prohibition: "I forbade to make an unprovided *nadītum* enter the Cloister". As a decree the order would have read: **nadītam lā ṣuddûtam abuša u ahhūša ana gagûm lā ušerrebū(ši);* incorporated into a law collection it might have become: **šumma nadītum abuša u ahhūša lā uṣeddūšima ṭuppam lā išṭurūšim ana gagîm ul ušerrebūši.*

38 *Asak* (etc.) DN *u* RN *īkul ša*... See now D. Charpin, Manger un serment, in: S. Lafont (ed.), *Jurer et maudire. Méditerranées* nos. 10-11 (Paris 1996) 85-96, and earlier A. Marzal, Mari clauses in "casuistic" and "apodictic" styles, *CBQ* 33 (1971) 333-364 and 492-509.

39 See my remarks on this formula in *Vetus Testamentum* 22 (1972) 380f.

Ms. A was deposited somewhere (text broken) in the Cloister ([gá.gi].a), ms. C probably in the é.di.[ku$_5^!$.kalam.ma]. The name of this locale, "House of the Judge of the Land", is well attested as the name of the temple of Šamaš in Babylon, see A. George, *Babylonian Topographical Texts* (Leuven 1992) 327ff. no. 38. But several of the OB references quoted on p. 328 refer to his temple in Sippar. In *AbB* 3, 73:3', it is its [SANGA] who, together with other dignitaries of Sippar (including the *galamahhu* of Annunītum), has to travel to Babylon. In the judicial record CT 2,1 // 6, in a case dealing with property of a *nadītum* of Šamaš, the plaintiff declares himself ready to have the symbol of that temple and of the é.di.ku$_5$ brought to him to take the oath in the city-ward, obviously in Sippar. This is also the case in the unpublished record BM 96998, where these divine symbols are set up "in the Gate of Šamaš of the é.di.ku$_5$.dá" during a trial conducted in Sippar. This shrine of Šamaš, included in the "standard litany of temple names" in a balag,[40] also occurs in the text on a OB worshipper figurine dedicated to Šamaš, "king of the é.di.ku$_5$.dá", for the life of king Ammi-ṣaduqa by the judge Gimil-Marduk, known from a later copy on a tablet found at Sippar and edited by E. Sollberger (*Iraq* 31, 1969, 90). The statue was set up before "Šamaš who from the é.di.ku$_5$.da had heard his words" (lines 24f.). The shrine is perhaps also mentioned in BE 6/1, 6:10, where litigants, having arrived at the é.di.ku$_5$, presumably to swear the oath, come to an agreement [**Add.**: It also occurs in BM 97103:1, from Sippar, a list of bread, meat and beer that is entitled kaš.dé.a ^{d}utu *ša* é.di.ku$_5$.e.ne].

Sophie Lafont (1997, 27) may be right in concluding that "le droit élaboré par Samsu-iluna a donc été 'reçu' par les souverains postérieurs de la dynastie" and that "la présence de ces **[58]** tablettes dans la maison d'un dignitaire religieux montre que le rescrit de Samsu-iluna constituait un droit 'vivant', appliqué ...". But we do not know the position of later kings vis-à-vis this rescript, nor the reason why the copies ended up in Ur-Utu's archives.

The assumption that this letter is not a unique case raises the question whether such rescripts could be called *ṣimdāt šarrim*, "royal regulations". Could a later king have instructed officials in Sippar to handle a complaint *kīma ṣimdat nadiātim*, or *kīma ṣimdat šarrim*, to refer them to Samsu-iluna's letter? The king himself does not describe in this letter what he did as *ṣimdatam aškun*, "I issued a regulation", and none of the royal letters mentioning a *ṣimdatum* refers to it is "*my* regulation" (though servants of the king refer to it as "the regulation of my lord"). The use of *aqbi*, "I ordered", implies that its result was an *awāt šarrim*, "order of the king", rather than *ṣimdat šarrim*. But the difference is not very big, since royal '*mīšarum*-decrees' usually designated as *ṣimdat šarrim*, in Old Babylonian Larsa were also called *awāt šarrim*.[41] Perhaps, then, a ruling of the king, transmitted as an 'order' in an official letter, could be designated as *ṣimdatum* by those who received and had to implement it, without a further administrative step, such as its "publication", being necessary to officially stamp it as *ṣimdat šarrim*.[42]

In the absence of evidence that such decrees were "published" on a stone monument (as 'laws' were),[43] we might assume that the distribution of official letters containing such

40 J. Black, *ASJ* 7 (1985) 21 line 139; I see no reason to consider it here a temple in Babylon, as Black does in his comments on p. 41.

41 See Kraus 1984, 34ff.

42 The scribe of one late Old Babylonian copy of the Laws of Hammurabi, in the colophon calls them *ṣimdā[t Hammurabi]* (*JCS* 21 (1967) 42), although neither the prologue nor the epilogue of the laws use that designation.

43 The only example could be *UET* 5, 420, from the fifth year of king Samsu-iluna, where a man hired to supervise the exploitation of another man's field, has to deliver the owner a fixed amount of barley, "for the shortfall that may occur they will treat him according to the word of the stele" (discussed by Westbrook 1989, 213 note 46; see *CAD* N/1, 365a,1 for a corrected reading). Since LH lacks such a ruling and there is not evidence of post-Hammurabi laws, the reference could well be to a separate decree (*ṣimdatum*) published on a stela.

a ruling among those who had to implement it[44] was equal to 'publishing' it, just like a royal decision on the name of the new year was published by distributing it by letter over a variety of administrative centers. In this connection the different colophons of the two tablets, which identify them as copies of Samsu-iluna's letter, are interesting. If the proposal made above is acceptable, it would mean that one original was deposited in the Cloister, which was directly implicated by the decision, and the other in (a special locale of) the Šamaš temple, devoted to judicial activities, where documents important for jurisdiction might have been kept. This agrees with the conclusions reached by Janssen (1991, 20f.) on the basis of writing errors and corrections in the copies, that there were (at least) two archetypes of the royal letter, possibly duplicates made and sent out by the royal chancery. The references mentioned above, which state that *ṣimdātum* written on tablets were "available with/in the hands of" certain people, hence might refer to rescripts in the form of such official royal letters. Unfortunately, the absence of similar royal letters, dealing with issues on which *ṣimdātum* are said to be available, even in the archives of Sin-iddinam and Šamaš-hazir (as far as recovered and published), makes it difficult to prove this. Moreover, while the subject matter of the ruling on the *nadītums* explains the presence of Samsu-iluna's letters in Sippar, it is somewhat surprising to find no less than three later copies in the archives of a priest who was not directly involved in the administration of the 'Cloister'. Their existence could be due to scribal training, but might **[59]** also be linked with the status of the archive owner, who could have officiated as judge. But this is still no proof that copies of royal rescripts were distributed among persons and institutions which needed them for performing judicial duties and that their contents were designated as *ṣimdat šarrim*.

As the case of the "hungry *nadītums*" and the subject matter of some of the other royal decrees show, such royal regulations need not be completely new. There was older pre-Hammurabi common law on the *nadītums* and LH also contained stipulations on their property rights (§ 178-182).[45] Samsu-iluna's 'order' was therefore meant to clarify, supplement or correct existing law (notably LH § 180), in order to protect the Cloister against the influx of poor *nadītums* (which might become a burden to the palace) by securing their material independence, and to prevent violations of property rights (*habālum*) of these ladies by making them judicially independent from their family's obligations and liabilities. Such a decree also makes sense, since there is no evidence for a new or adapted Babylonian law collection during the *ca.* 160 years between the publication of LH and the destruction of Babylon. New or adapted legal rulings, required by social and economic developments in the later Old Babylonian period, apparently had to be met by issuing royal decrees, the texts of which remain to be discovered.

From ancient Assyria we have evidence that some verdicts (*dīnum*) of the city assembly could become or be applied as generally binding (and generally known) rulings (*awātum*), some of which also (by separate decision?) could become statutory law, "published" on a stone stele, as references in letters and verdicts to "the words of the stele" show.[46] Since, however, the Old Assyrian law collection itself is still unknown, we cannot decide whether this applied to all rulings (*awātum*) of the city. There is, for example, a rule about the procedures to be followed when an Assyrian trader, active in Anatolia, died. It reads (with some variation): "Nobody, either in Assur or in Anatolia, shall touch anything, all his silver shall come together in Assur. Whoever has taken anything shall give it back, who does not give it back shall be considered a thief".[47] But it is never referred to as "the words of the stele" and hence may have been a separate ruling or decree that had not yet been raised to the status of statutory law. Still, this

---

44 See on this aspect also Kraus 1984, 119f.

45 See the observations in Lafont 1997, 23 on pre-Samsu-iluna legal practice concerning *nadītums*.

46 See Veenhof 1995, 1717-1744, esp. 1735ff.

47 See Veenhof 1995, 1726f.

apparently did not affect its validity, since what it prescribed, as quoted in several practice documents, was considered a binding rule.[48]

Something similar may be true of the type Old Babylonian royal decrees we are discussing here, since they are referred to in letters and contracts as valid and binding. What then was their relation to the rulings contained in the so-called law collections, primarily LE and LH, which are roughly from the same period? If, as several scholars believe, these collections contain normative, positive law and some of the legal issues they treat are also covered by the decrees, why are the 'laws' never quoted or referred to in practice documents, contrary to the decrees and to what happened in ancient Assur?[49]

[60] 4. References to and identification of decrees

Nearly all references to these decrees are in letters and contracts. Those in contracts offer two advantages, because the text of the contract shows which legal issue is at stake and provides a date for the reference. The latter, even though we do not know when the decree in question had been issued, at least allows us to relate the time of its validity to the date of a law collection. References in letters present more problems. Some letters can be more or less dated, such as those sent by king Hammurabi to his administrators Sin-iddinam and Šamaš-hazir (from the last ten years of the king's reign, after the conquest of Larsa), but in many cases their dates remain unclear. Moreover, in most cases such letters first describe a legal problem or wrong committed and next request, order or report in general terms that the issue should be handled or decided "in accordance with the regulation". Several letters in this context use the expression "to pronounce a verdict for somebody" (*dīnam qabûm* with personal dative suffix),[50] many more prefer the expression *dīnam šūhuzum* with personal accusative suffix, which also implies that a verdict is rendered.[51] While there must be a link between the issue stated and the verdict demanded, the reference to apply the *ṣimdātum* usually comes in the place of a statement on the substance of the verdict. Apart from that, there are several cases where the description of the wrong to be punished is damaged, unclear or too laconic. An example is the broken letter *AbB* 7, 135, where a man expects to obtain a (favorable) verdict "on the basis of the text of a tablet with a verdict that I have in my possession, in conformity with the regulation". But without knowledge of the issue and the substance of an apparently earlier verdict, the nature of the regulation referred to remains mysterious.

We cannot exclude that the reference to "the regulation" occasionally refers to procedure. In some of Hammurabi's letters royal administrative directives rather than decrees with a specific legal substance may have been meant, especially in cases dealing with problems concerning servants and tenants of the crown in the newly conquered Larsa province. I may refer here to the king's order (in *AbB* 13, 10) to handle such a case "in accordance with the judicial practice currently applied in Emutbalum", discussed below in § 8. In the broken letter *AbB* 1, 120, a man, deprived of all the property of his paternal house, asks the judicial authorities to convict his opponents "in accordance with the

---

48 The formulation, with words like 'nobody' and 'whoever', may reflect its origin as decree or proclamation. [**Add**: However, a regulation about the behaviour of creditors of a trader who has died is quoted in one verdict of the city (Kt a/k 394) with, and in another (*AKT* 6, 294) without reference to "the words of the stele". Referring to the stele apparently not was necessary].

49 The two only references in OB documents to stipulations written one a stele are in *UET* 5, 420 (see note 43) and the letter A 3529, translated in Roth 1995, 6) cannot be convincingly connected with rulings contained in the 'law collections' we know, but the issues at stake (the wages of a hired worker and the responsibility for a field entrusted for exploitation) belong to the subjects they treat.

50 Examples are given in note 26; see also *AbB* 11, 101:24f.

51 See § 2; examples are *AbB* 2, 19:12; 6, 142:11f.; 7, 85:14f.; 9, 6:11 and 25:8 (both speak of "the regulation of my/our lord"); 10, 161:9';13, 27:14f. and 38:2'; *ABIM* 33:13ff. ("the regulation which is in your hands"); *TCL* 1, 2:24; 18, 130:8; *JCS* 11 (1957) 106 no.1:14; 17 (1963) 83 no.9:7'; MA 9649:2 (see Kraus 1984, 61). *AbB* 6, 80:11 omits the verb and in 13, 48:1'f. it is probably *apālum*, "to give a person what he is entitled to".

regulations". Here the use of the plural (*ṣi-im-da-a-tim*) might indicate that the reference is not to a particular ruling, but more in general to "applying the law", enforcing the rules.

In some cases, however, the reference to "the regulation" is more informative, in particular when it is linked with the contents of the verdict or its legal effects. A good example is *AbB* 9, 25, where the judges pass the verdict "in accordance with the regulation of our lord" that a dowry has to be returned to the mother of a bride, which suggests a regulation on an aspect of marriage law.[52] In *AbB* 11, 183, in a case perhaps dealing with the division of the **[61]** harvest,[53] the writer warns the addressee with the words: "Don't you know that according to the regulation of my lord a man shall not be deprived of even one quart of barley to which he is entitled on the basis of his sealed document?" This looks like a quote from a decree which forbids and presumably punishes giving somebody less than contractually agreed, but it remains unclear whether this was a general regulation on the paying of rent, hire or rations, or one on a particular contractual relationship, such as the division of the harvest. And in the latter case, as the provisions of LH §§ 42ff. and practice documents show,[54] one may again distinguish between a "normal" division and cases of a reduced harvest (due to disaster or negligence) or one of a pledged field. Moreover, was the mention of "even one single quart of barley" part of the original decree[55] or rhetoric of the writer of the letter? In *AbB* 13, 27 Hammurabi instructs Sin-iddinam, in a case of a merchant who refuses to return goods given to him for safekeeping (*ana maṣṣartim*), to render a verdict "in accordance with the regulation". But it is not clear what exactly the misdeed was, an outright denial of having received the goods or a dispute about their status.[56] Finally, I mention *AbB* 3, 86, whose writer warns the man who pursues him (because of a claim?) and tries to get his field, that he "will oust him from (the field in which) he has invested work (*ina mānahtika ušelli*) on the basis of the regulation". Ousting somebody from (*šūlûm ina*) a field, in particular one in which work has been invested, is attested in letters (also of Hammurabi and his chancery),[57] and considered a violation of rights to be redressed or punished. Hence, there is no difficulty in assuming a royal regulation on such actions, but it is impossible to reconstruct its contents, because the subject is not covered by LE or LH (although LH § 47 stipulates that an unlucky tenant should be allowed to recover his *mānahtum*). "Investments" can be of various kinds (also non-agricultural) and a legal measure has to detail the circumstances and probably also the penalty for illegal action, which remain unknown in our case. It might be compared with rulings on unauthorized exploitation of somebody's field, such as the LH § d (mentions fields and house-plots) and in particular LU § 30 (punished by forfeiture of the investments),[58] but this is not enough to identify the regulation referred to in this letter with LH § d.

In some cases the order to handle a case "in accordance with the regulation", without specifying which verdict is to be passed, may have been deliberate. The basic rule stated in the regulation had to be applied with due regard for specific circumstances, so that the final verdict could not be predicted or prescribed, as is clear in the case of the return of a

52 I do not follow Kraus 1979, 60, who quotes this case as an example of a reference to a type of judicial procedure, without any reference to the substance of the law to be applied.

53 Lines 17': "We inspected the field and on(?) the field he tried to reach an agreement about one fourth or one third" (of ...?).

54 Note in particular the case reported in the letter published by O. Tammuz in *RA* 90 (1996) 125f., with the observations by H. Petschow in *ZA* 74 (1984) 181ff. on LH §§ 45 and 46. [See below note 143].

55 This suggests a public proclamation or a royal order of the type attested at Mari, like *ARM* 1, 6:18f. ("The sheikh who leaves even one single man behind...").

56 Two Old Assyrian texts, a judicial record (*EL* 292) and a letter (*VAS* 26, 1), show that goods considered given for safekeeping by one party were considered pledges by the other.

57 See for references *CAD* E, 134,d, and *AbB* 4, 24:10ff., 65:9ff., 68:21ff., 154:14ff.; *AbB* 2, 11:13 and 29 (without address) qualify it as *habālum*, violation of (property) rights.

58 Sumerian á.ni ... e_{11}, the equivalent of *ina mānahtišu šūlûm*.

dowry, mentioned in *AbB* 9, 25 and discussed below in § 6.d, where the judges use some freedom in implementing the rule of the regulation.

Of the references which are too damaged, laconic or unclear to allow identification and classification,[59] some concern violation of rights of various kinds, for which the verb *habālum* **[62]** and the noun *hibiltum* are used. Both cover a variety of wrongs and crimes, all of which imply depriving a person of things to which he has a right and the resulting damage, where the standard verdict is that the item/damage has to be returned/compensated (*turrum*, with personal dative suffix). The person suffering from such a misdeed, the *hablum* (masc. and fem.), is the very person the king has to protect and help as programmatic statements in the prologue of LH and by the prophet of Adad of Aleppo show.[60] But verb and noun are rarely used in the law collections themselves (an exception is LH § 34), because they prefer rulings on specific cases over formulating general principles. *Habālum* and *hibiltum* occur in combination with a reference to "the regulation" in *AbB* 2, 19; 10, 161 (address missing), 7, 85 (damaged; see line 16) and *AbB* 11, 183:23' (possibly in connection with the division of the harvest). Cases of *habālum*, without reference to a regulation, occur in Hammurabi's letters *AbB* 2, 6 and 18. In the first it is used of an unfounded claim on a field, followed by the seizure of the harvest, the second does not specify the damage (*hibiltum*) caused. The culprit in the latter case, after the damage has been compensated, has to be sent to the king, presumably to be punished, which is explicitly ordered in the former case. Hence one might think of a pertinent regulation, which includes a penalty, but we cannot prove it. Also *AbB* 3, 82, a clear case of abuse of power against the legal owner of a house-plot (the question is asked whether the judges "will bypass the regulation for your sake", *ṣimdatam etēqum*), and *AbB* 3, 86, discussed above, could be classified as cases of *habālum*, but the scribes prefer more specific descriptions of the wrongs.

AbB 6, 80 demands the administration of justice "in accordance with the regulation" in the case of a girl who was kidnapped, sold and is kept as slave by a man notwithstanding the fact that she is proven to be a free woman. There is no link with a ruling in LH, but freeing of slaves is part of '*mīšarum*-decrees' and Charpin 1987, 43f., considers this letter an illustration of EA § 20.[61]

To get a better idea of the relation between 'laws' and decrees we may distinguish the latter, mentioned both in contracts and in letters and whose nature and contents are reasonably clear, into three categories: a) decrees whose subject matter is not found in the laws; b) decrees whose subject matter is found in and hence might have been incorporated in the laws; and c) decrees referred to in the texts of the laws themselves.

5. Decrees whose subject matter is not found in the 'laws'

a. Decree on revolting adoptive sons

The reference to a royal decree on a revolting adoptive son is found in the unpublished contract BM 96973, dated to the thirty-sixth year of king Ammi-ditana.[62] After stating the adoption and the adoptive son's obligation to support his new father as long as he lives, we read:

59 I.a. *AbB* 11, 101:14; 12, 194:17; 13, 38:2'; 47:6'; 48:1'(?).

60 See *RA* 78 (1984) 10 lines 53f.: "When a man or woman whose rights have been violated calls to you (king Zimri-lim of Mari), take action, render them justice".

61 See also *AbB* 7, 88:5ff. for a royal measure to bring about the liberation of particular slaves (*šubarūtam... iškun*).

62 Studied and used by kind permission of the Trustees of the British Museum. [**Add.**: This contract is edited in K.R. Veenhof, Some Old Assyrian and Old Babylonian Adoption Contracts, part. II, as text no.3, in a volume on adoption to be edited by G. Suurmeijer (in the press)].

14 'If Š. says to B., his son: "You are not my son!", he will forfeit all his property. 18 [If B. say]s to Š., his father: "You [are not my father!]", 21 in accordance with the royal decree 22 he will be put at his disposal/mercy'.[63]

[63] The penalty is unique and line 22 probably authorizes the father to do with his rebellious son as he wishes. The standard contractual penalty for revolting adoptive sons is being sold as slaves, and the use of the rather vague expression "he will be put as his disposal", may to leave the father various options; the son was at his mercy, but sale into slavery was not obligatory. The reference to a royal ruling, the only one in dozens of Old Babylonian adoption contracts, is rather puzzling. One could link it with the unique formulation of the penalty, but it is difficult to imagine that a reference to a royal decree was needed to allow the father to deviate from the common penalty. Moreover, the decrees we are dealing with fix standard penalties for frequent, common cases, they are not meant to make exceptions possible. The reference to the decree might have to do with the background of the contract, since it concerns the adoption of the *rakbum* B. by another *rakbum*, while the father is contractually forbidden to adopt another son in addition to B.[64] But syntactically the reference is linked with the penalty for rebellion only, not with the whole contract as such.

Whatever the reason for the reference to the royal regulation, it is impossible to link it with LH, because of its subject matter and because the contract is more than hundred years younger. Adoption is treated in LH and § 192f. indeed deal with adoptive sons who repudiate their parents.[65] But the cases are very specific, the parents are persons who are unable or forbidden to have natural children and the unusual punishments for the revolting sons seem to be meant as deterrent.[66] The possibility of the existence of an older royal decree on adoption, of which the rulings of the laws are a reflection or adaptation, also seems very unlikely because of the substantial temporal gap between the two. A royal decree on such a matter is anyhow rather surprising.

b. Decree on defaulting ox drivers

There existed a special type of contract by means of which an ox (or a team of oxen) together with its driver was hired, usually for one to three months, to work a field, to take care of deep-ploughing, breaking the soil, harrowing and seed-ploughing. Its key term is *inītum*, recently studied by M. Stol,[67] which can refer both to the hired ox and its driver and to what is paid for hiring them. The norm, as Stol has demonstrated, was to supply/pay for two *inītum*'s of fifteen days each, valued at 1/2 shekel of silver apiece, hence an amount of 1 shekel of silver or (*in natura*) 300 litres of barley per month. It was customary to contract such workers with their oxen well in advance and hence contracts can stipulate a fine if they fail to turn up. A few[68] stipulate a monetary fine, "he shall pay the silver of the *inītum*", hence presumably the sum of 1/2 shekel of silver per failed

---

63 [*B.*] *ana Š. abišu* [19] [*ul abī*] *attā* [20] [*i-qa-ab*]*-bi-ma* [21] [*k*]*i-ma ṣí-im-*<*da*>*-at šarri* [22] *ana pānišu iššakkan*, followed by a mutual oath.

64 *Š. eli B.* [*mari*]*šu / māram šaniam ul iraššī.* At the end the oath is sworn "not to change their agreement" (*ana awātišunu lā enêm*), a rare formulation (also *BE* 6/1, 116:22f., with *riksātum* as object, in a donation of slaves to a man's wife for life-long usufruct, Sd year h).

65 See R. Westbrook, The Adoption Laws of Codex Hammurabi, in: A.F. Rainey e.a. (eds.), *Kinattūtu ša dārâti. Raphael Kutscher Memorial Volume* (Tel Aviv 1993) 195-204.

66 They are a courtier who is an eunuch (*girseqqum*) and a *sekertu*-woman, who therefore shall not be robbed of their adoptive sons. The penalties are based on the principle of *talio*: the son who *says* to his father..., looses his *tongue*, the one who (looks for and) *identifies* his natural father's house looses his *eye*.

67 M. Stol, Constant Factors in Old Babylonian Texts on Ploughing with the *inītum*, in: H. Gasche e.a. (eds.), *Cinquante-deux réflexions sur le Proche-Orient Ancient offerts en hommage à Léon De Meyer* (*MHEO*, II; Ghent 1994) 229-236; see also his article "Miete. B. I. Altbabylonisch", *RlA* 8 (1994), 163ff., § 2c, "Tiermiete".

68 Stol, *op. cit.* 232.

inītum. Two others[69] write: "in accordance with **[64]** the royal decree" (*kīma ṣimdat šarri*). The earliest reference to "the royal decree" is in the first year of king Ammi-ṣaduqa (MAH 16.305), but the simple mention of a monetary fine occurs earlier, already in the 28th year of Ammi-ditana (BM 97463, unpubl.).

There is no link between this decree and the laws, because the rented ox driver does not occur in LH and the earliest reference to the decree is more than one hundred years later. The contracts we know may reveal a development in the rules for non-performance, first without sanction (which does not mean that no compensation was due), next a monetary fine based on common law, equal to the wage in silver the ploughman would earn by his work, and finally a royal decree which fixes the penalty. But it is remarkable that while MAH 16305 shows that the decree was already in existence in the first year of Ammi-ṣaduqa, *PBS* 8/2, 196, fifteen years later, does not refer to it, but simply mentions as fine "the silver of the *inītum*". Perhaps the scribe had the choice between mentioning the nature and size of the fine and simply referring to the decree. If this is true, it means that the royal decree amounted to turning a rule of common law into a royal regulation. But without the text of the decree or rescript itself we cannot exclude the possibility that the latter was more comprehensive or detailed, in treating various types of breach of contract. In this context we note that the penalty stipulated in the decree for "not coming" (*ul illak*, used in MAH 16305) to do the agricultural work with oxen is very similar to that stipulated for contracted harvesters who "do not come", treated below (§ 6.a). This means that it is not impossible that there existed one single royal decree of a more general nature, which applied to various hired but defaulting (agricultural?) laborers.

c. Decree on absentee 'field managers'

A decree on this matter is mentioned in the damaged letter *AbB* 6, 75. The writer reports on a man who has failed to present himself in Isin to the men for whom or under whose supervision he probably had to work. The writer's instruction to have that man brought before him is reinforced by reminding his addressee of the fact that "the decree concerning absentee 'field managers' is valid" (*ṣimdat* ENSÍ *duppurim baʾlat*, lines 6'f.).[70]

Kraus 1979, 61 considered the reference to this decree "ungeklärt", but Gurney[71] assumed that it refers to §§ 30-31 of LH "or something of its kind". Unfortunately, the damaged letter cannot be dated, though it must fall before the latter part of Samsu-iluna's reign, since the city of Isin is mentioned. The reference to the decree suggests that the culprit was an ENSÍ, but the institutional context and nature of his work remains unclear. The ENSÍ was an important figure in the Old Babylonian period in the exploitation of fields belonging to the crown,[72] which explains the existence of a royal regulation concerning (his duties and) the penalty for not performing them by disappearing.

Neither LE nor LH mention the ENSÍ; the latter only deals with service-men or "soldiers" (*rēdûm, bāʾirum*), who have received a house, field and/or garden of the crown in **[65]** exchange for performing service duties (*ilkum*). But it is significant that § 31, adduced by Gurney, when treating the case of such a service-man who gives up the property he holds in view of (to get rid of) his service duty, uses the same verb for "to absentee himself" as the decree (*eqelšu* etc. *ina pāni ilkim iddīma uddappir*). Problems with ENSÍs, their fields

69 MAH 16.305 (Szlechter, *TJDB* 119):10: "if he does not come/perform" (*ul illak*); *VAS* 7, 87:8: "if he lets the *inītum* stay idle" (*inītam ušrāq*; cf. *PBS* 8/2, 196: 14, GUD.HI.A *ú-ra-aq*, and BM 97278:6, *inītam ú-ra-aq*, which use the D-stem of *rāqum* in the same meaning and show that *inītum* here refers to the oxen).

70 I take *duppurum* as verbal adjective ("the absentee tenant") rather than as infinitive ("the non-appearance of a tenant"), because also "the decree concerning consignment" is not *ṣimdat* + infinitive (*šūbulim*), but + noun (*šūbultim*). Frankena in *AbB* 6 made the tenant farmer the object of the infinitive *duppurum*, hence a decree concerning "die Entfernung eines Kolonen", but I follow *CAD* B 2, 3,b and Š 195, 2,a, in taking the farmer as its subject. The context of the letter asks for a sanction against a man who absents himself.

71 O.R. Gurney, *WZKM* 77 (1987) 198.

72 See for this meaning, Kraus 1984, 338ff. I follow the translations used in *AbB* 9, 116:56 and 13, 9:5.

and performances are repeatedly mentioned in the letters of Hammurabi,[73] and it is possible that their numbers and hence also their problems increased after the conquest of the territory of Larsa, when more crown-land had to be given out and exploited. It seems likely that in handling their problems a basic jurisprudence evolved, similar to the "legal practice currently applied in Emutbalum" in the case of other servants of the crown who failed to perform their duties.[74]

While the subject matter of LH may have been related to that of the decree, and elements of the substance of the decree may have had precursors in the laws,[75] there is no evidence for an earlier decree incorporated in the law collection. It is more likely that some time after LH a decree was issued (by Samsu-iluna?), which may have borrowed terminology (*duppurum*) from LH.

d. Decree on the division of the harvest

In a letter of Hammurabi to Šamaš-hazir and his colleagues, to be published as YOS 15, 27, in a case where the tenants have refused to give the owner of a field his share in the yield (*mikis eqlim*), we read:

> "As for the barley, the share in (the yield of) the field he is entitled to, in accordance with the decree, they must carry out the division with his tenants and give it to him".[76]

Law collections, of course, deal with the renting of fields and the rights of owners and tenants. They also mention the division of the yield between the two (see Roth 1995, 53 VIII:16f., 26f.; LH §§ 42-47), at times even with the rates obtaining (LH § 47: 1:1 and 2:1; EA § 19), but they do not prescribe them and they are missing in the tariff with which LE starts. The relevant norms and tariffs were a matter of customary law, stipulated in various ways in the relevant contracts between owners and tenants.[77] Hence a royal decree to impose or reaffirm the universal right of the owner of the field to obtain his contractual share in the yield cannot be at stake. The owner in the letter was a servant of the crown, a cook, who apparently had obtained a large sustenance field, which is worked for him by "many tenants". When he sent his "boy" (*ṣuhārum*, son or servant?), no doubt to collect his share, the tenants violated his right[78] by dismissing his claim and presumably chasing away his "boy".[79] Perhaps the **[66]** "decree" concerned in particular the somewhat more complicated case of sustenance fields assigned by the crown to officials who, as absentee landowners, in turn had to contract tenants to exploit them.[80] We might even consider the possibility of a more general decree dealing with crown-land and the duties and rights of its owners and tenants (both ENSÍs and *errēšums),* in which case there might even be a

---

73 See the references in Kraus 1984, 339ff., to which we can add *AbB* 13,45:3ff., where two ENSÍs who do not perform what they have to do, have to be brought under guard to the addressee, who will judge their case. Arrears of ENSÍs are mentioned in 13, 9; hired laborers working under them in 13, 78; an ENSÍ who notwithstanding a *mīšarum*-decree forces a debtor to pay, in 13:89.

74 *AbB* 13, 10. The letter concerns persons connected with the *bāb ekallim*, who will be judged because they have deserted their post (*mazzaztum*). ENSÍs too were attached to the *bāb ekallim* and when they failed to come to their "post" (*mazzaztum*; see Kraus 1984, 339, 7 and 8), they were brought to trial.

75 Note also the reference in an Old Babylonian text from Ur, dealing with a person hired to supervise the cultivation of a field, who "will be treated according to the provisions of the stela for any negligence that occurs" (see *CAD* N/1, 365a,1, collated text), a ruling not found in the law collections we know.

76 *še'am mikis eqlišu / kīma ṣimdatim / itti errešīšu / limkusūma / liddinūšum.*

77 See the survey in G. Mauer, *Das Formular der altbabylonischen Bodenpachtverträge* (München 1980) 103ff.; examples which use *makāsum*, "to obtain as one's share", on p. 107.

78 The verb is *darāsum* (D-stem with plural subject), also used in *AbB* 11, 153:17f.

79 Something similar happened in the parable told in Matthew 21:33ff.

80 See for references to the *miksum* of such fields *CAD* M/2, 64.b. An added complication could be that the fields had been acquired by Hammurabi after his conquest of Larsa and were assigned to the king's servant together with the tenants that used to work them, who now have to acknowledge him as their new owner.

link with the case treated under c. Lack of background information makes it impossible to say what exactly the substance of the royal decree was. Perhaps it dealt (also) with the sharing of economic goods in such relations, since violation (*darāsum*) of such rights, *e.g.* on irrigation water, occurred according to *AbB* 4, 23:17f., 13, 119:10f., and 199:9 (where in the first and third letter tenants are involved).

e. Decree on groundless claims

Groundless (*ina lā idim*) claiming of property (*baqārum/baqrū*) is regularly forbidden in contracts, especially in those of conveyance of real property and slaves, and in verdicts, which may also impose or stipulate a penalty for it. There is even a verdict from Dilbat (*VAS* 7, 152), dated to Hammurabi's twelfth year, where the dismissed plaintiff, if he tries again, will receive "the penalty for who raises a (groundless) claim" (*aran bāqirānim*). This suggests the existence of a generally known penalty for such claims, perhaps including those raised after an earlier renunciation of claims.[81] Such a penalty may have been rooted in customary law, but the letter *AbB* 1, 14 (quoted in § 2) shows that there existed a written (royal) decree on how to punish such a wrong claim.

Of the Old Babylonian law collections only LH deals a few times with claims on property, in all cases in order to prohibit them in particular situations. Claims raised by previous owners or third parties on property bought only occur in connection with slaves, in § 279. Other claims treated are those by a husband on his dead wife's dowry, in §§ 162-3, those on children born from a marriage between a slave and a free person, in §§ 171 and 175, those by brothers on real property donated by their father to their unmarried sister, in § 179 and those on adopted children, presumably by their natural parents, in §§ 185-188.[82]

AbB 1, 14 deals with a lawsuit concerning the inheritance of an (unmarried) woman of the *nadītu*-class, "which Naram-ilišu, the brother of Ibbi-Šamaš, had acquired", and which was contested by "the men of (the town of) Durum". The latter lost the case, because the court upheld Ibbi-Šamaš's title to the inheritance, which must have meant that he had the right to sell or deed it to his brother. The men of Durum were punished for their action "in accordance with the text of the tablet with the decree, as if they had claimed what was not theirs". LH § 178-9 treat the question what happens, after the death of a father, with the real estate he had donated to a daughter who as a priestess, *nadītum* or *sekertum*, stayed unmarried. Without written authorization to deed the property to whom she prefers, the real estate returns to her brothers in exchange for a lifelong maintenance; if they fail to provide it, she retains its **[67]** lifelong usufruct, but the property ultimately will go to her brothers. But if (§ 179) her father had given her that authorization, "her brothers shall not claim (*baqārum*) it from her".

To make the link between *AbB* 1, 14 and LH, Matouš and Gurney[83] assume that Ibbi-Šamaš is the *nadītum* and N. her brother. According to Gurney the latter would have acquired her property in line with § 178 ("an excellent parallel") after the death of the lady or her father. Matouš, on the other hand, detects an application of § 179, because he assumes that her brother N. is the heir of her choice.[84] Kraus is sceptical about these proposals ("gekünstelt und bedenklich"), but does not analyze or refute them.[85] Without going into details, I believe that equating the (anonymous) *nadītum* of Šamaš (of line 7) with Ibbi-Šamaš is very unlikely, not only because it is strange that her name would

---

81 See R.A. Veenker, An Old Babylonian Legal Procedure for Appeal, *HUCA* 45 (1974) 1-15 and Dombradi 1996, I, 345ff., §§ 459-465.

82 See for a detailed analysis of this issue Dombradi 1996, I, 262-294, and on its occurrences in law collections, 278f., § 376, where she discusses the difference between *ragāmum* and *baqārum*.

83 L. Matouš, *ArOr* 34 (1966) 42, and O.R. Gurney, *WZKM* 77 (1987) 197f. (review of Kraus 1984).

84 A situation confirmed by practice documents, see R. Harris, *OrNS* 30 (1961) 167, an article to which Matouš refers.

85 Also not in his study Vom altbabylonischen Erbrecht, in: J. Brugman e.a. (eds.), *Essays on Oriental Laws of Succession* (*SD* IX; Leiden 1969) 14f., where he does not mention *AbB* 1, 14.

be mentioned only later, but also because no Ibbi-Šamaš occurs among the numerous *nadītums* of Sippar attested in our records, not surprisingly because it seems to be a typically male name. Why in *AbB* 1, 14 citizens of Durum, perhaps the town where the property was located or from where the *nadītum* or her heir originated, contested the transaction remains unclear. Anyhow, the decree referred to in the letter cannot be linked with §§ 178-9 of LH and hence implies the existence of a separate, written decree on groundless claims and the penalty they earned, which was implemented by a court-of-law.

An important feature of the letter is that the men of Durum have been punished "as if they had claimed what is not theirs" (*kīma ša ... ibqurū*), as I translate contrary to *AbB* 1, 14, which prefers "because of the fact that".[86] Their action, perhaps in order to support the claim of a plaintiff (a fellow citizen?), is considered similar too and hence punishable like a groundless claim. This means that judges could treat comparable or closely related wrongdoings as falling under one single decree. I know two additional examples of "as if" in penalty clauses. In the judicial record MAH 16506+:13[87] one party swears: "By Marduk and (king) Abi-ešuh, if your bride-in-spe is with me or will be seen with me, [*I may be punished by*] the decree, as if I had brought a slave-girl of the palace out through the gate of Babylon!" If the decree mentioned indeed refers to LH § 15, which uses the same terminology,[88] the speaker would swear: "You can kill me if...". In *AbB* 4, 11:31f. Hammurabi threatens officials of the crown who fail to carry out his orders that they will not be pardoned "as if they had crossed the great boundary". These references document the principle that (under certain conditions) particular wrongdoings could be considered to be equal to and punishable like closely related, well defined crimes, for which penalties had been fixed. It must have restricted the need of drafting too many separate penal decrees and have provided the judges with a guideline for imposing penalties *per analogiam*, a principle that may also have been applied by judges who used LH as a guideline for their verdicts.

[68] The substance of the decree on groundless claims probably was similar to and perhaps based on clauses prohibiting or condemning property claims found in many contracts and litigation documents, but such a general prohibition does not occur in the laws. Hence there is little reason to assume the existence of an earlier decree underlying or incorporated in the law collection. It is more likely, even though it is difficult to date this letter, that the decree reflects a later regulation, issued to supplement the very specific cases treated in the law collection by a more general or comprehensive ruling with a wide application. It must have included the most common case, not mentioned in LH, the claim by a seller or a third party of an item acquired by purchase, which is regularly stipulated, already before Hammurabi, in the 'Eviktionsklausel' of deeds of sale.[89] An example is in the unpublished sale of an ox (BM 97131, date missing, but late OB), whose seller "is responsible for claims on it in accordance with the royal decree" (lines 12-14). A reference to it might also be detected in *AbB* 6, 142, although we do not know the background of this case. Here the judges of Larsa inform the authorities of a town of the fact that a man in their territory has appealed to them because of a claim on the garden he had bought five years ago and ask them to judge the case "in accordance with the regulation". If we assume a more comprehensive decree on various types of claims, we might even find a reference to it in the OB letter *JCS* 11 (1957) 106, no.1, which deals with a creditor who sues (*gerûm*) somebody for silver, apparently due to him as compensation for damage to his

---

86 The latter translation would require *aššum* or perhaps simple *kīma*, while the normal meaning of the conjunction *kīma ša* is "as if" (see *CAD* K 365c, and *Akkadica* 94/5 [1995] 33f.).

87 See *JCS* 7 (1953) 98. I follow *CAD* K 80,b,1': *kīma ša amat ekallim bāb Babīlim ušāṣiam ṣimdat[i...]*. The OB letter *VAS* 22, 90 rev.:9'f. (see *AoF* 10, 1983, 61) speaks of a man who "stole another man's slave and brought him out through the city-gate".

88 Also suggested by R. Yaron, *Zeitschrift der Savigny-Stiftung für Rechtsgeschichte, Rom. Abt.* 109 (1992) 64, note 39. A similar provision in LE § 51.

89 Treated in San Nicolò 1974, § 4.

property. The writer states that the silver already had been paid and asks his addressee to decide the case *kīma ṣimdat šarrim.*

Unfortunately, the references to the decree do not tell us what the penalty for groundless claims was and we are also not helped by the mention in a litigation document (*VAS* 7, 152, mentioned above) of the existence of a "penalty for who makes a (groundless) claim". As Eva Dombradi points out, this was most probably a monetary fine, perhaps the double of the amount involved, which finds confirmation in the deed of sale of a plot of land, *SLB* I/2 no. 26. Who claims the plot sold (line 19, read *bāqirānum* É, written over erasures) has to pay a fine of 1/3 (sic) mina of silver, almost the double of the purchase price of 9 1/6 shekels. The decree may have raised a presumably customary fine from the level of contractual and judiciary practice to that of a binding ruling.[90] But several questions remain, because we do not know which types of claims the decree may have treated and distinguished, *e.g.* groundless claims by previous owners or third parties, claims after an earlier renunciation of claims, and claims by creditors who already had been paid back. This last type is implied (it does not use the verb *baqārum)* in LH § 107, where a moneylender or trader, who denies having received back the silver he had given to his agent as trust (*qīptum*) has to pay six times the amount at stake. While we do not know whether all the references we have refer to one and the same royal decree, this example anyhow makes it likely that a decree on such matters also stipulated a penalty for violating the ruling.

6. Decrees whose subject matter is found in the 'laws'

a. Decree on defaulting harvest laborers

The first is the decree that stipulates the penalty for defaulting harvest laborers, to which a number of contracts refer and which is also treated in § 9 of LE, presumably to be dated to around 1800 B.C.

[69] The earliest reference in a Babylonian contract to such a penalty "according to the royal decree" is in *VAS* 9, 3, dated to the 17th year of Hammurabi, hence before his laws were drafted. This regulation is probably also referred to in a contract from Hammurabi's 40th year,[91] which shows that the penalty was a fine, since the reference to the royal decree is expanded by the words "he will pay silver". Similarly, the contract *VAS* 9, 31, where 36 laborers are contracted, in line 15f. adds the so-called clause of joint liability: "he will take [the silver] from who is present/available".[92] These references show the existence of a decree on this matter from Hammurabi's early years, or even preceding him. The defaulting harvester, who had received part of his wage in advance, had to pay a fine, but the references do not reveal how much this was. If the decree linked up with common law, it may have been the *duplum*, to judge from an early contract of this type,[93] which stipulates a penalty of twice the amount (5/6 shekel of silver) received in advance.

This royal decree was not incorporated in LH, which does not treat this issue, but its substance is found in the somewhat older § 9 of LE. Here the harvester "who does not present himself to harvest at harvest time", has to pay tenfold the prepaid one shekel of silver,[94] an extremely heavy fine indeed, presumably meant as a deterrent. Two

90 Dombradi 1996, I, 346-349. I doubt whether the (rare) degrading and public corporal punishments for recidivists (Dombradi § 460, with note 525) had been fixed by decree.

91 Published in *JCS* 11 (1957) 28 no. 17. [**Add**. A reference to such a decree from Hammurabi's 26th year is found in F.N.H. Al Rawi and S. Dalley, *Old Babylonian Texts from Private Houses at Abu Habbah, Ancient Sippir* (*É-DUB-BA-A* 7; London 2000) no. 90:11-12, *ul illakma ṣimdat* LUGAL].

92 KI LÚ.GI.NA.[TA KÙ.BABBAR] / ŠU BA.AB.T[E.GÁ] (dated to Hammurabi year 27 or Samsu-iluna year 7); see J.G. Lautner, *Altbabylonische Personenmiete und Erntearbeiterverträge* (Leiden 1936) 185f. for the implications of this clause.

93 S. Langdon in *PSBA* 33 (1911) pl. XLV, no. xxv, with the verb "to harvest" and the whole clause in Sumerian.

94 See for the text Roth 1995, 60.

rather similar harvester contracts from the realm of Eshnunna (found at Tell Harmal = Šaduppûm), both from the reign of king Ibal-pi-el and hence somewhat later than LE, refer to the existence of a royal decree on this matter. They stipulate that if he (the middleman or one of the laborers contracted) "does not come to harvest (at harvest time), the royal decree (comes into effect), he shall pay silver".[95] It is very likely that the decree referred to is either identical with or reflected by LE § 9, the more so because one of these contracts shares with the 'law' the unusual construction of an adverbial accusative (*eṣēdam*) followed by a finite form of the same verb (*iṣṣid*).[96]

Although these contracts are only slightly older than the earliest references to "the royal decree" in similar Babylonian contracts, we cannot simply equate the two decrees of Eshnunna and Babylon. Their existence in both states only proves that this was an urgent problem, which was taken up by the royal administration, but it is very well possible that both reflect or were inspired by a still earlier decree, which formalized and sanctioned a rule of common law.

b. Decree on liabilities in connection with slave sale

The liability of the seller of a slave to offer warranty to its buyer is a better candidate for a royal decree incorporated in a law collection. LH §§ 278-281 deal with this issue and such liabilities are also regularly spelled out in slave sale contracts. These contracts, as shown by **[70]** Stol and Wilcke,[97] state (with minor variations): "three days investigation (*tebʾītum*), one month epilepsy (*bennum*), for claims on him (the slave bought; *ana baqrīšu*, variant *ana bāqirānišu*, "for who claims him") he is responsible in accordance with the royal decree". The first guarantee considers the slave's legal status, the second the possibility of a latent defect in the form of an infection, and the third eviction by a third person, who claims the slave as his. The duration of the last guarantee is usually not stated, but occasionally one adds "for future days" or "forever".[98] There are, however, several problems in linking the stipulations in the practice documents, which refer to 'the royal decree', with what we find in LH.

While LH stipulate a one-month guarantee for epilepsy (§ 278) and the seller's warranty for claims on the slave (§ 279),[99] they do not mention the warranty for the results of *tebʾītum*, 'investigation', scil. of the slave's identity and legal status. Stol (134f.), however, believes that §§ 280-1, which deal with slaves bought abroad and subsequently identified in Babylonia by their former owners, present a concrete illustration of such an 'investigation', but without using the technical term *tebʾītum* or mentioning the term of three (rarely two) days found in the contracts. This allows him to conclude that "the entire clausula of the contracts [is] neatly in line with § 279-281 of CH". The decree referred to in the contracts hence must have been "one containing these or similar provisions". But he assumes that it was "issued by a later king, specifying Hammurabi's ruling", because LH

95 The clause reads: *ul iṣṣidma ṣimdat šarrim kaspam išaqqal*, see *JCS* 13 (1959) 107 no. 7 (Ibal-pi-el year 9), and *JCS* 24 (1972) 51, no. 25 (probably from the same time or even year; see for the year-name "Year when the temple of Sîn was built", *JCS* 13, 75b).

96 LE § 9: *[e]ṣēdam eṣēdam la iṣissu(m)*, *JCS* 13, 107 no.7:5f. *eṣēdam ul iṣṣidma*. See for the meaning of *eṣēdam*, an infinitive in the accusative, M. Stol, *Studies in Old Babylonian History* (Istanbul 1976) 104ff., who also discusses the two contracts. The double *eṣēdam* in LE § 9 is a problem, according to Roth 1995, 68 note 3, perhaps dittography.

97 Stol 1993, 133ff. A survey and analysis of the relevant contracts is offered by Wilcke 1976, 258-262. [**Add.**: Several new contracts are found in K. Van Lerberghe and G. Voet, *A Late Old Babylonian Temple Archive from Dūr-Abiešuh* (CUSAS 8, Bethesda 2009) nos. 1-4, 6, 8-11. They date from the period between Ammi-ditana year 29 until Samsu-ditana year 11 and all have the full version, mentioning the three guarantees and ending with *ana baqrīša/u kīma ṣimdat šarrim izzaz*]

98 U4.KÚR.ŠÈ, *ana mātimma, ana mātum mātumma, ana māt mātma*, see Wilcke 1976, 261f.; note also *ana warkiāt ūmim* in IM 54684:14.

99 See Petschow 1986, 24f., who tries to explain why § 278 (warranty for epilepsy) stipulates cancellation of the purchase (by returning slave and silver), but § 279, contrary to many contracts that mention a fixed fine, does not quantify the warranty, in order to offer a flexible rule applicable in different situations.

lack some details of the last warranty and contracts recording this triple guarantee first appear *ca.* fifty years after LH, during the reign of king Abi-ešuh.

While I agree with this last conclusion and also believe in a royal decree that specifies or supplements the rules found in LH, the question remains which provisions it contained and why it was needed if all elements it contained were already found in LH. The first two liabilities mentioned in the contracts, as pointed out by Wilcke, are formulated as independent nominal sentences (with *teb'ītum* and *bennum* in the nominative) and it is only in the third, a verbal phrase, that the reference to the decree is embedded: "he is responsible for claims on him in accordance with the royal decree".[100] From a linguistic point of view this allows the conclusion that the decree only bears on the warranty for claims (*baqrū*) by a third party. This is perhaps confirmed by the fact that references to the decree, with one single exception (*VAS* 16, 206: "in the future"),[101] only occur when no term for this warranty is stated and that it is absent when it is said to be "forever", presumably because the scribe preferred mentioning the substance of the liability over simply referring to the decree. This suggests that the decree also dealt with the duration of this warranty.

Since warranty for claims (*baqrū*) "in accordance with the royal decree" is also stipulated in various other sale **[71]** contracts,[102] I prefer to take the references to a decree in slave sale contracts not (as Stol does) as evidence for a special decree on this issue in connection with slave sale, but as a general regulation on liability for eviction of goods bought. The need for such a decree may have been felt because civil warranty for eviction in LH (at its very end, in a 'chapter' dealing with what Petschow calls "acquisition of strange labour force") is only stipulated for slave sale and not for sale of real property. Stipulations dealing with sale occur in §§ 7ff., but only in the context of property delicts and LH lacks rulings on procedures and warranties for normal sales, especially those of real estate. They may have been omitted, because they were an accepted feature of common law, current in sale contracts already before LH was drafted, at times even formulated exactly as in LH § 279 (*baqrī irtaši*).[103] Nevertheless, I assume that, for various reasons, it was decided to specify and perhaps also broaden the rules on warranty for eviction of various goods sold (real property, slaves, animals, etc.) in a new, more comprehensive royal decree, which had to supplement LH. It also offered the opportunity to specify what "to answer/satisfy the claim" (*baqrī apālum*) implied, monetary compensation for the rightful owner based on the sale price, or returning him the slave while indemnifying the buyer, etc.[104] It also adopted and acknowledged terminological changes, such as the use of the verb *izuzzum ana*, "to be responsible for", instead of *apālum* with accusative,

---

100 *3 ūmī teb'ītum* ITU.1.KAM *bennu(m) ana baqrīšu* (etc.) *kīma ṣimdat šarrim izzaz*, see Wilcke 1976, 259ff. In the ca. 30 occurrences the preposition *ana* is added only two times before *bennum*, and I follow Wilcke in assuming that this rare *ana benni* should also be taken as subject of a nominal sentence.

101 Once also used in connection with the sale of an ox, *YOS* 13, 259.

102 Passim in sales of oxen, for a donkey in *YOS* 13, 322, for a plot of land in *MAOG* 4 (Leipzig 1928/29) 291 (Ammi-ditana of Babylon, year 22), for a door in *VAS* 7, 46 (Abi-ešuh year "p"), see Wilcke 1976, 261f.

103 See Petschow 1986, 26ff. On p. 33 he assumes "eine überlieferte und noch vorhandene gewohnheitsrechtliche Rechts- und Urkundenpraxis", which was (still) known to and used by the composer of LH, who incorporated a common legal praxis in his law collection, "nunmehr rechtsvereinheitlichend für das Einheitsreich konzipiert" (p. 73). Note also the unlimited (*ana māt mātma*) warranty for claims on a slave in *ARM* 8, 10, dated to the second(?) year of the reign of king Zimri-lim (ca. 1774 B.C.) and hence older than LH.

104 See for the legal questions raised by the liability for eviction, Petschow 1986, and H. Kümmel, Ein Fall von Sklavenhehlerei, *AfO* 25 (1974-77) 72-83.

"to satisfy", used in older contracts and in § 279 of LH.[105] Unfortunately, the text of this new royal decree is unknown and we can only get some idea of it from references in various contracts, especially of the sale of slaves and oxen, which show that it performed a useful function.[106] It seems most likely that one of Hammurabi's successors, presumably Abi-ešuh, building on the provisions contained in LH, drafted the regulation.

c. Decree on consignment (šēbultum)[107]

A comparable case is the ruling on the punishment for the fraudulent consignee in § 112 of LH. Thus far five references to a royal decree on this matter are known from practice documents, in chronological order *YOS* 13, 328, BM 78589 (courtesy Frans van Koppen), and *YOS* 13, 436, from the years 33, 36, and 37 of Ammi-ditana, CBS 1153 from Ammi-ṣaduqa year 6,[108] and the damaged BM 97222A (courtesy Els Woestenburg), date not preserved.

[72] LH § 112 treats the case of the consignee whose does not deliver (*nadānum*) the goods "where he had been commissioned to bring them" (*ašar šūbulu*), but appropriates (*tabālum*) what has been entrusted to him by a trader on a business trip for consignment (*ana šēbultim*). The culprit has to pay a five-fold compensation. Non-delivery of consigned goods is also the subject of BM 78589 (2 *gur* of barley and 1/3 shekel of silver), of *YOS* 13, 436 rev. (barley), and of *YOS* 13, 328 (silver, to be delivered to the consigner's principal, *ummiānum*). While the first two stipulate "if he does not deliver: in accordance with the decree on consignment" (*ul inaddinma kīma ṣimdat šūbultim*), the third instead simply refers to "the royal decree" [(*kīma*) *ṣimda*]*t šarrim*,[109] but none of them specifies which penalty the decree imposes.

We cannot exclude that "the decree" referred to in these contracts actually is (or has been incorporated in) § 112 LH, since it mentions the necessary penalty and because the terminology is very similar, also in describing the liability of the consignee by means of the stative *šūbul*.[110] Unfortunately, the late Old Babylonian copy of LH, which provides selected groups of legal rulings with headings of the type di.dab$_5$.ba (= *ṣimdatum*),[111] does not give one for § 112, so that we cannot use this as an argument that when these consignment contracts were drawn up § 112 could have been referred to as a (royal) *ṣimdatum*. Nevertheless, the decree in question cannot have been identical to LH § 112, because it deals with non-delivery in combination with appropriation (*lā iddinma itbal*), which is not mentioned in the contracts. One could assume that § 112 was an expansion of the original decree by adding appropriation, in line with LH's preference for treating specific cases and serious wrongs.

---

105 See Petschow 1986, 25ff. But note that some early contracts (*UET* 5, 184, from Ur, and *YOS* 8, 86, from Larsa) already use the Sumerian verb gub (inim.gál.la gemé ... in.na.gub.bu), the equivalent of *izuzzum ana*, which also occurs in the contract from Mari (see note 103), which antedates the publication of LH. The use of *bāqirānum*, "a person who claims", instead of *baqrū*, "claims", is attested both in early (e.g. *YOS* 8, 31 and *VAS* 13, 76, both from Larsa) and later texts. These developments in the terminology, as pointed out by Wilcke 1976, are connected with the differentiation between clauses used for the sale of movable and immovable property.

106 Its occurrence in a contract discovered at Terqa, on the Middle Euphrates (published in *Syria* 5, 1924, 272), dated to the reign of a local king from the later Old Babylonian period, is evidence of Babylonian influence in that area.

107 See for the meaning of this term, K.R. Veenhof, *Aspects of Old Assyrian Trade and its Terminology* (Leiden 1972) 140-144 and R.M. Whiting, *Old Babylonian Letters from Tell Asmar* (*AS* 22; Chicago 1987) 113-119.

108 Recently published by M. Stol in: B. Bock e.a. (eds.), *Munuscula Mesopotamica. Festschrift für Johannes Renger* (*AOAT* 267; Münster 1999) 583f.

109 See Kraus 1984, 8.

110 *YOS* 13, 328:6ff *šūbulti šūbulū inaddinū* [*šūbul*]*ti šūbulū* [*ul inad*]*dinūma*; BM 78589: 3ff. *šūbulti* PN$_1$ *ana* PN$_2$ PN$_3$ (consignee) *šūbul*; CBS 1153:10f. *šūbulti šūbulu ul inaddinma* ... The variation between *šēbultum* and *šūbultum* is no counter argument, since it is attested in the law collection itself, see *CAD Š*/3 189b, 2'.

111 *PBS* 5, 93, see Finkelstein 1967, notes 2 and 6; the heading of §§ 113-116 in col. v:38.

But this does not fit CBS 1153, which stipulates a penalty "in accordance with the decree on consignment" if the silver is not delivered in time, within the period of three days stipulated in the contract. Timely delivery is also the issue in *YOS* 12, 201 (Samsu-iluna year 6), where the consignee has to pay a penalty "if he lets the summer go by" (*ebūram ibbalakkat)* before delivering an amount of copper. The decree referred to hence must have treated two or three possibilities, non-delivery with or without appropriation and late delivery. Appropriation was a serious crime, comparable to theft, and LH accordingly stipulates a fivefold compensation, but late delivery of course was less serious, according to *YOS* 12, 201 punishable by double compensation (*tašna utār*), while according *TIM* 3, 118 (from the realm of Eshnunna) in such a case interest had to be paid.[112] Late delivery is also the subject of two pre-Hammurabi consignment contracts from Larsa, *TCL* 10, 98 and 125,[113] from years 42 and 43 of Rim-Sin and related to the tin trade on Susa via Eshnunna. Both deal with a consignment of ca. 1 1/2 mina of silver to be delivered (in Larsa?) within two and six months respectively and the consignee who "lets the due date pass by" (*šētuqum* / bal) has to pay a fine.[114] Even **[73]** though these commercial contracts are rather specific and their purpose was presumably not simple delivery of money,[115] they support the idea that late delivery was an important issue in consignment contracts and hence should not have been ignored by a royal edict.

Since all four contracts with explicit references to the (royal) decree on this matter first appear *ca.* one hundred years after Hammurabi, it is rather unlikely that LH § 112 reflects or incorporates this decree. It was probably one issued quite some time after Hammurabi, perhaps during the reign of Ammi-ditana, probably in order to supplement LH § 112, which only dealt with the most serious crime of appropriation. The new decree could make use of the formulation of LH § 112 and of elements of common law as reflected in the earlier contracts from Larsa.

d. Decree on the return of a dowry

The judges of Babylon, in the letter *YOS* 2, 25 = *AbB* 9, 25, order "the return of the complete dowry which the woman M. had given to her daughter and (which she) had brought into the house of I.", apparently her daughter's husband. This was the substance of a verdict passed "in accordance with the regulations of our lord" (*kīma ṣimdat bēlini*), in a lawsuit between M. and I. If the case, as Westbrook points out,[116] concerns the dowry of a wife that had died childless, we can take the verdict as an application of LH § 163. Westbrook, however, notes that the order to implement this verdict speaks of "to hand over everything which is intact and can now (still) be spotted" (*mimma balṭam ša inanna innaṭṭalu nadānum*),[117] hence "only covers the dowry in its present condition, *i.e.* excluding what has already been consumed". This is different from what LH § 163 formulates as a basic rule in such cases, "her dowry belongs to her father's house", but Westbrook rightly states that *YOS* 2, 25 is "an illustration of the basic rules ...*in practice*" (italics K.R.V.). The implementation of a "basic rule" apparently does not exclude the possibility of taking into account particular circumstances. This is indeed borne out by our letter, because

---

112 See for this text F. Reschid, *Archiv der Nūršamaš* (diss. Heidelberg 1965) 113 (10 *gur* of barley *šu*-BI-*ú*-*ul*-*tum*), where the verb *šētuqum*, "to let (the term) pass by", is used for late delivery.

113 Edited in W.F. Leemans, *Foreign Trade in the Old Babylonian Period* (*SD* 6; Leiden 1960) 57ff. The second has an Eshnunna (were it was drawn up?) year-name contemporary with Rim-Sin year 43.

114 In line with the commercial nature of the contracts the fine is weighing out silver plus profit (*TCL* 10, 98) or tin (*TCL* 10, 125), in accordance with the commercial exchange rate (? *qāti harrān Šušim*). A similar stipulation in found in *TCL* 10, 20 (consignment of 125 1/2 shekels of silver), where the fine for exceeding the term of 4 months is paying silver in Susa *qāti harrānim*.

115 The rather long terms suggest that the consignee or agent in the meantime could use the capital entrusted to him for doing business, which makes it a kind of commercial loan. Other consignment contracts from the same archive (all are called consignments of Sin-uselli) are *RA* 72 (1978) 133ff. nos. 21 and 22.

116 R. Westbrook, *Old Babylonian Marriage Law* (*AfO Beiheft* 23; Horn 1988) 92f.

117 The proposal of *CAD* N/2, 128, 13,b) to interpret the verb as "to be admired" is unconvincing and we better stick to *CAD* B 69a, b) "which can be seen" = "which is available".

the reference to "the regulation of our lord" applies to the basic rule "to return all of the dowry" (lines 10-16). But when the judges next ask the addressee to implement that decision, they only speak of returning the dowry in its present condition (lines 18-20). It would be unfair to force a husband, who had lost his childless wife after a few(?) years of marriage, to return the (value of the) original dowry in its entirety and not to make allowance for what had been used and consumed by the married couple. There was, after all, a difference between a non-completed or frustrated marriage and one which only later came to a tragic end, a difference which also LE § 18 acknowledges.

If we accept that this application falls within the range of the basic rule, we can maintain that "in accordance with the regulation of our lord" could mean "conform LH § 163". If not, we have to assume a new regulation, perhaps based on precedent, *e.g.* a royal verdict or rescript, which adapted or refined LH § 163 by limiting the liability in such cases to returning **[74]** what was still available of the dowry after a couple of years.[118] This requires that the letter is later than the law collection, but I have been unable to fix its approximate date by prosopographic means. This means that, theoretically, even the possibility of a reference to a (royal) regulation preceding LH and perhaps later incorporated into it, cannot be ruled out, but I consider this very unlikely.

f. Decree on the recovery of missing goods (hulqum)

A reference to a regulation concerning the penalty for a person in whose hands missing goods (*hulqum*) are found occurs in *ABIM* 33:13, a letter addressed to the mayor and elders of a town. The writer, whose "boys" (*ṣuhārū*) have been seized and are suspected of the crime, asks the authorities to render judgment "in accordance with the regulation which is in your hands". The case might well be one of those covered by LH § 9ff., which state the penalties of thief and receiver, but these rulings seem to be more interested in matters of procedure, especially the question of proof by testimony, and in the relation between the rights of the owner and the honest buyer (of stolen property). However, because date and place of origin of the letter (blessing by Šamaš and Marduk) are uncertain, it is risky to consider it proof of the application of LH and hence of the fact that *ṣimdatum* may refer to rules found in a law collection.

7. Decrees referred to in the text of the 'laws'

a. Decree on homicide

The first reference to a 'royal decree' is in § 58 of LE, which deals with the case of a man's son killed by the collapse of a wall of a house that had been neglected by its owner. It states: "(It is) a capital case: the royal decree" (*napištum ṣimdat šarrim*). Although there is a tendency to assign capital crimes to royal jurisdiction, this is probably not what the ruling means, because *ṣimdatum* refers not to procedure, but to substance of law. Moreover, that a crime comes under royal jurisdiction is expressed in a different way in § 48 of the same laws: "a case involving life goes to the king" (*awāt napištim ana šarrimma*). Applying the basic meaning of *ṣimdatum* we have to assume a decree, which is unknown to us, which deals with liability in case of homicide or a capital crime. The reference in § 58 is explainable because it is not a simple case of homicide, but of death by guilt and there are gradations in guilt.[119] Yaron suggests that the decree in question may have been

---

118 The existence of such a new regulation might even be used to explain the appearance of the clause about "five sheep that do not die" in a dowry-list and a donation by a father to a girl, both dated to Hammurabi's reign (year-names in both cases broken), *CT* 4, 1b:6 + L. Dekiere *Old Babylonian Real Estate Documents* (Ghent 1995) no. 328:5' + *CT* 45, 29:17. This contractual clause tries to make sure that the dowry will always include the (value) of the original five sheep (cf. A.L. Oppenheim, A Note on *ṣôn barzel*, *IEJ* 5 [1955] 89ff.). Could it be an attempt to prevent a reduction of the value of the dowry along the lines indicated by the letter *AbB* 9, 25?

119 See for the text and its interpretation, Yaron 1988, 121ff. and 300ff., and also S. Lafont, *Revue historique de droit français et étranger* 73 (1995) 500.

"an example of the proper law of Eshnunna itself, its *ius civile*", hence probably based on a specific royal verdict in the form of a rescript. But we cannot exclude the possibility of a more comprehensive decree, which differentiates various life-taking crimes according to circumstances, guilt and loss, and stipulates the relevant penalties.

[75] *b. Decree on paying debts in different valuta*

Two references to 'royal decrees' are found in LH. The first is in § 51, in a 'chapter' dealing with indebted farmers, and it stipulates that a debtor unable to pay back in silver is allowed "to give his creditor <barley or> sesame for his silver and the interest on it, according to their market value, in conformity with[120] the royal decree (*ana pī ṣimdat šarrim*)". The second, § u, occurs in a 'chapter' dealing with commercial and other loans and again stipulates that if a debtor has no silver his creditor shall accept barley "in accordance with the royal decree (*kīma ṣimdat šarrim*)". It has been suggested that the substance of this 'royal decree' is to be found in § t, which fixes the rates of interest for loans in barley and silver at 33 1/3 and 20 % respectively, and Kraus 1979, 62, understands *kīma ṣimdat šarrim* in § u as "gemäss diesem Paragraphen", which means § t. This implies that "'Gesetzgeber' gelegentlich den alten Ausdruck für eine königliche Sondermassregel auf eine Einzelbestimmung ihres Codex bzw. Ediktes angewendet haben". But identification of the 'decree' with § t is difficult, because both in § 51 and § u the main issue is payment in a valuta different from that in which the loan was rated or received. Interest is not mentioned at all in § 51, while in § u it is not the only issue.

Paying back an interest-bearing debt in a different valuta of course may have consequences for the rate of interest, but more basic are the mere right to pay back a different commodity and the question which rates of conversion are applied in such cases. San Nicolo 1974, 219, hence understands *ṣimdat šarrim* in LH as "dass von König festgesetzte Umrechnungsverhältnis zwischen Silber und den wichtigsten vertretbaren Naturalien des damaligen Verkehrs". We know the custom of rating barley loans in silver on the basis of the (for the debtor unfavorable) exchange rate obtaining late in the year, to be repaid "at harvest time according the by then current exchange rate" ('verhüllte Fruchtwucher'), which secures the creditor much additional income.[121] Issuing a decree to protect the poor and weak by stopping or curbing such habits and fixing rates of conversion certainly would be in line with the professed intention of the law-giver (col. I:27ff.).

A ruling dealing with the same issue occurs in §§ 20-21 of LE, where in both cases the creditor is the subject. That a barley debt can be converted into one in silver by the creditor is taken for granted in LE § 20, which intends to lay down that a conversion of a grain loan into a silver one (§ 20) does not reduce the original rate of interest current for barley, 33 1/3 %, to 20 %, current for silver. This suggests that the rule envisages a creditor who obliges his debtor who cannot pay in silver (as LH § 51 assumes). LE § 21 adds that on a loan which was from the outset (*ina pānišu*) in silver, only the original lower silver interest can be charged, **[76]** even (as I would like to interpret) when paid back in grain.

---

120 *Ana pī* is frequent in Old Babylonian letters in the combination *ana pī kanīkim/ṭuppim*, where it serves as a compound preposition expressing "in conformity with", "on the basis of" what is written in a document. Cf. the use of *ana pī riksātim*, "in conformity with the contract", in LH § 264:57 and *AbB* 12, 72:20. When the focus is on the amount of goods (to be delivered, etc.), one may write *mala pī kanīkim* (etc.), "as much as..." (*AbB* 9, 156:13). The difference with *kīma pī* (e.g. *AbB* 3, 92:6') is minimal. While *kīma* (in *kīma ṣimdat šarrim*) seems to refer to a standard, a norm to be applied, *ana pī* may focus more on the details of a stipulation (numbers and quantities recorded in a document of assignment [*ṭuppi isihtim*/*ṣidītim*)], a title deed [*šīmātim*, *VAB* 5, 269:28], or a contract [*riksātum*, *AbB* 12, 72:20]), which have to be implemented. This would make sense in LH § 52, if indeed compliance with fixed rates of exchange and interest is meant. Note *AbB* 11, 183: 21'ff., where *ina ṣimdat bēlia* a man shall not be deprived of the barley he is entitled to *ana pī kanīkišu*.

121 See D.O. Edzard, *Altbabylonische Rechts- und Wirtschaftsurkunden aus Tell ed-Dēr* (München 1970) 30ff. and A. Skaist, *The Old Babylonian Loan Contract* (Ramat Gan 1994) 192f., on the "rate of exchange stipulation".

This might be an attempt to prevent a creditor from earning "verhüllte Fruchtwucher". In § 20 nothing is said about the tariff for converting a debt in barley into one in silver, but it is contained in LE § 1, which equates 300 quarts of barley with one shekel of silver.

A similar rule may be detected in LH § u, if we can read, restore and emend its incomplete and partly corrupt protasis, not preserved on the stele and only available on two damaged tablets, as follows (differences with Roth 1995 in italics): "If a man, who has obtained an interest-bearing *silver* loan, has no silver to pay back, *but has barley*, in accordance with the royal decree [*the creditor*] will take as its interest per 1 kor (=300 quarts) only (*-ma*) 60 quarts of barley",[122] hence 20 percent interest, the standard interest for silver. And he forfeits his claim if he takes more. If this interpretation is correct, LH agrees with LE § 21 in helping the debtor by maintaining the low silver interest of 20 percent, even when the debt is repaid in a different commodity, barley.

For Kraus's idea, that the 'royal decree' of LH § u is the interest tariff given in § t, could speak that the words "in accordance with the royal decree" belong to the apodosis, which deals only with the interest rate. But the fact remains that the probably identical 'royal decree', to which LH § 51 refers, concerns the exchange rate (*mahīrātum*), that the how much barley or sesame has to be paid for a debt rated in silver and for the interest on it. This clearly suggests a broader decree, which might have contained several elements: perhaps *a*) the conditions under which a debtor has the right to pay a silver loan in a different commodity; certainly *b*) the rate of exchange to be applied for such a conversion (*e.g.* standard rate versus seasonal fluctuation), *c*) which interest rate obtains if the conversion mentioned under a) takes place, that of the original or that of the new valuta, and perhaps *d*) the interest rates themselves, as found in LH § t.

Considering LH § t alone the royal decree referred to in § u is also problematic, because it only states traditional and current rates of interest, which certainly were not introduced by Hammurabi. The same rates are prescribed in somewhat older § 18A of LE, they occur in a still older, anonymous collection of Sumerian laws,[123] and are already current in debt-notes dating from the period of the Ur III dynasty (21st century B.C.).[124] Moreover, as Skaist has pointed out,[125] the mode of expressing the 20% interest rate on silver loans ("1/6 of a shekel and 6 grains of silver per shekel") is unusual, attested only in a few older contracts, decennia before both LE and LH. Hence there was no need for Hammurabi to state or confirm them in a new decree, but including them in a more comprehensive decree on debts, payments and interest would be understandable.

We conclude that we can assume the existence of a royal decree on paying debts in a commodity different from that in which it was rated, which stipulated when and at what rates of exchange and interest this was possible. LH § t may have been based on, but was not identical to, this decree. It is referred to in LH § 51 and u, which may quote parts of it and use its formulations – and this may be true of LE §§ 20-21 too, – but they do not provide information on **[77]** the rate of conversion at stake in § 51. In an authoritative royal text like LH there was no need to support or argue for a ruling by referring to a royal decree. But such a reference was necessary when a decree contains stipulations that the law collection does not contain. Since LH did not contain a conversion tariff or a list of equivalents, as is offered by LE § 1, it refers to a royal decree that must have contained such data.

---

122 On the basis of manuscripts S and t (collated by Veysel Donbaz. [**Add**. See now K.R. Veenhof, The Interpretation of Paragraphs t and u of the Code of Hammurabi, in: Ş. Dönmaz (ed.), *DUB.SAR É.DUB. BA.A. Studies Presented in Honour of Veysel Donbaz* (Istanbul 2010) 283-293., where also the issue of the payment of mixed loans is treated] [= pp. 285-296 in this volume].

123 See Roth 1995, 36 § m.

124 See H. Lutzmann, *Die neusumerischen Schuldurkunden*, Teil I (Heidelberg 1976) 42-52.

125 *Op. cit.* (see note 121) 104ff.

c. More decrees incorporated in law collections?

If LE § 9 (and perhaps also in §§ 18A and 20-21) and LH §§ t-u incorporate or use (parts) of older, originally separate decrees, are they the only stipulations in both collections to do so? While (royal) law collections as a whole and also groups of paragraphs dealing with one subject could be called 'decrees' (*ṣimdātum*),[126] hard evidence that the same term is used to refer to individual stipulations of law collections, postulated by Kraus 1979, 62,[127] is not so easy to bring. In the preceding paragraphs we have mentioned some cases where subject matter and date allow matching references to (royal) decrees or regulations with rulings in LH. But the evidence is rather weak and in the absence of even one single tablet with the text of such a *ṣimdatum* it is premature to identify a paragraph of LH as such or as a stipulation incorporating an earlier decree.

Detecting a decree incorporated into a law collection is also difficult because it may have been recast in the traditional casuistic style, which dominates LH and so obscures the original 'setting in life' of its rulings. A possible decree on rates of interest may figure in its original form of a simple, authoritative ruling or proclamation in LE § 18A: "Per 1 *gur* (= 300 quarts) of barley one adds 100 quarts as interest".[128] But in § t of LH, if it reflects such a decree or tariff, we have a secondary, casuistic formulation: "If a creditor gives grain or silver as interest-bearing loan, he shall take 100 quarts of grain per 1 *gur* as interest". The same happened with other stipulations on prices and tariffs, such as the one about the hire of a boat. Whereas LE § 4 writes "The hire of a boat is...", in LH § 276 this has been turned into "If a man rents a boat its hire is...". The second formulation offers no linguistic clue for its origin,[129] which can only be postulated if its subject matter links up with a known decree or with clauses in contracts which do refer to one. Such references, unfortunately, are still not numerous and often laconic, but discovery of the original texts of decrees to which practice documents may allow us to detect more traces of them in the law collections. Such discoveries can confirm that social and economic developments required the promulgation of new decrees, which could build on elements already contained in the law collections. Such decrees – examples are those one on groundless claims, consignment, defaulting harvest labourers and perhaps on the rights of *nadītums* (if we may consider a royal rescript a decree) – remained separate **[78]** regulations, since during the more than one and a half century after the composition of LH no new law collection was 'published'. And apart from them there must also have been older decrees that, for whatever reason, were not incorporated in the law collections.

8. The impact of 'laws' and decrees

a. Nature and enforcement of 'laws'

That law collections were never intended to cover all possible cases and conflicts also makes it less surprising that evidence for links between them and decrees is limited. Law collections basically were selections of exemplary "righteous verdicts" (*dīnāt mīšarim*) of various origin, collected and 'published' to show and proclaim that the ruler lives up to his duty and reputation of being a just king,[130] and to encourage or convince its readers

126 See notes 23 and 42.

127 'Sehe ich recht, so haben "Gesetzgeber" gelegentlich den alten Ausdruck für eine königliche Sondermassregel auf eine Einzelbestimmung ihres Codex, bzw. Ediktes angewendet'.

128 See for this paragraph and its formulation, R. Yaron, *ZA* 83 (1994) 206-218, who translates "das kor wird Zins hinzufügen", making the kor measure the subject of the verb. But the writing *1* GUR-*um* (like *1* GÍN-*um* earlier), by adding the phonetic complement -*um*, indicates that a locative is meant, "per 1 *gur*", which then requires a personal subject of the verb. In § t of Hammurabi's laws both manuscripts use the preposition *ana* for "per": *ana 1* (ŠE) GUR.

129 The exceptions are a few paragraphs of the laws which lack a casuistic formulation, such as § 36, which prohibits the sale of field, orchard and house by state tenants and still exhibits the style or a royal decree or ukase ("shall not be sold").

130 See the literature quoted in note 4 [and most recently, Westbrook 2000].

that following them up and implementing them was wise and profitable. Evidence for royal enforcement and an obligation for courts-of-law to apply them is hard to find.

Hammurabi's instruction to his servant Sin-iddinam, in the letter *AbB* 13, 10:10ff., to handle a case and pass a verdict "in accordance with the legal practice (*dīnum*) that is currently applied in Emutbalum"[131] is fascinating, but not very clear. It concerns men who used to serve in the palace (*bāb ekallim*; at Larsa?), but had deserted their post and went away (presumably to Babylon) and are now sent (back) by the king to his governor. We cannot take the words "the legal practice applied/verdicts passed now", that is after Hammurabi's conquest of Larsa in 1762 B.C., as meaning that Babylonian law or LH is now also valid in the realm of Larsa,[132] because Hammurabi himself calls his law collection *dīnātum*, "verdicts". The letter obviously means the by now current administrative and judiciary practice and the case suggests that it concerned the position (employment, status, maintenance) of people who had been servants of the palace of Larsa, but had deserted their post (*mazzaztum*) in connection with the confusion due to Hammurabi's conquest of the city. This event and Hammurabi's taking over of the 'palace organization' of Larsa must have meant a lot of administrative arrangements and decisions (some of which are reflected in his letters) concerning old and new servants of the crown and their properties.[133] This must have given rise to certain administrative procedures and a set of rules or royal directives,[134] which Hammurabi wants to see applied in this case too. It is not warranted to call this 'Babylonian law', because it concerned primarily servants of the crown and aspects of the palace organization, not the population and common law at large. But it does show that the king could and did impose the application of a set of judicial procedures and rules, written down or not.

Basically, LH does not impose, prescribe 'laws', but describes them as being in existence, in force, as col. V:14-26 puts it: 'When Marduk had instructed me..., at that time: **[79]** (§ 1) "When a man..."'.[135] But is this a realistic description? The formulation is similar to that by means of which in royal inscriptions prices of the main commodities or daily wages of workers are quoted as being current at the time the king undertook the building operation commemorated in the inscription.[136] These wages are higher and prices are lower than what is known from contemporary records, which shows that the inscription offers an idealized picture of the economic reality to present the king's reign as a period of great prosperity. In the same way, the 'law collections', as public royal inscriptions tend to draw an idealized picture of the maintenance of justice and righteousness. This does not mean that the legal cases and verdicts are unrealistic, but in some respects and in various degrees they probably were more 'righteous' than forensic reality. Just like a king could not fix and impose prices and tariffs irrespective of the economic realities and the market, so the king, notwithstanding his divine mandate to maintain righteousness, could not simply ignore or supersede common law as applied by local courts. Still, as supreme judge to whom one could appeal, through his court orders and directives, and

131 *kīma dīnim ša inanna ina E. iddinnu.* Emutbalum is the northern part of the state of Larsa.

132 The chronological counter argument, that the stele with LH (because of col. II:32ff.) was only written after the conquest of Larsa, is not valid, because we do not know the exact date of the letter and the substance of the law collection may have existed somewhat earlier.

133 Hammurabi also issued a '*mīšarum*-act' after his conquest of Larsa, see D. Charpin, *NABU* 1991/102 and 1992/76.

134 Without further information on this case we can only speculate on the possibility whether such a 'set of rules' might have received the form of a royal *ṣimdatum*, such as mentioned in letters addressed to Sin-iddinam (see above note 24). But it is meaningful that the king does not use this term in our letter.

135 In this LH follows the examples of Ur-nammu's laws, where the word u_4.ba, "at that time", connect prologue and laws.

136 See for these prices and their evaluation, D.C. Snell, *Ledgers and Prices. Early Mesopotamian Merchant Accounts* (*YNER* 8, New Haven 1982) 204f. Šamšī-Adad, in the building inscription of the Enlil temple writes: "When I built the house of Enlil, the rate of exchange of my city Assur was: for 1 shekel of silver ... was indeed purchased on the market of my city Assur" (*RIMA* 1, A.O.39.1:59ff.).

by his main administrators and perhaps also by means of the 'judges of the king',[137] he did have an impact on the administration of justice, as Hammurabi's letters show. The rulings of the 'law collections' hence probably were more realistic than the commodity prices quoted in royal inscriptions (just like the prices quoted in the beginning of LE are much more realistic than those in royal building inscriptions), but we cannot simply take them as faithfully reflecting the forensic practice. Moreover, the fact that none of the numerous contracts and especially verdicts known from the Old Babylonian period ever refers to, quotes or seems to apply LH, at least not *verbatim*,[138] cannot be ignored. That Old Babylonian royal decrees and Old Assyrian laws are quoted or referred to in contracts and letters, the latter also in official verdicts,[139] makes this silence all the more remarkable.

Various explanations for this silence have been proposed. Old Babylonian judges would not have been accustomed to refer to 'the laws' and in general would not have given legal grounds for their sentences, at least not in verdicts and protocols of lawsuits.[140] Or, LH would not have possessed the status of statutory and positive law and hence could not have been referred to as authoritative and enforceable.[141] If some royal decrees had been incorporated in law collections, the latter should, at least indirectly, have had force of law, because the original decrees had it, and therefore might have been referred to or quoted, as the original decrees were. The Old Assyrian evidence shows that it is too simple to explain the absence of explicit references in verdicts or letters to the law collections from judicial practice or principles. **[80]** Since LH was a selective mixture of traditional lore, scholarly legal wisdom, royal ideology, exemplary verdicts, and authoritative decrees, the possibility of using and referring to it in concrete cases must have been rather limited. Rulings which were of practical importance, *e.g.* for drawing up contracts, apparently were better known and applicable and perhaps also more readily available[142] in the form of specific royal decrees or regulations (see the end of § 2), which indeed were quoted and referred to. The absence of an updated and revised collection of laws by one of Hammurabi's successors was also a factor. In the later Old Babylonian period his collection was still copied (and studied) in the schools, but it seems that in judicial practice royal decrees played a much more important role, since they allowed the king to react to developments in society and hence were more up to date and tuned to the practical needs of the administration of justice.

b. Old Assyrian laws and Babylonian royal decrees

Babylonian royal decrees make the best comparison with the rulings of Old Assyrian statutory law, as inscribed on stelae and quoted in verdicts and letters. The latter owed their existence not primarily to the headwork of the king's scholars, but to the consultations and decisions of the City Assembly. Their close link with the practice of the trade and hence applicability explain their reflection in practice documents. And this applies also to the Babylonian decrees studied above, which present readily applicable legal and penal rulings for important or frequent legal problems. This was different with the at times very specific or learned rulings, some of which concern rare or improbable cases, compiled in the law collections. In many of the cases treated in Old Babylonian judicial records an appeal to or verdict based on 'the laws' was simply

---

137 See for the occurrences and the meaning of this designation, Dombradi 2000, I, 225ff.

138 But see footnote 88.

139 See Veenhof 1995, 1725ff.

140 See Westbrook 1989, 214. The two 'facts' he quotes to refute these arguments are not convincing, because they do not prove that laws were quoted in contracts or judicial records, which is the issue at stake. The first is from a legal compilation, the Mishna, not from a Jewish marriage contract; the second is from a speech by Demosthenes, not from a verdict.

141 See the literature mentioned in footnote 4 and J. Renger, in: H.J. Gehrke (ed.), *Rechtskodifizierung und soziale Normen im interkulturellen Vergleich* (Tübingen 1995) 27-58.

142 See § 2, above; we do not know whether the known Old Babylonian tablets with parts of LH were made and kept for consultation by judges.

impossible. But this does not exclude the possibility that LH's "righteous verdicts" influenced judicial practice, probably also via scribes and 'intellectuals' trained in the schools, where the reading and copying of the 'laws' must have been accompanied by a teacher's oral comments. Such instruction may have included observations on the legal principles underlying the concrete examples and on procedures such as deciding cases *per analogiam* ("as if"; see above § 5,e).

The characteristics of the Old Assyrian law also apply to the royal decrees of debt release ('*mīšarum*-acts'), which had a great impact on social and economic life. An interesting example of their use, also in comparison with a possible appeal to 'the law', is found in a recently published letter from the Old Babylonian town of Lagaba, NBC 6311. Its writer quotes a stipulation in a decree of king Samsu-iluna of Babylon, which forbids the collection of (private, consumptive) debts.[143] He does so on behalf of a debtor who had given his creditor his field as antichretic pledge for a debt of (only) two shekels of silver. The debtor complains that his creditor had robbed him by appropriating the complete harvest,[144] without leaving him the remainder of the yield he was entitled to after deduction of the share for working the field, the debt and the interest on it. The plaintiff-debtor could have based his claim on § 49 of LH, which deals precisely with this case (and uses the same formula, "gather and take along"; *esip tabal*) and **[81]** stipulates that, even when the creditor has worked the pledged field, at harvest time it is the indebted owner who takes the whole yield and then pays his creditor what he owes him. Ignoring the debtor's complaint and approach, the writer quotes from a recent royal decree, apparently because its application offered more. An appeal to the law – on the assumption that the rather idealistic ruling of LH § 49 could be enforced – would have secured the debtor only a small part of the harvest, after deduction of what the creditor was entitled to.[145] An appeal to the '*mīšarum*-decree', however, would earn him the cancellation of the original debt, the return of the field, and a bigger share of the harvest, even when the creditor, as the one who had worked the field, still would have been entitled to the major part (usually two-thirds) of the harvest. The case is interesting because the debtor apparently tried to enforce the application of the rule formulated in LH § 49, although without referring to it as such. The writer prefers to use a relevant and presumably recent royal decree, of which the debtor may not yet have been aware, perhaps because it yields more, since the debt as such is cancelled. But this may be too simple an explanation, because there are more cases where plaintiffs do not appeal to a 'law', but more generally to the king's righteousness, his duty of restoring equity and helping people who rights have been violated.

c. Petitions and appeals to the king of Babylon

An example is the letter *AbB* 7 no. 153, a petition to king Samsu-iluna by a man whose deed of sale of a house had been highhandedly broken (to cancel its purchase) by an official, without due investigation and in the absence of judges and parties involved.[146] This had happened in connection with a royal decree of remission of debts, which included cancellation of forced sales of real estate by debtors. The writer complains that his purchase did not fall under that category and that therefore the injustice done to him

---

143 O. Tammuz, *RA* 90 (1996) 125f.; see already W.W. Hallo, in: Z. Zevit, S. Gitin and M. Sokoloff (eds.), *Solving Riddles and Untying Knots. Jonas C. Greenfield Memorial Volume* (Winona Lake 1995) 82f. [**Add.**: My public lecture, *Recht en Gerechtigheid in Babylonië* (Leiden 2000), an English version of which is included in this volume, pp. 15-25, deals more in detail with this letter].

144 Line 12, *īsipma itbal*, "he gathered (all barley) and took it along". The last line of the letter should be read *še'am tamašša'*, "you are robbing (him) of the barley" (from *mašā'um*, "to take away by force"; *mašāhum*, "to measure out", does not occur in Old Babylonian texts, which use *madādum)*. The preceding line is an ironic question that uses a perfect tense: "You – is this the way you have executed what my lord's decree prescribes?".

145 We cannot calculate the owner's share, since the letter does no state how big the field was.

146 See for an analysis of the letter, Kraus 1984, 69ff., "4.B.S-i 5".

should be redressed. The complaint concerns the procedure followed, the fact that the ruling of the decree had not been properly applied, and that he had become the victim of abuse of power. Referring to the royal decree, he appeals to the king as highest judge (in line 46 he even addresses him as "god"!), who has the duty to protect the weak and has a reputation to uphold: "My Lord, judge my case, so that all Sippar can see that in the presence of my Lord the weak is not surrendered to the strong and the strong is not [allowed] to oppress the weak" (lines 49-53). This emotional appeal comes very close to quoting Hammurabi's own statement in the prologue of LH, where he expresses the same concerns, and line 53 of the letter may actually be a quotation of col. I lines 37-39 of LH. The plaintiff does not base his appeal on a particular ruling, because there is none in the law collection that really fits his case, but on the king's programmatic assurance that he will maintain justice, which should apply in any situation.

The letter *AbB* 2, 111, whose writer complains that he has been deprived of half of a plot of land and of a field, shows a similar approach. In this case of presumably administrative injustice (the field has been given to somebody else by the elders of his city) the plaintiff again makes a general appeal to the king as supreme judge: "You, my Lord, must take action, (because the god) Marduk, who loves you, truly has created you to provide justice!" (*ana šutēšurim*). Though this last verb actually occurs in the programmatic statements in the **[82]** epilogue of LH (col. V:16, where it is said to be Marduk's instruction to the king; cf. also XLVII:62 and 73), it is difficult to prove that the writer of the letter actually quotes these words. The appointment of Babylon's king by Marduk and his duty of maintaining justice and restoring equity are essential and well-known elements of royal ideology, not restricted to the text of law collections.

These examples help us to appreciate the difference between laws and decrees. They show the concrete impact of royal decrees in social and economic life and explain why plaintiffs, even when appealing to the king himself and perhaps familiar with the wording of his laws, did not or could not refer to particular stipulations in the laws. They based their appeals for legal help on specific royal decrees and on general statements of the king's righteousness and his duty to redress injustice, which were the generally known ideological basis of both decrees and laws.

BIBLIOGRAPHY

Bottéro, J. 1987. *Mésopotamie. L'Écriture, la raison et les dieux* (Paris), 191-223: Le «code» de Hammurabi.

Charpin, D. 1987. Les décrets royaux à l'époque paléo-babylonienne. A propos d'un ouvrage récent, *AfO* 44, 36-44.

–. 2000. Les prêteurs et le palais: Les édits de *mîšarum* des rois de Babylone et leurs traces dans les archives privées, in: A.C.V.M. Bongenaar (ed.), *Interdependency of Institutions and Private Entrepreneurs* (MOS Studies 2, Istanbul 2000), 185-212.

Finkelstein, J.J. 1961. Ammiṣaduqa's Edict and the Babylonian "Law Codes", *JCS* 15, 91-104.

–. 1967. A Late Old Babylonian Copy of the Laws of Hammurapi, *JCS* 21, 39-48.

Janssen, C. 1991. Samsu-iluna and the Hungry *nadītums*, in: *Mesopotamian History and Environment, Northern Akkad Project Reports*, vol. 5 (Ghent), 3-39.

Kraus, F.R. 1958.*Ein Edikt des Könings Ammi-ṣaduqa von Babylon* (SD 5), Leiden.

–. 1960. Ein zentrales Problem des altmesopotamischen Rechtes: Was ist der Codex Hammu-rabi?, *Geneva* N.S. 8, 283-295.

–. 1979. Akkadische Wörter und Ausdrücke, XII. *ṣimdatum, ṣimdat šarrim*, *RA* 73, 51-62.

–. 1984. *Königliche Verfügungen in altbabylonischer Zeit* (SD 11), Leiden.

Lafont, S. 1994. Ancient Near Eastern Law: Continuity and Pluralism, in: B.M. Levinson (ed.), *Theory and Method in Biblical and Cuneiform Law* (JSOT Suppl. 181), Sheffield, 91-118.

–. 1997. Les actes législatifs des rois mésopotamiens, in S. Dauchy e.a. (eds.), *Auctoritates. Xenia R.C. van Caenegem oblata* (Iuris Scripta Historica XIII), Bruxelles, 3-27.

Petschow, H.P.H. 1986.Beiträge zum Codex Hammurapi, *ZA* 76, 17-75.
Roth, M.T. 1995. *Law Collections from Mesopotamia and Asia Minor* (SBL Writings from the Ancient World 6), Atlanta.
San Nicolò, M. 1974. *Die Schlussklauseln der altbabylonischen Kauf- und Tauschverträge* (München 1974, second edition with additions and corrections by H.P.H. Petschow).
Stol, M. 1993. *Epilepsy in Babylonia* (Cuneiform Monographs 2), Groningen.
Veenhof, K.R. 1995. "In Accordance with the Words of the Stele": Evidence for Old Assyrian Legislation, *Chicago-Kent Law Review* 70/4, 1717-1744 [= pp. 109-127 in this volume]
–. 1999. Redemption of Houses in Assur and Sippar, in: B. Bock e.a. (eds.), *Munuscula Mesopotamica. Festschrift für Johannes Renger* (*AOAT* 267), Münster, 599-616 [= pp. 211-223 in this volume].
Westbrook, R. 1989. Cuneiform Law Codes and the Origins of Legislation, *ZA* 79, 201-222.
–. 2000. Codex Hammurabi and the Ends of the Earth, in: L. Milano e.a. (eds.), *Landscapes, Frontiers and Horizons in the Ancient Near East* (Papers of the XLIVth RAI, Venezia 1997), part III), Padova, 101-106.
Wilcke, C. 1976. Zu den spät-altbabylonischen Kaufverträgen aus Nordbabylonien, *WdO* 8, 254-285, esp. 258-262.
Yaron, R. 1988. *The Laws of Eshnunna.* Second edition. Jerusalem-Leiden.

Fatherhood is a Matter of Opinion. An Old Babylonian Trial on Filiation and Service Duties*

In Babylonia, as in any traditional society, personal status was to a large extent conditioned by birth, by being the child of a specific father, whose property, rights, duties and often also profession his son would take over. Doubts about filiation hence could have serious implications and several documents from the practice of law deal with them. In the absence of written documents (usually only available in cases of adoption) oral testimonies played an important role, as in the case of a presumably kidnapped child,[1] a disputed adoption,[2] the contested filiation of a posthumous child,[3] and in deciding whether a child was a free citizen or a house-born slave.[4] Establishing the truth could require the reconstruction of interesting pieces of family history from individual testimonies, and when scribes present rather full accounts of them we can "study the texts as narratives and *cases*" (Roth 2001, 281).

While filiation was important because it granted rights, especially to an heir,[5] it also entailed obligations, because a son had to pay his father's debts and could be obliged to take over obligations. If service duties owed to the state were at stake, the administration might get interested in a person's filiation. This is the case in a new judicial record from the time of king Ammiditana of Babylon, which also offers interesting details on the swearing of the oath, which I found several years ago in London in the large 1902-10-11 collection. It is published here by kind permission of the Trustees of the British Museum and with gratitude to B. Ferwerda, who made the beautiful copy of the tablet published here, and to Dominique Collon, who contributed the drawings of three seals. It is offered to the jubilarian, whose interest in Babylonian family life and legal history figures prominently among the many aspects of the Mesopotamian culture he has studied.

1 G. Boyer, *Contribution à l'histoire juridique de la 1re dynastie babylonienne* (Paris 1928) 70ff., see the recent translation by D. Charpin in: Joannès (2000) 100f. no. 57.

2 ARN 174, see J.J. Finkelstein in ANET², Suppl. 544f.

3 PBS 5, 100, the most detailed record dealing with such matters, recently analysed by Roth (2001).

4 VS 13, 32:8f., cf. Dombradi (1996) II, note 2439), and BBVOT 1, 23, analysed by C. Wilcke in: B. Pongratz-Leisten [e.a.], *Festschrift für Wolfgang Röllig*. AOAT 247 (Neukirchen-Vluyn 1997) 413-429.

5 This probably also was the background of PBS 5, 100 (see note 3), since both parents of the boy are dead and no other sons are mentioned. This could also explain the wish of the uncles – whether they confirmed or denied the boy's filiation – for a legally valid "tablet of sonship", because in the absence of a son they might have become heirs. That the result of the "confirmation hearing" was to be reported back (*ṭēmam turrum*) to the Assembly (lines ii:7f.; see Roth 2001, 268) means that it was needed in a trial, which may well have involved the inheritance of the boy's father. Note that the same expression is probably used in ARN 174 (see note 2) rev. 6, where such a report allows the judges to reinstate the man whose adoption was disputed as son (*ana mārūt* A. *uterrūšu*).

* Originally published in: W. Sallaberger, K. Volk, and A. Zgoll (eds), Literatur, Politik und Recht in Mesopotamien. Festschrift für Claus Wilcke (Wiesbaden 2003) 313-332.

1. The text of BM 96998

1.1. Transliteration

BM 96998 (1902-10-11, 52; 125 x 65 x 20 mm.)

aš-šum ^{p}*ṣú-*⸢*ša*⸣*-rum* dumu ^{f}*ši-ma-at-ištar*
a-ḫa-at la-ma-sà-ni lukur ^{d}utu dumu.munus *ì-lí-iš-me-a-ni*
ìr-*ku-bi* ugula mar.tu *ša* érin *na-we-e* zimbir^{ki}
^{p}*qur-ru-du-um* ugula.gidri ^{p}*i-na-pa-le-šu* ugula.gidri (erasure *a*)
^{p}*ib-ni-*^{d}EN.ZU dumu.é.dub.ba.a *ù ši-bu-ut a-ri-šu*
ma-ḫar ^{d}marduk-*mu-ba-lí-iṭ a-bi* érin
^{pd}marduk-*mu-ša-lim a-bi* érin
^{p}*el-me-šum* pisan.dub.ba
ì-lí-i-qí-ša-am gal.ukkin.na érin ká.é.gal
i-na zimbir^{ki}*-am-na-nim*
i-nu-ma ši-ip-ra-tim ša zimbir^{ki} *ú-še-pí-/šu*
ki-a-am iq-bu-ú um-ma šu-nu-ma
^{p}*šu-mu-um-li-ib-ši* dumu *a-na-*^{d}utu*-li-ṣi* šà érin *ša qá-ti-ni*
^{pf}*ši-ma-at-ištar a-ḫa-at la-ma-sà-ni*
dumu.munus *ì-lí-iš-me-a-ni i-ḫu-uz-ma*
^{p}*ṣú-ra-rum ma-ra-šu ù a-bi-sú-*<*um*> *ma-*⸢*ra-šu*$^{?}$⸣
⸢*ša*⸣ érin *ka-aš-šu-ú il-qú-*⸢*ša*⸣
2 ma-ri a-na šu-mu-um-li-ib-ši dumu *a-na-*^{d}utu*- li-ṣi*
šà érin *ša qá-ti-ni ni*$^{?}$*-mu-ur*
i-na-an-na ^{p}*ṣú-ra-rum ma-ra-šu*
^{p}*la-ma-sà-ni* lukur ^{d}utu dumu.munus *ì-lí-iš-me-a-ni il-qé-*⸢*e-šu*⸣
ma-ah-ri-ša wa-ši-ib an-ni-tam iq-bu-ú-ma
^{p}*la-ma-sà-ni* lukur ^{d}utu *ù a-ḫi-a-ia-am-ši a-ḫa-ša*
dumu.meš *ì-lí-iš-me-a-ni*
a-na ma-ḫar a-wi-le-e ú-qé-er-ri-bu-šu-nu-ti
aš-šum ṣú-ra-rum šu-a-ti i-ša-lu-šu-nu-ti-ma
ki-a-am iq-bu-ú um-ma šu-nu-ma
^{p}*ši-ma-at-ištar a-ḫa-at-ni a-na mu-tim ú-ul ni-id-di-in*
a-li-ku-tam il-li-ik-ma
$^{lo.e.\,p}$*šu-mu-um-li-ib-ši* dumu *a-na-*^{d}utu*-*⸢*li-ṣi*⸣
it-[*t*]*i ma-du-tim i-te-er-ru-ub-ši-m*[a]
ri-ik-sa-ti-ša ú-ul ⸢*iš*⸣*-ku-u*[*n*]
ka-sa!-sà ⸢*ú-ul iš*⸣*-ku-u*[*n-ma*]
ter-ḫa-as-sà ú-ul ni-im-⸢*ḫu*⸣*-ur*

Obv. BM 96998 (1902-10-11,52)

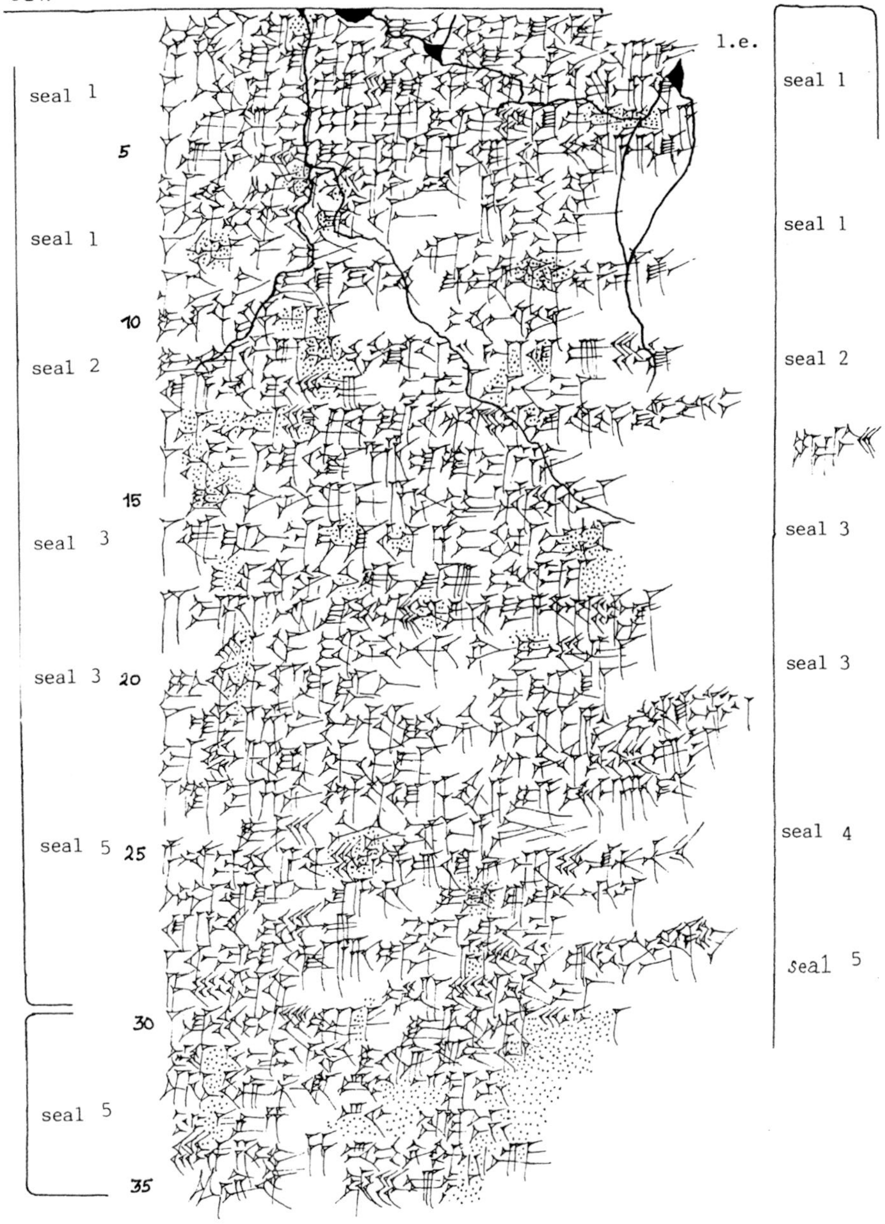

an-ni-tam iq-bu-ú-ma
$^{rev.}$ *ši-bi ša i-na ka-si-ša uš-bu i-⌈ri⌉-šu-šu-nu-⌈ti⌉*
ú-ul ub-lu-nim
a-wi-lu-ú a-wa-ti-⌈šu⌉-nu i-mu-ru-ma
a-na ká ^{d}utu *a-la-kam i-na ši-pa-ri-im*
ka-sa-a-am ù pa-ṭa-ra-am iq-bu-šu-nu-/ši-im
ki-ma a-wi-lu-ú iq-bu-ú
šu.nir ^{d}utu *a-lik maḫ-ra ša* é.di.ku$_5$ kalam.ma
šu.nir ^{d}utu *ša* é.di.ku$_5$.dá
i-na ká ^{d}utu *ša* é.di.ku$_5$.dá *uš-zi-zu*
^{p}ìr-*ku-bi* ugula.mar.tu *ša* érin *na-we-e* zimbir^{ki}
^{p}*qur-ru-du-um* ugula.gidri ^{p}*i-na-pa-le-e-šu* ugula.gidri x
^{p}*ib*!-*ni*-^{d}EN.ZU dumu.é.dub.ba.a *ù ši-bu-ut a-ri-šu*
a-na ši-pa-ri-im a-na sa-na-qí-im ú-ul im-gu-ru
^{p}*la-ma-sà-ni* lukur ^{d}utu *i-na ši-⌈pa⌉-ri-im ki-a-am ⌈iq⌉-bi-i-ma*
^{p}*a-bi-sú-um ù ṣú-ra-rum a-⌈na* ^{p}⌉*šu-mu-um-li-ib-ši ú-ul al-du*
a-na-ku-ma! ú-ra-ab-bi-šu-nu-ti-ma an-ni-tam iq-bi
u$_4$.kúr.šè ìr-*ku-bi* ugula.mar.tu *qur-ru-du-um* ugula.gidri / *i-na-pa-le-šu* ugula.gidri
^{p}*ib-ni*-^{d}EN.ZU dumu.é.dub.ba.a *ù ši-bu-ut a-ri-šu aš-šum a-bi-sú-um*
ù ṣú-ra-rum ma-re-ša a-na la-ma-sà-ni lukur ^{d}utu *ú-ul i-ra-gu-mu*
mu^{d}utu ^{d}marduk *ù am-mi-di-ta-na* lugal in.pàd.d[è.eš]
igi dingir-*šu-a-bu-šu* ugula.mar.tu igi ^{d}EN.ZU-*a-ḫa-am-* / *i-din-nam* ugula.gidri
igi ^{d}marduk-*mu-ba-lí-iṭ* sanga ^{d}nè.[e]ri$_{11}$.gal
igi *e-tel*-ka-^{d}utu dumu *i-ku-u*[*n*-^{k}]^{a} -^{d}utu
igi *si-ni-i* dumu sig-^{d}*a-a* sanga ⌈šu.nir$^{?}$⌉ ^{d}utu / é.di.ku$_5$.kalam.ma$^{!}$
igi ^{d}EN.ZU-*iš-me-a-ni* dumu ^{d}utu-[*nu-ú*]*r*-bar.ra
sanga^{d}utu é.di.ku$_5$.dá
igi ⌈*i*⌉-*din*-^{d}*bu-ne-ne* igi *i-b*[*i*-^{d}]nin.šubur
dumu.meš é.⌈dub.ba.a⌉
gìr *nu-úr*-^{d}iškur nimgir mar.tu
$^{u.e.}$ iti.ab.è u$_4$.*26*.kam
mu ⌈*am-mi-di-ta-na*⌉ lugal.e
^{d}⌈lama ^{d}lama bar.sù.ga.ke$_4$⌉
^{d}⌈inanna nin⌉.gal [kiš^{k}] ^{i}.a in.n[e].en.ku$_4$.⌈ra⌉

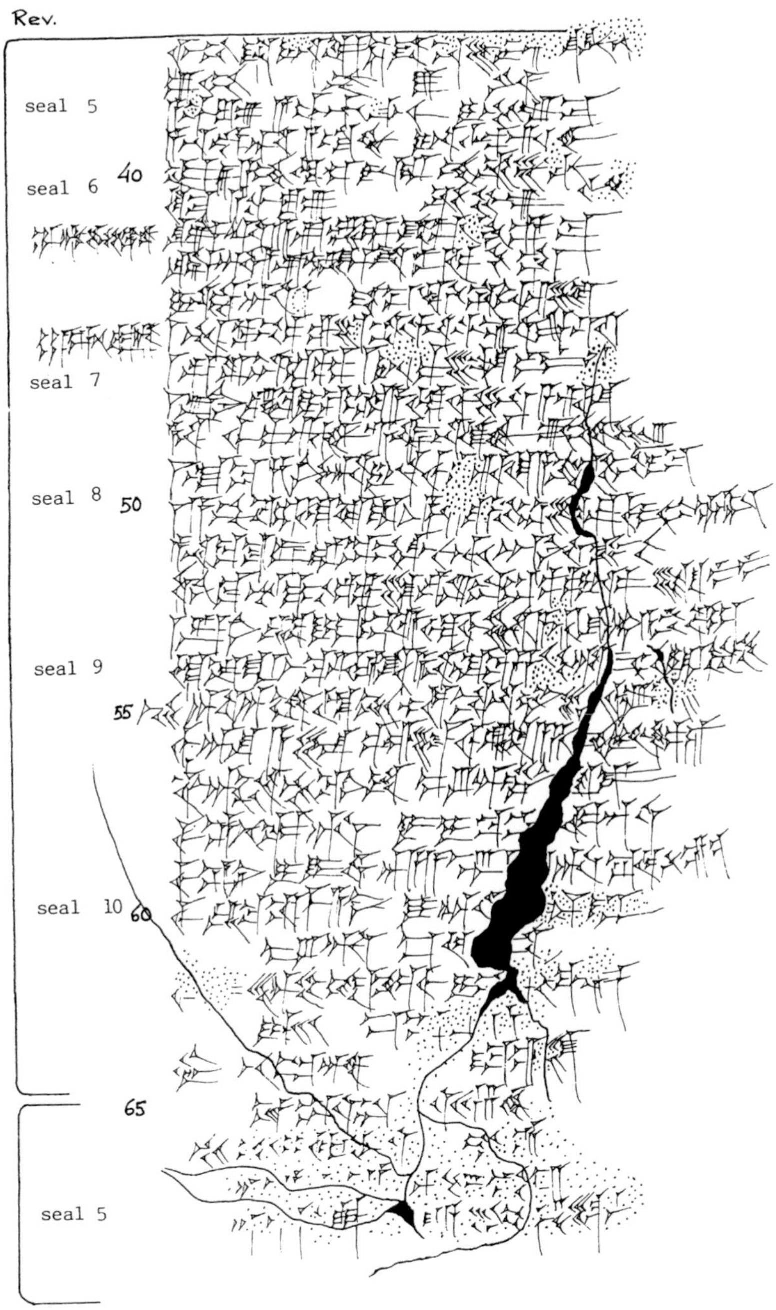
Rev.
seal 5
seal 6
40
seal 7
seal 8
50
seal 9
55
seal 10
60
65
seal 5

1.2. Inscriptions on seals and captions to seal impressions:

seal 1:inscription: *ṣíl-li*-[ ] / dumu *be-la*-[*nu-um*] / ir$_{11}$ ^{d}n[in.]
seal 2: no inscription, caption on r. e.: kišib *ib-ni-30*; drawing **a**
seal 3: inscription: *i-na-pa*-[*le-šu*] / [du]mu *k*[*a*$^{?}$-]
seal 4: inscription: [ ] x *nu* [ ] / [ ] x *ša*? [ ]
seal 5: [*i*]*p-qú*-[ ] / du]mu dingir-*šu*-[ ] / [i]r$_{11}$ ^{d} [ ]
seal 6: no inscription, caption on rev. // l. 7: kišib ^{d}marduk-*mu-ba-lí-iṭ*
seal 7: no inscription, caption on rev. // l. 10: kišib *e-tel*-ka-^{d}utu; drawing **b**
seal 8:inscription: ⌈^{d}iškur? -x⌉ [ ] / [dumu] ^{d}marduk-*mu-š*[*a-lim*] / ⌈ir$_{11}$⌉ ^{d}u[tu] / ⌈ù⌉ ^{d}*na-bi-um*
seal 9: inscription: *i-din*-^{d}[*bu-ne-ne*] / dumu x [ ] / ⌈ ir$_{11}$ x⌉ [ ]
seal 10:inscription: ⌈*x*⌉ *ba wa* x [ ] / [x] *ak*$^{?}$ *p a* [ ]/ ⌈ ir$_{11}$ ^{d}x [ ]; drawing **c.**

a

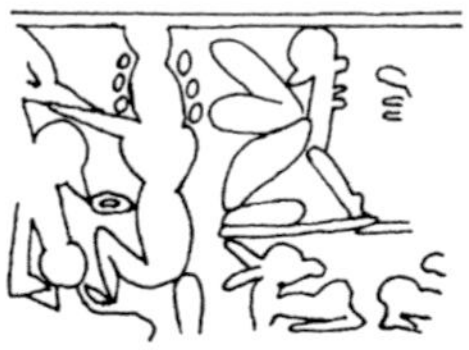

seal 2

b

seal 7

c

seal 10

1.3. Translation

Because of Ṣurārum, son of Šīmat-Ištar, sister of Lamassani, the *nadītum* of Šamaš, daughter of Ili-išmeanni, [3] Warad-Kubi, the general of the troops in the Sippar countryside, Qurrudum the captain, Ina-palêšu the captain, Ibni-Sîn the military scribe, and the elders of ... , [6] before Marduk-muballiṭ and Marduk-mušallim, two 'fathers of the troops', Elmešum, the *šandabakkum*, (and) Ili-iqīšam, the 'personnel director of the palace gate',[10] in Sippir-Amnānum, when they had to organize the work of Sippir, made the following declaration:

[13] "Šumum-libši, son of Ana-Šamaš-līṣi, who belonged to the troops under our command, married Šimat-Ištar, sister of Lamassani, daughter of Ili-išmeanni and [16] Ṣurārum is his son and Abisu(m) *his oldest son*, whom the Kassite troops took along. [18] *We*! have observed that Šumum-libši, son of Ana-Šamaš-līṣi, who belonged to the troops under our command, had two sons. [20] But now Lamassani, the *nadītum* of Šamaš, daughter of Ili-išmeanni, has taken his son Ṣurārum and he lives with her".

When they had stated this, [22] one brought Lamassani, the *nadītum* of Šamaš, and her brother Ahi-ajamši, before the gentlemen. [26] The latter interrogated them concerning the mentioned Ṣurārum and they made the following declaration: [28] "We have not married off our sister Šimat-Ištar. She became a philanderer and Šumum-libši, son of Ana-Šamaš-līṣi, like the many other men used to visit her. [32] He neither established a marriage contract for her, nor did he provide her ... , nor did we receive the bridal payment for her".

[35] When they made this declaration they requested from them (*the plaintiffs*) witnesses who had been present when he bound her by marriage, but they did not bring them. 38 The gentlemen thereupon considered their case and ordered them to go to the Gate of Šamaš, to bind or release in the throw-net. [41] As the gentlemen gave this order one made the emblem of Šamaš, 'The Vanguard' of 'The House-of-the Judge-of-the-Land', (and) the emblem of Šamaš of 'The-House-of-Judgment' take their stand in the Gate of Šamaš of the 'House-of the-Judgment'.

[45] Warad-Kubi, the general of the troops of the Sippar countryside, the captains Qurrudum and Ina-palêšu, Ibni-Sîn, the military scribe, and the elders of ... refused to approach the throw-net. 49 But Lamassani, the *nadītum* of Šamaš, declared as follows in

the throw-net: [50] "Abisum and Ṣurārum were not born as sons of Šumum-libši; I am the one who has raised them". This she declared.

[52] (That) in the future Warad-Kubi, the general, Qurrudum and Ina-palêšu, the captains, Ibni-Sîn, the military scribe, and the elders of … will not raise claims for Abisum and Ṣurārum against Lamassani, the *nadītum* of Šamaš, [55] they have sworn with an oath by Šamaš, Marduk and king Ammiditana.

[56] In the presence of Ilšu-abušu, the general, of Sîn-aḫam-idinnam, the captain,[57] of Marduk-muballiṭ, the priest of Nergal, of Etel-pī-Šamaš, the son of Ikūn-pī-Šamaš, [59] of Sinî, son of Ipiq-Aja, priest of Šamaš of the 'House-of-the-Judge-of-the Land', [60] of Sîn-išmeanni, son of Šamaš-nūr-barra, priest of Šamaš of the 'House-of-Judgment', [62] (and) of Iddin-Bunene (and) of Ibbi-Ilabrat, secretaries.

[64] Supervised by Nūr-Adad, the herald of the Amorites.

[65] On the 26th day of month X of the year "King Ammiditana brought the luxuriant protectives deities (which pray for his life, into her temple) to Inanna, the great lady of Kish" (= year 29).

2. Philological notes

3. érin *nawē Sippar*. See for the meaning of this expression F.R. Kraus, *RA* 70 (1976) 76ff., and for "workers" and the military organization in that area his comments on AbB 7, 46:11, *2* érin gi.íl *nawē Sippar*; 51:5f., PN_1 *nawē Sippar* níg.šu PN_2 ugula mar.tu; and AbB 5, 137:8ff., dumu é.dub.ba.a *šumma ina Larsam šumma in nawēm ša Larsam kališ wašbū.*

4. The traces at the end of this line and of line 46 are puzzling. Ferwerda considered a possible reading ugula dag_4.gi.a, but this is unlikely in view of clear ugula.gidri in line 52. Moreover, the plaintiffs belong to the military organization, where an "overseer of the ward" does not fit, while a general accompanied by two captains is not uncommon.

5. The meaning of *a-ri-šu* remains unclear, since its repetition in line 47 forbids emendation into *a-li-šu*. The preceding *šībūt*, "elders of", suggests a (thusfar unknown) place-name (the village of the disputed Ṣurārum's father?), but the absence of the determinative ki makes me hesitate. There is no lexical basis for the alternative "the elders of his (whose?) *arum*".

16. The reading of the damaged last signs, which qualify Ṣurārum's elder brother (see lines 50 and 53f.) Abisum, is not certain, perhaps a partially erased *-um {ša}* (with *ša* repeated at the beginning of line 17?) or ibila (DUMU.UŠ), "eldest son", or perhaps even aga.uš (*rēdûm*), "soldier", which would be interesting for the interpretation of this lawsuit.

25. Collective *awīlū* is used instead of repeating the names of the officials of lines 6-9, who serve as court of appeal. The verb *qurrubum* with personal acc. and dat. suffixes, "to bring (a person) before" (a court, an official), is rare.[6] While both parties and witnesses (ARN 174:12') can be its object, the question is who are its invariably plural subject. The form *aḫaša* in line 23 and comparison with BAP 42 (= VAB 5, 269):10-12, where in an identical construction the defendants must be the object, suggest that the situation in our text is the same (hence *-šunuti* refers to a man plus a woman). Since in ARN 174:13' the single defendant is ruled out as subject, we assume that in all cases the (anonymous) judicial authorities are the subject of the action.

29. The expression *ālikūtam alākum* is new, but must have the same meaning as *ālikūtam epēšum*, "to go philandering", attested in omen texts with a man as subject: he leaves his wive (CAD A/I 348b).

31. The pronominal suffix added to the verb must be in the dative, hence *īterrubšimma.*

32. See for *riksātim šakānum* VS 18, 1:57, CH § 128:38 and *ana ittišu* vii, ii:40.

---

6 See Dombradi (1996) II, note 430, AbB 6, 219:27, and 11, 158:30'.

33. "Depositing/arranging her (the bride's) *k.*", or (with double acc.) "providing her with her *k.*", mentioned alongside the marriage contract and the *terḫatum* must refer to a specific action. *Ka-sa*!(not NI, in view of the two horizontals)-*sà* = *kasassa*, must be a noun (an infinitive is unlikely) ending in a dental or sibilant, probably **kasātum*, but its meaning in unknown and connecting it with the verb *kasûm*, "to bind", used in line 36, is tempting but difficult.[7] Since both the marriage contract and the *terḫatum* primarily involve the father of the bride, it might refer to what the groom did to the bride herself, either a symbolic action or presenting her a marriage gift.[8] Or it might refer to a *de facto* maintenance of the girl (with food and clothing, as in VS 18, 1:58f.), which could be considered proof of a marriage.

36. The conclusion of a formal marriage is referred to by the single verb *kasûm*, "to bind". Taking it literally one might think of the symbolic tying together of the hems of the garments of groom and bride at the conclusion of the marriage, but this is rendered by (*sissiktam*) *kaṣārum*.[9] Nevertheless, *kasûm* nicely expresses the notion that marriage creates a "bond". I therefore take it as summarizing the effect of the various actions and ceremonies which together bind the partners together in "wedlock", creating a bond which is "severed" by divorce, when partners are "separated" (OA *naprusum*) and their hems are ceremonially "cut" (*batāqum*).

59-60. The only meaningful restoration of the break in line 59 seems to be šu.nir, but it is doubtful because of the traces and the space available. The restoration of the unusual name of the father of the priest in line 60 is inspired by MHET II/6 855: 28: Šamaš-*nūr*-barra sanga dutu, in Ha year 34, hence more than hundred years older, but perhaps from the same family.

64. See for the shape of late OB nimgir, YOS 13 191:17, 341:10, and 354:14, and for the combination nimgir mar.tu, Proto Lú 425 (MSL 12, 48).

66ff. Variant of the (abbreviated) name of Ad's 29th year, not yet registered in M.J.A. Horsnell, The Year-Names of the First Dynasty of Babylon, vol. 2 (s.l. 1999) 310ff.

3. Commentary

3.1. Archival and family background

The document belongs to a small family archive from Sippar-Amnanum, parts(?) of which were acquired by the British Museum in 1902. Apart from our text, which I call **A**, we can assign to it:

B. BM 96956 (1902-10-11, 10), from 25-V-Abiešuḫ year "5", records the division of the inheritance, "by order of the judges", of Ilī-išmeanni, son of Marum, son of Ilšu-bāni, between his three children, Aḫī-aj-amši, Ilšu-bāni and the *nadītum* Lamassani, and his widow Mārat-dA'ammâ.

C. BM 96980 (1902-10-11, 34), from the same day, a record of the share in the inheritance of the second son, Ilšu-bāni alone.

D. BM 96990 (1902-10-11, 11), from 30-VIII-Ammiditana 32, some 55 years later, which records the division of a large house (of ca. 113 m2) in "Sippar *rabium*". This may have happened after the death of the widow and/or Ilšu-bāni, second son, in whose place his two sons Iddin-Amurrum and Awīl-Sîn appear. But even then part of the family estate remains undivided and their common property (*ša birišunuma*).

---

7 *ki/asâtu*, "bindings", (CAD K s.v.) as a plural is excluded and there is no suitable derivative from *kasûm* apart from *kusītum*, a garment; an infinitive of *kasāsum* is impossible for semantic reasons.

8 This would fit the verb *šakānum*, see CAD Š/I, 123f. One might perhaps also think of veiling the bride, attested in Old Assyrian, in AKT 3, 80:22ff., "I will put a veil on the girl's head".

9 See Veenhof (2002), comments on text 3.

E. BM 96991, from 2-XI-Ammiditana 26, published in Veenhof (1989), where Aḫī-aj-amši and his sister Lamassani, marry off their adopted daughter Aḫatani to Bēlānum, the son of Rīš-Šamaš.

F. BM 97289 (1902-10-11, 343) = MHET II/6 898, from 6-I-Ammiṣaduqa year 21, where Awīl-Sîn rents out a field (adjacent to that of his uncle Aḫī-aj-amši) to the well-known Ur-Utu, the *galamaḫḫu* of Annunītum.

Texts B, C, and D are available in a transliteration by L. Dekiere, in NABU 1991/110, with corrections by E. Woestenburg and A. Jagersma in NABU 1992/28, p. 24, note 1. The existence of text F may indicate that the little archive ended up in the possession (and house) of Ilšu-bāni's son Awīl-Sîn, since text F, in which he rents out a field, must have belonged to his archive.

Of the *nadītum* Lamassani, who only inherited part of a house in the second division in D, in As 32 (and hence may have lived in the *gagûm*), little is known. Typical "*nadītu*-records" to throw light on her life have not been identified, which may be due to the fact that, as the record of the division of her father's inheritance, B:38 states, "her brothers are her heirs",[10] which may imply the end of her private archive. But text E shows that she was involved in family affairs, figuring together with her brother Aḫī-aj-amši (by that time her only surviving brother?) as the adoptive parents of a girl who is a *šugītum*. We do not know the background of this rather mysterious marriage contract, nor the reasons for the cooperation between brother and sister, but the girl adopted and married off (accompanied by her little(?) brother, line 13) may have been a relative (an orphan?), of whom they had taken care. According to our text Lamassani must have done something similar with the children of her unmarried sister Šīmat-Ištar, who she raised (her statement in line 51 does not speak of adoption) and who came to live with her, perhaps also in order to secure their help in her old age.[11] The emphatic *anākuma* in line 51 stresses that in this case she acted alone, but the plaintiffs also summoned her brother (line 23), probably because they knew of their cooperation revealed in text E.

Ili-išmeanni's other daughter, Šimat-Ištar is not documented in the other texts, not surprising, because as a marriageable girl she would not have received an inheritance and because a formal marriage, which would have yielded legal records, did not take place. Since she is also not summoned as witness she must have been dead, perhaps even many years ago (if she was a natural daughter of Ili-išmeanni she would have been born at least fifty years before this trial), which could be the reason why her sons came to live with their aunt. Equally absent are Ili-išmeanni's second son, who may have been dead by then, and Šimat-Ištar's presumed husband Šumum-libši, most probably also no longer alive. I have been unable to identify him in 'Sippar texts' and it is in general noteworthy that many of the persons appearing in our text are not attested elsewhere. Among the exceptions are the captain Ina-palêšu, the two "fathers of the workers", the general Ilšu-abušu (in CT 8, 7a, from Ad 32, together with the "secretary" Ibbi-Ilabrat), and the two administrative officials of the palace organization. The *šandabakkum* and the "manager of the personnel of the palace gate", mentioned in lines 9f., who function as judges, are attested in similar capacity in VS 7, 56:6-8 (Ad 24).[12] It shows that, however many "Sippar texts" we have, they only cover selected families and segments of the society.[13]

---

10 In BM 96990: rev. 9'ff. (Ad 32) she is authorized to give her inheritance "to that one of her brothers who loves and honours her" (does that include nephews, since she has only one real brother left?).

11 Note that *maḫriša wašib* (l. 22) can also mean "he serves her", see K.R. Veenhof, in: G. van Driel e.a. (eds.), *Zikir šumim, Assyriological Studies Presented to F.R. Kraus* (Leiden 1982) 375 note 42.

12 Ref. M. Stol and see Dombradi (1996) I 252 § 332. I am not sure that the text is from Dilbat; the two officials write letters to the authorities in Kiš in order to have the case treated.

13 Space does not allow detailed prosopographical investigations, which are also hampered by the fact that many persons, especially those with titles (in lines 3-9 and 56-59), lack patronymics.

3.2. The oath

With conflicting statements, in the absence of evidence, truth has to be established by oath. For this purpose the parties are sent to the "Gate of Šamaš" to swear before the emblems of Šamaš which have been placed there (*šuzzuzum*). The information on the oath is detailed and original, but presents lexical problems.

a. The place of the oath: *šipārum*

What does *šipārum* in lines 39 and 49 mean, to which the parties have to go (*sanāqum ana*) in order to "bind and/or loosen" *ina š.*? In such expressions *ina* may refer to the god or his emblem by which the oath is sworn (*tamûm, zakārum*), *e.g.* "by Šamaš's emblem" (*ina šurin* d*Šamaš*, CT 48, 5:29f.), "by Šamaš's bird trap" (*ina ḫuḫār Šamaš*, YOS 12, 325:11), "by the weapon of DN ..." (UET 5, 251:24f.), "by the drawing" (*ina uṣurtim*, AbB 5, 229:8'f.), etc.[14] But *ina* can also have a local meaning to refer to the locale of the oath,[15] where the judges send parties and witnesses,[16] usually the "Gate of DN", but also called "Gate of the oath by the god" (*bāb nīš ilim*).[17] Occasionally further local specifications are added: in CT 48, 1:20 the Nungal Gate is called "the place of the oath" (*ašar ma-<mi>-tim*), while CT 2, 9:9 adds "in (= standing within) the circle of flour" (*ina kippat qēmim*). Other texts speak of swearing "in front of the cella" *(ina pāni papāḫim),*[18] or "in the presence of" (*maḫar*) the god or his emblem.[19] Occasionally both meanings occur together, as in "he swore by [DN's] double-axe in the Dublamaḫ (building)" (PBS 8/2, 264:14f., from Ur). Since for the oath ceremony the divine emblem had to leave its normal location (presumably in the cella), to be moved to[20] the locale of the oath, its mention implies a reference to particular place, as is clear in Pinches, Peek no. 13:10, an agreement "in the house of the emblem" (*ina* é šu.nir). At times, hence, *ina šurinnim* has a local meaning, *e.g.* in CT 4, 47a: 8ff., where parties "come to an agreement" *ina* Šamaš's emblem in the old Šamaš Gate", which does not mean "by (means of an oath by)", but "at/before" the emblem. Hence, what does *ina šipārim* mean, (to swear) "in the *š.*" or "by the *š.*"?

CAD Š/III 56b, proposes two meanings for *šipārum*, which occurs here for the first time in OB: "ordinance, ruling" and "assembly". The latter is based on a commentary on *Šurpu* II 81, which explains our word in the phrase "to stand *ina šipāri* and speak untrue words" by the *puḫru*, presumably the assembly as court-of-law, since it occurs in a passage which continues by mentioning false oaths. "Assembly", however, is very unlikely in our passage, since parties are ordered to go to the *š.* from the place where the judges meet. The second meaning registered by CAD, "(divine) ordinance, ruling", must refer to that what was sworn, promised, ruled under invocation of the gods. In the Tukulti-Ninurta Epic the Babylonian king Kaštiliaš is said to have transgressed the *šipār ilī*, probably in concrete the oath sworn to the Assyrian king.[21] This also fits the bilingual

---

14 Cf. perhaps Gautier, Dilbat 13:8f., *iṣrat ša* d*Uraš.*

15 See the list drawn up by Dombradi (1996) I 322ff., table 33, which includes references to the "Gerichtsstätte" and the "Eidesstätte", which are not always well distinguishable.

16 In rare cases (e.g. CT 48, 2:11f.) the divine emblem is brought to the place where the court meets and the evidence is evaluated; they probably are cases where the judges convene in "the gate of the god". Note MHET II/1, 54A:17ff., where the judges in the temple of Šamaš *dīnam ina* ^{giš}šu.nir *ušāḫizū.*

17 See the analysis by Dombradi (1996) I 78ff., § 104ff. and 322ff., table 33, both in the "Eides-verfügung" of the judges and in the mention of the actual swearing of the oath.

18 Waterman BDHP no. 34:9; Pinches, Peek 53 no. 13; MHET II/2, 78:16 ; CT 45, 37:14, *ina* é ^{d}utu *ina* ká *papāḫim*.

19 E.g. BIN 7, 176:12. This must be the case in the unpublished letter A 337, quoted in translation by J.-M. Durand in: Lafont (1997) 62, "Que l'on apporte le Symbole de Šamaš et par devant lui, parlez droitement".

20 See for evidence Dombradi (1996) I 85 § 113, and for "to come out" (*waṣûm*), TCL 11, 245:6; YOS 12, 73:9f.; and AUAM 73.3193: 13ff. (unpubl., courtesy M. Sigrist), where "one brings out (*waṣûm*, Š-stem) the double-axe and the bird trap" (of Šamaš), but eventually the plaintiffs "made A (the defendant) come back from the bird trap" (*ina ḫuḫāri uterrūnimma*).

21 Cf. AfO 18 (1957-58) 42:32 as interpreted in CAD Š/III, 345, c).

prayer of Tukulti-Ninurta, which parallels "not transgressing the oath sworn" (*lā etēq* [*mamīte*]) with "observing (*naṣārum*) the *šipāru*".

This last text offers an important clue by equating *šipāru* with Sumerian sa.pàr, "casting net", used by gods and kings for catching enemies.[22] The literature on such nets focuses on them as a means of catching enemies,[23] and pays little attention to their role in the oath procedure. But it is well known, already from the "Vulture Stele" (XVII:30ff.), where Eannatum "gives" the man of Umma the great net (sa.šuš.gal) of various deities, whereupon the latter swears by these gods and accepts that, if he breaks his oath, "the great net of Ninḫursag (etc.), by which I swore the oath, may fall upon me", a fate visually depicted in the accompanying relief. In an inscription of Amar-Sîn, UET 1, 71:19ff., the dub.lá.maḫ, "the place of Nanna's judgment", is called "his casting net",[24] and this same dub.lá.maḫ is still in use as a place of judgment, where the oath had to be sworn, in Old Babylonian times.[25] A later ritual text (BBR 97 rev. 2; see *CAD* S, *loc.cit.* c) speaks of "arranging a net to serve as dwelling place for the divine judges", which evokes the image of a room where the net is visually ready to catch criminals and perjurers.

Helpful is that in MSL 11, 142 viii:40 the temple é.sa.pàr, "House-of-the-Casting Net", is glossed as é ^{d}nun.gal. For in OB texts from Sippar the "Gate of Nungal" is the place where people are sent to swear the oath, as is clear from CT 2, 9:10; 48, 1:19; 5:27 ([*a-n*]*a* ká$^{!}$. $^{d!}$n[un.ga]l; coll. B. Ferwerda); TIM 4, 42:14 (sic!); and VS 9, 142: 8f. In BM 80357:1-12 ten persons (presumably witnesses) are listed as "those who went down to the Gate of Nungal", and in CT 29, 41:12 the defendant has to swear a purgatory oath "in the Gate of Nungal".[26] Nungal's temple (gate) as the place of the oath, was apparently characterized by and called after the (his?) casting net which was somehow present there. This does not surprise for a god who, as the composition "Nungal in Ekur" shows,[27] is associated with judgement, punishment and prison. The link between oath and "casting net" is clearly borne out by BM 16764: 25f.,[28] where the judges order the defendant "to swear an oath in the Šamaš temple in Larsa in/by the casting-net" (*ina sa-pa-ri-im*; also line 35). But it is doubtful (see below § 3.2,b) whether in Sippar too the place of the casting net, and hence also the "Nungal Gate", was part of the main Šamaš-temple.

The presence of the net as an instrument of divine punishment at the very place where the oath is sworn creates an almost physically awareness of the danger of perjury. Still, the texts mentioning that emblems and symbols of the gods are brought to and set up in the place of the oath never mention the "casting net". This becomes understandable if we may conclude from UET I 71, BM 16764, and our text that the locale of the oath itself was called "Casting Net". Such a name implies that the net was visually present, either a real or a painted one, perhaps even over the heads of those who had to swear, ready to clap down (*sahāpum*) on the perjurer. This latter idea is suggested by "An appeal to Nanna" (UET 6, 402:19f.),[29] where an oath is sworn "in the Great Gate, underneath (*šapal*) the divine weapon". The numinous nature of the oath was further enhanced, as VS 8, 71:1f. informs us,[30] by ritually cleansing the person who had to swear there, by sprinkling him with water

22 See CAD S *saparru* A, a loan from Sumerian sa.bar / pàr / par_4, see note 24.

23 E.g. W. Heimpel, Netz. A. Philologisch, *RlA* 9 (1999) 235-39.

24 See P. Steinkeller, A Note on sa.bar = sa-par_4/pàr, "Casting Net", ZA 75 (1985) 39-46.

25 See D. Charpin, *Le clergé d'Ur au siècle d'Hammurabi* (Genève-Paris 1986) 332 with note 2 and Dombradi (1996) I 324, s.v. Ur.

26 See for the "Gate of Nungal" as a topographical feature in Sippar, mentioned to describe the location of a house, da ká ^{d}Nun.gal, CT 8, 13c:1 and VS 8, 105 = MHET II/5 634:2.

27 Edited by A. Sjöberg, AfO 24 (1973) 19-46. See P. Steinkeller ZA 75, 40, for references in this composition where Ekur (in Nippur), as a place of judgment, is called a "casting net".

28 Edited by M. Jursa, RA 91 (1977) 135-45. Note also the "seven nets" (written *šaparrē*, with initial *š*!) which, according to ARM 26, 192, the god Addu(?) sent to Zimrilim "in order to overwhelm the Elamites".

29 Latest edition by Charpin, Clergé d'Ur (see note 25) 326ff.

30 Line 2 is difficult (but the copy is correct according to a collation by J. Marzahn) and surprising, since Marduk is mentioned, but the sign before his name is not dingir; *me*$^{!}$*-e* is clear.

(in line with the practice described in *ana ittišu* VI i:39-45),[31] while he was standing in a sacred area, demarcated by a circle of floor or a reed fence (see below § 3.2,b).

The frightening aspect of the net is also present in the "symbols" of Šamaš used during the oath ceremony, his "weapon", "double-axe" (*pāštum*), "saw (or sickle)" (*šaššarum*), and especially his "bird trap" (*ḫuḫārum*).[32] The "Great Šamaš Hymn", too, praising Šamaš as god of justice, in connection with the oath (lines 83ff.) mentions the god's *šuskallu*-net, *šētu*-net, snare (*kippu*) and bird trap (*ḫuḫāru*).[33] As visual representations of the god's power they must have been effective means of frightening potential perjurers, just like the weapon of Zababa, which in VS 22, 28:40 is appropriately called ᵈ*Ka-mi-ta-mi-šu*, "Binder-of-his-(per)jurer".

These data in my opinion indicate that *šipārum* must be a by-form of *saparrum*, notwithstanding its surprising first vowel (initial *š*- is no serious problem; note the spelling *ša-pa-ar-re* in ARMT 26/1,192:8). They also suggest that *šipārum* refers to the locale of the oath and this is also likely of BM 16764: 25f.,35, where *ina saparrim* specifies the place in "the temple of Šamaš" where the oath has to be sworn.

b. The ritual of the oath: the "emblem of Šamaš"

Our text is one of the few to give more information on the "*šurinnu*-emblem" of Šamaš, which turns up in many sources, usually in the singular. We are told that those to swear are "assigned to it" (*nadānum ana*) and/or have "to pull it out" (*nasāḫum*), perhaps of its standard or its casing or sheath. Pinches, Peek no. 13:7 (é šu.nir kù.sig$_{17}$) and AbB 12, 64:6.8 show that it was of gold. In oath ceremonies it almost never occurs together with what we call Šamaš's "symbols", such as his double-axe, stone, and bird trap, which are found in records from Larsa such as TCL 10, 4:28ff., 34:11ff., YOS 12, 73:9f., and 325:11. Only in CT 2, 47:18f. the *šurinnum* appears alongside Šamaš's saw (*šaššarum*), while in VS 9, 130:6 the "emblem" of Sîn occurs alongside Šamaš's saw. This suggests that we have to differentiate "emblems" from the "symbols" and that there may have been differences between Larsa and Sippar.[33a]

Lines 42f. of our text show that there were two different emblems of Šamaš, which is confirmed by CT 2, 1:28 ("both *š*.-emblems", ᵈšu.nir.meš ... *kilallē*) and BE 6/1, 103:32 (2! ᵈšu.nir *ša* ᵈutu, which went down to a field), all in texts from Sippar, which do not mention the god's "symbols". This is also not the case in CT 2, 9:8f., where the defendant has to go "to the *š*.-emblem of Šamaš *ina kilkillī*, in the Nungal Gate, in the circle of flour". Contrary to CAD K 359 s.v., *kilkillū* does not mean "the *k*.-symbols" (by which one swears), but as shown by K. Reiter,[34] a special place in a temple, before the cella, demarcated by a reed fence or screen, within which the oath was sworn.

The two *š*.-emblems according to our text are:

1. the Šamaš emblem called *ālik maḫra ša* é.di.ku$_5$.kalam.ma, "The Vanguard" of "The-House-Judge-of-the-Land", accompanied by Sinî, son of Ipiq-Aja (line 59), "priest of the [emblem of?] Šamaš of the "House-Judge-of-the-Land".
2. the Šamaš emblem *ša* é di.ku$_5$.dá, of "The-House-of-the-Judgment", with Sîn-išmeanni, son of Šamaš-nūr-barra, priest of Šamaš of "The-House of Judgment".

---

31 The effect of this ritual is that the man in question "became afraid and did not dare to swear". Note the new Old Assyrian evidence for "purifying" (*qaddušum*) those who have to swear, in K. Hecker [e.a.], *Kappadokische Keilschrifttafeln aus den Sammlungen der Karlsuniversität Prag* (Prag 1998) I 681:26, with commentary.

32 See Dombradi (1996) II 92, notes 423ff., and for *ḫuḫārum* also my footnote 20.

33 See W.G. Lambert, *Babylonian Wisdom Literature* (Oxford 1960) 130.

33a See for *šurinnum* also ARM 18, 54:14 and 69:14, *pīt pīm ša šurinnim* (cf. *pīt pī ša kakkim ša* DN).

34 NABU 1989/107 and NABU 1991/84, using both philological and archaeological evidence. In 1989/107 she writes: "Dies muss ein Raum aus/mit Rohr gewesen sein. In diesem war ein Symbol des Šamaš, das *šurinnum*, aufgeplanzt oder irgendwie eingetieft, woraus der Beklagte es herauszureissen hatte".

They are also mentioned in CT 2, 1:28f. // 6:38f., where both are called "Vanguard" ([d]šu.nir. meš *a-lik ma-aḫ*[!]*-ra kilallē*), but in inverted order (and with the simple spelling é.di.ku$_5$). In ARN 174 rev.:1 (from Sippar) the witnesses take their stand in é [d]utu [d]šu.nir kù.sig$_{17}$ *ālik maḫ-ra-*[*ti-na*], "the temple of Šamaš *of* (= which houses?)/*at* (= before?) the golden emblem 'Vanguard'...", but it is not certain whether this text also mentions two emblems.[35] Two emblems does not surprise, since Nanna (UET 6, 402:25) knew the pair [d]Nanna-palil and [d]Nanna-á.daḫ, "Nanna-Vanguard" (= *ālik maḫra*!) and "Nanna-Support", and in the Ištar ritual from Mari her two emblems are carried from their "houses" to be placed right and left in the temple.[36] The nature and functions of such "emblems" or "standards" and their differentiation from what we call "divine symbols" still needs a special investigation.[37] But set up in a temple or carried in a procession they must have shown and embodied aspects or items considered typical of a particular god, who was conceived to be present in or represented by them. Our texts only mention their "functional" name, "Vanguard" (a predicate applied to several gods in the form *pālil* or palil = IGI.DU). Being made of gold they may have been the sun disc or a golden torch, just as Sîn's "emblem" must have been the moon crescent.

The two emblems are said "to be of", hence housed in, two separate buildings called é, hence a sanctuary or chapel (the word is also used in the Mari ritual, see note 36), each with its own priest-manager (sanga). The place of the oath itself, for reasons unknown to us, is "the house" of the second emblem, the "Gate of the é di.ku$_5$.dá". This shrine in Sippar is known from OB references which call Šamaš "king of the é.di.ku$_5$.dá" and "the god who hears from the é.di.ku$_5$.dá".[38] It also occurs in BM 97103, a list of bread, meat and beer, which is entitled kaš.dé.a [d]utu *ša* é.di.ku$_5$.e.ne. In UET 1, 71 the comparable name ki.di.ku$_5$.da.ni, "the place of his (Nanna's) judgment", is given to (part of?) the dub.lá.maḫ, which was a separate building, outside the great Nanna temple, specifically used for judiciary and administrative purposes.[39] In Sippar too, the é di.ku$_5$.dá, which follows the E-babbar in litanies, may not have been a chapel within the E-babbar, but a separate chapel, which explains the existence of an é di.ku$_5$.dá-street in Sippar-Amnānum.[40] This fits the evidence that the é di.ku$_5$.kalam.ma too was a separate sanctuary or chapel. Šamaš, both a great god in the pantheon and the city-god of Sippar venerated in the E-babbar, had many aspects and functions. His specific relation with justice may have resulted in special chapels where he was venerated as supreme judge, in whose cellas the appropriate emblems were kept and where (at least in the case of the é di.ku$_5$.dá) the oath ritual was performed. The mention, in an early judiciary record from Sippar, BE 6/1, 6:10, of litigants "going to the é di.ku$_5$", might refer to our chapel, unless it simply means the place where the judges convene.

Unfortunately, judiciary records from Sippar throw no further light on these chapels and on the priests administering them. The latter are mentioned as (court) witnesses in our verdict, no doubt because they had performed the oath ritual and had heard the statements given under oath. This must have happened many times, but no other

---

35 The reading of the last two signs is certain according to ARN p. 69 ad Ni. 1291, so that *maḫ-ra-ti*[!]*-šu*[!], suggested in ANET[2] Supplement 544 no. 9 and accepted in Dombradi (1996) II, note 422 (who also suggests the emendation šu.nir.<meš>), is excluded. More in agreement with the copy and in line with *kilallān* of CT 2,1: 28 and "2" of BE 6/1, 103:32 would be a reading [*ši-na*] "the two".

36 J.-M. Durand/M. Guichard, in: *Florilegium Marianum III. Mémoires de NABU 4* (Paris 1997) 54, ii:4'.

37 Šamaš's weapon and double-axe are signs of power, the trap a means of catching criminals, his "saw" may have a mythological background, his "(weighing?) stone" (*abnum*) and "great abacus" (*nikkassū rabûtum*, see CAD N/II s.v. 229,4) may reflect the role of the Šamaš temple checking weight standards and providing clearance by settlement of accounts.

38 According to the inscription on the statue of the judge Gimil-Marduk, published in Iraq 31 (1969) 90; see the discussion by the writer in JEOL 35-36 (1997-2000) 57.

39 Whether the é di.ku$_5$.dá in Isin(?), rebuilt by Damiq-ilišu during his seventh year, was a separate sanctuary is unknown.

40 See C. Janssen [e.a.], in: *Cinquante-deux rélexions sur le Proche-Orient Ancien offertes en hommage à Léon de Meyer*. MHEO II (Leuven 1994) 93 (ref. M. Stol).

judiciary record mentions them, at least not by title. We know that priests accompanied the "symbols" of the gods when, in conflicts about real estate, they went to wards, houses and fields in order to establish the truth, *e.g.* in MHET II/1 199:10: "the sanga of Sîn went down to the field". But evidence on the role of such priests in the oath ritual in a sanctuary – which is different from serving as judge or witness,[41] – is very meagre. In TIM 4, 35:6, in a conflict about herds, hence not a "religious" issue, the judges sent parties to Marduk's Gate where "the *ērib bīti*-priests of Marduk's temple took their stand", apparently in view of the oath.

c. The contents of the oath: *kasûm* and *paṭārum*

In the absence of factual witnesses and written evidence an oath by the parties has to establish the truth. What they have to do is called *kasûm u paṭārum*, "to bind and/or to loosen", without expressed object. A virtual personal object seems likely, because both verbs usually are construed with one,[42] and it could be both the other party and the disputed boy. But the focus is less on the persons themselves (their reliability) than on what parties have declared, on which the claim on the boy depends. We may compare the Old Assyrian pair *ka''unum* – *nakārum* in a standard phrase in court proceedings, when one party has to answer the allegations of the other: *ikrī ula ka''inī*, "confirm or contest/deny me!", where the personal object is expressed. But it may also be omitted, *ikir ula ka''in*,[43] which leaves room for making the facts stated its object. "Binding and/or loosening" without object could be swearing an oath to confirm one's own or the other party's statement and/or to deny the latter, and *paṭārum* might also mean withdrawing one's own statement by refusing the oath.

This use of both verbs was thus far unattested, perhaps apart from an occurrence of the D-stem of *paṭārum* in CT 48, 6:10'. In a lawsuit involving a claim on property the judges, in the absence of written evidence (*kanīkum*), order the parties to swear an oath. "The gentlemen (= the judges) took their stand in the gate of the oath by the god, *upaṭṭirūšunuti* and they obliged A. to pay 2 shekels of silver to B.". With the judges as subject and the litigants as object of the verb, it probably expresses that the judges – whether oaths were actually sworn or refused and whether a last moment agreement was reached or not – arranged the solution mentioned and thereby "released them" or "made them give up their claims".

Fortunately there is a good parallel to the wording of our text in an unpublished judicial record from Kiš, AUAM 73.3095:8ff., which I can use by kind permission of and on the basis of a copy by M. Sigrist. It records a lawsuit concerning the division of an inheritance between three children, in which the eldest brother, L., is sued by his younger brother A. and sister(?) S. The judges give the following order: "In the gate of Zababa A. and S. will 'bind' (*ikassû*) ᶠM. and her son and L. will 'loosen' (them?; *ipaṭṭar*) and L. will also (*-ma ù*) set their minds at ease[44] concerning the 21 shekels of silver of their mother". L. said in the gate of Zababa: "I will not swear an oath for you, take the slave-girl and her son along. You shall not claim the 21 shekels of silver from me and I shall not obtain a share of the slave-girl and her child together with you". By their mutual agreement A.

---

41 See for temple officials in judicial records Dombradi (1996) I 254, § 338ff.

42 *Paṭārum* can be used in the basic and in the double stem with impersonal objects, such as "obligation" (*e'iltum*) and "rulings" (*riksātu*). CAD P s.v., meaning 3.b, registers OB *tatmāma lā tapṭur* under "to release from an oath", apparently in absolute use, since other occurrences have the preposition *ina/ištu nīš ilī*. But *kasûm* with such objects is not attested.

43 See for examples of both CAD K 169, b) 1'. Note also OAss *kasûm* with personal object, registered in CAD K 252, 4, which means "to oblige somebody (to do something)", "to make somebody abide by (a decision, promise)".

44 Cf. AbB 6, 153:12f., where an oath serves to put somebody at ease.

and S. obtained ^{f}M. and her child, because L. did not share her with them."[45] "Binding" the disputed slave-girl presumably means that plaintiffs establish/confirm their claim on her under oath, and "loosening" that L. by his oath undoes, refutes their claim in combination with (in exchange for?) waiving his claim on the silver his mother left behind. But L., for whatever reason,[46] refuses the oath and hence does not refute, undo their claim; he accepts a compromise by yielding the slave-girl and keeping the silver.

If we apply these findings to our record, *kasûm* would mean confirming under oath a statement of facts made (like OA *ka''unum*) and hence (as in the text just treated) the claim made (on the boy), while *paṭārum* means denying, refuting that made by the others. The plaintiffs, confronted with the clear statement of the defendants and unable to produce proof of a marriage, refuse to do both. In combination with Lamassani's readiness to confirm her statement under oath this settles the case. The plaintiffs give up their claim and Ṣurārum was not be conscripted.

3.3. The service duty of the son

The issue of the trial is whether Ṣurārum can be recruited as labourer in the Sippar countryside, because he belongs to the "work force" under the authority of general Warad-Kubi and his staff. While the designation érin, unfortunately, is too general to reveal his task,[47] the expression *šiprātim ša Sippar šūpušum*[48] may offer a clue, since *ša Sippar* qualifies his work as "public works". In OB *šiprātum* (apart from unspecified *šiprātum* in AbB 12, 90:8) is thus far only attested in the combination *eqel šiprātim*, "worked field", but there is no reason to restrict it to agricultural labour. A *ṣābum ēpištum* (also qualified as that of a particular city, AbB 2, 7:7f.; TCL 1, 3:6ff., or district, ARM 3, 6:5) can also be engaged in maintaining the irrigation system (AbB 2, 4:7) and in building operations. Since there is no question of land held by Ṣurārum (anyhow unlikely since he was living with his aunt), his status seems to have been that of simple worker of the state.

The general's claim is based on Ṣurārum's filiation, which apparently would oblige him to take over his dead father's obligation, presumably also because his elder brother had been kidnapped during a Kassite raid.[49] The general's claim links up with what is known from other data, that such service or corvée duties were incumbent on families and hence would pass from father to son, including a possible remuneration for its performance, as was the case with the *rēdûs*.[50]

When the aunt in whose house the boy lived rejects his claim, the commander with his staff appeals to the local(?) personnel chiefs (*abbū ṣābim*) and the main royal or palace administrators, the *šandabakkum*, and the "personnel director of the palace

---

45 Lines ^{8}ff.: *ina bāb* ^{d}*Zababa* M. *ù mārassa* ^{9} *A. ù S.* ^{10} *i-ka-as-sú-ú-ma* ^{11} L. *i-pa-aṭ-ṭa-ar-ma* ^{12} *ù aššum ⅓ mana 1 šiqil kaspim ša ummišunu* ^{13} L. *lib[baš]unu unappaš* ^{14} *ki'am iqbû* ^{15} *ina bāb* ^{d}*Zababa* L. ^{16} *ki'am iqbi umma šūma* ^{17} *ul atammâkkunūš[im]* ^{18} *amtam ù mārаša tablā* ^{19} *ana ⅓ mana 1 šiqil kaspim lā tarag[ga/umā]* ^{20} *ù amtam ù mārassa ittiku[nu]* ^{21} *ul azâz*.

46 The costs of the oath ritual, the weakness of his claim, the value of the slave, or in order to realize his preference?

47 See for the variety of public servants and workers which fell under the category érin, CAD Ṣ s.v. *ṣābu*, *c*, and most recently P. Mander and F. Pomponio in JCS 53 (2001) 38.

48 The Š-stem is typical for managing a work force, cf. AbB 13, 111:14.

49 See for Kassites in OB texts, W.A.J. de Smet, Akkadica 68 (1990) 1-19, and K. Van Lerberghe, in: K. Van Lerberghe and A. Schoors (eds.), *Immigration and Emigration within the Ancient Near East. Festschrift E. Lipinski*. OLA 65 (Leuven 1995) 379-93, esp. 384ff. on raids by Kassite bands. The absence of references to looting "Kassite troops" during Ammiditana's reign must be accidental.

50 CH § 28 stipulates that the son of a missing or dead *rēdûm* can only retain the field or orchard held from the palace if he is able to take over his father's *ilkum*. If he dies without offspring, according to AbB 2, 111:14ff., his holding will be given to somebody else in order that the service, which was the state's real purpose of the arrangement, would continue to be performed. See also F.R. Kraus, Vom altbabylonischen Erbrecht, in: J. Brugman [e. a.] (eds.), *Essays on Oriental Laws of Succession*. SD 9 (Leiden 1969) 9f., and for the corvée as a family obligation, M. Stol, Old Babylonian Corvée (*tupšikkum*), in: Th.P.J. van den Hout – J. de Roos (eds.), *Studio Historiae Ardens. Festschrift Ph.H.J. Houwink ten Cate* (Istanbul 1995) 295f.

gate", who then act as kind of law-court.[51] While the behaviour of his mother would allow for Šumum-libši's fatherhood, the plaintiff's failure to bring witnesses and the oath of the defendants mean it could not be accepted as a fact. While Šīmat-Ištar's motherhood was a matter of fact, Šumum-libši's fatherhood remained a matter of opinion and saved Ṣurārum a recruitment as "worker". Ṣurārum's aunt or perhaps Ṣurārum himself may have obtained this record as proof of the fact that he did not belong to the "workers" and via them in must have ended up in the little archive described in § 3.1.

According to the end of the record (l. 64) "the herald of the Amorites" in this case functioned as gìr. Normal law-suits lack such a note, but it is understandable on the level of public administration, in connection with representation and delegation of authority.[52] The herald may have arranged this trial or, more likely, have been charged with "publishing" and implementing the verdict. The involvement of the "herald of the Amorites" with the personnel of the palace (érin ká.é.gal) is also attested in AbB 12, 9:6ff., where (together with another "herald") he is stationed in the city-gate of Sippar to check the departure of the plow teams.[53] He may also have had the task of summoning persons for their service duties and of dunning those whole failed to meet their obligations, as is indicated by AbB 11, 43:14f. and ARM 14, 48:9 and was also the case much later.[54] Our verdict meant that he had to leave Ṣurārum and his aunt alone.

BIBLIOGRAPHY

Dombradi, E. 1996. *Die Darstellung des Rechtsaustrags in den altbabylonischen Prozess-urkunden*, I-II. FAOS 20/1-2. Stuttgart.

Joannès, F. (ed.). 2000. *Rendre Justice en Mésopotamie. Archives judiciaires du Proche-Orient ancien (IIIe-Ier millénaires avant J.-C.* Saint-Denis.

Lafont, S. (ed.). 1997. *Jurer et maudire: pratiques politiques et usages juridiques du serment dans le Proche-Orient ancient.* Mediterranés 10-11. Paris-Montréal.

Roth, M.T. 2001. Reading Mesopotamian Law Cases. PBS 5 100: A Question of Filiation, *JESHO* 44 (2001) 243-92.

Veenhof, K.R. 1989. Three Old Babylonian Marriage Contracts Involving *nadītum* and *šugītum*, in: M. Lebeau and Ph. Talon (eds), *Reflets des deux fleuves. Volume de mélanges offerts à Adré Finet.* Akkadica Suppl. 6. Leuven, 181-189 [= pp. 355-365 in this volume].

–. 2002. Three unusual Old Assyrian Contracts, in: G. J. Selz (ed.), *Festschrift für Burkhart Kienast.* AOAT 274. Münster.

Westbrook, R. 1988. Old Babylonian Marriage Law. *AfO Beiheft* 23. Horn.

51 The *šandabakkum* and the "manager of the personnel of the palace gate", as their occurrence in VS 7, 56 (see above, note 12) suggests, may have had regional authority. See for these functions and in particular the "manager of the personnel of the palace gate", N. Yoffee, The Economic Role of the Crown in the Old Babylonian Period. BiMes. 5 (Malibu 1978) chs. 3 and 4, with D. Charpin, JAOS 100 (1980) 462ff.

52 We also find it in the severely damaged judicial record BM 80701, which deals with the collection of dues (*šuddunum*), where the decision (rev. 4': *ul igerrû*), after a ruling, is followed by: gìr *Sin-idinnam* ugula.d[am.gàr] / *ù* di.ku_5.meš zim[bir^{ki}]. In CT 48, 32, a deposition before three judges to the effect that some ox drivers had failed to perform their duties is followed by gìr PN, and after the date by two more persons introduced by gìr.

53 In AbB 12, 115:12, in a case dealing with érin.aga.uš, he plays a role in the assembly.

54 See the references quoted in CAD N/I 117, b 1'.

The Dissolution of an Old Babylonian Marriage According to *CT* 45, 86*

The undated document *CT* 45, 86, from Sippar, is one of the rare legal records dealing with the dissolution of a marriage. Unfortunately the text is seriously damaged on the obverse, while the writing of the reverse – according to collation – is at times rather indistinct, partly due to numerous erasures. The understanding of the document is moreover hampered by some lexical problems and by the peculiar style and structure of the protocol. In a recent study, "Cutting the *sissiktu* in Divorce Proceedings" (*WdO* 8/2, 1976, 236 ff.), the late J. J. Finkelstein – to whom we owe so many stimulating studies in the field of Babylonian law – has treated the text. While he reached a partial understanding of the document and thanks to collations could improve upon the reading of the final lines (30 ff.), a satisfying overall interpretation of the text is still missing, and lines 33 f. have so far remained obscure. On the basis of several collations, kindly undertaken for me in 1973 by C. B. F. Walker of the British Museum, and stimulated by Finkelstein's observations, I hope to have gained more insight in this interesting document.

Text

On the basis of Walker's collations (preceded by W in the notes to the following transliteration) and those carried out for Finkelstein by Sollberger and Walker (Finkelstein, *op. cit.*, 238; preceded by F), and anticipating the subsequent interpretation, I propose the following reading (the first 15 lines contain the names and patronymics of presumably 8 witnesses, for the greater part broken away or seriously damaged):

16 *ma-ḫa-ar ši-bi* 17 *an-nu-ti* [P]*A*[!]*-ḫa-am-nir-ši* 18 *i-ša-lu-*(erasure)*-ma*[!] *a-wi-il-tum* 19 *an-ni-tu as-ša-at-ka-a* 20 *um-ma šu-ma i-na si-ka-tim* 21 *ul-la-ni-in-ni-ma mi-iš*[a]*-re-ti-ia* 22 *pu-ri-sa ú-ul a-aḫ-ḫa-az* 23 *an-ni-tam iq-bi* 24 *aš-ša-sú i-ša-lu-ma um-ma ši-i-ma* 25 *mu-ti a-ra*[b]*-a-am ki-a-am i-pu-ul* 26 *šu-ú ú-ul im-gu-ur* 27 *si-si-ik-ta-ša ik-ṣú-ur-ma* **[154]** 28 *ib-ta-ta-aq-qi* 29 *a-wi-lu-ú i-ša-lu-šu-ma* 30 *[u]m-ma šu-nu-ma a-wi-il-tum*[c] 31 *ša i-na* É *a-bi-ka uš-b[u-m]a*[d] 32 *aš-šu-sà ba-ab-ta-ka*[e] *i-du-ú* 33 *ki-a-am-ma it-ta-al-la-ak* 34 *ki*[f]*-ma i-ru-ba-ak mu-uš*[g]*-ši-il-ši*[h]

[a]W: all written over erasures, so the extra wedges in *iš* need be no problem; [b]W: *a-la*[?]*-a-am* is all written over erasures and the first two signs are damaged. The *la*[?] is almost all gone, but *a-am* is still clear; [c]F: sign very doubtful; reads *-tum*(??); W: very indistinct; I cannot improve upon the copy; copy: as upper part of *ki*; [d]F: reading *uš-b[u]-ú*: reading confirmed by collations; W: exactly as the copy, so *uš-bu-ú* (my proposal – K. R. V.) unlikely; copy: at least 5 "Winkelhaken" followed by a sign ending with a lower horizontal and a vertical; [e]F, who proposed the reading given above: *-ta-ka*, both readings doubtful; copy: first sign like extended *du*, second: *zu*; [f]F: preferable reading by collation; copy: restored *šu*; [g]F: *uš* confirmed by collation; [h]F: *ši* last sign.

* Originally published in Revue d'assyriologie et d'archéologie orientale 70 (1976) 153-164.

Translation

'In the presence of these witnesses they questioned Aḫam-nirši: "Is this woman (still to be considered) your wife?" He declared: "(You can) hang me on a peg, yea dismember me – I will not stay married (to her)!" Thus he said. They questioned his wife and she answered: "I (still) love my husband." Thus she answered. He, however, refused. He knotted up her hem and cut it off! The gentlemen questioned him: "A woman, who has come to live with your family (ancestral house) and whose status of married wife is known to your ward, is she to depart simply like that? Fit her out exactly as (she was when) she moved in with you!"'

Philological notes

21 f. The form *ul-la-ni-in-ni-ma* has presented serious problems. Finkelstein opted for *elûm*, D, giving more or less the correct meaning. But this is not acceptable because – as he admits – the verb is not used in the sense required by the context (cf. only *ina zaqīpi šūlûm*, NAss), and especially because this derivation would require *ulliā*. Finkelstein rightly compares our text with *BE* 6/2, 58, 12 f., where in a comparable case – also a husband absolutely unwilling to continue his marriage – the man states: "I will not stay married to her! Let them rather hang me and so (or) make me pay (divorce) money." The verbal form *li-iḫ-lu-lu-ni-in-ni-ma* cannot be separated from our form in my opinion, but Finkelstein did so because there are morphological problems. We can derive *ullā(ninni)* from *(ḫ)alālum* in two ways:

a) *ullā* < *ullilā*, due to elision of the short *-i-*. In general such a development with a verb mediae geminatae, in a phonetic context where the consonant *l* figures predominantly, and perhaps in connection with the phonetic effect of the stress (on *-ā-* or the next syllable?) seems conceivable. There are some examples of vowel elision in this class of verbs, cf. *GAG Erg.* § 101 *e*; one might compare a phonetic development as in OAss *Šallimāḫum* > *Salmāḫum*. Convincing parallels, however, in particular of imperatives of the D-stem, are missing. Vowel elision, especially after a double consonant, is not common. The few verbal forms which might be used as arguments hardly have demonstrative force. The variant *ḫubbanni* alongside *ḫubbibanni*, "caress me" (*CAD* Ḫ, 2 *b*, *ḫabābu* B) is considered a mistake by Biggs in *TCS* 2, 33 no. 14, 8, on the basis of his manuscripts B and C. The form *ḫulli*, considered an imp. D by *CAD* Ḫ 34 *a*, *ḫalālu* A, should be an imp. G, as the verb always occurs in that stem. The unique form *ú-da-ab-ba-an-ni* (*PBS* 7, 55, 16), **[155]** called to my attention by M. Stol, presumably a durative, could very well be a mistake. In the absence of more systematic investigations of this phonetic feature (such examples of vowel elision with concomitant reduction of the double consonant might reflect spoken language, as the OAss personal name suggests) it is unwarranted to assume a development as postulated for this solution. The fact that the parallel *BE* 6/2, 58 uses a G-stem in exactly the same context also argues against a D-stem.

b) *ulla* is a plur. imp. of the G-stem. We have to assume the normal development for verbs mediae geminatae *'ulul* + vocalic ending > *'ull-* (cf. OAss *šuddā*, *EL* 305, 10; NAss *dubbā*, *ABL* 571, 3; NB *mundā* < *muddā*, *TCL* 9, 139, 14). With verbs initial aleph, however, we would expect *'alla* instead (GAG, § 97 *d*). This rule, however, is not completely without exceptions; cf. the imp. *ubut* in Lambert-Millard, *Atra-ḫasis* 88, 22. A possible explanation is the fact that the root in OB is normally *ḫalālum*, cf. the references in *CAD* A/1 s. v. *alātu A*. The only exception – apart from our text; *ḫalālum* from *BE* 6/2, 58, due to uncertainty about its meaning is quoted under *ḫalālu* C in *CAD* Ḫ 34 *b;* cf. also Hallo, *Studies Oppenheim*, 1964, 99[34], and Landsberger, *Symbolae M. David II*, 1968, 92[3] – is *YOS* 10, 16, 1: *ú-lu-la-at*. Starting from the normal *ḫalālum* the plur. imp. would be *ḫullā*. It seems probable that the occasional dropping of initial *ḫ* in OB would not automatically bring about a change of the initial vowel of the imperative.

The meaning of *ḫalālum*, narrowed down by the addition *ina sikkatim* (missing in *BE* 6/2, 58), is confirmed by the new reading of 21 *b: mešrētia purrisā*. Next to being suspended Aḫam-nirši mentions another brutal corporal punishment: being dismembered.

This reading is suggested by the occurrence of this expression in *AfO* 8, 184, 33, in an inscription accompanying a historical relief of Ashurbanipal: *uparrisū mešrētišu* is the treatment meted out to Dunānu, the rebellious chieftain of the Gambulaeans.

25. The reading *a-ra-a-am* seems possible because traces of *la* might be confused with *ra*; perhaps the writer of the tablet made a mistake. A similar confusion of *la* and *ra* occurs in *AbB* 1, 128, rev. 9', also in a form of the verb *râmum* (*LA-i-im* for *ra-i-im*). The statement of the wife makes excellent sense if read in this way. The renewed ref usal of the husband in line 26 asks for a preceding positive statement on the part of his wife. Moreover *râmum* nicely contrasts with *zêrum*, "to hate" > "to repudiate", the terminus technicus for the feelings which bring about the dissolution of a marriage, e. g. in *CḪ* § 142, 60. The co-occurrence of *râmum* and *zêrum* as a contrasting pair is not uncommon, cf . the texts quoted in *CAD* Z s. v. *zêru*, notably Gilg. XII, 23 f. The shortness of the wife's answer could suggest that her words are of a formulaic nature.

28. The form *ib-ta-ta-aq-qi* has been dealt with by F. R. Kraus, "Ein altbabylonischer '*i*-Modus'?" (*Symbolae ... Böhl,* 1973, 253 ff.), where it figures as no. 26. The form is one of "type A" (-VCCi), which in general is used to indicate "gewollte, inhaltbezogene und gefühlsgeladene Betonung" (264). The translation given above means that I cannot share Kraus's characterisation of our passage as "Schlusswort ... einer Parteienaussage in direkter Rede". Lines 26-28 contain a descriptive statement of what happened in the presence of witnesses and judges, as part of the protocol. The special emphasis given by the scribe to the form of *bataqum* is not without importance and makes sense in this phase of the proceedings, as will be shown below.

30. The reading *awiltum* is almost dictated by the context, and is needed as antecedent of the pronominal suffix in *aššūssa* and as subject of *ittallak.* Neither *awiltam* nor *awīl* + noun in the gen. make sense. The wife in question already had been referred to by *awiltum* in l. 18.

31. The reading *uš-bu-ma* is not excluded by the traces; in fact a final *-ma* seems more likely than *-ú.* A *-ma* is moreover required because lines 31-32 are in conjunction and together provide the argument why the question put in line 33 has to be answered negatively.

32. I follow Finkelstein in reading *ba-ab-ta-ka.* It makes excellent sense, as indicated by Finkelstein (*op. cit.*, 239). In the document published by him (*op. cit.*, 236 f.) the witnesses "who were in attendance at her divorce" (line 18), *i.e.* who witnessed the record he publishes, "had been present at the marriage agreement of ᶠT" (lines 20 f.). It is quite possible that the witnesses mentioned on the obverse of *CT* 45, 86 represented Aḫam-nirši's *bābtum*, "ward", and acted in **[156]** the same capacity. In that case *bābtaka* in line 32 would in fact be equivalent to: the witnesses here present.

33. This line is taken as a (rhetorical) question, with Finkelstein (*op. cit.*, 240); a direct answer by Aḫam-nirši is missing. Crucial for the interpretation is the meaning of *kīamma. Kīam*, "thus", with enclitic *-ma*, occurs in different functions and meanings, cf. *AHw* en *CAD* s. v. We can leave out of consideration combinations in which *-ma* functions as copula in a nominal sentence *(šī lū kīamma, šumma lā kīamma)*, *kīamma* after prepositions (*ina, ana, aššum*), and *kīam(ma)* introducing direct speech (preceding *qabûm*, *šapārum*, etc.).[1] Two possibilities remain: *a) kīam-ma* in which *-ma* lends special emphasis to *kīam*, allowing a variety of translations, among others "likewise" (*AHw* s. v. 2 ; *CAD* K *s. v.* 1, *b*), 2'; especially well attested in OAss); *b)* an interpretation suggested only by *CAD K s. v.* 2: "How (as interrogative and interjection)."

---

1 The only OB example of *kīamma* mentioned in *CAD K s. v.* 1, *b*, 1', is not correct; read in *TCL* 18, 113, 8: *ma-ti*!-*a-am-ma*, "is missing for me". *Kīamma* after prepositions is well attested in lexical sources but rare in OB contexts. *Aššum kīamma* (*CAD K s. v.* 1, *a*, 4', *c*') is attested in *ARM* 1, 36, 30 and *YOS* 2, 109, 28; it may essentially be a nominal phrase, "because it is thus...".

Applying *b)* we would get a straightforward question: "How is the woman to leave?"; that this question is not answered – as earlier questions in this protocol are – speaks against this translation. In fact a meaning "how" for *kīamma* is rather ambiguous. *Kīam* is not an interrogative but an adverb, to be kept distinct from *kī* and its combinations. In interrogative sentences it may receive enclitic *-ma*, which in such cases is regularly added to adverbs, which frequently have the main stress of the interrogative intonation, as is indicated by writings with added vowel: *-ma-a*, well attested in Mari (cf. GAG, § 123 *b* and Finet, *L' Accadien des lettres de Mari*, 1956, § 79 *c*; cf. an example like *ARMT* 1, 18, 9 f.: *aš-ra-nu-um-ma-a ana gamrimma tastakkanšu*?[2] As, however, *-ma* is by no means limited to interrogative sentences and serves a variety of semantic functions, phrases with *kīamma* in the absence of clear question markers (such as e. g. the lengthening of a final vowel; cf. *aššatkā* in *CT* 45, 86, 19), may be taken as positive, at times exclamative statements. Two of the examples quoted in *CAD* K *kīam* 2, *b*, "how", *EA* 13, 36 and *MRS* 6, 14, 6, are in fact translated differently by Knudtzon and Nougayrol respectively. The first example quoted by *CAD* under 2, a (*kiam*, "how") is translated in the lexical part as "so beautiful..." (= "how beautiful!").

Of the two OB examples quoted in *CAD* under 2, *b*, the first, *TCL* 1, 32, 6, is difficult to evaluate, for lack of an informative context. We might in fact also translate: "Should they just measure out?". *ARM* 1, 123, 7 is much clearer, occurring in a letter from Išme-Dagan to Jasmaḫ-Addu. Instead of CAD's: "How can I stand by and watch him?", I do prefer the rendering by Dossin, accepted by Finet (*loc. cit.*): "Vais-je, moi, simplement le regarder?" (*anāku kīammā anaṭṭalšu*). The king of Ešnunna has in mind to fortify a town, which is a threat and an act of hostility towards Išme-Dagan. The latter asks the rhetorical question whether he should be *just* looking on, passively. Of course not, for, as he continues: "I will in exchange deal a blow to his country!". In this case *kīam(mā)* is closely linked with the verbal form and questions not the way in which something is to be done, but the action as such: "just, simply".[3]

This use of *kīamma* is also attested in positive statements, as can be shown by some OAss examples. In the letter *CCT* 3, 23 *b*, the writer, a lady, states that her addressee "just keeps sending her consignments (of silver)" (*šēbulātim kīamma tuštenebbalam*), while she has been unable to send him, in return, textiles as merchandise. In the contract of service, *ICK* 2, 105 + 108, unfortunately damaged, the servant hired eventually, after having served the time of **[157]** the contract, "can simply leave" (*kīamma ittallak*, rev. 4'; cf. similar statements, e. g. *ICK* 2, 107: *ašar libbiša illak*). In the letter *BIN* 4, 38, 18, the writer complains that he has nothing to do, "is idle, and is *just* staying" where he is and keeping himself alive (... *rāqākuma kīamma wašbāku u šalmam akkal*). The same function has *kīamma* in my opinion in *CT* 45, 86, 33: is the woman just to leave, to depart without further ado? Are all obligations met when she simply departs, as the transporter can depart in *ICK* 2, 105 + 108, after having served his contract?

34. The rhetorical question is answered by the judges themselves. The woman should not depart empty-handed. The point apparently is how much she is entitled to take along. The verb *muššulum* (already recognized by *AHw* 624 *a*, D, end: "unkl.") means "to make equal". Normally it is construed with *ana* or a dative suffix: "to make equal to", but here the construction is different, as *kīma* is used. This combination is also attested in *AbB* 2, 171, 18 f. (*BB* 268): *meḫer kanik ... kīma šaṭru muššil*, "make an exact duplicate of the deed ... just as it has been written". Here *kīma* + permansive describes the example, the standard which should be equated: a situation or object present. In *CT* 45, 86, however,

---

2 I do not follow FINET, *op. cit.* § 79 *c*, when he distinguishes between enclitic *-ma-a (-mâ)* and the normal enclitic *-ma*, and identifies the former with independent *mâ*, introducing sentences (e.g. in OA, cf. HECKER, *GKT*, § 106 *d*). Cf. for an OB example of *-ma-a* in a question: *AbB* 1, 18, 22: *ba-lum-ma-a*.

3 Cf. the use of the same verbal form (without *kīammā*), with the same meaning, in S. DALLEY, B. F. WALKER, and J. D. HAWKINS, *The Old Babylonian Tablets from Tell al Rimah* (London, 1976), no. 5, 11, where the editors translate *inaṭṭal* with "will he (be content simply to) look on".

we have *kīma* + punctual, and this should be an abbreviated rendering of "as (she was when) she moved in with you". Perhaps lack of space on the left edge accounts for this compact formulation; perhaps also the fact that *kīma* may serve both as a temporal and as a comparative subjunction. As the reference is presumably to the dowry she is to take along, we might reconstruct perhaps something like **kīma šeriktam šarkat inūma irubakkum*; hence my rendering of *muššulum* by "to fit out exactly as...".[4]

The form *irubak* is also remarkable. In the first place the dative suffix is reduced to *-ak*. There are more examples of such shortened forms, e. g. *TCL* 1, 32, 15: *šu-li-a-aš* (also on a left edge!), and Walters, Water for Larsa (*YNER* 4, 1970), 67, 21 *(-ku-nu-ut)* and 68, 12 *(-ši-na-at)*. We might also compare the PNs of the type *DN-iddinaš* (Kraus, *JCS* 3, 1949, 58; Walters, *op. cit* ., nos. 39, 11 and 32, 5(!)). Again we might ask the question whether such forms do reflect spoken language. Also remarkable is the construction of *erēbum* with personal dative suffix, instead of amply attested *erēbum ana bīt* ..., also in marriage contexts. Forms with personal dative suffix are occasionally attested, cf. *i-te-ru-bu-ku-um* in *TCL* 17, 38 rev. 13'; *i-ru-ba-akkum-ma* in *UET* 5, 27, 9; *i-te-er-ba-ak-ki YOS* 2, 16, 12 f. Cf. also *šēp irubakkum* in OB omina (*YOS* 10, 44, 30 ff and 50, 11) and some examples quoted in *CAD* E. Perhaps lack of space again forced the scribe to use this less common construction. We can also suppose that he was influenced – in this marriage context – by the comparable expression *ana mutim wašābum*, "to go to live with a husband", attested in MAss and Nuzi (*CAD* A/2, 402, 2'), but which has now also turned up in OB: TR. 4251, 7 (S. Page, *Iraq*, 30, 94).

General comments

The text concerns a married couple, the male partner of which wants to get rid of his wife. Finkelstein (*op. cit.*, 239 ad 21) supposes that the couple was legally married (the marriage had been contracted some time before), but that the marriage had not yet been physically consummated. The scribe could use words like *aššatum, mutum* and *aššūtum* on the basis of the contract, but *aḫḫaz* should be translated: "I don't want to consummate the marriage". Recently (in *Symbolae M. David II*, 1968, 85 ff., especially 87[1]) Landsberger has convincingly demonstrated that *aḫāzum*, **[158]** whatever its basic meaning,[5] does not mean "to take carnally". As the parallels quoted by Landsberger (to which we may add *TCL* 11, 246, l'-4', discussed by Greengus in *JAOS* 89, 1969, 518[62]) show, we have to translate: "I don't want to stay married (to her)", or, with Greengus: "I won't have (her) any longer as wife". Our text confirms this interpretation. While its first part is still compatible with Finkelstein's interpretation, the second is not: the woman "has come to live with her husband's family" and even "has moved in with him". The marriage had not only been contracted but to all appearances was also consummated in consequence of the *domum deductio*, which is implicitly mentioned. This state of affairs also explains the wife's answer: "I still love (want) my husband" (durative).

The first part of the text, after listing the witnesses, starts with an interrogation of the couple by *awīlū*, "gentlemen" (see below). Their questions serve to establish the mutual feelings of the couple. The first one, *awiltum annītu aššatka*, reflects the formulaic language, the *verba solemnia* of marriage and divorce. They are an interrogative third person transformation of an original, reconstructed *(lū) aššatī*, inaugurating a marriage, and of *ul aššatī attī*, the divorce formula. Cf. the full discussion of the evidence – also on

---

4 *Muššulum* + *kīma* (preposition) is also attested, e. g. in *Idrimi*, 81. *VAS* 10, 214, V, 37 ff., mentioned in *AHw* s. v. D, 2, is different, because the phrase beginning with *kīma* depends on the following *šipṣet* (cf. B. GRONEBERG, *Untersuchungen zum hymnisch-epischen Dialekt der altbabylonischen literarischen Texte*, 1972, 48).

5 Cf . *op. cit.*, p. 87: "In das Wort *aḫāzu* kann nichts von Geschlechtsverkehr hineingedeutet werden." Perhaps the basic meaning, in view of OA *rābiṣam aḫāzum* and OB *wardam aḫāzum*, comprises both the ideas of "to acquire, to obtain" and of "to hold, to have, to engage" in a more lasting relationship. The second element seems to be important, also in distinction to *leqûm* and *ṣabātum*, and is not restricted to the durative. The translation problem is that "to marry" is punctual, inchoative, while we need something meaning "to acquire and have as wife".

the use of the second or the third person in such statements – by Greengus in "The Old Babylonian Marriage Contract", *JAOS* 89, 1969, 505 ff., especially 514 ff., sub II. Here the words are a question whether the husband is willing to continue his marriage.

The answer is not the formulaic statement *ul aššatī šī*, presumably because the husband is unable to deny her status of married wife and because the moment for the pronunciation of the divorce formula has not yet arrived; the "gentlemen" first want to be sure about his feelings. The answer of the husband is an outright and unconditional expression of his unwillingness to continue the marriage. Even in the face of the most brutal punishments he would refuse to stay married to his wife. His words, of course, do not imply that such cruel punishments actually threatened a husband in case of malicious desertion; neither are they really indicative of his dislike of his wife. They are also used (in a comparable situation, but in an abbreviated form) in *BE* 6/2, 58, and presumably represent a not uncommon figure of speech, used to underline by exaggeration – as in self imprecations – the firmness of a decision.

The wife in return clearly states her will to continue the marriage. She does not **[159]** "hate" her husband – the *terminus technicus* for repudiation – but still "loves", "wants" him (see above on *râmum*). The husband, however, does not give in; he wants divorce and immediately gets it. He performs the symbolic action of cutting off the hem of his wife's garment, discussed by Finkelstein, *op. cit.* (cf. also the references in Greengus, *op. cit.*, 515[44], including the unpublished OB text A 7757, partly communicated in 517[57], and *RlA* III, 321). Cutting the hem he symbolically cuts the bond of marriage. From our text, from Newell 1900, and presumably also from A 7757 (which mentions this symbolic rite but not the divorce formula; see Greengus, *op. cit.*, 517[58]) we might perhaps conclude that actual divorce documents regularly mention the performance of this symbolic act, while marriage deeds, which only consider divorce as an eventuality, refer to divorce by means of the divorce formula. In front of witnesses a divorce presumably was effectuated by both the act and the formulaic words; the mention of one of them apparently was deemed sufficient by the scribes. In our text the symbolic action is preceded by some statements, which are very short and almost formulaic (*mutī arām*; *ūl aḫḫaz)* and this could well have been the normal order of things.

Thus far nothing is said about a financial arrangement in connection with the divorce. There is no proof that this was necessary. A marriage agreement could contain advance stipulations on the financial consequences of a divorce or these matters may have been solved according to common law. Newell 1900 only records the factual divorce. The short text *BAP* 91 (= *VAB* 5, 7), mentioned by Finkelstein, is an exception, recording the divorce, the cutting of the hem and the payment of divorce money. This document, however, served special evidentiary purposes and was not a simple divorce record. It could protect the former husband against new claims of his ex-wife, serving as receipt for the divorce money; or rather, as the final clause indicates, safeguard the ex-wife against her former husband: the facts mentioned are written proof that the divorce had taken place, so that the wife was free to marry again. Newell 1900 may have served a similar purpose.

CT 45, 86 contains the record of the effectuation of a divorce, but the text is more than that. The divorce is preceded by an interrogation, which, at force, could be considered part of the standard procedure of divorce. The speaker of the witnesses or the chairman of the ward may have asked for public declarations on mutual feelings before the ceremony of the divorce proper. But this is hard to prove, and *CT* 45, 86 does not end with the ceremonial cutting of the hem. The questioning continues, and in addition to the witnesses "gentlemen" (*awīlū*) are present, who conduct the session. The text requires a different interpretation, which should explain its purpose and account for its remarkable form and contents.

The text begins with the names of eight (?) witnesses. Because they are mostly **[160]** missing or broken, because the wife remains anonymous,[6] and because the patronymics of the husband are not mentioned, we remain ignorant about their relations. They may have been members of Aḫam-nirši's ward (the *bābtum* is mentioned in line 32), called in because of their knowledge of the facts and acquaintance with the couple (cf. the qualification *awīlū mārū bābtim mudûšunu* in *VAB* 5, 279, 17 f.); this at least was the case in Newell 1900, where it is also mentioned that they earlier on witnessed the marriage agreement.

The questions are put by the *awīlū*, "gentlemen", local authorities, perhaps officials or aldermen (cf. the quotation above from *VAB* 5, 279; also A. Walther, *Gerichtswesen*, 67 f.). It is not easy to define their function. Like judges they conduct an interrogation *(šâlum)*, but they don't pass a formal verdict. They conclude with a reproaching question and a serious injunction, more in the way of arbitrators or wise elders. They apparently don't try to reconcile the partners, nor do they have to decide whether in this particular case a divorce was justified (unless this is the implicit meaning of the questions asked in order to establish the mutual feelings of the couple). They do not intervene when the husband's absolute unwillingness to continue the marriage materialises in the effectuation of the divorce.

Judges were not normally involved in a divorce procedure, unless having been appealed to because of legal problems or when one of the parties considered himself wronged. Such a case may have been the one mentioned in *BE* 6/1, 59 (= *VAB* 5, 232), where we read that the judge "pronounced her divorce" (*ezēbša iqbû*), to wit of a wife affected by a serious ailment. This special circumstance may have brought the judges in, or perhaps there were other problems in connection with the status of the wife or her son from an earlier marriage.

In our text the "gentlemen" appear to be concerned not so much with the factual divorce as with its correct settlement: the safeguarding of the financial interests of the wife. In so far their final question and injunction appear to provide a clue for the understanding of the text: they remind the husband of his financial obligations to his ex-wife. In this connection the verbal form *ibtataqqi* in line 28 becomes interesting. The scribe using the "i-mode" calls for special attention to, puts strong emphasis on, what the husband does: "... and he cut off – mark you! – the hem." As this symbolic action in itself is not remarkable he must have meant either the moment at which or the conditions under which the husband performed his act: *immediately* after his **[161]** final "no" or *just/simply*, without further ado. This seems to link up with the interpretation proposed above for *kīamma ittalla.* In concrete it could mean that the scribe called special attention to the fact that Aḫam-nirši divorced his wife without having first promised a financial arrangement, trying to send her away empty-handed. As the text does not mention the reasons why he wants to get rid of his wife, and she still loves him, the divorce may well have been one of gratuitous desertion without guilt on the part of the wife. Of course he had no right to send her away empty-handed in that case!

This brings us to the question of the nature of the procedure and the purpose of the text. Three possibilities present themselves: *a*) it is the protocol of legal proceedings involving a divorce; *b*) it is a self contained, immediate record of a divorce; *c*) it is a witnessed protocol of a divorce procedure and interrogation, drawn up to be used as evidence in a lawsuit between Aḫam-nirši and his ex-wife, the issue of which were the ex-wife's rights to part of the property of the couple. The first possibility would fix the role of the "gentlemen" as judges and make their interrogation understandable. As, however,

6 The wife is called *awīltum*, translated "woman", in order to avoid "lady", which might suggest class membership, which cannot be determined in our case for lack of any point of reference. I doubt whether she was called *awiltum* because of her marriage to an *awīlum*, as *CAD* A/2, 47, 1, *c*, suggests. Rather *awīltum* is a polite or neutral way of referring to her, just like the wife whose divorce is impending is called *awīltum* in *AbB* 5, 249, 7'. The use of *awīltum* of course poses the same problems as that of *awīlum*, ranging from the use of *awīltum* for slave-girls (*TIM* 2, 16, 18 f. and rev. 6) to *awīltum* as a free citizen, qualified as *mārat awīlim* (*AbB* 6, 80, 1-6).

the text also records the symbolic cutting of the hem, and the "judges" do no seem to pass a verdict, it can hardly be the protocol of a trial. The second possibility is unlikely because the record would give too much information, the purpose of which is not readily understandable. Why record the final question and injunction (if not: all questions), and not simply the factual divorce (as e. g. in Newell 1900)? The third possibility provides the best explanation. The mention of the fact that the husband already had been warned to meet his financial obligations – together with the circumstance that the wife was willing to continue the marriage (and by implication: was not guilty) – would be important for an evaluation of Aḫam-nirši's subsequent behaviour: he would prove guilty of intentional negligence towards his ex-wife.

If this is indeed the purpose of our text, its contents nevertheless remain most remarkable. The close connection between the interrogation and the divorce proper means that both occurred in one and the same session. The special purpose of the protocol probably accounts for the unusually detailed and direct record of what happened. As stated above the first series of questions is not too difficult to explain; they may have been asked in normal divorce procedures, though never recorded in the material we have. They are important in this case, shedding light on matters of motive, initiative and guilt. The second series, starting in line 29, is, however, rather unexpected. We cannot assume that such questions normally followed the effectuation of the divorce. The "gentlemen" must have had special reasons to ask them, and the most likely interpretation is that they knew – either as members of the ward, acquainted with Aḫam-nirši's affairs, or having been informed or instructed by the **[162]** party of his wife – that he was likely to evade his obligations. His rash cutting off of the hem of his wife's garment, without proposing any financial arrangement – perhaps nicely indicated by the scribe by means of the "i-mode" – triggers off their final question.

Form and content of this final question and its answer again require special attention. The rhetorical question they ask, together with the answer they themselves give, comprises a ruling together with its consideration. The substance of the ruling is that a wife, divorced without being guilty, cannot be sent away empty-handed. It is a rule phrased also in *CḪ*, § 156: *mimma ša ištu bīt abīša ublam ušallimšimma mutu libbiša iḫḫassī*, "he will compensate her whatever she brought along from her paternal home and a husband of her choice can marry her". This apparently was a generally accepted rule and the accurate description of the dowry, at times with the monetary value of special items, in written marriage contracts – some of them were little more than expanded receipts for bridal gifts or dowry, to quote Greengus, *op. cit.*, 512 with note 33 – was given in view of eventualities like divorce. The use of the verb *atlukum*, "to depart", is attested elsewhere in connection with the dissolution of a marriage. In both texts the point in question is what the divorced wife will take along, when leaving: her dowry, because she is not guilty, in *CḪ*, § 142; her adopted "sister", given to her husband as substitute wife or concubine, in *BIN* 7, 173, 22.

That the ruling just mentioned applies in this particular case is made clear in lines 31 f. Negatively, in so far as no misconduct is mentioned; positively by two connected arguments, which prove the status of the woman: she is a legal wife, because she lives with the family of her husband (marriage agreement sealed by *domum deductio)* and because her husband's ward is aware of her married status. The second argument is not simply the logical conclusion from the first (the people of the ward have seen her arrival and know how she lives; fact and reputation). I would rather follow the suggestion implicit in Newell 1900: the members of the ward – presumably now present as witnesses or aldermen – have been witnesses to the marriage agreement. In the absence of a written marriage contract – not referred to – they can testify that the marriage was contracted.

The way in which the "gentlemen" remind Aḫam-nirši of his obligation is remarkable. Its syntactical form is so unique that it must reflect what was actually said and cannot be a stylistic creation of the scribe. If that is true this document shows us that the objective style of protocols and verdicts – using 3rd person duratives – was not necessarily a reflection of what was actually said. Subtly formulated, rhetorical questions and injunctions were also used.

The rhetorical question is interesting because on the one hand it refers **[163]** to the concrete case – twice the possessive suffix *-ka* is used -, but on the other hand implies – as stated above – a rather general ruling. It starts with *awīltum*, "*a* woman", just like the rules in the so-called laws, but the following *ša* identifies it as an example of the so-called "relative formulation", one of the variants of the casuistic formulation, alternating with the conditional *šumma* formulation, *e.g.* in the "Laws of Eshnunna" and in the "Edict of Ammiṣaduqa" (cf. R. Yaron, *The Laws of Eshnunna*, 1969, 66 ff.).

I will refrain from entering the interesting discussion about the origin and use of the various legal formulations, furthered by Yaron's important observations, and limit myself to some remarks in connection with the text under discussion. The more general, less particular nature of the relative formulation makes sense in *CT* 45, 86; the rhetorical question phrases a fairly general rule. As to the origin of this formulation – found in (official) proclamations and decrees by Yaron; partly confirmed by A. Marzal in *Catholic Biblical Quarterly* 33, 1971, 333 ff. and 492 ff., cf., especially 500 ff. – and hence the background of the rule of *CT* 45, 86, no conclusions seem possible. There is no evidence of proclamations concerning family law, and we cannot exclude the possibility that it was based on litigation or precedent. All we can say is that the "gentlemen" introduce it as a customary rule, as common law. As pointed out by Yaron himself the form of a ruling is not always a safe guiding principle to establish its original "Sitz im Leben"; legal sentences could be adapted by scholars or compilers to their tastes or models. Not to be disregarded, in my opinion, is the linguistic aspect. The relative formulation is easy and natural when, as in *CT* 45, 86, there is no change of subject between protasis and apodosis: *awīltum ša ... ittallak*? When there is a change, the conditional formulation is easier, e. g. in *AbB* l, 18, 20 ff.: *šumma amtum ... uqtallal ... ušaqbāši*? Both texts deserve a comparison, because both use a rhetorical question in a legal argument. It may be meaningful that there is a marked difference in speaker and situation. In *CT* 45, 86, the aldermen or arbitrators phrase a generally accepted ruling (relative formulation), settling a case. In *AbB* l, 18 a lady approaches the *šāpirum* and in seeking justice asks a rhetorical question, which phrases her case, still to be decided by the judges (conditional formulation).

By means of their rhetorical question the "gentlemen" in *CT* 45, 86 confront Aḫam-nirši with a generally accepted rule, which the community is supposed to consider fair and hence cannot be ignored by him. He is almost forced to answer: of course not! They do not impose a decision, forced upon him, but confront him with a fair consideration, which must appeal to his sense of justice. But at the same time the question is a reproach: how could he try to evade such common obligations? To use the words of Jacobsen ("An Ancient Mesopotamian Trial for Homicide" in: *Toward the Image of Tammuz,* 1970, 194), they confront him with "common law ... being essentially a body of ethical rules backed by the pressure of public opinion". **[164]** It is not necessary for Aḫam-nirši to answer the question. It is a consideration from which the "gentlemen" draw their own conclusion: an injunction, stating how much he has to give to his divorced wife.

The procedure followed by the "gentlemen" in our text is, as far as I know, without parallels in legal texts. The only parallel I could find is in a letter by king Ḫammurabi. The king repeatedly gives air to his indignation by asking angry questions followed by strict orders. Normally specific problems are involved, and the questions refer to what his correspondents have done or neglected, or serve the clarification of facts. In *AbB* 4, 16, however, the situation is different. Here a clearly rhetorical question, expecting a negative answer, phrases a legal or administrative rule of general application, a principle of justice and wise administration. The ensuing order first asks to ascertain whether the case is indeed covered by that rule, and, if yes, to act accordingly. Kraus translates: "Wird eind Feld (mit) Dauer(widmung) jeweils weggenommen? Behandle die Angelegenheit, und falls besagtes Feld das seiner Familie ist, gib dem S. besagtes Feld zuruck!" The order is the logical application of the general rule, and the question implicitly reproaches Šamaš-ḫāzir of not being aware of it or not having applied it. The king in fact does not give an authoritative decision, but simply applies a rule of wise administration.

The situation in *CT* 45, 86 is comparable. The very wording of the injunction by the "gentlemen", *kīma irubak muššilšī*, as compact as meaningful, contains an inner logic: give her back what she brought along. It is a ruling just and wise, almost a council of wisdom. It is perhaps not accidental that comparable orders or injunctions and sentences with relative formulation (starting with independent *ša*; cf. e. g. Lambert, *BWL* 119, 8 ff.; 130 f., 85 ff.) occur in the so-called wisdom literature. In both cases the relative formulation is used to phrase general rules of normative behaviour, and the imperatives are councils of wisdom, which should be applied, because they are convincing and recommend themselves.

If there is some truth in these observations, *CT* 45, 86 may give us some insight in the way in which wise aldermen and judges phrased their considerations and formulated their orders or injunctions, to ensure their application. New texts should correct, confirm or refine these conclusions, admittedly built on a rather small textual basis.

Three Old Babylonian Marriage Contracts Involving *Nadītum* and *Šugītum**

In the course of its ample treatment of marriage and matrimonial property the Laws of Ḫammurabi, in several paragraphs (§§137, 144ff., 178-184) pay special attention to the status, rights and duties of a small group of 'religious' women. Foremost among them are the *nadītum*-priestesses – those of Marduk being singled out again in § 182 – and in their wake also women called *šugītum*[1] appear.

The traditional search for evidence in Old Babylonian legal records that reflects the stipulations of the laws or at least deals with similar issues has yielded much valuable comparative material on the *nadītum*s, but has been only partly successful in the case of the still rather enigmatic *šugītum*. The relevant literature (*Renger*, *Westbrook*, *Wilcke*) shows that we have evidence for her receiving a dowry, being married and having children (BE 6/1, 95; 101; PBS 8/2, 252), while there is both indirect (CT 8, 2a:12; CBS 1214:17) and direct (CT 45,119) proof of her position as secondary wife alongside a *nadītum* as main and first wife, who at times is her (natural or adopted) sister.[2] The amount of data would increase if we were to consider women in similar polygamous marriages alongside *nadītum*s or main wives who are their sisters always as *šugītum*s (*e.g.* in BE 6/1, 84:30 and TIM 4, 47). But this is not justified, since such marriage-arrangements are not limited to cases where the main wife is a *nadītum* (in CT 48, 57 she is a *qadištum*, while the secondary wife is the daughter of a *kulmašītum*) and in view of the variety in status and background of the secondary wives, who can be (adopted) slave-girls, sisters, or women without any apparent relationship to the main wife (*Westbrook* II ch.vi).

In this situation additional evidence on the *šugītum* in connection with her marriage and her relation to a *nadītum* is welcome.[3] It is available in the form of three new

---

1 Written ^{mí}*šu-gi$_4$-tum*, but note the variants ^{mí}ŠU.GI in BE 31, 22 (Late OB) and *šu-gi-tum* in PBS 5, 93 (OB), both in the text of § 145. In Proto-Lu (*MSL* 12) we have ^{mí}šu.gi$_4$ in 58:710 and 65 III:2, and ^{mí}šu.gi$_4$.a in 66:2, a writing also attested in Römer, *SKIZ* 130:70.

2 We should perhaps add BE 6/1, 95 (Sippar, Aṣ 13), dealing with a donation by I. to his *šugītum* wife H. The donation includes a house I. had inherited from A., a *nadītum* of Šamaš. *Westbrook* (I,74) reads: [8] *[ap]lūt A.* [9] *[ša] I...* [10] *[ap-lu-u]s-sà ilqû*, "the inheritance of A..., which I. has taken as her heir" (following Kraus *SD* 9, 46 note 103), calling it a "colloquial expression" and citing a few other occurrences. But since in none of them the (awkward) combination *aplūt ... aplūssa* occurs and the space for the missing first signs of line 10 according to Ranke's copy is too small for *[ap-lu-u]s-sà*, we better read *[mu-u]s-sà*, "her husband". This would mean that I. had inherited from the *nadītum* A. who was his first and main wife, and had subsequently made a donation to his (secondary) *šugītum* wife that had already born him children. The record thus would reflect the well-known triangular relation between husband, childless *nadītum* and *šugītum* with children.

3 Laws nor records shed any light on the presumed cultic status or functions of the *šugītum* (Finet, *Le Code de Hammurapi*, 1983[2], 107: possibly belonging to "le personnel subalterne du temple"). The only hint in this direction could be the passage of an Iddin-Dagan hymn, *SKIZ* 130:70, where "maidens, šu.gi$_4$.a, coiffured, walk before Inanna" in the procession of the New Year's Festival, alongside (line 68) "young men, carrying hoops" (D. Reissner, *JCS* 25 [1973] 287). The parallelism does not demand a cultic function for šu.gi$_4$.a,which seems to be in apposition to ki.sikil, perhaps only describing their role or outward appearance at this particular occasion. ARM 22,16:11, women *ša* É *šu-gi-tim*, is not helpful.

* Originally published in M. Lebeau and Ph. Talon (eds), Reflets des deux fleuves. Volume de mélanges offerts à André Finet. Akkadica Supplementum 6. Leuven, 1989, pp. 181-89.

marriage contracts, which I identified among unpublished Old Babylonian tablets from Sippar in the British Museum. I am grateful to Mr. C.B.F. Walker for making the group of texts to which they belong available for study, and to the Trustees of the Museum for their permission to publish them. It is a pleasure to make them known in the first place to Professor Finet, whose continuing interest in the Laws of Hammurabi is well known, in particular from his handy and lucid edition of the Laws, by which he put Assyriologists and many others in his debt.

A. BM 96991 (Sippar, 2-XI-Ad.26)

[O.1] ^{mí}*A-ḫa-ta-ni* ^{mí}*šu-gi-tum* [2] DUMU.MÍ *A-ḫi-ia-am-ši* [3] *ù* ^{mí}*La-ma-as-sà-ni* LUKUR ^{d}UTU [4] ^{p}*Ri-iš-*^{d}UTU DUMU ^{d}EN.ZU-*be-el-ma-tim* [5] *it-ti A-ḫi-ia-am-ši a-bi-ša* [6] *ù* ^{mí}*La-ma-sà-ni* LUKUR ^{d}UTU *um-mi-ša id-bu-ub-ma* [7] ^{p}*A-ḫa-ta-ni* ^{mí}*šu-gi-tum* [8] *a-na* É *Ri-iš-*^{d}UTU DUMU ^{d}EN.ZU-*be-el-ma-tim* [9] *a-na Be-la-num ma-ri-šu* [10] *a-na aš-šu-tim a-ḫa-zi-im* [11] *ú-še-ri-bu-ši* [12] 1 ^{giš}NÁ 2 ^{giš}GU.ZA 1 ^{dug}ŠAGAN [13] *ù I-lu-ni a-ḫa-ša a-na ma-ru-ti-ša* [14] *id-di-nu-ši-im* [15] *5* GÍN KÙ.BABBAR *te-er-ḫa-at* ^{mí}*A-ḫa-ta-ni* [16] *i-na qá-ti Ri-iš-*^{d}UTU DUMU ^{d}EN.ZU-*be-el-ma-tim* [17] ^{p}*A-ḫa-ia-am-ši* DUMU *Ì-lí-iš-me-a-ni* [E.18] *ù La-ma-as-sà-ni* LUKUR ^{d}UTU [19] *ma-aḫ-ru* [R.20] U$_4$.KÚR.ŠÈ *Be-la-nu-um* DUMU *Ri-iš-*^{d}UTU [21] *a-na* ^{mí}*A-ḫa-ta-ni aš-ša-ti-šu* [22] *ú-ul aš-ša-ti at-ti i-qá-ab-bi-ma* [23] 1/3 *ma-na* KÙ.BABBAR Ì.LÁ.E [24] *ù* ^{mí}*A-ḫa-ta-ni a-na Be-la-nu mu-ti-ša* [25] *ú-ul mu-ti at-ta i-qá-ab-bi-ma* [26] *i-ḫa-aš-šu-ši-ma a-na me-e i-na-ad-du-ši*

---

[27] IGI ^{d}UTU-*na-ṣi-ir e-ri-ib* É DUMU *Šu-mu-l[i-i]b-ši* [28] IGI *Šu-mu-li-ib-ši* DUMU *A-[ḫ]i-ša-gi-iš* [29] IGI *Ib-ni-*^{d}IŠKUR DUMU DINGIR-*šu-ba-ni* [30] IGI ^{d}X(U+MAŠ)-*li-ì-lí* DUMU *Ì-lí-ma-*DINGIR [31] IGI ^{d}ZA.BA$_4$.BA$_4$-*mu-ša-lim* DUMU *Ku-ub-bu-tum* [32] IGI *Šu-mu-li-ib-ši* DUMU *I-bi-*^{d}NIN.ŠUBUR [33] IGI *Ib-ni-*^{d}MARDUK DUB.SAR.

[L.E.34] ITU.ZÍZ.A U$_4$.2.KAM [35] [MU *Am*]-*mi-di-ta-na* LUGAL.E [36] ALAM.A.NI IGI.RÁ ERÍN KA.KÉŠ.DA.KE$_4$

[1] Aḫatani, the *šugītum*, is the daughter of Aḫi-ai-amši and Lamassani, the *nadītum* of Šamaš. [4] Rīš-Šamaš, son of Sîn-bēl-mātim, came to an agreement with Aḫi-ai-amši, her father and Lamassani, the *nadītum* of Šamaš, her mother, whereupon [7] they brought Aḫatani, the *šugītum*, into the house of Rīš-Šamaš, son of Sîn-bēl-mātim for [9] Bēlānum his son to marry her as wife. [12] One bed, two chairs, one storage jar and also Iluni, her brother as her son they gave her. [15] Five shekels of silver, the bridal gift for Aḫatani, from the hands of Rīš-Šamaš, son of Sîn-bēl-mātim, [17] Aḫi-ai-amši, son of Ili-išmeanni, and Lamassani, the *nadītum* of Šamaš, have received. [20] If in the future Bēlānum, son of Rīš-Šamaš, says to his wife Aḫatani "You are not my wife", he shall pay 1/3 mina of silver. [24] And if Aḫatani says to Bēlānum, her husband, "You are not my husband", [26] they will bind her and throw her into the water.

[27-33] six witnesses, the last one being the scribe.

[34-36] 2-XI-Ammiditana year 26.

This rather puzzling contract exhibits some uncommon features.

1. The parents of the girl to be married off, as we know from other records of their archive, certainly are brother and sister, children of Ilī-išmeanni. Lamassani must have adopted her niece, not uncommon among *nadītums*, perhaps after Aḫatani's own mother had died, unless the former was an adopted child of Aḫi-ai-amši. From texts belonging to the archive we know that her father must have been at least 60 years old when this contract was concluded, since he already figures in the division of the in-

heritance of his father (who must have died early) in the year Abiešuḫ 5.[4] Adoption by Lamassani has a parallel in a judicial record of the family archive, which shows that Lamassani had (also) adopted and raised (*rubbûm*) two sons of her younger sister, Šīmat-Ištar, born from extra-marital relations (*alikūtam illik*, "she had gone philandering"). The special relationship between daughter and parents is perhaps responsible for the syntax of the beginning of the contract, where lines 1-3, as my translation shows, figure as an independent non-verbal clause with declarative force, rather than as proleptic object of the main verb (*šūrubum*), which follows in line 1 l.

2. The wording of the contract is abnormal. It is neither a contract in which the act of the marrying off the bride is the main verb (*īḫussi*), nor one of those "expanded receipts for bridal gift and dowry" (*Greengus* 512a; cf. BE 6/1, 84; 101; CT 8, 2a; 47, 83; 48, 55). The latter start with an enumeration of the dowry, followed by the words "(all this) which her father (parents) gave her and (together with which) they brought her into the house (of the future groom or his father)". In our text the main verbal action is the bringing into the house of the father-in-law (*šūrubum*, line 11), while the marrying itself is mentioned only in the prepositional phrase as a goal (*ana aḫāzim*). After that the (extremely modest) dowry is listed, followed by the statement that the *terḫatum* has been (paid and) received. As to its structure, our contract most resembles CT 48, 50 (*Westbrook* I,1 60f.), where the dowry is listed after the mention of the act of the marriage[5] and the stipulation of the penalties for divorce. A unique feature is the inclusion of lines 4-6, mentioning a discussion or better an agreement between (*dabābum itti*) the father-in-law and the parents of the girl, for which I know no parallel.[6] It is unlikely that these words refer simply to the negotiations and arrangements which must have accompanied every marriage (asking permission of the parents, agreement on dowry, bridal gift and the contribution to the costs of the marriage ceremonies, *biblum*), which to some extent are reflected in the text of the written contracts (*riksātum*). Since lines 4-6 are linked to 9-11 by means of *-ma*, the contents or result must have been the *in domum deductio* in view of an intended marriage. It is possible that problems had arisen after an earlier marriage promise, for which we can only guess. On the basis of *Westbrook* II, 153ff., one might think of a betrothal turned into a formal inchoate marriage. It might even be a kind of *kallūtum* contract (though the term is not used), since it meets the conditions listed by *Westbrook* II, 77, and penalty clauses considering divorce (lines 20ff.) do occur in such a contract (see CT 8, 7b, *Westbrook* I, 129f., where the main verb is *ḫiārum*). In our text the future groom remains in the background and his father acts for him (cf. BE 6/1, 84:38f.; CT 47, 83:20'f.; CT 48, 55:11ff: *ana bīt A ēmiša ana B mārišu mutišaušēribū)*, which might indicate that immediate consummation of the marriage by the son was not intended.

3. Curious, finally, is the fact that the girl was given her brother as son (line 13). We might explain it from the family situation: a younger brother, whose mother was dead and whose father was of advanced age, was entrusted to his (older) sister as mother and guardian. The obvious link between sonship and inheritance rights might also be used as an explanation, even with an extremely modest dowry, since the girl probably was the prospective heir of her aunt, the *nadītum*. Finally the adoption could be taken to indicate that the girl herself was not expected to bear children, which in

4 *RlA* 2, 185, no. 188, Abiešuḫ, "e", with Goetze, *JCS* 5, 99 II (giš.aš.te bára.zag,etc.).

5 Read in line 5: *[i-ḫ]u-uz*$_x$, where *uz*$_x$ = AZ, also attested in YOS 8, 141:12: *i-na uz*$_x$*-ni-ša.*

6 Cf. perhaps TIM 4, 45:1ff.: *A u B ina migrātišunu mututtam u aššutta idbubū*, from a different period. Saporetti, The Status of Women in the Middle Assyrian Period (*Sources and Monographs. Monographs on the Ancient Near East*, 2/1, Malibu 1979), 14, believes the woman of this Middle Assyrian marriage contract to have been completely free, without family ties, presumably a widow.

turn might be one of the reasons why a special arrangement (lines 4-6) was necessary before the marriage was effectuated. We cannot choose.

The contract accordingly poses many questions for which we can only suggest hypothetical answers. This obtains also for what interests us here in particular, the question whether all the special features of this contract are somehow related to the fact that the girl was a *šugītum*. The only other contract where a *šugītum* is married off, PBS 8/2, 252 (*Westbrook* I, 220f.), does not exhibit any of these special features and provisions, while for the rest being fairly similar to our contract (the amount of the *terḫatum* and the penalty for the husband in case of divorce are identical to those in our contract, but we meet them in other contracts too). This makes it unlikely that the girl being a *šugītum* is the reason of the idiosyncrasy of our text, which must link up with the atypical structure of the family or particular events unknown to us.

[*Addendum*: See for the archive of the family to which this contract belongs my article Fatherhood is a Matter of Opinion, in: W. Sallaberger *e.a.* (eds*), Literatur, Politik und Recht in Mesopotamien. Festschrift für Claus Wilcke* (Wiesbaden 2003) 312-332 [= pp. 329-344 of this volume], especially 321-322, § 3.1. Archival and family background, with a list of the texts belonging to the archive.

B. BM 97057 (Sippar, 30-IV-Ad.37) (see the copy on pp. 366)

O.1 p*Ṣi-ḫa-a-li-*[*ša*?*-ra*]*-bi* [Š]U.GI 2 DUMU.MÍ *Bu-la-ṭa-tum* 3 p*Bu-la-ṭa-tum um-ma-ša* 4 pdENZU*-na-di-in-šu-mi* 5 p*I-din-Ištar* 6 *ù* SIG*-An-nu-ni-tum aḫ-ḫu-ša* DUMU.MEŠ DINGIR-*šu-ib-ni* 7 *a-na I-nu-úḫ-*É.SAG.ÍL [LUKUR dMARDUK] 8 *a-ḫa-ti-šu-nu* 9 *a-na it-ti-ša E-mu-u*[*q-ì-lí-ši-it-mar*] 10 *a-ḫa-zi-im id-d*[*i-nu(-ši)*] 11 5 GÍN KÙ.BABBAR *ter-ḫa-*[*as-sà*] 12 *i-na qá-ti E-mu-u*[*q-ì-lí-ši-it-mar*] 13 *ù I-nu-úḫ-*É.[SAG.ÍL] 14 LUKUR dMARDUK *a-ḫa-*[*ti-šu-nu*] 15 p*Bu-la-ṭa-tum um-*[*ma-ša*] 16 pdEN.ZU*-na-di-in-šu-m*[i] 17 p*I-din-Išt*[*ar*] E.18 *ù* SIG*-An-nu-ni-*[*tum*] 19 *aḫ-ḫu-ši-na* 20 DUMU.MEŠ DINGIR-*šu-i*[*b-ni*] R.21 *ma-aḫ-r*[u] 22 *e-zi-ib I-nu-ú*[*ḫ*-É.SAG.ÍL] 23 LUKUR dMARDUK DUMU.MÍ D[INGIR*-šu-ib-ni*] 24 *Ṣi-*[*ḫa-a-li*]*-*[*ša*?*-ra-bi*] 25 *i-iz-z*[*i-ib*] 26 *a-ḫi-iz I-nu-úḫ-*É.[SAG.ÍL] 27 p*Ṣi-ḫa-a-li-š*[*a*?*-ra-bi*] 28 *i-iḫ-ḫa-az* 29 MU dUTU dMARDUK *ù Am-*[*mi-di-ta-na* LUGAL] 30 IN.PÀD.DÈ.MEŠ

---

31 IGI *I-ku-un-*KA-dEN.ZU DUMU [ ] 32 IGI *Be-el-šu-nu* DUMU DINGIR-*šu-ba-ni* 33 IGI ÌR-d*I-ba-ri* DUMU SIG-*An-nu-ni-tum* 34 IGI d*Na-bi-um-mu-ša-lim* DUB.SAR

E.35 ITU ŠU.NUMUN.A U_4 30 KAM 36 MU *Am-mi-di-ta-na* LUGAL.E BÁD.DA UDINIM.KI.A 37 *Da-mi-iq-ì-lí-šu-*K[E_4]

1 Ṣīḫa-ālišа-rabi, *šugītum*, daughter of Bulaṭātum – 3 Bulaṭātum her mother, Sîn-nādin-šumi, Iddin-Ištar and Ipiq-Annunītum her brothers, children of Ilšu-ibni, have given (her) 8 to Inūḫ-Esagil, the *nadītum* of Marduk, their sister, 9 in order to be married together with her to Emū[q-ili-šitmar]. Five shekels of silver, the bridal gift for her, from the hands of Emū[q-ili-šitmar] and Inūḫ-E[sagil], the *nadītum* of Marduk, their sister, 15 Bulaṭātum, her mother, Sîn-nādin-šumi, Iddin-Ištar and Ipiq-Annunītum, their (fem.) brothers, children of Ilšu-ibni, have received. 22 Who divorces Inūḫ-Esagil, the *nadītum* of Marduk, daughter of Ilšu-ibni, divorces Ṣīḫa-āli[ša-rabi], 26 who marries Inūḫ-E[sagil], marries Ṣīḫa-āli[ša-rabi].
29 They have sworn the oath by Šamaš, Marduk and [king] Am[miditana].

---

31 In the presence of Ikūn-pī-Sîn, son of [ ], of Bēlšunu, son of Ilšu-bāni, of Warad-dIbāri, son of Ipiq-Annunītum, of Nabium-mušallim, the scribe.

---

35 30-IV-Ammiditana year 37.

Seals, captions and inscriptions[7]

1. KIŠIB [*Bu-la*?]-[*ṭa-tum]*
2. ᵈEN.ZU-*na-di-i[n-šu-mi]*, DUMU DINGIR-*šu-ib-n[i]*, ÌR ᵈx
3. KIŠIB *I-din-Ištar*
4. KIŠIB SIG-*An-nu-ni-tum*
5. KI[ŠIB *I-ku-un*-KA-ᵈEN.ZU](?)
6. KIŠIB ÌR-ᵈ*I-ba-ri*
7. KIŠIB *Be-el-šu-nu*
8. ᵈMAR.DÚ, DUMU AN.NA, KUR SIKIL.LA TUŠ.A

C. **BM 97025** (Sippar, x – y – Aṣ. 1) (see the copy on pp. 367)

O.1 ᵖI-*nu-úḫ*-É.SAG.ÍL 2 LUKUR ᵈMARDUK 3 DUMU.MÍ DINGIR-*šu-ib-ni* 4 DAM *E-mu-uq-ì-lí-ši-it-mar* 5 DUMU *Bur*-ᵈIŠKUR! 6 ᵖ*An-na-bu* ᵐⁱŠU.[GI?]-*t[um?]* 7 DUMU.MÍ *Sa-bi-tum* 8 DUMU.MÍ DINGIR-*šu-ib-ni* 9 *a-na it-ti-ša a-ḫa-zi-i[m]* 10 *a-na E-mu-uq-ì-lí-ši-it-m[ar]* 11 DUMU *Bur*-ᵈIŠKUR 12 *mu-ti-ša* E.13 *il-qé-e-ši* 14 5 GÍN KÙ.BABBAR *ter-ḫa-as-sà* 15 ᵖ*Sa-bi-tum um-ma-ša* R.16 DUMU.MÍ DINGIR-*šu-[ib]-ni* DI.KUD 17 *i-[na qá-ti I-n]*[*u-úḫ*]-É.SAG.ÍL LUKUR ᵈMARDUK 18 *ù [E-mu-uq-ì-lí-ši-it-m]ar* 19 *m[a-aḫ-ra-at]* 20 M[U] 21 I[N.PÀD.DÈ.MEŠ]

---

22 IGI ᵈE[N.ZU-] 23 IGI x [ ] 24 [I]G[I] 25 [I]GI x[ ] 26 IGI [ ]

---

27 ITI [ ] E.28 MU *Am-mi-ṣa-du-q[á* LUGAL.E] 29 ᵈUTU.GIM.KALAM.MA.NI. ŠÈ 30 ZI.DÉ.EŠ ÍB.TA.È.[A]

1 Inūḫ-Esagil, *nadītum* of Marduk, daughter of Ilšu-ibni, wife of Emūq-ili-šitmar, son of Būr-Adad, acquired 6 Annabu, the *šugītum*(?), daughter of Sabitum, daughter of Ilšu-ibni, 10 for Emūq-ili-šitmar, son of Būr-Adad, her husband, 9 in order to be married together with her. 14 Five shekels of silver, the bridal gift for her, Sabitum her mother, daugher of Ilšu-ibni, the judge, 17 from the hands of Inūḫ-Esagil, the *nadītum* of Marduk, 18 a[nd Emuq-ili-šitmar] 19 [has] rec[eived].
20-21 [They] have [sworn the] oa[th by]

22-26 In the presence of S[în-], of [ ], of [ ], of [ ], and of [ ].

---

27 Month [, day], 28-30 Ammiṣaduqa year 1

Seals, inscriptions, captions

1. KIŠIB *I-nu-ú[ḫ* – É.SAG.ÍL]
2. ᵈENZU-*i-din-n[am]*, DUMU *Nu-úr*-ᵈ[ ], ÌR *ša* DINGIR x (six-leafed rosette)
3. KIŠIB DINGIR-*Šu-ib-ni*
4. ᵈUTU-*b[a-ni]*? / DUMU *A-wi-il-* [ ] / ÌR ᵈNIN-x [ ]
5. Left half lower edge, impression rolled over the text
6. Right half lower edge, impression rolled over the text

7 Texts B and C are so-called "Quasihüllentafeln" as defined by C. Wilcke, *Zikir šumim* (Festschrift fur F.R. Kraus, Leiden 1982), 450ff., Exkurs B. I owe a debt of gratitude to Dominique Colon for helping me with the identification and demarcation (indicated by dotted lines in the copies) of the many, partial seal impressions. In the damaged text C they are also rolled over the cuneiform inscription which makes identification of them difficult. In B, seal 5 is a problem, since it must have been identified by the damaged caption at the top of the reverse of the tablet. But the impression below it is no. 6, which seems to be identified by a separate caption.

S 1-5. Impressions of seals rolled over the text, difficult to identify or damaged, not necessarily all different from each other and from nos. 1-6. S 1 is not identical to 1, as might be expected.

Notes on the texts

B. 1. The reading of the damaged name is not quite certain. It would mean "Great is the smiling upon her (scil. the goddess's) city", comparable to Taṣāḫ-ana-ālīša (name of a secondary wife in CT 4, 39a:1; note also Ṣīḫtī-līmur, the name of a *šugītum* in PBS 8 / 2, 252:9).
19. *aḫḫīšina* instead of expected *aḫḫīša*, referring either to the mother of the girl and the main wife, or to the girl and her aunt.

Seals. The seals on the obverse are those of the parties to the contract, beginning with the mother of the bride, who acknowledges the receipt of the bridal gift. Those on the reverse and lower edge are those of the witnesses, the last one, no. 8, belonging to the scribe. See for parallels to its inscription J.-R. Kupper, *L'Iconographie du dieu Amurru* (Bruxelles 1961), 65 note 5 (there is room on the seal to restore the missing [a]), D. Collon, *Catalogue of Western Asiatic Seals in the British Museum. Cylinder Seals* III (London 1968), no. 226, and B. Buchanan, *Catalogue of Ancient Near Eastern Seals in the Ashmolean Museum* (Oxford 1966), no. 528 (read the last two signs tuš$^{!}$.a$^{!}$).

C 6. The qualification of the bride is damaged, ŠU is clear, GI (or GI_4) is possible, and the final sign is doubtful (it resembles NA). In view of the parallel in A and in the absence of a better alternative, I have restored *šugītum*.

Seal no. 2. The last line of the inscription is exceptional. ÌR *ša* is uncommon and the god seems to be designated by a symbol, a six-leafed rosette.

In Texts B and C we meet the same married couple, Emūq-ili-šitmar, son of Būr-Adad, and his wife Inūḫ-Esagil, daughter of Ilšu-ibni, a *nadītum* of Marduk. The latter's family can be mapped as follows:

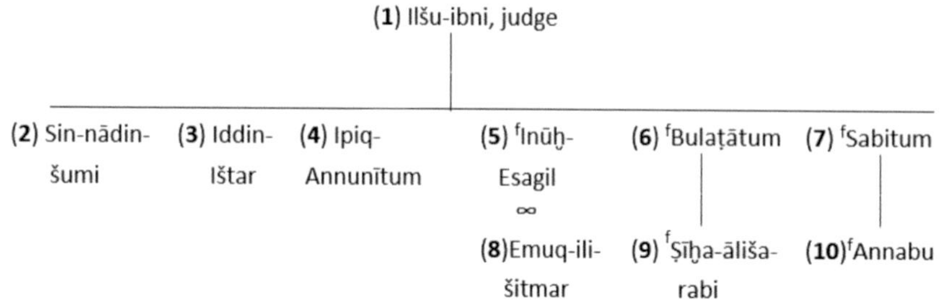

In text B, from 30-IV-Ad year 37, **(2)**, **(3)**, **(4)**, and her mother **(6)** "give" (*nadānum*) the girl **(9)**, a *šugītum*, to her aunt **(5)**, a *nadītum* of Marduk, "in order to be married together with her" (*ittiša*) to her husband **(8)**. In text C, from Aṣ year 1 (month and day broken), the same lady **(5)** "acquires" (*leqûm*) the girl **(10)**, her niece, probably also a *šugītum*, from the latter's mother, her sister **(7)**, for exactly the same purpose. Lady **(5)** hence provides herself and her husband, twice within at most 21 months,[8] with a secondary wife, a *šugītum*, to all appearances – in view of what we know from Codex Ḫammurabi § 145 and some *nadītum*-marriage contracts – in order to have children by her, since she herself was not permitted to bear them.

8 See F.R. Kraus, *SD* 11 (1984), 170, § 4, and for the year-name 198f.

Such and similar polygamous marriages could be contracted in two ways (*Westbrook* II, 315ff.). The husband could marry both wives simultaneously or the one (the secondary wife) after the other. The latter way seems the natural one when a normal marriage after some time proved to remain childless. The former recommended itself when it was clear from the outset that the wife had to remain childless since she was a *nadītum*. Both procedures indeed are known from marriage contracts, but the distinction is not as easy as that. We have contracts of simultaneous polygamous marriages without any indication that this was due to the wife's particular status, *e.g.* TIM 4, 49. In this and other cases where both wives are sisters, *Westbrook* II, 316 sees "an archetypal occasion for polygamy: the disposal of two daughters to the same son-in-law". In some of these cases, however, involving both *nadītum*s and wives without special status, sisterhood was artificial, through adoption of the secondary wife by the main wife, as sister (BIN 7, 173; TIM 5, 1; UET 5, 87) or as daughter (CT 48, 57).[9] This was also true in "the case of three Babylonian marriage contracts" (TCL 1, 6l; CT 2, 44; BAP 89) analysed by *Harris*, where it is only thanks to the last text that we know that the sister was an adoptee. We may suspect something similar in other cases, *e.g.* TIM 4, 46, where the singular DUMU.MÍ.A.NI, "his daughter", in line 2' is revealing, and in the unpublished contract BM 97159,[10] where *abiša*, "her father" (instead of "their father"), is noteworthy, also in the light of the apparently deliberate singular DUMU.MÍ in CT 2, 44:3.[11]

The case of the three related contracts, just mentioned, warns us against simple conclusions from single existing contracts. On the basis of BAP 89 alone we would have assumed a case of simultaneous adoption and marriage, on the basis of CT 2, 44 alone one of simultaneous marriage without adoption, and on the basis of TCL 1, 61 alone a simple marriage of the *nadītum* only. But in fact, as pointed out by *Harris*, the texts reflect three subsequent stages which, unfortunately (only the last text has a year-name) cannot be dated exactly. Between CT 2, 44 and BAP 89 a few years may have elapsed, since

---

9 For the contract CT 48, 57, see *Westbrook* I, 178f., and *Wilcke* 2, 261 note 268.

10 BM 97159 reads: [0.1] ^{p}*In-ba-tum ù Ri-ba-tum* [2] KI ^{d}EN.ZU-*ga-mil a-bi-ša* (sic) [3] ^{p}*Sa-mi-ia* DUMU *Ma-x* [4]*a-na aš-šu-tim ù mu-[t]u-tim* [5] *i-ḫu-uz* [6] 10 GÍN KÙ.BABBAR *te-er-ḫa-sí-na* [7] ^{p}*Sa-mi-ia a-na 30-ga-mil* [8] IN.NA.AN.LÁ [9] *u*$_4$*-um In-ba-tum ù Ri-ba-tu[m]* [10] *a-na Sa-mi-ia mu-[ti]-ši-na* [11] *ú-ul mu-ut-ni [at-ta]* [12] *iq-ta-[bi-a a-na me-e / iš-tu* AN.ZA.KÀR*]* [E.13] *[i]-na-ad-d[u]-ni-[ši-na-ti]* [14] *u*$_4$*-um Sa-mi-ia* [R.15] *[a-n]a In-ba-tum ù [Ri-ba-tum]* [16] *aš-ša-ti-i-šu ú-ul [aš-ša-tu-a at-ti-na]* [17] *i-qá-bi-ma* 1/3 *ma-na* KÙ.BAB[BAR Ì.LÁ.E] [18] ^{p}*Ri-ba-tum ze-ne In-[ba-tum]* [19] *i-ze-ne sa-la-mi-ša i-[sa-lim]* [20] ^{pd}UTU.TAB.BA-*we-di-im* [21] DUMU *Sa-mi-ia ù In-ba-tum* / MU ^{d}MARDUK (added between the lines) [22] *ù 30-mu-ba-lí-iṭ* (erasure of one line), followed by 9 witnesses and a broken year name MU BÁD I$_7$ x [...].
The restoration of the end of line 12 is uncertain, as *Wilcke* 2, 289, note 110 shows; in the unpublished marriage contract BM 97156:11, *ištu dimtim nadûm* is still attested during Ḫa year 12. [See the Addendum at the end of this article]. Lines 20f. state that Šamaš-tappa-wēdim is the son of Samia and his main wife, Inbatum. They might be taken to affirm the status and (hereditary) rights of the natural son of the main wife on the occasion of his father's marriage with a secondary wife, which meant the possibility of more sons. This would imply that the husband took a secondary wife notwithstanding the fact that his first wife had born him a son. This is not impossible, of course, but suggests an alternative interpretation, which I prefer. The son in question actually was a son raised by Samia with Ribatum, when she was his concubine, not formally married to him. After his birth he officially married her as secondary wife. The contract records this marriage, but not with her alone. Due to the specific relation between both wives it is at the same time a (partial) novation of the original, earlier, marriage contract with Inbatum. And it also serves to legitimate the son born by Ribatum, who now becomes legally the son of the main wife (in fact the goal of such a polygamous marriage). This means that also BM 97159 cannot serve as proof that both wives actually were married simultaneously

11 Speleers, *Recueil* no. 230, need not be considered here. Against the editor, Koschaker *JCS* 5 (1951) 114 note 28, and *Westbrook* I, 234f., the contract is not one of a polygamous marriage. On the basis of a collation one has to read: [0.1] ^{p}*A-bi-ku-ur-ra* [2] DUMU.MÍ *La-ma-sí* [3] K[I] *L[a-ma]-sí um-mi-ša* [4] DUMU.MÍ *Šar-rum-*^{d}IŠKUR [5] ^{pd}UTU-*re-ṣú-šu* [6] *a-n[a] aš-šu-tim ù m[u-t]u-tim* [7] *i-ḫu-sí te[r-ḫa-as-sà]* [8] *i-na* MU 1 KAM [ ] [9] [ ] x ÁŠ x [ ] [10] *[a-na La]-ma-s[í]* [11] [ ] x (remainder obv. broken). If my reading of line 7 proves to be correct, the *terḫatum* would consist of annual provisions to the mother, presumably a *nadītum* of Šamaš (in view of her name and the first two witnesses, Sîn-Bāni and Nannatum!, both "overseers of the *nadītums* of Šamaš"). Line 9 could mention the quantity, in *sūtums*.

the secondary wife now has children (unless she already had children from her future husband at the time of her marriage in CT 2, 44, which were legitimated when she herself was formally adopted as sister of the first wife and a blood relationship was created).

The texts also indicate that a double marriage right from the beginning was not obligatory for *nadītums*. It may have happened, of course, and TIM 4, 47 may be an example (note DUMU.MÍ.MEŠ in line 3). Moreover, CT 8, 2a indicates that at an early stage all necessary arrangements already had been made. The text records that the dowry of a young girl, designated as a *nadītum* of Marduk, was assigned to her at the time she was dedicated in the temple, some (considerable?) time before she was actually married off. Already then it included her sister, a *šugītum*, to all appearances in order to provide her with children. Perhaps the possibility of choosing between various methods of acquiring children (Codex Ḫammurabi § 144: by means of a slave-girl or by marrying a *šugītum*) allowed for some respite, which is also implied in Codex Ḫammurabi § 145, where the husband in due time is entitled to take the initiative, if the *nadītum* has failed to take the necessary measures. Several contracts (BIN 7, 173; CT 48, 48; CT 48, 57; TIM 5, 1; UET 5, 87), none of which seems to concern a *nadītum*, show us that the main and first wife was already married to her husband when she arranged the second marriage, acquired the secondary wife and gave her to her husband,[12] and this happened also with *nadītums*. In our texts B and C, Inūḫ-Esagil was already married when she provided her husband with a secondary wife. The *nadītum* of Marduk, married off in CT 47, 83 and the *entum* of CT 48, 55 in due time must have taken similar measures.

The purpose of the polygamous marriage in many cases, as mentioned, must have been to provide the couple with children. In general, marriage contracts from various periods (also from Nuzi and Alalach) stipulate that childlessness of the first wife is the necessary condition for permission to take a second wife. But it was a rather complicated and risky solution, compared with that of acquiring children by adoption or by legitimating those born by a slave-girl or a concubine. The relation between both wives was delicate, since the secondary wife, in general younger and the mother of the children, could easily become the favorite of the husband, as stipulations in laws and even an omen show.[13] The secondary wife is occasionally designated as *ṣerretum*, "rival", and it does not surprise that the plan to take a second wife once was subjected to an oracular inquiry (*tamītum*).[14]

This solution was nevertheless preferred in several cases, because, paradoxically, it granted the first wife a more important role. The children of the secondary wife, as mentioned explicitly in some contracts (CT 48, 47:13f.; VAS 8, 15 / 16:9f.), were to be considered her children. This was possible on a legal basis. By acquiring (buying, adopting or paying her *terḫatum*) the secondary wife and subsequently presenting her to her husband, the first wife became the co-owner (together with her husband) of the children born. Hence the emphasis in several contracts from the Old Babylonian (mentioned above) and from other periods[15] on the fact that it was the first wife who acted, which is also assumed in Codex Ḫammurabi § 144f. This is also true in our texts B and C, though

---

12 In CT 48, 67, the brother of a *nadītum* provides her with a secondary wife, adopted as sister. In CT 8, 22b, husband and wife (not a *nadītum*) together buy a slave-girl to serve as secondary wife.

13 Codex Ḫammurabi § 146. See for Laws of Šulgi § 25, Römer, *TUAT* I/1, 22 and the interpretation proposed by A. Falkenstein with C. Wilcke, *Das Lugalbandaepos*, 182 on line 179. [**Add.**: The meaning of this paragraph is different, see now M. Civil, The Law Collection of Ur-Namma, in: A. George (ed.) *Cuneiform Royal Inscriptions and Related Texts in the SchØyen Collection* (*CUSAS* 17, Bethesda 2011), 248, § 30, who translates: "If a slave girl insults someone who is acting as (or: on behalf of) her mistress ..."]. The omen is CT 20, 39:10: *amtum bēlša irāmšīma mala bēltiša imaṣṣi.*

14 ABRT I no. 4, I: 12ff.: [*PN šá* M]Í *annannītu aššassu ašibti ṣillišu ištu umē [ma']dūtu ... sinnišāti ittanalladūma ... zikāru ja'numa ...* (II, 3) *tāmīt aššata šanītamma* [ ].

15 Old Assyrian, ICK 1, 3:7ff.: "If within two years she has not provided him with offspring, she herself (*šītma*) will buy a slave-girl...". Neo-Assyrian, J.N. Postgate, *Fifty Neo-Assyrian Legal Documents* (Warminster 1976) no.14:41ff.: "If Ṣ. does not get pregnant and does not bear a child, she will take a slave-girl and put her in her place, instead of herself, and (so) provide sons...".

with some variation. In text C it is Inūḫ-Esagil who "acquires" the girl, and in B the girl is given to her in the first place.

By adopting the secondary wife as sister or (more rarely) daughter, a relation of kinship was created which went beyond ownership and constituted the nearest approach to real motherhood. From stories in the book of Genesis we know that by having the secondary wife give birth "on the knees" of the first wife, the latter's motherhood and acceptance of the new-born as her child could be visualized.[16]

The same goal could be reached by taking as secondary wife a natural sister of the first wife, as was the case in some marriage contracts mentioned above. Or one could choose a close female relative of the first wife, as happened in texts B and C, where the girl to be married in both cases was a daughter of a sister of the main wife. Since kinship could be created by legal measures, we may ask the question whether the sisters in our texts were in fact natural sisters and their children natural children. The first question is justified, because the mother of the bride in C is not mentioned among the brothers and sisters of the main wife in text B. The second is based on the fact that the fathers of the girls to be married off are conspicuously absent in both contracts. The absence of Sabītum in text B, however, can be explained from the fact that her agreement with the marriage was not required (so that she does not appear among those receiving the *terḫatum*). The absence of the fathers is more serious, and it is possible that the girls, unless they had been adopted by their (unmarried) mothers, were orphans. This could explain why in text B the three brothers (2) – (4) join the mother, their sister, in marrying off the girl. They may have replaced the missing father as legal guardians. But in text C no such arrangement is evident. The tablet seems to bear seven seal impressions, probably those of the mother of the bride, who acknowledges the receipt of the *terḫatum*, of Inūḫ-Esagil who acknowledges the "receipt" of the girl, and of the five witnesses. Among the latter, broken in the text but identified from the caption to his seal impression, figures Ilšu-ibni, most probably identical to the father of both Inūḫ-Esagil and Sabītum. His presence at the transaction perhaps balances the absence of the uncles of text B. But, though *pater familias*, he is not the legal actor or guardian of the bride or her mother. She later herself receives the *terḫatum*. All these facts, which I cannot explain, point to complicated natural and legal relations, which are only superficially reflected in our contracts which deal with different matters.

The difference between texts B and C is indeed remarkable. The much shorter text C uses *leqûm* where B has *nadānum ana*. Alongside *ana marūtim* (CT 48, 57:5), *ana atḫūtim* (BIN 7, 173:7, in Sumerian, UET 5, 87:5), *ana marūtim u kallūtim* (CT 47, 40:8ff.), and *ana kallat leqûm* (*Waterman* 72:5), we also have simple *leqûm*, *e.g.* in CT 48, 48:5.[17] I would rather consider it the non-specific counterpart of *nadānum* (just like *ša'āmum* and *ana šīmim nadānum* both occur in deeds of purchase, phrased *ex latere emptoris* or *venditoris*) than take it as "to adopt". *Leqûm* is neither "to adopt" nor "to buy" (*ša'āmum*, used in CT 8, 22b:4), but simply "to acquire", specified by "for marriage" (*ana aḫāzim*). This neutral term is required, because the person acting is a woman who cannot be the subject of *aḫāzum*. We do not know how exactly the relation between the main wife and the secondary wife was, in particular since the latter belonged to a younger generation.

Text B:22-26 contains the "clause of solidarity" which C lacks. It is attested several times (BIN 7, 173:14ff.; TIM 4, 49:6f., with wrong plural suffixes; UET 5, 87:11f.) and defines the two women as inseparable. In concrete it prevents the husband from divorcing the older, childless *nadītum*, while staying married to the younger mother of his children. If

16 Genesis 30:3. By having her slave-girl bear children on her knees the main wife is "built out of her". M. Stol, *Zwangerschap en Geboorte bij de Babyloniërs en in de Bijbel* (Leiden 1983), 94 with note 587, points to a possible Babylonian parallel, an Old Babylonian contract from Nippur (3 NT 225) which mentions that a father "pushed off his knees" (*ina birkēšu iddû*) a small child, the son of his daughter.

17 A doubtful case is TIM 4, 49:6, where *Westbrook* I, 251, restores [*il*?-*q*]*é*?. Note also *leqûm* together with *rubbûm* in VAS 18, 114:3.

the husband wishes to divorce his first wife, she is entitled, as BIN 7, 173:16ff. and TIM 4, 47:16ff. specify, to leave after having taken the hand of her "sister". Both "enter and leave" together, as another version of the solidarity clause puts it (*erēbiša irrub waṣēša uṣṣi*, CT 4, 39a:16f. and CT 48, 67:6f.). These two versions of the solidarity clause refer to acts only. A third version, more frequent (BAP 89:7f.; CT 2, 44:21ff.; 48:9ff.; 57:16; 67:8f.; TIM 4, 47:11f., and BM 97159:18f. quoted in note 10), includes relations and feelings (*zenûm* and *salāmum*). The use of the first version in text B is understandable, since marriage was the purpose of the transaction. Since neither text is a marriage contract with the (future) husband himself, the omission of the third version is understandable. Text C actually is little more than a record in which the mother and the future mistress and co-wife of the bride *in spe* acknowledge the mutual receipt of a sum of money (*terḫatum*) and a girl, for the purpose of marriage. Further clauses could be inserted in the contract whereby Inūḫ-Esagil actually had her husband marry the girl "together with her". Such a contract could have resembled a text like CT 2, 44 and have contained a clause bearing on divorce and stipulating the relation between both women, which in the case of *nadītums* usually includes a clause obliging the secondary wife to serve the main wife by carrying her chair to the temple and washing her feet.

Our texts shed additional light upon the ways in which *nadītums* provided their husbands with secondary wives in order to obtain offspring. They show a marked, repeated preference for female relatives that, moreover, are designated as *šugītums*. They do not help us, unfortunately, in understanding what *šugītum* means, unless it is not by coincidence that this designation is used of nieces of *nadītums* meant to provide them with children. The etymology of the word, recently discussed by *Wilcke* 1, 175, remains a problem. Neither his nor Jacobsen's recent explanation ("old man's darling") have convinced me.[18] Another question which cannot be answered is why the same *nadītum* had to "acquire" a *šugītum* as co-wife twice within a relatively short period. Where text C gives no explanation (unless its completely different structure is no accident), we can only speculate about problems in the family or some kind of tragedy (the risks of childbirth?) better done in a novel than in an article on an aspect of Old Babylonian social history.

Addenda:

The OB marriage contract BM 97156, mentioned above in note 10, reads:

$^{\text{obv. 1}}$ $^{\text{[p]}}$*Be-el-ta-ni* ^{2} KI *Be-el-šu-nu a-bi-ša* ^{3} ^{pd}MAR.TU-*ba-ni* ^{4} DUMU ^{d}UTU-DI.KUD ^{5} *a-na aš-šu-tim i-ḫu-us-sí* ^{6} *10* GÍN KÙ.BABBAR *te-er-ḫa-sà* ^{7} *ma-ḫi-ir li-ib-bi a-bi-ša* DÙG-*ab* ^{8} *u$_4$-um Be-el-ta-ni* ^{9} *a-na* ^{d}MAR.TU-*ba-ni mu-ti-ša* ^{10} *ú-ul mu-ti iq-ta-bu-ú* ^{11} *iš-tu* AN.ZA.KÀR *i-na-ad-du-ni-ši* $^{\text{le.e.12}}$ *u$_4$-um* ^{d}MAR.TU-*ba-ni* ^{13} *a-na Be-el-ta-ni aš-ša-ti-/šu* $^{\text{rev.14}}$ *ú-ul aš-ša-ti* ^{15} *iq-ta-bu-ú 16⅓ ma-na* KÙ.BABBAR Ì.LÁ.E ^{17} MU ^{d}UTU ^{d}*A-a* ^{d}*Marduk 18 ù Ḫa-am-mu-ra-bi* ^{19} *it-mu-ú*. There follow nine witnesses; on the left edge: [I]TU EZEN-^{d}IŠKUR MU GU.ZA ^{d}*Ṣar-pa-ni-tum* (=Hammurabi year 12).

See for *šugītum* now also Stol 2012, 112-115. He suggests that *šugītum* means "the old one" (Sumerian šu.gi$_4$.a = Akkadian *šībtu*), taking it as a 'taboo word', meant to deceive demons and to keep them away from the young mother and her child, while in actual fact the *šugītum* is the opposite, the young woman who gets a baby. *Šugītum* is also treated in Barberon 2012, 81f., 'Le titre particulier de *šugîtum*', with a chronological list of their occurrences. The book contains many comments on the texts edited in my article and it includes OLA 21 (1986) 73 (time of Ammi-ṣaduqa), where she finds in l. 6' the girl Ahassunu

18 Th. Jacobsen in J.H. Marks and R.M. Good (eds.), *Love and Death in the Ancient Near East* (Guilford 1987), 57 note 2. There is no evidence that *šugītums* were married to old men, as Abisag was to David. The identification of the *šugītum* as a kind of concubine is based on the equation with lukur.kaskala, also discussed by *Wilcke* 1, 175, but the equation goes back to the sign list Ea and not to the OB Proto-Lu. How reliable are such later equations, if one notes that Ea also equates our word with simple lukur?

šu[!]*-g[i-tum]*, listed as last item of the dowry given along with a girl married off. The broken line 7', not treated by Barberon, presumably has to be read *ittiša na-a[d-na-at]*, "she is given along with her", comparable to text B, above, where the *šugītum* is "given to the *nadītu* ... in order to marry together with her E. (her husband)".

CAD Š/III, 200 s.v. lists the lexical equivalents and synonyms of *šugītum* (also referring to *šugû*, "old man") and registers two occurrences in texts from Mari. In the letter ARM 10, 124:4-18, king Zimrilim writes to his queen Šibtu about "the girl, a daughter of Ibal-Addu, the *šugītum*', who is the subject of rumors. The queen has to find out whether there are complaints about her (*nuzzumat*) or not, which has consequences for where she must live. In letter 123:27-29 he writes that Šibtu has to "keep her there (in Mari?) and must not send her". One of the lists from Mari, ARM 22, 16, registers ten women summarized as (l. 11) *10* SAL[?].PA *ša bēt šu-gi-tim*, followed by 10 women who are female court sweepers (*kisalluḫātum*; from ARM 13, 17:19 we know a *bīt kisalluḫātim*).

Bibliography

[L. Barberon, *Les religieuses et le culte de Marduk dans le royaume de Babylone* (Archibab 1, Mémoires de NABU 14; Paris 2012)]

Greengus: S. Greengus, The Old Babylonian Marriage Contract, *JAOS* 89 (1969) 505-532.

Harris: R. Harris, The Case of Three Babylonian Marriage Contracts, *JNES* 33 (1974) 363-369.

Renger: J. Renger, Untersuchungen zum Priestertum in der altbabylonischen Zeit, *ZA* 58 (1968) 110-188; 59 (1969),103-230.

[M. Stol, *Vrouwen van Babylon. Prinsessen, Priesteressen, Prostituees in de Bakermat van de Cultuur* (Utrecht 2012)].

Westbrook: R. Westbrook, *Old Babylonian Marriage Law*, I-II. Dissertation Yale University 1982. University Microfilms 8221763 [since published as *Old Babylonian Marriage Law*, AfO Beiheft 23 (Horn 1988), which, however, does not contain the transliterations of the Akkadian texts of the documents presented in its Appendix].

Wilcke 1: C. Wilcke, CT 45, 119: Ein Fall legaler Bigamie mit *nadītum* und *šugītum*, *ZA* 74 (1984) 170-180.

Wilcke 2: C. Wilcke, Familiengründung im alten Babylonien, in: E.W. Müller (ed.), *Geschlechtsreife und Legitimation zur Zeugung* (Freiburg/München, 1984) 213-317.

TEXT B

BM 97057

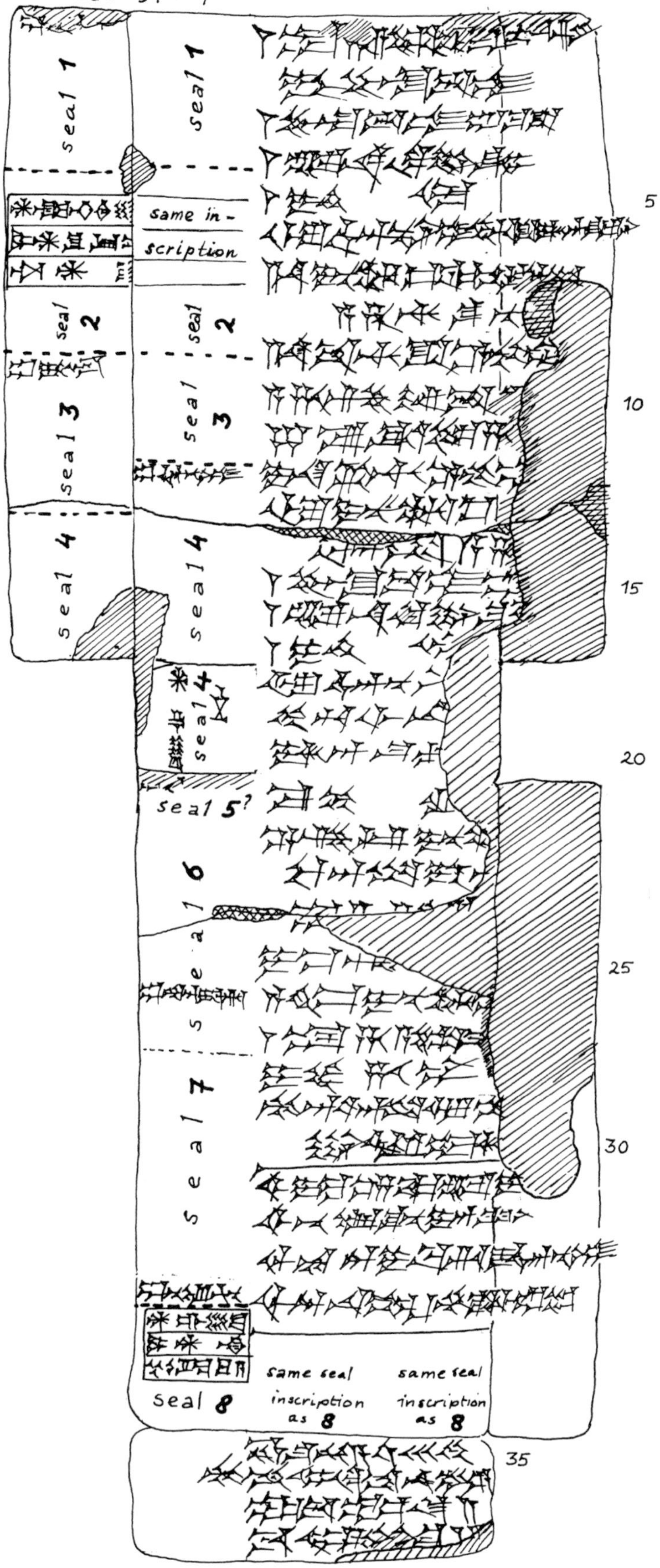

TEXT C

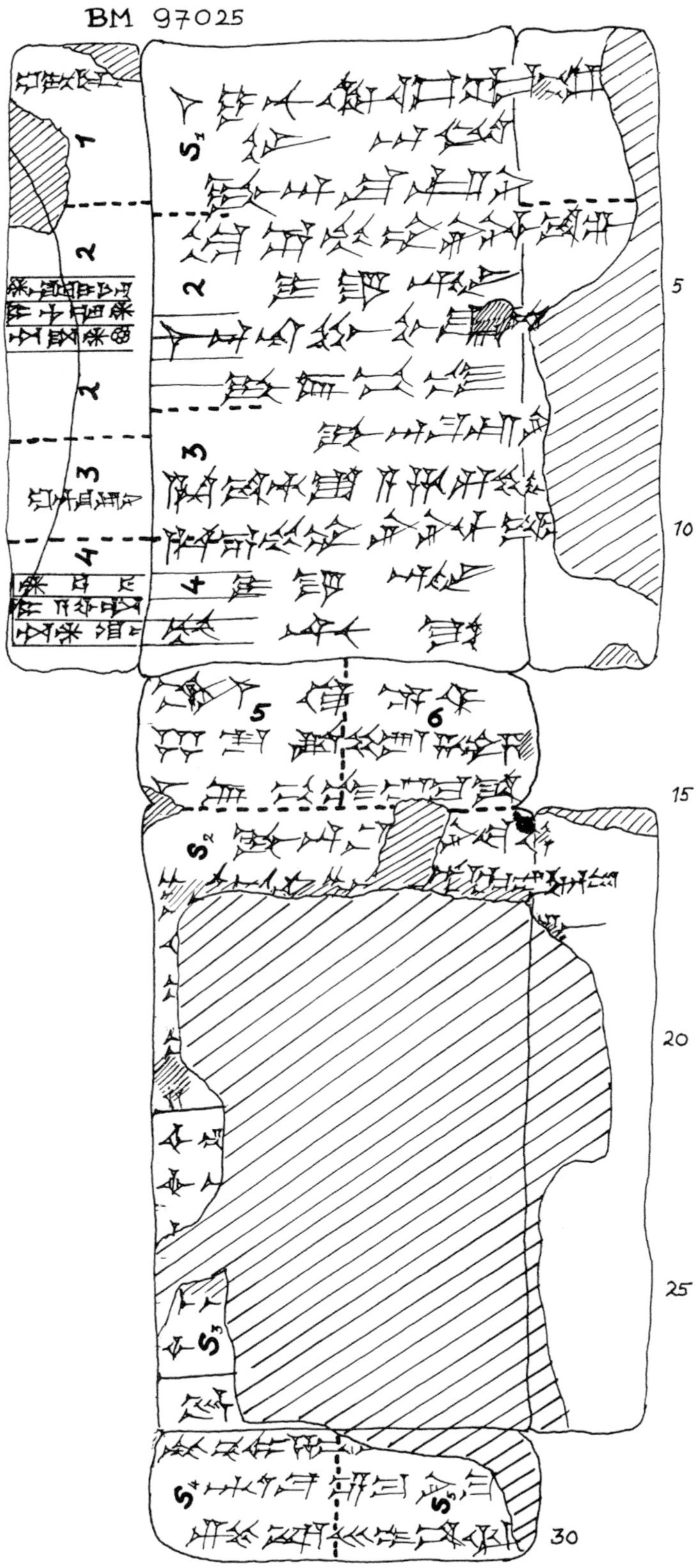

Trade with the Blessing of Shamash in Old Babylonian Sippar*

Temples in ancient Mesopotamia, which functioned as households of the gods, could not ignore trade. They needed products, materials and finished goods for the running of the institution they were, for the rites and ceremonies centering on the god, the master of the household, and for the needs of his servants, the personnel of the temple, who lived from its property and income. Much of what a temple household needed was produced by itself, by personnel working in agriculture, husbandry and in various workshops. It could also generate income by renting its fields, by using its funds for interest bearing loans (usually in barley or silver) or investment in business, and by charging payments for the specific services it could offer. In addition, temples received donations and votive gifts, not only from the rulers, who considered the care of the god and his house their duty, but also by a variety of individuals. Some needs, however, had to be met by acquiring materials and goods from outside. This could be done by exchange, either directly, using the temple's mainly agricultural surpluses and craft production, or indirectly, when part of these surpluses was converted into silver by merchants contracted for that purpose. The latter could supply the temple with the silver earned, which it then could use as it saw fit, or be commissioned to use it for acquiring materials and products the temple needed.

1. Commercial activities of temples

The evidence from Sippar on the commercial activities of the temple of Šamaš during the late OB period (mainly the reign of Ammiditana) was analyzed long ago by Charpin. He noted that in late OB times the temple sold mainly wool and oxen (and no longer in barley and sesame) and that the system, as documented in the few surviving contracts, was very similar to that of the palace.[1] The temple practised credit sale by entrusting merchandise to one or more traders who were contracted to sell it for silver (*ana* ŠÁM KÙ.BABBAR), which they would pay "when the temple asked for it", usually after one or two years. The price (not stated in the contract, but known from records which document its payment) was the normal one, gradually rising from 6 to 10 shekels of silver per talent in the period from Hammurabi until Ammiṣaduqa, with higher prices for smaller quantities.

The temple also gave out loans, both charitable ones, extended to people in distress, and loans of a business character, the interest on which provided the temple with income.[2]

---

1 Charpin 1982: 49-57. The few texts available to him, to which we can now add *BBVOT* I, 1 (from 10-vii-Ammiditana 3) and some unpublished records, identified by F. van Koppen, show that the temple converted the wool into silver via the *kārum*, which "received it in the temple of Šamaš". In CT 8, 30c the silver earned (47 shekels) was made available to a merchant for buying oxen for the temple, no doubt to work its fields, in other cases such silver was given to merchants who had to provide the temple with offering sheep (e.g. CT 45, 47, Ammiditana 9). Note also UET 5, 476: 1-5, "1 2/3 mina of silver, by the weight of Šamaš, from the silver, the price for wool of normal quality, which the temple of Nanna had given to the merchant of the fishermen". Note below footnote 5, on two texts from Ur, which reveal a similar mechanism of the temple of Nanna.

2 See Harris 1960: 126-137, Veenhof 1987: 55-62, and Skaist 1994: 172-180.

* Originally published in: J. G. Dercksen (ed.), Assyria and Beyond. Studies Presented to Mogens Trolle Larsen. PIHANS 100. Leiden: Nederlands Instituut voor het Nabije Oosten.

Votive gifts received, called a.ru.a or *ikribū*, could be of various kinds, including persons ("temple oblates"), but they frequently were precious objects of silver or gold and semi-precious stones, promised or donated to honor, obtain the favor of, or thank the god.[3] They could be hoarded as treasure or used for sumptuous display, but also function as bullion, as temple funds used for maintaining the temple household and for business, including trade.

According to Dercksen 1997: 94f. "The OA *ikribū*-system emerges ... as a balanced attempt to promote trade and prosperity by making temple funds available for commercial purposes" to a trader for whom they "constituted a credit on very attractive conditions" (long duration, perhaps lower interest rates, and fiscal advantages). In due time he would have to pay back the original amount, with "the covert obligation to present valuable offerings (hence the name *ikribū* – K.R.V.; they would be part of the profit made, see p. 84) to the god as a token of gratitude". Such offerings to the temples "enhanced their wealth and status" and "confirmed the merchant's social status as respectable member of the community".

Votive gifts are well attested for the Old Babylonian period, but evidence on how they were used is very limited. Texts which state or imply that temple funds were used for business purposes do not indicate their origin, *e.g.* by designating them as *ikribū*. Many valuable items, votive gifts donated "out of free will" (šà.gi.gá.gá) by a variety of people, including a few merchants,[4] are attested in Old Babylonian Ur, with precious objects mostly found in early records (until the middle of the reign of Nur-Adad). These donations are frequently labeled as "the tithe of Ningal" (zag.10 ᵈNingal), but occasionally they are also given to the temple of Nanna, and several are said to derive "from (the yield of, šà) an expedition to Tilmun". There is, however, thus far no evidence that such temple assets were used for commercial purposes,[5] unless one assumes that the tithe given by the traders was an obligatory ten percent share in the proceeds of a business venture, to which the temple was entitled on the basis of its investment, which is difficult to prove.[6] If the temples in Ur, like many individuals, did invest in the trade, they may have done so in two ways. By making capital, especially silver, available to traders as "money" for making specific purchases,[7] but also by providing them with "merchandise", such as woollen textiles, hides and oil, possibly produced by the workshops of the temple itself, to be exchanged for goods the temple needed or to be sold for silver. The latter form is attested during the preceding Ur III period, when temples supplied textiles, wool, palm-fibers, sesame oil, and hides as "merchandise for buying Makkan copper" (níg.šám.ma urudu Má.gan^{ki}).[8] There is no obvious reason why this could not have continued after the Ur III period, even when the economic power of the temples had become less, since this was also the way in which private investors supplied traders with merchandise on

---

3 Note YOS 14, 298, "1 mina of silver, 1 shekel of gold, 16 minas of copper, the weight of (KI.LÁ) (a statuette?) of S., (and) 1 slave, votive gift (ŠÙD.DÙ = *ikribū*) of Šallurtum. For the life (NAM.TI) of S. she has given it to Nanna on 21-I of Sin-eribam year 1". Th. Richter, *Untersuchungen zu den lokalen Panthea Süd- und Mittelbabyloniens in altbabylonischer Zeit* (*AOAT* 257, Münster 1999) 339, tentatively translates KI.LÁ by "Bildnis".

4 Among the objects donated were small silver boats: UET 5, 532:7f.; 551 iii:6'f.; 553 i:17, iii:10'f.; 561:4, 23; 563 iii:2, iv:11, 13; 566:4', rev.:3', 5', 8'; 567 I:2', 4'.

5 Butz 1979: 368, "ich bin mir nicht ganz sicher, ob der Tempel nicht doch den grössten Teil der gestifteten Halbedelsteine, etc., wieder verkaufte, um homogenes Material zu haben".

6 See Van de Mieroop 1989, with comments on earlier interpretations by Oppenheim 1954 and Butz 1979, and Heimpel 1987: 83ff. nos. 56-58 and 60-1 for transliterations and translations of the main texts.

7 Butz 1979: 365 assumes that the temple preferred the first method, but in the contract which would prove this (UET 5, 367) the temple is not involved. Note rare occurrences in the UET 5 lists of silver qualified as "price (paid for)" a product, e.g. UET 5, 558:IV 30f., "11 1/2 shekels of silver as price of (paid for the purchase of, mu šám) ivory" (see for this text also Appendix 2. comments on no. 6).

8 See the evidence presented in Leemans 1960: 18-21, with Heimpel 1987: 80ff.

credit, as consignment or in partnership.[9] The evidence, however, is very limited, which may be due to the nature and origin of the textual record. Van de Mieroop 1992: 82, in his "flow chart of goods in the temple economy", mentions trade in connection with the production of the temple workshops, in particular woollen cloth, which accordingly would in part have been produced for commercial purposes, but he does not document this in the following analysis. He states that trade at Ur (ch. 3.6) "was organized by private merchants", who "collected investments from numerous individuals", and "were also able to collect capital by taking out loans". But among the temple loans attested and discussed (94f.), part of which in his opinion reflect business and were a source of income, such commercial loans and investments do not figure. He believes that "large institutions of temples and the palace maintained some control over it" (the trade; 192), apparently by taxing it, but the instrument of credit and capital investment is not mentioned. But there is some evidence for trading operations which involve goods of the temple. In view of the large temple herds, wool a priori seems a likely surplus product to be put to commercial use, as Butz 1979: 365 already suggested, and he could refer to a text where wool was "given" to traders in exchange for/to be exchanged for silver.[10] And part of the woollen textiles, consigned or sold to private Tilmun traders as exchange goods, as recorded in UET 5, 367 and 848, might also originate from temple workshops, whether they were sold to traders or given to them in consignment.[11]

Commercial use of temple funds

Old Babylonian contracts which record loans or debts of property of a god, hence temple funds, are attested from various cities, especially from the temple of Šamaš in Sippar,[12] but the term *ikribū* is extremely rare. Some consider them real loans, others promises of votive gifts formulated as debts.[13] And if they are loans, one may hesitate between charitable consumptive loans to people in distress, and business loans, including those for commercial purposes. Without discussing these questions again,[14] we can say that a number of temple

---

9 E.g. in UET 5, 367 (Leemans 1960: 36 no. 14) and much earlier in YBC 5447 (reign of Gungunum), where a man gives staple goods (wool, wheat and sesame oil) in commission to a Tilmun trader (he uses a "Persian Gulf" seal and clearance will take place "at the safe conclusion of the journey"), see W.W. Hallo, *AS* 16 (1965) 199ff. This was probably also the reason why J.N. Postgate, *Early Mesopotamia* (1992) 135, writes "at Ur, the Nanna Temple supplied at least some of the trading capital for the Tilmun traders in Ur III and Old Babylonian times".

10 He refers to the damaged record UET 5, 558, rev.:10'ff., which mentions "2 talents of copper ..., its equivalent in silver 5/6 mina [...] the price of/paid for wool, de[livered? by] PN" (see Leemans 1960: 30). Note also two texts which record the delivery of silver (100 and 53 shekels), described as "from the silver, the price paid for (šám) normal wool, which was given to traders from the temple of Nanna" (UET 5,430; 476 has "which the temple of Nanna gave to the trader of the fishermen"). Van de Mieroop 1992: 91, translates "among the silver to buy ordinary wool", which wrongly suggests that the silver was given to buy wool, while it was acquired by selling wool belonging to the temple (é^d^Nanna.ta) through the services of traders.

11 See for the textile production at Ur, K. Butz, *WZKM* 65/66 (1973/4), 35f., III.2

12 Elsewhere too the temple of Šamaš was prominent in providing small, usually charitable loans, not surprisingly in Larsa, but also in cities without an important temple of his, such as Nippur and Ur, see Richter, *op. cit.* (note 3) 131f., 294, and 435f.

13 Examples of the latter, called *ikribū* are the first two texts quoted in *CAD* I/J, 64, b (both for the tiny amount of one-sixth grain of silver). In addition: YOS 12, 532 (16-II- Si 29): "3 shekels of silver, votive gift (*ikribū*) (vowed) by Š., Š. owes to Sîn (UGU M. *Sîn* IN.TUKU); when he goes to his town he will give the silver", and AUCT IV, 63, which records the promise that a man will give "1 2/3 shekel of silver, *ikribū*, silver of Šamaš". Assets called *ikribū*, possibly used for business purposes, are mentioned in CT 4, 27b, where Lu-Ninsianna promises to pay what he still owes to Šamaš (from the illegal sale of an ox of the god) "when I have returned to my town and my place, together with my many *ikribu*'s, the record of which is in the countryside and which he himself will search" (see *CAD* I/J *loc.cit.*, and Veenhof 1987: 61 with note 70). The "many *ikribū*" probably were items which, like the ox sold, belonged to Šamaš and which L. had borrowed from or or managed for the temple.

14 See my earlier observations in Veenhof 1987: 55-62, with those by Skaist 1994: 172-180.

loans, judging from the size of the loan, the terminology used, stipulations on interest or profit, and occasionally the identity of the debtor, must be of a business character.

A commercial purpose of a temple loan is clear when payment is due "upon the successful completion of the business trip" (*ina šalām ḫarrānim, e.g.* in YOS 14, 350, 8 3/4 shekels if silver, Ešnunna, reign of Naram-Sin). The amount (*e.g.* 70 5/6 shekels, interest bearing, in Edzard, *Tell ed-Dēr* no. 16)[15] and the quality of the silver (*ṣarpum*, "refined", in VS 9, 83:1, 5 shekels, and 183:1, 3 1/4 shekels) probably also indicate a commercial goal. This is very clear when the loan states that payment will be made be from the "profit" (*nēmelum*) which the debtor is assumed to realize (at times said to be due to the mercy of the god; BAP 9; Scheil, *Sippar* no. 76; CTMMA no. 52, *nemēlētum*)[16] and when the silver is designated as "partnership's silver" (KÙ. BABBAR TAB.BA; VS 9, 182:3 and Strassbourg 31). Revealing for the commercial character are also statements about the liability of the debtor for cash payment irrespective of whether he has sold on credit and has outstanding claims (VS 9, 183:7ff.), and about payment in "the *kārum* where he is seen" (VS 9, 83:7ff.).

A commercial background also seems possible for BM 14007 (M. Anbar, *RA* 72, [1978] 122, no. 8, RS year 55), because of the amount borrowed, 1/2 mina of silver, the identity of the debtor, the trader Šēp-Sîn, and the payment clause, "the day the principal asks for it", which is well attested in commercial loans and partnership investments.[17] But such an explanation is less certain for VAS 9, 148/9 (Sippar, Ham. 39), although the amount of 13 gur of interest bearing barley, borrowed by three persons, is fairly substantial.[18].

A difficult case is HE 147 (Boyer, *Contribution*, pl. xvii = *RA* 12, 68, 68, Si 3), which records a debt to Šamaš of "25 shekels of silver, *mitḫarum*" (1-2), to be paid back "when Šamaš will have shown him love and he will have experienced the mercy of Šamaš (so that) silver has come into his hands". There are, apart from the amount of silver involved, some features which might support a commercial interpretation. The seal of *A-lí-tum* SANGA, apparently the head of the temple and representative of the divine creditor, is unusual on a debt-note, and may have been impressed to record his acknowledgment of the financial arrangement and the friendly terms granted to the debtor. *Mitḫarum* is difficult, but Dombradi 2000: 66f. (a), is right in pointing out that the context excludes a meaning "duplum" as a fine. If we take it as "equivalent", it implies that the debtor had originally received something else, the counter-value of which is now rated as a liability in silver. And if it was commercial, the temple might have supplied the debtor "merchandise" as capital, perhaps in a situation (as in texts a) and b) below) where god and man were partners in a common fund. When the human partner proved unable to pay his due (part of the principal, if the temple was the main supplier of capital, and a share in the proceeds), Šamaš granted him extension of payment or additional means. This resulted in a liability recorded in this debt-note (IN.TUKU, not ŠU BA.AN.TI), with generous payment conditions, which of course are not by definition restricted to consumptive loans, but might also apply to people which had a special relationship with the temple.

An interesting case is also "P 2" (M. Anbar, *IOS* 6 [1976] 61f.), "For the silver of Sîn, as much as there is, Ku-Ninšubur has no claim on Sîn-līdiš and Ilī-išmeanni. With 3½ minas of silver, his share, he has been satisfied" (3 witnesses, month of Abum of an unknown year, sealed by Ku-Ninšubur).[19] The large amount of "silver of Sîn", which Ku-Ninšubur receives

---

15 Cf. also A.K.A. Aḥmad, *Old Babylonian Loan Contracts in the Iraqi Museum* (Diss. 1964) no. 40: nearly 30 shekels of silver, interest bearing, borrowed from Šamaš. Perhaps also the two loans of ca. 10 shekels of silver recorded in OECT 13, 13 (creditor Nanna) and 211 (creditor Šamaš, 4 debtors).

16 See Skaist 1994: 179 on these clauses, which appear in later texts, after Ammiditana.

17 It does not fix a date, but leaves the initiative to the principal, no doubt also because the return from a business trip is difficult to predict. See for attestations TCL 10, 75:6f.; HSM 7519:8f. and 7622:6f. (see G.F. Dole, *Partnership loans in the Old Babylonian Period*, unpubl. diss. Harvard 1965), and AUCT IV nrs. 39-41.

18 Cf. the very similar contract VAS 9, 201 (MU GIBIL), witnessed by Sîn and Šamaš, where the same two debtors, together with Nanaya-imdī, borrow 8 gur of barley from Ur-Kalkal, who is presumably a manager of the Šamaš temple.

19 KÙ.BABBAR ^{d}EN.ZU [2] A.NA.AN.GÁL.LÁ.ÀM [3] UGU ^{d}EN.ZU-*li-di-iš* [4] *ù Ì-lí-iš-me-a-ni* [5] KÙ-^{d}NIN.ŠUBUR [6] NU.TUKU.ÀM [7] 3 1/2 *ma-na* KÙ.BABBAR ḪA.LA-*šu* [8] Ì.DÙG ... 13 MU BÁRA.GUŠKIN ^{d}*Ḫu-ma-at*.

it as "his share", suggests a division, probably in the framework of a partnership which may have worked with silver (or merchandise rated in silver) supplied by the temple of Sin, of which, as Anbar proposes, Ku-Ninšubur may have been the representative or agent (though the inscription on his seal does not bear that out). If so, the large amount of silver he received would comprise both the principal and part of the profit made to with the temple was entitled.

Five commercial records

In the following five contracts the relation between god and men as commercial partners is beyond doubt.

a) CT 48, 99 (Sippar, Si 3 or 4)

18½ G[ÍN] KÙ.BABBAR	18½ shekels of silver,
ŠU.TI.[A *Ib-ni*]*-É-a*	received by Ibni-Ea
i-na l[*i-ib-bi k*]*i-si-im*	from the purse
ša ^{d}U[TU *ù Ib*]*-ni-É-a*	in which Šamaš and Ibni-Ea
tap-pu-ú [KÙ.BABBAR?]	are joint partners, [*the silver*]
ši-li-ip ti Ib-ni-É-a	is a withdrawal by Ibni-Ea.
ki-ma Ib-ni-É-a	As much as Ibni-Ea
il-qú-ú	took
^{d}UTU *i-le-eq-qé*	Šamaš will take.
IGI ^{d}IŠKUR	In the presence of Adad,
IGI ^{d}EN.ZU	of Sîn,
IGI ^{d}UTU*-be-el-ì-lí*	of Šamaš-bēl-ilī,
IGI *Ì-lí*-SUKKAL	of Ilī-šukkallī,
IGI *Ku-bu-lum*	of Kubbulum.
ITI APIN.DU$_8$.A U$_4$ *4*.KAM	4 – VIII
MU I$_7$ *Sa-am-su-i-lu-na* LUGAL.E	Samsuiluna, year 3 or 4

On the left edge a design in the shape of a pin with a round eye at the top, also found on some temple loans. The reading at the end of line 5 is conjectural, but makes good send as the beginning of a new sentence. See for withdrawal ABIM 20:73f.: "Do not release (*wuššurum*) to him the silver about which PN wrote concerning our purse, you must keep it!" *Šiliptum*, "withdrawal" from a capital is also attested the next text.

12. One might be tempted to take this witness as the god Šamaš, provided with the epithet "Lord of the gods", inspired by the honorific title "Enlil of his land", given to Šamas in text B:16. But it is better to read the personal name Šamaš-bēl-ilī, attested elsewhere (see note 32 below), perhaps of a member of the staff of the temple.

b) CT 48, 105 (Sippar, undated)

5/6 ma-na 2 GÍN KÙ.BABBAR	52 shekels of silver,
KÙ.BABBAR ^{d}UTU*-mi-tam-ú-ba-li-iṭ*	the silver of Šamaš-mitam-uballiṭ,
^{pd}EN.ZU*-re-ma-an-ni*	Sin-remanni,
ù Mi-nam-[x x]*-be-el-ti*	and Minam-...-belti ,
ši-li-ip-ti	withdrawal
^{p}*An-na-tum*	by Annatum,
iš-tu ṭe$_4$-em-šu	after he had delivered
a-na ^{d}UTU	his full report
ú-ga-me-ru	to Šamaš.

4. None of the names starting with *mīnam*, "what" (*-ēpuš, -ašēṭ, -aḫṭi*) fits the traces.

6. Annatum is not one of four partners, who withdraws his share in a joint capital, after having submitted a report (and settled accounts) before and with an oath by Šamaš, as trading partners did, who "entered the temple of Šamaš and made their report" (*ana bīt Šamaš īrubūma ṭēmšunu īpušūma*, CT 2, 28:4f.). Annatum does not figure as co-owner of the capital in lines 2-4, and the report is not delivered *maḫar Šamaš*, but "to Šamaš", hence as recipient and partner. The "silver of Š., S., and M." therefore cannot be their assets, but what they yielded, the proceeds from their sale. And indeed, two of the names are typical for slaves (see the literature quoted below, in the note on text C:10-30), and 52 shekels fits well as the price of three slaves. The record attests a partnership between a trader, Annatum, and the god Šamaš, which involved slaves, but probably much more, as in our texts A-C, since this a specified interim withdrawal of part of the capital, comparable to text a), which, however, does not specify the source of the silver withdrawn.

c) YOS 8, 145 (YBC 4337; Larsa, RS 37)

20 ma-na KÙ.BABBAR	20 minas of silver,
NAM.TAB.B	Ajoint venture capital,
6 ma-na KÙ.BABBAR *ta-ad-mi-iq-tum*	6 minas of silver, a *tadmiqtu*-loan,
ŠU.NIGIN *26 ma-na* KÙ.BABBAR	in all 26 minas of silver,
KI ^{d}UTU	from Šamaš
ù ^{d}EN.ZU-*iš-me-a-ni*	and Sîn-išmeanni
^{p}*Sú-ba-bu-um*	Subābum
ù ^{d}EN.ZU-*iš-me-a-ni*	and Sîn-išmeanni
ŠU BA.AN.TI.EŠ (case: MEŠ)	have received.
i-na ša-la-am ḫa-ra-nim	When the journey is completed
KÙ.BABBAR *ù né-me-el-šu*	they will weigh out
Ì.LÁ.E.NE	the silver and the profit on it.
Six witnesses.	14 – VII – Rim-Sîn year 37.

The first witness, Šamaš-muballiṭ, is also the first witness in text c), which, as the YBC numbers show, must come from the same lot or archive, probably that of the Šamaš temple in Larsa. The temple of Šamaš provides a substantial capital as investment in a joint undertaking, but we do not know how much the human partners contributed, apart from making the journey and actually conducting the trade. Alongside the investment it supplies a *tadmiqtum*, a commercial loan based on venture and trust, where the return of the capital is secured, but the amount of profit (see line 11) depends entirely on the success (*dammuqum*) of the business.

d) YOS 8, 96 (YBC 4335; Larsa, RS 31)

1 ma-na KÙ.BABBAR	1 mina of silver
NAM.TAB.BA.ŠÈ	as joint venture capital
KI ^{d}UTU *ù A-bu-wa-qar*	from Šamaš and Abu-waqar
^{pd}EN.ZU-*ga-tum*	Sîngatum
ŠU BA.AN.TI	has received.
u_4-*um um-me-a-nu-um i-ri-šu-ú-*[*ša*]	When the principal asks him for it
KÙ.BABBAR *ù ne-me-el-šu*	he will weigh out
Ì.LÁ.E	the silver and the profit made on it.
um-me-a-nu-um $ba^{!}$-*ab-t*[*a*]-*am*	The principal will not acknowledge
ú-ul i-la-ma-[*a*]*d*	outstanding claims.
7 witnesses	20 – X – Rim-Sîn year 31.

See for the payment clause note 17 and for the clause in 9-10, *AOATT* 419f. and HSM 7510:10f., *ummiānum bābtam ula idē*.

e) Di 258 (K. Van Lerberghe and G. Voet, *Sippar-Amnānum. The Ur-Utu Archive*, vol. (*MHE, Texts* 1; Ghent 1991), 22ff. no. 7)

a-na ^{d}UTU	For Samaš,
be-li-šu-nu	their lord,
i-na tap-pu-ti-šu-nu	when out of their partnership,
im-qú-ta-šu-nu-ši-im-ma(profits)	accrue to them,
Nu-úr-^{d}UTU	Nūr-Šamaš,
[*ša*] $^{[d]}$UTU-TAB.BA-*e*	son of Šamaš-tappê,
ù [^{d}EN].ZU-*e-ri-*[*ba*]-*am*	and Sîn-erībam,
[DUMU] *Bur-*^{d}EN.ZU	son of Būr-Sîn,
½ [*ma*]-*na*	will deliver
ú-še-re-bu	½ mina (of silver).

Taking the final verbal form as a present-future tense, the text (an undated, old and sealed tablet) records a conditional promise made by two persons, which reads like an indirect prayer to Šamaš to make the undertaking successful, so as to earn an amount of silver from the grateful traders. The preterite *imqutaššunušim* is taken as conditional, without *šumma*, and the neutral verb *maqātum* denotes what "accrues" to them, income, profit (cf. *CAD* M/I 247, 3'; but in others also losses, cf. *miqittum*). This is not a partnership and therefore the text does not speak of "profit", and since we do not know how big the capital was, we cannot quantify the gift in relation to it.
10. Note the use of the same verbal form in Boyer, *Contribution*, 212:6, referring to the remainder of a debt to Šamaš still to be paid, and in BE 6/1, 91:9f. (see Charpin 1982:51 note 59), where the silver due for wool obtained from the temple of Šamaš is collected and "brought into the temple of Šamaš".

These texts state that god and men are "partners" in business, speak of "partners", "partnership", and of "joint venture silver" (*tappû, tappūtum*, and *kasap tappūtim*),[20] which is also designated as their (joint) "purse" (*kīsum*, a). One partner can withdraw capital (*šiliptum*, a) from it, if the other (divine) partner receives the same amount, of course in addition to his share in the remaining capital and the profit made (b, c), when the business is terminated. As usual in such contracts, no date for payment is stipulated, since it depends on the completion of the journey (c). Text d) contains clauses known from commercial loans or investments, which have to protect the principal and money-lender (*ummeānum*) against his partner's or debtor's failure to pay back, due to "outstanding claims" (*bābtum*), because he had given merchandise in commission or granted credit (usually indicated by the verb *ezēbum* and *qiāpum*).[21] These terms and stipulations are not different from those in contractual arrangement between human partners; only the votive gift, promised in e) if the expedition is successful, is different.

Evidence from Old Babylonian Susa

Additional and similar evidence on the commercial involvement of the temple is found in some contracts from Old Babylonian Susa, which is not surprising in view of the importance of that city in the trading network, which probably also was the main reason for the Babylonian presence there. We have three contracts (MDP 22, 124; 23, 271 and 273) in which silver is borrowed from the god Šamaš together with a person (presumably the agent of the temple). The first states that the loan of 5 minas of silver is "for partnership" (*ana* TAB.BA), which could also apply to the three debtors alone, but in the second

20 I believe that in text d) the "partnership" refers to the two co-operating traders and not to them in relation to the god, for if the latter were the case there would be no question of a gift, because the god was entitled to his share in the profit.

21 See for these clauses in commercial contacts, Veenhof 1972:419ff.

one man "received partnershipsilver" (KÙ.BABBAR TAB.BA *ilqe*) for commercial purposes from Šamaš and his agent, which means a partnership between temple and trader. This must also be the case in the third contract, where *tappūtum* is not used, but where the stipulation that profit has to be divided equally (*nēmelam ibbaššû malla aḫ[mami izuzzū]*) between the single debtor and Šamaš implies a business partnership. The existence or perhaps renewal of a commercial partnership between Šamaš and a man is recorded in

MDP 22, 119

i-na URU.KI *ù* EDEN *i-na* KÙ.⌈BABBAR⌉	In city and countryside, for silver
ù GUŠKIN ^{pd}UTU *ù* ÌR-*Ku-bi tap-pu*	and gold, Šamaš and Warad-Kubi
⌈*ki*⌉-*ma a-bi-šu šà pa-ni-im*$^{?}$	are partners. As his father *previously*
a-bu-um i-pu-uš-ma	did, he will do what is
⌈*šà*⌉ ^{d}UTU *i-pu-uš*	(in the interest) of Šamaš.
⌈IG⌉I ^{d}MÙŠ.EREN IGI ^{d}IŠKUR-*ib-ni-šu*	Before Inšušinak, Adad-ibnišu
IGI ÌR-^{d}MAR.TU	Warad-Amurrim.

While there are some problems of interpretation,[22] it seems clear that the text records that Warad-Kubi will continue his father's partnership with the temple of Šamaš and thereby will promote the god's interests or follow his instructions. The text uses *ša Šamaš epēšum*, to express the obdediance demanded in a partnership with the god, see below on the interpretation of texts A:13f. and B:22f..

2. Sîn-išmeanni and Šamaš: BM 97032, 97048, and 97065.

Against the background of this evidence on commercial involvement of the temple and shared interests between a god and a trader, we must understand the following three records from Old Babylonian Sippar. The first, A, a perfect tablet, was selected and published long ago (1912), the other two, B and C, were identified by me in the same acquisition (1902-11-10), together with text D (see Appendix 1), and are published here with kind permission of the Trustees of the British Museum. They speak more in detail both of the merchandise involved and the relation between god and men, not only of the obedience demanded and the shared interests, but also of the blessing of his commercial activities, which the trader expects and asks from the god.

The texts

A) BM 97048 (1902-10-11, 102 = CT 33, 39)

5 ma-na KÙ.BABBAR	5 minas of silver,
148 ŠE.GUR *na-aš-pa-kum*	148 kor of barley, in storage
40 ŠE.GUR *ba-ab-tum*	40 kor of barley, outstanding claims -
ni-ik-ka-as-sí-šu	the accounting, which
ša ma-ḫa-ar ^{d}UTU *i-pu-šu*	he would carry out before Šamaš
^{pd}EN.ZU-*iš-me-an-ni i-pu-uš*	Sîn-išmeanni has performed -
e-zu-ub SAG.GÉME.MEŠ	apart from the slave-girls,
SAG.ÚRDU.MEŠ *ù mi-im-ma*	the slaves and whatever
ša i-ba-aš-šu-ú	(else) there is.
^{d}UTU DI.KU$_5$ *ki-na-tim*	Šamaš, righteous judge,
i-ṣú-um a-na ma-di-im	may what is little

22 I am grateful to Léon de Meyer for comments on this text. In line 3 *ša pānim* could be in apposition to *abišu*, "his late father", or belong with the verb at the end of line 4, "did previously"; the double *abišu* ... *abum* might be due to problems with *kīma*, as preposition (*kīma abišu*) and/or as conjunction (*kīma abušu ipušu* ..). De Meyer notes that the witness Warad-Amurru acts as Šamaš's agent in MDP 23, 271 and 273 (loans from Šamaš and W.), but also borrows from Šamaš (MDP 22, 198, 2 kor of barley and 10 shekels of silver).

li-tu-ur-ma	rev.	turn into much, so that
ša qá-bi ^{d}UTU ^{pd}EN.ZU-*iš-me-an-ni*		Sîn-išmeanni may do
li-pu-uš		what Šamaš orders.
IGI ^{d}EN.ZU	15	In the presence of Sîn
IGI ^{d}IŠKUR		of Adad,
IGI ^{d}MARDUK		of Marduk.
ITI KÙ.GA U_4 *12*.KAM		Month …, day 12,
MU ^{d}*Taš-me-tum*		year: Tašmetum (Ham. 41)

B) BM 97032 (1902-10-11,86)

5 ma-na KÙ.BABBAR	15	minas of silver,
60 ŠE.GUR *na-aš-pa-kum*		60 gur of barley, in storage,
80 ŠE.GUR *ba-ab-tum*		80 gur of barley, outstanding claims,
4 TÚG.ḪI.A *8* BAR.SI.ḪI.A		4 garments, 8 sashes,
4 sa-ap-pu ZABAR	5	4 bronze bowls,
1 URUDU.ŠEN *ša 13 ma-na*		1 copper cauldron weighing 13 minas,
1 ša-an-da-lum ša ZABAR		1 bronze *šandalu*-container,
14 ma-aš-ka-nu-um 1 ne-eḫ-li-tum		14 chains, 1 sieve,
1 ḫa-zi-nu-um 2 pa-at-ru		1 axe, 2 daggers -
eš-re-et KÙ.BABBAR *eš-re-et še-im*	10	the tithe of the silver, the tithe of the
eš-re-et SAG.ÚRDU.MEŠ		barley, the tithe of the slaves,
eš-re-et SAG.GÉME.MEŠ		the tithe of the slave-girls,
ù mi-im-<erasure >*-ma*	e.	and of whatever (else)
ša i-ba-aš-šu-ú		there is,
be-el ma-ti-im	rev.	the Lord of the land,
^{d}UTU *i-li-il ma-ti-šu*		Šamaš, the Enlil of his land,
KI ^{pd}EN.ZU-*iš-me-a-ni*		from Sîn-išmeanni,
DUMU *Za-ba-ia-tum*		son of Zabayatum,
i-le-eq-qe		he will obtain.
i-ṣú-um a-na ma-di-im li-tu-ur-ma	20	May what is little turn into much so that he \can
i-na ma-di-im ^{d}UTU *li-pu-ul*		satisfy Šamaš with what (has become) \much.
mi-im-ma ša ^{d}UTU *i-qá-ab-bu-šum*		Then he must do whatever Šamaš will
li-pu-uš-ma ^{d}UTU *li-pu-ul*		order him and satisfy Šamaš.
eš-re-tum KA DUB DINGIR		Tithe. The text of the tablet of the god.

C) BM 97065 (1902-10-11, 119)

3 ma-na KÙ.BABBAR	1	3 minas of silver,
21 ŠE.GUR ŠE *ta-ak-ši-tim*		21 gur of barley, barley for profit,
5 TÚG.ḪI.A *10* TÚG.BAR.SI.ḪI.A		5 garments, 10 sashes,
2 ša-an-da-la-tum		2 *šandalu*-containers,
3 sà-ap-pu	5	3 *sappu*-bowls,
1 URUDU.ŠEN *ša 13 ma-na*		1 copper cauldron weighing 13 minas,
14 ma-aš-ka-nu-um		14 chains,
1 ši-im-li-tum		1 *šimlītum*,
1 ḫa-zi-nu-um		1 axe,
1 SAG.ÚRDU *Na-ḫi-iš-ma-gi-ir-*^{d}UTU	10	1 slave, Naḫiš-māgir-Šamaš,
1 SAG.ÚRDU *Ša-*^{d}UTU*-dam-qá*		1 slave, Ša-Šamaš-damqā,
1 SAG.ÚRDU *Sa-ka-ar-*^{d}UTU*-ra-bi*		1 slave, Sakar-Šamaš-rabi,
1 SAG.GÉME *A-na-*^{d}*A-a-tak-la-ku*		1 slave-girl, Ana-Aya-taklāku,
1 SAG.GÉME ^{d}*Nu-ub-tum-um-mi*	e.	1 slave-girl, Nubtum-ummī,

1 SAG.GÉME ^{d}*A-a-ba-ni-ti*		1 slave-girl, Aya-bānitī,
1 SAG.GÉME ^{d}*A-a-re-me-ni*	rev.	1 slave-girl, Aya-remēni,
1 SAG.GÉME ^{d}*A-a-la-ma-sí*		1 slave-girl, Aya-lamassī,
1 SAG.GÉME *Na-ar-ba-tum*		1 slave-girl, Narbatum,
1 SAG.GÉME ^{d}*Ištar*$^{?}$*-um-mi*		1 slave-girl, *Ištar*-ummī,
1 SAG.GÉME ^{d}*A-a-mi-tám-gi-im-li*		1 slave-girl, Aya-mītam-gimlī,
1 SAG.GÉME ^{d}UTU*-la-ma-sí*		1 slave-girl, Šamaš-lamassī,
1 SAG.GÉME *Aš-tum*		1 slave-girl, Aštum,
1 SAG.ÚRDU ^{d}*Še-rum-ì-lí-a-bi*		1 slave, Šērum-ili-abī
1 SAG.ÚRDU *A-bu-um-ba-ni*		1 slave, Abum-bāni,
1 [SAG.ÚRDU] *Be-el-ti-a-bi-qí-ši-im*		1 slave, Bēlti-abī-qīšîm,
1 SAG.ÚRDU *Lu-ša-lim-ba-aš-ti*		1 slave, Lu-šalim-baštī,
1 SAG.ÚRDU *Ka-ab-ta-at-a-na-ḫa-mi-ri-ša*		1 slave, Kabtat-ana-ḫāmiriša,
1 SAG.ÚRDU *S[a]-ni-iq-*KA*-be-el-tim*		1 slave, Saniq-pī-Bēltim,
1 SAG.ÚRDU *Ma-am-mi-šar-ra-ate.*		1 slave, Mammi-šarrat,
1 SAG.ÚRDU *Aš-šu-mi-ia-li-/ib-lu-uṭ*		1 slave, Aššumia-libluṭ.
mi-im-ma ša i-šu-ú /	l.e.	Whatever
^{pd}EN.ZU*-iš-me-an-ni*		Sîn-išmeanni has
ša ^{d}UTU		belongs to Šamaš.

Notes on the texts

A:2f., B:2f., C:2. The amounts of barley are qualified by appositions. *Našpakum*, "granary storehouse, storage jar", must be short for "what is in store, in the silo" (hence *ša našpakim*), a meaning also attested in AbB 6, 8:9-13 ("he did not entrust to me *našpakī*", "I will make him pay the silver *našpakī*"). *Takšītum*, "profit, gains", also attested in Old Assyrian (cannot be realized, ICK 1, 17:39f, BIN 4, 67:14; has to be divided among partners ICK 1, 83:6f. // 2, 60: 2', with the corresponding verb *kaššu'um*, which is also used alone. In Mari it may denote both the profit from (foreign) trade (*WZKM* 86 [1996] 480:19'f.) and the earnings from seasonal labor (harvesting, ARMT 27, 26:24, read: *t. ...[ul ib]aššima..*; 80:44). In Ammiṣaduqa's Edict, § 15, the royal cancellation of debts is said to apply to barley due to the owner of a field as rent or as share in the harvest, but not to *še šīmim* and *še takšītim*, presumably barley (produced) to be sold or to be exchanged with profit (Kraus 1984: 248). The latter applies in our texts and I assume that C uses the term to cover both categories distinguished in A and B.

A:5f. To make this a meaningful statement I take the first *i-pu-šu* as subjunctive of the present tense. Settling accounts "before Šamaš" is not necessarily because of the involvement of the god in this commercial enterprise, for trading partners regularly settled accounts in a temple by clearance under oath (*tēbibtum*),[23] since not all transactions yielded certified records and various claims (travel costs, expenses, losses, etc.) were based on oral statements. Cf. CT 2, 22:6-13 (*ana bīt Šamaš ... īrubūma E. nikkassīšu maḫar Šamaš īpušma ..*); CT 2, 28:4f (*ana bīt Šamaš īrubūma ṭēmšunu īpušū*); VS 8, 8 5-8 (*ana Sippar ikšudamma ina bāb Šamaš nikkassam īpušūma.*); and Tell Sifr 37:4-8 (*ana tazkītim dajjānī ikšudūma ana bīt Šamaš īrubūma ina bīt Šamaš ummeānam īpulūma ...*). The words of our text seem to say that in making the accounting before Šamaš, Sin-išmeanni carried out what he had promised. A formal accounting of the assets provides a basis for calculating the tithe owed to the god according to text B.

A:15-17. Gods frequently occur as witnesses in loans extended by other gods (cf. Inšušinak in MDP 22, 119, and Adad and Sin in CT 48, 99, presented above).

A:18. A rare month name, also attested in CT 33,19:18 and VAS 9, 201:5 (also the record of a temple loan), both from Sippar; the position of this month in the calender remains unclear, cf. S Greengus, *JAOS* 107 (1987), 219, (4).

---

23 See W.W. Hallo in *AS* 16 (1965) 200, YBC 5447: 8-10.

B:4, C:3. As regularly in dowries, twice as much *paršigū* than garments, apparently because one *ṣubātum* and two scarfs make one set.

B:4, C:5. OB references to *sappu*-vases (which the dictionaries, following *Diri* V:70, equate with DUG.ŠAB = *šappu*), outside Mari (cf. *CAD* Š/I, 479 a), and ARM 22, 203 i:15f.; 204 ii:28'; ARM 25, 347 rev.2; 488:5; 499:8, 520:3 [see now ARMT 31, 292-285 and 32, 172]) are rare, but in MHET II/6, 921:11ff. the shares in an inheritance comprise each time 2 *sà-ap-pu* of bronze (see for bronze for making *sappu* also ARM 25, 697 and 704:1-6). They were relatively small, used for precious oil, and could be sent as gift ("as ointment for my lord", ARM 13, 16:27ff.). Data on their weight or size are rare (ARM 25, 704:6, 1 mina each; ARM 10, 18:13f. and ARM 22, 203 i:15f. are damaged).

B:6. The final vertical separates this line from the end of line 21on the edge.

B:6ff., C: 4ff. The objects in the two lists (A: 8f. simply writes "whatever (else) there is") probably were all made of copper or bronze, also the "sieve". All these objects were used in households, the "chains" (*maškanum*, in the singular), weighing several minas each, could be put to various uses, also as fetters to restrict the movements of slaves; perhaps they were meant to be sold together with the slaves listed in our records.

B:8, C:8. Instead of *neḫlītum*, spelled with initial NE, C has *šimlītum*, an unknown word, most probably (suggestion of M. Stol) a scribal mistake for *ši-iḫ-li-tum*, derived from *šaḫālum*, "to sift, filter, strain". These two new words occur alongside the more common names for sieves derived from the same roots, *maḫḫaltum* (= GI.MA.AN.SIM NÍG.ÀR.RA) and *mašḫalum* (DUG.NÍG.GILIM.MA, DUG.AL.ÚS.SA.SUR.RA). As the use of the determinatives GI and DUG shows, the difference was that the first is for solids and the second for liquids. The difference between *neḫlītum/maḫḫaltum* and a third word for "sieve", *nappītum/nappû* (= GI.MA.AN.SIM, GI.Š.ŠÀ.SUR, see *CAD* N/I s.v.), alongside which its occurs in inventories, is more difficult and both are made of reed. NÍG.ÀR.RA (= *mundu*, "groats"), in the logogram of the first, suggests a use for ground cereals, but the second also occurs as ^giš^*nappû ša* ZÍD, "a (wooden) sieve for flour", and alongside pestles, and may have been finer (note lexical GI.MA.AN.SIM IGI.TUR.TUR, "with very small openings"). The former may have been used in particular to clean cereals after the harvest, as is clear from TCL 1, 17 [AbB 14:17]:7f., where winnowing (*zarûm*) the barley is followed by "sifting" (*naḫālum* = LUḪ, ŠE.SU.UB, DU_6.DU). Cf. also the meaning of *neḫlum*, "what is sifted out", the quantity to be deducted in order to arrive at a net amount of clean barley (see my remarks in *Miscellanea Babyloniaca, Mélanges offertes à M. Birot* [Paris 1985] 289, on line 3; in one case the *neḫlum* deducted amounts to 1/15th of the quantity). The use in parallel records of *neḫlītum* and *šeḫlītum* for what most probably was the same tool, shows that even for native speakers the differentiation was not obvious, because such tools could be put to different uses, a *maḫḫaltum* also to sift ashes.

C:10-30. This is not the place to comment in detail on the names of the slaves, some of which are new or rare (lines 10, 12, 14, 20, 23). The reading of the divine name in 19 is not certain; the sign is neither a good LÁL nor a good Ištar. See in general Stamm 1939:126 and 307-314, Harris 1977 (for Sippar), and Stol 1991: 208f. It is important to note that all are good Babylonian names, many composed with the names of the gods of Sippar (10-14, 15-18, 20-21; ^d^*Nubtum* in 14 is a new "minor god" and I don't know which goddess is meant by "honeybee"). Some names are typical "slave names" (names in which a goddess is called "my mother", nos. 25-28, 30), given to children born as slaves (*wilid bītim*) or by their owners on acquisition. Harris assumes that slave-girls with the goddess Aya in their name "were owned and named by *nadītum*s of Šamaš with names that reflect the piety of their owners". The situation in our text is different from that in the late OB slave sale texts, recently studied by Van Koppen 2004: 24f., which include many slaves imported from areas north and north-east of Babylonia, with non-Babylonian names (the four slaves from Elam have Babylonian names). The trader of our text dealt in native Babylonian, partly Sipparian slaves, which were born as such, had become slaves through debt-servitude, or perhaps had been captured during the conquests of Hammurabi's later years. In the absence of evidence for "slave markets", we may assume that several of them were acquired from their owners, possibly also from *nadītum*s and from the temple of Šamaš itself. A slave-girl with the rare name Bēlti-abī-qīšim also occurs in CT 48, 33:4' (Ham. 34); she might have been sold by her mistress some years later.

Interpretation

The trader of these records, Sin-išmeanni son of Zabayatum, according to A:19 was active around the end of Hammurabi's reign, but his very common name makes it difficult to find evidence on him when his patronym is not mentioned. He must be the subject of the unusual record BM 97041 (from the same accession as text A-C, 1902-10-11), from Hammurabi 7, which seems to deal with his status, but provides no information on the background of texts A-C.[24] This unusual document is presented in Appendix 1 as **text D**.

Texts A and B record what Sin-išmeanni promises to give the god Šamaš if he makes his enterprise successful. B first states that the god will receive the tithe of everything, and both texts speak of giving what is due to the god (*apālum*). A:4-6 mentions the drawing up an account (*nikkassī epēšum*), which is necessary to establish to which assets the promise applies and all three texts list them:

text	silver (minas)	barley (kor)		textiles (sets)	metal objects total number	slaves	
		store	claim			male	female
A	5	148	40	?	?	x	x
B	5	60	80	4	24	x	x
C	3	21		5	22	11	10

Notwithstanding variation in numbers and specification, all three most probably concern the same basic assortment, in view of the similarity between B and C in the stock of metal objects and the fact that all three comprise slaves. In A:7ff. "and whatever there is" must include textiles and metal objects, and the words "apart from ..." only make sense if the nature and quantity of the other goods not mentioned was known. The differences must reflect the flow of goods at various moments, presumably during a limited period.

The merchandise listed suggests local or regional business, because large quantities of barley were not used for overland trade. Barley and the other items – garments, copper and bronze objects used in households, and slaves – could be sold on the Babylonian market. But what was the role of the silver, the first item in all three texts? The round figures suggest that is was commercial capital, "money", owned or borrowed,[25] rather than silver earned by earlier sales and still in stock, but how could one calculate the tithe on capital not yet used (explicitly promised in B:10)? Perhaps the trader at a later time would again have to account for what he had bought or earned with it, and this might explain the differences in the lists of assets, which were drawn up at various moments. those figures where differences had occurred, notably in the amounts of silver and barley.

It is difficult to determine the chronological sequence of the texts.[25a] A may have been the youngest, since, as noted above, the words "apart from the slaves" suggest that the composition of the merchandise was known. C could also be late, since the number of textiles is smaller and the amount of barley it lists could be what remains after successful sales of the stock mentioned in A and B. But if so, the mention of less silver (as yield of the transactions?) than in A and B is strange. If C is the earliest text, recording what was left

---

24 The name of his father Zabayatum is rare. He might be identical with the man whose daughter Marat-Erṣetim in CT 47, 40 (Sippar, Hammurabi 25) is adopted by a *nadītum*, and/or with son of Nur-Šamaš of CT 47, 32:19, witness in the year Hammurabi 11.

25 F. Al Rawi and S. Dalley, *Old Babylonian Texts from Private Houses at Abu-Habbah, Ancient Sippir* (*É.DUB. BA.A* 7, 2000) no. 103, lists assets of in all 5 minas and 34½ shekels of silver, consisting of various products and commodities (with their value in silver), plus three minas of silver. The liquidation of a commercial partnership in the temple of Šamaš in CT 2, 28 (*VAB* 6 no. 172, time of Hammurabi) meant dividing "silver, outstanding claims, slaves and slave-girls, both with the caravan and inside the city".

25a [**Add.** The next paragraph has been rewritten, but the conclusions remain tentative].

at the end of the previous accounting period, the smaller number of textiles is curious. We cannot regard the much larger stocks of barley in A and B as acquired for silver from the capital, because the latter in both texts was also bigger. It seems likely that the enormous stock of barley in A and B was hoarded soon after the harvest, when it could be bought cheaply, and if so, A might be earlier, with more in store and less sold on credit (*bābtum*), while according to B in due time credit sales had increased. That B lists in all 48 gur of barley less than A may reflect sales after A was drawn up, although this did not affect the amount of silver listed, which is the same as in A. This suggests that the capital in silver, available for transactions, was not affected by sales and profit made. This would be understandable if the merchandise had been given to Sîn-išmeanni on credit and was recorded as his debt, which stimulated him to pay back as soon as he had earned some silver,[26] which would suggest a late date for C. In that case a sequence A>B>C seems also possible, with A as the basic contract, B as an interim report, and C as a final balance of what was still in stock.

Text C allows a calculation of the total value of the merchandise in stock. In doing so we have to realize that the last years of Hammurabi were a period of economic prosperity, certainly in the core area of the state,[27] that barley and especially slaves (in consequence of Hammurabi's conquests?) were relatively cheap, and that there were differences between the purchase price paid by the trader (to people who wanted to get rid of slaves or when he bought barley soon after the harvest) and the sales paid by his customers, elsewhere or later in the season, which are better known. With this in mind we may estimate the price of the barley in C at ca. 20 shekels of silver, the sets of garments at perhaps ca. 20 to 30 shekels, and the twenty-one slaves, nearly half male and half female, depending their age, at at least ca. 4 to 5 minas of silver. The price of the metal objects is more difficult for lack of data and specifications on material (copper or bronze) and capacity or weight.[28] But most objects, apart from the heavy cauldron, considering their "normal" weight and the exchange rate of copper and bronze for silver, may have cost only a couple of shekels each, so that we may put the value of objects at perhaps ca. 1,5 to 2 minas of silver. This adds up to ca. 7 minas and together with the capital of 3 minas Sin-išmeanni's assets in C must have amounted to ca. 10 minas of silver.

The merchandise must have been of local origin, acquired from individuals (farmers, craftsmen) or institutions (palace, temple), who had surpluses and produced goods. Slaves became available when private or institutional owners sold them to raise money, because

---

26 In accordance with the procedure prescribed in Hammurabi's Laws §§ 104f., and comparable to what happened in CT 48, 72 (Charpin 1982:43f.), where the delivery and receipt of silver due for wool, consigned to merchants by the palace, is a continuous process, in various instalments (note *ina suddurim nadānum* in line 4, and the iterative forms of the verbs *maḫārum, nadānum* and *ana nikkassī šakānum* in the next lines).

27 Cf. the analysis of prices by H. Farber, A Price and Wage Study for Northern Babylonia during the Old Babylonian Period, *JESHO* 21 (1978) 1-51, and for slaves also Harris 1975: 342f. Mean prices for slaves and slave-girls in Hammurabi's time were ca. 16 and ca. 9 shekels of silver. Note also the average price of ca. 17 shekels in text b) above.

28 We have "cauldrons" ranging in capacity from 10 litres to 3 gur and weighing between 5 minas and 1 ½ talent, but *ruqqum* may also designate a sheet of metal, as in ARM 25, 385:1-4, one weighing 36 minas for making pegs. The capacity of *šandalums*, a smalle type of cauldron, ranged from 1/3 to 3 litre and its weight was often ⅓ or ½ mina. See for the evidence K. Reitner, *Die Metalle im Alten Orient* (*AOAT* 249, Münster 1997), Anhang VI, and for the cauldron, *CAD* R s.v. *ruqqu* [and ARM 31, 289-292]. Prices in silver vary considerably for cauldrons, from 3 to 6 shekels (AUCT IV no. 5, 6 shekels for a heavy one weighing 16 minas of copper) to 14 to 15 shekels (ARM 25, 603 rev. 12 and 609 ii:6, both presumably made of bronze). See for *sappu*-vases the note to B:4 /C:5; according to ARM 25, 704:6 a *sappum* could weigh 1 mina [and see now ARM 31, 292-295].

they could no longer employ them, or because their numbers became too big.[29] Captives acquired as booty by the military may have been subsequently sold to convert them into silver. There must also have been a local or regional market for Sin-išmeanni's merchandise and the barley would be sold in due time to people who did not grow their own crop or were confronted with shortages. The occurrence of *bābtum*, "outstanding claims" (A/B:3), does not imply overland trade, but reflects local or regional credit sales, perhaps also barley loans, which yielded silver as interest and additional profit when payment in silver at harvest time (at the by then prevailing rate of exchange) was stipulated.

All three texts indicate that Sîn-išmeanni took pains to obtain the help of Šamaš, but they are rather different in content and format. A is a witnessed record of Sîn-išmeanni's assets as established on the basis of an accounting (under oath) before Šamaš, in the temple (with other gods as witnesses), and continues with a prayer for Šamaš's blessing, followed by a conditional promise to the god. B and C, without mentioning the accounting, also start with a list of his assets, but are different. B is a memorandum which ends with essentially the same prayer and promise as A, but they are preceded by the promise (10-19) that Šamaš will receive the tithe (*ešrētim ileqqe*) of all the silver and merchandise, a fact not stated in A and C. The subscript indicates that the record essentially is about the tithe (promised) and identifies the tablet as written "in accordance with the text of a tablet of the god", hence probably as a copy of the original record made for and kept in the temple as proof of Sîn-išmeanni's promise.

Note that all three texts are objective, third-person records, which establish facts (A:6., B:19, C:31ff.) and formulate wishes and that in none of them Sîn-išmeanni himself speaks. He may have pronounced the prayers of A:11f. and B:20ff. and stated what he would do if his wish were granted, but he may also have only promised the tithe (B:10-19), while a representative of the god/temple then formulated the wish for profit and its ensuing liability. But Sîn-išmeanni's obligation to obey Šamaš's orders and to give him what he was entitled to could never have been recorded if he had not made a formal promise to that effect. Anyhow, A and B are objectively styled records of what happened in the temple, where an accounting and promises were made and prayers uttered. Text C, after a detailed listing of all assets simply states: "Whatever he has, Sîn-išmeanni, belongs to Šamaš", the meaning of which will be discussed below.

The words which describe Sîn-išmeanni's relation to Šamaš need a closer analysis:

A:10ff. *Šamaš dajjān kinātim īṣum ana mādim litūrma ša qabi Šamaš S. līpuš.*

B:10ff. *ešrēt kaspim ...* [15] *bēl mātim Šamaš illil mātišu ileqqe* [20] *iṣum ana mādim litūrma ina mādim Šamaš līpul, mimma ša Šamaš iqabbûšum līpušma Šamaš līpul.*

C:31ff. *mimma ša išû S. ša Šamaš.*

A and B, like a prayer, contain the following elements:

a) *An invocation of Šamaš.* Clear in A, but in B embedded in the promise of the tithe, in apposition to the god as subject of the verb. In A Šamaš receives a traditional title, *dajjān kinātim*, "the righteous judge", which does not seem to be specifically related to the subject of our text, but may imply a warning to be honest in these matters. The titles in B, "Lord of the land" and "Enlil/supreme god of his land", are remarkable in professing Šamaš's superior authority and power. Qualifying the god as subject of "he

29 We lack an overall study of slavery in the Old Babylonian period, but see Harris 1975: 332-350, also on ideas about numbers (biggest number 32, as part of an inheritance, mentioned in AbB 5, 244) and slave sales (341 on a family "which concentrated its wealth in slaves"). She mentions the possibility (336) that some slave owners, with equal numbers of male and female slaves, practiced slave breeding, which may have entailed the sale of young house-born slaves (with appropriate names, as documented in the list in text C). Note also *OLA* 21, 21:4ff. (Abi-ešuḫ), "10 5/6 minas of silver which was paid to the palace for the purchase of slaves" and "5 minas and 10 shekels, the price of 14(?) slaves which entered the palace", which must refer to the purchase and sale of slaves in/from the palace.

will obtain", they express that as supreme lord he is entitled to the tithe from a human subject. Indirectly, as a kind of *captatio benevolentiae*, they affirm that Šamaš has the power to grant Sîn-išmeanni's wish and as such are a strong appeal to the god to live up to his reputation.[30] The combination of "Lord of the land" and "Supreme god of his land", even if we can differentiate between "the land" and "his land", looks overdone and may betray the trader's urge to honor and please the god in order to earn his favor. But "his land", as the territory over which Šamaš as main god of Sippar had authority, have been chosen because this is where Sin-išmeanni intends to sell his merchandise.

Bēl-mātim may occur as designation of various major deities, who are "Lord of the land", cf. W.G. Lambert, *MARI* 4 (1985) 529, note 4, and J.-M. Durand, *MARI* 5 (1987) 611f. It is a self-designation of Šamaš in the mouth of his prophet in Andarig (ARMT 26/1, 194:3), by means of which he presents himself as a universal god, but in a speech which "offers a curious mixture of nationalism and universalism" (D. Charpin, *FM* 6 (2002), 29f., 3.4.2).

Illil mātišu, "Illil of his land", uses the name of the god Enlil, spelled phonetically, with initial *-i-* (as in a few syllabic spellings of in Old Babylonian and Old Assyrian personal names),[31] to qualify Šamaš as "supreme god of his land". Samsu-iluna in *RIME* 4, 381:14/15 calls Marduk "Illil of his land", after Anum and Enlil had "given him the sovereignty over the four quarters of the world", and Hammurabi in his laws (I:11) states that the *illilūt kiššat nišī* was given to Marduk. While this is understandable in view of the status of Marduk as main god of the capital, it is less so with Šamaš. Although as sun god and god of justice a universal god, his status as supreme god does not rest on a political development, sanctioned by Anum and Enlil, but in invocations and hymns meant to honor a god and to obtain his favor, his power and status may be exaggerated. In an inscription commemorating the building of the wall of Sippar (*RIME* 4, 334:2-4) Hammurabi addresses Šamaš as "the great lord of heaven and earth, the king of gods", and a devotee of Šamaš in Sippar could give her slave the name Šamaš-illil-ilī (CT 6, 40a:1).[32]

b) *A request*. Traders live from what they earn and need "profit" (*nēmelum*), by "converting what is little into much". This can be predicted in an omen, YOS 10,35:21 ([*makkūr awī*] *lim īṣum a<na> mādi<m> itā*[*r*]), but since trade always involved hasards and the market could be unpredictable, an Old Babylonian retail merchant may ask the gods to reveal him by extispicy "whether the retail goods he had bought will be sold with profit in the market street" (and the answer is favorable).[33] But gods could not only predict the outcome of the business, they could also help to make it succesful, as the man knew who called Marduk on his seal "the one who turns my few possessions into many" (*Marduk mutīr īṣi ana mādi*, AP no. 37). This same conviction must have inspired Sîn-išmeanni to enlist the help of Šamaš by means of a prayer which uses the same expression for making profit.

---

30 See for this function, W. Mayer, *Untersuchungen zur Formensprach der babylonischen "Gebetsbeschwörungen"* (Rome, 1976) 44f., where he quotes W. Beyerlin and E. Gerstenberger.

31 See for OB, *CAD* I/J 85 s.v. *illilu*, and for Old Assyrian, BIN 4, 119:11, kt 89/k 313:7, and Kayseri 291(!; published in C. Michel, *Innāya* II no. 175): 3 (*Šu-I-li-il*$_5$).

32 This PN also in BM 97021:1; *MHET* II/3, 375:18; VS 18, 8:15; VS 7, 20 seal, etc., and cf. names such as Šamaš-bēl-ilī, CT 48, 99:13 (above text a); *MHET* II/2, 140:2, 339:17; YOS 12, seal no. 216, etc., according to Stamm 1939:226, "Ehrentitel, welche dem Gott zum Dank gegeben wurden". King Sin-iddinam of Larsa (*RIME* 4, 169,3f.) calls Šamaš "the foremost of heaven and earth, the pre-eminent one among the Anunna gods" (sag.kal.an.ki,dirig ^{d}a.nun.ke$_4$.ne).

33 YBC 11056:2-4, *ana saḫerti ša išām*: *ina sūqi šimāti ana nēmeli innaddin*?, see A. Goetze, *JCS* 11 (1957) 91 and 93 note 21, B.Landsberger in *Suppl. Vetus Testamentum* 16 (1967) 184, and Veenhof 1972: 354.

c) *A promise of thanks*. This promise is conditional, as indicated by the use of two connected precatives, which link what Šamaš has to do directly with what Sîn-išmeanni will do in return. His deed is the logical effect of Šamaš's granting of his wish (*litūrma* ... *līpuš*/*līpul*) and we may render by "so that he will...", or "and then he will ...". Instead of the simple wording of A, *litūrma* ... *līpuš*, B has a double statement, *litūrma* ... *līpul*, "and then he will give to Šamaš what he is entitled to", followed (in a new sentence) by *līpušma* ... *līpul*, "then he will do what Šamaš orders him and give to Šamaš what he is entitled to". The interpretation of B raises two questions. Does B mean two different actions, first simply *apālum* (what was due or had been promised) and next *apālum* in obedience to an explicit order of the god? On the basis of A, the word order in B:23 (*epēšum* – *apālum*) and the repetition of *līpul* in B, I assume that B wishes to specify what simple *apālum* of 21 actually meant, "to do what the god orders", hence "meeting the god's legitimate demand" (*CAD* A/II, 155f.).[34] The second question is how this obligation relates to the tithe, which is the substance of B:1-19 and apparently also the main subject of this record, considering the "label" *ešrētum* in line 24. Could *apālum* actually mean the payment of the tithe and could this promise be the essence of the whole arrangement, notwithstanding the fact that B:1-19 is syntactically independent of what follows? Or does B imply that first the (traditional) promise of the tithe had been made and that subsequently (for whatever reason) a prayer was uttered to secure the god's blessing, which, when granted, would result in an additional obligation, the nature of which would be revealed by a word of the god. One could argue that giving the tithe was only feasible if profit was made and that the added prayer for the god's blessing was meant to bring this about. But then "doing whatever Šamaš orders" (B:22; A:13 has simply *ša qabê Šamaš*, cf. *CAD* Q 21,c) is strange and why should Šamaš give an order about the tithe, which had already been promised and whose nature and size must have been clear? The words used are similar to those in BIN 2, 85 (Si. 27), where 11 shekels of silver are borrowed from Šamaš, with as interest an offering meal (*mākalum*) and the debtor "will do as Šamaš tells him" (*kīma Šamaš iqabbû eppuš*) [35] One wonders what this could mean such loan, apart from meeting the request to pay back at a particular time, perhaps in a particular valuta. In our texts one might think of a particular wish uttered by the god and made known by extispicy.[36] But perhaps the orders of Šamaš could also concern the management of the trade, the use of the capital for the acquisition of goods the temple needed.

This raises the question of the ownership of the assets, capital and merchandise. Here the last lines of C, "everything Sîn-išmeanni has belongs to Šamaš" are important and the question is what they mean. One could imagine that Sin-išmeanni was in such big problems that he declared all his assets the property of Šamaš, in the hope that this would secure him the god's blessing, so that he could recover (*balāṭum, bulṭam kašādum*) economically. But there is no indication for it in the text nor any parallel, and how could our trader himself benefit from such a step? It is better to take these words as the acknowledgement that all Sîn-išmeanni's assets listed, which he managed as trader, in fact belong to Šamaš. This could mean two things. The temple, as a silent partner could have entrusted them to Sîn-išmeanni, who was contracted as a business partner (*tappûm*) of the god, as was the case in some of the contracts quoted at the end of § 1. But this is unlikely, because

34 The verb is also used in loans granted by Šamaš, where payment means meeting the debt claim of the god as creditor, e.g. in Boyer, *Contribution* 212:4, *ištu* ... *še'am* ... *ša Šamaš ina muḫḫi PN išû Šamaš īpulu*, "after PN had satisfied Šamaš with x barley which she owes to Šamaš ...".

35 See Harris 1960:132. These words remind me of the stipulation in MDP 22, 119 (quoted at the end of § 1) on a partnership between a god and a trader, where the latter's only promise is that "he will do what is (the wish/in the interest) of Šamaš" (*ša Šamaš ippuš*). This unspecified obedience to Šamaš is understandable in this basic agreement, devoid of any details, which presumably is a continuation of a partnership with the trader's father, the rules of which must have been known.

36 According to apodoses of Old Babylonian omina and some other texts (see *CAD* E 284f. 1,b, 2'-3', and 3) gods may request a priestess, a *nadītum*, a sacrifice, a precious garment, a wigg, a sun-disc, "something valuable", unspecified votive gifts (referring to vows which had not been fulfilled), and even the tithe.

the terms "partnership" (*tappūtum*) and "profit" (*nēmelum*), which characterize such relationships, are not used, while what the god will receive is called the tithe, ten percent (of the proceeds?), which is different from and less than what a silent partner might expect (in Old Assyrian partnership contracts the investing partners receive at least one third). I rather believe that Sîn-išmeanni's assets were a commercial loan from the temple, for which he had to pay back in due time (*ina šalām ḫarrānim*). While the trader could consider the assets he managed his own, they were also the property of the god. Acknowledging this fact must have been useful as a means of obtaining the god's blessing for the enterprise, the success of which would benefit both the god and his trader.

How does this relate to the promise of the tithe? I assume that the trader working with assets of the temple, in addition to paying back his divine principal what was normally due,[37] would also give him the tithe of the proceeds, which may have been a tradition in such a relationship. The Old Babylonian occurrences of the tithe, presented in Appendix 2, suggest that (in a commercial context) it was a gift to a god/temple, based on the tradition of letting the (local) temple share in the proceeds, or on a vow which promised the temple a round share (one-tenth) of what was earned in an undertaking for which the god's blessing had been invoked. Something similar is apparently assumed by Dercksen for temples which supplied Old Assyrian traders with assets designated as *ikribū*. He avoids the notion of a tax or a fixed share in the profit, and speaks of "a covert obligation to present valuable offerings to the god as token of gratitude" (quoted above, p. [2], hier p. 370). The tithe promised by Sîn-išmeanni may have been similar and the readiness to offer it may have been instrumental in obtaining temple assets as a commercial loan.

Conclusion

If all this is correct, the tithe in our texts has to be kept separate from the other liability which Sîn-išmeanni assumed. Having obtained his assets, which made him a trader for and a debtor of the temple of Šamaš, he must have wished to improve his chances of commercial success, presumably for specific reasons which remain unknown to us, but which may explain why our texts and their arrangements are thus far unique. He made a vow that if Šamaš blessed his undertaking and he made a good profit, he would give the god, in addition to the tithe already promised, also whatever the god would ask from him. The whole arrangement was agreed upon and recorded in the temple, which must have been helpful in doing so, since it would benefit from Sîn-išmeanni's success. The records which have survived – A a contract without its sealed envelope, B the copy of a temple record, and C a private memorandum – must have belonged to Sîn-išmeanni's archive and it is unfortunate that we have no records which document the role of the temple or the outcome of this remarkable arrangement. It only shows that our knowledge of Old Babylonian trade still is incomplete and that we need sizable merchant's archives, comparable to those found in *kārum* Kanish, to understand more.

---

37 Either the capital plus interest or a fixed sum at a fixed time, based on the value of the goods and the length of the credit term (with default interest if payment is too late), as attested in Old Assyrian and Old Babylonian Larsa credit sales and commercial consignments.

Appendix 1. BM 97041

Text B. BM 97032 (1902-10-11,86)

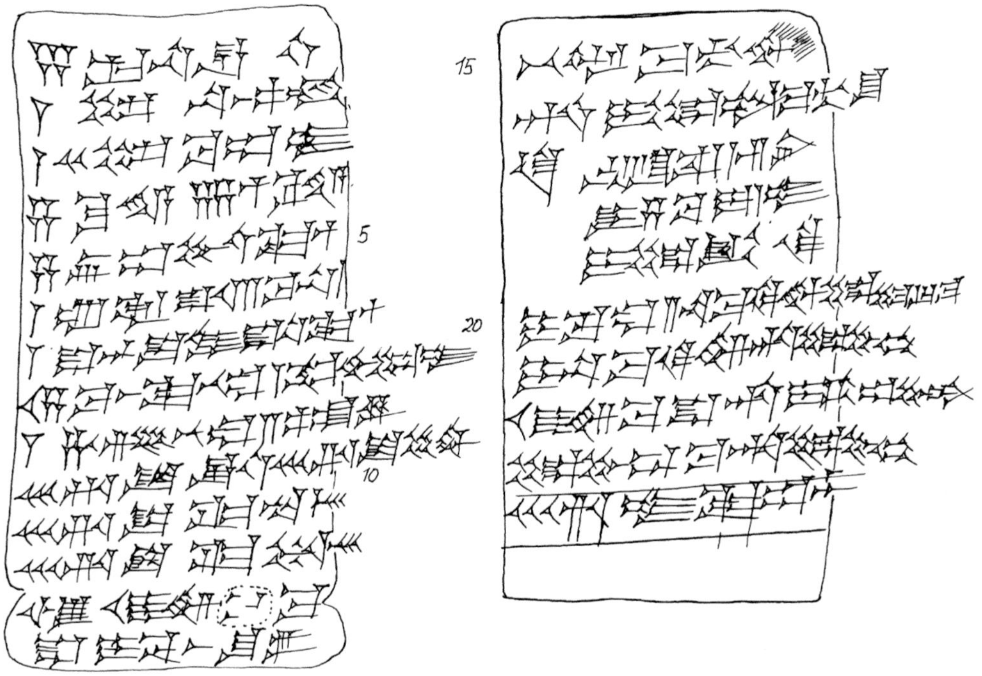

Text C. BM 97065 (1902-10-11,119)

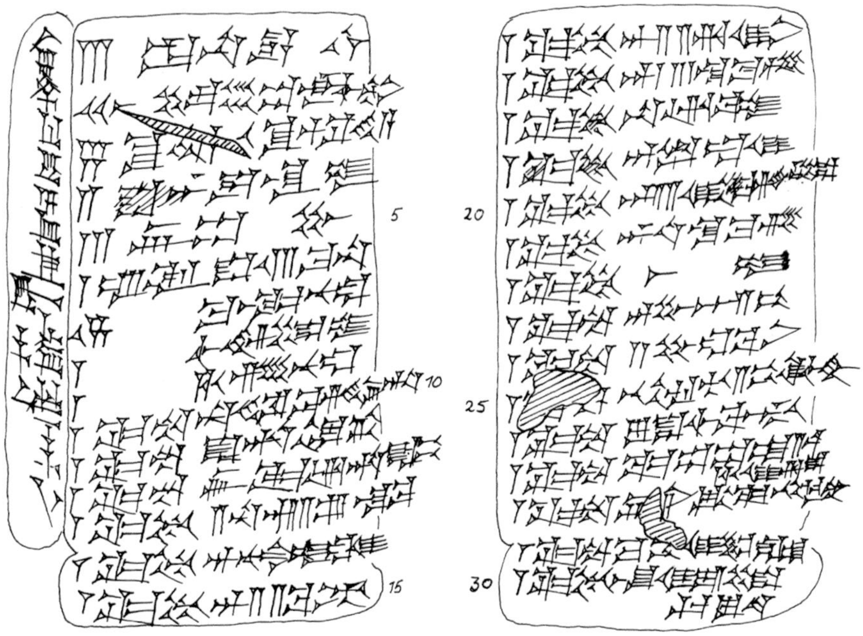

Text D. BM 97041 (1902-10-11,95)

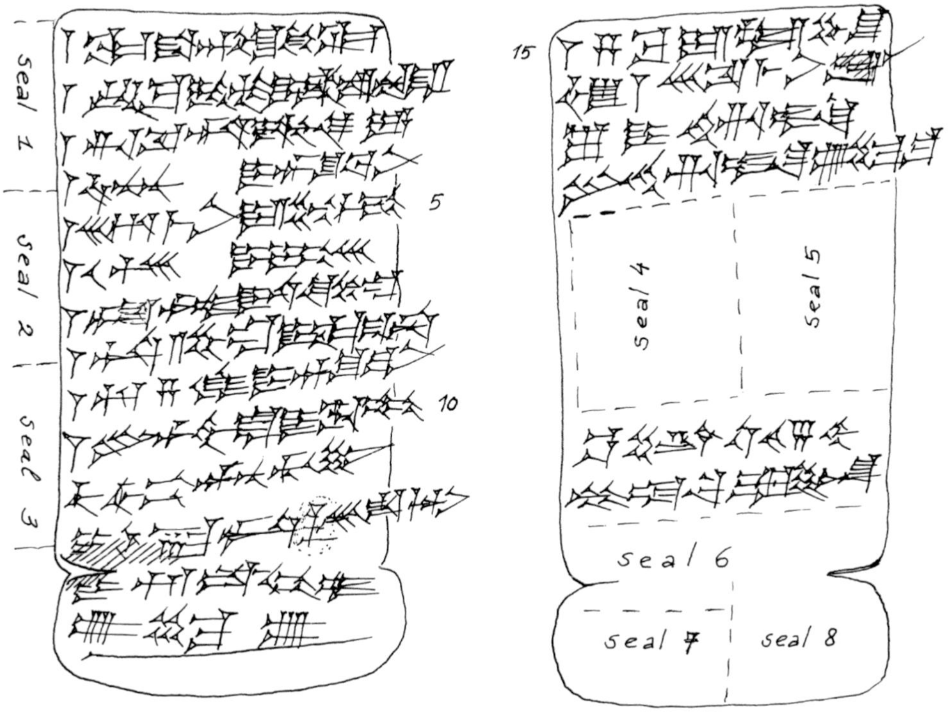

D. BM 97041 (1902-10-11,95), sealed tablet.

Text D belongs to the same museum accession as A – C and must have been part of Sîn-išmeanni's archive, since it deals with his person. The unique subject and the unusual formulation make its interpretation difficult, but assuming that "Sin-išmeanni, son of Huddultum" of lines 12f. is the same as Sîn-išme<a>nni of line 16, mentioned after "his father Zabayatum", the text probably deals with his status or identity (note the verbal suffix third pers. sing. in line 18). The verb *watûm*, "to find", could refer to the actual finding of an exposed child, a foundling, but perhaps also to the findings of an investigation. Sîn-išmeanni's identity must have been established by the testimony of witnesses, given under oath in the temple of Šamaš (line 12), that Sîn-išmeanni (known as?) the son of a woman called Huddultum (*CAD* H, 223a, also CT 45, 3:11, 21), was truly the son of Zabayatum. We do not know the reason for this legal action, but there may have been questions about Sîn-išmeanni's identity or status (legitimation of a bastard, disputed adoption?). Once his status was established, he counted – as his father – as citizen of the town of Hiritum, situated ca. ten kms. northwest of Sippar on the Irnina,[38] and was recognized as such by its citizens (taking LÚ in line 18 as collective).

^{p}PUZUR$_{4}$-^{d}NIN.ḪUR.SAG	Puzur-Ninḫursag,
^{pd}EN.ZU-*i-din-nam* DUMU *Ig-mil-Ìr-ra*	Sîn-idinnam, son of Igmil-Irra,
^{p}*Ri-iš*-^{d}UTU DUMU *Akšak*^{ki}*-ia*	Riš-Šamaš, son of Akšaya,
^{p}SIG-*Nu-nu* DUMU DINGIR-*šu-ba-ni*	Ipiq-Nunu, son of Ilšu-bani,
^{p}30-*re-me-ni* DUMU *A-bu-wa-qar*	Sîn-remenni, son of Abu-waqar,

38 See now S.W. Cole and H. Gasche, *Changing Watercourses in Babylonia* (*MHEM* V/1, 1998), 21ff., with map 7.

^{p}*U-bar*-30 DUMU *I-bi*-30	Ubar-Sîn, son of Ibbi-Sîn,
^{p}AN.KI-*an-tum* DUMU *Na-qí-mu-um*	Annum-pi-antum, son of Naqimum
^{pd}UTU-*a-bu-um* DUMU PUZUR$_4$-^{d}UTU	Šamaš-abum, son of Puzur-Šamaš,
^{p}*Ḫu-za-lum* DUMU DINGIR-*šu-ba-ni*	Ḫuzalum, son of Ilšu-bani
^{p}LÚ-^{d}IŠKUR.RA DUMU *Da-qu*	Lu-Iškura, son of Daqqum -
IGI *ši-bi an-nu-ti-in*	in the presence of these witnesses
i-na É-^{d}UTU $^{p!}$30-*iš-me-an-ni*	in the tempel of Šamaš
DUMU *Ḫu-du-ul-tum*	they found Sîn-išmeanni *(to be?)*
ú-tu-ú	the son of Ḫud(d)ultum.
^{p}*Za-ba-ia-tum a-bu-šu*	Zabayatum, his father,
ù 30-*iš-me-<a>-ni* DUMU.A.NI$^{?}$	and Sîn-išmenni, *his son*$^{?}$,
lu DUMU *Ḫi-ri-tum*^{ki}	indeed are natives of Ḫiritum.
LÚ *Ḫi-ri-tum*^{ki} *ú-tu-šu*	The citizens of Ḫiritum found him
ITU ŠE.KIN.KUD U$_4$ *25*.KAM	(to be so). 25-XII of the year
MU UNUG^{ki} *I-si-in*^{ki}“	Uruk (and) Isin” (Ham. year 7)

7. See for the reading of this name, M. Stol, *SEL* 8 (1991) 192, “Writing”.
12. “Personenkeil” over erased DUMU.
16. End of line difficult due to damage and some overlap with the end of line 12.

Inscriptions of seal impressions:

1. [*A*]-*bu-um-wa-qa*[*r*] / DUMU NANNA.MA.AN.SUM / GALA UD x [x], same seal on VS 9, 18 (delivery of barley *ana* ŠUKU É ^{d}EN.ZU, Hammu-rabi year x]
2. PUZUR$_4^{?}$-[ ] / DUMU *Ma*-x [ ] / ÚRDU *I*?-[ ];
3. Illegible, apart from *Ištar* at the end of line 3;
4. [x ...] *a*$^{?}$ – x .../ DUMU DINGIR-[*šu-ba-ni*] / ÚRDU ^{d}[MAR.TU]$^{?}$, witness 4?;
5. Illegible, apart from line 2: DUMU *Ta*$^{?}$-[ ];
6. ^{d}*Na-bi*-[ ] / DUB.SAR / É [ ];
7. PUZUR$_4$-^{d}NIN.TU.KE$_4$ / DUMU *A-lí*-ILLAT-*ti*, the first witness, also attested in CT 47, 17a:17’f. (Sm), *Puzur*$_4$-^{d}NIN.ḪUR.SAG.GÁ DUMU *A-li-<ti>-la-ti*;
8. [*Ri-iš*] ^{d}[UTU] / DUMU *Ak*-[*ša*]-[*ia*] / ÚRDU *Ḫa-am-mu-ra*-[*bi*], witness 3, presumably the same man as Rīš-Šamaš, son of Akšak-idinnam, in VS 8, 66 (Sm).

Appendix 2. The Tithe (*Ešrētum*)

“Tithe” (zag.10, *ešrētum*) is a numerical term which can refer to any share of ten percent. In Babylonia it can be the ten percent extra assigned to the oldest son and heir, the one-tenth of the proceeds of a trading expedition(?) which the gods Nanna and in particular Ningal in Ur in received (see below 5), and the one tenth share of the harvest which a tenant had to give to the owner of the field (níg.ku$_5$.da zag.10 = *miksi ešrēti* in *ana ittišu* IV iii:8). The tithe as tax is well known in Old Assyrian trade, where it is the percentage of the imported textiles which Anatolian palaces could pre-empt and also the tax levied by the Assyrian authorities on iron and lapis lazuli traded by Assyrians.[39].

The following OB occurrences need our attention:

1. King Išme-Dagan of Isin, according to *RIME* 4, 32ff., no. 5:5ff. and no. 6 cols. ii and vi, claims to have taken the following measures to improve the life of his subjects and especially of the city of Nippur. He freed Nippur and its subjects from taxation and obligatory service (gú du$_8$; dumu/éren kaskal.ta zig), making them (*thereby*) available for the temples of Nippur’s

39 See for lapis lazuli, VS 26, 12:4ff. and for iron kt n/k 67:28-37 (Donbaz, *Studies Veenhof*, 84), kt 92/k 200: 12f., and 221:12f. (see J.G. Dercksen, *Old Assyrian Institutions* (*MOS Studies* 4; Leiden, 2004) 114f.).

gods.[40] To this the longer inscription, no. 6 ii: 8-10, adds: "he cancelled the tithe of Sumer and Akkad" (ki.en.gi [ki.uri] zà.u.[bi] [m]u.[un.du$_8$]), and this same measure is mentioned again in col. v: 7'ff. (after the exemption from dues or taxation, gú du$_8$).

This last measure widens the scope of his action far beyond Nippur, but it remains unclear, since we do not know what this tithe was. Assuming that such a general "tithe" was levied on basic products, we may think of a tax on barley. We might then link it with Enlil-bani's reduction of the grain tax from twenty to ten percent (*RIME* 4, 89 vi:12-15), but this is only a hypothesis, since we lack data on general taxation of the population.[41]

2. BE 6/1, 66 (reign of Abi-ešuḫ): *1.1.4* ŠE.GUR ^{2} ^{giš}BÁN ^{d}UTU ^{3} IGI.*10*.GÁL ^{4} *ik-ri-bu* ^{5} *ša* ^{d}UTU $^{6\ edge}$ *i-na qá-ti* ^{7} ^{p}*Ma-an-nu-um-ki-ma-*^{d}⌈UTU⌉ $^{8\ rev.}$ (four lines destroyed) ^{12} *i-*⌈x x⌉ [x x] $^{13\text{-}16}$ 19-VI^{ii} Ae 6, "1 1/3 gur of barley, the tithe, votive gift of Šamaš, from the hands of Mannum-kima-Šamaš ... [*received*?]."

The interpretation is difficult because we lack the last five lines. Some may have registered witnesses, but we also need a verbal form, probably ŠU.TI.A / *imḫur*, "he received", and there might have been a second person who received the barley from M. It could be a loan, if M. acted as agent of the temple of Šamaš (which would match his name), from whom the missing debtor had received the barley. Its designation as "votive tithe" in that case could indicate that the temple kept a separate fund into which such donations went (see the comments on 4). It could also be a quittance, stating that the tithe vowed by M. (why and how remains unclear), recorded as a debt, is paid and [received by NN], who represents Šamaš. This is more likely, since the odd figure of 1 1/3 gur of barley suggests a capital of 1 gur increased by the normal annual interest (33 1/3 %) on barley.

3. TCL 10, 120 (date destroyed), a long list of valuable objects, semi-precious stones and pieces of furniture, their value frequently expressed in silver, in lines 34ff. ends with the subscript: *an-nu-um ša* IGI.*10*.GÁL ⌈x x (x)⌉ ^{35} ^{d}UTU *il-qú-ú* $^{36\ edge}$ *i-na né*$^{!}$*-me*$^{!}$*-li-im ša ib-ba-áš-šu* ^{37} I[GI].*10*.GÁL ^{d}UTU *i-le-qé* (followed by a broken dating), "This is what (of which?) as the tithe ... Šamaš received. From the profit which will be made Šamaš will take the tithe".

The slight emendation in line 36 (for my *né-me* the copy has SILA$_3$) is suggested by clauses in loans from Šamaš, that they will be repaid from the profit (*nēmelim* and the plural *nēmelētišu*) the debtor will make / which Šamaš will give him, see Skaist 1994:177. The lines quoted first identify what is enumerated as what the god has (already) received *as* tithe (or rather the tithe *of which* he received) and continue by stating that the god will also receive his share from future profit. It is a settlement of accounts of a completed journey, concluded by a promise of a tithe on the next one or its continuation.

4. CT 6, 40c (Sabium 2): *1/3 mana 4* GÍN [KÙ.B.] ^{2} *eš-re-tum* KI ^{d}[UTU] ^{3} ^{p}*Ki-šu-šu-ú* ^{4} ŠU BA.AN.TI ^{5} *ana Ilum-rabi* ^{6} *ana ipṭirīšu* ^{7} *iddin* ^{8} *ūm ebūrim še'am* ^{9} *ana* ^{d}UTU ^{10} *inaddin* $^{11\text{-}18}$ five witnesses and date, "24 shekels of [silver] is the tithe, Kišušū received/borrowed it

---

40 The interpretation of the last statement is based on the wording of a hymn of the king, where he describes the effects or purpose of his measure as making the men of Nippur (free and) available for (service to) the temple of Enlil, Ninlil and Ninruta (é ^{d}en.líl.mà.šè éren.bi ḫa.ba.ra.an.gar), cf. Kraus 1984: 18, I-D 3. Compare also the Sippar inscription of Hammurabi, *RIME* 4, 335f. : 58ff, *Sippar*^{ki} *āl ṣiātim ša Šamaš ṣābašu ina ṭupšikkim ana Šamaš lū assuḫ* // éren.bi^{giš} dusu.ta ^{d}utu.ra ḫé.bí.zi.

41 The argument that it cannot be the tax mentioned by Enlil-bani, because the tithe had been abolished a century earlier by a predecessor, ignores the ideological nature of such claims of social justice and economic prosperity.

from Šamaš. He gave it to Ilum-bani as ransom. At the time of the harvest he will give Šamaš barley".

I follow Edzard, *Tell ed-Dēr* (1970) 33, in assuming that the temple of Šamaš had loaned silver at favorable conditions (no interest, payment in barley at harvest time) to a man without means, who had to pay back the person who had ransomed him. The designation of the silver as "tithe" has nothing to do with the purpose of this loan, but probably shows that the temple kept a separate fund consisting of tithes received, but it would go too far to to deduce from our text that this fund was used in particular or only for charitable purposes.

5. AbB 8, 88. A severely damaged letter (address missing), which deals with the question why a woman by the name of Karanatum is suffering. A diviner has diagnosed a.o. the failure to bring the funerary offering for her father, and women who communicate with the gods (*šā'ilātum*) deny that her suffering is due to the "hands" of particular gods. Then follows: 11' x x *iš-re-e-tim il-ti-*[*e-qé*] 12' *libbašu ṭāb mim*[*ma* x x] 13' [x x x (x)-*ti* dUTU *ú*-[x x x]. 14' *Karanatum* [x x x] 15' *anumma ḫaṭṭum* [x x x] 16' *napšat* x [x x x] ..., " ... the tithe he has now received, he is satisfied, anything ... Šamaš [will not?]. As for Karanatum ...the staff is now ...the life of..."

The letter reminds me of Old Assyrian cases, where women suffer the anger of the gods, fall ill and are plagued by demons and evil spirits, because the traders, their male relatives, have not delivered the *ikribū* to the gods (see *CMK* nos. 323-325). Cf. also the omen in MDP 57, 242 III:5, *qāt Šamaš qāt ikribīšu*, where the (maleficent) "hand" of Šamaš is linked with the negative effect of an (unfufilled) vow. In line 15' *ḫaṭṭum* could be positive, a scepter or staff which protects (perhaps used metaphorically), but also an instrument to punish, cf. AbB 1, 18: 23 (*ḫaṭṭam nadûm eli*).

6. A "tithe (zag.10.kam) of Ningal" occurs in eight OB texts from Ur, which list valuable items, donated as votive gifts (a.ru.a) by a variety of people, including a few merchants,[42] often labeled as "from (the yield of, š à) an expedition to Tilmun".

Van de Mieroop 1989:399 distinguishes the tithe as votive gift, donated out of free will as an expression of gratitude (possibly in fulfillment of an earlier vow) for a successful business trip to Tilmun,[43] from the tithe which occurs in three texts (once also said to derive from an expedition to Tilmun) in combination with níg.ku$_5$ = *miksum*. The latter would be a levy of ten percent, "the amount of tax raised". But this

42 Among the objects donated were small silver boats: UET 5, 532:7f.; 551 iii: 6'f.; 553 i:17, iii:10'f.; 561:4, 23; 563 iii:2, iv:11,13; 566:4', rev.:3', 5', 8'; 567 I:2', 4'. Precious objects are mostly found in early records, until the middle of the reign of Nur-Adad.

43 With comments on earlier interpretations by Oppenheim 1954 and Butz 1979. Items qualified as "tithe of Ningal" occur in the texts edited by Heimpel 1987: 83ff. as nrs. 56-58 and 60-61, and possibly in UET 5, 524 rev.: 3'. In addition there are a few cases where Ningal receives "the tithe", which is ten percent of what Nanna gets (UET 5, 529:15f.; 557:7; and perhaps 564 III:1-4). In view of the quantities mentioned, I find it difficult to believe that all items designated as "tithe of Ningal" only represent one tenth of what had been given to Nanna and hence only one percent of the proceeds of the trade and I assume that there also existed a "independent" tithe, donated to Ningal alone. If not, UET 5, 546 and 678 (Heimpel 1987: 83f., nrs 56 and 61) would imply enormous donations to Nanna, of respectively ca. 16 and 170 talents of copper, ca. 6 and 50 minas of ivory, ca. 70 and 81 litres of kauri-shells, etc., which in turn would be only one-tenth of the total yield or profit of the trade. Although some texts mention vast amounts of copper acquired in Tilmun (UET 5, 796 more than 611 talents), and some of the records are summations of donations by "various persons who went on their own initiative" (lú.didli nì.ne.ne.ta du.a) and may cover several years (292, iv:5ff.), it is difficult to assume that what Ningal received represented only one percent of the yield of the trade.

distinction is problematic,[44] because the tithe is not equated with the tax, although both apparently were delivered to the temple of Ningal and both could consist of what the traders imported from abroad, such as semi-precious stones, ivory and gold. "One mina of copper, *miksum* of ivory", mentioned in UET 5, 678:13, in the middle of a text with the subscript "tithe of Ningal", could mean that the person who gives the tithe, instead of offering ten percent of his ivory (which might have required the splitting of a tusk), paid his due in copper, based on the exchange rate of ivory. Something similar happened in Old Assyrian trade (VS 26, 12:4ff.), where a trader would rather pay the tithe on lapis lazuli in silver, than cutting the lump of twelve pounds to pieces. If so, the use of *miksum* does not identify what was given as a "tax", but simply as an appropriate share due to the goddess. While *miksum* in some cases, presumably by decree or agreement, was a levy or tax, there is no proof for a fixed tariff.[45] An inscription of Enlil-bani (*RIME* 4, 89 vi:12-15) states that he reduced amount of barley due as *miksum* (še níg.ku$_5$.ra,which thus far had been twenty percent, to ten percent,[46] and this warns us against simply equating tithe and *miksum*. This also applies to the combination *miksi ešrēti*, "a *miksum* of one-tenth" (in *ana ittišu* IV iii: 7f.), where *miksum* is the contractually fixed share of the harvest due to the owner of his field, which according to this schoolbook might also be 50, 33 1/3, 25, 20, and 10 percent, hence no fixed percentage. Basically *miksum*[47] is that part of what somebody has acquired which he has to give to somebody else on the basis of a contract (*e.g.* for renting a field), a traditional arrangement, or a ruling (to be assumed for Larsa and Mari (see note 45).[48]

7. The undated administrative record Kienast, *Kisurra* no. 98, an account of oxen delivered for various purposes, ends with the laconic words "22 (oxen) for the temple of Nanna as tithe" (*22 ana* É ^{d}NANNA [15] *ana ešrētim*).

We know nothing of its background and 22 is neither the sum of the previous entries nor ten percent of the total of number of animals listed.

---

44 Main evidence in UET 5, 549 (see Heimpel 1987: 85, no. 60): precious stones "from (the yield of) an expedition to Tilmun, the tithe of Ningal, from what was delivered M. has delivered it to the temple of Ningal as (MU) the *miksum* (NÍG.KU$_5$) of various individuals". See also UET 5, 558 rev.10, at the end of a list of objects and goods, "21 minas of copper, *miksum* (NÍG.KU$_5$) of [various] persons (LÚ [...])", and in line 15, NÍG.KU$_5$ M[Á ...], but this text does not use the term "tithe".

45 Two occurrences in Larsa, *RA* 72 (1978) 132f., nrs 21:18f. and 22, where *miksum* was a levy on commercial shipments (*šūbultum*), give amounts in silver, but without mentioning a rate, which we also cannot calculate from the data given. In the complete no. 22, with a shipment of 1 talent of leek (*kàr-šum*), 4 shekels of silver are given "to the *mākisum* and for the boat", hence tax and transport costs. In Mari an import tax or rather transit duty in silver was levied (*makāsum*) on merchandise arriving by boat via the Euphrates (ARM 13,58-99, with *Syria* 41 [1964] 67-103 and *LAPO* 18, 2000, 25-39) and there are some indications that it could amount to ten percent (ARM 13, 90 and *LAPO* 18, no. 877) or at least that there existed a fixed tariff (the *miksum* on boats carrying oil and wine nearly always amounted to 1 shekel of silver per jar), but we cannot prove that this applies always and to all merchandise. ARM 7, 233:15'-19' states "Of 4 minas of silver of the palace and 1 mina of silver, a gift of RN, at an exchange rate of 14 :1, the *miksum* was 5 1/2 minas of tin", which means nearly eight percent or ca. ten percent if we assume that no *miksum* was levied on the gift to the king. [**Add**. See for the *miksum* levied on Old Assyrian caravans passing a town in the Jazira and its importance for the local ruler, mentioned in the Mari letter A. 3064, M. Guichard in: J.G. Dercksen (ed.), *Anatolia and the Jazira During the Old Assyrian Period* (*OAAS* 3, Leiden 2008) 46].

46 Probably rather the share in the yield of crown land which was due as rent than a general tax. J. Renger, in M. Hudson and M. Van de Mieroop, *Debt and Economic Renewal in the Ancient Near East* (Bethesda, 2002) 109, paraphrases as "The barley-dues (to be delivered on the basis of field rentals) which so far had been one-fifth, I reduced indeed to one-tenth (of the yield)". Note AUCT IV, 76: "114 gur of barley which S. owes to the palace as *miksum*" (*še miksi* UGU S. *ekallum išû*).

47 See the analysis by Kraus 1958: 133-143, with the data registered in *CAD* M/II. 63f.

48 Note also YOS 14, 313:9ff., summation, "52 sheep, their value in silver 2/3 mina, sheep as *miksum* of P[N] (UDU NÍG.KU$_5$ *Di-ib*-[...]), delivered to..." (Isin, Iddin-Dagan).

8. The apodosis of an OB omen text (CT 3, 4 rev. 22) simply states "Šamaš demands the/a tithe" (*Šamaš ešrētim erriš*).

Since the nature of the tithe is not specified, it must have been clear to those involved. It may have been the tithe traditionally donated to Šamaš (as was the tithe of Ningal in Ur), but more likely the tithe which the man consulting the oracle (who is addressed by the omen) had promised but had failed to give. This may have led to which made him decide to consult the oracle, which reminded him of his obligation. Cf. the OB omen apodoses where the god asks *ikribū* but also "*his ikribū*" (*CAD* I/J 65, c), that vowed by the person for whom the extispicy is carried out.

9. "[Year] when he ... the t]ithe of [Na]nna of Ur", occurs in Kienast, *Kisurra* no. 132, and is attested in its full form in OECT 13, 7 and 12: MU.ÚS.SA ZAG.10 ᵈNANNA URIM^{ki}(.ŠÈ) *Ibni-šadû* MU.UN.DÍM, "when Ibni-šadû ... the tithe of Nanna to Ur".

> This is a problematic reference, since what Ibni-šadû, a minor ruler of the city of Marad,[49] did with he "the tithe" is expressed by the verb DÍM, in OECT 13, 7:9 construed with a terminative/directive postfix. Kienast renders it by "heranschaffen", but the verb means "to fashion, build, create". Is ZAG.10 here (a valuable object donated as) tithe or rather used for ZAG = *a/ešertum*, "sanctuary, chapel", which the ruler built?

Abstract

In this contribution a set of three related texts (one of which was published long ago) from Old Babylonian Sippar are published and interpreted. They deal with a trader, who probably managed assets (silver and carefully itemized merchandise, consisting of barley, textiles, metal objects, and slaves) with a total value of ca. ten pounds of silver, made available to him by the temple of Šamaš. He had promised the god the tithe (of the proceeds?) and in addition the blessing and assistance of Šamaš are invoked to make his enterprise profitable. If so he promises to do what the Šamaš orders him by satisfying the god's demands. To understand these unique sources a survey is given of what we know about the commercial involvement of temples in the Old Babylonian period, with special attention for records which document commercial co-operation between a trader and a god, the role of votive gifts, and (in an Appendix) the tithe.

BIBLIOGRAPHY

Butz, K. 1979. Ur in altbabylonischer Zeit als Wirtschaftsfaktor, in: E. Lipinski (ed.), *State and Temple Economy in the Ancient Near East*, I (*OLA* 5, Leuven) 57-409, esp. 361ff., 3. Fernhandel, Import und Export nach Tilmun.

Charpin, D. 1982. Marchands du palais et marchands du temple à la fin de la Iʳᵉ dynastie de Babylone, *JA* 270, 25-65.

Dercksen, J.G. 1997. The Silver of the Gods. On Old Assyrian *ikribū*, *ArAn* 3, 75-100.

Dombradi, E. 2000. Studien zu *mitḫārum/mitḫāriš* und die Frage des Duplums, I, *ZA* 90, 40-69.

Harris, R. 1960. Old Babylonian Temple Loans, *JCS* 14, 126-137 (with Harris 1975, 206-208).

–. 1975. *Ancient Sippar. A Demographic Study of an Old-Babylonian City* (*1894-1595 B.C.*) (Istanbul)

–. 1977. Notes on the Slave Names of Old Babylonian Sippar, *JCS* 29, 46-51.

Heimpel, W. 1987. Das Untere Meer, *ZA* 77, 22-91.

Koppen, F. van. 2004. The Geography of the Slave Trade and Northern Mesopotamia in the Late Old Babylonian Period, in: H. Hunger and R. Pruszinszky (eds), *Mesopotamian Dark Age Revisited* (Öst. Akad. d.Wisss., Denkschr. Bd. 32, Wien), 9-34.

49 See for this year-name and the king to which it belongs now M. Stol, *AfO* 27 (1980) 162, § 13 and OECT 13, p. 1.

Kraus, F.R. 1958. *Ein Edikt des Könings Ammi-ṣaduqa von Babylon* (*SD* 5, Leiden).
–. 1984. *Königliche Verfügungen in altbabylonischer Zeit* (*SD* 11, Leiden).
Leemans, W.F. 1960. *Foreign Trade in the Old Babylonian Period as Revelead by Texts from Southern Mesopotamia* (*SD* 6, Leiden).
Oppenheim, A.L. 1954. The Seafaring Merchants of Ur, *JAOS* 74, 6-17.
A. Skaist, A. 1994. *The Old Babylonian Loan Contract* (Ramat Gan).
Stamm, J.J. 1939. *Die Akkadische Namengebung* (*MVAeG* 44, Leipzig) 307ff., § 41. Sklavennamen.
Stol, M. 1991. Old Babylonian Personal Names, *SEL* 8,191-212.
Van de Mieroop, M. 1989. Gifts and Tithes to the Temple in Ur, in: H. Behrens e.a. (eds), *Dumu-e$_2$-dub-ba-a. Studies in Honor of Åke W. Sjöberg* (Occ. Publ. S.N. Kramer Fund, 11, Philadelphia), 397-402.
Veenhof, K.R. 1972. *Aspects of Old Assyrian Trade and its Terminology* (*SD* 10, Leiden).
–. 1987. 'Dying Tablets' and 'Hungry Silver'.Elements of Figurative Language in Akkadian Commerical Terminology, in: M. Mindlin e.a. (eds.), *Figurative Language in the Ancient Near East* (London), 41-75.

Assyrian Commercial Activities in Old Babylonian Sippar Some New Evidence*

In 1980 C.B.F. Walker published a two column tablet (BM 97188), presumably from Sippar and written "in a clear Babylonian script", listing fourteen different loans, involving at least 9 minas of silver and some other items.[1] The dating of one of the loans by means of an Assyrian year eponymy and the fact that amounts of silver are twice qualified as "according to the weight-stone of the city-house" (*bīt alim*), he took as indications that the transactions recorded had taken place in Assyria. The first loan, involving silver used for commercial purposes (*kasap tappūtim* and *tadmiqtum*), was issued by a certain Warad-Sin, son of Ilī-asūni (KI *W. PN* ŠU BA.AN.TI), whom Walker took as "presumably an official of the institution, whether temple or palace, which makes all the following loans..., which apparently has a well organized book-keeping system, is involved in financing foreign trade, making loans to Assyrians and perhaps even having a representative at Aššur". Another loan (lines 49ff.) "of a large quantity of vegetables to an Assyrian, presumably for human consumption, hints at the presence of a large Assyrian family or possibly even a small trading colony at Sippar".

These observations, introduced by a survey of the evidence in Old Babylonian texts for Assyrian commercial contacts with or involvement in Sippar,[2] suggest an institutional framework for the commercial relations between Aššur and Sippar, which does not go beyond the bounds of what is feasible for this period, judging from the Old Assyrian commercial system and the role of the *kārum* of Sippar. But it is to a large extent based on the interpretation of a single text, BM 97188, and hence is in need of confirmation. The discovery, in the British Museum, of two texts, BM 96968 and 97097, belonging to the same acquisition (Bu 1902, 10-11) as BM 97188, and related to it by their contents, offers the opportunity of checking and revising the interpretations proposed by Walker. Additional information can also be derived from some of the letters recently published in AbB 12, belonging to the same collection, which Assyriologists in Leiden studied in the framework of our Old Babylonian Letters Project. I hope that these commercial texts, though lifting only a tip of the veil and raising more questions than they can answer on the activities of Assyrian traders in Sippar, will be of interest to the jubilarian, whose *Les Assyriens en Cappadoce* (1963) assured the Old Assyrian traders their by now well established place in ancient economic history and convinced me that the study of their archives and business would be a fascinating and rewarding pursuit.

In what follows text A = BM 97188, B = BM 97079, and C = BM 96968.

* Originally published in: D. Charpin and F. Joannès (eds), Marchands, diplomates et empereurs. Études sur la civilisation mésopotamienne offertes à Paul Garelli. Éditions Recherche sur les Civilisations. Paris 1991, 287-303.

1 C.B.F. Walker, Some Assyrians at Sippar in the Old Babylonian Period, *AnStud* 30 (1980) 15-22.

2 See for earlier interpretations of these data W.E Leemans, *SD* 6 (1960) 96ff. and *JESHO* 11 (1968) 20lff .

BM 97079 (Bu 1902,10-11,133)

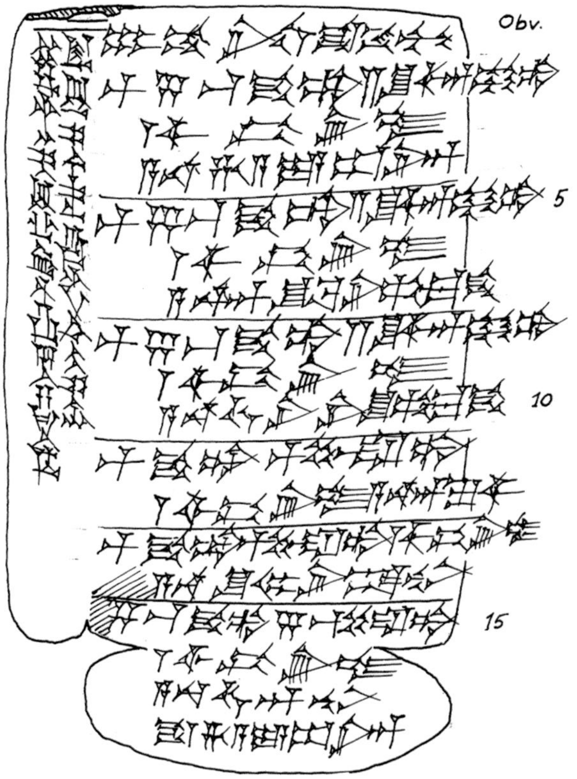

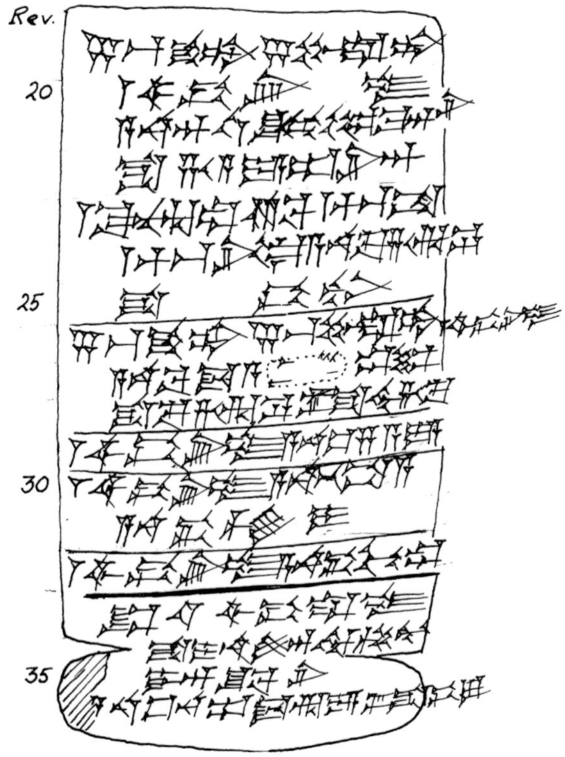

[289] 1. The texts

BM 97079 (B)

6 GÚ ^{na4}ša-am-mu
0,0.1 5 SILA$_3$ *kàr-šum 2 šu-ši an-daḫ-šum*
1 ši-pí-ir-tum
a-na Ḫa-a-ia-ab-ni-ìl

0,0.1 5 SILA$_3$ *kàr-šum 2 šu-ši an-daḫ-šum*
1 ši-pí-ir-tum
a-na DINGIR-*šu-ba-ni* UGULA DAM.GÀR

0,0.1 5 SILA$_3$ *kàr-šum 2 šu-ši an-daḫ-šum*
1 ši-pí-ir-tum
a-na SIG-*ì-lí-šu* UGULA DAM.GAR

0,0.1 kàr-šum 0,0.1 bu-ra-šum
1 ši-pí-ir-tum a-na DINGIR-LU-ŠI

0,0.1 kàr-šum 0,0.1 bu-ra-šum 1 ši-pí-ir-tum
a-na Šu-mi-er-ṣe-tim

---

5 SILA$_3$ *kàr-šum 5* SILA$_3$ *bu-ra-šum*
E. *1 si-pí-ir-tum*
a-na SIG-DINGIR-*tim*
ša Ḫa-a-ia-ab-ni-ìl

R *5* SILA$_3$ *kàr-šum 5* SILA$_3$ *bu-ra-šum*
1 ši-pí-ir-tum
a-na ^{d}UTU-*šu-ul-li-ma-an-ni*
ša Ḫa-a-ia-ab-ni-ìl
1 KUŠ *nu-ḫu-um* ŠÀ.BA 1 ½ SILA$_3$ LÀL
1 ½ SILA$_3$ Ì.ŠAḪ *a-na ṣú-ḫa-re-e*
ša bi-tim

---

5 SILA$_3$ *kàr-šum 5* SILA$_3$ *bu-ra-šum 1 ši-pí-ir-tum*
a-na Ba-da-a DUB.SAR
ša ṣú-ḫa-re-e ú-ša-aḫ-ḫa-zu

1 ši-pí-ir-tum a-na Iz-za-a-ia

---

1 ši-pí-ir-tum a-na Be-ta-a
a-na ga-gi-i

1 ši-pí-ir-tum a-na ga-gu-um

ŠU.NIGIN$_2$ *11 ši-pí-ra-tum*
ša i-na KASKAL ^{d}ISKUR-ZI.MU
DUMU DINGIR-*šu-ba-ni*
a-na É *na-ap-ṭa-ri-ia ú-ša-bi-lu*
L.E. ITI *ša sà-ar-ra-tim* U$_4$.24.KAM
li-mu Ḫa-bíl-ke-nu-um DUMU GE$_6$-*lí-Ištar*

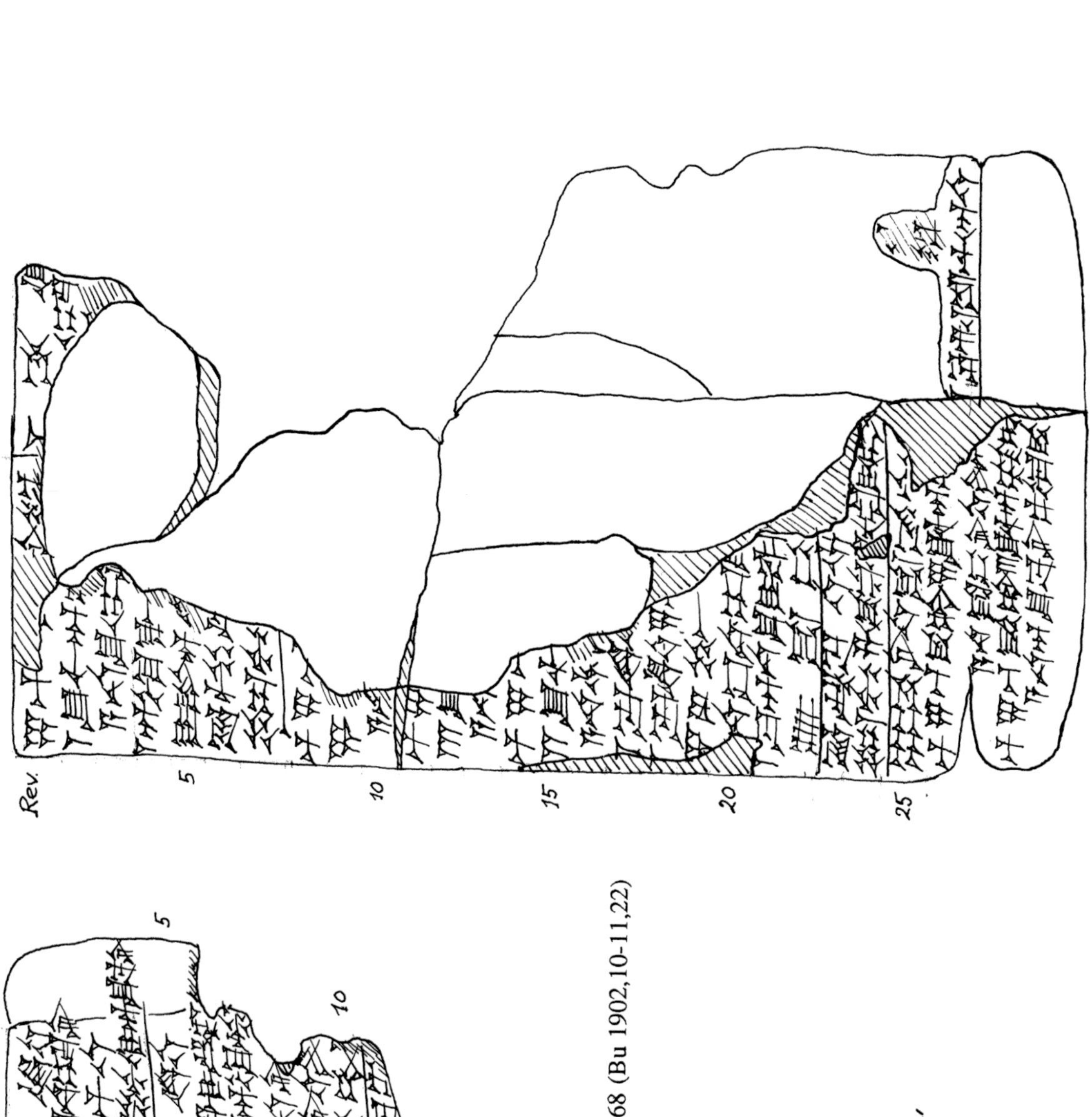

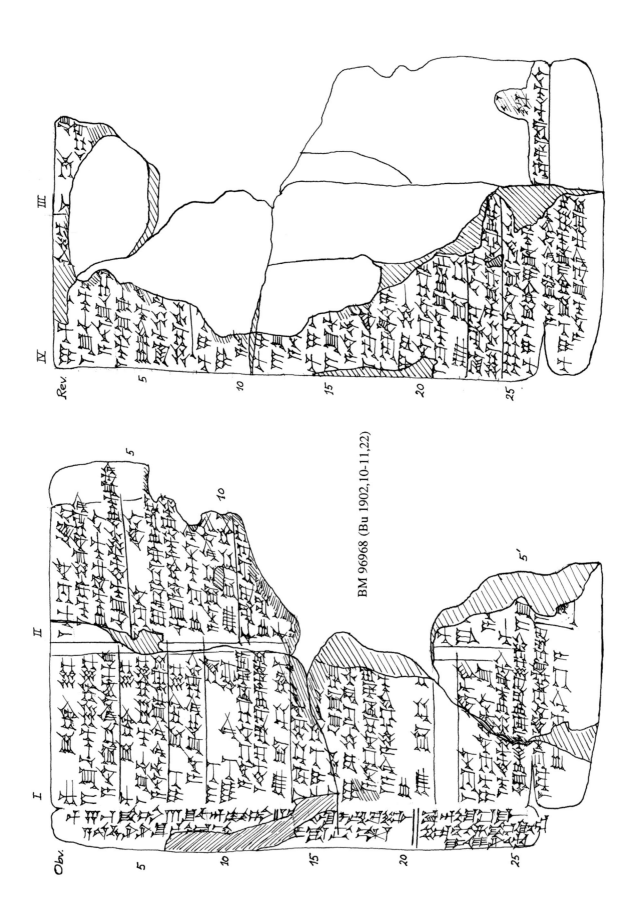

BM 96968 (Bu 1902,10-11,22)

[291] *BM 96968 (C)*

I *0,0.2 kàr-šum*^{sar}
šu-ši an-daḫ-šum^{sar}
a-na ša-pí-ir ZIMBIR^{ki}

0,0.1 kàr-šum^{sar}
1 šu-ši an-daḫ-šum^{sar}
a-na SIG-*ì-lí-šu* UGULA DAM.GÀR

---

5 SILA$_3$ *kàr-šum*^{sar}
a-na Šu-mi-er-ṣe-tim

---

3 SILA$_3$ LÀL
8 SILA$_3$ Ì.ŠAḪ
a-na É na-ap-ṭa-ri-a
^{p}*Im-gur-*^{d}EN.ZU DUMU *A-ḫu-wa-qar*
ú-ša-bi-il

---

1 e-bé-el t[i-na-tim]$^{?}$
0,0.1 5 SILA$_3$ x x []
1 UZU *ki-ša-dum*
6 NINDA *bu-ur-ru-m*[u]
a-na É na-ap-ṭa-ri-a
^{p}*A-lí-a-bu-um* LÚ ^{d}[ ]
DUMU (blank)
ú-ša-bi-i[l]

---

1 ma-na GUŠKIN
4 ½ ma-na KÙ.BABBAR-*šu*
^{pd}IŠKUR-ZI-MU DUMU DINGIR-*šu-*
ba-ni
ù DUMU-*eš-re-e* DUMU ^{d}EN.ZU-
šar-ma-tim
1 ⅔ ma-n[a] KÙ.BABBAR *Ma-num-ki-*
ma-^{d}EN.ZU
DUMU *Ib-ni-*^{d}*É-a*

II *1 ½ ma-na* KÙ.BABBAR
^{pd}MAR.DÚ-*na-ṣi-ir*
DUMU AN-KA-^{d}UTU
ù ^{d}IŠKUR-ZI-MU DUMU DINGIR-
šu-ba-ni

[*1*] *ma-na* KÙ.BABBAR
^{p}*Lu-uš-ta-mar* DUMU ^{d}EN.ZU-*[iš-me-*
ni]
ù A-wi-il-^{d}NIN.ŠUB[UR]
DUMU *Ma-an-na-ni*
a-na ša-pí-ir ZIMB[IR^{ki}]
ú-ša-bi-il

IGI ^{d}EN.ZU-*e-ri-ba-am*
DUMU ^{d}EN.Z[U]
IGI x[]
D[UMU]
(lacuna of ca. 7 lines)
0,0.1 []
4 S[ILA$_3$]
a-n[a]
0,0.1 [5 SILA$_3$ *kàr-šum*^{sar}]
2 šu-ši an-daḫ-šum]
^{p}[]
D[UMU$^{?}$]

III 11 UZU *ki-[ša-dum]*
[] x *ṣi* []
(lacuna of ca. 23 lines)
[] x []
^{p}*E-ri-iš-ti-*^{d}UTU

IV *5* SILA$_3$ [*kàr-šum*^{sar}]
1 šu-ši an-d[aḫ-šum]
a-na Šu-mi-e[r-ṣe-tim]
^{pd}NIN.GAL-*[e-re-eš]*
DUMU LUGAL-^{d}UT[U *ú-ša-bi-íl*$^{?}$]
ITI *sí-i[p-um* U$_4$...KAM]
li-mu []

0,0.1 5 SI[LA$_3$ *kàr-šum*^{sar}]
5 [šu-ši an-daḫ-šum]
a-n[a ša-pí-ir ZIMBIR^{ki}]
0,0.1 5 SI[LA$_3$ *kàr-šum*^{sar}]
3 š[u-ši an-daḫ-šum]
a-na [DINGIR-*šu-ba-ni* UGULA
\\DAM.GÀR]
0,0.1 5 S[ILA$_3$ *kàr-šum*^{sar}]
2 šu-ši [an-daḫ-šum]
a-na SIG-*[ì-lí-šu* UGULA \\DAM.GÀR]
[*1*] GÍN KÙ.BAB[BAR]
[*1*] GÍN KÙ.BABBAR *5 x*[]
5 NINDA *bu-[ur-ru-mu]*
[a]-*na* É *na-ap-ṭ[a-ri-a]*
^{p}*Ma-an-na-šu* DUMU *Ka-[lu-mi]*
ú-ša-bi-[il]

ITI ^{d}EN.ZU U$_4$ 1[4] [KAM]
li-mu Ḫa-bíl-k[e]-*nu-um* DUMU GE$_6$-*lí-*
I[štar]

---

6 GÚ ^{na4}*ša-am-m*[u]
0,0.1 5 SILA$_3$ *kàr-šum 5 šu-ši an-d[aḫ-*
šum]
a-na ša-pí-ir ZIMB[IR^{ki}]
0,0.1 5 SILA$_3$ *kàr-šum 3 šu-ši an-daḫ-*
šu[m]

a-na DINGIR-*šu-ba-ni* UGULA
\DAM.GÀR
L.E. *0,0.1 5* SILA$_3$ *kàr-šum 3 šu-ši an-daḫ-*
šum
a-na SIG-*ì-lí-šu* UGULA
\DAM.GÀR
^{P}[x] x *la* DUMU ^{d}EN.ZU-*šar-rum*
[*ú*]-*ša-bi-il*

ITI ^{d}NIN.É.GAL
li-mu Ḫa-bíl-ke-nu-um
DUMU GE$_6$-*lí-Ištar*

[292] *Translation*

B [1]6 talents of emery, [2]15 quarts of leek, 120 *andaḫšu*-bulbs, [3]one order, [4]for Ḫajabnil;
[5]15 quarts of leek, 120 *andaḫšu*-bulbs, [6]one order, [7]for Ilšu-bāni, the overseer of the merchants;
[8]15 quarts of leek, 120 *andaḫšu*-bulbs, [9]one order, [10]for Ipiq-ilišu, the overseer of the merchants;
[11]10 quarts of leek, 10 quarts of juniper, one order [12]for Ili-lu-ši;
[13]10 quarts of leek, 10 quarts of juniper, one order [14]for Šumi-erṣetim;
[15]5 quarts of leek, 5 quarts of juniper, [16]one order [17]for Ipiq-iltim [18]of Ḫajabnil;
[19]5 quarts of leek, 5 quarts of juniper, [20]one order, [21]for Šamaš-šullimanni [22]of Ḫajabnil;
[23]1 leather bag containing 1 ½ quart of honey, [24]1 ½ quart of lard, for the boys [25]of the household;
[26]5 quarts of leek, 5 quarts of juniper, one order, [27]for Badâ, the scribe, [28]who teaches the boys;
[29]one order for Izzaja;
[30]one order for Betâ, [31]for the *gagûm*;
[32]one order for the *gagûm.*

---

[33]In all 11 orders [36]which I sent to my quarters [34]with the caravan of Iškur-zimu, [35]son of Ilšu-bāni.
[37]The month *ša sarrātim,* 24th day, [38]eponymy of Ḫabil-kēnum, son of Ṣilli-Ištar.

C [I,1] 20 quarts of leek, [2]120 *andaḫšu*-bulbs [3]for the governor of Sippar;
[4]10 quarts of leek, [5]60 *andaḫšu*-bulbs [6]for Ipiq-ilišu, the overseer of the merchants;
[7]5 quarts of leek [8]for Šumi-erṣetim;
[9]3 quarts of honey, [10]8 quarts of lard, [12]I had Imgur-Sin, son of Aḫu-waqar [13]bring [11]to my quarters;
[14]one string of f[igs], [15]15 quarts of..., [16]one cut of "neck meat", [17]6...breads, [19]I had Alī-abum, the man of ... [20], son <> [21]bring [18]to my quarters;

---

[22]1 mina of gold, [23]its (equivalent in) silver 4 ½ minas: [24] Iškur-zimu, son of Ilšu-bāni [25]and Mār-ešrê, son of Sin-šar-mātim; [26]1 ⅔ mina of silver: Mannum-kīma-Sin, [27]son of Ibni-Ea;
[II,1]1 ½ mina of silver [2]Amurru-nāṣir, [3]son of Anum-pī-Šamaš, [4]and Iškur-zimu, son of Ilšu-bāni;
[5]1 mina of silver [6]I had Luštammar, son of Sin-[išmenni], [7]and Awīl-Ilabrat, [8]son of Mannani, [10]bring [9]to the governor of Sippar;
[11]in the presence of Sin-erībam, [12]son of Sin-..., [13]of ..., [14]son of ... *(lacuna of ca. 7 lines)*
[22]10 quarts... [23]4 quarts... [24]for ... ; [25]1[5 quarts of leek], [26]12[0 *andaḫšu*-bulbs], [27 P]..., [28]...

[III,1] 1 cut of "neck [meat]", [2]... *(lacuna of ca. 23 lines)*
[1']... [2']Erišti-Šamaš;
[IV,1] 5 quarts [of leek], [2]60 *andaḫšu*-bulbs [3]for Šumi-erṣetim [4][I had] Ningal-ereš, [5]son of LugalUtu [bring].
[6]Month Sip'um, [...day], [7]eponymy of...

---

[8]15 quarts [of leek], [9]300 *[andaḫšu*-bulbs*]* [10]for [the governor of Sippar],
[11]15 quarts [of leek], [12]180 *[andaḫšu*-bulbs*]* [13]for [Ilšu-bāni, the overseer of the merchants],
[14]15 quarts [of leek], [15]120 *[andaḫšu*-bulbs*]* [16]for Ipiq-[ilisu, the overseer of the merchants],
[17]1 shekel of silver, [18]1 shekel of silver, 5..., [19]5... breads,
[21]I had Mannašu, son of Ka[lumi], [22]bring [20]to my quarters.
[23]The month of Sin, 14th day, [24]eponymy of Ḫabil-kēnum, son of Ṣilli-Ištar.

---

[25]6 talents of emery, [26]15 quarts of leek, 300 *andaḫšu*-bulbs [27]for the governor of Sippar,
[28]15 quarts of leek, 180 *andaḫšu*-bulbs [29]for Ilšu-bāni, the overseer of the merchants,
[293] [L.E.30]15 quarts of leek, 180 *andaḫšu*-bulbs [31]for Ipiq-ilišu, the overseer of the merchants,
[32]I had ...la, son of Sin-šarrum, [33]bring.
[34]Month Beltekallim, [35]eponymy of Ḫabil-kēnum, [36]son of Ṣilli-Ištar.

2. Philogical Notes

šammu (B: 1; C IV: 25, and also A: 49, written simply Ú, without NA_4) has recently been identified as emery *(JCS* 40, 195ff.) a very hard stone used in powder form as "scouring sand", for cutting, abrasing and polishing (see now also ARMT 26/1, no. 134: 9'). As powder it was weighed and we usually meet round figures, as is the case in our texts. In Mari the price was 5 shekels of silver per talent. The origin of imported emery is difficult to establish and imports both from the north (Syria and Anatolia) and the south are possible.

karsum (B and C passim) has been identified as "common leek" (Stol, *BSA* 3, 62f. with note 58 (add for OB, AbB 9, 112: 12 ;12, 94: 10 and RA 72, 134 no. 22: 1, in all cases written *kàr-šum*sar).[3] Its quantity is always indicated by measures of capacity, usually a number of quarts, especially when there is question of rations or kitchen provisions (ARMT 23, 368: 7; 371: 6; TuM NF 5, 32: 25). In commercial contexts the quantities are bigger, from five quarts (AbB 5, 220: 31, collated; VAT 721: 4, see *ZA* 6, 292; AbB 12, 94: 10; OBTR 122: 13, sent as gift to a sister in Aššur) to ten or twenty quarts (TCL 10, 71, passim; AbB 7, 16: 17; CT 43, 118: 15'). Exceptional is *RA* 72, 134 no. 22 (business of Šēp-Sin, related to AbB 9, 112: 12) with 9 kor, a text which also mentions a price: 4 shekels per kor.[4] Common leek apparently was appreciated as a kind of seasoning, added to various dishes in the upper class kitchen. It occurs frequently in the culinary texts YOS 11, 25-26 (see *JAOS* 107, 1987, 11ff.), where it is added, together with other condiments such as garlic, cumin, coriander and *samīdu,* to soups or stews prepared on a basis of meat, fat and flour (cf. *RlA* 6, 289f.).

andaḫšum (B: 2-8; C I: 2-5, II: 26, IV: 2-end) is rare in OB. Our texts, CT 43, 118: 19' (*1 šuši a.*sar) and AbB 12, 19 *(passim*; rev.2ff. shipment of "90 of the best possible" *a.*sar) are the only references, but it also occurs in the "culinary texts": YOS 11, 26 I: 39f.: *kàr-šum ḫa-za-na-a[m ù]* [40]*[an-da]-aḫ-ši tasâkma).* It is attested in Ur III texts, presumably also as

---

3 The distinction, in Ḫḫ 17, 277ff. and 312ff., between *karšum* (preceded by *andaḫšum*, cf. our texts) and *karašum* (GA.RAŠsar) suggests a difference, supported by the fact that OB and lexical texts, when referring to the seed, only speak of *zēr karašim (CAD* K 213b,c), "leek seeds", see discussion 214a.

4 OBTR 204: 11 mentions a jar of *karšum* and amounts referred to by their value in silver occur in TEBA 34: 7 and TLB 1, 65: 10. In CT 45, 41: 6 (Abi-ešuḫ) leek is among the items – gold, wax (LÀL.HAR!), cedar oil and sundry goods *(daqqātum)* – designated as *igisû*-tax to be delivered by (?) *kār* Sippar-Amnanum. This underlines its commercial importance.

indaḫšum (cf. *CAD* A/II, 112f.; add MVN 6, 59: 2 (*20 indaḫšum*), AUCT 1, 974: 2 (50)), where it is usually counted, as observed by *CAD* s.v., but note that it is measured in BE 3, 77: 14 (10 quarts; only occurrence of *andaḫšum* in Ur III texts). *CAD* suggests "the spring-flowering lily or crocus, the bulbs of which are edible"; Stol, *BSA* 3, 62, a kind of onion, noting the lexical equation ŠUM.TUR. The combination with *karšum* in our texts parallels their close association in lexical texts (*Ḫḫ* and Forerunner, see *CAD* s.v.). The use as condiment and as ingredient of medicines would fit the identification as saffron crocus (*crocus sativus*), but note that for those purposes one used the dried stigmas and part of the style, not the bulb itself which seems to be meant in our texts, since they are counted (note "bundles", *riksātum*, of *andaḫšum* in Gilgameš's fictitious letter, SST 41: 21, where it figures as exotic foodstuff).

burāšum (B: 15), "the aromatic substance obtained from the juniper tree" (*CAD* B s.v.), *i.e.* from the *juniperus oxycedrus* (Stol, *MEOL* 21, 1979, 16 note 58), occurs about a dozen times in OB texts. The quantities in general are not very big, between a few and 20 quarts (one *pišannum* and one leather bag of *b.* in the inventory text OBTR 204: 9f.; 14 quarts in *RA* 72, 125 no.12: 2), but AbB 9, 112 records no less than 9 talents of ŠIM.LI (line 36), together with 1 talent of "assorted aromatics" (ŠIM.ḪI.A). The much valued products of the juniper tree, either its "grains" or seeds (with oil bearing glands, contained in its "berries"; written ŠE.LI and rarely ŠIM.ŠE.LI, well attested in Ur III texts, later equated with *kikkirānu*) or the oil distilled from its wood, were imported from the north, Syria and Anatolia. We regularly meet them in commercial texts (TCL 10, 71: 18,48; 81: 16; AbB 2, 143: 11,24 [purchase for 5 shekels of silver and sale for one shekel]; *RA* 72, 125 no.12: 2), some of which explicitly mention caravan trade: CT 43, 118: 13'ff.: "When the caravan arrived I sent him, after his messengers (had left), 20 quarts of leek, 20 quarts of juniper ...";[5] AbB 12, 94: 13ff. "Since the caravan, which is staying in Emar, was not yet due to arrive, I did not sent you your gift. Now I have sent you five quarts of juniper by means of PN". According to Snell, *YNER* 8, 159f., the price of ŠE.LI ranged from 5 to 8 quarts per shekel of silver (quantities rarely bigger than 20 quarts). Note the combination of juniper and leek in OBTR 204: 9ff.; VAT 721 (ZA 6, 292): 4f., preceded by honey; CT 43, 118: 15'; AbB 12, 94: 10ff.

[294] *dispum*, "honey" (B: 23; C I: 9), an expensive delicacy, two quarts for a shekel of silver in the Ur III period (Snell, *YNER* 8, 124f.), three in TCL 10,72 :10 (Larsa, Rim-Sin), rather rare in OB texts and usually only in small quantities. Used in small quantities for "the king's meal" in Mari (ARMT 9, 281, § 60; frequently mentioned together with oil, see also ARMT 21, 162, 179, 180 and 187). In UET 5, 601 quantities of honey are each time combined with larger quantities of *kikkirānu*, assigned to important persons such as the *mākisum*, the *rabênum* and the *wakil tamkārī*. It originated in areas north and west of Mari, where it arrived as part of shipments from allied princes and high dignitaries (see ARMT 7, 261f. § 70 and 9, 270f., § 39). It does not surprise that the quantities mentioned in such contexts are matched by OBTR 204: 2, namely 11 jars.[6]

naḫum, Ì.ŠAḪ, "lard" (B: 24 and C: I 10), frequent Ur III texts (Snell *YNER* 8, 153f.), with quantities from ca. 10 quarts until 10 kor and a price of 12 to 20 quarts per shekel of silver, which equals the tariff in the Laws of Eshnunna (15 quarts for a shekel) and that attested at Larsa (Rim-Sin, TCL 10, 78: 6 : 0,0.2 or 0,0.3 and 6 ⅔ $SILA_3$ for a shekel and 144 grains). Large quantities in OBTR 204: 2f. (preceded by honey, as in our texts), 15f. and 205: 1 (in jars and in "homers" of 120 quarts), with a better quality in 204: 3: Ì.ŠAḪ *ruqqû*, perhaps "aromatic lard".

NINDA *burrum[u?]* (C I: 17 and IV: 19), unidentified. The spacing of the wedges at the end of I: 17 suggest a final *-m[u]* rather than *-t[im]*. Hardly to be connected with the cereal

---

5 *ḫarrānum imqutma* [14']*warki mārī šiprišunu* [15']*0,0.2 karšum 0,0.2* LI-I .. [20'] *ušābilšum.*

6 Note also *5* quarts in *Sumer* 23 pl. 17: 13 (early OB) and 10 quarts in VAS 22, 84: 22.

name *bur(r)um* in Mari (always written as logogram, without case ending). "Speckled bread" is nowhere else attested.

ebel t[īnātim] (C: I 14), "a string of figs", suggested by ARMT 7, 234: 5' *(eblu ša ti-na-[tim*]), AbB 12, 59: 25 (*3 ÈŠ ša ti-na-tim*), and CCT 6, 3b: 18 *(eblam ša ti-na-tim*), see also Gelb, *Zikir šumim (Festschrift Kraus)* p. 78.

UZU *kišādum* (C: I 16, III 1), not attested in OB thus far, but see *CAD* K 448b, 3'.

The item mentioned in C: I 15 is not clear. The sign after $SILA_3$ is different both from GAR and from UZU.

šipirtum (B passim) qualifies the various consignments, each with its own address (*ana*), and distinguished by indenting and interlining (lines 23-25, though indented, lack the term and the interlining). The summary speaks of *11 sipirātum*, a plural morphologically and semantically distinguished from *siprātum*, "work/tasks performed", presumably a *pirīst* formation. It is also attested in texts from Mari, where the combination *PN ša šipirātim* (ARMT 14, 110: 11 and 23, 85: 31) is rendered "PN du service des ambassades". *AHw* s.v. gives as its meaning "Nachricht, Anweisung", which is not concrete enough in our text. I assume that, just like OAss *têrtum*, it may also denote what is ordered, "the order", especially in commercial contexts. In AbB 7, 16: 13f. we may translate: "I will not neglect your order", the more so when we read in 11: 4ff.: "as for the textile you ordered (*šapārum* with acc. object, "to write for")..., I did not send it", and in AbB 1, 130: 22ff.: "Why don't you write all the things I have to send you each time – barley or silver or fine oil or wool – well specified (*awīlam u šumšu*) on a tablet and have it brought to me?" (cf. 7, 16: 1lf.: *idišam šuṭṭerima šubilim*; all letters between the same correspondents). Etymologically *šūbultum*,"consignment, shipment", frequent in commercial contexts (Old Assyrian: *SD* 10, 140f.; Mari: ARMT 21, 512ff.; Ešnunna: *AS* 22, 113ff.), starts from the idea that the goods are shipped overland by their consignor; *šipirtum* (cf. in OB also CT 43, 118: 24'; JCS 14, 55 No. 91 = YOS 14, 69: 32) focuses on the person that had ordered them (by letter or messenger). In practice this distinction may be less marked, since both words refer to goods sent from elsewhere, and our text B: 33ff. summarizes: "*11 šipirātum* which I shipped to ... with PN's caravan", using *šūbulum*.[7] For our text it is important whether the items called "*šipirtum* to/for the governor of Sippar, the overseer of the merchants" indeed had been previously ordered by these officials.

bīt napṭārim (B: 35; C: I 11, 18, IV 20). There is no doubt that the term refers to the "quarters, lodging", where people could stay in a city were they were foreigners or guests (Kraus, *RA* 70, 165ff., X; see for Mari references, discussed on p. 166, now ARMT 26/2, p. 42 on Nos 361, 368 and 369). From the perspective of caravan traders, briefly visiting a foreign city with their goods and animals, Kraus's comparison with a near eastern *han* is enlightening, but in our text we have to do with a foreign trader who seems to have had a more permanent pied-à-terre in Sippar, the seat of a household *(bītum*, line 25), and here Kraus's suggestion to think of an agency or branch-establishment hits the mark. The possessive suffix added to *napṭārum* in our text then could indicate its owner and boss. The OB letter AbB 13, 110 shows that a foreigner could buy and own a *bīt napṭārim* in a city, in this case in Sippar: [5]*ina panītim inuma ana* GN **[295]** [6]*qadu ṣābia šaknākuma* [7]*ina Sippar ittia tannamru* [8]*kiām aqbikum umma anākuma* [9]*ina Sippar bīt napṭārī* [10]*ul išû ištên bītam amramma* [11]*kaspam lušqulma lūšâm*, "previously, when you met me in Sippar, while I had been stationed in GN (Ḫirītum) together with my workers, I told you: 'I have no quarters of my own in Sippar. Find me one house, then I will pay its price and buy it'". Against the background of this possibility several of the OB references could be understood to refer to the *bīt napṭārim* owned in a foreign city by somebody, e. g. YOS 13, 101: 6; TCL 18, 91: 13, 23; AbB 2, 97: 2 (dunned for service obligations; line 13 simply: *bītī*) ; AbB 3, 52: 11; AbB

7 A consignment of *karšum*, delivered by a trader, is called *šūbulti PN* in RA 72, 134 no. 22.

11, 102: 13ff. (the housekeeper for the absentee, travelling owner?). See CAD N/1, 325, b) for the references. If a *b.n.* has an owner, some permanent occupants (BM 79979+80020, unpubl., mentions a *waššābtum* of somebody's *b.n.*), and can function as a household, it is understandable that, as is the case with *bītum, b.n.* may refer collectively or individually to members of that household.[8] A question which cannot be answered is whether such a *b.n., e.g.* in Sippar, was located in the *kārum* or in the city proper, which, after all, had streets called after foreign residents (See Harris, Sippar, 19 with note 48).

ḫurāṣum, GUŠKIN (C: I 22f.). The rate of exchange gold : silver = 4 ½ : 1 is not exceptional for this period, see H. Farber, *JESHO* 21 (1978) 3f.: variation from 5,5 : 1 to 3 : 1 during Rimsin's later years; in Mari, during Zimrilim's reign, *ca.* 4 : 1, cf. also ARMT 21, 194f., 22: 247: lff.; 24, 108, 109, 125; in Babylonia, under Ḫammurabi, once 3 : 1 (TCL 1, 101), cf. VAS 22, 86: 10 (golden sun discs). Some differences may also be due to difference in quality (TCL 10, 72: 2-4). [Cf. M.A. Powell, *AoFl* 7 (1990) 80-82].

šāpir Sippar (C: 3, II 9, IV [10], 27). The "governor of Sippar" in each case receives the biggest amount of goods, which tends to make him the highest local official. Comparison between the passages in C and B: 1-10 makes it almost certain that we may identify him with Ḫajabnil, who is most probably identical to his namesake in AbB 2, 63 (receives a letter from king Samsuiluna on the journey of the goddess Annunitum to Sippar-Edinna) and CT 29, 43: 19 (heads a group of judges). In BM 97067 (unpubl., Sippar, Si) he occurs in the same function (line 18: *Ḫ. u dajjānī ikšudu*). He could be identical to Ḫ son of *I-zi-na- x* ÌR *Ḫammurabi*, whose seal is impressed on OLA 21 no. 66, and we also meet him in the letter AbB 11, 49 addressed to Warad-Sin (the writer of our texts A-C, see below); Ḫ.'s attention is asked for the fact that the purse of a certain Imdī-Ištar, "your son", is since two years in the house of Warad-Sin in Sippar.

The *šāpirum* of a city (attested for various OB cities, most references for Sippar, Kiš and Dilbat)[9] was an important official, most probably the representative of the central authority, the king, whose servant he was (seal on OLA 21 no. 66) and who appointed him (AbB 5, 147). The nature of the written evidence is responsible for the fact that we have an incomplete idea of his function and tasks. There is no reason to limit them to the judicial and fiscal sphere, and it is a simplification to see in him the supreme judge. He is distinguished from the group of judges (BM 97067; BE 6/1, 60: 10f.; *RA* 9, 22; CT 2, 43: 4f., where we should insert "and"); see also CT 29, 41 (AbB 2, 173):8, 16.[10] and may head the court of justice as highest administrator. As such one could, to some extent, compare him with the *rabiānum*, "burgomaster", but Harris's idea (*Sippar*, 77) that he would have replaced the latter after Samsuiluna year 15 or 16, is refuted by our texts, which attest his presence already *ca.* 15 years earlier. This note is not the place to go into the difficult question concerning his responsibilities and sphere of action, also in relation

8 Additional references in AbB 12 are the following : 69: 35f.: "PN has greatly harrassed (?) me and the people of my *b.n.*" (*ša bīt napṭ[āria]*); 119: 6'ff.: "send me a report on yourself and on his *b.n.*"; 144: 15ff. "I sent PN to you in Sippar. He is no stranger to you, he is our brother, he belongs to our family! Provide him with a pleasant quarter" (*bīt napṭārim ṭābam šukuššum).* In 59: 21 we have *PN napṭārī* (transmits a letter), which could well be the equivalent of *PN ša b.n.* Just like a member/descendant of *bīt Ḫumri* in Akkadian becomes *mār Ḫumri,* so too the combination **mār bīt napṭāria* could become *mār napṭāria,* of which *PN napṭārī* could be an equivalent (construct state replaced by apposition). In the same way *bāb napṭārišu,* in ARM 2, 72 (= ARMT 26/2, 378): 36, does not mean "la porte de son hôte", but renders **bāb bīt napṭārišu,* "(est retenu) dans son auberge" (cf. 361: 16).

9 See the discussion of his function in M.J. Desrochers, *Aspects of the Structure of Dilbat during the Old Babylonian Period* (Diss. UCLA 1978, UM 78-20207) 392ff. (note the occurrence of an UGULA Dilbat in VAS 7, 113: 24). *Šāpirums* are also attested for Rapiqum and Larsa, and we know *šāpirums* of areas such as Emutbal, Suḫi and Amnān-Jaḫrur, probably with functions similar to those of the *šāpir mātim.* References to a *šāpir Sippar* are also found in AbB 1, 49: 18; 2, 173: 8, 16; 5, 147: 4, 6; 7, 88: 9; 134: 28; 143: rev.7.

10 See A. Walther, *LSS* 6, 4-6, 139. See also the remarks of Kraus ad AbB 10, 1: 1, where he revokes the identification of the *šāpir mātim* as "Land(es)-Oberrichter". Note the occurrence of a *šāpir* DI.KUD in UM I/2, 10: 4.

to the *šakkanakkum*, the *šāpir rēdī*, the *šāpir mātim*, and the *šāpir nārim*, which deserves a special investigation.[11]

wakil tamkārī. There is no need to analyse the function of the "overseer of the merchants", which has been well studied. It is important to note that he was not only the administrative head of the merchants, with **[296]** direct contacts with the palace, but also performed tasks in the city administration, i.a. in judiciary matters.[12] Quite recently, Charpin *(NABU* 1990, p. 6 no. 9) has shown that the two different "overseers of the merchants" in our texts may be identified as that of Sippar-Jaḫrurum (Ilšu-bāni) and that of Sippar-Amnānum (Ipiq-ilišu), both of which were served by Warad-Sin.

3. The nature of the texts

The first question to be asked is that of the origin and nature of these texts. Who is the subject of the repeated phrase "I had PN bring ... to my quarters" (B: 36, C: I 11ff., 18ff. and IV 20ff.)? Walker, discussing the first loan of text A, suggested that the person issuing it, Warad-Sin, acted as agent of an institution, presumably the palace. This would hold good also of the following thirteen loans, although his name (for brevity's sake?) is not mentioned again. We know that institutions act through their officials or agents, and it may not always be necessary to specify the institution involved. Old Babylonian temple loans, e.g., are issued both by the god alone and in conjunction with his agent.[13] But in a context where no institution is mentioned,[14] we cannot simply take a person issuing a loan as acting in an official capacity.[15] I take Warad-Sin as a successful trader and money-lender or capitalist, who extends credit and gives out loans for commercial and other purposes.

Text A seems to be a private memorandum in which he lists all his claims. He starts by quoting the underlying contract more fully (loan no. 1), limits himself to the essentials in the following seven cases, and becomes very brief with the last loans, where first the verb (ŠU.TI.A or ŠU.BA.AN.TI) is omitted and soon also the preposition KI/*itti* introducing the debtor. There are good parallels for such gradually more concise "Sammelmemorandums" in Old Assyrian, some of which also omit the dates of the individual transactions.[16] Fortunately the writer supplied a date for one loan: the year-eponymy of Ḫabil-kēnum, son of Ṣilli-Ištar (lines 46ff.), which links A with B and C, dated to the same eponymy. Elsewhere I have tried to prove that this eponymy should be dated to 1750 B.C. (middle chronology) plus or minus a few years.[17]

Texts B and C are also memorandums, equally using the first person singular. Apart from the date, there are other features which link all three texts, such as prosopographical data. The pair Luštammar, son of Sin-išmenni, and Awīl-Ilabrat, son of Mannani, occur in A: 22ff. and C: II 6ff.; Ningal-ereš, son of Lugal-^{d}Utu, is attested in A: 6f. and C: IV 4f.; Mannasi, son of Kalumi, is found in A: 13f. and C: IV 21; Sumi-erṣetim figures in B: 14 and C: IV 3; and Iškur-zimu in B: 34f. and C: I 24 and II 4. A shipment to the *gagûm* in B: 31f.

---

11 See for some remarks on the relation *šakkanakkum* – *šāpirum* W.F. Leemans, *Symbolae ...Martino David Dedicatae*, II (1968), 125f. note 5, and for Dilbat, Desrochers, *op. cit.* (note 9) 363ff.

12 See R. Harris, *Sippar*, 71ff.; D. Charpin, *JA* 270 (1982), 6lff.; K.R. Veenhof, *JEOL* 30 (1987/8), and for his involvement in the local administration, F.R. Kraus, in A. Finet (ed.), *Les pouvoirs locaux en Mesopotamie et dans les régions adjacentes* (1982), 29-42.

13 See R. Harris, *JCS* 14 (1960) 128ff.

14 There is no reference to a palace or temple in text A and the mention of the "city-house" (43 and 61) only qualifies the weight used, not the institution involved.

15 Note F.R. Kraus's criticism of N. Yoffee's reconstruction of the functioning of an OB "crown bureau" by means of officials and subordinate personnel. According to Kraus *(OLA* 6, 1979, 433), Yoffee, by using records in which the palace is not mentioned and by considering middlemen, acting as private persons, subordinate officials responsible for disbursements, "verlegt ins Innere des 'Palastes', was sich ausserhalb von ihm abspielt".

16 See my analysis of such memorandums in *JEOL* 28 (1983/4), 10ff.

17 See my contribution : The sequence of the "Overseers of the merchants" at Sippar and the date of the year-eponymy of Habil-kēnum, in *JEOL* 30 (1987/88), 32-37, with the correction by Charpin *NABU* 1990, p. 6 no. 9.

may perhaps be linked with the occurrence of Erišti-Šamaš in C III: end, presumably the name of a *nadītum* living there.

Text A records only outstanding claims (*bābtum*), text B lists a long series of shipments (*šipirtum*), and both are linked by C, which lists shipments (PN *ušābil*) and claims in silver and gold, amounts borrowed or entrusted for transport to a number of people (I 22 – II 10) before witnesses (II 11-14). The amounts, obviously due to Warad-Sin, are such (between 1 ½ and 4 ½ minas of silver) that they must reflect commercial operations. Quite a number of the shipments mentioned in B and C are addressed to the same persons, officials in Sippar: two *wakil tamkārī* and the *šāpirum*. Even though the **[297]** figures for the number of *andaḫšum* are different, the correspondence between B: 1-10 and C: IV 25-31 is quite remarkable. Note also the occurrence of *šammu* stone in all three texts (A: 49[!], B: 1 and C: IV 25).

Texts A gives a dating for one transaction only: month V (of the Assyrian calendar). All shipments mentioned in B are dated to one and the same day, 24-II. The first dating preserved in C is month VII (IV 6), followed by month X (Sin replaces *ti'inātum* in later OA; IV 23f.), and by month I (L.E. 5) all presumably of the same year. We could consider the last dating (together with the transaction recorded, from IV 25 to end) as an appendix, and assume that the text was meant to cover one complete year. But the breaks in columns II and III make such speculations uncertain. A comparison between B and C makes it clear that the former is not simply a daily record used as a source for a "Sammelmemorandum" summarizing a whole year.

4. The persons

The main figure, the writer/speaker of all three texts, is Warad-Sin, son of Ilī-asūni (A: 4f.), also known from Waterman no. 63: rev.8 (witness ; Si year 1(?)), PBS 8/2, 227: 8 (read [ÌR]-30); among a series of persons supplying each one worker; Si 8), and CT 33, 47a: 11 (witness; Si year 8, a leap-year). There is additional evidence for his activities and family relations in a number of (undated) informative letters addressed to him. Occurrences in legal and administrative texts, apart from those just mentioned, are rare. I can only refer to CT 48, 11b (Ḫamm. year 42), recording a law suit between Warad-Sin and Šamaš-rabi, solved by payments by the former to the latter. The text records a mutual renunciation of claims bearing on "1 mina of silver of (due from?) the palace, silver of the caravan and inside the city, silver of (due from) Rīš-Šamaš's house (firm?), tablets and anything else belonging to the paternal household".[18] Among the witnesses we meet the "Overseer of the merchants" Ilšu-bāni. The documents show his commercial activities (probably a partnership, cf. text A: 1) and indicate that his career at Sippar spanned at least ten years.

Two women are associated with him. Tatūr-mātum, who addresses him as "my lord" (AbB 2, 110; 140; 141), greets him with a blessing by Šamaš and Aja *kallatum*, and begins by reporting that "the house and the boys (children? *ṣuḫārū*) are well". This shows that she lives in Sippar and writes to somebody temporarily absent, for whom she takes care of the house(hold).[19] The other woman is Tarīša, who has left us three letters: two addressed to Tatūr-mātum (AbB 12, 60 and AbB 7, 129, whose first line has to be restored accordingly), and one to Warad-Sin (AbB 12, 59), basically identical to the one (AbB 12, 60) addressed to Tatūr-mātum. Tarīša invokes for Warad-Sin the blessing of Šamaš and Aššur, and for Tatūr-mātum that of Ištar and Tašmētum. She is obviously living in the city

---

18 *ana warkiāt umī ana 1 mana kasap ekallim* [7]*kasap gerrim u libbi ālim* [8]*kasap bīt Rīš-Šamaš ṭuppātim* [9]*u mimmê bīt abim* [10]*ištu pê adi ḫurāṣim ...* [13]*ul iraggamū.* Cf. also CT 2, 28: 6f. (commercial, termination of partnership): *kaspam bābtam wardam amtam la ḫarrānim u libbi ālim* ..., and CT 48,1 : 32: *ana tappūtim kīsim ša ḫarrānim u libbi ālim ...* [35] *... ul iraggamū.*

19 She takes care of the house (hires a builder, has the roof plastered, 110: 13ff. 140: 13ff.), acts on information that Warad-Sin has silver available, and gives advice to her husband. That these letters, of a different acquisition (Bu 91-5-9), are written by "our" Tatūr-mātum is clear from a reference to Aššur-asu (141: 11). Cf. also her remarks on legal action (? 141: 14; cf. Kraus, *AoF* 10, 60 ad 6') against *awīlū*, to be compared with 7, 129: 22.

of Aššur (AbB 12, 60: 26), where Ištar and Tašmētum had a cult.[20] She calls herself "your daughter" in her letter to Warad-Sin, but writes to Tatūr-mātum as "your sister". In her letter to Tatūr-mātum, AbB 12, 60: 25ff., we read: "The whole city heard that you are (now) my sister and they will pray for you (masc. plur.) and I, too, will pray for you (masc. plur.) before Ištar and Tašmētum". The same words occur in her letter to Warad-Sin, but now with the masc. sing. suffix, while in her other letter to Tatūrmātum, shortly later, she tells her that the news the latter had sent her had made her very happy and that she keeps praying "for you" (fem. sing.), as does "the whole City". What was the happy occasion which made the two women sisters, gave rise to prayers for Warad-Sin, for Tatūr-mātum and for the two together? The most natural conclusion would be to assume that Warad-Sin had married Tatūr-mātum, **[298]** and we could derive support for that from AbB 7, 129: 1', where Tatūr-mātum is advised, in a certain matter, "to take counsel with the one who loves you" (*rā'imki šutāwi*). However, two objections could be raised: a) Would a man's daughter address his (admittedly young) second wife as "my sister"?; b) Would a wife address her husband as "my lord" and call herself "your servant" at that? At first sight a) seems unlikely, but we have to admit that we know little of the way relatives addressed each other, and "brother" and "sister" have a rather wide scope.[21] Moreover, Tarīša refers to Tatūr-mātum as *ṣuḫārtum*, "girl" (AbB 12, 59: 25ff. compared with 60: 22ff.). As for b), we observe that queen Šibtu of Mari starts her letters addressed to her husband, king Zimrilim, with *ana belia qibima umma Š. amatka* (ARMT 10, lff.). The use of *bēlum* is not necessarily conditioned by the rank for the husband. Kraus[22] believes that an address *ana bēlia* is also possible in other cases, and we could recall the fact that a husband having legally acquired a wife was a *bēl aššatim* (CḪ § 129).

Two alternatives are conceivable. The first is to consider T. an adoptive daughter of Warad-Sin, the second to make her the wife of his son, perhaps his *kallatum*, "a young woman acquired by master of the household as wife for his son living in this household" (*CAD* K 82b).[23] The first alternative would explain the use of "sister", but almost certainly requires a letter address *ana abia*. Also T.'s responsibilities in the household (see note 19) are rather unexpected for an adoptive child. The second alternative could presumably explain the address *ana bēlia* and perhaps also *rā'imki*, "your lover", but those words would fit better in the mouth of her husband, who is mysteriously absent.[24] In this case,

---

20 See for Tašmētum, Hirsch, *AfO Beiheft* 13/14² (1972) 26, and Add. 14b. Frankena, *SLB* 4, 54, showed that women in the greeting formulae of their letters invoke their own gods: that of their city and their personal god. In the same way Tatūr-mātum invokes, in Sippar, Šamaš and Aja *kallatum*.

21 See provisionally C. Wilcke, in E.W. Müller, *Geschlechtsreife und Legitimation zur Zeugung* (1985), 227 with note 14. But note that there is a difference between how one refers to a relative and how one actually addresses him, and here again one may distinguish between a formal address (in a letter) and an informal one, in private conversation. There are no letters addressed *ana emia, ana mutia*. Daughters of the king of Mari write to him addressing their letters "to my star", to which they may add "to my father", "to my lord". In Gen. 18 :12 Sara refers to Abraham as *'adonī*, "my lord".

22 See Kraus on AbB 7, 109: 1 (the woman in question refers to "your house") and AbB 7, 125: 3f. ("Ist sie die Ehefrau des Adressaten, wie Adresse und das Fehlen von Grussformeln zu verraten scheint?"). In general, without prosopographic data, it is difficult to decide who "my lord" could be. It could be a superior asked for help (e.g. AbB 1, 34) and frequently it is not clear (AbB 5, 23; 6, 147; 7,8 1). Note also AbB 12, 165, a letter by a woman to *bēl bītim*, the head of the household (not her father), in which she reports that the house and the children (*ṣuḫārū*) are well. Such statements are rather typical for letters addressed by women to their absent "masters" (AbB 2, 110: 7f.; 141: 5f.; 7, 81: 25ff.; 11, 168: 15). The last reference is from a letter by Zinû to her husband Šamaš-ḫāzir, whom she twice addresses with *ana awīlim* (AbB 11, 168; 14, 166).

23 See for *kallatum*, F.R. Kraus, *Vom mesopotamischen Menschen der altbabylonischen Zeit und seiner Welt* (1973), 50ff., and the remarks by Wilcke, *op. cit.* The address *ana bēlia* would have been used by a *kallatum* in AbB 2, 150 (see line 14), if we take *be-lí-ia-a* as *bēlia* and not as a PN, as Kraus (AbB 10, p. 13 note n) prescribes.

24 There is no way of proving that the Warad-Sin, receiving a letter from his son Puzur-Dagan (AbB 10, 203) is "our" Warad-Sin (Kraus : "Nordbabylonisch"). The writer of AbB 7, 76, Ibbi-Adad, calls Warad-Sin "my father", but the letter deals with business, and we cannot exclude that "father" is used for "boss" (see below on AbB 11, 49).

too, her responsibilities would be rather big and the tone of her letters to her father-in-law (note AbB 2, 110: 24ff.; 141: 11ff.) indeed rather frank. Considering all facts I prefer to regard Tatūr-mātum as Warad-Sin's young, second wife, married in Sippar when he was a man at middle age (with a grown-up daughter, from his first marriage, in Aššur). This is not impossible since he is attested at Sippar for at least ten years.

Four other letters addressed to Warad-Sin shed some light on his commercial activities (two mention a purse, *kīsum*; some refer to documents left behind, received, to be sent or used; one mentions silver due to him) and his contacts, but are insufficient to yield a coherent picture. AbB 7, 120 (Bu 91-5- 9), from Šamaš-mušēzib (blessing by Šamaš and Aššur), deals with records left behind by W. and reports on a "purse" which is safe. AbB 7, 76 (same acquisition), from Ibbi-Adad, "your son", (blessing by Šamaš and Marduk) reacts to W.'s repeated complaint that he has not yet received silver due to him. The writer states that, according to information he received, 10 1/3 shekels of silver had been paid to a man from Tursu/i; in the city of Assur (end damaged). According to AbB 2, 155 (Bu 1902-10-11; hence the same acquisition as texts A-C), written by Aššur-asu and Šalim-puti (blessing by Šamaš, Marduk and Aššur), W. will receive a letter from the City (of Aššur) and is urged to act in accordance with it (thus refuting the accusation that he is keeping the letter back in his house).

[299] AbB 11, 49 (CBS 1326), from Aššur-asu (cf. AbB 2, 141: 11), who blesses by Šamaš, Marduk and Aššur, is interesting but difficult to understand . The issue is the "purse" (*kīsum*) of Imdī-Ištar, which is since two years in W.'s house in Sippar (*ina bīt W. šaknat*, 12f.; cf. *maḫrika šaknat*, 6). A. has confronted Ḫajabnil with (*maḫar Ḫ. aškun*) the facts and urged him to take action to secure that purse (*šulum kīsim epēšum*). He now informs W. that he has just sent a letter to Ḫ., and asks W. to remind Ḫ. (of his promise/obligation). A. calls I. Ḫ.'s "son" and W.'s "brother", while Ḫ. is his "father". With Stol (note b. *a.l.*) we take these terms as referring to commercial relations, which could imply that all persons belong to the same firm or commercial community. A., I., and W. are more or less each other's equals, while Ḫ, "father", is their superior, principal or boss. It is virtually certain that Ḫ. is identical with his namesake in text B: 4, the governor of Sippar. Why and where was his help enlisted by Assur-asu? The wording of lines 11f. indicate that "here" was not in Sippar, but most probably in Aššur, where A. was active. This would imply that Ḫ. had travelled to that city, presumably for commercial reasons. Now that he is back in Sippar, A. takes action to secure that he abides by his promise. It is a moot question whether we have to see Ḫ. in this letter only as a wealthy and powerful entrepreneur, asked to promote the interests of some (minor) partners, or also as a high government official, with administrative powers. Both can very well go together in the Old Babylonian period, but I hesitate to consider his (postulated) stay in Aššur as "official business" (*e.g.* in the name of the city or *kārum* of Sippar). The problem he was asked to solve is also not clear. That I.'s purse remained for so long in W.'s house, apparently was not W.'s fault, since he was asked to intervene so that Ḫ. could solve it. Why was I.'s purse endangered? Was the capital not freely available, blocked, invested in outstanding claims or bad debts? What does it mean that this capital was "placed before W.", "in W.'s house/firm"? Presumably a commercial relation (they were "brothers"), *e.g.* facilities granted to I. by W. in his *bīt napṭārim*, or perhaps some kind of partnership (see text A: lff. and CT 48, 1, quoted in note 18), with cooperation or investment. We can only guess, and I would not even exclude the possibility that the "securing of the purse" might refer to other than strictly commercial problems, which would make it understandable that Ḫ. was called in. The other reference to a purse which has been secured (*kīsum šalmat*), in AbB 7, 12: 18f., is not very informative, because of breaks in the text. The statement is followed by: "I will send the tablet of ... and one will interrogate the gentlemen", which suggests some kind of legal action. Since we have only scattered remains of Warad-Sin's archives, many questions must remain unanswered and interpretations are tentative only.

Most of the other persons occurring in texts A-C and in the letters to Warad-Sin quoted above are unknown to us from other sources. They cannot be identified (in a number of cases also because occurrences without patronymics of well-known names defy identification) with people attested in Old Babylonian texts from "Sippar", and even some names (*e.g.* Šamaš-šullimanni) are thus far not attested at Sippar.[25]

But there are some exceptions. Ningal-ereš, son of Lugal-Utu, trading partner of Warad-Sin (A: lff.) and delivering goods for him (C: IV 4f.), is the recipient of the letter AbB 12, 133. He may well be the brother of the overseer of the merchants of Sippar-Ammānum, Ipiq-ilišu, son of Lugal-Utu (mentioned above). In AbB 12, 133 written by Irra-gamil and dealing with a law-suit which involved the sending of silver by a certain Ibbatum (most probably identical to the writer of the letters AbB 12, 38-42, all addressed to Nanna-intuḫ, in which Ibbatum figures as trader travelling abroad) Imgur-Sin, son of Aḫuqar known from C I: 12, figures alongside Ningal-ereš as recipient. He is also attested in PBS 8/2, 199 (Si 6), where it is recorded that the parents of a man, ransomed (?) and brought back by ImgurSin from his creditor in Jablia (where Ibbatum traded, cf. AbB 12, 40: 6), are responsible for indemnifying Imgur-Sin.[26] Babylonian traders abroad were supposed to (CḪ § 32) and in fact did ransom fellow countrymen, and perhaps the loan extended by Warad-Sin to Aššur-ṣulūlī (A: 16f.) may be **[300]** viewed in this perspective (although debt bondage is, of course, not excluded). One of the witnesses of PBS 8/2, 199 is Mannum-kīma-Sin, son of Ibni-Ea, who according to C: I 26f. received a loan or credit from Warad-Sin, worth 1 ⅔ mina of silver. He also occurs in YOS 13, 470: 17 (Si 18), as owner of a field bordering one bought by a *nadītum* in "Sippar". Whether, finally, Luštammar, son of Sin-išmeanni, occurring as witness in CT 48, 52 rev. l, in Sin-muballit year 20, hence *ca.* 40 years before our texts, is identical to his namesake in A: 22f. and C: II 6f., is difficult to decide. A grandfather with the same name and patronymic could be envisaged. Whether he could be identical to the writer of the letters AbB 11, 46-48, cannot be decided.

5. Interpretation

Our texts acquaint us with the merchant Warad-Sin, son of Ili-asuni, based in Sippar, where he had a house, also called his *bīt napṭārim* – perhaps because of his status as foreign resident or because of its specific function and facilities – which could be used by others. He had married a local girl, Tatūrmātum, presumably when middle-aged and, according to the texts which must have been discovered in his house in Sippar, was active between Hammurabi year 42 and Samsuiluna year 8. His records and the letters addressed to him bear witness of a variety of commercial activities and of contacts with many persons in "Sippar" and elsewhere.

As trader and capitalist Warad-Sin had entered into various relationships with others. He may have been an investor in other people's trading capital ("purse", *kīsum*), which could explain why two letters (AbB 7, 120 and 11, 49) tell him that somebody's capital is safe or should be secured (*šalamum, šulmum*); one of them is called "his brother". It is certain that he had entered into partnerships with some traders. According to A: lff. he made funds (amount broken off) available for a "partnership's capital" (*kasap tappūtim*) to Ningal-ereš, presumably the brother of the local "overseer of the merchants"; the wording of the contract as excerpted suggests that he was a limited partner. Similar arrangements may have existed with Šamaš-rabi, according to the settlement CT 48, 11b, which gives some idea of the range of the cooperation. The fact that AbB 11, 49 states that the "purse" of "his brother" Imdī-Ištar had been "placed before him", in his house in Sippar, may indicate a fair degree of integration. If Imdī-Ištar was an Assyrian, we could envisage a situation whereby he had decided to use W.'s *bīt napṭārim* as a base of action or even had

25 The "Sippar onomasticon", used with great profit, was compiled by Drs E. Woestenburg, incorporating data collected by B. Ferwerda, M. Stol, material of the Old Babylonian Letters Project in Leiden, and names from unpublished OB "Sippar tablets" in the Bu 1902-10-11 group.

26 The structure of the text is : *A ... itti B ummēnišu C ina Jablia itrušu, atappul D abīšu u E ummišu ina qāti* C.

become associated with W.'s firm. One might perhaps compare the situation which Old Assyrian texts describe as "to bring one's goods/capital into somebody's 'house'".[27]

Other operations resulting in claims of W. for amounts of silver or (less often) goods, recorded in texts A and C and hinted at in some letters, can be explained in different ways. W. may have acted as money-lender, he may have sold goods on credit, or he may have entrusted merchandise to agents or travelling traders (*šamallûm, tamkārum*). When records give only excerpts of the original bonds, omitting details, the choice is difficult. Bigger amounts of silver, registered as claims, usually have a commercial background, and our texts record no less than ten cases of more than half a mina of silver. From the Old Assyrian period we know that agents and regular customers, buying on credit or receiving merchandise as trust, simply signed bonds which mentioned only the amount of silver they had to pay in due time. This may be the case in texts A and C, too. But simple loans, against interest, are not excluded, *e.g.* A: 16ff. (½ mina of silver, for a ransom) and the much smaller amounts in A: 21ff., 36ff. Persons known as regular contacts of W. are more likely to have been trusted agents or clients who received credit. This certainly was the case when persons received loans called *tadmiqtum*, A: 3, 12, 65, where in all three cases the transaction was more complex, comprising silver and goods (textiles, a slave girl), some with interest free.[28]

[301] The total assets of W. recorded in texts A-C, as rated in silver,[29] of one single year, amount to *ca.* 20 minas (the no doubt important amounts of A: lf are missing), to which we may add several minas for the goods listed without their value in silver. The products he delivered vary from emery powder, used for industrial purposes (in all *ca.* 1000 pounds, worth at least *ca.* 1 ½ mina of silver), to a variety of less common edibles, some in large amounts, ranging from a specific kind of bread, meat and lard to expensive and more exotic products such as leek (*ca.* 250 quarts), *andaḫšu*-bulbs(1860 pieces), juniper oil or seeds (35 quarts) and honey (4,5 quarts). Most of them were delivered to persons and institutions in Sippar, but the emery recorded in A: 49f. was an asset to be supplied by an Assyrian. This fact and the data on the presumed origin and movement of the goods enumerated (excepting bread, meat and lard) suggest imports from the north, either along the Tigris (Assyria and beyond) or along the Euphrates, all the way from Syria. It is difficult to be more precise, also because we do not know whether Warad-Sin or his agents imported these goods directly from their place of origin, or simply bought them from caravans arriving from the north (see the procedures mentioned in letters such as AbB 5, 220: 15ff.; 13, 52: 7ff.; JCS 14, 55 No. 91: 9ff. and the record CT 43, 118: 13'ff.). In view of Warad-Sin's Assyrian connections import from that area is a serious possibility. A text such as OBTR 204 (Tell Rimah) shows that most of the products mentioned in our records were available and obtainable in the Sindjar-Ḫabur area.

Warad-Sin's Assyrian connections are clear from our sources and from the names of a number of his contacts (Aššur-asu, Aššur-mušallim, Aššur-ṣulūlī, Aššur-tajjār, Kurara, to mention only the most obvious ones). His daughter Tarīša, who lives in Aššur, writes him that the whole city prays for him/them (on account of their marriage), which means that he must be known there. Her letters reveal that there were regular contacts between Aššur and Sippar; men, women, silver and goods travel in both directions, i.a. as gifts

27 See *SD* 10, 398f., on TC 3, 129: 6ff. (correct the transcription to read : *ana bītia ... šūt ūšibma)* and CCT 3, 14: 7ff.

28 *Tadmiqtum* is an interest free loan, consisting of silver or merchandise entrusted to somebody for commercial purposes, in order to make the best possible profit (*dummuqum*), without stipulations on guaranteed yield and risk sharing. See the combination of *tappūtum* and *tadmiqtum* (A: lff.) also Kraus, *Edikt* (*SD* 5), § 6' (= § 8) with p. 63 note 1, and EG no. 36 = YOS 8, 145 (20 + 6 minas of silver).

29 No less than five of the loans recorded in text A mention "refined silver" (*kaspum ṣarpum*). While the term is not unknown in OB (see *CAD* 113a, 1, a, and CT 47, 33: 13; VAS 18, 2: 2; AbB 7, 123: 18f. // 2, 161; 12, 173: 8), it is relatively rare, also in loan contracts (though most of the occurrences are in loans and commercial contexts), which contrasts with its frequent use in loans from Mari (ARMT 8, 22ff.) and the ubiquitous use of *kaspum ṣarrupum* in Old Assyrian loans. See for the quality of silver also Stol, *JCS* 34 (1982) 150f., on *kaspum kankum* and its circulation (also AbB 12, 36: 15ff.).

(*tāmartum*) and "packets" (*riksum*).[30] Business contacts are clear from the excerpts of those bonds in text A that mention the use of the Assyrian "weight-stone of the city-house" and use Assyrian datings. They must have been drawn up in Aššur, with Assyrian partners or clients (A: 42ff., with Kurara, son of Ajāja; A: 60ff., with Warad-Kubi and Ipiq-Annunītum). AbB 7, 76 refers to the payment of silver, due to W., in Aššur to a man from Turšu/i, and AbB 2, 155 reports that W. will receive an (official?) letter from the City of Aššur. In AbB 11, 49 his Assyrian contact Aššur-asu informs him about an action there, meant to secure the capital of "his brother" Imdī-Ištar. One might venture the conclusion that Warad-Sin was an originally Assyrian trader, with regular contacts with Northern Babylonia, who eventually settled in Sippar, where he acquired his own *bīt napṭārim*, from which he organized the import and sale of products for which there was a local demand. Though based in Sippar,[31] he must have travelled regularly, since the letters of his wife were written from Sippar when he was away. He must have taken them home in due time, where they were found as part of his archives. The same must be true of texts A-C, also found in Sippar. Since B and C state that the items mentioned were "shipped to Sippar", they must have been drawn up elsewhere, presumably in Aššur, in view of the eponymy datings. Walker *(op. cit.,* note 1, p. 16) already observed that A "is written in a clear Babylonian script" and the same is true of B and C, which also lack orthographic and linguistic "Assyrianisms".[32] It is possible that W. or his scribe (see the information in A: 26ff. on scribal training **[302]** given to the boys in Sippar), or a scribe from the trading community in Aššur which much have comprised Babylonians (see *e.g.* AbB 11, 49, on the presence of Ḫajabnil in Aššur) wrote these records.[33] W. may have taken them home in due time (he occasionally left tablets behind in Aššur, see AbB 7, 120); text B may have accompanied the caravan transport which brought the goods to Sippar. Perhaps the use of Assyrian datings can be taken as proof of accountability in Aššur, if Warad-Sin's business was a branch of a firm with its seat in Aššur. It is difficult to reach final answers when the sources are so few and laconic.

The destination of the goods shipped to Sippar varies greatly. Some of the items – honey, lard, figs, meat and bread – most probably were meant as gifts (cf. the strings of figs sent as gift, *tāmartum*, in AbB 12, 59)[34] or for private consumption by the members of the *bīt napṭārim* (C: I 9ff., 14ff. ; IV 17ff.). Others were delivered to officials, such as the governor of Sippar (four times) and the "overseers of the merchants" of both Sippars (three times together, once only to Ipiq-ilišu) and to the *gagûm* (B: 32, contents not mentioned). Others again were meant

30 The packet in question (AbB 12, 60: 35ff.) was sealed by a named person and by the "overseer(s)", and most probably contained silver, perhaps resulting from a commercial transaction. This meaning is also suggested by the new reference AbB 12, 54: 16ff. (commercial letter): "divide the *riksum* and whatever there is in two". While this use of *riksum* is very rare in OB, it is common in Old Assyrian, where the word denotes packets of silver (normally less than 2 minas), cf. *SD* 10, 32ff.

31 This may also be deduced from the greeting formulae used in letters addressed to him, which always start with Šamaš.

32 See for such "Assyrianisms" my observations in *Zikir šumim* (*Festschrift Kraus*, 1982), 362ff [= pp. 245-265 on this volume]. Cuneiform tablets from the younger phase of the "later Old Assyrian period" (*kārum* Kaniš, level lb, post Šamši-Adad) as to shape, style and paleography are very similar to Babylonian tablets of the period from which our texts date, but they must be classified as "Assyrian" on the basis of the language, orthography and syllabary. Cf. e.g. T. Özgüç, *Kültepe-Kaniş* II (1986), pl. 48, 3a/b; pl. 49, la/b; pl. 58, 2a/b, and also pl. 45, 1 and 2 (disregarding the seal impressions).

33 See the evidence for contacts between Assyrians and Babylonians in this period collected by Walker, *op. cit.* (see note 1), 15f. See also AbB 2, 107: 7; 3, 60: 8; 6, 202: 3' (translate: "given to an Assyrian"). We can now add some interesting references from commercial letters published in AbB 12, such as 54: 7; 56: 28 (sale of slave in Aššur); 57: 9. All these references show that Babylonian traders went to Aššur, but we (still?) have no evidence for a Babylonian trading post there, not unlikely in view of the political situation around the middle of the 18th century B.C.

34 See the instructive letter AbB 12, 94, whose writer acknowledges the receipt of the addressee's attention (*zikir šumim*), consisting of a gift of 5 quarts of leek. To reciprocate he has just sent off as a gift (*tāmartum*) 5 quarts of juniper. See for gifts in the OB period, C. Zaccagnini, On gift exchange in the Old Babylonian period, in: *Studi orientalistici... Franco Pintore* (1983) 189ff.

for individuals mentioned only by name (Šumi-erṣetim, three times; DINGIR-LU-ŠI; Izzāja), or to individuals belonging to or ranging under an institution (the *gagûm*, B: 30f.; "boys of the household", B: 26f.) or official (two persons *ša Ḫajabnil)* or identified by their task (the scribe, B: 27f.). They arrived in various lots (C mentions at least six different shipments with different transporters). Those listed in B arrived as one shipment, with one caravan, at the *bīt napṭārim*, from where they were distributed over their destinations.

Taking the use of *šipirtum*, "order", in text B seriously, we have to assume that he supplied customers in Sippar with goods ordered before. That similar deliveries are never qualified as "order" in text C is not strange, if we compare the Old Assyrian evidence where we have records where each item or packet is called *šēbultum*, "shipment", and others where this qualification is omitted, without difference in purpose. Orders as such, either in the form of requests or as formal orders, are attested in many OB letters, where people "write for" certain goods, ask to buy them in certain quantities, at certain prices or for a specified value (*ša x kaspim*, "for a value of x silver").[35]

It is interesting to note that the governor of Sippar and the two "overseers of the merchants" were among Warad-Sins customers and regularly received their "orders". The governor received in one year at least four very similar deliveries (between 15 and 20 quarts of leek and between 120 and 300 *andaḫšu*bulbs), twice comprising also 6 talents of emery. This suggests the idea of "standing orders".[36] Since the leek and bulbs were most probably meant for consumption in their households, there is no clear evidence that W. somehow was involved in the commercial operations organized by the "overseers of the merchants" (perhaps also by the governor) by means of which they traded for the palace and for the temple, selling surpluses and buying goods needed.[37] But we note that the dispute between Warad-Sin **[303]** and Šamaš-rabi (CT 48, 11b) also involved "silver of the palace". The contacts with these officials seem to have gone further than simply supplying customers. As noted before, the son of one of the "overseers of the merchants" probably was W.'s partner.[38] Tarīša's letter to W.'s wife, AbB 12, 60, moreover, ends with the interesting request: "send me the packet *(riksum)* which Awīl-Adad and the *waklu* sealed, and the garments» (35-37). Since the packet is to be sent from Sippar, the *waklū* (plural, or perhaps sing. without mimation) could be the "overseer(s of the merchants)", but there are of course other UGULAs which could be meant.[39] As for the governor of Sippar, we learned from AbB 11, 49 that he visited Aššur and was commercially involved, since the fate of the capital of a man qualified as "his son" was at stake, capital deposited in W.'s house. Text C: II 5ff., moreover, registers the shipment by two agents of 1 mina of silver to the governor, presumably the yield of a transaction in which he had participated, realised by W., in whose business he could have invested or whom he could have given goods on consignment.

However small and casual these indications are, they suggest that the commercial activities of Warad-Sin were rather complex and many-sided, too complex to deduce from the sober listing of orders and shipments in a few memorandums from one single year, which thus far are our main source.

---

35 See the references in J. Renger in: A. Archi, *Circulation of Goods in Non-Palatial Context in the Ancient Near East* (1984) 100ff., with note 270. Quite a number of requests or orders to buy are of purely private nature, but some clearly refer to trade. Note e.g. AbB 12, 182: 8'ff.: "You wrote me: Buy wherever you can (! *šitajjam)* [goods] for 10 minas of silver and send them to me". Cf. also AbB 12, 82; 84: 8ff.; 149: 8'ff.

36 Their existence has been inferred, for the Ur III period, from the repeated occurrences of the same quantities of certain products in balanced accounts, cf. D. Snell, *YNER* 8 (1982) 96ff .

37 See for these activities F.R. Kraus, *OLA* 6 (1979), 423ff. and D. Charpin, *JA* 270 (1982) 25ff. The palace required from traders taking part in these activities that they supplied half of the good/funds out of their own pocket.

38 We cannot exclude the possibility that Iškur-zimu, working for/with Warad-Sin, son of Ilšu-bāni, actually was the son of the "overseer of the merchants" of that name which occurs in our texts.

39 It is unlikely to think of the Assyrian *waklum*, a designation of the ruler of Aššur, since the packet was sent from Sippar. The *waklum*/UGULA of course could be an UGULA É (cf. AbB 12, 65: 36ff.).